GENERAL JAN SMUTS AND HIS FIRST WORLD WAR IN AFRICA, 1914–1917

GENERAL JAN SMUTS AND HIS FIRST WORLD WAR IN AFRICA, 1914–1917

DAVID BROCK KATZ

CASEMATE

Philadelphia & Oxford

Published in the United States of America and Great Britain in 2022 by
CASEMATE PUBLISHERS
1950 Lawrence Road, Havertown, PA 19083, USA
and
The Old Music Hall, 106–108 Cowley Road, Oxford OX4 1JE, UK

Hardcover Edition: ISBN 978-1-63624-017-6
Digital Edition: ISBN 978-1-63624-018-3

A CIP record for this book is available from the British Library

Printed and bound in the United Kingdom by TJ Books

Typeset in India by Lapiz Digital Services, Chennai.

For a complete list of Casemate titles, please contact:

CASEMATE PUBLISHERS (US)
Telephone (610) 853-9131
Fax (610) 853-9146
Email: casemate@casematepublishers.com
www.casematepublishers.com

CASEMATE PUBLISHERS (UK)
Telephone (01865) 241249
Email: casemate-uk@casematepublishers.co.uk
www.casematepublishers.co.uk

✡

To strangers
To Russel Claude Brock
To Saja who knew me not
To adversaries who make me strong
Jack, you knew me—but for too short a time
And dear Miriam who knew me better than most
To Adina, best friend, companion, and love of my life
To Jacqui
And all my memories

Contents

Contents

List of Maps

List of Abbreviations and Acronyms

ACF	Active Citizen Force
Brig-Gen	Brigadier-General
Capt	Captain
CCF	Cape Colonial Forces
CGF	Coast Garrison Force
CIGS	Chief of the Imperial General Staff
C-in-C	Commander-in-Chief
CMR	Cape Mounted Rifles
CO	Colonial Office
Col	Colonel
DHQ	Defence Headquarters
DODA	Department of Defence Archives
FO	Foreign Office
GEA	German East Africa
Gen	General
GOC	General Officer Commanding
GSWA	German South West Africa
HCT	High Commission Territories (Bechuanaland, Basutoland, Swaziland)
KAR	King's African Rifles
Lt	Lieutenant
Lt-Col	Lieutenant-Colonel
Lt-Gen	Lieutenant-General
Maj	Major
Maj-Gen	Major-General
NASAP	National Archives Pretoria
OC	Officer Commanding
OFS	Orange Free State
PEA	Portuguese East Africa (Mozambique)
PF	Permanent Force
QMG	Quarter Master General
RA	Rifle Associations (mostly former Republican commandos)

SADF	South African Defence Force
SAMR	South African Mounted Rifles
SANDF	South African National Defence Force
SAPF	South African Permanent Force
TNA	The National Archives United Kingdom
TVL	Transvaal
UDF	Union Defence Force
ZAR	South African Republic (Zuid-Afrikaansche Republiek)

Acknowledgements

The production of a book of this nature is both an arduous and a rewarding venture. The research process has delivered me to wonderful museums and repositories both locally in South Africa and the United Kingdom. Along the journey I have met generous people who are expert in their job and willing to share their knowledge with enthusiastic strangers. My gratitude and thanks to the people who man the South African National Archives in Pretoria, the South African Defence Force Archives in Irene, the Ditsong Military History Museum in Saxonwold, the Libraries of the University of the Witwatersrand, University of Cape Town, University of South Africa, and Pretoria University. I received a professional welcome from The National Archives in London and the Imperial War Museum. Conducting research in London is always a joy.

Historia, *Scientia Militaria*, *The International Journal of Military History and Historiography*, and the *Journal of African Military History* supplied the opportunity to test my theories and submit pertinent articles before rigorous panels of peer reviewers. These were fundamental to the writing of this book. Academic conferences are a valuable resource in formulating and testing ideas. I am grateful to the Great War in Africa Conference (2014), the 120-year Commemoration of the Anglo-Boer (South African) War International Conference (2019), the Historical Association of South Africa and the Southern African Historical Society for providing wonderful platforms. Another institution very dear to my heart is the Saldanha Military Academy which serves as the faculty of Military Science for Stellenbosch University. Dr Fankie Monama, Professor Abel Esterhuyse, Professor Sam Tshehla, Mr Andries Fokkens and the late Professor Deon Visser, who all hail from this precious node of academic military excellence, went out of their way to make possible this publication.

Thank you, Ruth Sheppard and Casemate, for taking the decision to publish this work. Ruth's professionalism has eased the path to publication tremendously. My gratitude to Dr Evert Kleynhans who has given his unstinting support even in my darkest hours and has stood by me offering encouragement and advice at every turn. Lastly, to my long-enduring wife Adina, who has had to live with Jan Smuts every day for six years. The delivery of final product owes much to your encouragement and unbridled support. You inspire me to new heights, and you are the courage, and the drive behind all my enterprise. I dedicate this book to you.

Introduction

Jan Smuts is a subject as vast as it is contentious. Simply put, the 50-year political space Smuts occupied is a vigorously contested period of history. He was both admired, and much reviled, during and after his lifetime. His memory continues to trigger strong emotions decades after his death. He engendered mistrust and stirred a fierce loathing among great swathes of Afrikanerdom who labelled him 'Slim Jannie', a pejorative term referring to his slyness and cunning. Standing in stark contrast was the admiration and confidence most South African English-speakers felt for him, inspired by his loyalty to the United Kingdom and its empire. Smuts's lengthy career included a bitter struggle against British oppression during the South African War, followed later with his becoming one of the British Empire's most loyal sons. Unsurprisingly, his capricious political nature invited much controversy. Smuts, the victim of naked British imperialism, would later become, not only a willing participant in, but a skilful operator of the imperial machinery. Even when the sun began to set on the age of empire, and Britain's hold over its dominions and colonies began to waver, Smuts nevertheless remained the champion of the Empire. His career mirrors his complex, rich and very human charisma, and like his character, it contains many contradictions.

Smuts's remarkable half-a-century political career presents any would-be biographer with a mammoth challenge. His life traversed periods of enormous change and important aspects of his beliefs, philosophy and political outlook changed in tandem. Judging a man by modern standards for the acts and thoughts he committed in a distant past era presents a problem. Contemporary historians who are unable or unwilling to transport their minds into the past, fall into the trap of anachronism. Historians have a duty to account for their subject's historic conduct in terms of the standards of the time in which it occurred. Smuts's tardy and aloof policy toward his fellow black citizens' political aspirations, his ruthlessness in suppressing political dissent, his hunger for territorial expansion, and his unequivocal support of Empire and colonialism are attributes that historians cannot easily defend or explain with the hindsight afforded to those whose feet are firmly planted in the 21st century. A nameless British historian recently warned that, "I worry that an impartial view of Smuts is difficult in today's world".

Bill Nasson, a pre-eminent South African historian, poses a challenge to the would-be Smuts biographer that, "the challenge of writing a biography about the remarkable life and career of this remarkably ambitious Afrikaner soldier-statesman, is in conveying what it was that he amounted to".[1] Those attempting to meet the 'Nasson' challenge are faced with a moving target, not only due to the longevity of Smuts's career but also due to his evolving personality over time. Nasson goes further when he asks, "But what, though, was the *essence* of Jan Smuts? Or, how are we to take his measure?"[2] Attempting to capture the 'essence' of this multifaceted man who lived in complex times is not an easy task, often resulting in a one-dimensional portrayal of a multidimensional man. Smuts played several roles during his lengthy career, each with varying degrees of success. Faced with an enormous and intricate life, biographers face an impossible task when attempting to reduce the impact of its entirety into a single slim volume. The complexity of his character and the times he lived in, coupled with his political longevity, demand either a voluminous and detailed study, or a more focused approach on aspects of his career in order to unravel the "essence" of the man. This book, *General J.C. Smuts and his First World War in Africa, 1914–1917*, seeks to unravel the essence of Smuts in his role as a general during the First World War in Africa.

Smuts has been the subject of over 30 biographies which vary greatly in quality.[3] An Australian, Keith Hancock, delivered a two-volume product that remains unsurpassed in its scholarship and *locus classicus* 60 years after its publication.[4] Hancock's unreserved admiration of Smuts gives the book a tone that is overly sympathetic but not entirely uncritical of the statesman. In his own words, "[He] has tried not to write about Smuts *and* his times, but to write about [Smuts] *in* his times."[5] Early biographers such as N. Levi tended to produce amateurish hagiographic works.[6] Sarah Millin enjoyed access to Smuts's personal papers but her work is diminished by being published when Smuts was still alive and revised as to its facts (not its opinions) by Smuts.[7] Smuts has not been the favourite subject among Afrikaner authors but E.S. Crafford lays claim to be the first in 1943.[8] The most modern Afrikaner biography is collaborationist work of 17 Afrikaans authors who seek to reclaim Jan Smuts as an Afrikaner role model.[9] True to works of collaboration, the quality of the various submissions vary greatly. Only a miniscule portion of each of these biographies is devoted to his role during the First World War, and most predate 1968. Significantly, there are no dedicated books about Smuts as a general on campaign in the First World War.

In 1999, Albert Grundlingh optimistically predicted a 'Smuts renaissance' in South African studies. He quoted Saul Dubow and Shula Marks, who, reflecting on Keith Hancock's two-volume biography on Smuts, identified "Renewed interest via—his theories of holism, his environmental and scientific concerns and his exemplification of a particular tradition of white South African identity—suggest that Hancock's Smuts will be continued to be studied with profit." Grundlingh optimistically sees that the end of South Africa's isolation and her rejoining the Commonwealth would usher in an era where Smuts's political role on the world stage would be highlighted.[10] Unfortunately, not much of Grundlingh's predictions about a resurgent interest in Smuts have come to pass. Smuts's holism has been largely debunked, and he is all but written off as irrelevant in the post-1994 democratic South Africa. Even the most recent attempts by Afrikaner scholars to claim Smuts for Afrikanerdom have been stillborn.[11]

Although interest in Smuts has fallen well short of Grundlingh's hoped for 'renaissance', there are a handful of contemporary authors who have enjoyed limited success when reintroducing the subject. Richard Steyn delivered a journalistic account of Smuts and, at the outset, openly states his methodology. Rather than "bury [himself] in research for the next few years and produce a thick tome that would gather dust on the shelves", he was guided by "an academic of renown to produce a short and less daunting book".[12] Following the 'renowned academic's' advice has resulted in a work of popular history, "a sort of journalism about the past in which the story and the characters are the key elements and the argument is secondary". The path Steyn chose to travel may have resulted in an easy read, but it has amounted to nothing more than a rehash of the secondary sources. His approach leaves little chance of discovering the 'essence of the man' as demanded by Nasson,[13] and as a result, adds truly little to the existing pool of knowledge. Steyn's book will ultimately gather dust in the historical landfill, while students of history will profitably read Hancock's enormous tome, nested in primary sources, for centuries to come.

Working closer to Smuts and the First World War, Anthony Lentin has produced a book which focuses on Smuts's role at the Paris Peace Conference of 1919.[14] While Steyn dispenses entirely with primary documentation, Lentin manages to rely heavily, if not exclusively, on two published primary sources, *The Smuts Papers* and the *British documents on foreign affairs—reports and papers from the Foreign Office*. His book contains a rather thin bibliography which is devoid of any reference to academic articles, such as those of Shula Marks,[15] Saul Dubow,[16] and Martin Legassik[17], the most vociferous critics of Smuts's character and career. By ignoring academic articles, he misses an opportunity to deal with the cutting edge of research on Smuts and their harsh criticism, and by doing so, the book becomes a hagiography at worst and a eulogy at best. Needless to say, these works are not dedicated to nor give further insight into the military Smuts during the First World War.

The initial port of call when seeking information on the military Smuts in the First World War are the South African and British official histories. The first one dealing with aspects of the First World War in Africa, appeared in 1924 and was compiled by a team of historians, one of whom was Major J.G.W. Leipoldt, a land surveyor who served as an intelligence officer during the war.[18] This general history remained the only single volume dealing with South Africa's entire war effort during the First World War up until the publication of Nasson's *Springboks on the Somme* in 2007.[19]

The book deals briefly with the 1914 Rebellion, the German South West African (GSWA) campaign and the German East African (GEA) campaign. It also covers the actions of the Union Defence Force (UDF) in Egypt and France.[20] Nineteen years passed before the South Africans produced another official work, authored by Brigadier-General J.J. Collyer, South African Chief of the General Staff at the end of the First World War. Significantly, he had served in both GSWA and GEA campaigns with Smuts and had an intimate knowledge of the day-to-day operations from a South African perspective. His first book was *Campaign in German South West Africa, 1914–1915* (1937)[21] and then another on the campaign in GEA titled, *The South Africans with General Smuts in German East Africa 1916* (1939).[22]

The most comprehensive work to date on GEA appeared in 1941 as part of the British official histories. The authors relied in part on the work of the South Africans Leipoldt and Collyer and made good use of both publications.[23] Lieutenant-Colonel Charles Hordern originally meant the official history to consist of two volumes. However, only one volume made an appearance covering East Africa from August 1914 to September 1916. Volume two, never published (but available for researchers to scrutinise at the National Archives in Kew), left a lacuna for the period after September 1916 to the end of the war. A further shortcoming of the entire series of British official histories was the absence of any material on the campaign in GSWA. Appearing somewhat belatedly in the early 1990s, as part of the Ashanti series, were three semi-official histories dealing with the First World War in Africa. Controversially, the South African government funded their publication primarily for political reasons to curry favour with the West.[24] The first deals with the South African campaign in GSWA and is heavily reliant on the official histories in general and that of Collyer specifically. The author, Gerald L'Ange, an accomplished journalist, offers few new insights or critical analysis.[25] The second book in the series, by J.A. Brown, deals with the South African campaign in GEA in 1916.[26] Again, he relies heavily on the official histories produced 50 to 60 years earlier and rehashed published secondary sources. Both works show little evidence of archival sources, and they fail to build on the foundation laid by the official histories produced decades before. Ian Gleeson's book on black, Indian, and coloured (mixed-race) soldiers courageously covers a hazardous aspect of the war, neither well researched nor reported on before that time.[27]

Official histories have all too obvious shortcomings in that they tend to protect the reputations of the participants and paint a glorified picture of the events. The official histories were designed to teach the lessons of war and explain the sacrifices which the population was called on to make. However, these publications were somewhat limited in scope and critical analysis due to restricted access to records and the often-amateur nature of the authors. Some have described official histories as little more than narrow military chronicles.[28] However, despite their limitations, official histories occupy an important place in the historiography, offering the foundations stones which historians that follow are meant to build and expand upon. Unfortunately, in many instances, the official histories have become the last word on military events rather than the first word. South African historians are not alone in relying too heavily on the official histories and succumbing to some of their deliberate political obfuscation.

As a natural progression and building on the foundations of official works was the surge of campaign histories in the 1960s. The earliest of these followed a drum-and-trumpet style of military history, were typically Eurocentric, and barely concealed their admiration for the GEA Schutztruppe (lit. Protection Force) commander, Paul von Lettow-Vorbeck. They were equally dismissive of the Allied efforts to subdue him in general, and Smuts in particular. As a result, these books appeared as popular history instead of scholarly works based on military expertise. These authors also placed heavy reliance on two books which continued to play a major role in denigrating Smuts and shaping negative perceptions of his military fitness for future historians. Harold Courtney Armstrong published a most damaging biography, and he bears the dubious honour for creating an enduring negative legacy reflecting on the supposed poor generalship of Smuts in the First World War.[29] The importance of his book, lies not in its depth of research, for there is little evidence of this, but for the fact that many historians, including renowned contemporary ones, have come to rely on Armstrong for his views on Smuts as a general. When Armstrong is read together with the diaries and memoirs of Richard Meinertzhagen, an intelligence officer who served under Smuts in German East Africa, a picture emerges which depicts Smuts the general as impetuous, amateurish, and woefully inexperienced, and furthermore, inept at commanding large forces in the field.[30] Many historians have relied heavily on the work of these two gentlemen. The only antidote to unravelling the web of mischief Armstrong and Meinertzhagen have spun—exacerbated by the endless and incestuous cycle of cross citations prevalent among modern Smuts commentators—is this book's keen interrogation and wide and deep research of the documentary evidence housed in the British and South African archives.

Among the first of the campaign histories was Brian Gardner's *German East: The Story of the First World War in Africa* (1963),[31] followed a year later by Leonard Mosley's *Duel for Kilimanjaro* (1964).[32] Next to appear in a similar vein, short on bibliography and footnotes but long on sensationalism, was J.R. Sibley's stirring but inappropriately named, *Tanganyikan Guerrilla* (1973).[33] Again, the author liberally applies Meinertzhagen to his narrative influence, especially his take on Smuts's performance. The most readable of all these works, but not the most scholarly, is Charles Miller's *Battle for the Bundu* (1974).[34] The author makes no pretensions to drawing on any scholarly or military expertise. He admits to "drawing heavily on the literary licence and educated guesswork". Continuing to propagate the now-popular guerrilla theme is a book by Edwin Hoyt appropriately titled *Guerrilla* (1981). The author describes Lettow-Vorbeck as the 'German David'. The fact that

Lettow-Vorbeck's typical German way of war had little to do with guerrilla warfare did not deter this author nor those previous or after him from propagating that illusion.[35] Byron Farwell published the first book covering the entire war in Africa in a single volume titled, *The Great War in Africa* (1986).[36] His piece on Botha's conquest of GSWA contains vast swathes from Trew's *Botha Treks*.[37]

Two scholarly works, that of Hew Strachan and Ross Anderson, which deal in part with Smuts as a general on campaign in Africa, appeared in the early 2000s. Refreshingly, they drew heavily on primary documents revealed by archival research. Strachan produced a book on the entire First World War in Africa, and, as such, this thin volume describes military operations in a broader context, rarely delving into the details of individual battles.[38] Strachan debunks some of the decades-old mythology surrounding Lettow-Vorbeck, and repudiates that he fought genuine guerrilla-type warfare, or that he achieved his goal of tying up Entente troops destined for Europe. However, Strachan's treatment of Smuts lacks the same enlightened revision, and like Ross Anderson, he relies heavily on the myths created by Meinertzhagen and Armstrong. It seems the passage of time has done little to remove controversy surrounding Smuts's appointment as a colonial, to command British generals and an imperial force in East Africa, and Anderson and Strachan have questioned Smuts's suitability or ability for the position. Strachan describes Anderson's campaign history, *The Forgotten Front*,[39] as superseding all the preceding popular histories of GEA.[40] The book is derived from Anderson's doctoral thesis and relies on primary sources to a greater extent than previous GEA campaign histories.[41] Anderson describes Smuts's GEA appointment as "highly unusual, with a colonial officer in supreme command of Imperial troops". He assesses Smuts as "not a professional soldier, and [lacking] experience of higher command in war".

Emerging 'new history' has thrown light on the enormity of the calamity that befell Africa in the First World War. Africa's contribution to the overall human cost of the war has emerged from it being considered as a mere sideshow until recently. The competence of Smuts's adversary, Lettow-Vorbeck, long regarded as the doyen of guerrilla warfare, has also come in for welcome revision. His cynical but ultimately futile approach led to the deaths of hundreds of thousands of black civilians and the devastation of the African countrywide. Black participation in the conflict was central to the war in Africa as the major portion of the fighting and the logistical support was undertaken by blacks on both sides fighting a surrogate war for their European masters. Smuts, and his conduct during the First World War, has not attracted the same level of revision and the opportunity exists, through rigorous research, to make a contribution in that field.

Smuts's outstanding career shaped the map and politics of southern Africa and left an indelible stamp. He fortified, vigorously defended, and galvanised the British Empire. He served and inspired the international community. Smuts the general commanded forces in the Anglo-Boer and First World wars. He became Prime

Minister of South Africa twice and, when not at the helm, held various cabinet posts. He was a member of the Imperial and British War Cabinets during the First World War and was instrumental in the founding of what became the Royal Air Force. He played an essential role in the drafting of the constitution of the League of Nations and later went on to his primary achievement, the drafting of the Covenant of the United Nations. He was a field marshal in the British Army in 1941 and served in the Imperial War Cabinet under Winston Churchill from 1939. His career as a peacemaker was equally impressive, having shaped the Peace Treaty of Vereeniging in 1902 and being the only man to have signed both treaties ending both world wars. He was an energetic intellectual giant, the first student in Cambridge University's 600-year history to have achieved a double first, and a botanist of some repute, giving the world the philosophy of holism. Anyone of his career highlights could fill a thick volume.

One expects that a man of such high international stature and influence, who created and then shaped the politics and territory of South Africa, would form part of an enduring part of the national fabric. However, Smuts's memory has not endured the test of time. Smuts, seeking a role for South Africa within the British Empire, alienated a large proportion of the Afrikaners and, unfortunately, deferred dealing with an equitable political solution inclusive of South Africa's black community. His emphasis on empire and international affairs, at times to the detriment of affairs on the home front, has resulted in a lasting and negative impact on his memory. His enormous stature and central role within the Empire often outshone that of the other dominion leaders. His dominance in that role has attracted much adverse opinion from many quarters at home and abroad which persist up to modern times. Smuts has received rough treatment at the hands of contemporary British, Commonwealth and South African historians.

His principal failing was his avoidance of tackling the issue of black political aspirations within his creation the Union of South Africa. His bequest, through the formation of the Union of South Africa in 1910, are the borders of the modern democratic South Africa. Although, one can justifiably argue that although modern democratic South Africa shares the same borders as the Union of South Africa, it is not the same country. His bequest may have translated into a legacy had he displayed greater sympathy and not ignored the plight and aspirations of the black community. Nasson is alert to the "big contradiction embodied by [Smuts]".[42] Many are perplexed by Smuts's ambivalence to black aspirations at home, in contrast to his quest for freedom abroad. His pursuit of racist policies at home has allowed some to label him as a high-handed hypocrite. Placing Smuts squarely in the context of his times goes some way to explain this apparent contradiction but fails to exonerate him completely. There were those who lived in his time, such as John X. Merriman and Jan Hofmeyr (Smuts's Deputy Prime Minister and nephew of Onze Jan) who in positions of power acknowledged the problem and proposed solutions, however inadequate. Smuts's view of freedom was very much linked with the civilising influence of Christianity and the order and hierarchy of the Empire.[43] The spread of Western civilisation was central to and the driving force behind his political vision. He dedicated a considerable portion of his career to combatting the racial inequalities in South Africa, except for the fact that the racial issues at the turn of the nineteenth century involved the fraternal struggle between Boer and Englishman. It was only much later, after the Second World War, that the racial emphasis shifted firmly to issues of black and white.

Smuts was a profoundly intellectually gifted man who impacted massively during his lifetime. However, he possessed flaws which damaged his legacy. He could be aloof and stubborn, but it is his ruthlessness that receives the most contempt from those that would denigrate him. He did not hesitate to execute those convicted of treason or use excessive force in bringing dissident communities to heel. He could be just as magnanimous and forgiving to his enemies and former enemies and could comfortably wear the garb of 'conciliator', just as he could don that of a ruthless oppressor of dissent. The passage of time has not been kind to Smuts's reputation, with many choosing to highlight his flaws and thereafter diminish his contributions. Any assessment of his abilities or lack thereof as a general has to pierce the thick veil of decades of adverse opinion and penetrate the shadows cast by his tarnished legacy.

This book focuses on Smuts and his First World War in Africa, describing and analysing his role as a general in the Afrikaner Rebellion of 1914, GSWA campaign of 1914/15 and the GEA campaign of 1916/17. The period under scrutiny represents Smuts at the peak of his military abilities where he enjoyed some of his most significant achievements. However, it is also the period when the seeds of his eventual demise and alienation were sown. Focusing on a shorter span of his lengthy career, especially one as significant and seminal as the First World War, allows an opportunity to explore and capture the essence of the military Smuts.

Smuts's military role and his campaigns in Africa have remained relatively obscure. To the extent that historians have neglected the war in Africa in general, so too has Smuts's military career in that war received scant coverage, despite his fundamental role in the GSWA and GEA campaigns and the peace process thereafter. The little attention he has garnered has been mostly adverse, amounting to synography based on thin evidence and mostly propagated by those holding a certain political agenda. The historiography reflects the general disregard that the war in Africa has suffered in the wake of the torrent of material produced on the European and especially the Western Front. However, the war fought in Africa was far from insignificant to those who participated in the conflict. The war devastated the local population and the countryside in which the battles were fought. In the case of South Africa these events were especially significant. The First World War shaped South African politics for decades afterwards, especially Afrikaner nationalism and later black nationalism.

South Africa's conquest of GSWA and Smuts's failure to acquire Delagoa Bay gave impetus to setting South Africa on a political trajectory from which she was only to emerge in 1994.

The Union entered the First World War as a dependency automatically drawn into the conflict—although she remained at liberty in determining the extent of involvement.[44] In the 12 years between the South African War and the eve of the First World War, Louis Botha, the first Prime Minister of the Union and Smuts, his defence minister, had resolved much of the naked Afrikaner–English conflict.[45] Nonetheless, despite their best efforts, a significant portion of Afrikaners longed for an independent South Africa divorced entirely from British influence. The risk of fracturing fragile South African unity by awakening Afrikaner nationalist militancy, should the country adopt anything more than a purely defensive posture in the First World War, was a very real one.[46] The fact that South Africa went to war for the British Empire was due in part to Botha and Smuts's loyalty towards the British for the grant of self-government to the former Boer Republics in 1907/8 and the creation of the Union as a self-governing dominion in 1910. The deep underlying reason for placing South Africa at Britain's side was the opportunity to acquire German territory for the Union.

When Britain declared war on Germany on 4 August 1914, Botha and Smuts seized the opportunity to suggest that the British South African garrison should be withdrawn to aid the fight directly against Germany. The prospect of an early departure of British forces was attractive to both Botha and Afrikaner nationalists. The prospect of an invasion of neighbouring territory, especially one perceived by many Afrikaners as having been friendly to the Afrikaner cause, was not as straightforward. The campaign against GSWA could only be conducted at the expense of the unity of the new South African nation. This was manifest in the Afrikaner Rebellion that took place within a few weeks of the decision.[47] Botha seized the military helm and with the help of Smuts, put down the rebellion and went on to conquer GSWA in a campaign that was not without its fair share of military mishaps.[48]

Why was Smuts willing to risk South Africa's precarious unity in the pursuit of military adventures? Botha and Smuts's decision to risk the unity of South Africa went beyond loyalty. They harboured a deep-seated desire, shared by many white South Africans, to expand the territory of the Union. For South Africa, the war in Africa carried Smuts's hopes and aspirations of building a vast and expanded greater South Africa that would dominate the British Empire in Africa. South Africa's sub-imperialism found congruity with the British desire to create an unbroken string of colonies from Cape Town to Cairo. There were those who believed that First World War presented South Africa with an opportunity to forge unity amongst a divided population and bring about a coming of age of the Union.[49] The furnace of conflict also ran the real risk of dividing a fractured population even further. In the final analysis, South Africa fell short of her territorial claims when Smuts failed to deliver at the Paris Peace Conference of 1919. The war accentuated the political rivalries on the home front and alienated a large proportion of the Afrikaners who preferred a narrow, Afrikaner republican nationalism to reconciliation.

Smuts's expansionist desires played a significant role in shaping the grand strategic and the strategic military decisions on the conduct of the campaign against the Germans. Smuts's expansionism was central to South Africa's participation and conduct in both world wars. He was at the forefront of South African sub-imperialism and championed her expansionist cause. Britain's and South Africa's desire for expansion in Africa, often, coincided, and sometimes the distinction between the two blurred. Smuts considered that the creation of the greater South Africa ought to have been "one of the cardinal points of British imperial policy". Smuts, while seeking an extension of the borders of the Union, was sincere in his endeavour to increase the influence of the British Empire at the same time.[50]

The UDF's competency and capability did not match Smuts's enormous territorial ambitions at the outset of the First World War. The formation of the UDF in 1912 owed much to Smuts as its founding member, chief architect, and the Union's first minister of defence. He was determined to create a modern defence force based on Western methods. However, it was designed mainly for enforcing internal stability and was not suitable for combatting a major European power such as Germany. Furthermore, the UDF reflected a fractured nation forced to compromise on many military matters in the name of unity. Politics took precedence over function and many appointments were conciliatory rather than based on ability. The result was the uneasy fusion of three military traditions of Boer, colonial forces and British instructors.[51] Smuts accomplished much despite the obvious challenges of forming an effective army out of former enemies speaking different languages, but at the outbreak of the war, despite much progress, it remained a blunt instrument.[52]

Smuts masterminded an ambitious plan to conquer GSWA by taking advantage of South Africa's long tradition of manoeuvre doctrine. The subsequent landward and seaborne invasion, designed to present the Germans with a dilemma of several swiftly advancing forces simultaneously converging on their capital Windhoek, quickly became unstuck. The UDF's lack of a credible general staff and suitable staff officers resulted in chaos at the various landing grounds and a fatal delay of the invasion of the port of Walvis Bay/Swakopmund. The timetable of Smuts's original plan was finally wrecked on the outbreak of the Afrikaner Rebellion. He had a major hand, together with Botha, in swiftly suppressing the rebellion, and getting the invasion of GSWA back on track. The successful, if not swift, conclusion of the GSWA campaign under the generalship of Botha and Smuts raised the image of the UDF's military ability within the Empire. South Africa supplied a welcome, much-needed, and rare victory for Britain in the face of the deadly stalemate on the Western Front. The South African use of manoeuvre warfare resulted in the capture of vast swathes of German territory with relatively little human cost. This was in stark contrast to the enormous losses suffered on both sides in the trenches of France and Flanders for little territorial gain. The UDF emerged from the GSWA campaign as a far more formidable force than the one which initially went to war.

The successful conclusion to the GSWA campaign allowed the British an opportunity to capitalise on South Africa's regional military power and expertise to bolster their weak forces in East Africa. British East Africa was the cause of much embarrassment as it was one of the few instances where the Germans occupied British territory. The British found the situation of German occupation of British soil intolerable. They had spent much of the war thus far unsuccessfully attempting to evict the Germans from British East Africa, with several unsuccessful operations in the Taveta Gap after a disastrous seaborne operation against German East Africa at Tanga in 1914. In January 1916, Smuts accepted the position of supreme commander of the East African force after the sudden illness of the newly appointed commander, Lieutenant-General Sir Horace Smith-Dorrien.[53] On arrival, Smuts immediately conducted a lightning operation of manoeuvre which conquered vast amounts of territory at Taveta and Kilimanjaro with few battle casualties.

Smuts's penchant for manoeuvre over attrition warfare yielded much territorial gain but failed to eliminate the German forces who traded space for time using a skilled and wily defence. Smuts's operational art undoubtedly saved casualties on the battlefield, only to lose the major portion of his fighting power to disease and poor nutrition due to logistic difficulties. By May 1916, a short three months after their arrival in GEA, South African units lost up to 50 per cent of their manpower to disease.[54] Despite vociferous criticism by the British generals and senior officers serving under him, Smuts could boast that by December 1916 he had conquered 80 per cent of the colony and 90 per cent of its infrastructure.[55] By securing a strategic victory, Smuts fulfilled his aim of territorial conquest (a prerequisite to expansion) and enhancement of South Africa's position within the Empire. There remains much confusion, even to the present day, whether he in fact could claim victory. A substantial portion of the criticism levelled at Smuts is due to the differing strategic goals of the British generals who served under him and even the government of the United Kingdom. His campaign ended in January 1917 when he was called to London to represent South Africa in the Imperial War Cabinet.[56] His conduct of the campaign, initially warmly commended, came in for much criticism after the war. This criticism has persisted and has become pronounced among contemporary historians. Not only was he responsible for grand strategic policy but he also assumed the role of a frontline operational commander implementing his vision at the helm of a military machine. The world had not witnessed this type of leadership (except for Botha) since Napoleonic times.[57]

The statesman's co-option into the British War Cabinet crowned the already considerable influence he enjoyed over British policy in Africa.[58] Smuts was the arch-manipulator who created a linkage between British imperialism and South

African sub-imperialism, and he managed to reconcile the expansionist aims of South Africa with the preservation of Empire.[59] Most modern researchers have either failed to draw reference to this point or have relegated South African expansionism to a few terse paragraphs. Few studies of the First World War in Africa correctly place Smuts in a central role conducting and orchestrating an expansionist policy.[60]

Smuts reached the pinnacle of his achievements during the First World War. He played a significant role in force preparation of the newly formed UDF in 1912. He served as Defence Minister and Deputy Prime Minister to Louis Botha. He was instrumental in ruthlessly putting down the Afrikaner rebellion of 1914 and offering the magnanimous hand of conciliation to the surrendering rebels. He commanded forces in conquering GSWA in 1915 and went on to command the entire British contingent in GEA in 1916. He emerged from conquering most of GEA to accepting a post in the Imperial and British War Cabinets in 1917 and 1918. His contribution in that post was significant as was his service as a signatory to the Peace conference of 1919. Smuts presided over South Africa's coming of age during the First World War. This book will seek to restore the balance through a detailed re-examination of the battles commanded at the operational level by Smuts, using new archival material and revisiting primary evidence.

CHAPTER I

Smuts Emerges:
From Scholar to Intellectual—From
Adversity to Reconciliation, 1870–1910

Early Years, 1870–1895

Smuts was born on the family farm, Bovenplaats, near Riebeeck West in the Cape Colony on 24 May 1870. He shared his birth year with a future adversary, the commander of the Schutztruppe in German East Africa, Paul von Lettow-Vorbeck (1870–1964). He was the second son of Jacobus Abraham Smuts (1845–1914) and Catharina Smuts (1847–1901). The Smuts family were typical Cape farmers who had inhabited the land in that area for many generations. One can assume that the Smuts family was relatively satisfied with their lot under British rule. The Cape Dutch settlers lost their colony permanently after succumbing to the British conquest of the Cape during 1806. Despite some friction under the British yoke, most of the early Cape Afrikaners readily or reluctantly accepted British rule. In time, they were prepared to build a unified South Africa under the British banner.[1]

Jacobus Smuts took a leading part in the religious, social, and political affairs of the Riebeeck West Valley. He was elected as the Member for Malmesbury in the Cape Parliament in 1898.[2] His community did not define itself in opposition to the British or the United Kingdom, unlike the Boer Republics to the north.[3] The Smuts family remained unmoved and substantially uninfluenced by the nationalism that led to the Great Trek and the formation of the Boer Republics in the northern regions of South Africa.[4] The majority of Cape Afrikaners stayed loyal to the British Empire despite encouragement from the Boer Republics to rebel and join the Boer cause in the South African War (1899–1902).[5] Those Cape Afrikaners imbibed British culture and became steadily anglicised despite attempts to retain Dutch as their language. Smuts was born into this contested environment brought about by a clash of Afrikaner cultures. Boer republicans, British colonists and Cape Afrikaners all competed for the soul of the Afrikaner.[6]

Cape Afrikaners, over time, formed alliances with the British and were represented by organisations such as the Afrikaner Bond (hereafter the Bond) under Jan Hofmeyr (1845–1909), 'Onze Jan'.[7] The Bond was formed 11 years after Smuts's birth, as an association of all *Afrikanders* or people who considered their fatherland as Africa.[8]

Jacobus Smuts, member of the Cape legislature, pledged his support to Hofmeyr and the Bond. After the Cape had received self-government in 1872, there was an incentive to work toward a united South Africa, undivided by nationality. Initially mildly anti-imperialist, the Bond grew more inclined to cohabit with indirect British rule.[9] However, a nationalistic strain in Cape Afrikanerdom began to take root especially after the British annexation of the Transvaal in 1877 and the First Anglo-Boer War of 1880/1.[10] Cape Afrikaners experienced a complicated and ambiguous material relationship with British rule and a sentimental and ethnic link to the Afrikaners in the republics. We can assume that Smuts and his family were not immune to the political atmosphere and harboured many of these political and sentimental ambiguities.[11]

In 1882, the 12-year-old Smuts, second son of the family, attended school for the first time owing to the death of his brother, who as the eldest son, was the only child designated to receive a formal education. Smuts, a late starter, made exceptional progress, completed his schooling, and gained admission to Victoria College in Stellenbosch in 1886. A letter to his professor, C. Murray, revealed his seriousness when he referred to himself as "retired and reserved". He displayed none of the flippancies typically evident in an 18-year-old youth.[12] Smuts met his future 16-year-old wife Sybella ('Isie') Krige (1870–1954) on his way to class. Isie was as serious and formal as Smuts, and, like him, enjoyed poetry. The two seldom mixed with other students, and neither enjoyed sporting activities. This marked the beginning of a 53-year marriage which saw them exchange romantic poetry and immerse themselves in languages and literature. Smuts expressed a weakness for women which he described as an "inner affinity and appeal". Smuts would strike up enduring friendships with many women during his lifetime, and he described his female friends as "more interesting".[13]

Smuts first made acquaintance with Rhodes in 1888, when the mining magnate and politician was on the verge of becoming Prime Minister of the Cape Colony. Hofmeyr had by then forged strong ties with Rhodes and shared the vision of expanding 'white civilisation' into the vast expanses of Africa, under the banner of a unified South Africa. It was not a straightforward alliance and reflected the complexities of Cape Afrikaner politics. Bond members tended to seek a united South Africa under one flag, just as Rhodes did, but under British rule.[14] The links between the Bond and Rhodes, at first tenuous and distrustful, strengthened as time passed, with their goals seemingly congruent on the surface. Smuts, as leader of the debating society, delivered the welcoming address on the theme of pan-Africanism. He was developing a political outlook typical of his time at Stellenbosch. His moderate political upbringing in Riebeeck West, his family's close ties with the Afrikaner Bond and rejection of Afrikaner exclusivism, and his philosophical pursuit of the embodiment of unity that would develop into his philosophy of holism, shaped his outspokenness as a supporter of South African unity.[15] Two essays he produced during his time at Stellenbosch reveal his penchant for a unified South Africa.[16]

His departure from a path of studying divinity marked a pivotal moment in his intellectual development. The years at Victoria College broadened his mind to other intellectual possibilities. His membership of the Victoria College Volunteer Rifle Corps is of some significance. There he received military training and wore a British uniform and received his first exposure to military structure and discipline.[17] Smuts graduated in 1891 with first-class honours in literature and science. His strong academic record gained him the Ebden scholarship through which he studied law at Christ's College Cambridge in Britain. An early indicator of Smuts's penchant for expansionism was his interest in Delagoa Bay. In an essay written in 1891 on the 'South African Customs Union' where he referred to Lourenço Marques (present-day Maputo, the capital of Mozambique) as the "finest natural harbour in South Africa" and the possibility that it may become part of the Zuid-Afrikaansche Republiek (ZAR, or South African Republic) should they join the customs union.[18] Smuts attributes the writing of this essay to his early political awakening and his realisation that he was a member of the "great South African community".[19] He graduated in 1894 with double first-class honours and was in the process the recipient of many prestigious academic awards. After graduating, Smuts passed the examinations for the Inns of Court and entered the Middle Temple. His academic performance was lauded in 1970 by Lord Todd, Master of Christ's College, who placed him among John Milton and Charles Darwin.[20]

In June 1895, despite the prospect of a bright future in the United Kingdom, a homesick Smuts journeyed back to the Cape Colony. His return coincided with the heyday of the Bond and Rhodes's tenure as Prime Minister of the Cape Colony.[21] He attempted to build a law practice but received few briefs and sought other means to supplement his meagre income. He involved himself in politics and journalism to make ends meet and soon acquired a taste for it. His association with the Afrikaner Bond drew him closer to the ideals of Rhodes.

> When Mr Cecil Rhodes appeared on the scene in 1889 as Premier of the Cape Colony under Bond auspices, with a platform of racial conciliation, political consolidation of South Africa and northern expansion, my natural bias as well as the glamour of magnificence which distinguished this policy from the 'parish pump politics' of his predecessors, made me a sort of natural convert to his views. I began to dream of a great South Africa in which the English and the Boer peoples would dwell together in happy concord.[22]

The Bond laid claim to representing all those who considered Africa to be their home, rather than Europe, and sought the federation of South Africa into one independent state. Rhodes envisioned a fusion of English and Afrikaner culture where white ranks would close against the "majority of prolific barbarism" and a white South African nationhood would be proof against inter-European rivalries.[23] These political views ran like a golden thread through Smuts's long career and persisted long after Smuts came to despise Rhodes and the jingoes.

Rhodes shared a dream with those of the Bond of a united South Africa where English and Afrikaans-speaking white South Africans would govern themselves, free of the British government. His vision extended beyond the borders of South Africa and included the territories right up to Egypt. A statue of Rhodes in Cape Town shows him pointing north with the inscription, "Your hinterland is there".[24] In these formative years, the unified and expansionist ideals of the Bond attracted Smuts over the isolationist policies of Paul Kruger (1825–1904), the third President of the ZAR, one of the independent Boer Republics north of the Vaal River from 1852. He embraced Rhodes and his ideas with vigour, to the point of becoming obsessed.[25] Smuts, although blinded with admiration for Rhodes, still harboured some empathy for Kruger and the ZAR. He understood the conflict between the pastoral values of the Boers and the new industrialists installing themselves in Johannesburg; however, he was at odds with the methods employed by Kruger to retain hegemony for the Boers in the ZAR.[26] Kruger deployed a strategy of divide and rule which ultimately set the ZAR Boer against the Cape Boer and Englishman against Boers. He was against Kruger dividing the South African nation that he would have preferred to emerge from the disparate factions.[27]

In October 1895, Hofmeyr approached Smuts, tasking him to speak at a meeting in Kimberley where he would defend Rhodes and his policies. There he defended the government of Rhodes as "progressive", and stated his support for its aims. Smuts identified the two fundamental issues facing South Africa as the consolidation of the white race (English and Afrikaner) and the relation of the white to the 'coloured' community. Smuts pointed out the challenge whites faced in forging their destiny against overwhelming numbers and "lifting up and opening up that vast deadweight of immemorial barbarism and animal savagery to the light and blessing of ordered civilisation". Faced with this "threat", Smuts offered white consolidation based on a "great South African nationality and pervading national sentiment" as the answer. Smuts's ideas on nationality coincided with that of the Bond where national unity was prerequisite to a political union: "There must be a people before there could be a state." Smuts identified that the new material wealth of the ZAR divided its people into capitalists who owned the mines and Afrikaners who ran the government. Material wealth divided instead of bringing together the people of the ZAR. The relationship of Rhodes representing commercial and territorial interests, and Hofmeyr of the Bond representing a national movement, set the groundwork for future South Africa. Smuts saw the ZAR as dangerously ambitious and increasingly alienated from the Cape through courting European continental support.[28]

The Kimberley speech provided a deep insight into Smuts's somewhat paternalistic views on how white South Africans would deal with their black compatriots. Whites had a civilising obligation toward blacks and held a position of guardianship over them. His view was that even where whites and blacks mingled commercially, the latter came off worse than before the encounter. He favoured blacks receiving "more physical and manual than intellectual" education, and he was not beyond discriminatory legislation in the form of "class" differentiation. Smuts was not a firm believer in democracy until people reached a stage of political development which allowed them to be entrusted with the responsibilities of self-government.[29] When not contextualised within the times he lived, these views can be jarring to the modern ear. Samuel Cronwright-Schreiner (1863–1936) witnessed Smuts's Kimberley delivery to a half-empty hall and described him as a "pallid, slight, delicate-looking man with a strong Afrikaans accent". He describes Smuts's attempt to demonstrate via a "torrential flow of words", the "admiral alliance" of capitalists (De Beers)[30] and Labour (the Afrikaner Bond). Smuts was not yet the pre-eminent political speaker he was to become, and Cronwright-Schreiner decided that it was "so amusing that we decided it was not worth replying to".[31]

Behind the scenes, unbeknown to Smuts, Rhodes was growing increasingly impatient with Kruger and felt threatened by the ZAR's budding ties with the Germans, who were rapidly building their own African empire to the north.[32] According to Smuts, Rhodes skilfully and cynically drove a wedge, via his links with the Bond, between the colonial Afrikaners and the Republics. Kruger distrusted the Bond and pursued an increasing isolationist policy. Rhodes, feeling that he had driven the wedge far enough, and out of desperation, hatched an ill-conceived plan which resulted in the infamous and abortive Jameson Raid—designed to effect regime change in the ZAR.[33] The intrigues behind the plot are beyond the scope of this book, but it was born out of the rivalry of competing interests to control the gateway to Greater South Africa. The Jameson Raid, a complete debacle, took place on 29 December 1895. One of the many casualties of this political fiasco was Smuts's relationship with Rhodes, and it drove him and other Afrikaner Bond members into the arms of Afrikaner republicanism.[34] His own words described his apparent *volte-face*:

> How shall I ever describe the sensations with which I received the news on New Year's Day of 1896 of that fatal and perfidious venture. [. . .] When during the political storms that arose after the Jameson Raid I quietly asked myself whether I had really been wrong in striving so hard for the national fusion and concord of the white races. I came to the conclusion that I had not been wrong, that my ultimate political lodestar was not a will-o'-the -wisp and was worthy of being followed in the future even more seriously than I had done in the past. In the course of 1896, it became clear to me that the British connection was harmful to South Africa's best interests that I feared my future position as a Cape politician would be a false one.[35]

According to Smuts, the Jameson Raid was the catalyst that mobilised slumbering Afrikaner nationalism and "sent an electric thrill direct to the national heart". He continued, "Now or never! Now or never, the foundation of a wide embracing nationalism must be laid. This was now the opportunity for a United South Africa on the soil of pure and all-comprehensive national sentiment."[36] Smuts rejected the ugly face of imperialism and sought political solace in an Afrikaner-led united South Africa. The complete lack of policy or guidance from the Bond in the wake of the

Jameson Raid completed Smuts's estrangement from Rhodes. No one convened a special conference nor a special session of parliament to discuss the raid. The Bond leadership seemed paralysed, and its lack of direction at a crucial moment may have left Smuts in a political wilderness.[37]

Historians have wrestled with this 'road to Damascus' moment in Smuts's life, and explanations range from epiphany to the more cynical and even conspiratorial. The broad range of offerings demonstrate just how enigmatic the figure of Smuts appears to both contemporaneous and modern historians. Piet Meiring, a former political journalist, and Union of South Africa Director of State Information, knew Smuts personally from the early 1930s and was one of the few Nationalist Afrikaners who attempted to reclaim Smuts back into the Afrikaner fold. Meiring, while acknowledging Smuts's English-influenced Cape Afrikaner heritage, draws attention to his youthful immersion in 'Afrikanership' via 'Onze Jan's'—'our Jan's'—readily available publications.[38] Meiring describes Smuts as a student in Stellenbosch, embracing the concept of a South Africa free of all foreign bonds and British domination. He speaks of Smuts's patriotism and his drive to place the Afrikaans language on an equal footing with English. However, Meiring stretches Smuts's obvious embracing of Afrikaner cultural enthusiasm into some type of early support for Afrikaner republicanism, paving the way for his expeditious political transition from Rhodes to Kruger.[39]

It is not a stretch to define Smuts's lodestar as nothing less than a united white nation living harmoniously in Greater South Africa. Rhodes's political demise in the wake of the Jameson Raid temporarily removed the British as a force for unification and expansion. Smuts was left little option but to seek a new political vehicle in the form of the ZAR.[40] Mordechai Tamarkin believes that the Rhodes betrayal was more than just a personal tragedy and loss to Smuts. It was "a crashing failure of a grand political strategy". One must measure the effect of the raid against "a great promise broken, of a wonderful dream turned into a nightmare".[41] Smuts's decision to abandon Rhodes was not an immediate one. He was at first reluctant to join the crowds in condemning Rhodes but waited for the facts to emerge. Smuts held on until the evidence of his complicity was irrefutable, for he had invested heavily in Rhodes's dream and there were not many alternatives on the South African political horizon.[42] Smuts's eventual political choice bordered on pan-Afrikaner nationalism where his intellect, education level, and exposure to continental nationalism set him apart from the prevailing ideological mood of the Cape Afrikaner and the Bond. Embracing Afrikaner nationalism, Smuts went further than most Cape Afrikaners.[43] He believed that the Jameson Raid was the real declaration of war in the South African War, not only due to Rhodes's treachery, but a new form of aggressive British imperialism.[44]

His rupture with the dream of a united Greater South Africa within the British Empire was short-lived and lasted for the duration of the South African War, where he fought tenaciously under the colours of the ZAR. Smuts defined the Boer aims of 1899 with the slogan: "from Zambesi to Simon's Bay: Africa for the Africander". His dream of expanding South Africa's borders northward remained constant despite his political capriciousness. Roger Hyam describes Smuts as the most committed and persistent expansionist of them all. Smuts addressed his commando in 1901 on entering the Cape Colony and spoke of the flag of the great Republic floating from the Equator to Simons Bay.[45] Smuts's political switch of allegiance can be viewed as a tactical manoeuvre, while still retaining the overall strategic aim of a unified Greater South Africa.

From Bondman to Republican, 1895–1897

The capricious nature of Smuts's various political about-turns challenges the historian. However, the essence of Smuts's political opportunism becomes somewhat more transparent if one identifies his political *schwerpunkt*.[46] Smuts's relationship with Rhodes and their shared idea of a united South Africa is well documented in the secondary sources. Less well documented is the explanation for Smuts's enthusiastic support of the Boer Republics and his Anglophobic ranting in his book *A Century of Wrong*.[47] The true extent and profound nature of his disillusionment with Rhodes and his altruism in deciding to defect to the ZAR is open to question. Smuts offers a far more pragmatic take on the Jameson Raid and the fall of Rhodes in his eyes.

> He alone, of all remarkable men of his generation, could have put the copestone to the arch of South African unity ... He spurned the ethical code ... The man that defies morality defies mankind, and in that struggle with mankind not even the greater genius can save him.[48]

It is almost as if Rhodes and British policy reached the end of their usefulness in achieving Smuts's overriding objective of unifying South Africa.

Smuts identified a shift in Britain's policy to South Africa where the relationship was previously based on a "spiritual, an ethical, a sentimental influence in the colonies ... not ... of material force but the ties of a community of ideas of sympathies". It seemed to Smuts that the British were now bent on using material force, witnessed by the increasing number of regiments arriving in South Africa, to impose her will. The Jameson Raid polarised politics in the Cape and undid the careful work of Hofmeyr and Rhodes in drawing together the English and Afrikaner toward a common South African identity.[49]

Sarah Gertrude Millin, an early Smuts biographer, suggests Smuts felt deeply betrayed, fooled, soiled and shamed, and this is the principal and logical reason for a committed pan-Africanist to switch his allegiance suddenly.[50] Millin eventually concedes that the idea of a unified and Greater South Africa was an idea that was bigger than Smuts's relationship with Rhodes and bigger than Rhodes's betrayal. She wholeheartedly agreed with the *Fortnightly Review*[51] describing Smuts as "Rhodes

Redivivus".[52] There are clues, however, that Smuts was able to subordinate his political allegiances to the higher objective of a unified Greater South Africa. He fought tooth and nail for the Boer cause, culminating with his daring raids into the Cape Colony. Smuts, during the South African War, remained a *Bittereinder*—a 'bitter ender'—when many Boers threw in the towel after the fall of the Boer capitals of Pretoria and Bloemfontein in 1900. Then in a reversal of his staunch opposition to the British, he took a leading role in the peace negotiations to end the war, resulting in the Peace Treaty of Vereeniging on 31 May 1902. The event marked Smuts's resumption of a pro-British/imperial trajectory which led to the obtaining of self-government for the two former Boer Republics in 1906, and the unification of South Africa in 1910. One can discern the heavy thread of pragmatism in Smuts which always trumped any display of extreme political zealousness on his part.

Pure economic reasons also feed fickleness and need to be considered.[53] Smuts had accumulated debts as a student in the United Kingdom,[54] and his earnings as a journalist in the Cape precluded him from marrying Isie Krige.[55] His unsuccessful application for the Lectureship in Law in the South African College provided further impetus for his seeking financial fortune in the ZAR.[56] Smuts faced accusations of being in the pay of Rhodes and De Beers and once that relationship ceased, so too did his source of income. Smuts vehemently denied the accusation but conceded to receiving some travel reimbursements but never a stipend.[57]

Smuts provides clues on how he and fellow Cape Afrikaners were able to switch from a tolerant attitude to British imperialism to support of republicanism. He questioned the loyalty of Cape Afrikaners to Britain and disputed the fact that this loyalty was deep-seated or permanent. Where the British viewed the granting of responsible government as a favour, the Afrikaner viewed it as a right. Smuts spoke too of the absence of blood ties between the British and the Afrikaner and that he considered "blood was thicker than water". Smuts identified that "loyalty" to Britain rested on one conviction only, that Britain was a force making for "righteousness, fair play and freedom within the widest limits consistent with the public good".[58]

The formation of the Bond demonstrated an undercurrent of republicanism in the Cape when it included in its programme of principles a clause in favour of a united South Africa under a republican flag. Rhodes managed to win over the confidence of the Bond and subdued their tendencies toward republicanism with a movement toward patriotism and South Africanism.[59] Once Rhodes revealed his imperialist tendencies, a bitter Smuts referred to him as a "false idol I once worshipped". Smuts referred to Rhodes as the Afrikaner's Moses who came to lead them to the promised land. The Afrikaner invested in Rhodes, and one cannot underestimate the disappointment of his betrayal.[60] Smuts may have overestimated, even at this early stage, the willingness of Cape Afrikaners to convert their sympathy for the republics into overt military resistance. His belief in their support would shape his initial military strategy to invade the Cape to provoke an uprising in the opening phase of the South African War and thereafter in the guerrilla phase.[61]

In the final analysis, it seems that Smuts found that Kruger's republicanism became less repugnant due to a shift in policy after the Jameson Raid. Kruger felt less threatened by the Bond and the Cape Afrikaners, and their shift in sentiment emboldened him to curtail his isolationist policies. This took the form of renewal and extension of the alliance between the two republics in March 1887, which resulted in a closer union of the two. Smuts believed that Kruger was now emboldened to pursue a policy of internal economic reform and an external South African rapprochement. This enabled Smuts to board the ship of South African unification albeit sailing under the republican wind rather than that of the imperial.[62]

Carroll Quigley suggests that Smuts never gave up on his ideal of a united South Africa and later, a united Empire. All his actions were directed to that end even if some of them seemed to take Smuts in a different direction. The motivation behind Smuts's vociferous criticism of Rhodes and the British was to elevate his importance in South Africa. Smuts desired to be at the helm of the unification of South Africa, and the best route to elevate his profile was via support of the Boer cause. His supposed contradictory manner of advising Kruger to make concessions to Alfred Milner (1854–1925), Governor of the Cape Colony and High Commissioner for Southern Africa, and then drafting the final ultimatum which led to the outbreak of war, was a clever strategy to increase his profile. He was a *Bittereinder* but was instrumental in encouraging acceptance of the British Vereeniging peace terms without delay. He later launched frequent attacks on Milner and 'his Kindergarten', but then cooperated with them after obtaining self-government in 1906. Quigley concludes that Smuts was quite cynical in choosing a pro-Boer path to achieve prominence on the South African stage. Smuts was pro-Boer on all non-essential matters and pro-British on all the essential ones. He realised that he would have to play a role in South Africa before he could play a role on the world stage.[63]

Quigley's hypothesis proposes that Smuts sought a prominent role in South Africa to achieve his objective of a united South Africa, an expanded South Africa and thereafter a united British Empire. Millin describes a young Smuts as "full in those days of the predestined greatness of South Africa".[64] He hitched his wagon to Rhodes, who was the rising star in the Cape political scene from 1890 when he served as Prime Minister of the Cape Colony. Smuts was a keen supporter of the Rhodes–Hofmeyr partnership on his return from Cambridge University in 1895, and he was employed by the two as a minor acolyte with an ability to write and debate the Rhodes–Hofmeyr vision. The fall of Rhodes after the Jameson Raid in 1896 left Smuts without a powerful political benefactor, but his objective in seeking a unified South Africa was intact. He was a man possessed of a vision in search of a political vehicle to carry his dreams to fruition. Rhodes's folly irreparably damaged the alliance between Boer and Brit in the Cape, and politics began to polarise so that the jingoes and supporters of the Boer Republics began to hold sway. "For the future, the line was to be sharply drawn, and there was hardly any alternative for the Dutch-speaking colonial than to look with a friendly eye on his brothers across the Vaal."[65] Smuts found himself pushed by the jingoes and pulled by the allure of better political prospects towards the ZAR. Hancock paints a picture of altruism, with Smuts unable or unwilling to deliver his contribution in half-measures. In an article in *Ons Land* Smuts transferred the task of unifying South Africa under the British banner and a fusion of the two white races, and he sought solace in Afrikaner rapprochement and a united South Africa under an Afrikaner Republican banner.

> A new feeling has gone like a wave through all South Africa. The feeble and insipid imperialism which had already begun to dilute and emaciate our national blood, is gradually giving way before the fresh new air blowing upon our people. Many who, weary of the slow working of the national idea, had surrendered to imperialism, have repented and have asked themselves what imperialism has achieved in South Africa. [...] Now or never the foundation of a comprehensive nationalism must be laid. [...] Mr Rhodes has been a sort of the dividing wall between the Colonial Afrikaners, and their brothers in the Republics. [...] let us lay the cornerstone of a truly United South Africa on the foundation of a pure and comprehensive national feeling.[66]

Smuts undertook an intellectual trek toward Afrikaner republicanism, and he followed this up with a physical trek from the Cape northward into the heart of the Boer republic in the Transvaal. He settled in Johannesburg in January 1897. He practised at the Johannesburg Bar until June 1898 where he became the state attorney for the ZAR.[67]

Smuts versus Alfred Milner, 1897–1900

Smuts immediately drew attention once he settled in Johannesburg. He was fabulously qualified and possessed intellectual powers that were somewhat of a rarity in his newfound home. Unlike the Cape, where he waited in vain for a brief, he was able to build a steady legal practice quite rapidly. Smuts was entering the eye of a perfect storm developing in South Africa. The re-election of Kruger in February 1898 by a substantial majority marked the end of British hopes of policy reform from within the ZAR and of a more progressive Boer leadership. The next blow to British political prestige came in the form of Gordon Sprigg's ousting in favour of William Schreiner and the Progressives' defeat by the Bond at the polls in the Cape Colony in September 1898. The chief justice in the ZAR, John Gilbert Kotzé, was dismissed soon after Kruger's re-election.[68] The political climate was polarising, and 'Hands off the Transvaal' was the cry of the Bond. The ZAR and the Bond shaped political sentiment across South Africa.[69]

Smuts gained the attention of Kruger when he sided with the ZAR President in a legal wrangle where he accused the chief justice of concerning himself with politics. His intervention took the form of a cleverly devised document which quoted at length from the Roman-Dutch Law.[70] Hancock believes that the role played by Smuts in this affair has been exaggerated; however, what is important, is that his strong position on the side of the executive gained Kruger's attention.[71] One needs to consider whether Smuts's actions leading him to Kruger were by design, or if indeed he acted out of pure conviction. The scales tip toward the former if one believes that Smuts inserted himself in the centre of events to gain prominence to reach his objectives. Smut's vigorous defence of Kruger resulted in his appointment as state attorney on 22 June 1898 at the tender age of twenty-eight.[72]

Smuts, deploying considerable administrative skills, proceeded to sweep clean the corruption which surrounded the ageing Kruger and his regime and gradually began to assume a role that took him beyond the duties of state attorney.[73] Added to his duties were requests by the Executive Council and the Volksraad (People's Council, the ZAR Parliament), to attend and advise all their meetings and he soon found himself advising many government departments on matters of policy and administration. Smuts busied himself with drafting new legislation, among which would be the controversial franchise bill central to the outbreak of the South African War. He removed prostitutes, dismissed corrupt officials, ended illicit gold buying, and harassed counterfeiters and illegal liquor sellers. Among his numerous victims was Chief Detective Robert Ferguson who Smuts dismissed in November 1898 and after that took personal control of the detective force in June 1899.[74] Smuts delivered so much change through his prodigious work ethic and powerful intellect that Hancock believes that by the new year, 1899, he was the leading personality in the ZAR, barring Kruger. Kruger possessed high regard for Smuts referring to him as "one of the cleverest lawyers in South Africa and a man of versatile attainments besides".[75] Smuts enjoyed the confidence of Kruger and wielded more influence, apart from Willem Johannes Leyds (1859–1940), ZAR envoy in Brussels and former state attorney of the Transvaal, than many of the more experienced Kruger entourage.

However, the deteriorating Anglo-Boer relationship was to take the primary spot and demand all his attention. Rhodes was hell-bent on war against Kruger, and he used the vast machinery of the English-speaking press, which he controlled, to magnify what was known as the *Uitlander* (lit. outlander, i.e. foreigner) grievances out of all proportion in the ZAR.[76] Rhodes's goal was to induce the British to come to the rescue of the 20,000 Uitlanders living in the ZAR.[77] Adding to the ZAR's woes was the appointment of Alfred Milner as Governor of the Cape Colony and High Commissioner for Southern Africa on 5 May 1897. Milner, calling himself "a civilian soldier of the empire", made a slow and cautious start to his tenure and took the opportunity to familiarise himself with the circumstances.[78] A grand strategic goal possessed Milner, which he saw as fundamental to the salvation of the British Empire. He considered that civilisation came about with good governance, and it was the duty of an advanced people to elevate those on the lower rungs of civilisation. Britain was approaching a situation when she could no longer perform this task without the aid of the self-governing colonies. Kruger's republic stood directly in the way of Milner and his ambition to unite South Africa under the British flag.[79] Milner enjoyed the same vision as Smuts in seeking a unified Greater South Africa, except that he desired this under British control.[80]

He adopted a far more pragmatic approach to the problem than Rhodes and was mindful that while the British military in South Africa was understrength, bold demands were out of the question for fear of Boer military action.[81] He travelled extensively through the Cape Colony, Bechuanaland, Rhodesia, and Basutoland and took the trouble to learn both Dutch and Afrikaans to gain a better understanding of the Cape Dutch points of view. Before the trip, he believed that colonial Afrikaner sympathies ultimately lay with the Republics, and only a strong military presence would maintain British supremacy.[82] Resulting from his journey, he concluded that there was no hope for peace as long as the ZAR remained independent and stood in the way of the British ambition of controlling Africa from the Cape to Cairo.[83] Milner judged that the increasingly unfriendly political climate in South Africa coupled with a favourable shift in sentiment toward the ZAR posed a threat to British hegemony in southern Africa. He began, in February/March 1898, to test the water with Joseph Chamberlain (1836 –1914), Secretary of State for the Colonies, for what he considered was the inevitable looming conflict. Chamberlain was determined to keep the peace and wrote "our greatest interest in South Africa is peace".[84] However, the British intent was clarified by Lord Selborne (1859–1942), Under Secretary of State for the Colonies, who insisted that it could not be "peace at any price". He offered that, "Our object is the future combination of South Africa under the aegis of the Union Jack".[85]

British intentions became clear to Smuts when he granted the British Agent in the ZAR, Edmund Fraser, an audience over the alleged ill-treatment of coloured British subjects, on 22 December 1898. Fraser told Smuts that Britain was unhappy with the maladministration in the ZAR and the mistreatment of her subjects, and the time had come to show "the Boers that England is master in South Africa". Smuts connected Fraser's assertions with rumours in the press of a strengthening of British forces in South Africa.[86] Thereafter, he assumed an ambiguous role as both war- and peacemonger in the months leading up to the outbreak of the South African War, but in the main, from April to August 1899, he did everything in his power to remove the causes of war.[87] Smuts maintained well-established communication channels with Hofmeyr, Schreiner, and John Xavier Merriman (1841–1926), senior politician and Treasurer General of the Cape in the ministry of W.P. Schreiner from 1898 to 1900.[88] He used these levers to judge the mood of the colonial Afrikaners and attempted to bring pressure on the British via mobilising the republican cause among them. The Boers sought to retard the process on the chance that a delay could usher in a friendlier British government. In the meantime, leaving nothing to chance, they seized the opportunity to stock their armouries.[89]

Various quarters, alarmed with the deteriorating political climate, extended peace feelers. The Orange Free State (OFS) government, under President Marthinus Steyn (1857–1916), facilitated a conference, held in Bloemfontein on 30 May 1899, where Milner and his aids faced Kruger and Smuts. On the eve of the conference, Germany intimated that she was unable to assist the ZAR in the event of war due to Britain's overwhelming sea power. Germany urged the ZAR to concede as much as was necessary to maintain her independence.[90] The threat of the rapidly waning international support substantially weakened the Boer hand.

During the conference, Smuts always remained at Kruger's side to "restrain and advise". According to Smuts junior, Milner came to know that it was Smuts, not Kruger with whom he must deal.[91] Smuts entered the conference with considerable confidence of securing peace, unlike Hofmeyr, who cautioned him and Kruger that war was unavoidable.[92] Kruger attended reluctantly: his strategy was to negotiate for the incorporation of Swaziland, the formal recognition of ZAR sovereignty, and a modification of the London Convention of 1884.[93] In turn, he would concede a small modification to granting the franchise for the Uitlanders if he could achieve these aims.[94] Milner came to the conference in an intractable mood bent on forcing the ZAR to concede the Uitlander franchise and its sovereignty or face war.[95] He cautioned Selborne that he was not very hopeful about the outcome of the conference and sent him a long telegram advising on the strategic considerations of war.[96]

Kruger was the immovable object, reluctantly taking Smuts's advice and cajoling.[97] Armstrong describes Smuts as being at Kruger's elbow, "prompting him, cadaverous, pugnacious, vibrating energy, putting new energy into Kruger and stiffening his obstinacy".[98] The first two days were dominated by Kruger who matched Milner's focused demands and intellect with bluster and obstinance. Smuts could see that Milner was driving Kruger into a corner.[99] Smuts did his best to outmanoeuvre Milner by offering concessions, but to no avail, as Milner would accept nothing less than his original demands.[100] Kruger, well past his physical and mental prime, relied on Smuts to enable him to put up a decent show of defence in the face of a wily and confident adversary.[101] The Bloemfontein talks were doomed to failure and disbanded after a week of inconclusive discussions. Smuts then turned to Hofmeyr and the Bond and tried to secure Afrikaner solidarity as a means to diverting the British from their course of war, and in return, he received a deluge of advice from the Cape to make the concessions that would hopefully avert the conflict.[102]

The seeming inevitability of war changed the Boer strategy from seeking peace to delaying the conflict for as long as possible. There was much to do in preparing the Boer forces, and a delay would also bring closer the possible election of the Liberals in the United Kingdom led by Henry Campbell-Bannerman (1836–1908), Leader of the Liberal Party from 1899 to 1908. Concessions would feed delay with a twofold effect. Smuts strongly believed a Cape rebellion was a possibility especially in the face of generous ZAR concessions on the franchise. Smuts and Francis William

Reitz, State Secretary of the ZAR, correctly gauged the mood of the British, with Chamberlain and Selborne concerned that public opinion was not ready for war. Selborne informed Milner that "The idea of war with the [ZAR] is very distasteful to most people". Selborne took pains not to outrun public opinion. Chamberlain was adamant in the policy of exhausting moral pressure before proceeding to extremities.[103] Therefore, any concessions made by the ZAR were sure to keep the lid on British public opinion, and this sound strategy was adopted.[104]

In the coming months, Smuts seized every opportunity to avert war. Hancock places Smuts as Kruger's chief minister, especially so in the crucial July/August 1899 period during Reitz's leave of absence on a coastal holiday with his family.[105] The young state attorney faced considerable pressure from Hofmeyr, Merriman and Schreiner who encouraged him to make concessions and produce a settlement of the franchise and satisfy the claims of Milner and the British.[106] Smuts drafted a franchise bill for presentation to the Volksraad as a result of these discussions, and in turn, pleaded for Afrikaner solidarity from Hofmeyr and the Cape Colony Afrikaners.[107] The Volksraad passed the bill on 18 July 1899, with resulting approval from the Cape friends.[108] These new concessions nearly resulted in the resignation of Milner who grew frustrated with the British government's eagerness to embrace the ZAR's overtures.[109] Smuts's far-reaching measures and tireless efforts almost averted a disaster when *The Times* announced that the crisis was over.[110] Smuts astutely delivered sufficient concessions to win over British public opinion, and the breakthrough seemingly enthused Chamberlain.[111] Milner furiously set about reversing this disaster to his plans of war and managed to convince Chamberlain and the British government to keep on track. Once again, Milner outflanked Smuts, when on 27 July 1899 he demanded that representatives of the two governments submit the new franchise bill to a joint inquiry. If Smuts accepted, it would result in the surrender of the ZAR's legislative authority.

Smuts, on 12 August 1899, launched one last initiative to save the peace when he entered unofficial negotiations with Pretoria-based British agent, Sir William Conyngham Greene.[112] There was also a considerable military incentive in delaying an outbreak of war during the Transvaal's dry season of August and September.[113] Greene was favourably disposed toward Smuts, regarding him as "genuine" while distrusting Kruger and Leyds.[114] Milner also favoured Smuts, and stated on a previous occasion, "I rather wish I could get hold of Smuts just now. I still believe I could do something with him."[115] Leo Amery too believed that Smuts held good intentions, describing him as "a young man in an exceptionally high position, with everything to gain and nothing to lose by the preservation of peace". Amery believed that Smuts possessed a better appreciation of Britain's power than his "adopted" countrymen and considered his efforts as genuine.[116]

The thrust of the radical proposal hammered out by the two men for a comprehensive settlement required that the British withdraw their demand for a joint inquiry in return for far-reaching franchise concessions. The concession after the debate with Greene looked like those demanded by Milner at the Bloemfontein conference. Intuitively, Milner felt that Smuts was leading Greene into a trap and that the ZAR was playing for time and would repudiate the concessions on some spurious grounds. Greene received a reprimand from Milner for his "irregular methods", but Chamberlain felt that if the proposals were genuine, they constituted a considerable concession.[117] However, Kruger gradually whittled down the original proposal initialled by Smuts with demands regarding suzerainty and arbitration—for which the British could not possibly concede. The ZAR executive failed to endorse Smuts's assertions to Greene.[118] Milner was able once again to retrieve the situation by taking advantage of Smuts's naïve diplomacy.[119] Smuts became a pawn in the political game played between Kruger and Milner, and the Volksraad repudiated all of Smuts's verbal assurances to Greene.[120] British impatience was adequately expressed by Chamberlain on 6 August when he declared that "the sands of time are running out [and Kruger] dribbles out reforms like water from a squeezed sponge".[121]

Frustrated at every turn and not able to bend destiny to his will, Smuts turned his eyes to war.[122] He expressed his confidence to Hofmeyr that the two republics could field 50,000 men with no equal in the world. The British would have to deploy 150,000 men to equal the Boer forces.[123] Smuts had lost all faith in British statesmanship, and adopted a defiant stance in the face of what he believed was a British desire to destroy South Africa.[124] His new belligerent disposition manifested during one of the last peace initiatives led by Arthur Guy Enock, a member of the Society of Friends. In a cablegram to his Quaker friends in London, Enock described Kruger as willing to continue negotiations and make further concessions. He sought an audience with Kruger to endorse the cablegram, which after a long and challenging process, was finally secured by appointment for 4 p.m. on 3 October 1899. Enock felt he was making progress with Kruger until Smuts joined the meeting and released a tirade against the British which swayed the other men there. Enock believed that Smuts wrecked his peace plan.[125] The die was cast, and Kruger delivered his ultimatum, relieving the British of having to explain to the people of England why they were at war.[126]

The South African War

Smuts opened his war against the British with a political treatise chronicling the evil of British aggression against the Afrikaner. *A Century of Wrong*, an unabashed propaganda piece, attempted to unite Afrikaners, especially those living in the Cape Colony, behind the republican cause.[127] Besides its call to rally reluctant Cape Afrikaners and to elicit anti-British overseas sympathy, it also provides an insight into Smuts's deep feelings of betrayal by jingoistic imperialists and the capitalist mine magnates.[128] Once peace had finally evaporated, he threw himself with customary zeal into war planning. He produced a memorandum for the ZAR executive council detailing a strategic plan for the future conduct of the war. The plan was even more remarkable for his relative lack of military experience except for a brief sojourn with the Victoria Volunteer Rifle Corps back in his Stellenbosch student days.[129]

Boer war planning tended to be superficial and inadequate at the strategic level. Smuts expressly stated that "no comprehensively planned war plans were prepared", only "the broad outlines of such a plan".[130] General Piet Joubert, the Transvaal Commandant-General, had given no thought to a war plan even up to the eve of the war, and neither had the Orange Free State.[131] However, the Boers had devised a shrewd strategy in the First Anglo-Boer War, where they commenced the campaign using the strategic offensive coupled with the tactical defensive. The Boers, by laying siege to British-held garrisons in the Transvaal, had enticed the British to move a cumbersome column from Natal along the only viable road through to the Transvaal in an attempt to relieve the besieged towns.[132] British logistics, restricted to the railway or road networks, made predictable their route of attack. The Boers ensconced themselves at the eminently defensible Laing's Nek, astride the only road providing a practical route into the Transvaal. The siege of the British garrisons formed the strategic offensive. The enticing of the British onto Boer choice of ground where they enjoyed considerable defensive advantages, had formed the tactical defensive.[133]

Smuts offered a different more daring strategy in 1899, at the start of the South African War, designed at the outset to take advantage of Boer mobility and numerical strength.[134] He proposed a lightning strike using deep offensive strategy, necessitating offensive tactics and advancing far into Natal and ultimately seizing the port of Durban.[135] The seizure of the port would prevent rapid reinforcement of British troops in Natal and cut off the communication routes to Rhodesia.[136] He hoped that a successful operation along these bold lines enjoyed a reasonable chance of igniting a rebellion among the Cape and Natal Afrikaners who, Smuts hoped, would be inspired to rise in sympathy with the audacious Boer victory.[137] Furthermore, a bold early victory such as this may have tempted foreign powers frustrated with Britain to take a more bellicose stance, thereby persuading Britain to sue for peace to avoid the intervention of a third power. (See Map 1.1)

The Boer leadership chose to replicate the less ambitious strategy of the First Anglo-Boer War and laid siege the towns of Ladysmith (Natal), and Kimberley and Mafeking (both in the northern Cape). However, the Boer plan was not devoid of strategic cunning, and it forced the British to split their forces to relieve the besieged towns.[138] The British faithfully followed the script and chose political reasons over military ones, dividing their army into three columns in the hope of relieving the beleaguered towns. Their fighting power thus divided, the Boers forced them to attack entrenched prepared positions. Heavy tactical defeats followed during the so-called 'Black Week' at the battles of Stormberg (10 December 1899), Magersfontein (11 December 1899), and Colenso (15 December 1899).[139] However, as Smuts predicted, the British possessed sterner resolve than in the First Anglo-Boer War and departed from the script. Instead of suing for peace, they consolidated their forces and waited for reinforcements to arrive from the United Kingdom, which flowed unhindered from the ports of Cape Town, Port Elizabeth, and Durban. They soon garnered an overwhelming numerical advantage. (See Map 1.1). Boer tactical success did not translate into strategic success.

The Boers threw away the slim chance of a strategic victory by adopting the less imaginative tactical defensive stance demanded by the conservative generals.[140] They faced the almost certain prospect of being ground into defeat by facing an overwhelming British numerical and economic advantage.[141] They skilfully forced the British to fight on ground not of their choosing and thereby enjoyed significant tactical victories. However, assuming a defensive posture does not win wars and offensive strategy is an essential element of winning a war. Defensive stances are a temporary measure allowing for an advantage to develop, which will eventually result in offensive action to secure combat success.[142] Smuts laid the blame squarely on the shoulders of Commandant-General Piet Joubert describing him as "passé" and "hopelessly incompetent".[143] However, Smuts later cast doubt on whether the Boers at that early stage of the war were indeed capable of launching an offensive of the magnitude he had proposed.[144] (See Map 1.1)

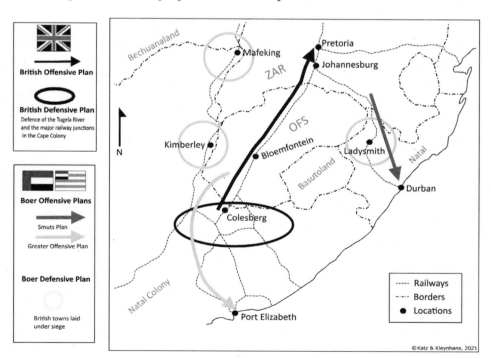

Map 1.1. The Boer and British strategic plans at the outset of the South African War

Smuts played a marginal military role in the early conventional phase of the war. Louis Botha replaced Joubert, who died on 28 March 1900, as Acting Commandant-General, but his appointment was too late to influence the conventional war decisively. Smuts, during this time, busied himself with running the government and paying frequent visits to the front. He reported back to the government, but they ignored his exhortations to greater military feats directed at the ageing generals.[145] Once Botha assumed the position of Acting Commandant-General, so began his enduring relationship with Smuts. In Smuts's first communication with Botha, he implored him to take the offensive in Natal and not assume the defensive. Smuts possessed a keen strategic grasp of the situation as he made good use of the Boer internal lines of communication to suggest a switch of forces from Natal (once the British are defeated there) to the western front of Mafeking to meet the British column under Lieutenant-General Frederick Carrington making its way from Rhodesia.[146] Botha, a consummate fighting general, wholeheartedly and enthusiastically agreed with Smuts.[147]

Before he grabbed a chance for a combat leadership role in the guerrilla phase of the war, Smuts busied himself with foreign affairs and other organs of state including logistics for the war effort. He attempted to rally Boer forces who were melting away with instructions to those in charge to use persuasion or force, to get Boer burghers back on commando.[148] The government made the strategic decision to abandon a static defence of Pretoria in preference to conducting manoeuvre warfare on the vast "illimitable" veld.[149] A raiding strategy would substitute a persisting strategy.[150] Smuts urged the Boer generals to fight on and rejected British peace initiatives (once the capitals of the Boer Republics, Bloemfontein and Pretoria, fell in 1900). However, even he began to realise that the Boer cause was tenuous and hopes of winning dwindling.

What did Smuts hope to achieve by extending the war beyond the fall of Pretoria in what amounted to an emotional decision devoid of military or economic logic? It was the accusation from President Steyn of the Orange Free State of cowardice by the Transvaalers where he expressed his unalterable opposition to peace in the face of the ruin brought down on the Free State and the colonial rebels. Smuts wrote that it boiled down to self-respect for the burghers and future generations of Boers.[151] Furthermore, with sure signs of British war-weariness, the continuation of the war offered the possibility of foreign intervention. The threat of destroying the mines would sow dissension in the ranks of the jingoes. The greatest hope remaining was the recruitment of Cape Boers sympathetic to the cause.[152]

Smuts ruthlessly seized the Transvaal's gold reserves and, in a plan narrowly averted, sought to destroy the gold mines.[153] The Boers fought a final battle marking the close of the conventional phase, at Donkerhoek to the east of Pretoria in the Magaliesberg on 11/12 June 1900. There under Botha, heavily outnumbered, they put up a brave but fruitless defence.[154] The surrender of Pretoria served as a signal to many Boers to abandon their commando and return to their farms. Against the tide of defeatism, Koos de la Rey (1847–1914) revived the abandoned Western Transvaal as an operational area under his command.[155] Smuts described De la Rey as an old friend, and he grabbed the chance to accompany the general to the Western Transvaal. The ZAR government installed Smuts and De la Rey as the leaders of virtually a separate government of the western districts.[156] There Smuts made the transition from civilian to soldier under the able tutelage of De la Rey, and soon the two busied themselves with clearing the western districts of the British occupation.

Two advancing British columns under Major-General Ralph Arthur Penrhyn Clements soon tested Smuts who commanded 600 burghers during one of De la Rey's absences in late 1900. In a deadly game of cat and mouse, Smuts and his men survived to rejoin De la Rey. The young Smuts learnt his soldier's craft under De la Rey's watchful eye, the wily general issuing him with varying military tasks as and when the opportunity arose.[157] During these exploits, Smuts, De la Rey, Botha, Steyn, and others of the Boer hierarchy attended a war council at Syferfontein in September 1900. The ravages inflicted by the British within the republics rekindled the idea of taking the war to the colonies in the old hope of mobilising the colonial Afrikaners. Foremost in the mind of the participants was the improvement and fighting spirit of the Boer leadership and the men under their command.[158] They decided to launch an operation in January or February 1901, targeting for destruction the mines and mining property on the Witwatersrand. Smuts devotes much time to the role of the capitalist mining magnates in his South African War memoirs. He stresses the military soundness of mine destruction and barely conceals his contempt for the role the mining magnates played in the Jameson Raid and in enticing the British to act against the republics.[159] He is often at pains in his memoir to demonstrate that the Boers possessed a plan of action in the latter part of the war and that they did not just wander across the veld aimlessly. However great his intent, the Boer plans came to nought when faced with their huge numerical disparity, professional military force and the unlimited resources the British deployed.[160]

Smuts, while operating in the Magaliesburg region, undertook military tasks whenever the opportunity arose and assumed command on De la Rey's visits to other fronts. He made acquaintance with and befriended Christiaan Beyers (1869–1914)[161] and Christiaan de Wet (1854–1922).[162] He was a natural leader and soldier and in Kruger's words, "Although scarcely 30 years of age, and without the slightest previous experience of military affairs, he developed in the latter phases of the war, into a most brilliant general, so that he added to his position as State Attorney that of an [Assistant Commandant-General] of the South African Republic."[163] Smuts, on his suggestion to De la Rey, was given the command of the south-western districts. His task was welding disparate commando units roaming the countryside into one effective force and restoring discipline and efficiency much neglected by their respective commandants.[164] Smuts made good use of his administrative skills in overhauling his new command, the Potchefstroom Commando.[165] His first action was a success when he stormed the British camp at Modderfontein on 30 January 1901 and beat off a determined counterattack, inflicting heavy casualties and taking over 200 prisoners together with a sizeable booty.[166]

Despite inflicting tactical successes with their raiding strategy, the Boers found operational conditions in the Transvaal and the Orange Free State increasingly untenable. The persisting British strategy combined with a scorched-earth policy presented ever-increasing logistical challenges. Smuts cast his eyes to the richer prospects of raiding the Cape and Natal.[167] The signs that the Cape Afrikaners were growing weary with the protracted war encouraged the political Smuts, while the military and expansionist Smuts was keen to take the war to the British colonies, not only for the restoration of the republics but for the vision of a united South Africa under control of the Afrikaners.[168] A perfect political storm was brewing comprising Cape Afrikaner uneasiness, British public and political opinion (which was not unsympathetic to the Boer suffering), and increasing foreign displeasure at the effects of British tactics on civilians.[169] Sound military and logistic opportunities in an unscathed Cape awaited a daring and resourceful commander.[170]

The Waterval *Krygsraad*, or council of war, was held on 20 June 1901 (attended by Smuts)[171] on whether to continue with the war or to negotiate peace terms. It was decided to send Botha into Natal and Smuts into the Cape Midlands. Interestingly, the decision was the exception in that both the Republican governments seldom acted in military concert as they lacked a supreme command.[172] Smuts junior states that his father, far more than other Boer leaders, always considered the Cape as paramount to the Boer cause. He placed the failure to rouse Cape Afrikaners to the cause on the same level as poor military decisions in the first part of the war. Smuts junior has no hesitation in describing Smuts's foray into the "unscorched" Cape at the head of 362 hand-picked men as the most "daring" and "brilliant" of the war.[173] Smuts envisaged that the excursion into the Cape would be a joint venture between him and Beyers, each commanding 500 burghers who, moving separately, would fight in unison. His discovery that Botha recommended Beyers as commander of the expedition with Smuts under his instructions met with his strenuous objection. He pleaded that he did not deserve a placement under Beyers due to his questionable tactics.[174] Smuts respected Beyers's military skills, but his disdain is apparent in describing his methods in his memoirs as a "unique combination of praying and fighting".[175] Smuts was equally vociferous when he wrote to Botha saying that as the state attorney he could not be placed under the orders of any general as he was responsible to the government and, as a military officer, to De la Rey.[176] However, it was to N.J. de Wet, military secretary to Botha, that Smuts opened up and revealed the true nature of his objection, describing with barely concealed disdain Beyers's dubious "war policy" and "wonderful combination of praying and looting".[177] These early encounters set the tone for Smuts's later relationship with Beyers.

Smuts, where De Wet failed in an earlier attempt, succeeded in penetrating the Cape with his handpicked men.[178] Smuts junior gives an account of his father's journey of 3,200 kilometres, which tied up 35,000 British troops and eventually attracted 3,000–4,000 men to his command. The impressive tactical successes enjoyed by Smuts, with a £1,000 price on his head, were testament to the aggressive and offensively minded raiding strategy adopted by the Boers. The younger, more disciplined, innovative and energetic leadership opened new possibilities for the Boers but was eventually unable to deliver the promise Smuts dearly hoped for throughout the war.[179] By the time he attended the Vereeniging Conference, he had realised that there was little hope left for the prolongation of the war.[180]

Historians are apt to cite the minuscule size of Smuts's force as proof of his inexperience in commanding large forces and his unsuitability when given overall command of the British forces in German East Africa in the First World War.[181] During the South African War, Smuts gained extensive experience at the operational and tactical levels of war—all this while operating under extreme geographic and logistical conditions against a numerically superior enemy. He was involved at the lowest and highest levels of action, more so than most of the men who later came to criticise his military acumen in the First World War.[182] He showed excellent acumen at the strategic level with his plan at the outset of the war to capture Durban and deny the port to the British. His invasion of the Cape in the guerrilla phase showed a brilliant political and strategic grasp. That he commanded relatively few men is not an indication of his lack of operational ability. His bold excursion into the Cape showed a keen grasp at the operational possibilities within a raiding strategy. De Wet appointed Smuts to command all the Orange Free State forces in the Cape in February 1902, as a testament to his ability as a general.[183] The last words on Smuts's military ability come from his most prominent critic, Armstrong, barely able to disguise his obvious contempt, yet showing an unwitting, albeit grudging, respect.

> Almost at once he showed a remarkable ability as a raider. He was as physically brave as he had been insolently brave before Kruger and the old men in Pretoria. He was as crafty and as full of ruses in attacking isolated detachments of English troops as he had been in fooling Conyngham Greene and wasting time.[184]

An unlikely source attesting to Smuts's bravery was P.J. du Toit, who kept a diary and later became a National Scout. He relates an incident where General de la Rey attacked a British convoy at Elandsdrift with some success and Smuts "showed distinguished bravery" in charging cannon to within "70 yards".[185] Smuts added to his already formidable character and considerable academic record, his experience of government and a keen sense of the political astuteness. The South African War added yet a further dimension with the provision of an excellent, practical, military education coupled with actual combat experience. The art of manoeuvre and the skilful practice of a raiding strategy became ingrained in his makeup. He was able to meld the grand strategic art to the low-level tactics of the battlefield. Not many men in history have acquired and mastered these different skills by the age of thirty-one.

The Peace Treaty of Vereeniging

The skill and dogged perseverance which Smuts and his compatriots displayed in the last phase of the war was insufficient to tip the balance in their favour. Victory slipped from their grasp, and the price paid for continuing the battle became too high. The Boers' plight was desperate, and as the third winter of the war approached, they would have to endure another season of diminishing supplies. Each day their numbers dwindled and those of the National Scouts increased. The areas of operation became smaller as the British extended the blockhouse system.[186] It was time for peace, and here too Smuts was to play a prominent role.

Peace initiatives were not something new during the war—the first being attempted in March 1900. After that, both sides led initiatives at various times, including an offer of £10,000 each to De la Rey and Botha if they surrendered. Botha met with Herbert Kitchener (1860–1916) on 22 February 1901 at Middelburg in the Transvaal, and both men left the meeting having failed to secure peace but gained mutual respect. Botha's relationship with Kitchener grew after the war to the extent that he invited Kitchener to advise on the Union's military affairs. Peace overtures failed because the Boers insisted on independence, while the British were bent on annexation. Furthermore, the Boers were dead set against any extension of the Cape franchise for blacks and coloureds in the Transvaal and Orange Free State. The fate of the Cape rebels was also a significant area of concern for the Boers who had encouraged them to join the Boer cause. With no peace agreement, the war dragged on for another 14 months with the Boers eventually obtaining much of what they demanded at Middelburg.[187]

Peace talks were reconvened when 60 Boer delegates and members of both Republican governments met in Vereeniging in April 1902. London agreed to grant the former republics early autonomy within the Empire, and the Cape rebels would be treated leniently with only suffering disenfranchisement. The participants postponed the question of black and coloured enfranchisement. The Boer pro-war lobby opposed these generous terms, leaving the pacifists to dismantle their objections until they all agreed to peace.[188] Smuts and General James Barry Munnik Hertzog (1866–1942)[189]—both lawyers educated at Victoria College—were instrumental in removing initial stumbling blocks by defining the status of delegates as plenipotentiaries who could vote in respect of their opinions without having to refer back to their constituents.[190] Smuts was keen to negotiate a peace with the best possible terms before the British crushed the Boers and forced unconditional surrender on them. He could see that although they had avoided complete defeat and it was possible to continue the war, to do so was tantamount to political suicide. Finally,

Smuts joined a committee consisting of Botha, Hertzog, De Wet and De la Rey representing the Boers in the Vereeniging negotiations.[191]

Smuts met his old adversary, Milner, at the conference, and the Englishman was just as immovable and intransigent as he had been at the Bloemfontein conference. However, this time Smuts found an unlikely ally in Kitchener, who weary of the war, held more pragmatic opinions than Milner regarding the way forward.[192] Where Kitchener favoured conciliation Milner demanded unconditional surrender.[193] Smuts was unable to move Milner despite strenuous arguments that the Boer proposals were not in conflict with the British ones laid down in Middelburg. Milner, proof against Smuts's ingenuity, was unwilling to concede at the table what the British had painstakingly won on the battlefield. Smuts failed to gain traction via an informal meeting with Milner and Kitchener on further concessions.[194] The turning point was provided by Kitchener who pulled Smuts aside and gave assurances that a new British Liberal government was in the offing two years hence, and once they gained power, they would grant a constitution for South Africa.[195]

Smuts was willing to accept a short-term disadvantage for the prospect of a united South Africa within the Empire. Most of his peers lacked his clarity of vision, and the peacemakers had a hard time convincing the *Bittereinders* in accepting the peace terms.[196] Smuts concluded that although the prospect of continuing at the military level existed, the continued suffering of Boer civilians in the concentration camps was unsustainable. The promised amnesty for the Cape rebels also gave the impetus for ending the war.[197] Smuts, although winning few concessions in the process, played an essential role in negotiating an acceptable formula and drafting the final agreement.[198] Much to Milner's later regret was clause 8 of the treaty which delayed the question of the black franchise to when the British would grant self-government. Thus, the participants, who successfully settled the dispute between the white races, sowed the seeds of future race conflict between black and white.[199] Smuts, even if he had possessed the vision or the inclination, was unable or unwilling to include any clauses which would cater to black political aspirations. On 30 May 1902, the terms of surrender, "one of the strangest documents in history" according to Milner, were signed.[200]

Winning the Peace and the Attainment of Self-government, 1902–1906

The Boers sacrificed their republics on the altar for peace and settled on much the same terms as the British offered soon after they had surrendered their capital in June 1900. However, Smuts had benefitted from extending the war as he had grown in political and military stature. His exploits in the guerrilla phase of the war and his high profile at the peace conference boosted his political prominence. The war had gifted him the opportunity to be a soldier, and under the guidance of

De la Rey, he had become a keen and spirited proponent of manoeuvre warfare. He practised this with much skill, dexterity, and bravery. He built enduring links with the younger Boer leaders, especially Botha, and with them, he forged a new path toward a united South Africa. He began the war as the talented attorney, very much in the background. He ended the war recognised by the Boers as a leader, and by the British, as a formidable opponent and a possible future ally. He was able to cast himself in the role of the honourable opponent instead of a bitter enemy, which stood him in good political stead, and paved the way for his political future.

The implacable Milner had battled and bested Smuts on two previous occasions at Bloemfontein and Vereeniging. As peace broke out, they squared up for a final battle. Milner took over the two defeated Boer Republics and administered them as occupied territory. He gathered a group of young British officials and administrators whom he had recruited during the South African War. These young administrators, famously known as 'Milner's Kindergarten', busied themselves with reconstructing and invigorating the devastated Boer territories.[201] Milner's grand design consisted of rapidly defeating the Boers in a short sharp war with minimal damage to the infrastructure (here he failed as the war was protracted and devastating) and thereafter, instituting a gigantic exercise in physical and social engineering. Milner hoped to attract thousands of British immigrants to the Transvaal, thus creating a sizeable English majority as a counterpoise to the demographic dominance the Afrikaners enjoyed in the Cape. A necessary part of Milner's plan for federation and anglicisation was to abrogate the power of the Bond in the Cape by suspending the constitution there and manning the Executive with loyalists. A combination of Chamberlain's caution, Gordon Sprigg's (1830–1913)[202] desperate clinging to power, and Rhodes's untimely death, conspired against Milner and the Cape Parliament was returned with Sprigg at its head with the aid of the Bond. The Cape remained the Achille's heel of Milner's grand design even though Leander Starr Jameson (1853–1917) and the Progressives in 1904 ousted Sprigg and the Bond.[203]

Armstrong wrote that Smuts emerged from the aftermath of the war as a nervous, resentful, bitter and a rather reclusive man, who sank into depression for lack of purpose. He credits Botha for shaking Smuts out of his dark, sombre mood and restoring his shattered confidence.[204] Hancock paints a more believable picture of a man fully in control of his destiny and determined to "start afresh, working along the lines opened by the new conditions".[205] Smuts took advantage of his lack of office in the immediate wake of the war to organise his matters and acquire several properties, all enabled by the many lucrative briefs he received.[206] Many Boer returnees were vehemently against the new order of things, but instead of vocal or open defiance, they showed their displeasure indirectly.[207] The immediate aftermath of the war found the Boers preoccupied with rebuilding their personal lives and restoring their property.[208]

The first challenges to Milner's plans came from Uitlanders who found his administration heavy-handed and expensive. They resented the Kindergarten filling the prime positions of authority rather than the 'spoils of war' being shared. The quest for representative government began to gather momentum in these former jingo, capitalist, Uitlander circles. Despite steady and growing opposition, Milner set about building railways, establishing municipalities, launching a forestry department, forming the Rand Water Board and a native commission to coordinate policy, and coordinating the resources of the former republics.[209] Despite Milner's best efforts and the Kindergarten's boundless energy, the economy remained flaccid, and the expected and needed immigration of English-speakers never materialised. Milner stood, caught between rampant dissatisfaction of delaying federation—or bringing it about prematurely before achieving British dominance and allowing South Africa to fall under Boer dominance.[210]

The next issue to rock the Kindergarten plans was 'Chinese slavery'. Milner proposed indentured Chinese labour to overcome the shortage of black labour on the mines. His expedient approach to a labour problem caused havoc in British politics and divided the British in the Transvaal, allowing Smuts and Botha to re-enter politics. Hancock asserts that Smuts was at the centre of the Boer attack.[211] He used the occasion of Chamberlain's visit to South Africa on 8 January 1903 to head a deputation of 100 leading Boers to raise the issue of amnesty for the Cape rebels where he addressed Chamberlain, raising issues of concern.[212] Although Chamberlain steadfastly refused to re-open the Treaty of Vereeniging or negotiate beyond its terms, these encounters with British authority raised his status among Boers and British.[213] Smuts was firmly in the centre of the politics surrounding Milner's rule, and Hancock states that "not a single memorandum or a letter of any political importance to which Botha put his signature [...] did not originate in draft by Smuts".[214]

In 1903, Milner attempted to garner Boer support for his programme and offered De la Rey, Botha and Smuts seats on the Legislative Council and advisory body to the Executive Council crewed with Milner acolytes.[215] Shrewdly, the offer was rejected in the knowledge that collaboration with the benevolent autocracy of Milner would devalue their political standing with the people, the *Volk*.[216] Milner took steps to install English as the primary medium of communication. He imported 300 teachers from England to wean Boer children from their mother tongue, and he believed that he could win over the Boers to British culture with modernisation, education, efficient administration and developing the economy. The Boers were not prepared to cooperate in the extinction of their language and continued to advocate for its equal status in South Africa.

Smuts and Botha were astute with their use of the 'Chinese Affair' to build bridges with the Transvaal British and undermine their support for the Kindergarten.[217] Thus began a quest for the steady erosion of support for Milner both at home and abroad.

Smuts positioned Emily Hobhouse (1860–1926) to propagate the Boer version of the state of the Transvaal in the British press. Hobhouse paints a role for Smuts as the lone spokesman for the Afrikaner cause:

> Perhaps nature intended you for a philosopher rather than a fighter, but circumstances made you that … Perhaps you hardly realise that you are the only Afrikander [. . .] who has the power of expressing on paper the sentiments, moral and political, of your people. For the most part the Afrikander people are still dumb, only able to express themselves in deeds, and one longs for one of them to speak and make England and the world know what they think and feel.[218]

No holds were barred when condemning Chamberlain's visit to South Africa and the shortcomings of Milner's government in the Transvaal.[219] Smuts conducted Boer politics outside of Milner's government to the extent of communicating with the Secretary of State directly, thereby delivering criticism without official responsibility.[220]

The Boer trio gave Milner sufficient rope to perform the increasingly unpopular duties of government while they distanced themselves and made inroads into Milner's support base, keeping Boer grievances under the yoke of the British government. Smuts and Botha used the time to organise politically and when they were ready, courteously informed Milner that they would be holding a series of political meetings.[221] Milner and Alfred Lyttelton, the Colonial Secretary, attempted to retrieve their deteriorating political power and offered the Boers a watered-down or transitional form of representation that fell short of responsible government in 1904.[222] It was an effort to buy time to gain a numerical advantage through immigration to South Africa or win over enough Afrikaners to the British cause. Milner recognised that Smuts and Botha were at the head of a new political movement which aimed at the "keeping up of [political] discontent with the present form of government" and, at a later date, agitating for responsible government.[223] Smuts's dream of a united and Greater South Africa was never far from his mind, and he eagerly waited for the Liberals to get into power which he saw as a chance to push in the direction of federation.[224]

The formal inauguration of the Het Volk (The People) Transvaal political party followed in January 1905, under the leadership of Louis Botha and his deputy, Jan Smuts. Smuts was also building bridges with Merriman in the Cape, and the two kept up a friendly correspondence.[225] The details of the Lyttelton constitution were published at the end of March 1905 which provided for representative and not responsible government and never took effect before the Unionist government fell at the end of 1905.[226] Smuts and Botha devoted themselves to the introduction of full self-government in its wake. In February 1906, the new British Liberal cabinet announced its decision to grant self-government to the Transvaal colony. Het Volk graduated from a political association to a political party only after the establishment of self-government by letters patent on 6 December 1906.[227]

The modus operandi of Het Volk was one of conciliation which was not born of philanthropy but of necessity in securing enough votes amongst the Afrikaners but also among sympathetic Englishmen. In 1905, Botha and Smuts feared that the British in the Transvaal would outnumber the Afrikaners and they set about securing the goodwill of both.[228] They vigorously promoted Boer unity by integrating the 'hands-uppers' and National Scouts back into the ranks of the *Volk* and exploited the fissures in the Transvaal English by making concessions that would win some over. Smuts could exploit the issue of Chinese labour in attracting the English labour class to the cause. The English working class saw the import of Chinese labour as a direct threat to their job security while the Afrikaner saw it as an unnecessary complication to the already complicated racial issues in the Transvaal. Het Volk opened its membership to disaffected Englishmen with success.[229] With a keen eye for strategy, Smuts and Botha gave assurances that a united South Africa would remain permanently within the British Empire.[230]

Milner's retirement as High Commissioner on 31 March 1905 ended his grand scheme of a transformation of the Transvaal into an English outpost. Botha and Smuts ensured the Boer organisation was better than ever before. When Lord Selborne succeeded Milner in 1906, Smuts wrote a most generous letter to his former arch-enemy, Milner, on his departure for London.

> Will you allow me to wish you 'Bon Voyage' now that you are leaving South Africa forever? I am afraid that you have not liked us; but I cherish the hope that, as our memories grow mellower and the nobler features of our respective ideals become clearer, shall more and more appreciate the contribution of each to the formation of that happier South Africa which is surely coming, and judge more kindly of each other. [...] History writes the word 'Reconciliation' over all her quarrels.[231]

Hancock finds the letter to Milner as nothing less than astonishing. He sees it as the magnanimous act of a man towards his defeated foe and describes his way with enemies as unusual.[232] Milner failed in achieving his grand design when he overestimated the prowess of the British army to defeat the resolute Boers quickly and decisively.[233] These words to Milner reveal Smuts's commitment to a united South Africa and a recognition that both men were fighting for the same ideal but from different sides. Although Smuts shared the same ideals as Milner and Rhodes, he abhorred their quest for British dominance.

> I was fighting for a United South Africa, in which there would be the greatest possible freedom, but from which the disturbing influence of Downing Street would have been finally eliminated. I was not fighting for 'Dutch' supremacy or predominance over English Afrikanders.[234]

The Liberals in the United Kingdom ushered in a more amenable political dispensation in December 1905 when they achieved office. Smuts took the opportunity to visit England and press for self-government in a bold and audacious move. He produced a document that acknowledged the annexation of the former Boer

Republics but appealed for self-government for a defeated foe.[235] Smuts was effectively asking for the restoration of the country to the Boers less than five years after their total defeat, but in his memorandum to the Colonial Office, he was at pains to demonstrate that the Boers would acquire only 23 of the 50 available seats.[236]

Smuts stands accused of being oblivious to the plight of the blacks at various times in his long political career. Those seeking to protect his legacy insist that he be judged by the standards of his times and his peers. Merriman was quick to point out that Smuts's memorandum was devoid of any ideas for the political aspirations of the black majority.[237] Smuts, replying to Merriman, reveals the key to his thoughts on black political aspirations.

> I sympathise profoundly with the Native races of South Africa whose land it was long before we came here to force a policy of dispossession on them. And it ought to be a policy of all parties to do justice to the natives and to take all wise and prudent measure for their civilisation and improvement. But I don't believe in politics for them. [...] I would therefore not give them the franchise [...] When I consider the political future of the Natives in South Africa I must say that I look into the shadows and darkness; and then I feel inclined to shift the intolerable burden of solving that sphinx problem to the ampler shoulders and stronger brains of the future.[238]

Therefore, Smuts adopted a non-policy toward black political aspirations which even judged by the standard of the time seemed short-sighted and placed an unnecessary burden on future generations. Merriman with much foresight told Smuts, "Do not flatter yourself that you can push this question off. The very existence of our race in this country depends on our native policy."[239]

Although his requests seemingly fell on deaf ears when he met with members of the British Cabinet, Smuts was able to pursue Campbell-Bannerman, the newly elected Liberal Prime Minister, with better results. He offered Boer friendship in return for recognising Boer aspirations for equality and freedom under British rule. Bannerman cajoled to magnanimity, committed his country, despite his colleagues' doubts, to a position of trust with the Boers.[240] Smuts, regarded with suspicion as the most dangerous of Boer leaders by the British, accomplished a considerable feat.[241]

Het Volk's election manifesto and their programme was the work of Smuts and Frans Engelenburg (1863–1938), the editor of the *Volkstem* newspaper. They emphasised cooperation between the white races and proposals on unification. Smuts aimed to create an organisation sufficiently broad to appeal to 'British' voters in the Transvaal. Smuts and Botha struck a delicate political balance in securing self-government and their compromise cost support amongst the Afrikaner nationalists. They accommodated the British while suppressing republican leanings and Afrikaner interests began to take a back seat. The Colonial Office characterised Het Volk as a weapon in the hands of an organisation "so constituted as to coerce rather than represent Boer opinion". The stance of conciliation led to a surprise Het Volk victory in the Transvaal, winning 37 of the 69 seats at the polls on 20 February 1907. Smuts proved his commitment to conciliations which included a member of the opposition in his ministry and a minimum of retrenchments of British officials in the civil service[242]

Het Volk owed much of its spirit and constitution to the Afrikaner Bond. The statutes of Het Volk were primarily the work of Smuts who, with his father, were former members of the Bond. However, Het Volk was not a mere copy of the Bond as Smuts simplified and added to the constitution as he saw fit. There is little doubt that all power was vested in Botha and Smuts and those that opposed them from time to time, the most prominent being Beyers, enjoyed insufficient prestige to do so effectively. Beyers caused Botha some embarrassment in 1905 with his outspoken attacks on the Lyttelton constitution. He was reined in during the 1906/7 election campaign, and then, omitted from Botha's Cabinet and sent to the wilderness by being made speaker of the assembly. The party secured its mouthpiece, the *Volkstem*, under the editorship of Engelenburg. The Transvaal held the first election for responsible government in 1907 where the Boers obtained a large majority. Botha, with Smuts as his Colonial Secretary and Minister of Education, formed a government while Abraham Fischer (1850–1913) became Prime Minister with a substantial Boer majority in the Orange River Colony. A year passed that saw the Bond win a sweeping victory in the Cape. Except for Natal, the volte-face was complete.[243]

The Union of South Africa: A Vehicle for Smuts's Expansionism, 1910

Smuts harboured a belief, emanating from and bolstered by his holistic philosophy, in the expansion of South Africa within the Empire; and incorporating the British territories to the west, east and north of South Africa.[244] The South African War interrupted these dreams for the duration, but after that, and after reconciling with the British, he embraced the concept of a Greater South Africa within the British Empire with renewed vigour. Smuts again revealed his interest in Portuguese East Africa (Mozambique) early on in 1907 when he encouraged Boers to make inquiries regarding land settlements in the Beira area. In 1908 he was thought to have promoted a trek into southern Mozambique to establish an Afrikaner presence as a pretext for a subsequent takeover.[245]

The Portuguese were alert to Smuts's overt designs on their East African territory, and their jumpiness was apparent in their diplomacy and media. An agent for 500 families from Harrismith, Bethlehem, and Vrede called upon Colonel A.J. Arnold, a British officer in the service of the Portuguese Chartered Company at Beira, in May 1908, stating their interest in settling in the Portuguese East African highlands. A Mozambican newspaper article in 1909 spoke of a proposed assault by 400 Boers on the port of Lourenço Marques in Delagoa Bay.[246] The article, combined with Smuts's visit to the region, served as reliable indicators of the Boer intent to settle and eventually establish themselves in the area. In a letter which demonstrated the congruency and rivalry between British imperialism and Smuts's sub-imperialist ambitions, Arnold encouraged the British to beat the "Dutch" to the gun and move on Portuguese territory without delay. He cites Portugal's miserable financial and political plight as offering that "never in the past nine years has the situation been more favourable to a change of flag".[247]

Sir Edward Grey (1862–1933), the British foreign secretary (1905–1916), stated in 1908 "the Union of South Africa will never rest so long as she [Portugal] has Delagoa Bay".[248] Lord Herbert John Gladstone (1854–1930) the first governor-general of (the Union of) South Africa (1910–1914) identified Smuts as one of the prime motivators behind any attempted Mozambican land grab. He compared the idea to "a Jameson raid on a larger and more effective scale".[249] Botha too was at the forefront of an effort by the Transvaal government in 1908 to obtain a lease for a fixed term of years for the harbour and railway to Lourenço Marques. Botha busied himself negotiating a lease on Lourenço Marques on behalf of the Transvaal while simultaneously engaging with participants of the National Convention. He did so despite the risk of raising the ire of the other participants who were negotiating a "closer union".[250]

Smuts was the driving force behind the formation of the Union in 1910. Keith Hancock describes Smuts as "preeminent" amongst the many men who worked together to construct the Union of South Africa. His strategy and tactics dominated the entire process.[251] Soon after its birth, he cast his eyes on the territories within and to the north of its borders. The Union inherited all the expansionist conceptions and interest in territories from the previous era, dominated by Rhodes, Kruger and the British Empire.[252] The first phase of his intended expansion was the acquisition of the High Commission Territories (HCT) consisting of Bechuanaland, Basutoland, and Swaziland and then the territory of Southern Rhodesia. After that, his ambitions stretched farther north even beyond the Cunene (modern-day Kunene) and the Zambezi rivers.[253] His territorial appetite also included the long-coveted Delagoa Bay.

From the British imperialist point of view, the Treaty of Vereeniging signed on 31 May 1902 enabled the British to consolidate their interests in southern Africa. A further benefit of the treaty was that it allowed the British to gain control of the region without having to expend enormous amounts of blood and resources, as previously done.[254] The Union presented an opportunity for the defeated Afrikaner to achieve self-government and partial control over their future aspirations without having to fight a war. For English-speaking South Africans, the Union provided stability, where Afrikaners and Englishman could join in a joint endeavour, to exploit the abundant natural resources of the country and build an economic future and further the aims of the British Empire in Africa as a civilising force. Lord Selborne, one of the architects of a united South Africa, envisaged something more in what he called 'National Expansion'. He saw the South African situation as similar to the American and Canadian experience where union allowed them to control and develop their vast hinterlands. He urged South Africans to look north to the Zambezi and gain control of Southern Rhodesia. He pointed out the danger of the "unwisdom [sic] of allowing the political organisation of the northern countries to take place in utter independence of the community already established to the south".[255] Selborne unequivocally set the expansionist tone behind the formation of the Union and lit the path to territorial acquisition for Smuts and Botha.

The former enemies held a National Convention in 1908 in a spirit of conciliation and a rare meeting of minds to formulate a common goal. Smuts played a huge role in placating key players such as the sceptical Merriman. It was he, together with Merriman, who set the tone for the new constitution and both agreed they wanted it unitary and flexible, not federalist.[256] The parties negotiated the terms and constitution of a governmental, together with legislative, and economic union. The British government ratified these proposals, and they became the South Africa Act on 20 September 1909, leading to the establishment of the Union of South Africa on 31 May 1910, with Louis Botha as its first Prime Minister. Importantly, the Act made provision for the incorporation of Rhodesia as a fifth province and the eventual inclusion of the HCT. The black inhabitants of all three HCT preferred exclusion from the proposed Union in 1909. The British government assured them that although they made provision for possible eventual transfer in the South Africa Act 1909, such transfer was subject to certain conditions designed for the protection of 'native' rights and interests. Once again, in a similar fashion to the Vereeniging Peace Treaty, the question of the black franchise was deferred, arguably an essential reason for the war in the first place. Article 8 of the treaty signed at Vereeniging provided that: "The question of granting franchises to natives will not be decided until after the introduction of self-government".

The initial exclusion of the HCT from the Union also served to provide an imperial balance/counter-balance against the newfound independence of the Union.[257] The British did not intend for the retention of imperial responsibility for Rhodesia, Nyasaland, and the HCT to be a permanent arrangement. The HCT became a lever which the British government could use to press the Union to accept the British policy of black enfranchisement.[258] Thus the two issues, incorporation of the HCT and the extension of the 'Native' franchise, now became interdependent. London and Pretoria expressly regarded the borders of the newly formed Union as provisional.[259] Botha, the Union Prime Minister proclaimed in 1913 that "the Union would never be complete before Rhodesia and all the protectorates were included".[260] The final borders of the Union were neither defined nor limited, providing an elucidating glimpse into the underlying expansionist intention of the new-born Union.

The South Africa Act failed black South Africans, in that although it retained and entrenched the liberal Cape qualified franchise system of the Cape Colony; it failed to extend this system of a multiracial franchise to the rest of South Africa. 'Native Affairs' was passed into the hands of the national government and thus

Britain effectively sidestepped her responsibility to the black population of South Africa.[261] The Peace Treaty of Vereeniging, the National Convention, and the South Africa Act, leading to Union marked a remarkable period of conciliation between Englishman and Afrikaner. The failure to immediately incorporate the HCT in the Union's formation was due to British wariness of South African attitudes and 'native policies' as they stood in 1908.[262] There was no provision for the extension of the Cape 'native' franchise, although the South Africa Act entrenched it. Merriman was the champion of the limited franchise. Smuts had to walk the tightrope of British expectations in this regard and the Transvaalers' refusal to grant a limited franchise to blacks.[263]

The new dispensation left blacks outside the Cape with no vote and no vehicle to cater to their political aspirations. It was left to the Union to formulate some type of acceptable 'native policy' and the transfer of the HCT would be contingent on that process. The British deliberately left the HCT out of the Union in 1910 to encourage the new South African government to adopt a "more acceptable native policy". Instead, the opposite happened as successive nationalists rolled back the Cape franchise and the Union inevitably and inexorably removed blacks from the voters' rolls in 1936. Under the Representation of Natives Act, 1936, three white members represented black voters in the Cape province, but eventually, these too were abolished.[264] Present-day democratic South Africa would have drawn her borders far farther northward had the formation of the Union stimulated inclusiveness towards all the population groups.[265]

CHAPTER 2

South Africa's Entry into the First World War, 1910–1914

The formation of the Union was the culmination of an arduous journey for Jan Smuts. At its heart was the reconciliation of the two white nations who together would form a common South African identity in a united South Africa under the British flag. Integral to the Union was the provision for its future expansion whereby it would become the central vehicle for British interests in southern Africa. However, Smuts's dream of an unfettered expansion began to unravel even before the formation of the Union in 1910. The British were reluctant to hand over the High Commission Territories until they were satisfied that the Union catered for black political aspirations. Heated by Smuts's conciliation policy, Afrikaner nationalism bubbled below the surface and finally boiled over with the declaration of war in Europe in 1914. Political fissures did little to stop Smuts from casting an eye at territorial expansion. However, one should contextualise South Africa's entry into war within Smut's broader war aims.[1] (See Map 2.1)

An opportunity occurred in 1910/11 elevating Smuts's hopes of acquiring Delagoa Bay. The significant republican movement in the Portuguese colony of Mozambique, coupled with rumours of a possible annexation of the area by the newly formed Union, fuelled unrest among the local white Portuguese population. A local revolt leading to the declaration of an autonomous state became a distinct possibility.[2] The Governor-General of Mozambique, Alfredo Augusto Freire de Andrade (1859–1929), suggested the possibility of the colony joining the South African federation.[3] The Portuguese October 1910 Revolution caused significant instability in the Portuguese African colonies.[4] Riots broke out in Lourenço Marques on 21 February 1911, causing much alarm to the British Consul, Reginald Maugham, who reported to Gladstone the regime's apparent inability to quell the disturbances and thus endangering British interests.[5] A British ship, the *Forte*, loitered near the port of Lourenço Marques ostensibly to protect British citizens and assets if the need arose.[6]

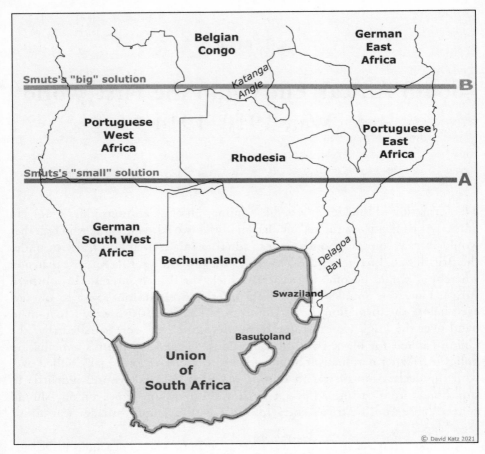

Map 2.1. Smuts and his vision for a Greater South Africa[7]

It was possible that because of the fragile political climate in Portugal, Mozambique would be tempted to declare its independence and either throw in its lot with South Africa by joining the Union or be subjected to land grabs by Germany and Rhodesia.[8] Smuts, with a well-practised eye for opportunity, inserted himself into the crisis. It seemed that Maugham, against protocol, had directly informed Smuts and kept him abreast of the situation, much to the consternation of the British. Gladstone was confident that Smuts and Louis Botha would not hesitate to intervene militarily should there be an outbreak of severe disorder. Maugham's words to Smuts left little to the imagination as to the opportunities that the unrest in Mozambique presented. "It seems to me that the present and immediate future may hold out possibility of consolidation of British interests here" and again "Consider favourable opportunity to obtain more control over Delagoa Bay Railway".[9] Botha even raised the bogey of a German occupation regarding the secret German–British Treaty of 1898 and sought assurances that this would not happen.[10]

Britain feared that unsanctioned action by the Union government, who were champing at the bit to intervene, would unsettle the delicate political balance in the region and Europe. Gladstone reported that Botha and Smuts felt, "public feeling would require the forcible occupation of Lourenço Marques".[11] British caution prevented the Union from occupying Portuguese territory on the pretext that it would prompt Germany to enact the 1898 agreement. Smuts was informed of the contents of the secret Anglo-German convention to dissuade him from any "police action".[12] In the event, cool heads prevailed, the Portuguese authorities restored order, and the Union took no action, much to the relief of the British.[13]

The restoration of relative political stability in the area did not deter Smuts for long. Reports showed him to have declared at a banquet in October 1913, attended by the Acting Governor-General of Mozambique, Augusto Ferreira dos Santos, that "the day was not far distant when most, if not all, of the country of Africa south of the equator would be in the Union of South Africa". Gladstone obliged Smuts to "clarify" his intent to allay Portuguese (if not Belgium and German) sensitivities.[14] Smuts attempted to make the best of the situation in December 1914 when the Portuguese Consul-General secretly approached him seeking a loan of £500,000 to finance Portuguese operations against German South West Africa (GSWA) and elsewhere. Smuts saw this request as an opportunity to strengthen the Union's position regarding Delagoa Bay. It was left to the British to quash his enthusiasm as they correctly saw that it would be nearly impossible to enforce the repayment of the loan in case of default, or practically seize Delagoa Bay as compensation.[15]

Botha was not far behind Smuts in his desire for land and declared in a speech delivered in Nylstroom in the Transvaal on 1 November 1913 that the Union was more than an interested spectator as to the events taking place in Rhodesia and "this greatest object of ours—to get a united South Africa as far north as possible".[16]

> You will remember even when the time when our Union was being established I stated repeatedly that in my opinion the Union would never be complete until Rhodesia and all the Protectorates had been included. In regard to the Protectorates … Special arrangements were entered into. In regard to Rhodesia, however, no such agreement exists.[17]

Botha was most insistent on including Swaziland, and as early as 1906 he threatened that his party, Het Volk, would take no part in the institution if the British separated Swaziland from the Transvaal.[18] The desire for Swazi territory was not new and stretched back to the old Boer South African Republic (ZAR). In 1897 Smuts was behind moves to swap Swazi territory with the Portuguese and in turn gain access to the sea.[19] As premier of the Transvaal in 1909, he again urged for the transfer of

Swaziland. He was said to be "obsessed" with the idea of Rhodesia at the time of the National Convention in 1908/9.[20] Both Smuts and Botha reported that they intended, "to stand in the shoes of the Company as soon as they can get them".[21] Again in 1911, Botha, as Prime Minister of the Union, insisted on the incorporation of Swaziland.[22] Botha wrote a letter to Gladstone in 1913 expressing his uneasiness at the representations made by the Chartered Company[23] in respect of incorporation of Bechuanaland into Rhodesia. Botha took the opportunity to lodge an objection and to remind Gladstone of the expectation that all the protectorates would be transferred to the Union sooner or later. Using this incident as ammunition, Botha pressed for the immediate transfer of Swaziland and Bechuanaland—a claim rejected out of hand by the British.[24]

Territorial expansion aside, Smuts and Botha presided over the birth pains of a new country struggling to become a united nation. The political space was a three-way contest between Afrikaners, the English, and the blacks.[25] The period between the formation of the Union and the First World War is a story of a struggle for the soul of the white man and the measures taken to mitigate the black man's overwhelming numerical superiority. The formation of the Union did not silence strong Afrikaner sentiments toward language equality nor those who sought distance from the United Kingdom even in the form of a republic. It did not help Smuts's cause that he had acquired a certain notoriety for political deviousness even among those who acknowledged his brilliance such as John X. Merriman:

> If our friend John [sic] Smuts was only as full of high principles as he is of brains! He is the man who has most outlook, but often saddens me by his infernal shiftiness. It is such a pity, for he has more brains than all of the Government put together—but whether it is ambition of not I do not know—somehow or another his character does not keep pace with his ability [...].[26]

Conciliation represented the hope of melding the English and Afrikaners into a single nation, but it came at the cost of steadily eroding Afrikaner support. Initiatives allowing blacks access to rudimentary political rights would alienate large sections of the white population. Smuts and Botha walked a political tightrope which swung in the wind of growing Afrikaner nationalism and isolationism. Conciliation also meant the sacrifice of black political aspirations with the dream of a Greater South Africa deferred.[27]

The firm hand of Smuts was found everywhere in shaping the form and setting the direction of the Union. Three essential milestones marked South Africa's path into the First World War and presented challenges to the unity of the nation. Smuts oversaw the formation of the Union Defence Force (UDF) in 1912, the ousting of Hertzog from the Cabinet in 1912, and finally quashed the labour unrest of 1913 and 1914. His strength and resolve, even though heavy-handed at times bolstered the flagging spirits of Botha, quieted the naysayers, and destroyed the militants.

The Formation of the Union Defence Force, 1912

The United Kingdom, victorious from the South African War in 1902, was able to dismantle the Boer Republics and impose a Pax Britannica on the region. However, the colonies of the Cape, Natal and the former Boer Republics of the Transvaal and Orange Free State faced military challenges of an internal and external nature. Political unrest within the colonies was a real and ever-present danger. Disgruntled Afrikaners sought the reinstatement of the Boer Republics, and restless blacks provided the Union with a constant threat of uprising with the added possibility of encouragement by external forces. The task of the colonial militia was to counter these simmering internal threats. The military thinking of the period, based on imperial policing as a priority, was dominated by Colonel Henry Timson Lukin (1860–1925), Commandant-General of the Cape Colonial Forces[28] (CCF) who produced an influential pamphlet on *Savage Warfare*.[29] Also influencing doctrine were Brigadier-General George Aston (1861–1938), serving on Field Marshal Paul Sanford Methuen's staff, Major Percy Silburn (1876–1929) of the Natal Militia, and Lieutenant-Colonel Hugh Wyndham (1877–1963), the commander of the Southern Mounted Rifles of the Transvaal Volunteers.[30]

South Africa faced new threats in the wake of the disastrous South African War, and it became necessary to coordinate its fractured defence mechanisms.[31] Military challenges were not only confined to ensuring internal stability. There was the landward threat from Imperial Germany and Portugal who shared common borders with South Africa through GSWA and Mozambique respectively. This threat would materialise in the event of a European war involving the United Kingdom, an event that was becoming more and more likely. Hostile powers were also capable of launching a seaward threat and possibly seizing a port—not a likely prospect given the United Kingdom's overwhelming sea power in the southern oceans. More likely was the prospect of unfriendly neighbours inciting and supporting either an Afrikaner or a black rebellion in South Africa.[32] France and Belgium, as African colonisers, presented an unlikely threat to the security of South Africa. These European powers had few qualms in arming and training black troops for combat, a prospect abhorrent to South Africa.[33]

A short-term solution was the formation of volunteer units within the colonies, replacing a dwindling British military presence in South Africa. Both Afrikaners and Englishmen joined British-style volunteer regiments exposed to the ever-present threat of a black uprising. The threat eventually manifested with the Zulu Bambatha Rebellion in 1906. Colonial troops serving under the command of Colonel Duncan McKenzie (1859–1932)[34] stifled the rebellion in an unequal battle. They deployed machine guns and artillery against Zulus armed substantially with spears and cowhide shields.[35] Although McKenzie quickly subdued the rebels, the campaign highlighted deficiencies in the disparate colonial militias and defence organisations and policies within the colonies. Military necessity brought about closer cooperation between the colonies. The process ensured greater military cooperation, resulting in the creation of a regional military force, which was a precursor to the UDF.[36]

The proclamation of the Union in 1910 contained no provision for the defence of the new country. The overall responsibility of defending the Union remained with the Imperial government. Botha appointed Smuts as the first Minister of Defence in May 1910 as well as the Minister of the Interior and for the Mines. In turn, Roland Bourne (1874–1932)[37] became the Under Secretary for Defence as an aid to Smuts.[38] Even with Bourne's help, the trio of portfolios assigned to Smuts was always going to tax his abilities to the fullest. That Botha assigned these portfolios to Smuts is testament to the trust he had in him (or the dearth of talent available), his recognition of Smuts's superlative abilities and prodigious work ethic, but also the precarious nature of the politics of the period.

The creation of the UDF in July 1912 was far from a simple matter. Afrikaner nostalgia for the lost Boer Republics persisted as did the mistrust and antagonism toward the British military. Occupying the other extreme were the Unionists demanding a defence force designed to deal with internal matters, but also able to be deployed within Africa in support of British forces. Smuts felt compelled to accommodate those wishing to maintain a British military connection and those who yearned for the restoration of the Boer military and political traditions. The dissent took on many and varied forms and emanated from ordinary citizens to the commanding heights of the political spectrum. Former President of the Orange Free State, Marthinus Theunis Steyn, and John X. Merriman were cautious that the UDF should not encourage a policy of militarism and that South Africa should not participate in European quarrels.[39]

The question of a defence system was first raised in the Union Parliament on 1 March 1911. The house greeted Smuts with cheers when he identified that the threat to South Africa was within its borders and one can safely assume that he received their full backing. However, he stood on less firm ground when drawing the house's attention to South Africa's strategic role in the world. He then dealt with the "lines of cleavage" along language lines and among rural and urban dwellers and how an equitable system of defence needed the support of the entire community. Therefore, although the seeds of equitable representation began to encroach on qualification and efficiency, Smuts was determined that any system of defence had to be efficient, economical, practical and finally effective. He foresaw a small permanent force supplemented by a citizen force in times of need. He anticipated the day British forces would withdraw from South Africa, leaving South Africans to fill the void.[40]

Small, rapid-reaction forces with an artillery component would fulfil the dual roles of police as well as military. The Cape Mounted Rifles (CMR) with its artillery corps attached was the ideal example of what Smuts envisaged.[41] Such mounted rifle units could be replicated throughout the country, making for economic and efficient use of resources. Smuts favoured compulsory military service over a volunteer system for the future Citizen Force. However, he realised that a compulsory system would yield too many soldiers and come at too high an economic and political cost. Therefore, he proposed a system of taking volunteers first to harness those who were most keen to offer service.[42]

The Boer Republics lacked highly trained officers and experienced poor discipline in the rank and file, which robbed the Boers of fighting power despite being the "best fighting material in the world". Smuts insisted that new army would have to address these two issues and "not merely rely on the self-devotion of the people of South Africa".[43] The Cadet system proposed by many was efficient in urban areas but substantially less so in the more sparsely situated rural areas from where most of the recruits would emanate. Military districts would divide the country, with a permanent officer who would register all those eligible for military duty in his area. Short period camps in which the youth of the district would be called up would teach recruits to shoot, ride, cooperate with each other, and show obedience to officers. These camps could be repeated at an optimal number of times to achieve a reasonable degree of training. Everyone who possessed any military training would enrol in a veterans' reserve via a rifle club or some other system. The Swiss system inspired Smuts by calling up the youth once a year in the vacation for two weeks.[44]

Smuts proposed a military college to train officers and redress past problems of an insufficiently qualified officer corps. Permanent officers would become instructors, ensuring that future trainers and officers were all South Africans, thereby reducing reliance on the United Kingdom. Smuts, almost harking back to the old commando leadership system, sought trustworthy officers drawn from their districts and associated population. He explicitly excluded British officers for rural areas. Smuts emphasised the South Africanisation of the whole process, and he looked forward to a time when South African graduates of the military college would command the army.[45] Drawing Citizen Force officers from the ranks and their native districts ensured the UDF would perpetuate language divisions. "We are not going to have an alien system of officers imposed—English officers on the Dutch-speaking section or Dutch officers on the English-speaking section."[46] Smuts's words describe the process that would ensure a divided UDF on language, structural and doctrinal lines. The result was two army types eventually deployed to GSWA—a mounted Boer-type infantry and an English-type mounted and regular infantry. The former, substantially Boer in character and doctrine and staffed with Afrikaans officers, and the latter English in character and doctrine, and staffed predominantly with English officers.[47] This was despite earlier attempts at the South African Defence Conferences in Durban and Pretoria in 1908/9 to institute a single military doctrine based on Cape Mounted Riflemen.[48]

The opposition and backbenchers agreed that the main threat to the Union was the "large semi-barbarous population which might easily become unfriendly and give considerable trouble".[49] There were only a few dissenters.[50] Wyndham was concerned that Smuts had announced the replacement of the volunteer system without putting forward an alternative. His next concern was for the formation of an intelligence department.[51] Merriman disagreed that the blacks were the "natural enemy" and he instead thought that "They ought to be our natural friend". His concern was that blacks would only become a problem if mismanaged, and he called on the government to "govern the natives properly". Merriman turned to the external threat posed by Germany and Portugal who were neighbours to South Africa. T.L. Schreiner saw that the destiny of South Africa "was to be both a white and a black man's country". He saw an opportunity to raise a military corps amongst the "coloured people" whom he believed had no better in the world and if led by a "proper" European they would follow him to their death.[52]

The notion of arming blacks drew antagonism from much of the house. General Tobias Smuts (1861–1916), a distant relative to Jan Smuts, hoped that South African troops would never fight on behalf of the Empire. The training of coloured troops and placing them on the same footing as white troops would be immoral and they would be a menace. He also represented old-school Boer military thought in cautioning against too much discipline and drill. His emphasis was on good riding and shooting skills.[53] Smuts explained for the second reading that although the Bill placed no compulsion of coloureds for military training, it did not exclude them from volunteering their services.[54] At the time of passing the Bill, coloureds were already serving in the CMR and the Cape Mounted Police (CMP). Charles Preston Crewe pointed out that the House had no right to exclude any volunteer and he referred to the excellent service blacks had provided as scouts in Basutoland on campaign in 1881.[55]

Race divided the UDF.[56] Smuts was determined to reduce blacks to support roles. The mere thought of arming blacks to fight against white Germans in GSWA conjured up deep-seated fears in most white South Africans of black soldiers returning to the Union and posing a threat to white hegemony. Nevertheless, blacks played crucial roles in the GSWA campaign, and their contribution peppers the record for those who delve into the archives. Major-General C.W. Thompson, the commander of the South African (Imperial) Military Command in 1915, described the essential work of black labourers in keeping the ever-shifting sands from enveloping the newly laid railway tracks of Lüderitzbucht as well as laying and repairing railway lines throughout GSWA.[57] The South African Engineering Corps and its black members were fundamental in the sinking of essential boreholes, establishing a telegraph, telephone and wireless system, the erection and maintenance of water condensing plants, the conversion of buildings into hospitals, and essential sanitary work.[58] In all, 35,000 blacks were recruited from the Union in service in the GSWA campaign.[59]

Sir George Farrar (1859–1915) foresaw a problem that became a reality in the Afrikaner Rebellion, GSWA and German East African (GEA) campaigns. He cautioned Smuts on drawing exclusively upon the rural, mostly Afrikaner, population to supply the mounted infantry and the predominantly English urban population to provide the infantrymen, technical personnel, and signal capabilities. Smuts addressed the question of discipline and assured the House that the UDF would not simply take over the British military code but modify its use to suit South African conditions.[60] Botha, supporting Smuts, assured the House that the racial divisions belonged to the past and that all (white) citizens had both a role and a duty to defend South Africa. Botha believed the defence force was a powerful nation-building tool. His predilection for Boer tactical-level thinking was revealed in the debate when he stressed that shooting skill and judging distances receive priority. Botha raised the critical issue of discipline and the need for good officers but stressed economy and made no mention of a formal college for officer training. Botha urged the forming of a defence force to step in should the "Mother Country" withdraw its troops and leave South Africa defenceless.[61]

Smuts as Defence Minister set about building a Union defence establishment. British officers such as Lord Methuen (Commander of military forces in South Africa), and Colonel Henry Lukin (Commandant-General of the Cape) profoundly influenced the committee. These men supported a Swiss-style system where all adult males had a military duty and once trained were allocated to a reserve. However, the costs were prohibitive, and Smuts relied on a strong ethic of military volunteerism which was especially present among the English-speaking sectors of South Africa. The Imperial Conference of 1911 decided that South Africa should be responsible for its defence in the context of growing tensions in Europe. Financial constraints assured only the partial application of the Swiss concept.

Smuts set about creating a modern defence force, capable of engaging a modern enemy, modelled on European lines and called upon Captain John Johnston Collyer (1870–1941)[62] to assist in preparing the Defence Act for the Union. Certain Afrikaner quarters greeted the introduction of the South Africa Defence Bill with much criticism and scepticism in February 1912. There was considerable resistance to compulsory training, British military discipline, British-style uniforms and the fact that Smuts considered questions of defence to be an imperial matter.[63] Smuts was also not constrained by the geographic expression of "South Africa" in the Act, and he assured the Governor-General, the Right Honourable Viscount Herbert John Gladstone (1854–1930) that "it would surely cover any part of the continent of Africa south of the equator".[64] The Defence Act inextricably bound up the UDF with imperial defence by recognising that South Africa was dependent on the Royal Navy to protect the country from a seaward invasion by a foreign power.[65] On 13 June 1912, the Governor-General approved the Act, and it was officially promulgated in the *Government Gazette* the following day. The South African Defence Act gave birth to the UDF in 1912. The Act allowed for compulsory cadet training for all white youth aged 13 to 17; white males between 17 and 25 were obliged to report for military service, although instituted via a lottery due to financial constraints. In the event of war, all male citizens aged between 17 and 60 were eligible to be called up for military service.[66]

Smuts's challenges had only begun when he created a defence force comprising former enemies with different military systems. Integration into the UDF involved former Boer Republican armies, colonial forces from the Cape, Natal and Transvaal, and the British Army, each bringing its unique battle doctrine and hoping its culture would become the mainstay of the fledgeling UDF.[67] Each military system had its strong supporters, and while English-speakers wished to maintain links to Britain, Afrikaner nationalists supported a restoration of the old Boer military system. Then there was the language and cultural barrier of English and Afrikaner. Bitter enemies a mere 10 years previously now needed accommodation on an equitable basis in the new structure. The Boers saw an opportunity to revive the Republican spirit and Boer way of war in the UDF while the English had an eye on their military obligations to the defence of the Empire even beyond the borders of South Africa. All too evident was the fact that South Africa, on the formation of the UDF, was a mere geographical expression rather than a politically homogenous nation.[68]

At the strategic and planning level, Smuts wanted a modern army based on western military methods. He opted not to simply recreate the old Boer armies and their way of war and recruited those who possessed talent and experience rather than pander to pure political appointments. Smuts's hand-picked staff officers included former enemies such as Lukin,[69] Bourne, Collyer, and assistance from Methuen and his chief of staff, Aston, who stayed on in South Africa until 1912 at Smuts's request.[70] He displayed progressive military thinking as he was prepared to challenge the traditional Boer ways and discard the ideology that would hinder the modernisation of the UDF. Smuts welcomed senior and warrant officers from the British Army in training the new UDF. He visualised that the UDF would become a capable modern fighting force only through the recruiting and assistance of expert, battle-hardened, militarily trained personnel, most of whom would come from the former colonial and British forces.[71]

The Structure of the Union Defence Force: An Exercise in Compromise

The UDF, when established on 1 July 1912, consisted of the SA Permanent Force (SAPF), the Active Citizen Force (ACF), the Coast Garrison Force (CGF), the Rifle Associations (RAs) (or resurrected commandos), the South African Division of the Royal Naval Volunteer Reserve (RNVR), and the Cadet Corps.[72] (See Figure 2.1) Roland Bourne had to explain to the Colonial Office that the post of Commandant-General was not the sole and supreme military command of the UDF.

In an exercise that defied one of J.F.C. Fuller's immutable laws of warfare—the unity of command—the posts of Inspector-General Permanent Force, Commandant of the Cadets, and Commandant-General Citizen Force, were three independent and distinct executive commands.[73] The Defence Act mandated the UDF to defend "South Africa" which for Smuts extended past the Unions borders and included all territory south of the equator.[74] The small Permanent Force (PF), consisting of a headquarters, instructional and administrative staff and five regiments of the South African Mounted Rifles (SAMR) (each regiment reinforced with an artillery battery), would be supplemented in times of conflict by the Citizen Force component. The permanent structures of the UDF housed the artillery component, which alluded to the excellence of the Permanent Force artillery of the ZAR and the OFS and the outstanding service they rendered in the South African War. Smuts doubted that volunteer artillery units would be able to reach the level of expertise of a Permanent Force unit.[75] The SAMR was a military constabulary modelled on the CMR and tasked primarily with police work in their respective geographical areas. The strength of the SAMR had grown to 103 officers, 348 non-commissioned officers, and 1,565 riflemen by May 1913, while the black component consisted of nearly 2,000 black and Indian constables.[76] (See Table 2.1) This mounted constabulary with their artillery support would form a strike force into the "Native Territories" in times of need.[77] Smuts saw the SAMR as an efficient and economical way of internal policing coupled with a trained permanent artillery component.

Table 2.1. Union Defence Force strength, December 1913[78]

Structure	Compliment
SAMR (PF)	2,016
SAMR (PF) Black and Indian Constables	2,000
ACF and Coast guard Garrison	23,462
Cadet Corps	11,318
Rifle Associations	42,000
	80,796

The formation of the ACF contained the seeds of divisiveness which at best perpetuated parallel doctrines within the same defence force, or at worst, fed a sense of 'otherness', leading to the internecine conflict culminating in the Afrikaner Rebellion of 1914. On 1 July 1913, the ACF incorporated into their first line at least 26 former volunteer regiments, all of whom possessed a distinct colonial or British flavour.[79] None of the former Boer Republic commandos were incorporated in this way and instead, almost by default, they found a home in the second-line Citizen Force Reserve, known as the Rifle Association (RA). The intent was for the RA to soak up those who were eligible for the four-year military training but not drafted into the ACF due to budgetary constraints. The popularity of the RA was demonstrated by the 42,000 citizens who joined in the first year, each issued with a government rifle and bandolier with free ammunition.[80] (See Table 2.1 and Figure 2.2) Unlike the ACF, members of the RA were not subject to compulsory military training, but the intention was for them to keep up their rifle shooting skills at informal shooting meetings. As an unwitting result, the doctrine, military skills, and discipline of the new UDF were wholly or partially absent from the RA.[81] Geyer suggests that the 1914 industrial strike which saw the government deploy the commandos presented "an opportunity for the traditional Boer leadership to rebuild their suppressed political networks".[82] However, it is not a far stretch to imagine that, left to their own devices, the RA accommodated the rebuilding of old Boer commando leadership and networks during 1913/14.

Imperial commitments shaped defence policy and the need to protect South Africa's borders and to prevent an internal uprising. Political expediency and the need to dispense equitable representativity between Englishman and Afrikaner through all UDF structures tempered the commitment to modernise doctrine and create a professional, efficient well-trained army. Therefore, implementation fell short of planning as ability gave way to expediency. The Defence Council headed up by the Secretary of Defence, Bourne, was formed to advise Smuts.[83] It was staffed by four councillors, two English and two Afrikaans, eminent ex-soldiers, and representing the four provinces.[84] The council, in the absence of a General Staff structure,[85] oversaw the amalgamation process, the protection of language, and could intervene to resolve conflicts of a sectarian nature. It was an advisory and a consultative body which had nothing to do with the ordinary administration of the UDF but would assist with the drafting of regulations, the arrangement of areas and distribution of forces.[86] Crewe found himself on the Defence Council and suggested the submission of the majority of first appointments to the council.[87]

Measures to equitably balance British and Boer military systems compromised the efficient operation of the UDF, including the fastidious maintenance of balance between English and Afrikaner representation. The Parliamentary Select Committee for Defence approving the Bill in March 1912 was equally split on language and political lines. Van der Waag states, "The UDF was a consensus, a product of a combination of systems, but nonetheless a thoughtful combination."[88] Van der Waag shows that the High Command was also split almost evenly between 1912 and 1920 along language lines.[89] The first course held in 1913 at the newly established Military School in Bloemfontein hosted 51 officers from the erstwhile British colonies and Boer Republics.[90] The course adhered fastidiously to an English/Afrikaner split of 25:26 and eventually posted those qualifying as staff officers to the various military districts.[91]

Lukin became Inspector-General of the SAPF while the ACF fell under Colonel Christian Frederick Beyers (1864–1914). Lukin attempted to engender an environment that was agreeable to both language groups, and his endeavour was reasonably successful.[92] In contrast, Beyers rid the organisation of its English component and proceeded to fill its ranks with political allies. One of Beyer's victims was Hugh Wyndham whom he forced out in 1912. Wyndham had been forewarned of the danger of the divisiveness of this "very violent Boer".[93] Beyers would later resign and become part of the Afrikaner Rebellion in 1914. Smuts's wisdom in appointing him to this crucial post—given his negative experience of the man stretching back as far as the South African War—is questionable.

Beyers showed early signs of discord with Smuts's vision of a first-class modern army based on the best European standards. His first complaint was against the opposition benches who showed a lack of respect for the Afrikanders and their military history. According to Beyers, the English had shown contempt for everything Dutch, and this had led to their humiliation at Majuba (1881), the Jameson Raid (1896), and the lengthy extended South African War (1899–1902). He felt the opposition did not embrace the policy of conciliation and cooperation. He accused Smuts of failure to consult the ex-officers and men of the Republican forces regarding the formulation of the Defence Bill, while he consulted with English officers. According to Beyers, the Defence Bill was too reliant on a foreign model which was unsuitable to South African conditions. He also argued against the ballot system as it would extinguish patriotism and too much discipline which would kill the Boers' natural initiative. Lastly, Beyers was opposed to the Defence Council as being an unnecessary additional body between the Minister and the General in Command.[94]

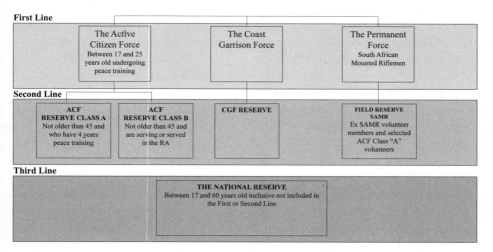

Figure 2.1. The Union Defence Force structure as of 1912 on its inception[95]

However, Beyers, once appointed to the UDF, seemed to embrace the position wholeheartedly. He visited Switzerland on Smuts's instruction to observe their annual manoeuvres, taking note of their organisation and methods. His trip included visits to French, German and British military establishments, and the newly established Aviation School on Salisbury Plain which would be a guide to establishing a similar school in South Africa. An enthralled Beyers revelled in the role of aircraft and their reconnaissance capability. He intuitively realised that aircraft would be a gamechanger and would pose challenges to concealing movement by ground troops.[96] Beyers may have misled Smuts with his newfound enthusiasm for his role in the UDF, leading Smuts to believe that Beyers had at last subdued his strong nationalistic tendencies.

The UDF was unsuited for waging war against a European power. The small Permanent Force component of mounted infantry and artillery was structured for internal police duties, very much aligned with British military thought and discipline, and principally officered by Englishmen.[97] The ACF comprised a mix of infantry and mounted infantry housed in traditional colonial regiments, trained along British lines and led by Englishmen.[98] The RA made up the bulk of the Citizen Force and consisted primarily of mounted infantrymen of Afrikaner origin, many of whom were veterans of the old Boer commandos and officered by Boer Republic veterans of the South African War. These formations, forming the bulk of Botha's northern offensive in GSWA in 1915, would not have looked out of place in the South African War. (See Figure 2.4) As mentioned, the UDF effectively fielded two distinct armies with two different military systems.[99] Hugh Wyndham, the chief intelligence officer, described this in a letter in December 1914 where he spoke of a divided command and a complete absence of organisation. (See Figures 2.1, 2.2 and 2.3)

> We have at the present time two entirely different military organizations operating side by side in the field. One is the commando system, which in reality is no system at all, and the other is a somewhat faint copy of the British system. However we are getting along all right.[100]

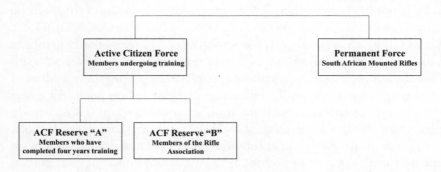

Most units in the UDF were mainly ex-colonial and volunteer formations. The majority of the regiments were led by Englishmen and followed colonial/British military doctrine. The exception was ACF Reserve "B" which consisted mainly of Commando formations from the ex-republics. The majority of the members and leadership of this section of the UDF were Afrikaners, and they ascribed to the Afrikaner Commando doctrine of mounted infantry.

Figure 2.2. Structure of the UDF August 1914: one army containing two doctrines[101]

Furthermore, adding to the confusion was lack of consensus with respect to the Union threat perception, or an exact scope of the UDF's mandate in southern Africa in the event of war.

Figure 2.3. *The Cape Times* of December 1913 indicates the eclectic nature of the UDF.

Hertzog and the Growth of Afrikaner Nationalism

Hertzog always stood in opposition to Botha and Smuts's policy of conciliation. He favoured Merriman over Botha to assume the position of the Union's first Prime Minister, a stance Botha may have found difficult to forgive or forget.[102] Hertzog introduced the Education Act in 1908 as Minister of Education in the Orange Free State. His bilingual policy in the OFS advocated equal status to both English and Afrikaans, and stance on language equality threatened to wreck the National Convention. English opposition to 'Hertzogism' spread throughout the Union and embarrassed Botha's ministry. Hertzog opposed (English) immigration, the imperial connection, and Botha's policy of conciliation and concessions to attract English votes. Attempting to side-line Hertzog, Botha used Smuts as an intermediary to try and persuade him to accept a position at the Supreme Court. Despite all Smuts's efforts, Hertzog insisted on remaining in politics and Botha reluctantly installed him as the Minister of Justice in the Cabinet. His inclusion, like most things about the Botha–Smuts regime, amounted to pure political expediency. Botha and Smuts's wish to secure a comfortable majority in the House of Assembly depended on gaining the majority of Afrikaner and a significant proportion of the English votes. Smuts blamed Hertzog when Botha lost his seat in the first Union election, although the party won a comfortable majority.[103]

Jan Hofmeyr and the Bond had in the past preached Hertzog's brand of Afrikaner nationalism when they too sought racial and language equality. The difference was a matter of approach. The Bond was inclusive while Hertzog was accusatory and maligned those who did not put South Africa first beyond imperial ambitions. Where Botha considered that the Liberals redressed the wrongs of the South African War, Hertzog believed in continuing the fight until the Afrikaners attained equality. Botha pandered to English and Afrikaner supporters while Hertzog sought support exclusively from Afrikaners or anti-imperialist Englishmen.[104] Hertzog embarked on an anti-imperialist mission and accused the leader of the opposition of being a "foreign adventurer". He considered that South Africa was conscious of its destiny and would not be governed by "aliens".[105]

Botha feared that Hertzog's shenanigans would jeopardise the Grahamstown by-election results set for 9 December 1912. The seat was a test for Botha's conciliation policy in a constituency holding a sizeable English majority. Hertzog was dismissive of Botha's conciliation policy as "giving in gracefully to all demands made by the opposition with sufficient arrogance". Hertzog presented the final straw in a speech delivered at De Wildt on 7 December 1912:

> I am not one of those who always talks of conciliation and loyalty: they are idle words which deceive no one. I have always said that I do not know what this conciliation means.[106]

Hertzog's belief that South Africa's interests must take precedence over those of the Empire was revolutionary at the time. Botha, on the other hand, saw no conflict between South African interests and those of the Empire. Botha expected and received the worst when voters, wary of Hertzog, humiliated Botha's candidate for Grahamstown at the polls. Defeat raised a din from the English press for the immediate removal of Hertzog. Smuts, sensing the devastation Hertzog's removal would cause to Afrikaner unity, tried to extract a written apology from Hertzog—but failed. Botha found it intolerable to continue with Hertzog in the Cabinet, but Hertzog refused to leave. Botha, abandoning conciliation for the moment, went ahead and handed in his resignation as Prime Minister to the Governor-General. He received an invitation from the Governor-General on the same day to form a new government. Botha wasted no time in forming a new cabinet which excluded Hertzog.[107]

Hertzog's exclusion from the Cabinet would have far-reaching consequences in breaching the veneer of Afrikaner unity under Botha and Smuts.[108] The removal of Hertzog solved one problem for Botha but created a bigger one which would cause considerable strife for Botha and Smuts during the First World War.[109] Initially, Hertzog found only five members of the 121-member Parliament to support him. He could count among his supporters Christiaan de Wet and M.T. Steyn who would later play a prominent role in the Afrikaner Rebellion. Beyers and De la Rey at first chose to maintain the unity of the party over openly supporting Hertzog. However, in March 1913, Hertzog gathered an overwhelming vote of confidence (47–1) at the party congress in Bloemfontein. He attracted 90 of the 221 votes at the National Conference in November 1913, receiving the backing of Daniël François Malan and Tielman Roos. Hertzog, bolstered by his growing support base, formed the National Party in January 1914, setting the scene for the final dissolution of short-lived Afrikaner unity.[110] Smuts's troubles were not confined to the political front alone. Labour issues began to brew on the Witwatersrand, adding fuel to an already volatile situation.

Labour Unrest: The 1913 and 1914 Strikes

The UDF's first operational test came in the form of a violent industrial strike called by the South African Federation of Trades on the Witwatersrand in January 1914. Once the strike turned violent, Smuts declared martial law for the first time since the establishment of the Union.[111] He deployed PF and ACF units when the police were unable to contain the situation. Deploying the UDF marked a pronounced shift from the 1913 strike where the Union government relied on the services of the imperial forces, the South African Police, special police constables, and the SAMR.[112] The PF, recently formed in July 1913, was unable to quell the riots alone and the UDF called on the Rifle Associations, almost exclusively manned by the former Republican commandos, for assistance.[113]

Smuts unwittingly, by deploying forces of the old Boer Republics under the command of General Koos de la Rey, briefly revived the old traditional commando system with future adverse consequences.[114] Notwithstanding that the deployment was within the context of the new UDF milieu, it contained apparent risks such as revitalising powerful nationalist elements and rebuilding Boer leadership networks. Key nationalists used the foundations built during the strike deployment to conjure up the rebellion a few short months later.[115] One questions the wisdom of utilising the commandos during a fragile and formative phase of the UDF along the lines of the old Boer systems, considering the apparent risks involved.[116]

MOUNTED BURGHERS.

A squadron of Burghers going on relief duty to the mines.
(See page 64.) —Photo from "Natal Mercury."

Figure 2.4. The Boer commandos ride once again, 12 years after the South African War[117]

The process of modernising the UDF had little time to take effect before the strikes. Burghers in the RA had received minimal modern training, no uniforms, and knew little of the new UDF rank structures. The commandos kept their old Boer leadership system as well as their informal rank structures.[118] There was more than a passing resemblance to the traditional Boer commando system, where each man reported for duty with his horse and rifle. Thereafter, every successive deployment of the RA would adopt some of the modernising influences demanded by Smuts through the Defence Act.[119] The commando action against the strike supplied a feeling of nostalgia for many Afrikaners and an opportunity to fight against the Englishmen, albeit in the form of an urban striker. (See Figure 2.4) Deneys Reitz (1882–1944) reported that Beyers, whilst addressing the commandos during the strike said, "the English townspeople have forgotten what a Boer commando looks like, and … [it is] time to refresh their memories."[120] The strike offered the traditional Boer leadership an opportunity to rebuild the old military and political networks and give many youngsters a taste of commando life which they had missed in the South African War.[121] The riots of 1914 greatly facilitated the organisation of the rebellion that would shortly follow.

South Africa Tentatively Enters the First World War, August 1914

War clouds were gathering over Europe while Botha was visiting Southern and Northern Rhodesia in early August 1914. It was fortuitous that Botha did not find himself as a surprise captive when he hastily cancelled his booking on a German ship destined to pick him up in Beira and return him to South Africa. He chose instead to return via a safer overland route. South Africa remained rudderless in the opening moments of the First World War with the absence of a Governor-General due to the early resignation of Gladstone in July. His replacement, Sydney Buxton, delayed his departure to South Africa due to the outbreak of the war. The Lord Chief Justice, John Henry de Villiers, temporarily stepped into the breach only to die two days before Buxton arrived on 2 September.[122] At the outbreak of the war, South Africa contained all the combustive elements suitable for a political inferno. Divisions along pro- and anti-British lines would deepen as the events unfolded in the coming weeks and months.

The British government forewarned South Africa of impending war on 1 August and at a very early stage requested that the UDF provide Walvis Bay with guns and a garrison manned by "local troops".[123] Britain's formal declaration of war on Germany on 4 August bound South Africa automatically and precluded any thoughts of remaining neutral.[124] Smuts and Botha seized the opportunity afforded by war and made an unsolicited offer to take over the duties of the imperial garrison in South Africa, consequently relieving them for duty in Europe.[125] The removal of British troops fulfilled an objective of Smuts to elevate the status of South Africa, and many South Africans welcomed the opportunity to rid the country of "foreign forces". Others greeted the British departure with more nostalgia such as Piet van der Byl who "felt that it was the end of a period that would never recur".[126]

Britain never doubted Botha and Smuts's loyalty, and although Hertzog agreed that South Africa was *ipso facto* at war once Britain was involved, doubts existed whether they would be able to elicit the same amount of loyalty from their fellow Afrikaners. Hertzog was dead set against an invasion of GSWA and sought a limited role for South Africa in defending its territorial integrity. Botha left it to Smuts to persuade the Cabinet that Germany was the aggressor and Britain deserved the Union's unmitigated support.[127] However, at this early stage of the conflict, Botha and Smuts, cognisant of certain deep reluctance to the war had no inkling of the future rebellion.[128] The reality was that Afrikaner unity, always a shaky prospect, was shattered with the exclusion of Hertzog from the Cabinet in 1912 and Botha and Smuts no longer enjoyed the support of most Afrikaners.[129] They would have to look to the English opposition benches to bolster their parliamentary numbers in future elections.

There was little indication of the trouble brewing. The most vociferous in the opposition benches could accept that South Africa was at war and had a duty to defend herself. Smuts and Botha had yet to commit to any adventure, and the removal of the imperial garrison, if not welcome in all sectors, was undoubtedly not contentious. Botha, ever the leader, took the opportunity of calling all the commandants together to clarify the government's position of having taken over the duties of the British imperial garrison. He also sought to assure those present of his intention to conduct the war "without commandeering the people".[130] This early reference to seeking volunteers for the military demonstrated Smuts and Botha's sensitivity to the possible unpopularity of a European war among large sectors of the Afrikaners.

Smuts and Botha saw clear opportunities for South Africa after Britain's declaration of war. South Africa's would enhance her status within the British Empire while the war also brought the opportunity for immediate territorial expansion in the direction of GSWA, Delagoa Bay, and the HCT.[131] Some Afrikaner nationalists also saw prospects for South Africa to take advantage of Britain's perilous circumstances to declare a Boer republic once again. M.T. Steyn barely concealed his *schadenfreude* when referring to Britain's discomfort.

> Is it not a strange Nemesis that the same persons and influences who caused South Africa so much suffering and misery are now also busy causing Great Britain, in the Ulster question, as much, if not more, worry and trouble. And yet, if one considers the matter, one can see that the troubles in England are the result of the South African War. One sees still more. This war has driven England out of her 'splendid isolation' into her 'ententes' and her yellow alliances and today she has fallen foul of Continental entanglements. The mills of Providence grind slowly indeed![132]

Large sectors of the Afrikaner community mirrored Steyn's sentiments on Britain's comeuppance and many, even though not overly sympathetic to Germany's cause, revelled in Britain's discomfort.[133]

Lewis Harcourt, the British Colonial Secretary, accepted Botha's offer of relieving the imperial garrison on 7 August but went a step further in asking them to "seize such part of German South West Africa as will give them the command of Lüderitzbucht, Swakopmund and the wireless stations there or in the interior".[134] German wireless stations posed a considerable risk to Allied shipping travelling around the Cape of Good Hope, and the prospect of denying GSWA ports to German shipping would enhance British sea power in the southern oceans.[135] At this early stage, perhaps anticipating a South African land grab, the British made their position quite clear as to the eventual fate of GSWA if conquered by the Union. The proviso was that German territory seized must be placed at the disposal of the Imperial government for purposes of an ultimate settlement after the war.[136] All but a few thought the war would last beyond Christmas and that territory seized from Germany would form a bargaining chip at any peace conference to follow.

The British possessed sound reasoning for involving South Africa as she was the only British dominion who shared a common border with a German territory which directly threatened British territory. No matter how remote the threat, it was exacerbated by divided loyalties within the Union. The British believed the Germans could foment the situation due to their proximity to South Africa. There was even a humanitarian concern in sectors of the British government over the harsh black policy of the Germans in their colonies. A further consideration cited by the sub-committee of the Committee of Imperial Defence was the decisive political effect of enticing South Africa to cooperate militarily.[137] Lastly, Smuts and Botha's sub-imperialist desires were wholly congruent with strong expansionist desires within the Imperial government, and all saw the opportunity to drive South Africa's borders northward.

Smuts agreed with the general sentiment that the war would soon be over by Christmas of 1914. Historians need to judge the alacrity with which Smuts reacted to the unfolding situation in this light. Smuts was not alone in predicting a short sharp war in Europe. Although Kitchener, appointed as Secretary of State for War, was cautious in predicting a three-year war in his first Cabinet meeting on 7 August 1914, Sir John French, the British Expeditionary Force (BEF) commander, believed it would be very short, as did his chief of staff, Sir Archibald Murray.[138] Winston Churchill, First Lord of the Admiralty, told the British Admiralty departments to proceed on the basis that the war would only last 12 months and that the greatest effort would be required in the first six months. The public expected a short war, and they were even more optimistic than the most optimistic among officialdom. As Hew Strachan puts it, "the long-war idea belonged in the imaginings of pessimists, while the short-war illusion reflected most of mankind's continuing optimism."[139]

Smuts, believing the opportunity to be fleeting, was anxious to waste no time in increasing South Africa's world status and grabbing territory.

Smuts's enthusiasm and British urgency met with mixed feelings in a Cabinet meeting held on 7 August. Botha urged the Cabinet to immediately accede to the British request, but opinions were split. He raised the spectre of Australian or Indian troops overrunning GSWA instead of the South Africans which would remove South Africa's territorial claim to GSWA. F.S. Malan, H.C. van Heerden, Hendrik Schalk Theron, and David Graaf were bitterly opposed to going beyond the commitment offered on 4 August, while Smuts, Thomas Watt, Nicolaas de Wet, and Henry Burton fully supported Botha. Once Cabinet reconvened on 7/8 August, Malan adopted a Hertzogvite position of "South Africa first and then the British Empire". However, some of his concerns were worth consideration. Especially pertinent was that the invasion of GSWA would further destroy Afrikaner–English unity. The invasion of GSWA was not in South Africa's interests, especially in the absence of any sign of German aggression from the territory. South Africa would weaken its internal defences against black insurrection in committing troops beyond its borders in some adventure. The campaign would be long and drawn out given the treacherous terrain it would have to traverse. The Union was also bereft of a fleet which would be necessary to launch an amphibious landing in GSWA. He raised a further point that South Africa would not even be able to annex GSWA due to the British policy as stated. Malan believed that South Africa should not go beyond its responsibilities to defend its territory, and should the Cabinet decision go against him—he would resign.[140]

Malan wavered on 9 August in a meeting held with the dissenters of the Cabinet. He was concerned that their resignations would be misconstrued by the population and lead to an Afrikaner uprising. Failure to comply with Britain would open South Africa up to accusations of dishonesty, especially after Botha had offered to relieve the imperial garrison. That evening, Botha reminded Malan of the German betrayal and treatment of Paul Kruger while he was in Europe. The refusal to invade GSWA would also lead to an alienation of English-speakers who expected the country to come to the aid of the United Kingdom. Botha's assurances that the war against a common enemy would further unite English and Afrikaners were less convincing to Malan.[141] During the Cabinet adjournment called until 10 August 1914, the British followed up with a second and more urgent request.[142]

Malan finally relented when Botha read the British telegram received on 9 August, and Smuts conceded that the invasion force would only consist of volunteers. All agreed that they would consult Parliament beforehand. Smuts's reply to the British government was an unconditional acceptance which made no reference to Parliament nor the exclusive use of volunteers. Smuts and Botha had presented an ambiguous stance of exclusively using volunteers for military business beyond the Union borders. This caused much confusion and alienation especially when

Lieutenant-Colonel Salomon Gerhardus 'Manie' Maritz (1876–1940) received contradictory orders on 23 September 1914. The fact was that the conquest of GSWA would not be undertaken solely by volunteers. Hertzog made the point that commandeering for the GSWA campaign would have led to people taking an immediate decision to rebel. He also pointed out that he could not see a way for the government to undertake the expedition without commandeering.[143] South Africa informed London on 10 August that they would neutralise the wireless stations at Lüderitzbucht and Swakopmund. However, this would leave remaining the massive wireless station in Windhoek which was capable of communication with Nauen in Germany without the aid of the other two stations.[144] An early indication as to German intentions was intelligence received on 11 August 1914 that the Germans had evacuated Swakopmund and Lüderitzbucht and destroyed the facilities there, leaving both ports deserted of their civilian population.[145]

Afrikaner Dissent Grows with the Prospect of War in GSWA

News of the British request for the invasion of GSWA began to attract further criticism and concern in other quarters. Hertzog and other senior politicians were not alone in their opposition to the invasion of GSWA. They were joined by Merriman, who was averse to risking a fragile South African unity over a GSWA campaign.[146] More worrying were the signs that all was not well with Beyers. He revealed his ambiguity on 2 August 1914 while attending a garden party at Roberts Heights, when asked who he thought would win the impending war. H.F. Trew describes Beyer's reply as filled with a "holy fervour" that unsettled him as to his trustworthiness. Beyers flung up his arms in a dramatic gesture and said, "The German armies will sweep across the world; there is nothing that can stop them."[147]

The wavering Beyers called a meeting of commandants attended by Smuts and Botha on 14 August 1914 and informed them that he had his own opinion regarding the invasion of GSWA but would wait for the decision of Parliament. Some of the commandants, including Major Jan Christoffel Greyling Kemp (1872–1946),[148] wished to discuss the issue of GSWA even after Smuts insisted it was not on the agenda. Beyers grabbed the opportunity to launch a personal attack on Smuts and accused him of withholding arms from the Afrikaner section of the community. It was evident that Beyers was insinuating that Smuts did not trust arming the Afrikaners, a spurious accusation as the military was awaiting the new issue of the upgraded Lee-Enfield. Botha found himself having to remind those present of their duties and loyalty to the will of Parliament. However, he was able to identify "a decided spirit of unrest and irritation" especially with Beyers, Kemp, Chris Muller (1865–1945), and Maritz. Smuts made Maritz a general when his raiding force made contact in January 1902. Maritz demonstrated his ruthlessness when he exterminated a coloured settlement suspected of supporting the British. After the war he went into voluntary exile in Europe and Madagascar. After a short stay in the Cape in 1904, he participated in the German suppression of the Herero in GSWA. He was deported from the Transvaal in 1905 for refusing to take the oath of loyalty to the Crown but was allowed to return in 1907. He became a major in the UDF in 1912 and together with Kemp vowed to use his position to re-establish a Boer republic when the opportunity presented itself. He maintained links with the Germans in GSWA and canvassed them for support for a Boer uprising should it take place. He does not seem to have secured any form of German commitment to the Boer cause.[149] Botha confirmed his fears that night when he met with individual officers who confirmed that rebellion was afoot.[150]

Smuts and Botha, having identified most of the ringleaders, failed to take decisive action despite irrefutable evidence of insubordination. Instead, Botha conducted several one-on-one interviews with unconvincing results despite Beyers denying any rebellion and Kemp writing off his blatant and boastful statements of insubordination as mere humour. They, together with Muller, gave assurances that despite differences of opinion, they would obey the wishes of Parliament whatever the outcome of the debate. Shortly before, Botha was confronted by a crazed De la Rey who, infused with the visions of the seer 'Siener' van Rensburg saw "that there would be independence given to this country without any bloodshed". De la Rey held enormous sway with the ordinary Boer who looked upon the old general as a hero and would gladly follow him into rebellion. Once again Botha trusted De la Rey when he said he would quell any dissension in the Boer ranks.[151] The whole affair was shrouded in an air of indecisiveness where Smuts and Botha seemed content to wait for events to take place rather than take decisive action. Merriman felt driven to send an angry letter to Smuts, where he called for all those who were lawless to be punished instead of parleying with them.[152]

Commandant F.G.A. Wolmarans of Lichtenburg went so far as to commandeer burghers with horse, saddle, bridle, rifle and ammunition, and food for four days and to appear at Treurfontein in the Western Transvaal that coming Saturday. Botha reacted to this clear sign of insurrection by instructing Wolmarans to retract the order and desist from any further moves to mobilise his commando. Wolmarans sought an interview with Botha at which he informed him that he was acting on the instruction of De la Rey. Evidence like this could have left no doubt in Botha's mind as to De la Rey's intention or the state of Wolmarans's loyalty given that De la Rey had no standing in, nor any authority to command members of, the UDF.[153] De la Rey continued to play a double game and once again demonstrated his opposition to the GSWA campaign by delivering a speech to the Senate. De la Rey then made his way back to Johannesburg/Pretoria where he met with Beyers.

Dissent seemed to be gaining traction across the board, and, on 15 August 1914, Beyers and Maritz were involved in a meeting near Lichtenburg. However, on this occasion, it appeared as if Beyers dissuaded De la Rey from taking any immediate action. Rumours were abounding of De la Rey possibly calling for a restoration of the former Boer Republics and the non-intervention in GSWA.[154] Smuts and Botha had got wind of the meeting and convinced De la Rey to instead call for calm. The crowd dispersed in somewhat confused state and a rebellion was narrowly averted. Smuts must have felt that his hopes were going awry and that acquiring GSWA would garner support amongst the Afrikaners and quell any idea of rebellion.

Beyers was an obvious target for recruitment by the Boer rebels. He held meetings with Kemp and Maritz in mid-August, during which they sounded him out for his commitment to a Boer rebellion. Maritz was certain of Beyers's support in a coup d'état to overthrow Botha with German support and install a new Boer republic. However, it seems that Beyers was less than enthusiastic and refused to meet with the German Governor, Theodor Seitz (1863–1949), on the GSWA border as arranged by Maritz. However, Beyers did lodge his resignation with Smuts on 15 September, citing his opposition to the government's war policy. He continued to refute his involvement in rebellion even after the accidental death of De la Rey on the same day at a police roadblock near Johannesburg. In the meantime, Maritz had gone into open rebellion on 9 October. Beyers, although attending various meetings and denouncing the government's war policy had yet to show his hand regarding the rebellion.[155]

Adding to Smuts's woes was the news of his father's death on 25 August 1914. Parliament, in recess, was summoned to a special session on 9 September, although military preparations were in full swing. Several ACF and PF units were called up for service "anywhere in South Africa, within or outside the Union".[156] The unavailability of naval resources precluded a planned amphibious invasion of Lüderitzbucht before a meeting of Parliament.[157] Smuts and Botha were hoping to present Parliament with a fait accompli, as it would have been impossible to undo the invasion once opposing sides were locked in combat. Botha admitted,

> We were going ahead with the expedition before Parliament had decided [...] In case parliament did not agree with our policy, then of course we would not remain in office any longer. We would have resigned, and the expedition would have been recalled. But in the meantime we went right along with the forces and trusted to Parliament endorsing our policy.[158]

Smuts and Botha ordered extensive military preparations and were willing to launch an attack on GSWA before gaining the approval of Parliament.[159] They had not seen fit to consult with some of the opposition role-players such as Hertzog or Steyn.

Smuts and Botha had thus far conducted South Africa's entry into the war with a 'fire, ready aim' approach rather than consulting with the various interest groups and bringing them on board before making major political and military decisions. Hertzog was not canvassed or included in any conversation before making important decisions. A consultation process with those most opposed to the war may have gone a long way to precluding an armed rebellion. Both men were driven by the confidence that they would obtain the necessary numbers in Parliament and that they could rely on the Unionist and Labourites for support.[160] It was evident by now that there was widespread Afrikaner opposition to the campaign in GSWA as witnessed in the Cabinet and a general outpouring of feeling in the population. Botha and Smuts could anticipate a hotly contested debate in Parliament. Smuts was undoubtedly aware that the ordinary Afrikaner harboured a genuine dislike for the GSWA campaign.[161] Despite many signs of Afrikaner discontent, Smuts remained confident that there would be no civil war and that the conquest of GSWA would form part of the Afrikaans heritage and quell all dissent.[162] Many Afrikaners felt a moral revulsion on invading a neighbour's territory being against their Christian values and tradition, especially in the light of the assistance the Germans had provided the Boers in the South African War. A further consideration was that some were reluctant to fight against Afrikaners who had sought and found refuge in GSWA after the South African War.[163]

All that was needed to formalise the invasion of GSWA was the rubber stamp of Parliament which was ready to sit again in September. Botha and Smuts were confident they would get Parliament behind the decision to invade GSWA, although the South African Party harboured many would-be nationalists that would split from the party in the 1915 general election. Parliament finally gave consent on 14 September to mobilise the UDF via a large majority of 92–12. However, no amount of positive numerical indicators could disguise the fact that the issue of going to war with Germany deeply divided the country.[164]

Soon after the parliamentary vote, while Smuts and Botha were still in Cape Town, they received Beyers's long-winded resignation via telegram on 15 September.[165] A further telegram informed that De la Rey had been accidentally shot at a police roadblock while accompanied by Beyers in a car apparently on their way to meet fellow conspirator Kemp. The death of De la Rey was grist to the mill of those seeking to sow discord and garner support for their anti-government stance. De la Rey's funeral on 20 September 1914 became a political statement, and Botha and Smuts's attendance was uncomfortable. Botha wisely withdrew all police presence from the funeral to diffuse the hostile crowd. At a meeting with commandants after the funeral, he called for their loyalty in the face of a possible rebellion and assured them that he would conduct the GSWA expedition exclusively with volunteers.[166] Botha himself replaced Beyers, putting the military operations back on track immediately. A sign that trouble was brewing was a report delivered by a Mr Botes, who had travelled from GSWA, which showed that Maritz was in communication with the Germans and had crossed the border to meet them.[167]

CHAPTER 3

The German South West African Campaign and the Afrikaner Rebellion, 1914

Jan Smuts and Louis Botha's designs on German South West Africa (GSWA) were part of a long-standing grand scheme to create a Greater South Africa. Botha made clear his commitment to invade GSWA at the Imperial Conference of 1911 where he revealed to David Lloyd George, "I will keep my word and stand by the Empire. As soon as war is declared I will lead 40,000 horsemen into German South West Africa and clear out the Germans."[1] The climate of war gifted Smuts and Botha the opportunity of meeting their obligations to the United Kingdom and simultaneously expanding the Union at the expense of the Germans. Smuts went beyond Britain's request to disable GSWA radio stations and deny ports to the Kaiser's navy, and shunning offers of foreign intervention, he sought an unfettered claim to the territorial spoils of war.[2]

Territorial expansion, although paramount, was not the only reason Smuts sought GSWA conquest. Loyalty to the United Kingdom was not negotiable, but altruism was not high on the agenda either. The conquest of GSWA would remove a potential (and later real) pernicious source of support for Afrikaner nationalism. Then there were substantial economic reasons. The territory offered attractive economic possibilities, including the best natural harbours on the west coast of sub-Saharan Africa. Equally attractive were the extensive mining operations producing an abundance of lead, copper, zinc, and other minerals. Enormous herds of cattle roamed the interior. Large diamond mines were an attractive prize for any conqueror.[3] Smuts cherished the opportunity to elevate South Africa's status within the Empire and place it on the world stage. With enthusiasm bordering on naivety and in direct contrast to Merriman, he presumed the prize of GSWA would galvanise the divided Afrikaner and English South Africans behind a common cause.[4]

Then there was the need for political expediency. Smuts and Botha had received a drubbing at the hands of the Labour Party in the Transvaal provincial elections in early 1914 in the wake of the 1913/14 Witwatersrand strikes.[5] Hertzog had formed his new party in January 1914 and indications were that it would attract significant Afrikaner support.[6] Further unwelcome pressure arrived after Mahatma Gandhi (1869–1948) mobilised the Indian masses and extracted concessions from Smuts.[7]

In the wake of these disasters, Botha and Smuts faced the uncomfortable prospect of losing much of their political power. Hertzog's break with the South African Party sank Botha into a deep depression where he expressed doubt that he was able to hold the government together. Botha, at his lowest ebb, was on the verge of resigning and letting Smuts take over. During these trying times, from Hertzog's eviction in December 1912 to the suppression of the Witwatersrand strikes in February 1914, it was the ever-energetic Smuts who ran the government.[8] Attending to the age-old truism, the prospect of war supplied a needed if not welcome distraction from the endemic internal political strife in the Union.

The Smuts Plan for the Conquest of GSWA, July/August 1914

Smuts differed fundamentally with the British on the scope and objectives of the GSWA campaign. Compared with Smuts, the British had limited strategic aims. Firstly, they wanted to secure the ports of Lüderitzbucht and Walvis Bay/ Swakopmund, thereby denying them from the German fleet sailing the Southern Ocean. Secondly, the British required the destruction of the powerful transmitters housed in the German wireless stations at these ports and in Windhoek. The complete territorial conquest of GSWA was not a British priority at this stage, unlike the territorial ambitions which drove the Smuts plan for the campaign from the outset.[9] Smuts, ambitious and in a typical act of sub-imperialism, was prepared to deliver the limited British objectives through conquering the entire territory for eventual incorporation into the Union. (See Table 3.1)

The invasion of GSWA was not a new concept considered by South Africa and the United Kingdom on the eve of the First World War. British plans to invade and annex the territory stretch as far back as 1902 shortly after the South African War was concluded. Here the British proposed to occupy and annex Damaraland (the entire territory to the north of and including Windhoek).[10] The scheme involved the occupation of Swakopmund by 1,500 troops supported by British naval fire.[11] The next evidence of British intentions to invade and occupy GSWA occurred in 1910 via a document titled 'Project for the despatch of an Expeditionary Force to GSWA the object being …'[12] The plan is reasonably detailed and is the work of Field Marshal Paul Methuen. It identifies six landing sites on the GSWA coast of which only Swakopmund, Walvis Bay, and Lüderitzbucht were suitable for invasion purposes. The British scheme favoured a landing at Lüderitzbucht and Swakopmund as a feint to attract as many German troops as possible while the main invasion force would be in the south along the GSWA/South African border with the first objectives of Warmbad and Kalkfontein. Interestingly, the British made provision for 2,500 to 3,000 mounted troops and two batteries of field artillery for the conquest of the southern half of GSWA, numbers quite similar to that eventually fielded by Lukin in the opening stages of the invasion.[13] Methuen was set against a defensive policy regarding GSWA in the event of war and he encouraged the necessity for an offensive policy, a position endorsed by Vice-Admiral George Egerton (Commander-in-Chief, Cape of Good Hope Station).[14] One can only surmise as to the change in British strategy to one of limited objectives concerning GSWA at the outbreak of the war in the absence of detailed documentary evidence.

Poor communication with the British and incongruent operational war aims made the fog of war dense. British ignorance of the details of Smuts's ambitions may have been part of a deliberate ploy on his part. Smuts was all too aware that the British were at pains to point out that any territory conquered in GSWA would revert to Britain rather than the dominions.[15] Furthermore, Smuts's ambitious objectives required increased force levels, a more substantial artillery component, more organisation and extensive logistics at the operational level. Smuts was surprised that in light of being "pressed to take active steps in German South West Africa", the British demonstrated reluctance to accede to his request for vehicles, equipment, and stores from the departing imperial garrison in the process of being repatriated.[16] The British were against any delay in the proceedings for lack of artillery and resources, and believed that German resistance at either port was improbable and that once Smuts seized them, their defence would be easy.[17]

The hand of Smuts was present in all phases of the GSWA campaign, from his involvement with trivial tactical or logistical details and operational concepts, to the broad brushstrokes of strategy. He formulated a bold plan which included the simultaneous seizing of Lüderitzbucht, Walvis Bay/Swakopmund, and the invasion of GSWA from its southern border.[18] Such audacity harked back to a time when Smuts planned to grab the port of Durban from the British in the opening phases of the South African War.[19] Once the UDF established bridgeheads at the ports and the southern GSWA border, these formations would simultaneously advance deep into the interior of the country, presenting the Germans with a dilemma of which wing to concentrate against. (See Maps 3.2 and 3.3)

The ambitious invasion plan, designed to deliver the entire GSWA territory into South Africa's hands, drove Smuts's feverish quest for military assets and manpower. The original seaborne invasion allowed for four separate columns to converge on Windhoek. (See Map 3.2). The plan called for 'C' Force under Colonel P.S. Beves (1863–1924)[20] with approximately 2,000 men to land at Lüderitzbucht, and with the help of the Royal Navy, its primary task to destroy critical infrastructure such as the wireless station. The next objective for this group would be to advance inland towards Aus along the railway line with the objective of capturing Seeheim/Keetmanshoop. Further south, H.T. Lukin commanded 'A' Force with 2,500 men, and would land at Port Nolloth and threaten the southern border of the colony. The capture of Sandfontein would provide Lukin with a gateway into southern GSWA, since this first staging post had excellent water resources. A further advance northward to Kalkfontein would take 'A' Force to the southern terminus of the

Table 3.1. The British and Smuts plans for the invasion of GSWA in August 1914

Plan	Strategic level	Operational level	Tactical level	Doctrinal Method
British Plan July–August 1914	**The British had limited objectives of securing their shipping lanes.** 1. Destroy the German Wireless Stations. 2. Secure/Deny the use of the GSWA ports of Lüderitzbucht and Swakopmund/Walvis Bay to the Germans.	Seaborne operation with small forces landing at and securing Lüderitzbucht, Walvis Bay/Swakopmund and destroying the wireless installations.	Ports would be seized and held with small forces supported with British naval assets giving offshore artillery support.	Strategic offensive in securing/destroying/denying strategic assets to the Germans, combined with a tactical defence of the ports. Raiding and limited persisting strategy.
Initial Smuts Plan 21 August–29 September 1914	**Smuts wanted to expand South Africa's borders northward (expansionism) and unite English and Afrikaners in a common cause.** 1. Fulfill the British objectives of destroying German wireless stations and securing/denying GSWA ports. 2. Conquest of the entire GSWA territory.	Seaborne landings on a large scale involving 8,000–10,000 troops/men seizing the ports of Lüderitzbucht, Walvis Bay/Swakopmund and also landings at Port Nolloth to initiate a cross-border land invasion of southern GSWA. The plan included the seizing of Windhoek and the destruction of the German forces.	Ports seized making them a base to build up forces for an invasion. Simultaneous advance of forces from southern GSWA, Lüderitzbucht and Swakopmund.	Persisting offensive strategy using manoeuvre warfare doctrine to advance simultaneously along external lines of communication. Concentration in time in order to overcome the German use of interior lines to concentrate in space.
Second Smuts Plan 5–8 October 1914	Conquest of the entire GSWA territory.	Resuming the aborted landing at Walvis Bay/Swakopmund with the aim of capturing Windhoek. Simultaneous advances from Southern GSWA, Lüderitzbucht and Swakopmund.	Use an overwhelming numerical advantage (40,00+ troops/men) to ensure that the Germans were unable to outnumber the UDF even through concentration in space.	Overwhelming numerical superiority. Manoeuvre warfare at the tactical level. Huge logistical requirements.

German railway system. (See Map 3.1) Lukin's next objectives were Warmbad and then further along the railway line, to join forces with Beves's column at Seeheim/Keetmanshoop.[21] Joining Lukin and protecting his right flank would be 'B' Force under Maritz with 1,000 mounted men. He would invade GSWA from the southeast, with Upington as his base of operations and he would protect Lukin's exposed right flank.[22] (See Map 3.2)

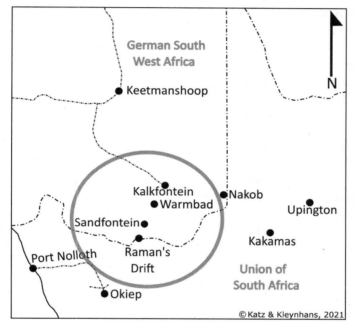

Map 3.1. Sandfontein: southern gateway into GSWA[23]

The most significant and crucial formation, in terms of size and the ultimate role it would play—written out of the history books—was 'D' Force commanded by Colonel Duncan McKenzie with 4,000 men. He was to effect a landing at Walvis Bay, capture Swakopmund, and then advance towards the final objective, the grand prize of Windhoek.[24] The capture of Windhoek would sever the rail links to Keetmanshoop in the south and render the German defence south of Windhoek untenable. (See Map 3.2) Opposing the 9,500 converging Union troops would be 5,000 *Schutztruppen* defending GSWA territory. (See Table 3.2) 'D' Force was fundamental to the success of the entire delicately balanced operation. Failure to land 'D' Force and seize Swakopmund would allow the Germans unfettered opportunities to concentrate their forces either against Lukin in the south or Beves at Lüderitzbucht. For as long as McKenzie held Swakopmund in force, thereby threatening Windhoek, the Germans would have to glance back over their shoulder should they have any intentions of attacking either Beves or Lukin. It is 'D' Force and its intended deployment that official historians have wittingly—and later contemporary historians unwittingly—written out of the history books. Its omission renders Smuts's original plan nonsensical and obfuscates the mechanics of the operational plan he intended. J.J. Collyer, in the official history, identified the need for close cooperation and for a "simultaneous" advance of 'A', 'B', and 'C' Force in order to overcome a concentrated enemy over any one of the advancing forces. Collyer also identified the need before any forward movement in the south of GSWA be undertaken until that force was either considerably reinforced or for "arrangements made and put into effect for a diversion elsewhere which would compel the enemy to detach heavily". The diversion Collyer refers to is of course the missing 'D' Force to be landed at Walvis Bay/Swakopmund.[25] (See Map 3.3)

Carl von Clausewitz (1780–1831) observed that strategic convergent attacks have an advantage in that an attack on any one enemy force has an impact on other enemy forces because of the insecurity delivered on the enemy army by a victorious army in its rear.[26] The commander must arrange for an effective convergent attack so that "the advance [is] made offensively from every point possible, and at the same moment exactly".[27] Smuts was cognisant that interior lines of communication afforded the Germans operating from a central position the ability to concentrate swiftly and at a greater tempo than the UDF operating on exterior lines of communication. The extensive German railway network facilitated their rapid movement of the *Schutztruppen* to meet each individual UDF threat in turn. It offered the Germans, a numerically inferior enemy, a chance to achieve tactical/operational superiority at a decisive point.[28] However, their use of interior lines did not in itself render a marked advantage to the Germans. Smuts knew the advantage his strategy conferred on the UDF by advancing using exterior lines and keeping the threat of envelopment constant.

Antoine-Henri Jomini (1779–1869) stressed the proviso that a successful operation using external lines of communication demands *simultaneous* (author emphasis) operation on all flanks.[29] Smuts's plan was somewhat optimistic in its requirement for numerical superiority (the most achievable of the requirements), good communication and coordination between the individual converging wings (an almost impossible task) and speed in executing movements (an equally difficult task). There was a further advantage to splitting the UDF into four almost-equal prongs in that the desolate and arid terrain lent itself to supplying smaller formations more easily.[30] Smuts's risky strategy carried with it the promise of not merely forcing the German *Schutztruppen* to retreat, but the prospect of cutting them off and eliminating them piecemeal.[31] (See Map 3.2)

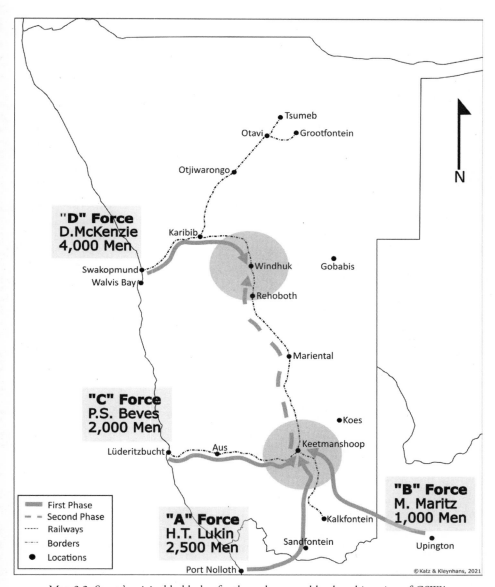

Map 3.2. Smuts's original bold plan for the seaborne and landward invasion of GSWA

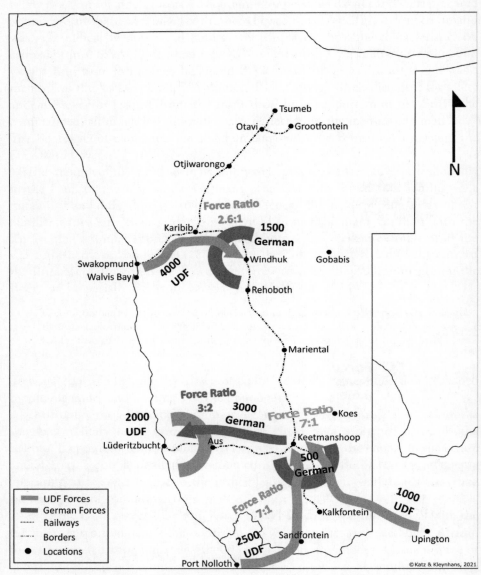

Map 3.3. The advantage of exterior over interior lines of communications[32]

The plan was not short of detractors. In September, Sydney Buxton harboured "grave doubts" on the likelihood of success for the operation and the lack of sufficient artillery. He was deeply concerned that any reverse suffered by the UDF would have grave consequences on the political situation in the Union.[33] However, the plan, although ambitious, was not reckless. Smuts predicated his strategy on sound manoeuvrist doctrinal foundations, shaped by the necessity of the UDF using external lines of communication. De la Rey had instilled in Smuts a firm and enduring grip on Boer manoeuvre warfare during the South African War, which he coupled with Clausewitz's observations on the superiority of simultaneous concentric advances on exterior lines (concentration in time) over interior lines (concentration in space).[34] (See Map 3.3)

The adoption of Smuts's brand of manoeuvre warfare carried the risks of the German ability to concentrate in space and garner a tactical numerical advantage over any one of Smuts's four prongs. (See Table 3.2) The *Schutztruppen*, at a considerable strategic numerical disadvantage, would have been severely challenged in achieving a tactical numerical superiority against any of Smuts's four prongs. Furthermore, doing so would severely weaken the fighting power of those opposing the simultaneous advance of the other prongs.[35] The Smuts plan allowed for UDF formations to exploit the advantages of the defence, or refuse battle, or retreat, while other formations advanced and threatened the enemy rear.[36] Contemporary historians have overestimated the advantages enjoyed by the *Schutztruppen* in operating on interior lines and overlooked the problematic logistics and exhaustion that rapid movement over vast distances would entail.[37] (See Map 3.2).

The German Plan to Defend GSWA

Comparisons of German military performance in GSWA with the protracted and heroic antics of their compatriots in German East Africa is tempting. The GSWA Schutztruppe commanding officer Lieutenant-Colonel Joachim Heydebreck and the Governor Theodor Seitz possessed limited options should the war in Europe prove to be a protracted one. However, German resistance in GSWA proved lacklustre and all too brief in comparison with that offered by Paul von Lettow-Vorbeck and his GEA Schutztruppe. The German semi-official history hints that the end of the operations in GSWA came somewhat "prematurely" because of South Africa's overwhelming superiority although the *Schutzruppen* remained unbeaten in the field.[38]

Botha's evidence before the commission of inquiry into the Afrikaner Rebellion bears out the observation that the Germans did not plan, nor had the intention or the wherewithal to invade South Africa. He blamed the rebellion for giving the Germans the impetus to resist. Vindicating Smuts's original plan, which used smaller force levels—Botha believed, but for the rebellion, the invasion of GSWA would have been a small, inexpensive, rapid operation:

Because it was quite clear to me that the Germans could not fight. The only fighting they did was where they found a few men, but when I went there with eight or ten thousand men, they surrendered without firing a shot. Over 5,000 surrendered at Otavifontein, and they surrendered without resistance. If they could do that later on, why not at first. [...] And I am satisfied that had it not been for this rebellion and the assistance they expected to receive from this side, and they talk about 50,000 rebels coming along to help them, I doubt very much whether they would have fired a shot in South Africa. [...] It was perfectly plain to me that they had no intention to fight.[39]

Botha in attempting to paint the rebels in a poor light may have embellished their role of bolstering German military resolve in GSWA. However, he insisted that the Germans showed little resistance when confronted with unfavourable numerical odds. Botha's pertinent remarks give a measure of credibility to the efficacy of Smuts's plan in the absence of the knowledge of the forthcoming rebellion.[40]

The German semi-official history attests to the unpreparedness of the Schutztruppe in GSWA with a tale of steady decline since the German Herero Wars (1904–1907). Despite the increase of the white population from 4,500 since that rebellion, to 15,000 in 1914, the Germans could field just 1,870 rifles. The military decline was so great that it put the internal stability of the colony at risk. The Germans were fully aware of South African territorial desires, especially in the light of recent diamond discoveries and great advances in farming and mining. In the event of war, they believed that the European battlefields would decide the strategic fate of the colony. The settlers would buy time and handle the short-term defence of the colony. Lack of military engineers further precluded the possibility of good field fortifications. A shortage of shrapnel artillery ammunition, portable machine guns suitable for mounted warfare, sensitive artillery unsuitable for desert conditions with too many calibres, complicated and exacerbated German woes. The Germans fared better with signals having plenty of good-quality equipment to ensure first-class communication between headquarters and the various formations in the field. Two old planes of dubious reliability gave the Germans an aerial reconnaissance ability.[41] The Germans with few motorcars in their inventory relied on mules and oxen for logistical transport where the railway was not available.[42]

At the outbreak of the war, the Germans temporarily increased men under arms to 6,000. However, they contracted to 3,000 frontline, and 2,000 second-line troops after health and economic considerations were applied.[43] (See Table 3.2) Many of those who reported for duty were of poor physical health, lacked previous military training, and could neither ride nor shoot well. These volunteers relieved better-quality personnel for frontline service. Some of those fit for service occupied essential economic positions and could not render military service. The Germans instituted immediate steps to conserve food stocks and ensure that despite a scarcity of all goods, the military and civilian population remained supplied with essentials for the duration of the campaign.[44] J.J. Collyer indicates that the Germans did enjoy some advantages in having a unified command, properly qualified staff in adequate numbers that were uniformly trained as regular officers, and lastly a homogenous force trained via the same system and fighting to the same plan.[45] Furthermore, the Germans enjoyed a significant advantage in artillery pieces.[46]

German forces in GSWA, after mobilising the reserve and the Landwehr,[47] were a fraction in comparison to that available to the South Africans. The Germans would be hard-pressed in suppressing an internal uprising—always a likely threat—let alone confronting the numerically superior UDF. Seitz suffered no illusions as to his unenviable predicament should war break out. He could expect no help from Germany and faced the real threat of internal rebellion endangering the safety of the German settler population. European battlefields and control of the oceans would ultimately decide the future of GSWA.[48]

Table 3.2. The German forces available at the outset of the GSWA campaign 1914[49]

	Available	Note	Combat Effective
Standing Army	**1969**		**1949**
Officers	90		90
Soldiers	1828		1828
Medical and Veterinarian staff	31		31
Civilian employees	20		0
Police and Police Auxiliaries	**1182**		**482**
Rehoboth soldiers	150	1	0
Officers	12		12
Troopers	470		470
German deputies	300	2	0
Black deputy police	250	2	0
Military Reserves	**4206**		**2526**
Active Reserve	823		823
Inactive Reserve up to age 45	803		803
Non-Standby Reserve	2580	3	900
Total Military and Para Military Forces	**7357**		**4957**

Notes. 1. Rehoboth used only for internal defence such as guarding prisoners.
2. Police deputies had received no miltary training and would also be expected to maintain internal law and order.
3. Only 900 of the Non-Standby reserves were fit for military service.

The German Colonial Office demanded that the German colonies in Africa submit their defence plans. The overall plan for the colonies was a strategic defensive stance trading space for time. The offensive initiative in GSWA would be surrendered to the South Africans and at the same time avoiding rash attacks against an invading force possessing great numerical and material strength. Keeping the fighting power intact for as long as possible entailed a slow retirement into the interior avoiding decisive defeats. The hope was for a swift German European victory while avoiding the surrender of a colony in the process. A further objective was redirecting as many Allied resources as possible and denying their use in Europe. The plan emanated from a position of relative German weakness compared to the vast resources available to the British via their colonies and an overwhelming naval superiority. On the outbreak of the war, German colonies would be isolated and cut off from reinforcements and left to their own devices.[50]

The German wildcard, outside of a quick German victory in Europe, lay in the possibility of provoking a rebellion and attracting thousands of Afrikaner rebels to cross into GSWA and join the *Schutztruppen*. The Germans showed interest in maintaining contact with anti-British elements in South Africa but were rather cautious about the prospect of invading the Union. They preferred to foster and then support a Boer rebellion using these forces to install a friendly government in the Union. Seitz considered that the encroachment of Union territory might swing Boer opinion away from Germany. Maritz who had maintained secret contact with the Germans for years concurred with Seitz's wisdom and requested the Germans not to attack Union territory. As a result, Seitz issued a direct order to Heydebreck that he must avoid cross-border attacks.[51]

The Schutztruppe's primary purpose was the maintenance of colonial law and order, and the suppression of internal disturbances. Its conventional military capabilities against a well-armed, numerically superior foe were limited, and its survival would depend on taking advantage of opportunities as they presented themselves. A rather lackadaisical political approach to forging links to South African republicans and nationalists such as Hertzog and Steyn ensured minimum influence on South African politics. The Germans failed to fully exploit the possibility that the Afrikaner Rebellion would swell the *Schutztruppen* numbers. The Germans were disappointed with the lacklustre resistance offered by the Afrikaners at the outbreak of the war and their seeming lack of desire for independence. The Germans issued a belated proclamation making the distinction between fighting against invading "British troops" and supporting the Afrikaners' cause. Seitz formalised an alliance between Germany and Afrikaners in a treaty signed with Maritz giving guarantee to Boer independence.[52] Needless to say, Maritz had no authority to commit South Africa to any agreement or treaty with the Germans in what amounted to an act of high treason.

It was feared that launching an attack (always the preferred option of the German officer class no matter how overwhelming the odds) would strip GSWA of soldiers and police and expose the entire colony to an internal uprising by the local black population. Ironically, these same fears of a black uprising circulated in South Africa where the UDF was distracted by GSWA. The Germans were known to have ruthlessly crushed internal rebellions on previous occasions with genocidal fervour and were now afraid of leaving their civilians unprotected. A large part of their planning gave priority consideration to the safety of their citizens. The threat of retribution by the local black population posed a greater risk than an invading South African army.[53] The prospect of a restless indigenous population troubled the Germans to such an extent that they relocated them into the interior of the country on the outbreak of the war. The South Africans eventually recruited GSWA blacks as scouts who revealed numerous locations of mines planted by the Germans.[54]

Therefore, political and practical strategic considerations shaped the operational and tactical battle the Germans planned to fight. They would adopt a delaying strategy using a vigorous mobile tactical defence/offence facilitated by their excellent railway network and internal lines of communication.[55] Numerical inferiority necessitated a concentration of forces when opportunities arose, allowing for successful counterattacks with superior local forces. The railway network, completed in 1912, was the cornerstone of the German military offensive and defensive plan. It was fundamental to rapid mobilisation and efficient troop movement either in retreat, advance, or concentration phases of the campaign. However, efficiencies deteriorated as the campaign dragged and the Germans eventually in desperation used wood instead of coal to fire their locomotive engines.[56]

The Germans excelled in maintaining the health of their troops and animals. Large-scale typhoid vaccinations prevented massive outbreaks of the infection. Rigorous measures were also employed to conserve scarce fodder, oats and corn supplies. The scarcity of water challenged both sides and curtailed all but the most basic movements and operations. The limited availability of water along the few routes well known to all forced combatants to conduct their operations along lines, limiting the element of surprise.[57] The hardship of war in this inhospitable climate eventually took its toll on the men and animals with many animals succumbing in the last days of the campaign.[58]

Seitz outlined the Schutztruppe mission in his mobilisation order: attacks must be made only in response to enemy actions, a defensive attitude would be adopted, and the borders with the Union would be secured. The opportunity to go over to the offensive was dependent on the successful outcome of an Afrikaner rebellion.[59] A resurgence of the Herero uprising of 1904–1908 was a distinct possibility if encouraged by the British. He tasked the *Schutztruppen* with securing rear areas against any uprising. The eastern border was secure as the Kalahari Desert provided an almost impassable barrier. The threat from the Portuguese on the northern border with Angola was an unlikely possibility, as they possessed neither the capability nor desire to take on the Germans. Heydebreck thus concentrated his main military effort along the southern border defined by the Orange River. The biggest challenge was the west coast with its two ports, Swakopmund and Lüderitzbucht, providing their only contact with the outside world. Walvis Bay remained a vital harbour—its capture from the British was easy enough. These ports, although a strategic lifeline, were surrounded by the formidable Namib Desert and could only be supplied by the vulnerable German railway line. They posed insurmountable defensive problems being unfortified, vulnerable to naval bombardment, and with the sizeable German civilian population at risk should they remain.[60]

Limited troops and the risk to the German population inhabiting the ports made for the pragmatic decision to abandon them to the South Africans. The retreating Germans, contrary to the sound requirements of war, left unharmed the houses and installations in the hope of soon returning. The Germans were content to withdraw into the interior and rely on their one-year supply of provisions and munitions to build a redoubt in the more environmentally friendly centre of the colony.[61] They too, like Smuts, were betting on a short decisive war in Europe, and, unlike Smuts, they banked on a German victory.

Seitz declared a state of war on 7 August, financing the military mobilisation of the colony by issuing Protectorate treasury notes. All exports of foodstuffs and cattle were banned with the colony enjoying three to five months' supply of food at the outbreak of the war. He eventually introduced food rationing in January 1915. One of Seitz's first acts was the removal and relocation of the radio station at Lüderitzbucht to Aus. The Germans allowed the repatriation of British citizens to the Union via a neutral ship that sailed to Cape Town.[62] The Germans, ever sensitive to an internal uprising, took extra policing measures and relocated the entire population of Bondelswarts from the south-eastern part of the colony to Otjiwarongo in the north in August.[63]

Heydebreck correctly assumed that the British would enlist the military support of the Union and deploy the might of the Royal Navy which would enable the invasion of the territory across the Orange River as well as the seizure of the coastal ports. Seitz instructed Heydebreck to take precautions to guard against a 'native' uprising and secure the borders against the UDF immediately on the outbreak of war—the order of priority was revealing. Seitz discouraged the invasion of the Union as politically incorrect but urged Heydebreck to defend encroachments of GSWA territory vigorously.[64] Unlike GEA, the Germans were unable to make use of black askari in large numbers, and their exclusion from the Schutztruppe in GSWA diminished Heydebreck's fighting power substantially. However, a few local black formations, drawn principally from the Rehoboth Basters, were established on 8 August to protect themselves from outside interference and free up Germans for military service.[65]

The Germans concentrated the initial defensive effort in the south, leaving the protection of the north to the police aided by the local militia. The south offered opportunities for local counterattacks which would threaten the Union and slow the advance. Heydebreck abandoned the coastal region after destroying the railway lines and the water resources.[66] The Germans relied on the inhospitable terrain of the Namib to slow down forces advancing from the ports. (See Map 3.4) Heydebreck thus planned to offer stiff resistance at Aus in the south and Usakos in the north.

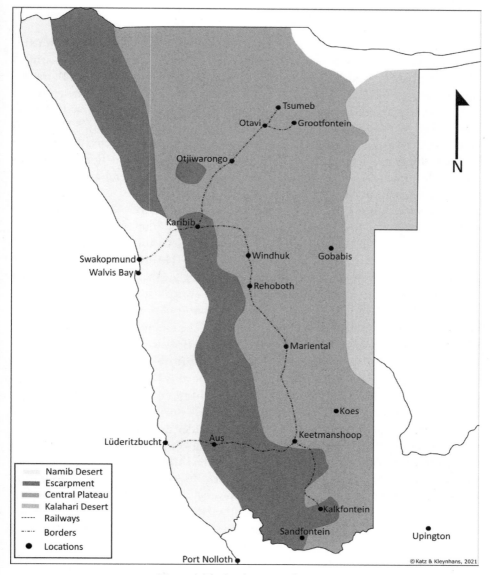

Map 3.4. The harsh terrain of GSWA

The radio stations would remain in operation until the last possible moment, only to be destroyed in the face of imminent danger.[67] Thereafter, Heydebreck planned for a slow, deliberate, contested retreat to the north with the last stand at the mining area of Otavifontein.[68] The railroad system would facilitate the rapid movement of German forces from one sector to the next and ensure a secure supply line.[69]

South Africa's Invasion Preparations

South Africa signalled its loyalty and a step towards greater independence when it offered to undertake the defence of its territory with the exclusive use of its army.[70] The Secretary of State of the Colonies, Lewis Vernon Harcourt (1863–1922), framed the British acceptance of Botha's offer with a request to invade GSWA, describing it as "a great and urgent Imperial Service". The words carried meaning for the British who wished the South Africans to complete the operation expeditiously.[71] The British could not accuse the South Africans of procrastinating, for within five weeks of the Union Cabinet decision taken on 10 August to invade GSWA, the first UDF troops crossed the Orange River under the command of Brigadier-General Tim Lukin. Two days later a seaborne landing took place at Lüderitzbucht.

Contemporary historians have criticised the alacrity of the GSWA invasion before sufficient preparation. Rodney Warwick admonishes "the Union' government's urgency to invade GSWA" as if it were a unilateral decision on the part of Smuts, but he ignores the British emphasis on "urgency".[72] He accuses Smuts of placing politics above pure military necessity when he hastened to present the Afrikaner nationalist with a fait accompli.[73] However, the British joined Smuts in seeking the same political advantage and saw the positive "political effect of inviting the cooperation of the South African Government".[74] The Union undertaking to destroy GSWA wireless stations was at the behest of the British and the primary aim of invading of GSWA was to secure several strategic British war objectives.

The concept of a seaborne invasion of GSWA ports was an idea which the British first suggested on 1 August.[75] However, the British stressed that the "military details must be left to the Union Government".[76] Botha, as early as 15 August, embraced a simultaneous landing at Swakopmund and Lüderitzbucht while concentrating a strong force on the Orange River.[77] Smuts laid out his plan for the invasion of GSWA on 21 August when the principal officers of the UDF met at Defence Headquarters (DHQ) Pretoria to finalise the plan.[78] Smuts presided over the meeting in his capacity as Minister of Defence. Present among the delegates were generals Christiaan Beyers (Commandant-General), McKenzie and Lukin, colonels Beves and P.C.B. Skinner (Chief Intelligence Officer),[79] and Sir William Hoy (General Manager of the Railways).[80] Smuts confirmed that the UDF would land troops at Port Nolloth, Lüderitzbucht, and Walvis/Swakopmund. Van der Waag and Strachan have incorrectly suggested that the meeting resulted in the modification of Smuts's plans, leading to the abandonment of the landing at Walvis Bay/Swakopmund.[81] Collyer is the probable source of contemporary misunderstanding when he suggested in the official history that Smuts's original plan for the simultaneous invasion of Lüderitzbucht and Walvis Bay did not survive the 21 August DHQ meeting in Pretoria.[82]

Extensive primary documentary evidence shows that the idea of the scuppering of Smuts's plan on 21 August is incorrect. Documentation shows the conversation centred around the Walvis Bay/Swakopmund landings for weeks after 21 August. Examples exist such as C.P. Crewe endorsing Smuts's arrangements for a landing at both Swakopmund and Lüderitzbucht on 24 August.[83] A minister's memo, dated 25 August, speaks of the delayed Swakopmund/Lüderitzbucht expedition rescheduled to 12 September due to lack of naval escorts.[84] Smuts's intention is evident when he replied to Merriman on 2 October on the latter's suggestion of a landing at Walvis Bay. Smuts confirmed that this had indeed been his original idea and that he had arranged the expedition on that basis.[85] Merriman wisely identified Swakopmund as the most direct route to Windhoek offering good ground for the invasion force after traversing 65 kilometres of the desert.[86] Secretary of State Harcourt sent a telegram to the Acting Governor-General (Sir James Rose Innes)[87] on 4 September which outlined the discretion afforded to the commanders of the Swakopmund and Lüderitzbucht expeditions.[88] The embedded journalists accompanying the invasion placed the abandonment of the Walvis Bay operation after the resignation of Beyers on 15 September.[89] Overwhelming evidence points to the complete adoption of Smuts's four-prong attack on 21 August. The cancellation of the Walvis Bay/Swakopmund landing only occurred at a much later date on 28/29 September.[90]

Confusion mired the opening phase of the operation. The British claimed that Smuts had failed to consult them about the best way to undertake the various operations even though they were indispensable in delivering the seaborne component with their powerful navy.[91] It was an ambitious plan fraught with danger and uncertainty for a fledgeling army such as the UDF. Strachan considers that hope of coordinating the three widely dispersed prongs of the southern force was fanciful when hampered by the tyranny of distance and the relative weakness of the forces deployed.[92] The UDF could muster forces totalling some 5,324 men by combining the 'A', 'B', and 'C' Forces against a similar number of German troops. However, absent from Strachan's arithmetic were the 4,000 members of 'D' Force destined for Walvis Bay/Swakopmund.[93] The risk of German ability to concentrate overwhelming numerical superiority against a UDF prong was remote due to the nature of the harsh desert terrain limiting logistics. The numerical balance of forces, although slim, offered the UDF a square chance of delivering the limited objectives of Lüderitzbucht and Walvis Bay/Swakopmund and holding them if counterattacked.

Strachan cites Britain's limited sea transport for forcing Smuts to choose either Lüderitzbucht or Swakopmund for a sea landing. Smuts never faced a choice as the decision to land at both locations remained intact until 28 September. However, many challenges to the British and the South Africans manifested in delays in getting operations underway. Botha grew increasingly impatient at the British with their lack of naval escorts, and on 8 September, threatened to call off the whole operation which included the landings at Lüderitzbucht and, more significantly, "the third and largest Expeditionary Force" at Walvis Bay.[94] Harcourt swiftly replied that he would prioritise the allotment of escorts for the Lüderitzbucht and Walvis Bay/Swakopmund expeditions and that he would not allow the evacuation of the Cape garrison to interfere with the invasion proceedings.[95] The delayed landing at Walvis Bay was a combination of an initial lack of British naval escorts, then the UDF's disorganisation at the staff level, and finally, the arrival of the Afrikaner Rebellion.[96] The German naval fleet roaming rampant in the South Atlantic in mid-December added to the heightened alarm later in the campaign but was not the principal reason for delays in August/September.

Strachan is extremely critical of Smuts's "muddled" choice of a first landing at the more southern and closer port of Lüderitzbucht. He argued that a landing to the north at Swakopmund would produce more decisive results in threatening to cut off the Germans holding the south along the Orange River.[97] Strachan fails to consider that Swakopmund is 450 kilometres from Lüderitzbucht, a considerable stretch further in the face of limited shipping resources in a hostile ocean. Once the operation became one of sequencing the landings rather than a simultaneous effort, then considering Lüderitzbucht over Swakopmund made good military sense. The landings at Swakopmund would be even more isolated than the one at Lüderitzbucht as the nearest South African forces would be a vast 800 kilometres away and busy fighting their way up the railway line without the benefit of supply through Lüderitzbucht. The Germans would undoubtedly have more time to concentrate their forces against a landing at Swakopmund, which was close to their military centre of communications at Windhoek (259 kilometres).

Sheer distance coupled with the sullen reluctance of crucial members of the UDF, which later progressed to rebellion, made the landings at Swakopmund a perilous venture. Furthermore, Swakopmund harbour consisted of a single jetty that could be and was neutralised by naval bombardment, whereas Lüderitzbucht was a natural harbour. The ports offered a natural landward defence in the form of an expansive desert zone which was difficult to traverse and offered good natural defences against sea bombardment. Expectations were that a South African force ensconced would be able to fend off a seaward or landward attack unaided.[98] Therefore, on balance, where a simultaneous landing became impossible, landing at Lüderitzbucht first, which was more defensible, was likely to divert German attention away from Swakopmund.

Another problem diverging from British expectations was that Smuts was preparing a larger operation with increased force levels. Smuts overtook the British idea of a small task force and expanded the operation to a full-fledged invasion. (See Table 3.1)

The intention after landing in force at Walvis Bay/Swakopmund was to proceed to Windhoek. Needless to say, that the staff officers, organisation and logistics needed for three simultaneous landings were lacking. Lack of communication left the British guessing and only suspecting that a bigger operation was underway. Admiral Henry Jackson (1855–1929), the adviser on overseas expeditions and planning attacks on Germany's colonial possessions, was concerned that the military forces Smuts accumulated were more than what was required to secure the ports and destroy the wireless stations in the face of weak opposition. He suspected that Smuts modified his plan to a full-scale invasion intended to capture Windhoek. Jackson sought clarification from Smuts as to the timing and extent of the new operation, and the naval escorts required considering the bigger operation.[99] The expanded force would require naval escorts and resources not foreseen in the original British plan, since all available escorts were needed to safeguard the transport of the imperial garrison forces returning to the United Kingdom.[100]

British anxiety grew with the delayed destruction of the wireless stations at Lüderitzbucht and Swakopmund.[101] The South Africans gave assurances on 24 August that the expedition was ready to sail on 5 September and that the increase in troop numbers was not the cause of delay. In the meantime, intelligence arrived that the Germans had abandoned Lüderitzbucht and Swakopmund, disabling the wireless stations and moving them further into the interior.[102] Now it was the chance of the British to delay the proceedings when it emerged on 26 August that the required naval escorts for the invasion force would only be available on 12 September.[103] A single armed merchant cruiser, escorting four or five transport ships, was not adequate for the task at hand, which included supporting the troops in capturing the ports should the landing be opposed.[104] Smuts, attempting to avoid any further delay, proposed that the GSWA expedition would sail in tandem with the naval escorts and transport ships repatriating the imperial garrison. The naval force would see the GSWA expedition safely landed and then loaded with the remaining imperial garrison, proceed to the United Kingdom.[105] Harcourt readily concurred, and the GSWA expedition was set to sail on 12 September, only to be rebuffed by Jackson who feared that the combined move would considerably delay the departure of the imperial garrison.

The Seaborne Invasion Proceeds, August 1914

The fog of war descended quickly, obscuring Smuts's plans of a simultaneous landing at GSWA ports. Lukin's expedition to Port Nolloth landed on 31 August and immediately experienced delays in disembarkation partly because of the state of the port and partly to disorganised staff work.[106] The UDF could expect the same or longer delays at Lüderitzbucht and Swakopmund.[107] Lack of planning, organisation, and experienced staff officers took an early toll.[108] Chaotic disembarkation procedures at

Port Nolloth—10 days to land the stores—delayed the rest of the GSWA expedition a few days beyond 12 September. The expectation was that disembarkation at the other ports would be a lengthy process too.[109] (See Figure 3.1) Roland Bourne, the Secretary of Defence, belatedly formed a Joint Operational Command in Pretoria on 9 September to alleviate the logjam, which was staffed by a senior naval and army officer, and a senior representative of the South African Railways.[110] Delayed timetables began to clash with the British efforts to repatriate their garrison forces using the same scarce shipping resources. The British informed the South Africans on 7 September that they would not delay the departure of the ships conveying troops back to the United Kingdom beyond 14 September. The South Africans were encouraged to make suitable arrangements to meet the deadline.[111]

The British determination on keeping to a strict timetable exasperated the South Africans. On Buxton assuming the role of Governor-General on 8 September, he sent an impassioned plea to the British that the non-availability of naval escorts would scupper the whole expedition with disastrous effects on public opinion. Smuts asked personally and informally whether the repatriation of the imperial garrison could be delayed by a few days to facilitate the GSWA expedition.[112] Political pressure forced the British to weigh up the cost of delaying the repatriation of the imperial garrison for a couple of weeks, against dampening enthusiasm for the expedition in the Union. Jackson concluded that the importance of the expedition outweighed any benefits of early repatriation of the imperial garrison.[113] The considerable benefits of destroying three German radio stations compared to repatriating one and a half battalions to the United Kingdom won the day.[114]

Figure 3.1. The slow pace of disembarkation at Lüderitzbucht[115]

The GSWA expedition was back on track, and with British patience restored, the next problem on the horizon was of the considerable delays at Port Nolloth. Large-scale disorganisation meant that the Walvis Bay part of the expedition would take place one week after the landings at Lüderitzbucht on 14 September.[116] Bad weather intervened leaving the timetable for Lüderitzbucht for 14 September but delaying the departure for the Walvis Bay/Swakopmund to 26 September.[117] The landing at Walvis Bay/Swakopmund would then only be complete by 11 October, causing considerable delay to the repatriation of the imperial garrison.[118] Further delays at Port Nolloth meant the naval transports were only able to get back to Cape Town by 17 September which delayed Beves's belated occupation of Lüderitzbucht to 18 September.[119] Before Beves set out for Lüderitzbucht, the political horizon became increasingly clouded following the resignation of Christiaan Beyers and Jan Kemp on 13 and 15 September respectively. Their resignation and the worsening political situation in the Union, which included the looming prospect of rebellion, cast a shadow on the GSWA campaign.[120]

Fiasco at Sandfontein, 26 September 1914

The failure to secure Walvis Bay/Swakopmund placed Beves at Lüderitzbucht in a precarious position. The occupation of Swakopmund would have placed the Germans on the horns of a dilemma, and in the absence of occupation, they could concentrate their forces on Lüderitzbucht. Smuts's predicated his plan on the ability to advance his forces simultaneously on exterior lines disallowing the concentration of German forces using interior lines.[121] Beves, facing the might of the Schutztruppe alone, would have to rely on Lukin ensconced at the southern border to create a diversion to distract the Germans. The threat of a flanking attack by Lukin prevented German concentration against the port. However, Lukin faced problems of his own beside the prospect of moving his troops over many kilometres of inhospitable arid terrain. Maritz with 'B' Force guarded Lukin's vulnerable right flank, but he was growing increasingly hostile to the whole idea of invading GSWA.

Maritz, the commandant of the northern military district bordering GSWA, was a physically powerful man and a *Bittereinder* in the South African War.[122] He agitated against the invasion of GSWA ever since receiving news of it via Beyers on 15 August.[123] Smuts was fully aware of the open secret that Maritz was vehemently hostile to an invasion of GSWA.[124] Maritz had also contacted the Germans sometime after 21 August and sought arrangements to acquire arms and ammunition. Seitz received his request favourably and proceeded to set up the Afrikaner Sudafrikanischen Freiwilligen-Korps (Vrijkorps) consisting of 300 Afrikaner settlers in GSWA under the command of Andries de Wet.[125] The Vrijkorps, assisted by support elements of Germans, launched an attack, capturing the Union police station at Nakob on

16 September, in response to the South Africans occupying Raman's Drift and seizing the German police post two days earlier.

A perfect storm was brewing which placed Beves in considerable jeopardy. The government took note of Maritz's recalcitrant behaviour and, coupled with delays in the seaborne operations, an uneasiness descended on the entire operation.[126] Smuts cajoled Lukin to proceed with his advance to discourage the Germans and keep Maritz onside. Maritz would protect Lukin's right flank and cooperation between these two forces was crucial. The advance along exterior lines called for Lukin to strike through Raman's Drift on the Orange River and successively capture the towns of Warmbad and Kalkfontein. The latter was the southern terminus of the German railway system. (See Map 3.1) Such a thrust by Lukin would fulfil the further objective of thwarting any German intentions of invading the Union.[127]

It soon became apparent that Maritz was not going to cooperate in covering Lukin's flank. Furthermore, strong indicators emerged that he was about to declare open rebellion. Instead of his force bolstering Lukin's right flank, it began instead to menace him. Maritz posed a real danger if he could add his force to the enemy, thereby destroying the delicate balance of fighting power. Smuts, instead of his usual decisiveness, took no action to remove Maritz immediately despite all the evidence of his wavering attitude.[128] An indication that Smuts underestimated the threat of rebellion as late as 22 September was his reply to Deneys Reitz's letter in which Reitz had pointed out the rebellious mood in the Orange Free State. Smuts replied that he was not afraid of revolution or civil war.[129] Instead, he ordered Maritz to advance to Schuit Drift from Kakamas and then head to Ukamas to assist and cooperate with the force under Lukin on 23 September. Smuts's decision to test Maritz's loyalty rather than replace him is testament to the difficult political climate where his usual decisiveness and indeed ruthlessness on occasion gave way to expediency.

Smuts pressed Lukin to advance to Sandfontein expeditiously to create a diversion to relieve Beves of pressure at Lüderitzbucht and allow for reinforcements to arrive at the scene.[130] The intelligence picture of a rapidly gathering German force in the south as painted below shows the threat to Beves as actual rather than Smuts merely perceiving a threat. The official history describes Smuts's request to Lukin as one verging on a request for "self-sacrifice".[131] Lukin was under no illusion as to the precariousness of the situation. He possessed reliable intelligence showing the enemy was determined to oppose his advance to Kalkfontein and that they would use the railway to concentrate considerable forces against him.[132] However, Lukin paints a different picture in his report, blaming his predicament on intelligence failure. He felt that scouts should have detected the enormous force of 1,800 Germans and 10 guns. If he had known of the impending attack by so large a force, he would have withdrawn the Sandfontein force within three to four hours. Lukin pointed out that the disaster would have been greater had the Germans delayed their attack and allowed him to advance on Warmbad.[133] When Lukin did advance, contrary to what Smuts expected, he did so with only a fraction of the force available to him. The doyen of manoeuvre warfare, Heinz Guderian, who cautioned some years later against attacking in penny packets offered the retort "*Klotzen, nicht Kleckern*" which adequately encapsulates Lukin's error.[134]

Inevitably and not unexpectedly, Maritz disobeyed Smuts's order to advance, leaving Lukin high and dry deep inside German territory. Instead of support, Maritz offered a long-worded reply which boiled down to offering his resignation should Smuts see fit to order him to attack GSWA. Smuts, still vacillating, sent Major Barend Enslin, an experienced and reliable officer, to investigate the circumstances of Maritz's clear insubordination. Captain P. E. Erasmus joined Enslin, and they hatched a plan to reveal Maritz's true intentions. It became increasingly clear to both men on 28 September that Maritz was in contact with the Germans and was cooperating with them. Maritz produced a letter from Seitz who undertook to assist in an Afrikaner uprising to restore their independence.[135]

Enslin's report to Smuts emphasised the fact that Maritz would not attack the Germans, but he inexplicably downplayed the fact that he was almost certainly cooperating with them. Maritz was aware that 2,000 German troops were advancing on Lukin's forces and he rebuffed Lukin's request for reinforcements. Smuts, acting on Enslin's evidence, immediately summoned Maritz to Pretoria on 30 September and instructed him to hand over command to Enslin. Maritz flatly refused to cooperate, and Smuts eventually transferred the command of 'A' and 'B' forces, including the men under Maritz, to Colonel Coen Jacobus Brits (1868–1932)[136] on 2 October. Maritz received his long-awaited discharge from the UDF on 9 October. He arrested his replacement Major Ben Bouwer on his arrival to take over command, thus signalling his formal act of rebellion. His action effectively deducted 1,000 soldiers from the UDF strength and added them to that of the Germans.[137]

On 26 September Lukin's 'A' force, unsupported by Maritz and understrength for the task allotted, suffered a serious defeat at the hands of the Germans at Sandfontein. German casualties amounted to 14 dead and 46 wounded, while the South Africans lost 16 men dead and 51 wounded. Although the numbers of casualties were not large nor the defeat of any strategic consequence, it was a blow to the prestige of the fledgling UDF with the possibility of serious political repercussions.[138] The advance in such small numbers to Sandfontein was an operational error considering the uncertainty of Maritz's allegiance, knowing that the Germans were in force in the vicinity, and contrary to the rules of concentration. Furthermore, Lukin committed grave tactical errors such as the lack of adequate reconnaissance. Smuts laid the blame for the reversal at Sandfontein squarely at Lukin's door.[139] He dispatched a telegram to Lukin on 28 September in which he admonishes Lukin for taking "too large a risk in leaving so small a force at Sandfontein and your main force so far away at Steinkopf". Smuts revealed the overall strategic concern of the operation when he pressed Lukin to hold the Orange River and not retire further south in the wake of the Sandfontein fiasco. Smuts was concerned that Lukin would no longer pose a threat to the German flank, thereby leaving them free to deal with the forces at Lüderitzbucht. Further communication instructed Lukin to move most of his forces from Steinkopf to the Orange River and adopt an aggressive posture to keep the enemy away from a vulnerable Beves. In the wake of these developments, Smuts finally abandoned the Walvis Bay/Swakopmund expedition on 29 September and dispatched McKenzie's 'D' Force, originally earmarked for Walvis Bay, to Lüderitzbucht on 30 September.[140]

Operation Walvis Bay Abandoned, 29 September 1914

Smuts together with Buxton concurred with the suggestion of the Vice-Admiral Sir Herbert King-Hall, the Commander-in-Chief (C-in-C) of the Royal Navy's Cape Station, to abandon the idea of the Walvis Bay/Swakopmund expedition on 29 September.[141] King-Hall believed that a landing would be untenable in light of the chaos experienced at Lüderitzbucht and the difficulty of protecting Walvis Bay from the sea because of its the vast defensive perimeter. Furthermore, he could not account for all German shipping in the area.[142] Collyer, the official history, and the contemporary accounts of Warwick, Strachan, Van der Waag and Garcia have a different version of events. Evidence reveals that Smuts did not exclude a landing at Walvis Bay/Swakopmund on 21 August as they have suggested. Reading Lukin's biography confirms that he executed his advance upon Sandfontein in terms of Smuts's original plan, which included the landing at Walvis/Swakopmund.[143] Further evidence is when Crewe expressed his satisfaction of Smuts's modified plan and suggested he increase the landing at Walvis Bay/Swakopmund to 20,000 men.[144]

Misidentification of the Walvis Bay/Swakopmund operation cancellation date—21 August instead of 29 September—has removed the operational context of the Sandfontein battle and has led contemporary historians to misunderstand some of Smuts's motives. Van der Waag postulates that the UDF achieved the objectives of the first phase of the operation when they successfully occupied Lüderitzbucht on 18 September and neutralised Swakopmund via naval bombardment. The problem is his assertion of a "first phase" before it even existed (reading history backwards) and his dismissal of the essential nature of Smuts creating a fourth prong to enhance the effects of using external lines of communication.[145] It is not surprising that once Van der Waag removes the operational context, there remains little reason, according to him, for the continuation of the advance by Lukin. Van der Waag incorrectly attributes the operational necessity for Lukin's hasty action down to a fear that the Germans were destroying precious water holes on their side of the border.[146] Incorrect assumptions that Smuts abandoned the Walvis Bay/Swakopmund seaborne landings well before the Sandfontein debacle have led historians down a rabbit hole of bogus tactical, operational, and strategical analysis.

It was the British in the form of King-Hall who pressed for the cancellation of the Walvis Bay/Swakopmund landing. The British were increasingly concerned with poor organisation and bungled logistics at Lüderitzbucht. The rapidly deteriorating political situation within the Union, coupled with the disastrous reversal at Sandfontein, also did not inspire confidence. The British suggested an alteration of the plan in the light of this on 28 September. Smuts concurred that all these factors together with a rapidly developing Afrikaner rebellion, which included Maritz's treachery, placed Lüderitzbucht in a precarious position.[147] There was thus little option but to bolster the defences of Lüderitzbucht with the disbanded 'D' Force formerly earmarked for Walvis Bay/Swakopmund. Smuts would only reinstate the expedition to Walvis Bay/Swakopmund on 25 November after he and Botha had registered decisive successes against the rebels.

The Afrikaner Rebellion

The First World War revealed/caused deep fissures in South African society which widened the barely healed rift between Afrikaner and Englishmen following the South African War. Many Afrikaners abhorred the prospect of siding with Britain against Germany in the First World War. Unreconciled Afrikaner nationalists looked to Germany as a possible ally in the restoration of the former Boer Republics, and the First World War provided an opportunity to test that notion. At the outbreak of the war, Afrikaner nationalists and pacifists accepted, albeit reluctantly, that South Africa had no option but to enter the war on the side of the British as a consequence of her dominion status. However, invading GSWA, instead of adopting a defensive posture, was a step too far for many Afrikaner nationalists. Afrikaner resistance to the war, at first only vocal, became increasingly menacing once Smuts let it be known of his territorial desires on GSWA.[148]

Smuts, confident that the opposition was under control, seemed oblivious to the rapidly deteriorating situation within the Union once the invasion of GSWA got underway. He noticed something was seriously amiss when Maritz became increasingly uncooperative and then openly defiant to the point of disregarding orders. Smuts displayed caution which was out of character with his typically decisive nature when confronted with difficult and ambiguous situations. He was reluctant to remove Maritz even when the available evidence suggested that the former Boer leader had joined the German side. When he eventually acted, it was too late to prevent the disastrous defeat at Sandfontein. The same cautious behaviour was present when it became clear that Beyers and Christiaan de Wet were secretly carrying on with the rebellion as reported by Buxton on 22 October. Smuts considered their arrest unwise and uncharacteristically wanted the two men to take the first aggressive steps.[149] Smuts held Beyers with special contempt for he was party to the decision to allow the British to withdraw their garrison, while simultaneously harbouring intentions to rebel. Adding to the treasonous soup, was the fact that Beyers was part and parcel of the planning to invade GSWA.[150]

It seemed that Smuts remained one step behind the rebellion. He waited for Maritz to openly revolt before declaring martial law even though he knew weeks beforehand that the conspiracy was well underway. On declaring martial law, Smuts preferred to pacify the rebels by appealing for them to be reasonable and not allow foreign agents to influence them. He was reluctant to spill the blood of former comrades of a recent past. Sarah Millin speaks of Smuts's policy of letting things develop, believing that his policy was one of an optimist who wishes for the matter to resolve amicably, rather than prematurely forcing the situation.[151] He carried this attitude well beyond the height of the Afrikaner Rebellion when he granted a blanket amnesty to all the rebels, including the leadership. Botha and Buxton took a harder line. insisting that the amnesty should not apply to leaders and persons who took a prominent or leading part in the rebellion.[152] The amnesty offered on 12 November which expired on 21 November excluded the leadership.[153]

The Afrikaner Rebellion was integral to the opening phase of the GSWA campaign. Botha and Smuts were not oblivious that an invasion of GSWA would carry the risk of awakening Afrikaner nationalists. Nevertheless, the prospect of gaining territory, and the demonstration of loyalty to the United Kingdom, outweighed the risks of dividing the nation. Smuts, naively, banked on the notion that conquering GSWA and adding its territory would unite Englishmen and Afrikaner behind a Greater South Africa. Smuts was genuinely taken aback by the betrayal of those who conspired to rebel.[154] With the Afrikaner Rebellion underway, Smuts reluctantly postponed the invasion of GSWA, giving birth to the notion of a first and second phase to the GSWA campaign. The Afrikaner rebels posed a more severe and immediate threat to the Union than the Germans. Placing the GSWA invasion on hold allowed Smuts to immediately switch some of his military resources to meet the rebel threats.

Botha acted decisively once the rebellion was underway. He took to the field as the head of the forces mobilised, thereby taking no chances in uncertain leadership of dubious loyalty. He was wisely cautious about the divided loyalties within the UDF. His decision to use loyal Afrikaner commandos to suppress the rebellion rather than English-orientated formations spoke to the sensitivity of the political situation.[155] Fortunately, an indecisive rebel leadership delivered a poorly planned and coordinated rebellion.[156] Lukin's force was an exception with Smuts taking direct control of him and ordering him and his 2,000 men to proceed to Bloemfontein to be available to intercept De Wet. Smuts believed that the rebels might attempt to break out toward GSWA where they would procure arms and munitions from the Germans and return to South Africa.[157] An important consequence of Botha and Smuts mobilising loyal commandos to fight the rebels, instead of relying on British offers of military support, was the unlocking of the Rifle Association mounted infantry. These predominantly Afrikaner commando formations were passed over for political reasons in the first phase of the GSWA campaign and would now become available for future operations in GSWA once the Afrikaner Rebellion was quashed.[158]

Botha delegated Smuts the role of organising the campaign behind the lines while becoming Botha's chief of staff. South Africa was divided into 15 military districts, with the staff in each district tasked to locate the rebel forces in their area, providing Botha and Smuts with accurate timely intelligence.[159] An expert telegraphist, who accompanied Botha in the field facilitated communication—Smuts having a similar device in his office. The two men often spoke directly to one another via this channel of communication.[160]

> General Botha and General Smuts were a perfect combination and appeared to have the utmost faith and confidence in each other. I have stood near the general. During the rebellion, when he was carrying on a conversation with General Smuts over the telephone telegraph. He always started in the same way, "Is that you Jannie? Now listen, this is my plan". He would then detail his plan, and wind up by saying, "What do you think of the plan?"[161]

This typical exchange described so eloquently by Trew epitomised the relationship between the two friends. It paints a picture of the support and encouragement Botha received behind the scenes, allowing him unfettered command of his forces in the field knowing Smuts guarded his back.[162]

The defeat the Germans handed to Lukin at Sandfontein, coupled with the internal political strife brought about by the rebellion, emboldened Seitz to declare that GSWA "could hold out another year".[163] The Germans placed some of their strategic hopes in taking advantage of an Afrikaner uprising to prolong their resistance in the face of overwhelming numerical advantages enjoyed by the UDF. Maritz was the first to rebel in the northern Cape and GSWA, followed by De Wet in the Orange Free State with Beyers and Kemp in the Transvaal, all commanding significant rebel forces. Faced with an uncertain strategic position and not knowing the full extent of the forces available to the rebels, Smuts and Botha decided to concentrate their military resources in the Pretoria area and strike out from this central position.[164] This sound strategy of operating from internal lines split the rebels and forced them to operate from external lines.[165] (See Map 3.5)

Botha relied heavily on Smuts to manage the administration back at Defence Headquarters in Pretoria and Smuts undertook much of the staff work involving planning, strategy, and the measures undertaken to suppress the rebellion.[166] Mobility, essential for the swift execution of manoeuvre war, would be enhanced with using the railways at the operational level, and horses and cars at the tactical level.[167] The question of mobility was so crucial that Smuts laid 227 kilometres of new railway lines between Prieska and Upington.[168] Well-armed and -armoured trains could rapidly deploy not only infantry, but complete formations of mounted infantry who, fully bridled and saddled, could speedily detrain and quickly go into action.[169] The identification of objectives was aided by a reasonably sophisticated intelligence network which garnered information from local police, magistrates and members of the Railway Rifle Associations.[170] Intelligence would identify the exact location of the rebels, their force strength and their intentions to focus planned attacks.[171] A motorcar contingent comprising 110 automobiles provided by the Transvaal Automobile Club, fitted with machine guns and manned by 500 soldiers of the 2nd Transvaal Scottish, enhanced the UDF's mobility and ability to deliver firepower rapidly to the objective. All the information gathered was processed centrally in Pretoria under the direction of Hugh Wyndham.

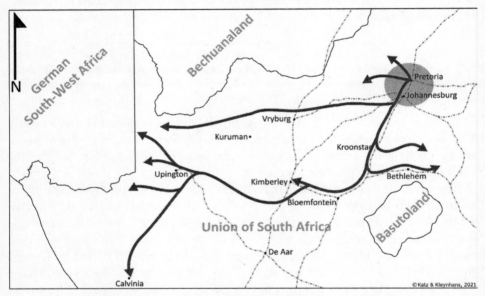

Map 3.5. The central position of operations during the Afrikaner Rebellion, 1914[172]

Smuts did not rely on military means alone to bring the rebels to heel and urged them on numerous occasions to desist from rebellious acts and return to their homes. Smuts was encouraged by reports that many rebels were disillusioned, fed up and desirous of returning home. He issued a proclamation on 30 October informing the rebels that if they surrendered their arms, they would avoid prosecution. The combination of mailed fist coupled with a velvet glove offering generous surrender terms yielded positive results.

Botha left nothing to chance and assembled a commando under his leadership to tackle De Wet, who was the largest and most dangerous threat. De Wet's commandos numbering 2,000 camped in a valley east of Bloemfontein for the night but failed to cut the telephone line from Mushroom Valley to Winburg. Sound intelligence via a government loyalist betrayed de Wet's presence. Botha managed to surprise the rebels on the morning of 12 November, but not everything went to plan. Brits and Lukin were at constant loggerheads, and their vendetta impacted negatively on their judgment and actions, with the result that they failed to arrive on time.[173] De Wet and a large part of his force made good their escape through a gap in Botha's encirclement. Although Botha inflicted a considerable defeat, he missed the chance of a knockout blow.[174]

The effect of the victory was immediate, and several small parties of disillusioned rebels made their way back home while others surrendered at the first opportunity. While rebel fighting power diminished, Botha's forces continued to grow with Buxton reporting that the numbers had swelled to 9,000 by 12 November.[175] Botha was able to report on 15 November that "many" rebels were surrendering as a direct result of the action at Mushroom Valley.[176] He set off in hot pursuit of De Wet who attempted to join up with Beyers and Kemp. Steyn sent a telegram to Botha on 16 November that De Wet and Beyers wanted to discuss a peace settlement. Botha and Smuts, seeking a decisive end to the rebellion, took a hard line and refused to parley.[177] Botha increased his efforts to pursue De Wet, calling on all commandos to combine and hunt him down relentlessly.[178] De Wet was finally captured by Coen Brits on 1 December, with the balance of his forces 200 kilometres north-west of Vryberg.[179]

Botha and Smuts believed the fight had left the rebels and they were anxious to surrender if they could obtain assurances that he would spare the lives of their leaders.[180] Further evidence was an appeal from rebel leadership to avoid further bloodshed. They sought an armistice to allow for a safe passage to confer with the captured De Wet and press him to negotiate with the government. Should De Wet not cooperate, they would take it upon themselves to end hostilities. Botha, in consultation with Smuts, took a hard line against these belated attempts to extract concessions from the government. Their reply pointed out that the responsibility for the bloodshed lay squarely with the rebels and the time for negotiations had lapsed, and the best course of action was immediate, unconditional surrender to prevent serious consequences.[181] Reports came in on 8 December that Beyers, while trying to cross the Vaal River at Greylingsdrift, had been shot and wounded and had subsequently drowned. The government offered a reward for the recovery of the body.[182]

Maritz, who had kicked off the rebellion, continued to battle the UDF well into January 1915. Reports indicated that despite extending peace feelers, Maritz and a force of 1,600 Germans were 80 kilometres north of Upington on 21 November.[183] Maritz conducted his last efforts against a tide of rebels deserting everywhere. On 22 November Buxton reported that the rebellion was "expiring" and "armed resistance to the government [was] approaching the end". De Wet, down to 40 men, desperately tried to evade his pursuers.

Kemp was approaching Upington, with worn-out horses and disheartened men.[184] Maritz and Kemp's forces finally made contact and surrendered to General Jacob 'Jaap' van Deventer (1874–1922) after their failed attack on Upington on 24 January 1915.[185] However, Smuts and Botha remained in some danger as evidenced by an uncovered assassination plot in April 1915[186] and the constant threat of industrial unrest while the UDF was campaigning in GEA.[187]

Contemporary historians, when dealing with Smuts's generalship and conduct of the German East African campaign, are prone to accusing Smuts of neither having the necessary expertise nor experience in conducting operations involving thousands of men. Few, if any historians, have considered Smuts's extensive involvement with the first and second phases of the GSWA campaign and his crucial support role in the Afrikaner Rebellion where he played a decisive role in all phases, with his handprint present in all the planning and strategic decisions. Restricting his experience of battle, as many do, to his exploits in the South African War at the head of 300 men, ignores his staff work internship in support of operations involving many thousands of troops in 1914 which required planning, coordination, communication, recruitment, procurement, equipment, logistics, intelligence, transport and mobility. Least quantifiable but fundamental was the moral and intellectual support which he extended to Botha during a particularly trying and tragic time. In Botha's own words:

> Nobody can appreciate sufficiently the great work General Smuts has done—greater than that of any other man throughout this unhappy period. At his post day and night, his brilliant intellect, his calm judgement, his amazing energy and his undaunted courage have been assets of inestimable value to the Union in her hour of trial.[188]

The rebellion was a testing time for both men, but their friendship and trust not only endured but grew stronger. Their skill sets were complementary to each other and brought a swift, successful resolution to the rebellion.

CHAPTER 4

The German South West African Campaign, 1915

When I returned to the Union from German South West Africa I found that many bloodthirsty civilians seemed disappointed at the smallness of our casualty list. It was hard to make them understand that it was only the strategy of a genius that made this result possible. General Botha never gave them a chance to fight. He disliked the direct approach, and frontal attacks—the only criticism I ever heard him make of British generals was that they were too fond of frontal attacks.[1]

The GSWA campaign's postponement allowed revision of the original Smuts plan between 5 and 8 October. The plan retained most of Smuts's original objectives, but this iteration contained a massive fourfold increase in numbers deployed.[2] (See Table 4.1) Increased force levels would adversely impact the tenuous logistical support system in the forthcoming months of the campaign. P.S. Beves at Lüderitzbucht received reinforcements from the disbanded 'D' Force and then further reinforcements from H.T. Lukin's unfortunate southern army.[3] Beves was replaced by Duncan McKenzie and the force redesignated 'Central Force'. Lukin's remaining force would stay on the southern border with GSWA and hold the Port Nolloth–Steinkopf railway line. Smuts reconstituted Manie Maritz's old 'B' Force with strong mounted commando elements under the command of Jacob Louis van Deventer[4]—now designated 'Southern Force'—to act in concert with Beves in simultaneously driving the Germans out of Keetmanshoop. A reconstituted powerful 'D' Force, now called 'Northern Force' under the command of Louis Botha, would land at Walvis Bay to advance in great strength from Swakopmund to seize the ultimate prize of Windhoek. Joining the Southern Force was the Eastern Force under the command of Lieutenant-Colonel C.A.L. Berrangé (1864–1922).[5] (See Table 4.1)

The prerequisite for launching an attack from Swakopmund in Windhoek's direction was building and rebuilding railway communications between Swakopmund/Walvis Bay and Karibib. The new plan called for large quantities of railway material and appropriate construction staff as part of the Walvis Bay combined force. The optimistically set schedule for Southern and Central forces to launch an attack as per the revised plan of invasion of GSWA was for the end of October. The Northern Force would be ready to launch their invasion by 16 November. The whole operation depended on the availability of Royal Navy ships to support the extended operation.[6]

Table **4.1.** Composition of UDF deployment to GSWA, March 1915[7]

Force	Commander	Doctrine orientation	Mounted	Infantry	Artillery	Admin	Total
Northern Force	Botha	Republican	13,265	5,046	742	1,141	20,194
Central Force	Mckenzie	Colonial/ British	3,853	5,792	528	777	10,950
Southern Force	Van Deventer	Mixed	9,309	-	112	664	10,085
Eastern Force	Berrange	Colonial/ British	1,957	-	40	331	2,328
Total			28,384	10,838	1,422	2,913	43,557
			65%	25%	3%	7%	100%

The new incarnation of the Smuts plan contained fundamental differences from the original. Apart from Maritz's former 'B' Force, Smuts initially relied mostly on the UDF's Active Citizen Force units. These possessed a distinct colonial/British structure and doctrine. They had a formal rank structure, were trained in British methods, and led by English officers with a distinctly British detailed command style. The Boer commandos were more informal, led by Afrikaners, with a less rigid structure and a directive command style that encouraged initiative and the devolution of decision-making down to the lower levels of command. Smuts boosted the invasion's second iteration with the addition of the Boer republican-style commandos of the second-line ACF Reserve (Class B) Rifle Association members. (See Figure 2.1 and 2.2) These units had played a significant role in extinguishing the Afrikaner Rebellion a mere few weeks before their deployment to GSWA. Predominantly Afrikaner, and veterans of the South African War, these mounted infantry forces were earmarked for deployment to Walvis Bay/Swakopmund (Northern Force) to be commanded by Botha leading from the front.[8] Botha and Smuts decided that the commandos, who had proved loyal in extinguishing the Afrikaner Rebellion, could now be used to good effect in GSWA. Smuts's plan, once nimble and manned by 10,000–12,000 colonial/ British-orientated units, became bloated with a cumbersome complement of 40,000 men.

Any one of the four forces deployed (Northern, Central, Southern, and Eastern) would vastly outnumber the entire *Schutztruppen* complement of GSWA. The new steamroller, accompanied by unwieldy logistics and employed bludgeon like, would replace the rapier-like thrusts which Smuts had originally conceived. Neither the official histories nor contemporary historians have addressed the cumbersome nature of the reconstituted Smuts plan of 1915, nor have they addressed the superfluous nature of the many infantry units deployed.[9]

The British greeted the revised Smuts plan positively, and wholeheartedly agreed that a railway line was the most suitable form of logistic communication for a modern war coupled with a port facility and overwhelming sea power. Smuts's original plan was devoid of any intention of building or restoring the railway. The British approved the increased force levels, agreed on Port Nolloth's unsuitability for launching a concentrated attack from the south, and preferred to launch the southern offensive from Lüderitzbucht. They raised concerns regarding the effectiveness and supply requirements for the commando forces situated at Upington (Eastern Force) and assumed that they would be self-sufficient and live off the land. Concerned, the British then deferred to Botha's greater knowledge of both the lay of the land and the campaign's operational conditions. Additional concerns centred around the UDF's weakness in artillery pieces and lack of trained, experienced gunners.[10] Availability of shipping, forever plaguing the early stages of the campaign, once again reared its head. The British planned to divert their scarce naval resources to intercept the German light cruiser SMS *Königsberg*, which threatened Allied shipping sailing on the African continent's east coast.[11]

Unlike the original plan, Smuts now consulted the British on matters connected with the expedition.[12] However, Maritz going into open rebellion on 9 October again delayed the intended landings at Walvis Bay. Historians have tended to blame lack of British naval support for delays.[13] However, there is a need to consider other contributing factors, including the rebellion, rampant disorganisation, and lack of high-level communication. Sydney Buxton reported that results from talks about naval arrangements for the GSWA operation were "quite satisfactory" between the British C-in-C Cape of Good Hope Station, Vice-Admiral Sir Herbert King-Hall and Smuts and Botha.[14] Buxton advised the British about the severe state of affairs in South Africa on 25 October, and they, considering the internal risks, recommended that the South Africans suspend operations against GSWA until they had suppressed the Afrikaner Rebellion. The consensus was that the rebellion was spreading rapidly, and that all of South Africa's resources were needed to deal with the perilous situation. The British wisely felt that the South Africans, thus far, had struggled with the operation, being "unaccustomed" to dealing with overseas expeditions even with their advantage of concentrated resources. The added complication of the rebellion would dangerously divide their attentions.[15]

Smuts was impatient about reinvigorating the stalled proceedings and proposed the launch date for the Walvis Bay expedition for 12 December. The British issued a cautionary note that the expedition should not start until the German naval squadron in the southern oceans was located and neutralised.[16] Smuts insisted that further delays would have severe repercussions for the campaign and morale on the home front.[17] Despite Smuts's obvious irritation, the British delayed the expedition by a further two weeks. In the interim Duncan McKenzie, commanding the forces at Lüderitzbucht, received a further 2,000 reinforcements.[18] Intelligence sources confirmed that the German fleet had set sail from South America for South Africa on 7 December.[19] However, the German naval threat was finally eliminated in the battle of the Falklands on 8 December when the SMS *Gneisenau*, SMS *Scharnhorst*, SMS *Leipzig*, and SMS *Nurnberg* were sunk by the Royal Navy.[20]

Although the UDF would now re-enter the fray with a significant numerical advantage, South Africa faced a formidable foe in the Schutztruppe. The Germans not only enjoyed greater artillery firepower than the UDF, but they were a homogeneous army led by veterans of their excellent *Kriegsakademie* and in possession of a dynamic command and staff system. What follows is an analysis of how the two sides would conduct their warfare in GSWA.

Toward a Union Defence Force Doctrine

South Africa, more than the other First World War Allied belligerents, possessed acute sensitivity to home-front opinions. Divisive politics, including the politics of exclusion, shaped war policy, strategy, operational art, and even tactics. The UDF, barely two years old at the outbreak of war, held a hybrid institutional belief system. Its doctrinal roots were an amalgamation of Boer, colonial, and British military systems. In this respect, the UDF was unlike the other belligerents fighting it out in the world's first global conflict. South Africa's otherness came about from the fact that the UDF comprised former enemies. A mere 12 years before 1914, Englishmen and Afrikaners were bitter foes, locked in mortal combat. The formation of the UDF in 1912 gave priority to nation-building rather than an effective modern military force. Smuts imbued the process with political compromises that underpinned the UDF's structures and appointments with an eye to soothing historical animosities rather than rewarding skill and expertise.[21]

Threat perception was fundamental in designing the UDF and its doctrine, emphasising the suppression of internal strife emanating from disaffected and disenfranchised blacks. Military planners composed the institutional belief system around the unlikelihood of foreign invasion by a European power. Indeed, the UDF's first action was against white organised labour in January 1914.[22] Significantly, the deployment relied heavily on the old Boer commandos who had been languishing as members of the Rifle Associations. A further noteworthy military test against South African citizens was when the UDF occupied itself in quashing 11,000 Afrikaner rebels, some led by former UDF members, between August and December 1914. Again, Boer commandos loyal to Botha and Smuts were used to suppress the rebellion. The fledgeling UDF could not field a modern army based on European military models but increasingly relied on the old Republican Forces' men and doctrine.[23]

Smuts began the invasion of GSWA with regiments belonging to the Permanent Force and the Active Citizen Force which displayed a strong colonial/British doctrine and which regiments were led by Englishmen such as Beves, McKenzie, Berrangé, and Lukin. The second phase of operations came to rely heavily on the Boer mounted infantry of the former Republican armies and its veteran commanders such as Botha, Van Deventer,[25] and Coen Brits. The UDF's relative newness severely limited training time and ability to equip sufficient recruits with modern British doctrine favoured by the fledgling UDF. When the second phase of the GSWA campaign got underway, Smuts, once

Figure 4.1. Two armies and two doctrines[24]

again, relied on the mounted infantry of the former Republican armies to fill the ranks. The challenge was that the UDF was not a homogenous force but effectively fielded two armies following differing doctrines, structure and discipline.[26] (See Figure 4.1)

The Northern Force under Botha fielded two commando mounted brigades and an infantry brigade. Veterans of the South African War led the two mounted brigades and closely followed the "Boer Way of War" which was a directive command style which relied on initiative and intuition down to the lowest ranks. They favoured a manoeuvre doctrine which they had practised for over a century and perfected by Botha in the latter phases of the South African War.[27] The Boer mounted infantry were highly mobile and preferred to manoeuvre to fight rather than conduct pitched frontal assaults. Through manoeuvre and high mobility, they often forced their opponents to attack under unfavourable circumstances. Their conventional doctrine, when adopting a persisting strategy in the opening stages of the South African War, favoured the strategic offensive coupled with the tactical defensive.

Beside the Boer mounted infantry, the UDF was also home to the more English-orientated mounted infantry and traditional infantry units. The mounted infantry was represented by the South African Mounted Rifles (SAMR). The mounted and traditional infantry had colonial regimental roots and were mostly led by Englishmen with a British-orientated detailed command style, conventional military discipline, a structured hierarchy of ranks, and adherence to British doctrine. The traditional infantry was made up of newly recruited Afrikaners and Englishmen but almost exclusively led by Englishmen. The Boer horseman had more affinity for the care of his mount having ridden horses from youth than his English counterpart who first learnt to ride on enlisting. Demonstrating this point were the horses of the Southern Force, made up predominantly of the more traditional English mounted regiments, which suffered excessive saddle wounds from lack of attention to saddlery.[28] Boer mounted infantry, less reliant of traditional logistics, endowed with a flexible command style based on individual initiative, were able to conduct their operations at a higher tempo than either their UDF comrades in the SAMR, or their *Schutztruppen* opponents.

At the tactical level, the UDF Boer mounted infantryman, more so than their English SAMR equivalents, rode much lighter than his German counterpart. The Germans were much heavier in cavalry saddle and equipment which made them slower on the march.[29] Mounted infantry fought dismounted much like conventional infantry. Their horses brought then into and took them out and away from the fight. The Boers trained their horses to stand still when they dismounted, dispensing with a horse-holder and allowing every man to contribute to the firing line. The Boers adopted a pace designed to produce maximum speed with minimum physical strain on the rider and the mount. Importantly, their frugal way of life on campaign reduced the mounted infantryman's dependence on the logistical chain to a minimum.[30]

Superior mobility permitted retreating out of harm's way should conditions on the battlefield warrant a withdrawal. The Boer style of command facilitated a generous amount of initiative on the battlefield compared with their opponents.[31] The Boer made skilful use of the terrain and his ability to be accurate at extreme ranges to get the most out of his marksmanship. No formal fire direction existed, and each Boer used his initiative in selecting a target. Complete reliance on individual initiative disallowed any subordination to the intention or will of a superior. It made conformance to a plan of a superior almost impossible after the battle was underway.[32] Freedom to exercise initiative was often unbridled and often practised out of the overall confines of an objective as prescribed in German doctrine. The lack of a formal conventional command structure often delivered unexpected results on the battlefield.

To some extent, their incredible mobility compensated for lack of depth in their formations, which allowed for a certain amount of flexibility to reinforce other sectors of the line. Fear of being outflanked persuaded them to overextend their defensive lines which exacerbated their lack of reserve. Early over-commitment of forces precluded the increase of firepower in areas of opportunity and severely curtailed any chance of going over to the offensive when the occasion arose. Therefore, Boer doctrine delivered powerful defensive results but was flawed in the tactical offensive. Commanders tended to be slow, or even reluctant, to take advantage of tactical opportunities as they arose, and the lack of reserve precluded fresh troops delivering decisive firepower. How Boers fought was a result of their lack of training, organisation, and complete absence of discipline.

The Germans found the Boer lack of will to annihilate their enemy incomprehensible.[33] Boers preferred to outflank or envelop an enemy rather than become involved in a costly frontal assault. The Boer mounted infantryman carried no bayonet in the South African War and neither in the GSWA campaign, and he was unlikely to engage in shock action.[34] The South African forces outnumbered the modest German force in GSWA, but this numerical advantage did not tempt them to conduct a costly war of attrition. They avoided pitched battles in favour of advancing on multiple fronts. Using the threat of envelopment, the UDF dislodged the Germans from their prepared positions and made them defend locations, not of their primary choice. The South Africans forced Victor Franke (1865–1936), the last commander of the Schutztruppe in GSWA, to surrender on 9 July 1915 with the German fighting capability almost intact. The campaign's successful conclusion at a relatively low human cost was a vindication of Boer manoeuvre warfare, carrying all the hallmarks of a developing South African "way of war".[35]

The final word on the UDF belongs to their adversaries who provide a useful insight into the unsettling nature of Boer manoeuvre warfare over the vast desert terrain of GSWA. The Germans acknowledged that the UDF comprised an amalgamation of disparate and even adversarial groupings. The paper-thin edifice of unity was vulnerable to setbacks that, if suffered, could tear the UDF apart. After the Afrikaner Rebellion, the South Africans relied on a massive numerical advantage to preclude the chance that the Germans could launch a strike against any of the offensive thrusts.[36] Very few opportunities arose for the Germans to gather a numerical advantage against the UDF. When the chance had presented itself at Sandfontein earlier, they seized it. Numerical strength and strategic manoeuvre throughout the campaign forced the Germans to give up good defensive positions rather than stand and fight and saved the UDF casualties by avoiding pitched battles. The Germans held the 'Boer' element of the UDF in high regard and considered them natural soldiers who had suffered poor leadership in the South African War. The mounted infantry displayed skill and resourcefulness in GSWA. They used "peasant cunning" and independent initiative while being doggedly persistent and frugal. Their fitness and resolve enabled them to march many miles through harsh conditions for days on end.[37]

The Germans were less flattering when it came to the UDF's face-to-face tactical fighting abilities and rated their performance in these encounters as moderate and the artillery as ineffectual.[38] On the defensive the Boers often applied concentrated firepower from well-prepared positions to overwhelm an often numerically superior opponent. On the offensive, Botha would advance in three columns covering a broad front, with the two flanking columns slightly ahead of the centre. A thick fringe of scouts at the front covered the advancing columns. Botha sought a military result through manoeuvre rather than a pitched battle. He seldom, if ever, resorted to frontal attacks and preferred to pin the enemy in the centre and then attempt a double or single envelopment. Botha had no fear of an enemy appearing in his rear, and, true to manoeuvre warfare principles, his army had no fixed lines of communication.[39] These were lessons that Smuts would apply during his tenure in German East Africa, on the offensive and the defensive.

The Germans were reluctant to deviate far from their communication lines and kept close to their railway lines, removing the element of surprise. Walker provides his insightful impression:

> Herein is found a cue to their ill-success in this campaign; for, unless they were compelled to do so, they did not leave the railways or roads, and never moved without ample transport and food. Whenever they attacked us, they came down the line or along the road. They prepared fortified positions, and built light railways up to them, and whenever we captured them, they had transport and food and drink in abundance. General Botha's men had quite different ideas about fighting. They trekked without transport and without sufficient food or clothing; they crossed deserts and mountains irrespective of roads; and the last thing they thought of was to make a frontal attack or fight when the Germans expected them to.[40]

There was some doubt in British quarters during the GSWA campaign about how the mostly Afrikaner mounted troops would fare when attacking entrenched positions. The Boer way of war was known for its penchant for manoeuvre, taking the path of least resistance, and not getting involved in costly frontal attacks. On a visit to GSWA, Buxton seemed pleased that the Boer elements of the UDF had shown extraordinary mettle in this type of entrenched situation; however, it remained the preferred Boer method to outflank the enemy and avoid a pitched battle.[41]

The Second Phase of the Invasion of GSWA, December 1914

The period from the declaration of war on Germany up to the Afrikaner Rebellion can be considered as the first phase of the GSWA campaign. The South Africans finally landed at Walvis Bay on 25 December which marked the beginning of the second phase. Buxton identified some advantages from delaying the expedition to Walvis Bay/Swakopmund. The size of the expeditionary forces grew exponentially, which ensured tactical victory by default based on an overwhelming numerical advantage. During the intervening period and Afrikaner Rebellion, the UDF acquired essential skills and experience previously lacking, especially in the area of General Staff work. Politically, the country stood on firmer ground, becoming familiar with, if not more amenable, to the idea of invading GSWA. Determined resistance waned somewhat by the time of implementing the second phase of operations in December 1914. A sign of Smuts's confidence was the paltry forces left in garrison in South Africa compared with those joining the campaign.[42] The most significant change was Botha taking supreme command of the GSWA operations. His frontline participation—one of the last heads of state to take to the battlefield—greatly enhanced the campaign's popularity among the Afrikaners.[43]

Colonel P.C.B. Skinner, on loan from the British Army,[44] with two infantry brigades under his command disembarked at the undefended harbour of Walvis Bay on Christmas Day, 1914.[45] Skinner oversaw the invasion until General Botha assumed overall command of the Northern Force.[46] The invaders immediately set about building a defensive line around Walvis Bay.[47] The landing surprised the Germans and was unopposed. The Germans, who had long since abandoned Walvis Bay/Swakopmund in favour of making their defence further into the interior, allowed for a bloodless occupation. South African patrols found no Germans for up to 30 kilometres distant from Walvis Bay. The first sign of the enemy was a two-man German patrol coming from Swakopmund. All indications were that the Germans had no idea of the South African landing. An inhospitable climate and severe lack of water posed a more significant threat to the invasion force than the Germans. The inadequate port facilities were improved together with the infrastructure in what became a massive logistical operation. In peacetime, the Germans had tried to isolate British-held Walvis Bay with the result that no road or railway links extended to the larger German towns in GSWA.

The South Africans soon learnt via wireless intercepts that Joachim von Heydebreck, in command of the GSWA forces since 1910, had perished in a training exercise on 12 November. His position was taken over by Victor Franke, who, like Heydebreck, was a veteran of the Herero Wars (1904–1907).[48] News of Heydebreck's death had little influence on the South African operations. The challenge remained to secure sufficient water resources for the South African troops' steady build-up in Walvis Bay.[49] The Germans had poisoned wells that fed the port's population, leaving the South Africans to devise another plan. Supply ships brought thousands of tons of water from Cape Town, a voyage of over 1,300 kilometres, in the ballast tanks. Engineers worked tirelessly improving the jetties and telephone lines and accumulating sufficient supplies to construct the railway as the troops advanced. All supplies had to be shipped in from Cape Town to sustain the thousands of troops and horses.[50]

Skinner set out with a patrol for Swakopmund on 13 January 1915 once he had safely secured Walvis Bay. His small party encountered German mines on the approach to the port, which killed two mounted infantrymen. Undaunted by their deadly encounter, the patrol proceeded to Swakopmund just in time to see the enemy garrison of approximately 25 beat a hasty retreat. The German inhabitants of Swakopmund had already deserted the town during September. What Skinner intended as a mere reconnaissance turned into the occupation of Swakopmund. The Germans poisoned the town's water supply with sheep dip on their departure, and until the South Africans managed to reinstate it, they would garrison the town with their infantry.[51]

The Germans decided to camp on the outskirts of Swakopmund at Nonidas and kept their distance, not bothering the South Africans as they steadily built up their forces.[52] Then the invaders hastily constructed a railway which extended from Walvis Bay to Swakopmund.[53] Botha took command of the Northern Force on 11 February when he arrived in Swakopmund with his commandos under Brits's command. There he set up his headquarters on the same day that the engineers completed the railway from Walvis to Swakopmund.[54] Barely two weeks passed before Botha was ready to engage the Germans. He could field, in addition to Skinner's brigade, two commando brigades which had been steadily assembling their numbers at Walvis Bay and amounted to 3,000 and 2,000 men respectively.[55]

Botha Breaks Out, February 1915

All the available mounted troops which included Brits's mounted brigades, the 1st Imperial Light Horse, and Grobbelaar's Scouts set off on the night of 22 February. They formed up in a wide enveloping movement north and south of the Swakop River towards Goanikontes farm. The operation would take the form of a double envelopment which became a trademark of Botha's campaign in GSWA. Botha believed the enemy had congregated in some force and so he conducted a night march over relatively unknown terrain, aiming at the arrival of the columns at their destination just before dawn. The difficulty of manoeuvring at night precluded Grobbelaar's Scouts and the Imperial Light Horse, who were advancing on the left flank, from reaching their objective by dawn. On 22 February, despite setbacks, Botha advanced directly into Nonidas which stood at the mouth of the Swakop River. He had with him his 3rd Infantry Brigade and artillery with HMS *Astrea* and her 6-inch guns in support. He launched the attack without the aid of the flanking forces which amounted to a frontal assault on the German defences. Failing to develop the flanking attack timeously allowed the Germans to make good their escape, leaving the South Africans with a deserted objective.[56]

Nevertheless, although an operational failure, Botha managed to secure a valuable source of water supply at Nonidas.[57] The Germans had little option in the face of overwhelming numbers but to trade space for time rather than conduct pitched battles. They were content to hinder the South African advance by laying massive mines and poisoning the precious water wells in their path.[58] Botha greeted the poisoning of wells with threats to bring the perpetrators of this "unwarlike" practice to book after the campaign. German mines were dealt with by driving herds of goats before the advance, hoping that the hapless creatures would set them off.[59] The Germans may have been responsible when Botha fell victim to a stomach ailment of an unknown source.[60] Botha's wife, Annie, and their daughter arrived via warship at Swakopmund to tend to his dietary needs and restore his health. They returned to South Africa on 17 March having restored Botha to health.[61]

Since 28 February, critical shortages of transport hampered Botha's advance. Impatient and not one to wait on developments, Botha scoured every corner for his transport needs, not hesitating in purloining it from headquarters staff, his bodyguard, the medical units and numerous other sources. He wrote letters to Smuts reporting "large deficiencies [in] transport [and] consequent[ly] supply difficulties", indicating the inadequate level of staff planning in the UDF.[62] Poor planning, coupled with increased force levels were crippling the logistics of the invaders.[63] Smuts worked frantically behind the scenes to rectify an almost insurmountable supply problem. At times, the frustration between the two men was palpable; however, their strong friendship and mutual trust endured despite the enormous difficulties.[64]

Botha requested more motor lorries from Defence Headquarters to bolster the meagre transport resources. He set up an advance supply base at Goanikontes to support further operations and pushed for the railway line extension to move ahead at full steam. Good news came in the form of securing decent water supplies at Husab on 8 March, but the lack of transport restricted the advance along the railway line to a few kilometres ahead of the repaired railway. The dire transport situation throttled intentions to swiftly advance along the Swakop River, thereby delaying operations against the enemy. Botha, attempting to breathe momentum into the advance via manoeuvre warfare, became ever more frustrated with the operation's lacklustre tempo. He laid the blame squarely on the shoulders of Colonel M.C. Rowland, the QMG.[65] Botha's intention of restoring manoeuvre and reducing dependency on the railway line by advancing along the Swakop River required many more transport vehicles than available.[66] The communication between the logistical arm, a pure staff function, and those conducting the operations at the 'sharp end' was less than optimal, leaving Botha and his ponderous armies languishing.

Roland Bourne, the Secretary of Defence, on behalf of the QMG, did not take Botha's criticism lying down and endeavoured to justify the reason why Botha now found himself in a transport predicament. Botha's arrival at Swakopmund on 11 February was without any plan of advance into the interior. He preferred to wait until he had assessed the situation first-hand on the spot in character with the Boer way of warfare. The good rains caused the Swakop River to flow, in itself, an infrequent and fortunate event. This good fortune spurred Botha to expedite the dispatch of the mounted units to Swakopmund "at all costs". The support services made great efforts to requisition additional ships with herculean measures to deliver three mounted brigades to Botha within five weeks of his request.[67]

The swift delivery of the mounted units came at the expense of transports, remounts, supplies, stores, and railway materials. The landing facilities at Walvis Bay and Swakopmund were overburdened, leading to inevitable delays and confusion. The responsibility for not informing Botha of the dire situation present at the landing facilities belonged to the staff handling those facilities. A complete failure at the staff level ensured that Defence Headquarters remained oblivious to logistical requirements, proposed dates, or transport needed for the advance on Windhoek. Botha and his staff never inquired whether the transport needs were feasible. The QMG, in the absence of contrary information, assumed that the advance would proceed along the railway at the pace of the railway construction (three kilometres per day). Bourne felt that the failure to supply Botha with adequate logistics fell on "woefully defective staff work" and that the staff had "hopelessly misconceived or neglected its elementary functions in failing to apprise [Botha] and keep insisting upon the essential conditions of time and means which it was their duty to lay before him".[68] Shoddy staff work coupled with lapses in communication between the operational arm and the QMG caused a logistical nightmare that crippled the Northern Force and its endeavours to manoeuvre. Witness to Botha's frustration are the numerous messages which flew back and forth between him and Smuts.

The South Africans built up a reasonable intelligence picture of the enemy dispositions. The exposed desert conditions made it difficult for the South Africans to spy on the German encampments. The South Africans, who always made good use of the local population for information, were denied this source by the Germans who removed all the locals from the direct line of advance. Nevertheless, Major J.G.W. Leipoldt (1877-1945) was able to garner a full list of the German officers and their commands by gathering every piece of evidence provided by German newspapers, postcards and carelessly discarded scraps of evidence.[69] Through the intelligence department's excellent services, Botha knew that the Germans were concentrating at Usakos and Jakkalswater and that there were one and a half artillery batteries at the latter position.[70]

Botha had two options of advancing through some of the most inhospitable terrain in the world.[71] He could advance along the railway line, thus ensuring a continuous supply via the railroad. The Germans, not willing to oblige, tore up yards of the railway as they retreated, forcing the South Africans to lay new line in its place.[72] The problem was that the Germans used a 2-foot narrow-gauge railway instead of the wider 3-foot 6-inch gauge deployed by the South Africans along this stretch of railway.[73] The decision was to replace the narrow German gauge with the wider South African one.[74] The railway provided a sure route to Windhoek but at the snail's pace—estimated at three months—of rebuilding the railway.[75] Although tempting from a logistical stance, advancing along the railway line was also predictable and would offer the enemy many opportunities to prepare defences or launch strikes in its path. Following the railways would likewise rob the UDF of the mobility advantage of its mounted formations.[76] One needs to raise the question as to the efficacy of replacing the German narrow-gauge railway with the broader Cape gauge. In his dispatch, Botha answers the feasibility question of taking the more expedient route of repairing and using the narrower gauge:

> I ordered Colonel Skinner to send a reconnaissance from Rossing to the Khan with an engineer party to decide if it was possible to do anything to repair the narrow-gauge railway to Jakalswater. This had been reported to me as undesirable and [an] extremely difficult undertaking, but, on finding an extension of this railway to Riet of which we were previously unaware, and realising that, unless some means were found to supplement my very slender means of conveying supplies, there was little prospect of making headway with the campaign, I determined to decide the matter by observation on the spot. The project proved to be quite feasible and at the time when this despatch is being framed the railway is almost finished.[77]

The insistence of changing the railway gauge when it was expedient to repair and use the German narrow-gauge, cost Botha time and the unnecessary expenditure of scarce resources. The discovery of 600 tons of rails unfit for use at Walvis Bay, sent up from Cape Town and rejected, was also a reason for delay.[78] Economic and contractual reasons overrode the temporary restoration of the narrow-gauge rail. It would according to the contract be upgraded to the 3-foot-6inch gauge permanently. What often happens in war is good business principles take precedence over sound military needs. In German East Africa in 1916, Smuts was able to use his pioneers to narrow the gauge of several heavy lorries, allowing them to operate on the railway line and carry 10 to 15 tons of precious supplies. Van Deventer was able to use this method to carry supplies from Dodoma to Kilosa, easing his logistical burdens.[79]

A bolder and shorter route meant leaving the railway and advancing along the dry riverbed of the Swakop River. A promising possibility was the availability of water along the dry riverbed of the Swakop. In many places, especially at Riet, the water lay just below the surface and required some digging to access it.[80] However, using the indirect approach came with its own set of problems. The route would require 400 mule-drawn wagons instead of the 40 on hand. Staff planning had centred around Botha adhering to the route along the railway and resources were allocated by divisional headquarters in accordance.[81] Botha characteristically favoured a war of manoeuvre and chose the riskier approach to restore surprise and mobility. His intention did not match his resources, and inadequate logistics would accompany any advance along the river.[82] The less mobile infantry units would accompany the rail builders, while the two mounted brigades, totalling 4,850 mounted infantrymen and eight artillery pieces would follow the route along the Swartkop riverbed. Opposing them were 2,000 Germans and four artillery batteries entrenched in the high hills of Riet and Pforte.[83]

Further motivation to advance without delay was the lure of good grazing grass beyond the small outpost of Riet. Reports of good inland rains spurred Botha into action. Grazing land would partially free Botha from the logistics and inadequate transport crippling his mounted troops' mobility.[84] He chose Husab, some 48 kilometres from Swakopmund, as the jumping-off point for his offensive. The final objective, Riet, lay an equal 48 kilometres from Husab. The infantry occupied the forward positions at Husab while the mounted infantry temporarily returned to Swakopmund for provisions.[85] In the meantime, vital provisions for the offensive were brought up to Husab and fortunately drew very little attention from the Germans. A more aggressive opponent might have used the opportunity to disrupt the UDF's forward deployment at Husab. Heydebreck's replacement, Franke, lacked his predecessor's vision and initiative. Botha used all his transport resources in accumulating supplies for five and a half days at Husab for his mounted infantry by 16 March.[86]

Botha hoped to launch his offensive simultaneously with McKenzie whom he urged to advance from Lüderitzbucht and capture Aus.[87] As Smuts had originally planned, a simultaneous offensive would place the Germans on the horns of dilemma and stretch their defensive resources. However, all intentions of a coordinated advance quickly evaporated. McKenzie, citing insufficient water supply at Garub and his newly arrived mounted brigade (his third) not having sufficiently acclimatised, insisted he was unprepared to advance. Botha would push forward alone.[88] McKenzie captured Garub on 22 February (on the same day Botha captured Nonidas/Husab in the north) and Lieutenant-Colonel George Farrar, the Acting QMG for Central Force, sent a report to Smuts on the water and logistical situation offered at the town. He was confident enough water existed at Garub to supply the entire camp (50,000–60,000 gallons per day) and the blockhouses further down the line. All he required was to build the necessary infrastructure and reservoirs.[89]

McKenzie's lack of urgency allowed two weeks to pass between the capture of Garub and the measures required to secure water. Correspondence highlights the painfully slow process of drilling boreholes and then testing them for capacity. Farrar, rather lackadaisically, requested an additional 14 days to determine the exact amount of water available.[90] Central Force established a decent waterpoint at Garub by 23 March, providing at least 50,000 gallons of water and extended the railway line to the town. Farrar, ever cautious, was determined to build a 100,000-gallon-capacity reservoir as insurance against one of the water pumps failing or the Germans damaging it in one of their air raids.[91] McKenzie's casual advance towards Aus frustrated Botha to the extent that he was hesitant to send artillery pieces requested which he felt could be better used by the Northern Force.[92]

Botha identified that the advance to Windhoek would bring the decisive battle. Contrary to the planned concept of advancing simultaneously on exterior lines, he advised Smuts not to expend undue effort on the southern front as their distance from Windhoek precluded them from playing a decisive role.[93] Botha did not have high regard for McKenzie's fighting abilities and lost all faith, preferring to leave the main push in the south to Van Deventer's wing, who by advancing from Upington and Sandfontein, would facilitate McKenzie progressing without much of a fight.[94] Botha's frustration culminated with his visit to McKenzie on 29 March where he subjected the commander to a "long and serious talk". Botha would tolerate no more delay and admonished McKenzie instructing him to "do more with such a big, costly army". Botha even offered to take command and attack Aus if McKenzie so desired. However, Botha stopped short of sacking him or forcing his resignation as he had an eye to the political situation. McKenzie commanded a force mainly made up of men who harked from Natal, and his resignation would cause unwanted political ructions at a delicate time in the campaign. Botha left McKenzie with strict instructions to move on Aus the next morning with no excuses.[95] (See Map 4.1)

Botha expected a vigorous defence at the waterholes at Riet and Pforte, and he planned, in the Boer way, to unhinge the German defences via a wide enveloping

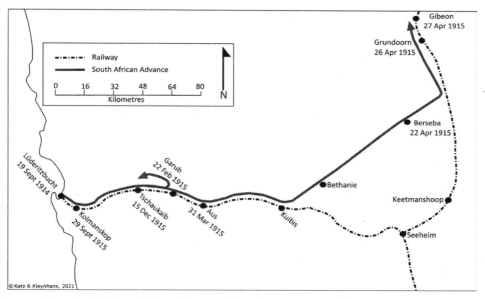

Map 4.1. McKenzie's Central Force and the advance to Aus and then Gibeon Station

movement rather than a head-on assault.[96] Botha relied on his two mounted brigades for the operation, while infantry would be left to guard the rear areas. Brits commanded the 1st Mounted Brigade of 2,289 men and four guns of the Transvaal Horse Artillery. They would form the right wing of the attack. Botha tasked half the mounted infantry on pinning the defending Germans while the other half would outflank the position and make for Riet. The outflanking manoeuvre was to be executed via a passage through the Langer Heinrichberg hills which would threaten Riet to the German defences' rear. Brits, ignoring an immutable concept of war, failed to reconnoitre the passage before the attack and instead relied on a map showing the route. The 2nd Mounted Brigade, under Colonel Johannes Joachim Alberts, consisting of 2,564 men and four guns of the 4th Permanent Field Artillery Battery was assigned to the left wing of the attack.[97] Half of Alberts's force would pin the Germans defending Pforte while the remainder would outflank the position and threaten Jakkalswater in the German rear.[98] (See Map 4.2)

Botha's advance was the first significant offensive undertaken by the Northern Force since the landings at Walvis Bay in December. Rugged terrain and the need to secure the next viable water supply en route limited Botha's offensive options.[99] Besides some minor probes to consolidate his position, the Northern Force did little more than build up its forces and logistics since occupying Swakopmund on 15 January. The route Botha chose to advance was evident to the Germans. The contention Garcia makes that the "speed" of Botha's advance "gave the Germans little time to finalise their defensive plans" is untenable. Botha achieved hardly any surprise at the operational level although some surprise was achieved at the tactical level using a combination of night moves and speed.[100]

Botha attacked during the early evening on 19 March in a bold night manoeuvre. The two mounted infantry brigades set off from Husab, reaching their objectives by dawn. According to Botha's intelligence, the Germans held Pforte with two mounted companies of approximately 400 men and an artillery section numbering two guns. The Germans held Riet with four mounted companies of approximately 800 men and a battery of four field guns. Their reserve remained at Jakkalswater and Modderfontein with four or five companies consisting of between 800 and 1,000 men and two artillery batteries with eight guns. German sources show that Botha overestimated the German strength by at least 50 per cent.[101] (See Table 4.2)

Table 4.2. Comparative strength of the opposing forces at Pforte and Riet, 19 March 1915[102]

	Botha's Estimate German Strength		German Records German Strength		Official History UDF Strength	
Positions	Men	Guns	Men	Guns	Men	Guns
Pforte	400	2	200	2	2564	4
Riet	800	4	400	4	2289	4
Jakkeswater/Modderfontein	1000	8	100	6		
Total per Botha	2200	14	700	12	4853	8
UDF/German strength ratio per Botha		2.2				
Actual UDF/German strength ratio		6.9				

Figure 4.2. Smuts and Botha in German South West Africa.[103]

Following the plan, Brits sent a force to pin the Germans at the foot of the Langer Heinrich Mountain. He detached the Bloemhof Commando comprising 300 men under the command of Bezuidenhout to the south, who skirted along the southern border of the mountain and attempted to locate the through route to Riet. The manoeuvre failed as the path clearly shown on the map did not exist. Scant maps do not substitute for thorough reconnaissance before undertaking an operation in unknown terrain.[104] At 0630, Brits with the remainder of the force engaged the German defenders who occupied strong defensive positions at the foot of the Langer Heinrich. Brits's pinning attack soon deteriorated into a stalemate. (See Map 4.2) The Swakop River's impregnable cliffs along its banks straddling Brits's northern flank put paid to the idea of a tactical outflanking manoeuvre. However, Brits had little incentive to press the pinning attack when he relied on Bezuidenhout's flank attack to unhinge the German defences. Only when it became clear that Bezuidenhout's outflanking manoeuvre was a failure did Brits attempt to attack the German left flank with 300 men. The attack became bogged down by the rough terrain and undiminished German firepower. Too few men remained in reserve to reinforce the attack because Brits had committed them all earlier in the day at the Langer Heinrich Mountain. The chance of using Bezuidenhout's men as reinforcements for the frontal attacks disappeared when he inexplicably returned to Husab without informing or joining Brits.[105]

Alberts commanding the left flank sent Colonel W.R. Collins (1876–1944)[106] forward with greater success. Collins's reconnaissance patrols quickly located the

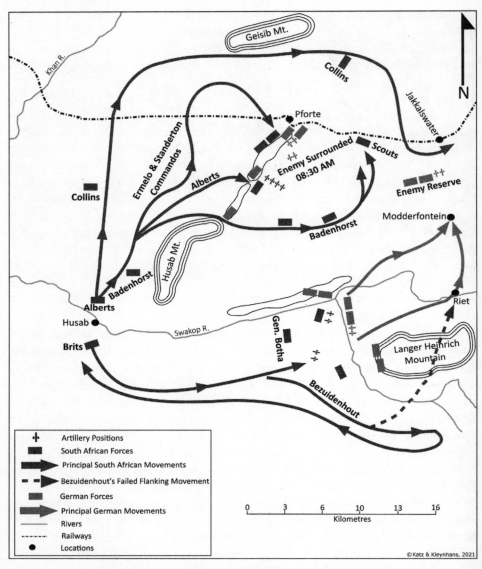

Map 4.2. Botha's offensive on Riet and Pforte, 20 March 1915

German positions at Pforte. The approach route to Pforte was over open ground under the observation of the Germans who commanded the heights. A night march ensured that the South Africans arrived undetected in front of the German positions at 0630. They were also able to detach the Ermelo and Standerton commandos, in a tactical enveloping manoeuvre, who then worked their way to the rear of

Pforte and cut the railway line between Pforte and Jakkalswater. The Germans found themselves in an uncomfortable predicament with their communications and escape route cut off. The surrender and capture of nine German officers, 200 men and two guns followed swiftly at 0830. Collins registered the only tactical victory for the day.[107]

Less successful was Collins's operational flanking manoeuvre sweeping to the north of Pforte. The deep flanking attack necessitated a gruelling 65-kilometre night march. The objective was to occupy Jakkalswater, thereby diverting the German reserves and ensuring that they could not reinforce Pforte and Riet. If successful, the envelopment would cut off German attempts to retreat from the area, delivering a decisive victory. As so often happens with the fog of war, things did not go exactly as planned. The German reserves met Collins on his approach on Jakkalswater at 0630, and his detachment lacking artillery support retreated for the loss of 43 captured.[108] Fortunately, after delivering this rebuff, the German reserves were content to cover their general retreat and took no part in any further attacks that day. Consolation for Collins's unsuccessful flank attack was that it managed to occupy the German reserves for the duration of the operation. A more energetic German commander might have used his initiative to severely punish the disorganised South Africans retreating from Jakkalswater.[109]

Losing Pforte meant the Germans now faced an enemy enjoying an overwhelming numerical advantage on one flank. Collins and Bezuidenhout's mounted infantry reserves waited in Husab. The South Africans were within easy striking distance of Riet and Modderfontein and threatened to cut off the Germans defending forward of Riet making their position untenable. Using the cover of darkness, the Germans gathered their forces and retreated out of harm's way. The South Africans were content to mask the retreat rather than attempt a bold manoeuvre to cut off the retreating Germans forces. Lack of aggression handed Botha a tactical victory and a territorial gain. He missed an opportunity to inflict severe losses on the enemy and gain a decisive operational victory. Occupying Riet provided a forward base with sufficient water to sustain Botha's advance on Windhoek. The promised grazing lands beyond Riet did not materialise; nevertheless, by crossing the formidable Namib, the gateway to Windhoek lay open.[110] Botha was confident that the Germans intended to make a last stand at Windhoek and their surrender would shortly follow once he occupied the capital. He reasoned, with much insight, that the Germans had angered the local black population to such an extent that they posed a constant danger and made it impossible to conduct guerrilla warfare.[111] On cue, the Rehoboth Basters went into open rebellion on 26 April 1915, after offering their military services to Botha. He turned the offer down for political reasons for it was anathema for the South Africans to arm blacks in a white man's war.[112] We shall see that the Germans had no such qualms in German East Africa where the majority of their fighting soldiers were black.

Lessons Learnt from Botha's Action at Pforte and Riet, 19 March 1915

Smuts was the central figure in the formation of the UDF, and its performance on the battlefield is testament to his role as its creator. The GSWA campaign can be seen as the furnace in which the UDF's disparate formations and doctrine were finally melded. The UDF which accompanied Smuts to GEA grew to be a truly united South African force. In many ways, at the outset of the GSWA campaign, the UDF was a blunt instrument suited to internal counterinsurgency operations, designed to placate old foes and build of a new nation. Smuts did not contemplate war with a first-rate European power. Examining Botha's battles in GSWA is relevant to the study of Smuts and his Great War in Africa because they demonstrate the doctrinal evolution of the UDF. Both men were mere products of a Boer way of war. Furthermore, many of the commanders and soldiers who fought in GSWA would go on to command and man the UDF formations in GEA. They and Smuts brought with them the lessons learnt in GSWA. Many of the cultural, structural, and doctrinal issues which Botha and Smuts faced in GSWA would have to be dealt with by Smuts in German East Africa.

The action at Pforte and Riet was the UDF's first test of manoeuvre warfare at the operational and tactical level. Botha had a direct influence on events, but Smuts certainly had an indirect share. Botha's operation in GSWA brought into sharp focus troubling doctrinal aspects which reduced South African fighting power. The UDF failed to combine the two divergent elements of predominantly English regular infantry and the Afrikaner mounted infantry into a single cohesive force. Together with the SAMR mounted units, the infantry followed traditional British doctrine incorporating their organisation, discipline, drills, and rank structures. The mounted infantry, comprised of and commanded by veterans of the South African War would not have been out of place in 1900. There was an inability, or even a reluctance, on the campaign, to combine these two arms. Often Botha would leave the regular infantry languishing well in the rear on garrison, logistical, or engineering duties, while he used the mounted infantry as the *arme blanche*. The UDF faced a massive logistical challenge due in part to its considerable and excessive numerical advantage over the Germans. The underutilised infantry consumed a substantial portion of the scarce resources which the mounted infantry could have used more effectively.[113] Botha was asked the question by a Boer commandant who saw little use for the footslogging infantry, and why he insisted on dragging the infantry and artillery along the campaign route. He was supremely confident that the mounted infantry was more than capable of finishing the job alone. Botha replied, "You see, I know you very well. One day you will find the Germans in a strongly fortified position prepared to fight, and you will come running to me saying 'we must wait for the infantry and big guns because we have no bayonets.'"[114]

South Africa's overwhelming numerical superiority did not always work in her favour when faced with tight logistical constraints and limited water availability. When visiting GSWA in March 1915, Buxton ironically noted that there seemed to be a lack of available Germans in allowing all the forces to do some actual fighting. "It is likely to be a case of one poor lion has not got a Christian."[115] Smuts conceived the original strategic concept of attacking the enemy on exterior lines using four columns of sufficient strength to cope with any concentrated opposition likely to be encountered. The second iteration of the plan left nothing to chance. Distrusting the power of simultaneous manoeuvre, Smuts reinforced each advancing column to the extent that each one alone outnumbered the entire enemy force substantially.[116] The second phase emphasis on gaining a substantial numerical advantage at the cost of manoeuvrability stands in stark contrast with what Smuts hoped to achieve with far fewer forces in the first aborted phase. A leaner, more aggressive force, relying on simultaneous manoeuvre and less married to logistical constraints, may have accomplished more in the way of manoeuvre warfare. After all, manoeuvre warfare is often the last resort of the numerically inferior with historically decisive results.

A case in point is the Pforte/Riet operation. Botha accumulated five and a half days' worth of provisions with the explicit intention of exploiting any German retreat. However, mention of these provisions mysteriously disappeared after the single day's operation and are not referred to again in the official history. When the Germans retreated, Botha could have halved his force and thus extended his provisions to nine days for the pursuing soldiers, fully exploiting the opportunity presented. Inexplicably, the operation ceased prematurely, and there was no exploitation phase. Neither Botha nor Smuts considered a reduction in excessive force numbers even when confronted with the reality of not finding the expected grazing fields beyond Riet.

Converting the German narrow-gauge railway to the wide South African gauge harmed the supply situation in the short term. It seems that long-term economic goals overrode short-term military considerations. It would have been more expeditious to rebuild and reuse the German railway and apply some ingenuity to modifying the engines and cars to the narrow German gauge. Doing so would have given Botha the option of advancing up the railway and the Swakop River, thereby alleviating his substantial logistical challenges. The combination of a force unnecessarily large for the task at hand, an underutilised infantry component, and the time-consuming decision to lay a wide railway gauge created the perfect logistical storm.[117] As mentioned, Smuts was able to later convert road lorries to run on the German narrow gauge in GEA with good effect.

The South Africans paid dearly for lack of reconnaissance before the operation. The UDF employed the old Boer method of deploying scouts forward of their main force, but they had more of an effect on the tactical situation and hardly influenced the operational level of war. Had Botha reconnoitred well before the operation he would have located the path through the Langer Heinrichberg and turned the German flank at Riet. The lack of prior reconnaissance saw the Bloemhof Commando lost to the battle when it failed to find the route to the enemy rear. Lack of reconnaissance led to the fiasco at Jakkalswater where Collins's mounted infantry, enjoying an overwhelming numerical advantage, was beaten back by a small German force. A reconnaissance failure resulting from an intelligence failure led to the overestimation of German troop strengths and available reserve forces.[118] It will be seen that time and again well laid plans came awry due to lack of reconnaissance.

The double envelopment performed at night was an over-intricate manoeuvre which had the effect of splitting the Union forces in half and then again splitting each half into a pinning and enveloping force. Botha could have used the infantry, left to languish in Swakopmund, as the pinning force that would have released a portion of the mounted infantry to serve as a reserve to exploit opportunities. Botha immediately committed all the available forces into battle. The lack of a reserve meant that reinforcements were not available to bolster success or take opportunities as they presented themselves throughout the day during the battle. The Boer armies did not possess a concept of a tactical or operational reserve and often threw their entire effort into the frontline immediately.[119] Given Botha's overwhelming superiority, a sounder option would have been to combine the entire force into one overwhelming thrust aimed at the decisive point or the centre of gravity that lay at Modderfontein. A small force could have occupied and pinned the defenders at Pforte and Riet along the foothills of the Langer Heinrichberg. The main force would have quickly overwhelmed the German reserve at Modderfontein and easily cut off the defenders by threatening Jakkalswater and Riet simultaneously. (See Map 4.2)

Leadership from the front was a hallmark of the Boer way of war, and Botha was one of its finest examples. The Boer style of command remained an enigma to the British throughout the South African War and even through the First World War.[120] The Germans, brilliant exponents of manoeuvre warfare, also coveted this leadership style. However, in this operation, Botha's move upfront had little effect on the battle's outcome. A bodyguard of 100 overly concerned mounted infantry accompanied him into battle, seemingly excessive compared to how Smuts would conduct himself ahead of his main force in GEA. The concept of a general leading from the front has its proponents as well as its detractors. One benefit of leading from the front is the inspiration given to ordinary soldiers to achieve greater efforts, gain a first-hand understanding of the enemy dispositions, and change the course of the battle through on-the-spot decisions. However, leading from the front can also reduce a general's viewpoint by looking through the keyhole, losing sight of the operational context and becoming embroiled in tactical aspects of the battle. Botha, leading from the front, found himself pinned down in a static situation after Brits encountered the Germans on the foothills of the Langer Heinrichberg. He remained there for the duration, missing the decisive events unfolding on Collins's flank at Jakkalswater and Pforte. Botha's presence at Jakkalswater could have bolstered flagging fighting spirits, and instead of retreating in disarray before a numerically inferior enemy, he could have engaged and defeated the German reserve. Weak command, control and communication plagued the operation when elements of both wings, Collins and Bezuidenhout, retreated to Husab without informing Botha of their intentions or making themselves available to join the battle at another point.[121]

Lack of aggression in a frontal attack was a hallmark of the Boer way of war.[122] They showed great initiative but lacked discipline and showed a reluctance to engage the enemy head-on.[123] This fact was drawn attention to in the German official history of the South African War and Collyer's account of the Pforte/Riet battle.[124] The Boer way of war displayed an aversion to needless losses, frontal assaults, and the exploitation of an advantage gained on the battlefield at all the levels of war. Sound reasons for this existed at the tactical level as the Boers, who performed as dedicated light infantry, were averse to shock tactics including the bayonet charge, but preferred to use their superior mobility to take advantage of a battlefield opportunity or retreat out of harm's way.[125] Smuts devised an aggressive strategic plan for the invasion of GSWA which was not carried forth with the required vigour at the operational level. McKenzie's sluggish advance and lacklustre levels of aggression showed that caution was a hallmark of the UDF in GSWA up to that date. Botha missed an opportunity to exploit the German defeat at Pforte to overwhelm a numerically inferior enemy at Jakkalswater. He missed the operational opportunity to exploit and press the German retreat, giving chase to a demoralised foe. Momentum would have carried Botha to the gates of Windhoek. Instead, Botha and his Northern Force played an insignificant role in the advance for the next few weeks, having reached his culmination point far too early in the operation. Having failed to unhinge the Germans in the north, he handed the initiative over to Smuts and his Southern, Eastern and Central Forces.

Smuts and the Southern Offensive Revitalised, April 1915

After Botha had captured Riet, the expected booty of good grazing land into the immediate interior failed to materialise. Although theoretically in possession of supplies for the next four and a half days, Botha sent his two mounted brigades back to Swakopmund for rest and provisions.[126] Botha's stalled advance coincided with the beginning of Smut's advance in the south which would culminate with the capture of Gibeon on 27 April. Botha did not resume his northern offensive until Smuts captured Gibeon, amounting to a hiatus of five weeks after the capture of Riet. (See Table in Appendix: Chronology of the GSWA campaign and Map 4.3) Botha's failure to aggressively pursue the enemy robbed the UDF of a chance to seize the critical rail juncture at Karibib, thus cutting the German southern defences as well as Windhoek off from the north. Botha was content to allow Smuts's advance to encourage the German forces in front of him to withdraw without a fight.

Smuts took command of the Southern, Eastern and Central forces on 11 April 1915.[127] His appointment was at the insistence of Botha who had written to Smuts to ask him to hurry through the parliamentary session and then get to the southern front to get things moving.[128] His immediate objective was surrounding and capturing Keetmanshoop and cutting the railway link north with a simultaneous advance of his three forces. His first obstacle was Aus, where Smuts favoured flanking attacks over a frontal assault.[129] McKenzie advanced on Aus at a leisurely pace, frustrating his officers and men. Smuts's enveloping manoeuvre planned to circumvent the strong German defences at Aus never developed as the Germans abandoned their stronghold without a fight. Van Deventer's and Berrangé's simultaneous advancing forces from the south and east unhinged the strong German defences at Aus by threatening to isolate the defenders.[130] (See Map 4.1) McKenzie belatedly occupied Aus on 31 March without a fight.[131]

Demonstrating the UDF's muddled command structure, Botha became incensed when Buxton spoke to McKenzie while bypassing him during the Governor-General's visit to GSWA. Buxton suggested that Central Force needed more guns which Botha saw as unwarranted meddling and a further excuse for McKenzie to delay the capture of Aus. Botha threatened to change the Defence Act in this regard.[132] In the event, Aus's capture motivated Botha to release McKenzie's force from following the railway line. He suggested an operational manoeuvre outflanking the Germans in the south. The land to the east of Aus was more hospitable and contained ample grass and water up to Bethanie. Smuts would strike out with Central Force via Bethanie/Berseba-/Gibeon and cut the enemy off. (See Map 4.1)

Botha urged Smuts to proceed to Lüderitzbucht and instructed McKenzie to command a single mounted brigade to undertake the manoeuvre. He believed that McKenzie did not understand infantry doctrine and therefore, Smuts should give him a smaller mounted infantry formation to command.[133] Pressurised to 'economise' the Central Force, which had achieved little with its relatively large size, led Botha to suggest the release of all the six-month-contract soldiers.[134] Smuts set about relieving McKenzie of his command as diplomatically as possible and installing him as commander of the mounted brigade.[135] As expected, McKenzie was upset with being relieved of his command when his forces had at long last reached suitable terrain for manoeuvre-type warfare. Attempting to protect his reputation, he asked that Smuts make the reasons for the change in command quite clear "in order it should not appear [as a] lack of confidence in me".[136] McKenzie had to wait nine days before resuming his advance while the engineers secured the water supply at Aus which the Germans had booby-trapped and poisoned.[137]

Windhoek, the central hub of the GSWA railway network, was vital to the German defence arrangements. Once deprived of Windhoek, the Germans would lose operational mobility and the advantage of concentrating on internal lines using their extensive railway network. Its capture would reverse the strategic situation by placing the UDF on internal lines and the Germans on external lines. Therefore,

Collyer identified that the main effort and concentration of resources should go to the Northern Force, it having the shortest and most direct route to Windhoek. Collyer's impression was that the UDF failed to concentrate enough resources in the Northern Force and placed too much emphasis on the Central and Southern Forces.[138] However, most of Botha's challenges were logistical, and a reduction in his superfluous infantry component would have had the same effect as denuding efforts in the south and directing them toward the northern offensive.

The retention of ineffective infantry formations meant Botha, despite an adequate water supply, would remain at Riet, content with a few reconnaissance missions until his supplies dried up on 24 March. Instead of a significant advance in Windhoek's direction, Botha withdrew his mounted infantry back to Swakopmund to the safety of the supplies provided by the ships docked there. There he languished for five weeks leaving Riet defended by 600 infantrymen while he waited patiently for replenishment. Botha instructed, against much opposition, that the narrow-gauge railway discovered from Jakkalswater to Riet be rebuilt, a task accomplished by 24 April.[139] Botha was content with allowing the Southern, Central, and Eastern Forces to advance northwards while he took a breather at Riet. He left it to Smuts to launch an offensive from 31 March to 27 April which led to the capture of Gibeon, making the intended German defence of Windhoek untenable.

Smuts achieved a remarkable feat in coordinating three converging forces over a considerable distance with rudimentary means of communication. McKenzie (Central Force) covered 264 kilometres, Van Deventer (Southern Force) advanced 343 kilometres, and Berrangé (Eastern Force) advanced 150 kilometres to Keetmanshoop. (See Map 4.3) On Botha's suggestion, McKenzie deviated from the railway line, outflanking Keetmanshoop and breaking the German defence. He reached Berseba on 22 April via Bethanie, with a wide flanking movement signalling typical manoeuvre warfare denied thus far in having to stay with the railway lines.[140] Collyer attributes a large portion of McKenzie's victory to pressure Botha exerted on Windhoek, but the timeline shows Botha stalled at Riet (290 kilometres from Windhoek) when McKenzie captured Gibeon on 27 April. (See Table in Appendix: Chronology of the GSWA campaign)

A combination of the speed of the southern advance and the proximity of Gibeon to Windhoek (338 kilometres) convinced the Germans to withdraw and abandon Windhoe's now untenable defence.[141] The Germans faced the unenviable possibility of being crushed by Smuts's advancing forces from Gibeon and Botha's Northern Force advancing on Karibib and then onto Windhoek. The primary threat to Windhoek was not Botha's forces lying immobile at Swakopmund, but Smuts's southern armies running rampant and advancing from Keetmanshoop. After lengthy deliberation, the Germans decided to abandon Windhoek and move their forces and headquarters through Karibib northwards utilising the railway network while it remained in their control.[142] After acting as a bludgeon for months, the UDF assumed the role of a rapier as they restored manoeuvre to their operational art.

Franke seized an opportunity to grab a tactical victory in what would be the last German offensive of the campaign. He set his sights on the South African positions at Trekkoppies on 26 April which Botha occupied along his line of advance to Karibib. Franke aimed his attack at stalling Botha's inevitable advance and not allowing him to accumulate provisions uncontested. The attack would cover the

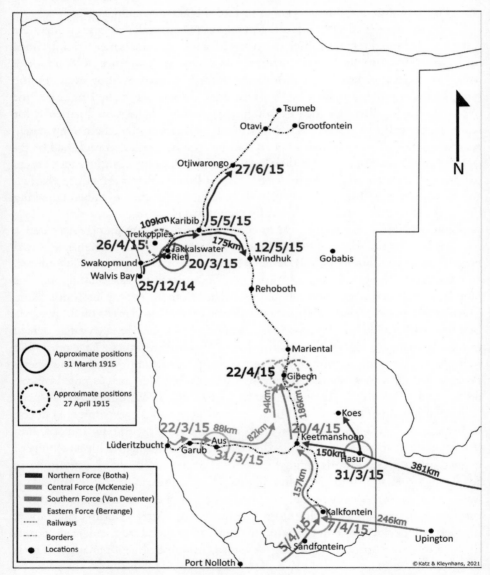

Map 4.3. The Union Defence Force manoeuvre timeline, 31 March to 27 April 1915

Germans defending Karibib and Windhoek, allowing their northward withdrawal in an orderly manner. The diversion would also buy time for the southern German forces facing inexorable pressure from Smuts to withdraw from harm's way. Extensive German reconnaissance using two aircraft revealed Trekkoppies as a suitable venue for an attack. The Germans hoped to overwhelm the defenders and inflict a tactical victory. Franke mustered 2,000 *Schutztruppen* against the 400 defenders using the railway line in the rear to rush up reinforcements.[143] The possibility of the Germans overrunning Trekkoppies was real, but a reconnaissance overflight on 25 April revealed that the South African defenders had strengthened their number to 1,000, considerably reducing the odds.

The South Africans were also able to deploy a single artillery piece and the machine guns belonging to five Royal Navy armoured cars.[144] With favourable odds swiftly evaporating, one of his front commanders urged Franke to cancel the operation. He refused.[145] From the start, the German attack suffered several mishaps. After manoeuvring into position, the main force found itself directly in front of the Union forces instead of facing their flank. The Germans mistakenly blew up the railway line in front of the South African positions instead of their rear and missed a chance to cut off their supply route. The defenders' numerical strength, combined with machine-gun fire from the Royal Navy armoured cars, suppressed the German attack despite their healthy preponderance in artillery pieces. The South Africans failed to use the armoured cars or their numerical advantage to launch a counterattack and exploit the German retreat in this final setpiece battle in GSWA.[146]

The End Game: Manoeuvre Warfare Restored

Smuts's original idea of simultaneous converging advances on the enemy's centre at Windhoek from all points of the compass expired in the morass of logistical problems brought about in no small part by the large increases in manpower over the original plan.[147] Nevertheless, the fall of Gibeon in the south enabled Botha to launch his attack on Windhoek after successfully addressing his debilitating logistical problems. His first objective en route to the capital was Karibib, which lay at the railway junction linking southern and northern GSWA. Cutting the railway threatened to trap the remaining German defenders in the south. Botha pleaded with Smuts for more transport in a letter on 3 March, after attempting to juggle his meagre resources between the mounted brigades with partial success.[148] He complained of the agonisingly slow progress of refurbishing the railway line.[149] The enormous forces at his disposal were too numerous to all be used in the combat zone, but they consumed his precious resources and stifled the tempo of his advance. Smuts responded to the transport crisis by scouring the country for wagons, mules, donkeys, and drivers.[150] The capture of Gibeon station coincided with extending the northern railway line to Trekkoppies, further alleviating Botha's supply problems.

The concerted efforts resulted in Botha once more accumulating five days' worth of supplies by 25 April, thereby allowing him to resume his advance.[151]

During the period between the battle at Riet on 19 March and 25 April, Botha's mounted infantry component doubled in size. Botha now commanded a mounted force of 8,868 men and 16 guns. The 3rd and 5th Mounted Brigades commanded by Brigadier-General M.W. Myburgh joined the 1st and 2nd Mounted Brigades under Brits. Botha's infantry component had also swelled, bringing the total forces under his command for the move inland to 13,000 men—a force three times the size of the one which attacked Riet.[152] Extending the infantry component is difficult to understand in the light of scarce logistical resources. The footslogging infantry, performing fatigue and garrison duties, and also undertaking strenuous marches in the wake of the mounted infantry, saw minimal action throughout the campaign.[153]

Once Botha's forces resumed their advance, and the Germans were forced to retreat towards Karibib, psychologically overwhelmed by their speed, numerical strength and the distance the South African forces covered. The Germans abandoned Karibib on 5 May, which effectively allowed the UDF to cut Windhoek's railway line to the north. Consequently, the Germans abandoned Windhoek on 12 May.[154] Smuts and Botha could now claim to have achieved the British objectives as requested. They occupied the coast and rendered the wireless stations, especially the one at Windhoek, inoperable. Seitz also believed it now opportune to seek an armistice and a negotiated settlement.

German military prospects in GSWA looked bleak. A ray of hope for Seitz and Franke was the prospect of a German victory in Europe with the German armies near the gates of Paris.[155] Governor Seitz sent Botha a letter on 13 May which called for a meeting for 21 May at Giftkuppe during a temporary armistice.[156] At the meeting Botha demanded the unconditional surrender of the Germans. He also brushed aside Seitz's suggestions for the establishment of a demilitarised neutral zone between the two forces, with the Germans remaining in occupation of the northern part of GSWA.[157] Smuts and Botha, harbouring an expansionist agenda, would be satisfied with nothing less than the occupation of the entire territory. Botha, carefully discerning Seitz's mood at the conference, believed the German forces, mostly unscathed and intact, would not make a fight of it or attempt a last stand. They had retired north, and any attempt to hold fast would invite an enveloping movement with Botha enjoying an overwhelming numerical advantage and greater mobility.[158]

The Germans, unwilling to surrender unconditionally, believed they possessed military prospects in holding nearly half the remaining territory north of Windhoek. Encouraging them was the undeniable South African sluggishness in the eight months of campaigning thus far. The Germans also retained the more hospitable portion of the territory regarding water availability, good grazing, plentiful wild game, and 160 kilometres of railway. There was also the possibility of waging a guerrilla campaign from southern Angola. Holding out until there was favourable news from Europe was a sound strategy for the Germans to adopt.[159]

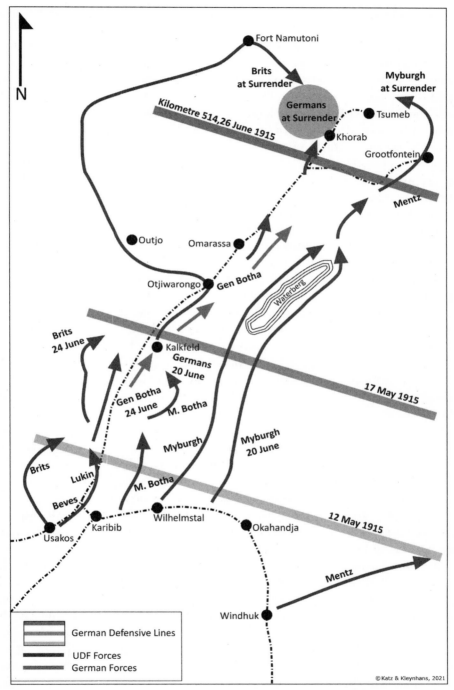

Map 4.4. The final battle of Otavifontein leading to the German surrender of GSWA[160]

The Germans took up positions to the west and east of Omaruru, while the South Africans with 20,000 troops held the Usakos–Karibib line. The two sides skirmished on this line with Union forces launching an attack on a German forward positioned just to the north on 12 May. (See Map 4.4) Franke, conscious of Botha's penchant for envelopment thus far in the campaign, and acknowledging that his position lacked natural defences, withdrew his force 65 kilometres back to the Kalkfeld–Osire–Waterberg Mountain line on 17 May. (See Map 4.4) Here he established a long defensive line in an attempt to preclude a flanking manoeuvre by the UDF. The Germans intended withdrawing to the line 'Kilometre 514' after resisting at the Kalkfeld line.[161] (See Map 4.4) After putting up a show of resistance, the Germans had options to continue the struggle via guerrilla warfare, flee to Angola, or even make for German East Africa. Botha, numerically powerful, was again hamstrung waiting for his supply columns to catch up with his main forces holding the Usakos–Karibib line. Engineers had partially built his railway network, and a mixture of German and standard Union Cape railway gauge necessitated much loading and reloading to bring supplies forward. After conferring with Smuts, Botha disbanded the Southern Force soon after the capture of Windhoek, and the remaining field forces reorganised with 32 artillery pieces and a complement of 13,000 men divided into six brigades, of which one was regular infantry. Botha was ready to resume his offensive on 18 June, having dispensed with the superfluous forces, and he set forth with a leaner, better supplied and more agile force.[162] (See Map 4.4).

Botha conducted his final phase of the campaign using the deep roots of operational manoeuvre type warfare within the UDF's bi-national doctrine. Botha's manoeuvrist approach was one Smuts and his command group would take to GEA. Smuts and his veterans of the Afrikaner Rebellion and GSWA campaign would replicate the double envelopment that Botha used in the final battle of GSWA with good effect. Botha fielded 5,250 mounted infantry, 4,750 infantrymen and 32 guns against Franke's 4,750 men. Botha's mere 2:1 numerical superiority bucked the trend of his bloated numerical advantage he had enjoyed thus far in the campaign.[163] The risk that the Germans could concentrate superior numbers against Botha's divided force as he advanced was real. For the first time in the campaign, Botha would rely on his superior mobility, enabling greater tempo and unleashing his latent penchant for manoeuvre warfare—rather than rely on sheer numerical superiority alone. Using combined arms operations, Botha finally managed to find a combat role for his footslogging infantry—reversing their relegation to safeguarding the rear areas vacated by the mounted infantry. With this configuration, the UDF was a far nimbler force. Secure supply lines in the rear emboldened Botha to risk cutting the advancing columns from their logistical constraints and allowing them to live off the land.[164] He appointed Skinner as the General Officer in Command (GOC) Lines of Communication, and together with Sir William Hoy who energetically directed work on the railways, there was a marked improvement in Botha's logistics—no doubt aided by the drastic reduction in the numbers of troops earmarked for the final assault.[165] A small and highly mobile force such as this is perhaps what Smuts had originally envisaged with the Smuts plan's first iteration back in August 1914.[166]

Botha conceived a plan which involved a wide turning movement. Brits would lead his mounted units on the left flank well to the west of the railway line making his way through Outjo to the south of the Etosha Pan. He would then proceed in an easterly direction on to Fort Namutoni where the Germans kept the majority of the 600 South African POWs, placing him well in the rear of the German defences at Kilometre 514. Myburgh's advance using highly mobile mounted infantry would move in an easterly arc tracking east of the railway line with the objective of capturing Grootfontein, and beyond that, a further advance to Tsumeb. Each wing would cover more than 300 kilometres in a matter of days—in stark contrast to the Allies manning trenches in France who measured movement over months in metres. The closing of the Brits-Myburgh pincers to the west and east of Tsumeb would cut off the German defenders facing Botha with his infantry in the centre.[167] (See Map 4.4)

The speed and distance of the flanking manoeuvres would mean that Brits and Myburgh would have to exercise their initiative in the absence of any reliable communication with Botha.[168] Their sheer tempo of both flank's advance would outpace logistical support necessitating the rapidly advancing commandos to live off the land. Botha was left with Lukin's 6th Mounted Brigade and Beves's footslogging 1st Infantry Brigade to advance up the German railway line and distract the *Schutztruppen's* attention from the enveloping wings. The entire operation bore all the hallmarks of the Boer way of war—expertly applied by Botha in the latter part of the GSWA campaign.[169]

Although outnumbered, the Germans enjoyed some advantages of being concentrated, having a numerical advantage in artillery and machine guns, and being familiar with the territory. Botha's advance met with little resistance and the 3,000 Germans holding the Kalkfeld line, which faced 12,000 South African advance troops beat a retreat to Kilometre 514 on 21 June, whereafter they reached Otavifontein on the night of 26/27 June.[170] The Brits–Myburgh advance on the flanks had achieved the desired result of unnerving Franke who had no desire to be surrounded. Brits advancing northward remained undetected until Franke learnt of their presence west of Etosha and realised he was the subject of a double envelopment.[171] Franke, realising his predicament, decided to defend Otavifontein and its wells—thereby denying water to Botha's central forces crossing a 65-kilometre arid stretch from Omarassa.[172] If Franke could deliver a tactical defeat on the UDF at Otavifontein, and deny them the water resources in the immediate vicinity, then he would force Botha to retreat back to the start line at Omarassa.[173] Here was Franke's opportunity to deliver a decisive tactical defeat on the South Africans, strengthening his hand at the negotiating table.

Furthermore, by forcing a South African retreat before Otavifontein, he could engage Brits and Myburgh in sequence with overwhelming numerical superiority. His forces enjoyed internal lines of communication and proximity, which allowed him to concentrate on Otavifontein rapidly, where he could achieve almost numerical parity with Botha's forces facing him.[174] Franke had every intention of making a last stand judging by an appeal made to his troops on 28 June. He justified his evasive tactics in the campaign thus far by avoiding any pitched battles, thus preserving his fighting power. Now he called for the preservation of the Schutztruppe until the conclusion of peace in Europe by delivering a decisive act.[175] He appealed to the *Schutztruppen* to deliver a final powerful blow to the South Africans. However, the constant retreat in the face of the relentless, albeit ponderous UDF had taken its toll on the ordinary German soldier's morale.[176]

Otavifontein also offered Franke strong natural defences. However, Botha's rapid advance threw the Germans off balance, rendering the defensive preparations at Otavifontein incomplete. Furthermore, the strategic importance of Otavifontein to the German defences was only realised by them at the last possible moment. The German official history records the poor state of the German defences at Otavifontein, explaining that effective defences would have taken several weeks more of preparation.[177] Without waiting for the infantry, Botha decided on an immediate attack with his mounted units on the German defenders at Otavifontein. He intended to distract the Germans' attention from his two rapidly advancing mobile columns of Brits and Myburgh.[178] Botha's conduct of the operational manoeuvre thus far was a delicate balance of advancing the flanks, and either delaying or expediting the centre, then pinning the German centre to enable the flanks to envelop them.

Botha launched his attack on Otavifontein on 1 July. He deployed a double tactical envelopment with Commandant Manie Botha and the 5th Mounted Brigade on the left of the railway line and Lukin's 6th Mounted Brigade to the right. Their rapid, and at times instinctive advance, at an unexpected tempo, managed to dislodge the Germans from their strong positions.[179] On the spot decisions driven by the commanders' initiative, unsettled the German defenders who could not dispose of their main force as they had planned.[180] Using his initiative, Manie Botha pressed the attack with all his forces in close country covered in dense bush, making visibility almost impossible.[181] Major Hermann Ritter, who commanded the German forces, retreated to Grootfontein, allowing Botha to secure the water supplies at Otavifontein. Some would ascribe the South African success to luck; however, rapid manoeuvre often brings forth opportunities which a wily commander can exploit to his benefit. The Germans lacked resolve, and Franke only committed a fraction of his available forces.[182] The German official history describes the low casualties suffered by both sides as "out of proportion to the importance of the task" of defending Otavifontein.[183] The Germans failed to identify the importance of the position in time, and the constant retreat in the campaign eroded the German resolve to fight aggressively. Had the Germans held Otavifontein and repulsed the South Africans as planned, they would have inflicted a substantial tactical defeat. A South African retreat south back to their water sources would have allowed Franke a few weeks respite to deal with the enveloping wings of Brits and Myburgh or retreat even further north.[184]

The developing threat of Brits and Myburgh enveloping his entire force unsettled Franke who requested a meeting with Seitz on 2 July 1915. Franke was pessimistic of the German prospects of facing a numerically superior enemy advancing on three fronts against his tired, worn-out troops. The Germans were at the lowest ebb of morale. Their horses were malnourished and unable to exert themselves, and food and clothing were in short supply. Regular retreats during the campaign's course had extracted a toll, and the situation looked hopeless.[185] Franke also did not believe that the Germans could escape the encirclement fast enough due to Botha's proximity and pressing of his forces in the centre. Franke failed to deliver the tactical victory Seitz sought to negotiate from a position of strength.[186] The speed of Botha's enveloping forces destroyed Franke's will to resist despite the cajoling of some of his junior officers wanting to attack one of the enveloping wings by mustering superior numbers. There was also the opportunity to counterattack in the centre and re-capture Otavifontein with all its supplies and abundant water, and the biggest prize of all, capturing Botha at the head of his troops. However, Franke did not believe his men were up to the task.[187]

Botha rejected Seitz's first attempts at a parley on 4 July by demanding unconditional surrender as he wanted a more favourable position to develop. A meeting was set for 6 July at Kilometre 500 just north of Otavi station. The ceasefire excluded Brits and Myburgh, which allowed them to complete their encirclement.[188] (See Map 4.4) The garrison of 110 Germans at Fort Namutoni surrendered to Brits on 6 July while Myburgh reached Tsumeb on the same day, a mere 32 kilometres north from the main German forces at Khorab. Both men taking full advantage of the fog of war, used the confusion to occupy Tsumeb while Botha negotiated with Seitz and Franke at Kilometre 500. The Germans, surrounded and demoralised, signed the final surrender on 9 July, ending the GSWA campaign.[189]

The UDF conquest of GSWA was accomplished with remarkably few casualties. The number perishing in combat was slightly lower than the casualties suffered during the Afrikaner Rebellion. Afrikaners suffered twice as many casualties killed and wounded in the Afrikaner Rebellion only to reverse the situation in GSWA. The Afrikaner/English ratio of casualties when compared over the Rebellion and the GSWA campaigns achieved a 1:1 ratio signalling that although the two language groups may have fought differently and with varying intensity—in death and injury, they achieved parity. (See Table 4.3). The most important consequence of the invasion of GSWA and the operations during the Afrikaner Rebellion was that the UDF had come of age in these campaigns.

Table 4.3. Casualties: Rebellion and German South West Africa, 1914–1915[190]

Showing figures for Afrikaner/English statistics

	Rebellion	GSWA	Total
Afrikaner			
Killed and Died of wounds	80	46	126
Wounded	183	92	275
Total Afrikaner casualties	263	138	401
English			
Killed and Died of wounds	51	76	127
Wounded	94	178	272
Total English casualties	145	254	399
Total			
Killed and Died of wounds	131	122	253
Wounded	277	270	547
Died other causes		181	181
Prisoners		782	782
Grand Total of all casualties	408	1355	1763
Ratio Afrikaner/English			
Killed and Died of wounds	1.6 : 1	0.6 : 1	1 : 1
Wounded	1.9 : 1	0.5 : 1	1 : 1
Total	1.8 : 1	0.5 : 1	1 : 1

CHAPTER 5

Salaita Hill and the Clash of Military Doctrine

The debacle at Sandfontein helped shape the UDF toward a unified command, better organisation and logistics coupled with the rudiments of a staff under Collyer.[1] The Otavifontein battle was an excellent demonstration of the Boer (and now rapidly becoming the UDF's) penchant for the operational double envelopment—using regular infantry as a pinning force, and then mounted infantry as a fast mobile enveloping force. Many South African combatants assembling in German East Africa (GEA) in 1915 were the same leader group and soldiers who participated in the GSWA campaign. The army Smuts took with him and commanded in GEA would repeatedly replicate the fast-moving manouverist approach of Botha's army at Otavifontein. After all, Smuts, who could trace his military lineage back to Louis Botha and Koos de la Rey, was merely a product of his nation's way of war.

Smuts would now face the GEA *Schutztruppen*, commanded by Paul Emil von Lettow-Vorbeck. Smuts's new adversaries were quite different from their GSWA comrades whom the UDF had conquered with extraordinarily little material and human cost. Lettow-Vorbeck was far more resourceful, determined, and resolute than Victor Franke. He was schooled in the German way of war, and unlike his compatriots in GSWA—and Smuts for that matter—had no qualms in recruiting thousands of black soldiers known as askari into the Schutztruppe. An understanding of the participants' doctrine reveals that Smuts, rather than a gifted amateur, unsurprisingly subscribed to and adhered to his nation's way of war, and similarly, Lettow-Vorbeck too was merely a product (albeit gifted) of the German *Kriegsschule* and *Kriegsakademie*.[2]

The British Doctrine

Examining how the protagonists fought via an examination and understanding of the military doctrine they subscribed to, can give historians greater insight into the decisions behind and eventual outcome of battles and campaigns. Adopting a doctrinal approach also has its limitations and researchers need to corroborate the evidence with other tools of military science. An understanding of the doctrine which propelled the UDF, the British, and the Germans, goes a long way to explaining some of the inter-Allied tensions in GEA, why Smuts fought the way he did, and why the Germans presented a dangerous foe even when they were substantially inferior in numbers. Military doctrine is a set of fundamental military principles designed to gain advantage and eventually overcome an enemy. It is a formal expression of military knowledge and thought to guide military forces as to how they should conduct their operational art and tactics, to achieve their strategic objectives. It is *descriptive rather than prescriptive*, outlining how the army thinks about fighting, but not how to fight. It is a *guide* to military activity and, as such, does not replace initiative and judgement on the battlefield.[3] The doctrinal lens needs continual adjustment to stay in focus with the introduction of improved and new technologies into warfare, thereby throwing the relationship between the different arms (artillery, air, armour, and infantry) out of synchrony.[4]

At the outbreak of the First World War, the British system of warfare had not advanced much nor learned the lessons provided by the South African War. At the outset of the South African War, the British used what Thomas Pakenham labels "the Aldershot set-piece in three acts". This one-day action comprised the first act—an artillery duel and a preparation of the ground—which could last several hours. It took place with little infantry activity who preferred to wait for the artillery bombardment to end. This phase of the action was devoid of combined arms warfare with the artillery and infantry engagements forming two distinct phases in the battle. The result of the first phase—more often than not—was for the enemy to dig in and keep his artillery concealed. The second act consisted of the infantry launching a frontal assault in open-order formation. The infantry approach to assault distance was accompanied by artillery fire but only up to the stage where it was felt that friendly fire would jeopardise the attackers. Artillery fire would cease at the most crucial moment as the infantry were closing on the enemy and were most in need of artillery support.[5] The final act was a cavalry charge to cut off the enemy's retreat.[6]

This anachronistic form of warfare cost the British dearly in the South African War. Of course, the set-piece action was devoid of operational art and lacked all the essential elements of combined arms warfare where cooperation between the three different arms (infantry–artillery–cavalry) was necessary.[7] The British relied heavily on frontal assaults using shock tactics. Their tactical manoeuvres sought to place their troops in a position close enough to ultimately charge an enemy position with fixed bayonets. However, during the South African War, the British often failed in developing superior firepower (a crucial factor in German doctrine) before launching their final assault. Therefore, often, they charged into the teeth of the unsubdued defender and suffered accordingly. The British failed to add reserves at the crucial point in time and space, and bent on keeping control, held close-order formations for too long and too close to the enemy. The result was that the British tended to deliver their frontal assaults half-heatedly and prematurely at half-pressure, without having gained the necessary superiority in firepower. The British, although adopting the German doctrine in theory of "the infantry fight is decided by fire-effect", did not develop superiority of firepower on the battlefield.[8] They failed to adequately manage their reserves, and instead of distributing them to specific areas for fire-effect, they committed them too hastily and inflexibly. It is obvious that the British had not fully resolved these issues as witnessed by the events as they unfolded at Salaita Hill.

However, after the South African War, British military doctrine did not stand completely still and evolved to a certain extent due to the expensive lessons learned on the battlefields of South Africa. Hard lessons resulted in the publication of the *Infantry Training Manual* of 1902.[9] The manual supported offensive action over defensive action but categorically rejected simple brute force and frontal attacks across the open, fire-swept ground.[10] The manual strongly suggested turning movements which would yield better results for far fewer casualties on the modern battlefield where defensive firepower could overwhelm even considerable numerical advantages. British doctrine identified the need for combined arms warfare and close cooperation between arms but offered minimal suggestions on a systematic implementation method.[11] The Germans took issue with this fresh British way of war because modern battlefields delivered withering defensive firepower. The Germans believed that no matter the nature of the terrain, no enveloping movement could be effective and decisive unless made in combination with an energetic frontal attack. According to them, a flank attack should always arrive at its destination when the enemy is most preoccupied with the attack on his front. Failure to carefully coordinate the arrival of the flank attack with the frontal assault would result in an enemy extricating himself from the envelopment in good time.[12]

The Russo-Japanese War of 1904/5 catalysed a revitalisation of the frontal assault for influential British military thinkers who once again emphasised willpower over firepower. The *Field Service Regulations 1909*[13] published after the *Infantry Training Manual 1902* began to reflect these subtle changes. It de-emphasised flank attacks and gave preference to the 'final assault' over developing superior firepower. The belief that courage alone could overcome defensive firepower began to take hold. The newfound preference for bold offensive action steadily eroded the cautious approach that had emerged directly after the South African War. The result was a downgrade in the belief in firepower and movement, replacing it with faith in moral supremacy and willpower.[14] Military theorists viewed the South African War as an aberration from European war conditions, believing that the lessons learned in South Africa were not completely transferable or applicable to European conditions.[15] Many of Smuts's British peers, and later on historians seeking to find explanations for Smuts's manoeuvrist approach in GEA, would judge his performance as a general in terms of the British doctrine as described above. When using this narrow British doctrinal lens, it is not surprising that Smuts falls short in their eyes and that his peculiar brand of operational art and tactics remained an enigma, and anathema, to the many senior British officers serving under him.

Developing a South African Manoeuvre Doctrine

There is a clear distinction between manoeuvre warfare, which is a doctrine, and mobility, which is not a doctrine, but an attribute best expressed in relative terms. Historians often use the two interchangeably, but they are not. Static or linear warfare, as practised on the Western Front in the First World War, is the exact opposite of manoeuvre warfare. Both sides in the South African War enjoyed mobility, but it was the Boers, who were all mounted infantry, who possessed superior mobility over the British infantry and cavalry. Furthermore, nations practise manoeuvre warfare differently with different objectives in mind. Applied manoeuvre warfare depends on a myriad of factors such as leadership styles and ultimately on changing terrain and battlefield circumstances. The Republican Boer armies were highly mobile being formed into mounted infantry formations. These Boer soldiers should not be confused with traditional cavalry who fought mounted and used swords and lances in epic charges which resulted in close-quarter shock action. The Boer mounted infantryman travelled to the battlefield on his horse and fought dismounted in the fashion of an infantryman. His horse was purely a mode of transport which brought him to and removed him rapidly from the battlefield.

The Boers favoured a war of manoeuvre. The combination of freedom of action devolved to the lowest levels, and the unsurpassed mobility enjoyed by the mounted Boer Commando, delivered a tempo on the battlefield greater than their adversary.[16] Using the superior mobility inherent in mounted infantry, the Boers chose to outflank or envelop an enemy rather than become involved in a costly frontal assault. Every Boer soldier owned and maintained his hardy horse or pony. He carried no bayonet and was unlikely to engage in shock action.[17] The Boers, who manoeuvred to fight, sought the most advantageous ground to do battle. The more cumbersome British fought to manoeuvre and were tied into their significant logistic needs serviced by more formal communication routes. Mobility coupled with a directive command style enabled the Boers to swiftly manoeuvre on the battlefield and, with great intuition, they were able to concentrate on taking advantage of a battlefield opportunity or disperse when faced with danger.[18] The Boers were able to change direction many times within a battle, unlike their enemies, who once they had unleashed their forces, were committed to a set sequence of action. The British had neither the mobility nor the flexibility to modify plans with the changing battlefield conditions.[19]

The South African mounted forces supplied to GEA were distinctly Afrikaner in origin, while the foot infantry tended to be predominantly of English extraction.[20] As a result, the UDF was an interesting combination of opposing doctrines and former enemies.[21] Smuts and the UDF adopted this way of war and put it into practice with good effect in GSWA and with mixed results in GEA. The UDF, under British command, was unable to exercise its manoeuvre doctrine at Salaita Hill as practised successfully in GSWA in 1915 under Botha and the Kilimanjaro operations in GEA in 1916 under Smuts.

Smuts and his UDF arrived in GEA with a well-developed South African way of war and not with his version of a new-fangled art of war. The UDF's military doctrine was a derivation of the combination of the forces that took part in the South African War. The UDF borrowed heavily from the Boer Republican, colonial regiments, and British forces that battled it out in the South African War.[22] The UDF entered the First World War with the incomplete integration of these former formations and their respective doctrines. As noted in preceding chapters, the UDF harboured two dissimilar armies and doctrines—the Boer-orientated mounted infantry and the British- and colonial-orientated infantry regiments. Partial integration of opposing military doctrine ensured that differing rank structures, command styles, and discipline levels existed within the UDF. However, the Afrikaner Rebellion and the GSWA campaign were the catalyst in melding the disparate groups within the UDF into a more homogenous army. The South African army Smuts fielded in GEA had taken on a distinctly South African way of war epitomised by Botha's last envelopment battle at Otavifontein. Unsurprisingly, the UDF owed much of its penchant for manoeuvre warfare to the Boer manoeuvrists such as Koos de la Rey, Botha and Smuts. Understanding how Smuts and the UDF fought necessitates a grasp of the Boer way of war which dominated the mounted infantry component of the UDF.

The Republican Boers, and subsequently the UDF, were naturally averse to conducting expensive and often futile frontal attacks and preferred their particular brand of manoeuvre warfare. Much of the criticism levelled at Smuts in GEA was his natural aversion to expending lives in futile frontal attacks. The British struggled to understand the South African preference for enveloping manoeuvres designed to dislodge and unhinge the enemy from their defensive positions and lure them onto ground not of their choosing. Richard Meinertzhagen (1878–1967), an observer, participant, and a bitter critic of the conduct of the war in GEA, gives some insight into the British penchant for frontal assault. Meinertzhagen served as chief of British military intelligence for the East Africa theatre from January 1915 through August 1916 and thus served under Smuts. He explained it thus:

Manoeuvre is a peculiar form of war which I do not understand and which I doubt will succeed except at great expense in men and money. [...] A series of manoeuvres will only drag operations on for years. Smuts should bring him [Lettow-Vorbeck] to battle and instead of manoeuvring him out of position should endeavour to surround and annihilate him, no matter what our casualties are.[23]

Different armies make use of their ability to manoeuvre to achieve different battlefield objectives. One form of manoeuvre warfare describes a strategy seeking to debilitate the enemy by incapacitating their decision-making processes through demoralisation or disruption. This was the position adopted by the British military philosophers B.H. Liddell Hart and J.F.C. Fuller during the interwar years after the First World War. It has also gained increasing favour in modern Western armies who seek dislocation rather than attrition to defeat the enemy. Manoeuvre warfare can also result in attrition whereby by concentrating forces at the decisive/focal point at the critical time enables the enemy to be overcome through superior firepower/ fighting power.[24] This is very much the objective of German manoeuvre doctrine which seeks a *Vernichtungskrieg* (war of annihilation) usually after effecting a double envelopment leading to a *Kesselschlacht* (cauldron battle).

Another permutation of manoeuvre warfare, favoured by the Boers, diverted, or lured, the enemy into doing battle on ground not of the enemy's choosing. Thus, the enemy is enticed to attack under unfavourable conditions over ground suitable for the defence. Botha in GSWA would often use the tactical offensive version of this to threaten an enemy with envelopment and force him to retreat off his prepared defensive positions. Attrition warfare is not the opposite of manoeuvre warfare but is often a necessary phase or even the last phase in manoeuvre warfare. The Boers were particularly averse to attrition-type warfare and were criticised by the British and the Germans for often not driving home the advantage given them by successful manoeuvre. Boer manoeuvre warfare was more orientated to dislocation than attrition and the UDF, a product of the Boer way of war, was similarly inclined.

A vital element of manoeuvre warfare depends on operating at a higher tempo than the opponent, and by so doing, achieving surprise. An indispensable component of achieving surprise and heightened tempo is a decentralised command structure allowing for initiative and intuition devolved down to the lower levels of command. Placing decision-making in the hands of those who are on the spot, usually junior commanders at company and platoon level, ensures the necessary flexibility to adapt to rapidly changing circumstances.[25] The Boers had the ability to deploy formidable fighting power at the crucial points and the right time due to a flexible command structure where initiative was encouraged at the lowest levels of command. Unlike the British who followed a detailed command structure where junior commanders often waited for instructions from higher up, the Boers, using a directive command style, often left decisions to those who were on the spot in the thick of the action which resulted in a higher tempo.

Between directive command and detailed command, there exists a plethora of variations. Bouwer compares the more prescribed training of the British officer to the Boers' "elastic methods with men and things".[26] The Boers tended to use a directive command system, whereby initiative devolved to the lowest levels in fulfilling a commander's objectives. The British used a detailed command system which called for obedience to orders at the expense of individual initiative.[27] The Boer style of command called for considerable initiative on the battlefield compared to their British opponents.[28] The Boer made skilful use of the terrain, and with his accuracy at extreme ranges, he made the most out of his marksmanship.[29] There was rudimentary fire direction, and each Boer used his initiative in selecting a target.[30] The Boer attained these qualities due to the "one long emergency in which he lived, [which] evolved the qualities of self-reliance, and individualism, horsemanship, and marksmanship, and fitted him to the changing conditions and equipped him for the strenuous struggles of his daily life".[31] Reliance on individual initiative disallowed subordination to the intention or will of a superior and made conformance to plan or wish of a superior impossible.[32] Freedom to exercise initiative was often unbridled and practised out of the confines of an overall objective as prescribed in German doctrine.[33] The lack of formal conventional command structure often resulted in unexpected results on the battlefield. There was no formal legal provision to maintain discipline in the field and no practical way of compelling or enforcing authority. The Boer commanders, chosen by the burghers they led, had no executive powers similar to the British officers.[34]

In the Transvaal War, the First Anglo-Boer War of 1880/1, and the first stages of the South African War, the Boers preferred to manoeuvre by conducting a strategic offensive and a tactical defensive. The Boers favoured the tactical defensive where they could make effective use of defensive multipliers and their keen marksmanship. Their use of artillery was different to the British and they preferred to disperse and conceal the guns among their defensive positions. The Boer artillery would only open up at the last minute when the British attacked. Therefore, there was more of a combined arms approach to the Boer use of artillery.[35] The Boers preferred to avoid an artillery duel, and the dispersal of the guns made them a difficult target for the British to destroy. They often forced the British to attack in circumstances unfavourable to the attacker using their advantage of manoeuvre and high mobility. Therefore, the Boers used their superior mobility to ensure that they would conduct a battle on ground of their choosing. Botha described the doctrine succinctly on campaign in GSWA to some senior officers.

> The greatest asset of our South African mounted troops is their extreme mobility. We must make the greatest possible use of this. We must never, if possible, fight the Germans in their

prepared positions; we must manoeuvre them out of them, and fight on ground of our own choosing.[36]

Many Boer commanders displayed contempt for personal danger and were prepared to undergo any hardships asked of the men they commanded. This style of command was exemplified by Botha and Smuts, who displayed the same characteristics on campaign in GSWA. Smuts had received some British-style military training and wore a British uniform when he attended Victoria College as a student and was a member of the Victoria College Volunteer Rifle Corps.[37] Their disregard for safety and insistence of leading from the front drew little support from the British he commanded, although his antics did earn respect from the men he commanded.[38] The Boer style of command remained an enigma to the British even through the First World War.

The strength of the UDF lay in its ability to bypass resistance and appear suddenly in the flank or the rear of the Germans. The Germans found this fighting style unfamiliar and difficult to get to grips with. General Botha, displaying a way of war familiar with many Boer leaders, and derived from their many conflicts with the Zulus, used a similar approach of body and horns. An excellent example of its use was at the battle of Isandlwana (1879) where the Zulus pinned and then surrounded the British, resulting in their destruction. Trew revealed the Zulu influence on the Boers, and especially Botha on campaign in GSWA in 1914:

> General Botha's favourite method of moving was in three columns covering a very wide front, the two flank columns moving in advance of the centre one. This I always thought was the result of his early experience with the Zulus, for it is an adaptation of the celebrated horns formation used by the Zulu Impis.[39]

Trew asserts that a fighting doctrine is often forged in the flames of battle and shaped by the ingenuity and craftiness of the opponent.[40]

The front of the advancing columns was covered by a thick fringe of scouts. Botha sought a military result through manoeuvre rather than a pitched battle. Botha seldom, if ever, resorted to frontal attacks preferring to pin the enemy in the centre and attempt a double or single envelopment. Neither did Botha fear for an enemy appearing in his rear as true to the principles of manoeuvre warfare his army had no fixed lines of communication.[41]

After the UDF successfully suppressed the rebellion, it was time to deal with the Germans ensconced across the border in GSWA. The fact that the South African forces numbered approximately 50,000 compared to the modest German force of about 7,000, did not tempt them to conduct a costly war of annihilation. They avoided pitched battles in favour of advancing on multiple fronts. By using the threat of envelopment, the UDF dislodged the Germans from their prepared positions and made them defend locations not of their primary choice. The South Africans forced the Germans to surrender on 9 July 1915 with their fighting capability almost intact. The successful conclusion of the campaign, at relatively low human cost, was vindication of manoeuvre warfare and carried all the hallmarks of a South African way of war.[42] Presenting even more of an enigma to the British than the Boer way of war was the Germans and askari of the Schutztruppe.

The Schutztruppe and German Doctrine

First World War Germany most probably fielded the best-trained and -disciplined army in the world. The Imperial German Army benefitted from 43 years of doctrinal development and rigorous training since the Franco-Prussian war of 1870. The Schutztruppe, or colonial Protection Force, delivered a strict regimen of discipline, combat readiness, professional ethos, and German customs and ritual on the askari who hailed from varying cultural backgrounds. The Germans drilled and trained the askari daily to achieve a level of competence and confidence that would allow them to perform even when heavily outnumbered. The Germans encouraged initiative, intuition, and independent thought among the junior officers and NCOs. Commanders expected their subordinates to take risks in the spirit of mission command tactics. The training continued daily even when the askari were on active deployment, reminding the soldiers constantly of Schutztruppe order and discipline even on the march. Repetitive training was accompanied by war games instilling in the askari the skills to handle a variety of potential military scenarios such as meeting engagements, assaulting fortified positions, and extricating themselves from engagements with an organised retreat—always a difficult procedure under the best of conditions.[43] Although the askari received training on the Schutztruppe's machine guns as well as rifle musketry, their performance in this regard was always felt to be below par by the German officers.[44]

Unlike European armies organised along corps, divisional and brigade lines, the largest formal unit of the Schutztruppe was the *Feldkompagnie* (field company). The strength of the *Feldkompagnie* consisted of 100–200 askari and between 10–20 German officers. Each *Feldkompagnie* was allocated a dedicated carrier unit of porters numbering up to 250 members. These carrier units were also a source of replacements for the company. Several *Feldkompagnien* could be combined into an *Abteilung* (detachment) under one commander for a particular operation and then disband once again into their companies. Each company had two to three machine guns, usually manned by Germans and supported by the rifle fire of the askari. Small unit tactics were based around the machine guns which were central to the firepower of the company.[45] Organising the structure of the Schutztruppe along company lines rather than the bigger battalions and brigades used by Smuts and the British gave the Germans unprecedented and unrivalled flexibility and mobility. However, such a structure depended on the skills of its officer corps' ability to act independently and intuitively to rapidly changing circumstances. The Germans were able to apply a skill set, not found in other armies, to avoid their *Feldkompagnien* from being overrun and destroyed piecemeal. Smuts has been criticised for not mimicking the smaller organisational structure of the Schutztruppe; however, critics have failed to consider the dearth of quality officers available to Smuts which was vital to ensure the survival of the German *Feldkompagnie* structure.[46] (See Figure 5.1)

German officers and NCOs formed the leader group of the Schutztruppe and were a small fraction (10–15%) of its complement. However, to gain an understanding of why the Schutztruppe presented such a formidable opponent one needs to gain an idea of German military doctrine. The German army took its training to heart and considered combat to be the ultimate step in their training programme. Germans considered that war was an art and decision-making and leadership in combat as creative acts, not a science that followed rigid rules and a set formula as in many other armies. The German army rejected *Normaltaktik* or a standard solution to tactical problems. Each tactical or operational situation had to be recognised for its uniqueness and evaluated on its own terms. A firm basis of history and doctrine supplied a foundation for the German soldier, but

Figure 5.1. A company of *Schutztruppen* comprised three platoons and three or four machine guns. (Bundesarchiv Bild 105-DOA5062)

on the day, he would have to rely on his intellect and determination to solve real-life tactical problems.[47]

The Germans were more flexible in their approach to warfare than the British. German military culture prized initiative down to the lowest levels of command. The changing nature of the battlefield meant that to survive the fire-swept killing zones, formations would have to be much smaller and act more independently. Lethal firepower meant that senior leaders would not have as much influence on the battle after the first shots were fired. Modern firepower made necessary the devolution of decision-making down to the lower ranks. Company grade officers and NCOs as well as the ordinary soldier were expected to think and act independently as well as use their own initiative to fire and move.[48]

Their mission-type tactics (*Auftragstaktik*) was a principal component of the German Armed Forces since the 19th century. This military culture allowed subordinates to make decisions on the spot down to the lowest levels of command, on condition that they followed the overall commander's objective.[49] The German army encouraged aggressive tactics and their default was to attack or counterattack from nearly every situation, even in the face of a numerical disadvantge, or even when circumstances seemed unfavourable. The Germans were also proponents of combined arms warfare and their frequent military exercises stressed cooperation between the different arms of service. They practised manoeuvre warfare (*Bewegungskrieg*) where they favoured mobility over remaining static (*Stellungskrieg*). The Germans sought to manoeuvre their forces to place them in the most advantageous position where they could overwhelm an unsuspecting enemy. Often they would attempt to encircle their opponent and after that, try to destroy him in a cauldron battle (*Kesselschlacht*). Colonel Paul von Lettow-Vorbeck was a product of this German military training and his conduct of the GEA campaign, as commander of the German forces, conformed to the prescribed German doctrine of the time.[50]

Smuts significantly outnumbered the Schutztruppe when he arrived in GEA. Lettow-Vorbeck often had to rely of defensive tactics in the face of a heavy numerical disadvantage. Nevertheless, his defensive strategy and tactics were not passive, and he encouraged an active defence which sought opportunities to counterattack whenever an opportunity presented itself on the battlefield. He relied heavily on his commanders' initiative to seek out opportunities and launch aggressive attacks using flanking and enveloping manoeuvres when possible.[51] The Germans, due to their training, leadership style and enhanced tempo were superior on meeting engagements and many British flank attacks such as those at Salaita Hill were met with vigorous and unexpected German counterattacks. Robust and regular training in German methods coupled with an officer corps steeped in the traditions of German military doctrine which encouraged aggression, intuition, and initiative, and combined with the resourcefulness and resolve of Lettow-Vorbeck, ensured that Smuts would be presented with a formidable enemy in GEA.

Salaita Hill

The battle for Salaita Hill took place on 12 February 1916, just weeks prior to Smuts's arrival in GEA. Its significance is the involvement of South African troops and how they fared under British command in the absence of Smuts. Salaita was the first occasion that South African troops, albeit under British command, engaged with the Germans in GEA. Conditions in GEA were unlike anything that the South Africans had encountered before. The UDF forces which took part in the battle were made up of regular South African infantry and excluded the mounted infantry brigades which had yet to, or were in the process of, arriving in GEA. The South Africans who fought in GEA were mostly veterans of GSWA and were all volunteers.

Thus far in the GEA campaign, the British, under Major-General Michael Tighe (1864–1925), had fared poorly and there was legitimate concern that this was "damaging to our prestige among the native races".[52] Most importantly, Salaita Hill was one of the only pieces of British territory that the Germans occupied in the First World War.[53] The political value of removing them from this piece of British real estate placed immense pressure on the military to do so as soon as it was possible. The arrival of strong South African forces in British East Africa in February 1916, presented the British with an opportunity to remove the Germans before the arrival of Smuts. The British conducted the Salaita operation in terms of a strategy to be undertaken before the onset of the rains in April, termed "Preliminary Operations". These operations would consist of capturing strong German outposts in British East Africa to restore prestige and provide sound jumping-off points when the rains ceased in June.[54] One has to question the Tighe's wisdom in conducting a major operation using South African forces just weeks prior to the arrival, and without the knowledge, of Smuts.

Salaita Hill was a significant strategic outpost constructed on British East African soil and held by the Germans as part of a deep defensive system stretching back to German territory. Salaita was the first in a series of defensive positions occupied by the Germans, which guarded the Taveta Gap, the gateway to British East Africa/ GEA. (See Map 5.1) Its forward position also facilitated German raids of the British railway and logistical infrastructure. The Germans adopted a defensive persisting strategy coupled with an offensive raiding strategy, an activity they engaged in often and with repeated success to the extreme irritation of the British.[55] Salaita Hill also gave the Germans a useful observation post providing the only high ground astride the single road leading to Taveta, on an otherwise flat almost featureless plateau. The impenetrable Pare Mountains in the south and the dominating Kilimanjaro to the north flanked the 25-kilometre Taveta Gap.

Brigadier-General Wilfrid Malleson (1866–1946) found himself in command of the British 2nd Division, which Tighe earmarked to launch the attack on Salaita

Hill. Malleson was a relatively inexperienced general, having seen very little in the way of combat and even less time in command. Meinertzhagen describes Malleson as having no knowledge of command and that he was

> a bad man, clever as a monkey, but hopelessly unreliable and with a nasty record behind him. He is by far the cleverest man out here, but having spent all his service in an Ordinance Office, knows very little about active operations and still less of the usual courtesies amongst British officers. He comes from a class which would wreck the Empire to advance himself. [...] [He] is loathed and despised as an overbearing bully, ill mannered, and a rotten soldier.[56]

Meinertzhagen was not alone in assessing Malleson's generalship as below par and Smuts would be less than complimentary when he canvassed for his removal on 15 March 1916 after Malleson asked to be relieved of his command "owing to serious indisposition". Smuts at his diplomatic best could hardly conceal his contempt:

> I regret to say that after the Salaita fiasco on the 12 February there is very little confidence in the fighting ability of Malleson and a change in the command of the 1st East African Brigade is also desirable; Tighe considers him a capable administrator and I hope his talents could be better employed by the war office in an administrative capacity.[57]

Tighe did not escape his fair share of criticism. The South African exploratory mission to GEA at the end of 1915 found Tighe to be of "nervous manner, lacking in strength of character and forcefulness, lacks experience of conducting operations of a large scale, cannot look at things from a big point of view [and] does not realise the use to which mounted troops can be put". Lieutenant-Colonels A.M. Hughes and Dirk van Deventer were even less complimentary about Malleson: "Neither of us were impressed by this officer ... he was not a big man in the sense of being strong and resourceful."[58]

On 1 May 1915, Malleson assumed command of the Voi area, which extended from the coast to Kilimanjaro. On 13 July 1915, he advanced on Mbuyuni with 1,100 men, eight machine guns, and three pieces of artillery. He launched an attack on the morning of 14 July against the entrenched German positions after a night march. It took the form of a frontal assault, supplemented with a weak flanking attack on the enemy left.[59] The entire operation harked back to the uninspired tactics employed by the British in the opening stages of the South African War. Malleson suffered casualties of 170 men and one machine gun in this unsuccessful action. He had delivered a frontal attack on a carefully prepared position against a numerically superior enemy and had no hope of success.[60] A.E. Capell sums up the result of the fiasco as "strengthening of the already fine morale of the enemy".[61] It was an inauspicious beginning to an unremarkable combat career.

With little success or experience, and one defeat behind his name, Malleson drew up operational orders on 11 February 1916 for an attack on the German positions at Salaita Hill. His motivation for the attack before the arrival of Smuts, according to Malleson, emanated from an order he received on 10 February 1916, which stated that he was to capture the hill before 14 February. These orders apparently originated from General Sir Horace Lockwood Smith-Dorrien (1858–1930) in South Africa and travelling en route to assume the command of the East African Force from Tighe.[62] The orders first took the form of a query issued by Smith-Dorrien on 4 February 1916 to Major-General M. Tighe, commander of the British forces in East Africa, asking when he would attack Salaita Hill. Tighe replied on 7 February that he would attack Salaita between 12–14 February. There is little evidence to suggest that Smith-Dorrien or anyone else informed Smuts of this planned attack on Salaita Hill when the latter replaced him on short notice.[63] It is unlikely that Smuts would have condoned a frontal attack of this nature.

Smith-Dorrien received his appointment as the General Officer Commanding of East Africa on 22 November 1915. On his voyage to South Africa, he unfortunately contracted pneumonia and was eventually unable to take up his new command. Prior to Smuts being appointed to replace Smith-Dorrien, he attempted to convalesce in Cape Town. The British appointed Smuts as Smith-Dorrien's successor on 6 February 1916 and he arrived in East Africa on the 19 February.[64] It seems strange that the British would launch a major attack before the arrival of Smuts on a query issued by Smith-Dorrien on 4 February. Logic dictates that the new commander would have wanted to be present at the scene, instead of languishing on a ship sailing for East Africa. The suggestion for the attack emanated from Smith-Dorrien who was no longer in command and the attack took place a day after Smuts departed for East Africa.[65] It seems that Malleson and Tighe were anxious for a victory before Smuts's arrival.

This was not the first time that the British had attempted to assail Salaita Hill. The previous effort took place on 29 March 1915 and took the form of a probing attack by two companies, two machine guns and a single artillery piece.[66] Meinertzhagen described the assault as "aimless, objectless and dangerous". Maj G. Newcome, true to prevailing British doctrine, executed an unimaginative frontal assault on the hill. A German counterattack on the right flank readily reinforced by the main German base at Taveta a mere 10 kilometres away, drove him back. The British attack failed miserably with five killed and two machine guns abandoned in the panic of retreat.[67] The way the Germans were able to reinforce Salaita rapidly and launch a flank attack was a precursor to what Malleson could expect when he attacked. According to Malleson's after-battle report, he expected the South Africans to encounter the German "hostile reserves" that he believed resided on the western side of Salaita Hill. Therefore, any flank attack could have reasonably anticipated stiff resistance at any time in their manoeuvre.[68]

Figure 5.2. South Africans in German East Africa.[69]

Malleson resolved to launch his attack with a bit more imagination and flair than that of Newcome. He was determined to remove the enemy on Salaita via a turning movement, which would envelop the German positions on the hill from the north. (See Map 5.1) The divisional war diary makes it clear that the intention of the attack was to remove the enemy and secure Salaita Hill.[70] The newly arrived, fresh (inexperienced) South Africans would conduct this flanking manoeuvre. The Germans would be pinned on their front by the veteran 1st East African Infantry Brigade, a formation which had seen most of the action in the campaign thus far. Thus, Malleson chose to leave it to the "green", recently arrived[71] South Africans, to execute a flanking manoeuvre against an enemy that had rebuffed similar assaults on two previous occasions at Salaita on 29 March 1915 and Mbuyuni on 14 July 1915.[72] Malleson comments on the South Africans; inexperience in a note he penned on 20 April 1917.

> So far as I am aware the South Africans were the only Overseas contingent put straight into the field. All other contingents had months of thorough training in England or Egypt before being sent into the field. Br[igadier] General Berenge [Berrange], Commanding 3rd S.A. Brigade, told me that the greater portion of his men had been given their arms and uniform on board the transport at Durban.[73]

The South African troops were woefully undertrained; the time between recruitment and seeing their first action, amounted to only a matter of weeks.[74] Although many of the officers were veterans of the South African War there was a shortage of experienced NCOs. Most of the men were hastily recruited, undertrained teenagers and there was little time to hone them into an effective fighting force.[75] (See Figure 5.2)

Malleson's decision to split his holding forces (1st East African Brigade) and his offensive brigade (2nd South African Infantry Brigade) equally, worked against the basic principle in warfare of concentration and economy of force.[76] The South African outflanking manoeuvre was clearly the point of maximum effort and as such should have attracted the bulk of the troops available. As it was, there was no discernible reserve placed under Brigadier-General P.S. Beves's command to reinforce success, or if necessary, to ward off an enemy counterattack. (See Table 5.2) It was counterintuitive to the principle of unity of command, whereby unity of effort develops by appointing a responsible commander and placing the necessary resources at his disposal to reach the objective. The flank attack could have achieved an overwhelming superiority had Malleson thinned out the static forces holding the western front of Salaita and creating a reserve for the flanking attack.

The brunt of the turning movement would be conducted by the 2nd South African Infantry Brigade under Beves, a veteran brigade commander under Brigadier-General Sir Duncan McKenzie in the GSWA campaign. Beves had served as a captain in the South African War in a regular British infantry regiment and saw extensive action at Lombard's Kop and the defence of Ladysmith. He went on to command a battalion from 4 September 1900 to 15 May 1901. After the war he commanded the Transvaal Volunteers until 1912 and then became Commandant of Cadets in the UDF.[77] Collyer describes him as, "an officer of Regimental experience, careful, and attentive to the comforts and needs of those whom he commanded".[78] Malleson is at pains to explain that he did not design the action, especially the flanking movement, to manoeuvre the Germans out of Salaita. To do so would have risked the intervention of the 6,000 German troops in the Taveta vicinity and he did not have the luxury of the extra 10,000 soldiers that Smuts would field a month later. He was fearful of "splitting up" an already inferior force that a deeper flanking attack would require.[79]

Common sense would dictate that Malleson should have assigned the more difficult role of enveloping Salaita Hill to the more experienced 1st East African Infantry Brigade rather than the relatively inexperienced 2nd South African Infantry Brigade. They had barely arrived in GEA and had little time to acclimatise or train in their new surroundings.[80] Malleson himself comments that the South Africans were the only contingent put straight into battle: "All other contingents had months of thorough training in England or Egypt before being sent to the field."[81] It would have been more prudent to allow the South Africans to assume the static role in front of Salaita, which would have afforded them a valuable learning experience against a veteran enemy that was the wily victor of many battles. However, Malleson in his wisdom seems to have felt that his veteran troops deserved a break after being continuously on campaign for many months.

The depth of Malleson's proposed tactical outflanking manoeuvre can also be called into question. The further north and thus the wider the manoeuvre (an operational rather than a tactical manoeuvre) described by the outflanking units, the more the German positions at Salaita would be unhinged. A manoeuvre designed to arrive in the rear of Salaita would have disrupted the supply lines to those defending the hill, forcing the Germans to either abandon their positions or launch a counterattack on a numerically superior enemy on ground of the enemy's choosing. The main weakness of Salaita was that it did not have a supply of water. The defenders of Salaita carried in every drop of water from the west and this supply line was extremely vulnerable to disruption, which could have made the defence of Salaita untenable.[82] As it was, Malleson's flanking attack was a very shallow affair, barely stretching two kilometres to the Germans' left flank on the hill. The lack of depth of the attack allowed the Germans the opportunity to extend their flank and meet their attackers from prepared positions close to Salaita. If one considers the South African flanking manoeuvre, it was even shallower that what Malleson had intended, and unintentionally developed into a frontal assault delivered well to the north-east instead of to the north-west. Malleson does offer his reasons for resorting to a tactical solution rather than launching a flanking manoeuvre at the operational level. He explains his motivation for adopting a shallow outflanking manoeuvre as follows:

> The information supplied by G.H.Q was to the effect that the enemy had in and around Taveta, which is in close supporting distance of Salaita, not less than 6,000 men. As I could not bring more than 4,500 rifles to the actual attack there could be no question of trying to manoeuvre the enemy out of Salaita, as was possible a month later with 10,000 additional troops, as to make any attempt would have involved splitting up an already inferior force, and thus risk defeat in detail.[83]

Therefore, using dubious numbers as an excuse not to launch a more imaginative attack, Malleson resorted to what turned out to be a costly unimaginative frontal assault on a well-prepared position without the element of surprise.

At the outset, the British underestimated the enemy forces facing them, despite the ground and air reconnaissance undertaken in the few days before the operation.[84] They estimated German strength to be in the region of 300 men entrenched with machine guns but with no artillery.[85] However, this flies in the face of a report produced by Malleson, shortly after the battle, where he speaks of intelligence reporting the availability of 2,000 Germans near Salaita.[86] One can compare this with the actual figures shown in Table 5.1. Malleson, despite the woeful underestimation of the forces in front of him (according to the British official history), did enjoy a substantial numerical superiority in men, machine guns, and artillery. According to Malleson's account directly after the battle and then again 14 months later, he expected there to be considerable German resistance when he attacked Salaita. The result of the battle would depend on the skilful use, or otherwise, of his numerical advantage in directing his forces to the centre of gravity of his attack (*Schwerpunkt*).

Table 5.1. The opposing forces present at Salaita Hill, 12 February 1916[87]

	German Frontline	German Reserves	German Total	British Total	Force Ratio
Rifles	1400	600	2000	6000	3 : 1
Machine Guns	12		12	41	3,4 : 1
Field Artillery	2		2	14	7 : 1
Heavy Artillery			0	4	∞
Armoured Cars	0		0	4	∞

Further to the poor intelligence on enemy numbers, was a gross underestimation of the enemy fighting power and his ability to rapidly move into battle reinforcements situated some seven kilometres away. The British plan depended on a preconceived notion that they could capture Salaita Hill before the enemy was able to send reinforcements. They also underrated the strength of the enemy defences after two previous unsuccessful attacks on the same positions. The Germans had occupied the same ground for many months and made good use of their time to build formidable all-around defences and thoroughly reconnoitre the area.[88] The South Africans too were guilty of making light of the resourcefulness and skill of the enemy, dismissing them as mostly 'native' troops. Their contempt for the enemy matched their low regard for the Indian soldiers who ironically come to their rescue in the aftermath of the fiasco of Salaita.[89]

Beves received his divisional order on 11/12 February, the night before the operation, stating that his brigade would attack the enemy positions to the north-east of Salaita Hill. He prudently sought further information as to the proposed action that would take place subsequent to the occupation of the enemy positions. Malleson informed Beves that no discussion would be entertained on the actual orders.[90] Beves took the opportunity to raise several concerns surrounding the execution of the operation. He was apprehensive at the lack of surprise because his brigade would be in full view from Salaita Hill from several miles distant. Furthermore, the enemy was able to reinforce his positions swiftly from Taveta some 11 kilometres away, allowing for a possible counterattack. Beves pointed out that he was short of a battalion—the 8th South African Infantry (SAI) Battalion had not yet arrived—and requested a replacement battalion to bolster his exposed flank. Finally, he requested intensive artillery preparation and after that, the full cooperation of the artillery during the attack. He was fearful that artillery cooperation would not be possible in the event of a counterattack launched by the Germans in the bush.[91] Malleson placated Beves when he gave assurances that he would make adequate artillery support available and that the assault would be over before the Germans could launch an effective counterattack. Belfield's Scouts, by conducting reconnaissance far in advance of the South Africans, would be able to alert them promptly of any enemy movement towards them that emanated from Taveta.[92] (See Table 5.2)

As it turned out, there was little in the way of a combined arms approach as the artillery was unresponsive to the immediate needs of the infantry on the changing battlefield. Malleson reduced the role of the artillery to that of softening up the enemy positions on Salaita in an opening bombardment reminiscent of the "the Aldershot set-piece in three acts" applied in the South African War. For the main part, the artillery was unable to respond to the German counterattack and give support to the South Africans. Once the infantry became mobile on the right flank and the battle became fluid, the South Africans were unable to communicate effectively with the artillery to call for close support. The artillery also failed to respond and alter their bombardment when they discovered that the enemy main defensive trench line was at the foot of Salaita rather than at the summit. The Boers had used the same tactic at Magersfontein on 11 December 1899 against the British and the South Africans should not have been surprised at the position of the German trenches.[93]

Table 5.2. The order of battle for the opposing sides at Salaita

German		British		
Colonel Paul von Lettow-Vorbeck		Brigadier-General Wilfrid Malleson		
1 FK		1st East African Infantry Brigade		
14 FK		2 Loyal North Lancashire Regiment		
15 FK	Major Georg Kraut	2 Rhodesia Regiment	(Lt-Col A. Capell)	
18 FK	(1400 men)	130 Baluchis Regiment	(Maj P.H. Dyke)	
30 FK				
6 Shutz K		2nd South African Infantry Brigade		
		5 SAI Regiment	(Lt-Col J.J. Byron)	Brig-Gen
6 FK	Capt Schulz	6 SAI Regiment	(Lt-Col GM.J. Molyneux)	P.S. Beves
9 FK	(600 men)	7 SAI Regiment	(Lt-Col J.C. Freeth)	
24 FK				
		Divisional Troops		
		Mounted Infantry Company		
		Belfields Scouts (60 men mounted)		
		61st Pioneers		
		Various artillery units		
		4 Armoured cars	(Lt-Commander Whittal)	

The Battle for Salaita Hill Commences, 12 February 1916

The two brigades set off at dawn on 12 February from the Serengeti camp. (See Table 5.2) They reached the Njoro riverbed two and a half kilometres apart at 0645 and there were issued with orders for the attack. Malleson envisaged enveloping Salaita Hill from the north while Belfield's Scouts and two armoured cars guarded the right flank, and the mounted infantry and a further two armoured cars guarded the left flank of the South Africans. The pioneers deployed in the riverbed to improve ramps and search for mines.[94] The South Africans had positioned themselves to the north-west of Salaita, when an hour later, two reconnaissance planes reported a sighting of newly dug German trenches, which extended northward from the hill.[95] The diary entry of an eyewitness, E.S. Thompson, brings the moment to life:

> Reveille 0230. Marched on to the road and waited for daylight when we advanced and struck off to the right through the bush. After we had advanced about an hour we halted and an aeroplane came flying overhead and flew round the fort. We again advanced and when we had gone about 400 yards [366 metres] Jock Young found that he had left his rifle behind and went back to get it but couldn't find it. We still advanced with the 6th Regiment on our right and the Armoured Motors and Headquarters Staff on our left. We had advanced into an open space when suddenly we heard shells whistling over our heads and bursting about 30 yds [28 metres] behind us. At first there was a momentary pause then we all scampered for cover and a few more shells came along. For my part I was too excited to be frightened. After 5 minutes we were given the order to advance through the bush. Our howitzers now began firing and it was a fine sight seeing the shells bursting round the trenches. When we got closer up they began firing at us with rifles so we got into cover and unpacked the guns. We kept on advancing and then the wounded began coming back.[96]

The South Africans continued their march and at 0800, the 5th, 6th, and 7th South African Infantry Regiments (SAIRs) deployed 1,000 metres from the north-west of Salaita Hill. (See Map 5.1) The artillery came into action at 0900 and began to bombard the German positions on the top and slopes of the hill. The artillery fire was mostly ineffective because the Germans had occupied the trenches on the base of the hill rather than on its slopes.[97] The 7th Battalion halted some 500 metres from the German entrenchments at the base of the hill and began to take effective fire from the partially cleared fields of fire.[98] Beves, in response, sent his 6th Battalion to extend his line and thus develop the enveloping movement on his right. He kept the 5th Battalion and his four remaining mountain guns in reserve. Beves lost touch with his mounted troops (Belfield's Scouts) as they disappeared out of sight to the north.[99] Captain James commanded the machine-gun battery, which Malleson had attached to the South Africans for the day. He reported, after the battle, that the South Africans did not build up a proper firing line and the men were reluctant to open fire because of the enemy attention it would attract.[100]

The attack hardly came as a surprise to the Germans who noticed the preparations as early as 9 February. One of these was an abortive reconnaissance in force against Salaita made by the 2nd Rhodesia Regiment and the 130th Baluchis and artillery elements on 3 February 1916.[101] The attack involved two South African regiments in support, as well as an artillery barrage against the fort at the top of Salaita. On 5 February, the 6th South African Infantry Regiment made another reconnaissance and drew fire from Salaita.[102] On 9 February, the entire South African Brigade demonstrated in front of Salaita.[103] It is not surprising that after all the British activity, which included numerous aircraft overflights, the Germans suspected an attack in the area.[104]

The element of surprise, often the factor in war that gives the attacker the edge, was lost. The overflights and various reconnaissance missions and demonstrations undertaken in the days before the attack had alerted the enemy as to Malleson's interest in the outpost. Salaita's dominant position also afforded the defenders a good observation post where they were able to spot an enemy attack a good distance away, giving them time to reinforce the position. The artillery barrage undertaken in the vain attempt to soften up the enemy defences would also alert the Germans prematurely that an attack was underway. It was always going to be a difficult ask to try and achieve the element of surprise and the better solution was perhaps the one Smuts instituted a month later when he bypassed the stronghold and forced the Germans to abandon it. Smuts revealed his attitude and Boer way of war in a sentence he delivered on visiting the area on 20 February 1916. After surveying the enemy territory by climbing a tree he said, "No necessity to attack Salaita."[105]

The Germans realised, at approximately 0900, that the British were launching a full-fledged attack and not merely demonstrating. They quickly identified that the main attack was developing in the north and was descending on the flank. They immediately responded and Major Georg Kraut ordered the 15th Feldkompanie to position themselves to attack the South African right wing at 0915. Captain Schulz did not need any orders and he acted on his initiative. He began to advance with three companies to meet the South Africans. Kraut issued the order for Schulz to attack at 1000. In the face of mounting casualties, Beves now ordered his 7th SAIR to fall back at about 1300,[106] at almost the same time that the Germans launched a counterattack against the 6th SAIR with their 15th Feldkompanie. The usual German aggressiveness accompanied their attack. The arrival of the Germans to the right of the South Africans threatened to envelop their exposed wing. (See Map 5.1)

To counter this, Beves sent forth his 5th SAIR to form a defensive flank. However, the 5th SAIR soon found itself outflanked in turn by the arrival of the 6th, 9th, and 24th Feldkompanies under the command of Schulz. The warning by Belfield's Scouts of the new German counterattack developing came too late for the 5th SAIR and took the South Africans completely by surprise.[107] In the face of the unexpected

German attack, the South Africans began to give ground and retreated in what was to become essentially a rout.[108] The Germans regrouped at 1400 and once again went on the attack, relentlessly pursuing the retreating South Africans, only to be stopped by the resilient defence of the 130th Baluchis.[109] It was 130th Baluchis who successfully covered the ignominious South African retreat, resisting a bayonet attack and restoring order to the British front.[110]

What had developed on the South African flank was a classic encounter battle or a meeting engagement where the opposing sides collided in the field, incompletely deployed for battle. All indicators point to the fact that the South Africans were preparing to assault fixed entrenched positions on the north-west flank of Salaita. They were surprised to see the Germans had abandoned their trenches and that these were dummy positions designed to deceive the enemy. What transpired was a manoeuvre battle where each side tried to extend its flank to meet the enveloping enemy. It was a battle in which the Germans held all the advantages. Their emphasis on devolving decision-making down to the lowest levels of command (*Auftragstaktik*) allowed junior officers to make on-the-spot decisions. The decisive factors in these types of battle are the initiative of the junior officers and the calmness and efficiency of the troops. German training encouraged their troops, when they were in doubt, to make for where the sounds of battle are the loudest and charge aggressively in that direction immediately. The Germans were veterans of many battles while the South Africans were newcomers to war in East Africa. Once the Germans derailed the South Africans from their set-piece attack by appearing on their flank, the South Africans became unhinged, then broke in the face of incessant aggressive attacks, and then ran.

The battle for Salaita exposed the weak C3I[111] that plagued all the phases and levels of the operation. There seemed to be little coordination of efforts between the two brigades, and it is inexplicable that Malleson only put the East African Brigade into action after the South Africans had been in a battle for over four hours.[112] The South Africans had no communication with divisional headquarters or with the East African Brigade and they were unable to direct the artillery fire to support them.[113] Beves lost control over his forces once the situation became fluid on the British right. The South African retreat turned into a panic and then into a rout. Retreating in the face of an aggressive enemy takes great skill and coordination and Beves would have done better had he ordered his regiments to attack instead of retiring.

Meanwhile, at 1045 the 1st East African Brigade was a sent forward. The British had inexplicably held it back up to this point, supposedly to support the South Africans if necessary. Their advance soon halted after emerging from the bush into comparatively open ground 1,000 metres in front of the German trenches. There they came under heavy fire. Confronted with the well-placed German defences, they were unable to make any further forward progress.[114] At 1200 orders were received to move the entire East African Brigade to the north to assist the South

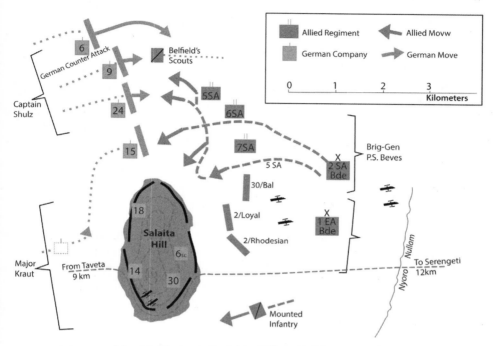

Map 5.1. The battle for Salaita Hill on 12 February 1916

Africans in their north-east attack. Before elements of the brigade could complete the manoeuvre, a countermanding order was given to attack Salaita directly.[115] It seems that Malleson intended the East African Brigade to attack only once the South African attack was well underway, according to one regimental history. They lay in their positions for more than an hour "subject to heavy shell and searching rifle fire". They were waiting for the South African flank attack to develop before advancing themselves. When eventually the order to advance was given at 1300,[116] there was a reluctance resulting in hesitation to move out of their relatively safe positions to ones that were closer to the enemy and far more vulnerable to their fire. Lieutenant-Colonel A. Capell, commanding the 2nd Rhodesia Regiment, objected to a verbal instruction to move forward, and asked for written orders. At that stage, it became apparent that the flank attack had failed, and Rhodesian regiment began to retreat.[117]

The last word describing the trauma inflicted on the South Africans is left for E.S. Thompson who graphically describes the impossible chaos of the action and the fog of war surrounding the battlefield:

> The 5th Regiment then began to retire and acted disgracefully, refusing to halt and lie down when ordered. Our Corporal then told us to retire right back so we retired till they began shelling us again so we lay flat down. It was at this point that I last saw Jock and Bob Thompson. We

retired further and got behind some tall trees but they again shelled us so we doubled across an open space to the right and got in amongst the Indian Mountain Battery. We lay down for about half an hour with bullets zipping past all the time. The firing seemed to be coming nearer, then the 6th retired behind us so we retired right back and then to the right. ... then the Baluchis who were guarding our rear got behind us so we retired further and got behind some trees but they began shelling us again so we got right out of it. By this time I had finished my water and was terribly thirsty and tired. Several men of 'D' Company of the 7th got into the first line of trenches but as the 5th would not support them had to evacuate the place. Hans Gosch was killed during the retreat. He was bending over when he was shot through the back, the bullet coming through his jaw and smashing it. Everybody reckons that although it was a very hard position to storm we would have won had it not been for the 5th retiring. On reading this entry recently, I would say that we had been rather harsh about the behaviour of the 5th SAI. As far as I recall it was a case of a few young chaps going into a panic and that should not be interpreted as a reflection of the whole regiment.[118]

According to Malleson, Beves, who narrowly escaped capture, was apologetic and told him, "I don't know what to say for letting you in [sic] like this; I can only deeply apologise. My men have gone; it is impossible to rally them here. I am very sorry." Malleson describes the South Africans he encountered as being without discipline and cohesion and the officers appeared helpless. Malleson reported that several other officers, beside Beves, approached him the next day and apologised profusely for their poor conduct and said that the men were, "kicking themselves with shame and disgust".[119]

The fiasco cost the South Africans 139 casualties in a matter of four hours of combat, whereas they incurred 288 casualties in the entire German South West African campaign.[120] German losses were considerably less with one German, six askari and three carriers killed and three Germans, 22 askari and eight carriers wounded. The Germans captured a considerable amount of booty including 40,000 cartridges, 14 7cm artillery shells and 14 mules.[121] The final scorecard fairly reflected the scale of the defeat inflicted on the South Africans.

An obviously shaken Tighe took four days to report the defeat to the Chief of Imperial General Staff, Lord Kitchener.[122] Kitchener, fully understanding the possible political repercussions for South Africa, censured Tighe. He cautioned him not to take premature operations that would deprive the newly appointed commander of the East African forces, General Smuts, of full liberty of action before his arrival.[123] Smuts, on his arrival in GEA shortly after the battle of Salaita, did not take immediate action against Tighe or Malleson. He gave both men another opportunity to prove their worth. Smuts sought and received permission from the British to carry out his major operation before the rainy season, on 25 February. Smuts whitewashed the defeat at Salaita in his dispatch by saying that the South Africans had learned "invaluable lessons".[124] Botha did his best to keep the extent of the fiasco out of the House of Parliament.[125]

Smuts launched an attack on 5 March, a mere three weeks after his arrival on 19 February. His wide enveloping movement forced the Germans to abandon

Salaita Hill with hardly a shot fired. During the afternoon of 11 March, the British launched an attack, which took them to the foot of the Latema-Reata hills where were enemy gunfire held them up. Malleson, the commander at Salaita, apparently suffering from dysentery and perhaps a dose of uncomfortable déjà vu, chose to sick report.[126] Tighe took over the command from Malleson. In the aftermath of the battle, these two generals were relieved of their command by Smuts who could barely conceal his contempt at their performance.[127]

CHAPTER 6

Smuts and the Kilimanjaro Operation in East Africa, March 1916

South Africa's successful conclusion of the German South West African (GSWA) campaign in 1915 encouraged Britain to seek further assistance in German East Africa (GEA). Despite vociferous Afrikaner nationalist objections to the war effort and the 1914 Afrikaner Rebellion, Louis Botha and Jan Smuts's loyal support of the Empire earned Britain's trust and gratitude. However, elevating South Africa's international status came at a steep political price. Smuts and Botha lost much ground to the Afrikaner nationalists who opposed South Africa's foreign military adventures. The October 1915 election results returned the ruling South African Party (SAP) to power with a much-reduced majority. The reduction of seats to 54 out of 130 forced the SAP to seek support from the English Unionist Party in the opposition benches to retain power. Barry Hertzog and his National Party gained 27 seats, splitting the Afrikaner vote down the middle. Smuts's hoped-for unification of English and Afrikaner in a common cause of conquering GSWA had instead divided the South African nation.[1]

An understanding between the governing SAP and the Unionists delivered an electoral mandate which cleared the way for a South African military contingent to be sent to GEA. However, as with GSWA, some individuals holding high office in the United Kingdom, such as Lord Kitchener, Secretary of State for War, saw GEA as a distraction and preferred to have the South Africans deploy to the main military effort in Europe.[2] Kitchener was outspoken in his opposition to an offensive policy in GEA in general and, particularly, to South African participation in the sideshow venture:

> This scheme for offensive operations in the centre of Africa is, in my opinion, a very dangerous project in the present state of the war ... The general military policy now advocated, may therefore, lead us to place South African troops in positions where they will be liable to disaster, from which we will not be able to extricate them, as our troops will be fully engaged elsewhere.[3]

Kitchener's concerns were an indicator of what several influential sectors of the British military thought of South Africa's fragile political situation and uncertain military abilities. However, despite Kitchener's reservations, and using his temporary absence on his departure to the Dardanelles, the British Cabinet sanctioned the use of 10,000 South Africans for GEA.[4] They also offered Smuts the position to command the imperial forces in East Africa, which offer he initially turned down while casting an anxious jaded eye toward the unsettled political situation in South Africa before the elections.[5]

Thus far British endeavours in East Africa had been a failure especially after Colonel Paul Emil von Lettow-Vorbeck had delivered a devastating defeat to the British at Tanga in November 1914. Since then, Lettow-Vorbeck was safely ensconced on British territory, holding the Taveta Gap where he spent 18 months profitably fortifying his position. From there he adopted a raiding strategy, interdicting the British Mombasa–Uganda railway line.[6] Out of desperation, the British appointed General Sir Horace Smith-Dorrien to take command of the East African Force in December 1915, hoping that he could revitalise their prospects of evicting Lettow-Vorbeck from British territory. British policy for East Africa was stated in bland terms of "The operations in East Africa are being conducted with a view to the reduction of the remaining enemy forces in the theatre in as short a time as the difficulties involved by the nature of the country and the climate will allow".[7] This rather obscure policy points toward a British attrition strategy rather than a territorial strategy.

Smith-Dorrien produced an 'Appreciation on the Situation in East Africa' in November 1915 which delivered a bleak verdict on the state of the British troops in their East African colony. Based on the East African commander Major-General Michael Tighe's report, he estimated that of the 15,600 British forces available under his command, only 7,600 were fit for offensive operations due to disease and "loss of morale". Some units were reported "useless owing to lack of morale" with the 13th Rajputs Regiment from India described as a unit that "will never be of any more use in the field".[8] Smith-Dorrien looked to the South Africans to boost his rapidly dwindling numbers. With Smith-Dorrien's health failing, Smuts could not refuse the position of Supreme Commander of the East African Force a second time around when it was offered to him in January 1916.[9]

Smuts Takes Command of the East African Forces

Smuts assumed his command of the East African forces on 12 February 1916 and set sail from South Africa the same day. He arrived in Mombasa on 19 February and immediately met with Tighe. The latter briefed him on the preparations undertaken for an operation in the Kilimanjaro area before the onset of the seasonal rains at the end of March after which operational manoeuvre became extremely difficult.[10] The British generals and officers whom Smuts was to command were not too charmed at the prospect of having a 'colonial' take charge over them. Despite their apparent reservations, Smut's appointment was a relief to his fellow South Africans who had first started arriving in GEA in December 1915[11] and the European colonial volunteers already deployed in the theatre.[12] The ordinary soldiers respected his knowledge of Africa and his willingness to share their hardship and dangers of combat.[13]

Smuts's acceptance of this prestigious military position was more due to opportunism than altruism. John X. Merriman agreed with Smuts that a South African contingent would better serve the Allied cause in taking GEA than being swallowed up in France. South Africa's mounted troops would serve little purpose in the static conditions of the Western Front.[14] A GEA victory, where the British were struggling, would elevate South Africa's position within the Empire. Thus far British efforts in East Africa were primarily a failure, and by October 1915 they faced a precarious situation. The British were concerned that this was "damaging to our prestige among the native races".[15] Most importantly, Taveta–Salaita was the only British territory the Germans occupied in the First World War. The political necessity of removing them from British real estate placed immense pressure on the military. Removing the Germans would not be an easy task, particularly since they had strengthened their numbers after successive and successful askari recruitment drives. Their reported numbers had swelled to 20,000, and they were adequately replenished with arms, ammunition, and equipment from blockade runners and the guns salvaged from the SMS *Königsberg*.[16] Smuts, if successful in removing this threat, would earn the admiration and gratitude of Britain. Then there was also Smuts's ever-present quest for territorial expansionism. He hoped to gain German territory in East Africa and exchange it with the Portuguese for Delagoa Bay.[17] There was congruency between the British and the South African war aims which both sought the destruction of German forces in East Africa, but whereas this was a priority for the British, Smuts's paramount objective was to occupy the entire German territory in the shortest possible time.[18] Furthermore, the occupation of GEA would remove all German aspirations of building a vast African empire stretching from coast to coast in the middle of Africa and competing with the British who sought a contiguous route from Cape to Cairo. (See Figure 6.1)

Reproduced by courtesy of the Royal Geographical Society.

The cover of a Map of the German plan for Central African Empire. Published by the Colonial Office, Berlin, 1917.

Figure 6.1. *Mittelafrika*: aspirations for a vast German African empire along the equator[19]

The passage of time has done little to remove controversy surrounding Smuts's appointment as a colonial, to command British generals and an imperial force in East Africa. Contemporary British historians such as Ross Anderson and Hew Strachan have questioned Smuts's suitability or ability for the position. Strachan describes Anderson's campaign history, *The Forgotten Front*,[20] as superseding all the preceding popular histories of GEA.[21] The book is derived from Anderson's doctoral thesis and relies on primary sources to a greater extent than previous GEA campaign histories.[22] Anderson also relies heavily on the work of H.C. Armstrong and Richard Meinertzhagen. He describes Smut's GEA appointment as "highly unusual, with a colonial officer in supreme command of Imperial troops". He assesses Smuts as, "not a professional soldier, and [lacking] experience of higher command in war".[23]

The "unusualness" of a colonial officer commanding British officers and colonial troops is essentially a non-point. Smuts, together with Botha, had conducted a successful campaign in GSWA. It is difficult to argue against the efficacy of appointing a South African commander to take charge of a force, the bulk of whom were South Africans, which deployed closer to South Africa than the United Kingdom. Furthermore, non-professionalism has not hindered capable amateur generals of exceptional ability. General Sir John Monash, a civil engineer, became an Australian military commander in the First World War on the Western Front. Field Marshal Bernard Montgomery considered Monash to be one of the best Allied generals of the war.[24]

Lack of professionalism aside, Anderson goes on to describe Smuts's inexperience of higher command as severely limiting. He insinuates an absence of operational and tactical skill, coupled with a precarious grasp of administration and supply. Anderson sees Smuts's position as a politician and a government minister as performance-limiting factors.[25] He bolsters his argument with a letter from Smith-Dorrien to Buxton where the ailing general states, "Concerning General Smuts' powers as an up to date General I know nothing and I certainly should not have selected him had there been time to get a General who had devoted His life to War from Home."[26] Nevertheless, Smith-Dorrien says the opposite in a memorandum in which he agrees that Tighe did not possess a "broad enough mind or sufficient experience in dealing with considerable bodies of mounted troops" to take the supreme command. He even goes as far as to say that some of Tighe's tactical skills were unsound. Smith-Dorrien found difficulty suggesting a remedy other than Smuts whom he describes as "on the spot and could reach East Africa quickly and is in touch with the military situation in that country".[27]

Smuts wasted little time once appointed as C-in-C of the East African Force. A mere three weeks passed from his arrival on 19 February to the launch of his first all-out attack on 5 March. Historians have expressed dismay at the alacrity with which Smuts launched his operation to clear the Germans from the Kilimanjaro area—although his swiftness of action conformed to a set of pre-existing instructions.[28]

On 18 December 1915, before Smuts arrived on the scene, Kitchener advised Smith-Dorrien regarding the objective of expelling the Germans from British territory and safeguarding it from further incursions before the onset of the next rainy season due in April which would put an end to all military operations and severely restrict logistical movement. (See Map 6.2). He spelt it out thus:

> General Sir Horace Smith-Dorrien to receive instruction in the sense that, prior to the next rainy season in East Africa, he is to undertake an offensive defensive with the object of expelling the enemy from British territory and safeguarding against further incursions. The decision as to the ultimate scope of the offensive operations to be undertaken against GEA after the rainy season should be postponed until General Sir Horace Smith-Dorrien has reported in the light of the experience gained before the rainy season.[29]

Anderson quotes the instruction verbatim in *The Forgotten Front*[30] but omits the words emphasised above. The omission of "prior to the next rainy season in East Africa" changes the paragraph's meaning and suggests that the operation to expel the Germans from British territory should occur only after the rains. Kitchener's instruction—with the original preceding sentence correctly included—has the opposite meaning. Kitchener expected Smith-Dorrien, and later Smuts, to launch an attack before the rainy season to dislodge the Germans from British territory. Further operations would occur after the rainy season. The Chief of the Imperial General Staff (CIGS), Sir Archibald Murray, almost encouraging Smuts, told him that he would reconsider launching an offensive before the rains based on Smuts's assessment of the situation on his arrival in GEA.[31] Anderson's omission casts Smuts in a reckless and impetuous light. He conjures up cynical political motives, depicting Smuts as hell-bent on launching an attack with untrained troops and unsuitable logistics before the proper preparations:

> However, Smuts had no intention of waiting for the dry weather and had been pressing for an early advance well before his appointment as commander-in-chief. [...] despite the shortness of time for detailed consideration of the situation and his lack of familiarity with the region, he signalled to London on 23 February that he wished to undertake an immediate offensive, receiving approval two days later. This sense of over-riding haste was to be typical of Smuts's time in command. While it was interpreted as part of his implacable willpower and desire for success, it can also be seen as part of his lack of understanding of the situation. He had pressed for an accelerated offensive timetable before he had been given all of Smith-Dorrien's campaign papers or had inspected the terrain. He made up his mind to attack in less than four days in the country, of which the better part of two were needed for travel, and before the all-important transport arrangements were put in place.[32]

Not only did Smuts's operation conform to Kitchener's instruction, but there was a set of perfectly sensible political and military reasons for wishing to launch the attack immediately, rather than waiting a few months for the cessation of the rainy season.[33]

Smith-Dorrien had identified the German occupation of the Kilimanjaro–Taveta area as the most profitable to launch an offensive operation against. A measure of success here would relieve the British of the fear of a German invasion of British East Africa and restore their damaged prestige. Faced with an absence of maps and meagre information regarding Lettow-Vorbeck's dispositions, Smith-Dorrien was reluctant to estimate the time or the forces necessary to evict the Germans from GEA. He saw that the only way to remove the Germans from their entrenched positions at Taveta would be a flanking manoeuvre from Longido to Arusha. (See Map 6.1) Smith-Dorrien could not envisage that he could complete the preparations for such an offensive before the March rainy season set in. He also felt that he should conduct the Kilimanjaro offensive simultaneously with a Belgian push to Tabora, a northern offensive from Rhodesia and an Allied landing at Tanga:

> I regard this advance on the enemy's stronghold by three lines as the best plan of campaign, but it should not be attempted until every possible arrangement has been made to ensure that when a forward move is made we shall not fail owing to the great difficulties of the country, and as such arrangements, especially on the vital line of advance (via Longido) cannot be made until the rains have commenced, *the actual move forward should not be attempted until the rains are over, namely, about the end of June.*[34]

At this early stage, before Smuts's arrival, any campaign objectives beyond the eviction of the Germans from British territory were vague. Smith-Dorrien outlined two differing objectives: occupy as much German territory as possible before peace negotiations as a negotiation lever, or to secure British territory and bottle up the Germans in their colony for the war's duration.[35] The difference in operational tempo between Smith-Dorrien and Smuts became all too obvious when the former insisted on at least three months preparing for the "thorough organisation of the transport", taking the launch date beyond April and well into the rainy season. "Operations would then have to be deferred until the rains ceased in June or July." Smith-Dorrien could not envisage decisive military success before August 1916, by which time Smuts had already conquered two-thirds of the territory.[36]

Smuts sent a telegram to the War Office on 23 February setting out his objectives for the operation before the rainy season.[37] He was keen to undertake the operation before the rains to deny the Germans their principal recruiting and supply area.[38] There was also the question of extending the railway once he had captured Arusha to aid logistics. The German threat to the Uganda railway line, which they attacked no less than 40 times in December 1915, had to be removed.[39] Then there was the risk that inactivity before the rains would delay an attack for many months, adversely affecting the health and morale of the idle troops, and more importantly, damaging the prestige of the government back on the South African home front.[40] The South Africans' morale was especially low after the drubbing they received at Salaita Hill on 12 February 1916, and even amongst the other troops, who had been mainly on the defensive for the entire duration of 1915.[41] An observer left an impression of how low the South African morale had sunk:

The South Africans talked a lot about the campaign they won in German South West, until they came across Salaita Hill, a nut they found 5% of casualties would not crack, so they dropped their kit and slouched back into camp, like a crowd from a football match.[42]

A victory would boost flagging Allied spirits and at the same time lower that of the victorious Germans.[43] There was merit in not wanting to wait out the rainy season having lost the first round. The Germans were aware of the military build-up and were expecting an offensive in the Kilimanjaro area.[44] Therefore, there was little chance of Smuts achieving a strategic surprise, but by launching the offensive in the teeth of the rainy season, he hoped to achieve an operational surprise.

There were sound strategic reasons for evicting the Germans from their well-prepared positions within British territory. The *Schutztruppen* had ensconced themselves in the only gateway into the interior of GEA, and their positions provided a perfect springboard to threaten the British supply and communication lines. Capturing the Taveta Gap before the rainy season would secure a good platform for the East African Force from which to launch offensive operations after the rainy season. Smuts's "alacrity and impetuousness" was nothing less than his attempt at wrenching the British out their deep-seated defensive-minded approach in the wake of their trouncing at the hands of Lettow-Vorbeck at Tanga in 3–5 November 1914. Defensive mindedness permeated to the top, including Kitchener, who considered Africa a mere sideshow: efforts made there detracted from the real war on the Western Front in Europe.[45] Smuts received permission to go ahead with his plan from Murray on 25 February, after being cautioned about the rainy season's proximity.[46] Not only has Smuts's appointment come under fire, but questions have persisted around his fitness to hold the position as C-in-C of the East African forces.

John Keegan in *The Mask of Command* recognised that a general might be much more than the mere commander of an army.[47] Louis Botha was simultaneously the head of his forces in GSWA and Prime Minister of the Union of South Africa. Similarly, Napoleon Bonaparte was head of state and the supreme commander, but unlike Botha, his tenure was less susceptible to his electorate's vagaries. The political situation back in the Union certainly influenced Botha and Smuts on campaign. Keegan recognises that an army is an expression of the society from which it emanates. The how and why of warfare is determined by what a society desires from war and the effort it is willing to expend in pursuit of its objectives.[48]

An Oxford dictionary definition reveals that generalship is the skill or practice of exercising military command.[49] The Collins dictionary defines generalship as the art or duties of exercising command of a significant military formation and further offers that generalship incorporates tactical and administrative skill.[50] The definitions paint a picture of generalship as a mixture of art and science. Significantly, generals accomplish great victories by displaying a firm grasp of the art and science of warfare. Art and science aside, a further essential element in battlefield command, is the quality of leadership, described as, "a process of social influence in which a person can enlist the aid and support of others in the accomplishment of a common task".[51]

The core of this book lies in the assessment of the military Smuts. Thus far the book has examined his growth as a military leader through the South African War, the formation of the UDF, his bold strategic plan for GSWA, the Afrikaner Rebellion, and the final stages of the GSWA campaign. The GEA campaign during 1916 provides another excellent lens to examine his military abilities and testing his effectiveness as a commander at the tactical, operational, and strategic levels of war. When one judges Smuts as a general, one swims against a tide of overwhelming, persistent views of his poor performance in GEA. There are abundant opinions that the German commander, Lettow-Vorbeck, 'out-generaled him'. There are encouraging signs emerging of researchers re-examining the myths surrounding Lettow-Vorbeck's prowess as a military commander. However, these tentative efforts at revision have not arrested the fanatical esteem which some quarters hold for Lettow-Vorbeck. His astonishing bravery and skilled resourcefulness have blinded his admirers to Smuts's considerable abilities. Denigrating Smuts, whilst singing the praises of Lettow-Vorbeck, is not a new phenomenon. One can trace it back to the time of the campaign, where even Smuts was prone to be over-complimentary about his adversary.[52]

Armstrong's *Grey Steel* was one of the first books offering an adverse opinion on Smuts's lack of generalship.[53] The book's subtitle, *A Study in Arrogance*, reveals much about Armstrong's agenda when building his biography of Smuts, and specifically in his assessment of his generalship.[54] It is peculiar that a man who busied himself with Turkish matters for decades turned his next work over to South African politics. Armstrong's motivation lies within his own words, "there remain untouched by the fury of the iconoclasts only four men—T.E. Lawrence of Arabia, Marshal Foch, Mustafa Kemal of Turkey, and the Jan Christian Smuts". Armstrong assumed the task of removing the "flabby nonsense" written about Smuts up to that date.[55] It is with the intention of an iconoclast that Armstrong sets about his task of dismantling the cherished beliefs held regarding Smuts. His assessments retain a significance well beyond the historical worth of his work. Contemporary historians, especially those contemplating Smuts's military skill, have continued to rely on Armstrong's heavily flawed work.

His first salvo reproaches Smuts for being a theoretician, in contrast to Botha, a general who considered the very human aspects applicable to warfare. Armstrong considered Smut's intellect as a driver for his arrogance which made him aloof and full of disdain and overly sensitive to criticism.[56] Furthermore, "Smuts had seen the fight as a chess-game on a board. He had not considered personalities, he had not realised how they counted: an army was to him a machine".[57] Armstrong builds a case for Smuts's impetuosity, amateurishness, and inexperience of commanding large forces in the field. Contemporary authors such as Anderson and Strachan have profited from this warped theme, even to the extent of using much of the same language.[58]

> He acted not so much as a general in command of a considerable force, but as he had acted when he was the leader of his three hundred men raiding full tilt across the Cape. He would take no excuses. The columns must hurry forward; supplies or no supplies, they must bustle. He sent McKenzie riding hard into the blue, without keeping contact, from Aus across the desert to Gibeon, to cut off the Germans retreating down the railway, and then messengers after him to urge him on. He himself pushed on with his tireless, fearless, and unreasoning impetuosity, and so rapidly that often his staff and even his personal secretary could not keep up with him, lost him, and found him again stranded away out alone on the bleak veld. Once he was captured and brought in by his own patrols.[59]

Armstrong, referencing Smuts's opening manoeuvres in the GEA campaign, builds steadily on the theme of an impetuous, inexperienced, and arrogant man, ignoring the advice of his more experienced staff officers. Without the necessary research, contemporary historians have adopted the same sentiment, if not the same language, and repeated the general theme:

> He was at heart a raider and not a soldier. His only experiences of war had been his guerrilla fighting and raiding in the Cape. In German South West he had treated his forces in the south as raiding columns. To dash ahead, each man carrying his own rations, fending for himself and his horse, overleaping difficulties: that was his experience, and he treated this campaign as a magnificent raid. He calculated to finish it in six, or at most nine, months and get back to Cape Town.[60]

And again:

> But Smuts would not listen to them. He knew nothing of scientific staff work and he despised it and the staff officers, who were, he considered, always making difficulties. He told them he would not be worried with details. "I am sick and tired of experts," he said. "The experts have hopelessly broken down in this war.".[61]

Smuts's command style is more compatible with that of German Field Marshal Erwin Rommel—both of whom are enigmatic to most British military analysts. The two men were similar in the way they conducted their campaigns and displayed leadership. Both lacked formal staff officer training and displayed a lack of interest in all matters beyond the frontline, including logistics.[62] Like Rommel, Smuts spent most of his formative military years leading small groups of men using the tactics of infiltration, flanking and rapid movement. To the extreme frustration of his superiors and those he commanded, Rommel often led from the front at considerable personal risk. He drove his men relentlessly and tirelessly, beyond their endurance, to achieve an objective. Like Smuts, Rommel displayed empathy for the ordinary soldier but was unforgiving of his senior officers. The two men favoured a war of manoeuvre delivered at a breath-taking tempo. The parallel continues when Rommel, like Smuts, was vociferously criticised for launching his initial attack too soon after arriving in the theatre before his forces were ready. History has judged these two men, who militarily had much in common, very differently. The irony is obvious, considering that Rommel was ultimately defeated while Smuts was ultimately victorious.[63]

Armstrong, not content, offered up entirely manufactured evidence on behalf of Botha. With no reference to any existing document, Armstrong quotes Botha having a conversation with one of his staff about an offer for Smuts to take command of the Middle East Forces:

> He telegraphed to Botha for advice. Botha understood Smuts. He knew that Smuts' great ambition was to be considered a great general, and Botha had no delusions about that. He knew that Smuts was an excellent guerrilla leader, a fine, bold raider, but no general.
>
> Knowing nothing about the Turks, Botha sent for one of his staff who did.
>
> "Tell me," he said. "Have the Turks any big generals?"
>
> "Surely," replied the officer. "Enver Pasha is there and many Germans, von der Goltz and others."
>
> "But are they really big generals?"
>
> "Yes," replied the officer, "they are".
>
> "Then," said Botha with a smile, "I don't think we had better let our Jannie go against them ... but I have something else for him. Something more in his line. They want him in the War Cabinet in England."
>
> And he sent a telegram to Smuts, a telegram which showed how close and intimate these two men were with each other, for both were sensitive men easily hurt. If anyone else had sent Smuts such a telegram he would have flown into a fury.
>
> "Advise you to refuse," it ran. "We both know you are no general."[64]

There is no evidence that such discussion ever took place, and in the face of overwhelming evidence that Botha admired Smuts's military abilities, one must dismiss the entire conversation as fiction. Hancock devotes some time to "killing a legend" and successfully debunking the myth behind this non-incident.[65] Fortunately, the full record is available showing what Botha thought of the Palestine proposal, which he considered an honour for South Africa and he urged Smuts to take it.[66] When it comes to contemporary opinion on Smuts's ability as a general, unfortunately, all roads lead back to the dubious Armstrong. Historians have come to rely on Armstrong, and few new insights exist since he was published in 1941.

Stuart Mitchell's effort brings a more balanced approach when assessing the generalship of both Smuts and Lettow-Vorbeck.[67] Mitchell, examining Smuts's performance within the political context of the time, concludes that Smuts's operational conception was fundamentally correct. Smuts was a product of his earlier experience in the South African War and later in the Afrikaner Rebellion and

GSWA, where he waged a successful campaign using superior mobility and rapid movement. Mitchell emphasises the congruency of Smuts's operational art to his political aim of rapidly securing GEA territory. Smuts's acquisitive goal, coupled with Lettow-Vorbeck's objective of surviving to tie down as many Allied troops as possible, conspired against a decisive battle of annihilation taking place. Mitchell's approach encourages one to question what constitutes victory, whether on the battlefield, or within a theatre, or for that matter, a campaign.

Smuts like Botha, and true to his republican commando roots, often chose to place himself in the frontline to assess the military situation for himself. Contemporary historians mirror Meinertzhagen's dismay at Smuts's penchant for leading from the front. Meinertzhagen reproaches Smuts for making

> the mistake in mixing himself up with local situations. They obscure the general and larger situation. During an advance, he is usually with or in front of the advance guard. During an action [he] is often in the firing line and loses control of the fight.[68]

The British theoretician J.F.C. Fuller held great store in a general who led from the front and showed great personal courage, sharing the battlefield's dangers with the common soldier. Fuller believed that a creative mind was one of the main pillars of generalship.[69] Finally, Fuller posited that a capable general needed to be physically fit to display courage and creative thought.[70] He recognised the attributes of a general who leads from the front:

> War with impersonal leadership is a brutal soul-destroying business, provocative only of class animosity and bad workmanship. Our senior officers must get back to sharing danger and sacrifice with their men, however exalted their rank, just as sailors have to do. That used to be the British way but, unfortunately, there was a grievous lapse from it in the late war.[71]

Accusations of being too brave and too close to the front directed at British generals are indeed rare, and here Armstrong does not disappoint:

> Smuts himself lived as hard as his men. He ate the same food, went as hungry and short of sleep, and was as ill as they were. He had malaria, filled himself up with iron and arsenic and quinine, and forced himself to keep going. He took many personal risks, and was often foolhardy; he did not realise that the commander of a large force had no right to risk himself as if he were leading a small raiding party. He would get up well in front, often ahead of his advance troops, and even of his scouts. His staff tried to keep him back, but that made him angry and petulant, and he pushed on the more. At the crossing of one small river there was a fight. He was up with the front line and through the river with the first men, under fire. On another occasion he went so far forward that a German patrol cut him off and he had to run for safety, and he got away down the back of a hill with his clothes ripped by the thick thorn of the brush and his face and hands cut with the sharp boulders.[72]

There is general agreement that Smuts was a man of great personal courage who preferred to lead from the front. On more than one occasion, this attitude found him in a situation of extreme physical danger. However, Smuts's displays of bravery in the face of the enemy have been condemned almost universally by British historians as being foolhardy and amateurish at best, and a breach of duty at worst. Lettow-Vorbeck stressed the importance of supplementing intelligence and reports with personal observation in the African bush, a task he often undertook at great personal risk.[73] Anderson is unimpressed with Smuts's predilection for the front, citing a too-close involvement with local battles and isolation from his staff—although conceding the facilitation of quick decision-making.[74] Shelford Bidwell offers a contrary opinion and speaks of British generals placing themselves well to the rear in 1915 and 1916 when, because of shallow objectives, rearward communication was more important than forward. When the situation restored movement, commanders had once again to shift their headquarters right into the battle.[75]

Of all the criticism levelled at Smuts, the accusation that he was a leader who led from the front is the most inexplicable. Unlike their British counterparts, German commanders made a habit of visiting the frontline and examining the battlefield first-hand. The German doctrine of decentralised command demanded that high-level commanders make considerable efforts to ensure they were well informed. This entailed frequent visits to frontline commanders as well as to the actual frontline. The Germans considered it essential for senior commanders

> to gain, by means of personal reconnaissance, a thorough knowledge of the ground and the trenches in his sector. Only thus will he be in a position to conduct the fight properly and maintain the necessary personal touch with the troops.[76]

Ironically, Lettow-Vorbeck was wounded at Kondoa Irangi on 13 June 1916, when shrapnel from a South African artillery shell struck his headquarters near the front. Lettow-Vorbeck peppers his account with examples of his undertaking reconnaissance close to enemy lines, including a solo bicycle trip into Tanga to assess enemy positions.[77] Intuitively, a man who sets an example by leading men from the front, sharing with them the dangers and deprivations that the proximity of combat brings, and risking life and limb together with his men, is an inspirational leader. Melvin Page captures the feeling of the ordinary soldier serving under Smuts:

> These men trusted him and felt that he, at least, understood Africa and Africans whereas the War Office fundis [experts] were generally deficient in such knowledge. Smuts, they were sure, knew how to command and control the African soldiers and laborers with whom they campaigned. Likewise, his willingness to share their suffering, in combat and in the African bush, added greatly to their respect for him. Out of both this respect and their need for some release from the awful task of war, they came to identify with him.[78]

Strachan is critical of Smuts's forward approach in placing himself well forward of his rear headquarters which rendered him a "bad tactician and strategist". Strachan concedes that Smuts supposedly impressed his troops but sacrificed effective command due to the difficulties of communications Smuts's absence from headquarters presented.[79] Unlike the Allied practice on the Western Front in France, Smuts divided his headquarters into two where he manned the advance headquarters while the administrative staff were ensconced further back. According to Strachan, this had the effect of separating field command and logistics. Strachan reproaches Smuts for following the same procedures ordained in the *Field Service Regulations* where he divided his headquarters, as was the procedure on the Western front, into advanced and rear headquarters, thus dividing the field command and logistics where their mutual dependence was paramount.[80]According to Strachan, Smuts could have mitigated this had he deployed competent staff to take care of logistics and administration behind the lines. His allegation is spurious and is discussed below in more detail. (See Table 6.1)

Armstrong sees a fatal flaw in Smuts, while Fuller would lament the lack of British leadership from the front on the Western Front and the South European front of Gallipoli. He maligned those generals who directed their men, safely ensconced in their chateaus many miles behind the frontline: "Should the general consistently live outside the realm of danger, then, though he may show high moral courage in making decisions, by his never being called upon to breathe the atmosphere of danger his men are breathing, this lens will become blurred."[81] Like Lettow-Vorbeck, Smuts was not averse to danger, and he undertook personal reconnaissance to assess the situation with his own eyes. Where historians praise Lettow-Vorbeck, they denigrate Smuts for undertaking the very same risks. The final irony is that the Germans would understand Smuts in terms of their doctrine, as they expected leadership from the front and personal reconnaissance.

Smuts, according to leading British historians, lacked the experience necessary to lead a large force. Strachan is more damning than Anderson in his criticism of Smuts's abilities, describing him as a general in command of 73,300 men in East Africa whose only experience thus far was leading a Boer commando of 300–400 men in the South African War. Strachan completely disregards Smuts's extensive experience in the Afrikaner Rebellion and GSWA. He accuses Smuts of dismantling the one structure that may have mitigated against his "inexperience", which was the staff created by Smith-Dorrien, and filling its ranks with equally inexperienced South Africans.[82] His assertion is incorrect because Smuts retained much of Smith-Dorrien's hand-picked staff (See Table 6.1) Jack Collyer replaced Brigadier-General Hugh Simpson-Baikie as the chief of staff, having gained valuable experience in GSWA in a similar position.[83] Furthermore, according to Fendall, Simpson-Baikie was "too young for the job", thought himself infallible, and was inexperienced with a bad manner which was likely to cause trouble.[84] Strachan cites three other officers whom Smuts replaced, namely Tighe, Malleson and Brigadier-General James "Jimmy" Stewart (1861–1943). However, they were not staff officers, and their removal was justified in terms of dismal performance as divisional commanders.[85] The bulk of the middle-ranking staff officers chosen by Smith-Dorrien remained in service under Smuts.[86] Strachan therefore grossly exaggerates Smuts's wholesale dismantling of the staff. (See Table 6.1 and Figure 6.2)

Table 6.1. A comparison of General Staff members employed by Smith-Dorrien and later by Smuts[87]

Title	Smith-Dorrien	Smuts
Chief of General Staff	Simpson Baikie	J.J. Collyer
Director Admin and QMG	Brig-Gen R.H. Ewart	Brig-Gen R.H. Ewart
Assistant Adjutant and QMG	C.P. Fendall	C.P. Fendall
GSO1	On Baikie's staff at Gallipoli	?
GSO2	From the KAR	?
GSO3	Captain Henry (Freddie) Guest	Captain Henry (Freddie) Guest
Director Supply and Transport	Col P.O. Hazelton	Col P.O. Hazelton
Director of Medical Services	Hunter	Hunter
Commander Royal Artillery	J.H.V. Crowe	J.H.V. Crowe
Commander Royal Engineers	J.A. Dealy	J.A. Dealy
Inspector General Communications	W.F.S. Edwards	W.F.S. Edwards
Director Railways	W.A. Johns	W.A. Johns
Director of Remounts	Previous SA service	?
Provost Marshall	KAR man	?
Chief Intelligence		P.J. Pretorious

Strachan describes Smuts's use of divisional and brigade structures as paradoxical, compared to the Germans, who preferred the more flexible and self-contained field company.[88] According to Strachan, Smuts's reliance on "the higher formations of European warfare" supposedly increased the logistical burden. Reading Lettow-Vorbeck's account provides enlightenment on the difficulties encountered when relying on a company rather than a brigade structure. He described scenes of utter chaos when attempting to gather his forces defending the Morogoro and re-concentrate them for an attack on Jaap van Deventer defending Kondoa Irangi many kilometres away. The complicated movement over roads, paths, and railways was further complicated when companies leapfrogged each other and hopelessly entangled their logistics and communication lines. Lettow-Vorbeck's company structure was unsuited to rapid concentrations when attacking a large force.[89]

Figure 6.2. Jan Smuts and his German East African Staff.[90]

The image of Smuts as a small-time guerrilla leader persists. Ian Liebenberg attempts to trace Smuts's political and more important military choices to his, "somatic experience as a guerrilla soldier and commander during 1900–1902".[91] Liebenberg treads a familiar path with, "Smuts was a strategist, but his commanding capabilities were those of the 'guerrilla-commander-in-action'". In describing Smuts's guerrilla experience in the South African War as fundamental and formative to his generalship, Liebenberg tries to explain his military conduct by referencing his guerrilla roots.[92] He uses a slightly different technique from the British historians but arrives at very much at the same conclusion: Smuts was a poor tactician in large conventional military operations.

As commander of the East African Force, Smuts commanded 73,300 men in unfamiliar and harsh surroundings against a capable enemy with extensive military experience. Strachan rates Smuts's previous military experience as "irrelevant" to the enormous task facing him in GEA. He does so without the slightest sense of irony that Kitchener and John French, as well as a raft of British generals saw active service in the South African War.[93] He dismisses Smuts with, "In the Boer War he had led a commando of 300–400 men with minimal logistical needs in a defensive campaign in a moderate climate over familiar terrain".[94] Strachan's figures are not entirely correct. Smuts may have indeed initially commanded 300 men when he first set out to raid the Cape Colony during the South African War. However, by war's end, his command had swollen to 3,000–4,000 men.[95] In January 1902, Smuts reported to Koos de La Rey that he had 19 commandos directly under him, each of approximately 100–150 men, making 1,900–2,850 men directly under his command.[96] He accumulated a fair amount of tactical and operational experience in command of a substantial number of men by the end of the South African War.

Smuts further demonstrated military erudition at the strategic level in the South African War. If the Boers possessed a grand strategy at all, it was due to Smuts. In the six weeks before the outbreak of the South African War, Smuts produced an insightful political warfare plan, economic mobilisation, and a plan of military operations. The final plan involved a daring thrust by the combined forces of the ZAR and Orange Free State to capture the whole of Natal and its ports, thus disrupting British supply and morale. He understood that assuming the offensive was advantageous to the aggressor and raised morale, while simultaneously lowering that of the defender. An attacker enjoyed the freedom to choose the time and place of battle, and by taking the fight into enemy territory, he could live off the enemy land.[97] He may not have personally led massive forces in the South African War, but he demonstrated a remarkable capacity to grasp big strategic ideas, which was a rarity among the Boer leadership. Besides his natural talent for war and some experience in the field, he devoted much of his time studying military history and was able to assimilate the theory he had learnt from his studies of war.[98]

Historians have ignored Smuts's role in the forming the UDF in 1912 with the resulting challenges of amalgamation and transformation and his skill in overcoming adversity in building a new defence force.[99] The UDF's creation confirmed his considerable skill and gave him experience structuring and commanding an effective force from a polyglot of forces. Smuts applied these same skills with good effect firstly in GSWA and then in GEA where he tackled the mammoth task of creating an effective imperial fighting force. Few historians have considered this aspect of Smuts's campaign in GEA.

An essential part of Smuts's military experience was his involvement in organising the suppression of the Afrikaner Rebellion of 1914. His actions were decisive when he advised Botha for the immediate declaration of martial law. His decision to use loyal Afrikaner troops rather than levies from Natal or the Cape was sound and helped stall the rebellion's spread.[100] He used the 15 military districts with good effect and gained vital intelligence on the formation and movement of the different rebel groupings. He was the originator of the idea of concentrating the UDF around Pretoria and using internal lines and rapid manoeuvre to suppress the Afrikaner rebels. Botha stole the limelight as the decisive, swashbuckling soldier, while Smuts used his considerable administrative skills to secure the railroads, mobilise loyalists, and marshal ammunition and supplies. He used the railway network and motorised transport to outflank the rebels and concentrate his fighting power at the decisive point.[101] The use of implements of the industrial age to wage a modern war was both innovative and imaginative.

Most accounts of Smuts's qualification to lead large armies glaringly omit the experience he garnered in the GSWA campaign in 1915. The strategic plan of a landward and seaborne invasion designed to make the most use of external lines of communication belonged to him. Smuts eventually commanded a substantial army in the campaign in April 1915, made up of the Central, Southern, and Eastern Forces. The men under Smuts's command amounted to over 22,000, which is a far cry from the 300 in the South African War, often cited by historians as the total of his command experience.[102] Smuts had to contend with a manoeuvre approach in conquering vast swathes of GSWA territory and deal with difficult transport and logistical problems exacerbated by the vastness of an incredibly harsh territory. He planned on using a manoeuvre type warfare in GEA, as practised in the South African War and in the GSWA campaign, except on a scale larger than had ever been undertaken by a South African general.

The Plan of Attack on the Kilimanjaro Position, 19 February–4 March

Smuts's opening battle in the GEA campaign is a first battle that carries a particular significance due to the lack of recent, relevant combat experience by both or one of the forces engaged. Organisation, preparation, expectations, predictions, and decisions are based on theory and doctrine without the comfort that battlefield experience brings. The precise circumstances of the new war and the terrain fought over are unique, and the capabilities and weaknesses of the enemy are unknown. According to Charles Heller and William Stoft in *America's First Battles*, political considerations seem to be of the utmost importance in shaping a first battle strategy. South Africa's performance during the Kilimanjaro operation via an assessment of their perceptions, planning, organisation, and strategic aims has been distorted somewhat by knowledge of the outcome. Reading history backwards can have the effect of destroying the past. The future participants in battle had no idea of the outcome, the exact dispositions of the enemy, their morale, force levels, equipment or the exact nature of the terrain. Smuts and his staff—before the operation and for some time afterwards—only possessed a vague idea of the state of development, communications, population, local conditions and terrain of GEA—a territory twice the size of Germany.[103]

Smuts deployed his operational art almost ignorant about his enemy as well as the capabilities of his forces. One should judge his first action against Lettow-Vorbeck as a first battle, where he was shrouded in ignorance and uncertainty, lacking the luxury of having a realistic appreciation of his calculations, predictions, hopes and aspirations as a commander. Smuts did benefit from a report produced by Lieutenant-Colonel Dirk van Deventer and a Lieutenant-Colonel A.M. Hughes. They conducted a military mission to East Africa in November 1915 in anticipation of the South African contingent's arrival.[104] Their first meeting was with Malleson who commanded the Voi area, and later with Tighe the C-in-C East Africa Force. There Smuts learnt that the Germans had entrenched in the only viable route into the interior, known as the Taveta Gap, which was flanked by two impassable obstacles, Kilimanjaro on the northern flank and the Pare Mountains on the southern flank.[105] (See Map 6.1)

They learnt that the Germans had considerably strengthened their defences in the Taveta Gap and the road and railway infrastructure supporting the logistics for a protracted defence. Presupposing a frontal attack on the German positions, the British noted a need for howitzers to dislodge the well-entrenched enemy. The Germans had also put to good use the four guns salved from the stricken SMS *Königsberg*, destroyed on 11 July 1915. The Germans managed to rescue the *Königsberg* cargo which yielded many modern rifles, eight maxims, six field guns and enough ammunition to last for the duration of the campaign. Tighe also reported that the Germans had trebled their manpower with recruitment drives and estimated their strength at 15,000–20,000 by the end of 1915.[106]

Van Deventer and Hughes concluded that the territory was suitable for mounted infantry operations primarily in the high country while the regular infantry was suited for operations in the low country. They insisted that the operational aspects of the campaign could only be practical with a strong mounted component. None other than Smith-Dorrien backed up their point of view and spoke of "the necessity of using considerable bodies of Mounted Troops for the subjugation of German East Africa".[107] Their reported underestimation of the abilities of the 'native' enemy, was equalled with an underestimation of the deadly diseases that awaited man and beast on the South African arrival. They declared that "horse sickness is not as bad [as] the low-lying districts of the Transvaal" and "mule transport is suitable to that country" as well as the fact that animals who fell victim to the tsetse fly could work a further six to eight weeks after being bitten.[108]

Interestingly, Van Deventer and Hughes, while assessing the situation in GEA, were being judged by the British. An insightful letter sent to Smuts by a Mr Papenfus tells of a Captain Frank Douglas of the British East African Rifles who on having met Van Deventer revealed some of his misgivings. He felt that Van Deventer underestimated the fighting power of Germany's black troops. He noted that the Germans would retreat "into the unhealthy and [tsetse] fly areas" of the territory when pressed. He noted that the Germans, along with their black troops and their porters were resilient to the local conditions, which would pose a problem to the less nimble or robust South Africans. Douglas foresaw the great difficulties the unacclimatised South African soldiers and their animals would have to face in GEA.[109]

Smuts would have learnt of Tighe's plan for the offensive once the South Africans completed their arrival in GEA. This was the plan (the details are below) that Smuts adopted on his arrival with some critical modifications. Tighe was confident of a successful outcome and believed that the offensive would terminate hostilities swiftly. The demoralisation of the 'natives' would rob the Germans of their greatest recruitment source. Van Deventer and Hughes were sceptical of Tighe's optimism and suggested a thrust to capture Tabora and deny the Germans the heartland of current and future askari recruitment.[110] Tighe underwhelmed both men, and they described him as having a "nervous manner, lacking in strength of character and forcefulness, little experience of conducting operations on a large scale", and little understanding of the mounted troops' role. They gained a better impression of Stewart although he would later prove to be a greater disappointment than Tighe. Malleson, they reported, also lacked in strength and resourcefulness, and here their judgement would prove to be spot on.[111]

Lettow-Vorbeck took charge of the Schutztruppe in GEA on 17 January 1914. The Schutztruppe's primary purpose was to maintain law and order among the blacks in that territory, and their training was not suited for fighting against a European power in a conventional war. One of Lettow-Vorbeck's first instructions was the change of training, especially using machine guns in the attack. The machine gun, operated by what the Germans regarded as competent whites, became the primary weapon in the Schutztruppe company. Lettow-Vorbeck shifted the Schutztruppe doctrine from a focus on internal stability and police work, to a force that would meet an external enemy on conventional lines.[112] The previously inward-looking force now considered taking a more aggressive stance by disrupting the Uganda railway and offering resistance before considering any retreat. Lettow-Vorbeck met with considerable resistance from those who believed that an uprising was inevitable and the real threat to the colony. Lettow-Vorbeck believed in taking action to the enemy and looked to an aggressive invasion of British territory in the Kilimanjaro region. His primary opponent was Heinrich Schnee, the civilian governor of GEA, who advocated a more passive stance, whereas Lettow-Vorbeck saw his role as distracting as many British resources to the colony and thereby subtracting them from the main effort in Europe. The colony entered the war with the views of Schnee and Lettow-Vorbeck misaligned.[113]

Among Smuts's substantial list of challenges, beside those of inhospitable climate and disease, was the considerable experience and skill of his opponent. (See Figure 6.3) The Germans put the 18 months before Smuts's arrival to good use in preparing their defences, especially in the Taveta Gap. Their extensive knowledge of the climate and terrain was unrivalled. Lettow-Vorbeck would operate from interior lines of communication and possessed a railway network that would greatly aid his troops' movement. The railway network would allow the swift reinforcement of areas under threat or to capitalise on opportunities that presented themselves. The Germans knew the tactics that Smuts would use against them, Lettow-Vorbeck having earlier gained first-hand experience when fighting side by side with Boers in the Herero Wars.[114]

> At that time I gained an abundance of personal experience [in the Herero and Hottentot Rebellion in South West Africa (1900–1901)], not only of the natives, but also of Boers, both on the staff of General von Botha [sic] and as an independent Company and Detachment Commander. The excellent qualities of this low German race, that had for generations made its home on the African veld, commanded my respect. That the Boers would later take a decisive—and in a sense tragic—part in anglicizing the German part of Africa I never dreamt.[115]

At the beginning of March 1916, the Germans were able to field a force comprising 3,007 white troops and 12,100 askari, which included administration staff. Not included in these numbers were several thousand auxiliaries, used as border, railway, and coastal protection as well as scouts and messengers.[116] Significantly, the Schutztruppe made use of hundreds and thousands of porters in their logistical supply chain.[117] Porters were an integral part of the Schutztruppe company, providing a ready source of fighting replacements, whereas the initial British version relied on unwieldy 1,000-man units separate from the fighting forces.[118] Traditionally, Boer forces often operated without transport and supplies, living off the land as they did in the South African War and the last stages of the GSWA campaign. Smuts, schooled in the Boer way of war, found his role reversed in GEA. Here the Germans, who recruited from the local tribes were very much in their home territory. They were able to gather intelligence and live off the land depleting local food supplies as they retreated before Smuts. On the other hand, the South Africans were dependent on long tenuous supply lines, much the same as the British in the South African War.[119]

Besides the two railway lines, the few developed roads ran almost exclusively in a west–east direction following the territory's old caravan tracks. Constructing railway lines lessened the importance of road networks. However, crisscrossing the territory were many paths and trails dependent for their use on the influence of the rain season. The rivers were not much use as waterways, due to the frequent rapids which interrupted the water flow. The Germans possessed few motor vehicles: at the outbreak of war, there were nine cars, eight trucks and eight motorcycles. Using ox-wagons was limited to an area in the eastern highlands due to the high incidence of the tsetse fly, rendering all but mules and donkeys inoperable as beasts of burden. Notably, the Germans had no use for horses, the mainstay of the South African mounted infantry, as they were too susceptible to disease. The Germans made almost exclusive use of black porters for their transportation; Ludwig Boell refers to "East Africa as the land of carrier transportation".[120]

The Germans organised their structure around a self-contained company with an integral logistical organisation. On average, a company's force amounted to three officers, one medical officer, two sergeants, one medical sergeant, and 159 askari troops. The army recruited officers and sergeants from all branches. They could retire to their original units at any time, after a commitment period of two and a half years. Askari troops had to commit voluntarily to at least five years' service but often stayed longer. The Schutztruppe recruited two-thirds of their members from the local tribes; however, the remaining third were foreigners, mainly Manjema, Sudanese, Waganda, Abyssinians, and Somali.[121] They were usually older than the average local recruit, and many had sons and fathers who served in the Schutztruppe. Each company carried three or four machine guns and up to three cannons of different calibres and varying modernity. A company had 30–50 'military' porters, usually called "permanent carriers" or "Rugaruga". (See Figure 5.1) They were more motivated and willing than the normal porters, used to discipline, and could be used as replacement soldiers when necessary. Due to their reliability, the company also utilised them as machine-gun carriers. Humans were not immune to the vagaries of disease, and except for the high mountain regions, deadly strains of malaria afflicted the territory. Local blacks enjoyed a modicum of immunity to malaria, and the Germans were adept to treating Europeans with quinine.[122] The Germans had obtained near self-sufficiency in fuel for their motors, "Ersatz Whisky", cloth for their uniforms, boots, and more importantly munitions factories producing both artillery and small arms ammunition. They were also able to manufacture quinine.[123]

SOME COLONY;
or why the Campaign continues.

J.C.S.: "Von Lettow offers to surrender on one condition."
L.B.: "Ja Jannie, en wat is dat?"
J.C.S.: "That the Colony be never given back."

Figure 6.3. With Jannie in the jungle, "Some Colony".[124]

A rampart of formidable mountain ranges buttressed the German frontline which ran for 200 kilometres from the coast to Kilimanjaro. The gateway to the interior lay in an eight-kilometre gap between the foothills of Kilimanjaro and the Pare Mountains. Blocking the pathway through the gap were the Germans entrenchments around Taveta and Salaita Hill for which they had spent the previous 18 months fortifying against attack.[125] Further back in the narrow Taveta Gap and constituting another formidable defensive bastion, were the twin hills of Latema-Reata. (See Maps 6.3 and 6.4) Stewart held the north-western sector of the British line in the Longido area. This force faced a gap between Kilimanjaro and Mount Meru guarded by Major Erich Fischer and 1,000 askari. The plan was for Stewart to force the Kilimanjaro–Meru gap and take the enemy positions at Kahe in the rear.[126]

Tighe's plan involved the advance from two directions – one arm from Longido (see Stewart on Map 6.1) and the other from Mbuyuni (see Malleson on Map 6.1) converging on Kahe to the south of Kilimanjaro. The distance to Kahe from Longido was 130 kilometres as the crow flies as opposed to 50 kilometres from Mbuyuni to Kahe.[127] It was possible to cut off the German forces with this strategic encircling movement; however, this depended on the westerly arm (see Stewart on Map 6.1) reaching Kahe before the Germans retreated in the face of the easterly arm (see Malleson on Map 6.1). Tighe gave Stewart's westerly arm a full two days lead start to reach Kahe by 11 March and trap the Germans.[128] The operations aimed to encircle the German forces via the pincer movement and eliminate them once the pincers had snap shut. Smuts looked for and received permission on 25 February 1916 to conduct the operation before the start of the April rainy season. The decision to launch an attack so close to the onset of the rainy season with so few good campaign days remaining has attracted vociferous criticism from Anderson and Strachan.

Before Smuts's arrival, Tighe ordered Stewart, who commanded the 1st Division, to occupy Longido on 15 January and Malleson, who commanded the 2nd Division, to occupy Mbuyuni on 24 January. Securing the jump-off points for the offensive's two wings coincided with extending the railhead inland and improving logistics to support the attack.[129] Smuts was generous in his praise for Tighe's efforts in preparing for the operation.[130] The abortive attempt to rid Salaita Hill of the Germans in the few weeks before Smuts arrived proved the futility of conducting a frontal assault against prepared German positions.

Smuts adopted Tighe's plan with a significant modification. He removed Jaap van Deventer's 1st South African Mounted Brigade from Stewart's right wing and transferred them to the left wing directly under his command (see Van Deventer on Map 6.1). He was able to complete the transfer with the aid of the railway by 4 March. He was determined to avoid costly frontal attacks against entrenched enemy positions hidden in the dense bush. Notably, he was concerned with maintaining the tempo of the operation and the speed of the advance, which he saw as fundamental to the operation's success.[131] The Germans assumed, via faulty intelligence, that the bulk of the South African mounted troops would operate from Longido, allowing Smuts to achieve operational surprise with his switch.[132] Stewart complained that the transfer out of "the purely Dutch elements" of his command stripped him of all but a small mounted contingent. He believed that the objective and terrain allotted to his command was more suited to cavalry action.[133] It becomes apparent from a reading of the German official history that the Germans possessed a good idea of the mechanics of the Smuts plan. They correctly identified the direction and intent of the east and west pincers and witnessed the build-up of troops through intelligence and reconnaissance. The plan would not unfold as a surprise to the Germans who intended to concentrate their forces and defeat each flank consecutively.[134] However, the plan's surprise element was Smuts's switch of Van Deventer's mounted infantry to the east flank.

Adding Van Deventer as a force multiplier to the east pincer unhinged the German positions at Salaita, and they withdrew without firing a shot. Van Deventer's advance threatened Salaita's sole supply of water situated deep behind the lines. Lettow-Vorbeck did not decide to abandon hard-won territory lightly. Had he not done so, the German forces' destruction would have swiftly followed. Van Deventer's flanking attack had the same effect on the strong German positions at Latema-Reata. (See Map 6.1) The threat of a flank attack by the South African mounted infantry forced the Germans to abandon their position despite rebuffing a strong Allied frontal attack on the position.[135] The German official history sets the scene:

> At noon on this day some older captains of Division Schulz appeared on Pantzier-Hill and asked the commander to start an attack. They did not understand why the troops remained idle, while convoy after convoy moved past the Front and the opportunities for attack seemed favourable to them. Besides, they outlined that constant retreat, without taking any opportunity for attack, threatened to undermine the confidence of the Askari. General von Lettow writes about this in his 'memories': "An attack which would find the enemy in fortified stations, not only far superior in numbers, but also in armament, held no promise success. Therefore, I did not give in to the pleas of several company leaders to attack. However, this expression of brave soldier-spirit strengthened and lifted me in this difficult situation that we found ourselves in.[136]

The mounted brigade was to execute a turning movement on the Germans holding Salaita and Taveta by taking a northerly route[137] (see Van Deventer on Map 6.1). The objective of this manoeuvre by the mounted brigade was first, to avoid, "frontal attacks against entrenched positions in the dense bush", (obviously with Salaita Hill still fresh in Smuts's mind) and secondly, to secure the rapidity of the advance before the onset of the rains expected at the end of March.[138] Smuts also created a reserve force to follow Van Deventer to a central position on the Lumi River where it would then be available to either reinforce Malleson or van Deventer as the situation required.[139]

Smuts grounded his plan to outflank Salaita Hill, rather than engage in a frontal assault, in sound reconnaissance of the area. Before the operation, he consulted with

Major Piet Pretorius (1877–1945)[140] about the best course of action to remove the Germans from Salaita. Pretorius supplied vital information revealing the fatal chink in the well-prepared German positions around Salaita. The area's arid nature forced the Germans to transport all water for the Salaita garrison from Taveta some 13 kilometres distant. There was not a drop of water in the vicinity surrounding the hill. Whoever controlled the Taveta area would control Salaita without having to fire a shot.[141]

Valuable insight (perhaps hindsight, as it appears some 20 years after the event) into Smuts's thinking appears in P.B. Blanckenberg's, *The Thoughts of General Smuts*:

> Von Lettow (in his book on the campaign) referred to the 'unskilfulness' of the tactics adopted in the attack on the Taveta positions. The facts are that Von Lettow had had eighteen months within which to prepare an impregnable line; that on my arrival I had only a few days for reconnoitring the position, that I at once detected the weakness of his line in that the Lumi River in the direction of Chala Hill was not properly defended, and that my use of that blunder of his enabled me to make his whole line crumple up in two days in spite of my 'unskilful advance'. If Von Lettow had arranged for a proper defence of the Lumi, which was a very formidable barrier, and had placed even a thousand men near Chala Hill, we could have been held up for days or weeks, and his swift ejection from his carefully prepared positions might not have taken place.

> The rainy season was nearing, and the occupation of the Kilimanjaro area might have been postponed till after the dry season had set in again. This was quite possible with skilful leadership on his part, and might have destroyed the prestige of his opponent at the very start. He was working on interior lines, could move men in all directions in the confined Moshi–Taveta area, and could in his prepared positions have put up a prolonged defence. His plan of defence was seriously faulty and his erroneous dispositions on the Lumi the cause of the swift disaster to his defence. I never saw a better defensive position than that held by the Germans on the Taveta lines and the blame for the sudden collapse must rest on the commander. It is true I did not keep in continuous touch with General Headquarters, but everything depended on the success of Van Deventer's flank move, and under the circumstances I decided (I submit quite rightly) to remain in close touch with him even at some risk of outraging the proprieties![142]

The school of thought pervasive amongst contemporary historians is that Smut's reluctance to engage in a frontal assault was the root cause of his inability to annihilate the enemy.[143] However, the British official history recognised the futility of direct assaults against well-prepared positions in the bush.[144] Meinertzhagen set the pace for other British historians by dismissing Smuts's predilection for manoeuvre warfare as:

> Smuts is quite determined to avoid a stand-up fight. He told me openly that he intends to manoeuvre the enemy out of positions and not push them out. He told me that he could not afford to go back to South Africa with the nickname 'Butcher Smuts'. Manoeuvre is a peculiar form of war which I do not understand and which I doubt will succeed except at great expense in men and money. Every man killed in action means ten invalided with disease, therefore it is all important to bring the campaign to a close as soon as possible. Moreover, it is essential that we are in possession of the German colony before hostilities cease in Europe, whenever that far-off date is. A decisive action in the Kilimanjaro area might finish the campaign, but a series of manoeuvres will only drag operations on for years.[145]

Meinertzhagen is the source of a myth which persists to the present day. Edward Paice,[146] Anderson, and Strachan[147] accept without question that there were but two choices on engaging Lettow-Vorbeck. The first, and preferable one, was his annihilation in a set-piece battle once Smuts surrounded him—assuming that the wily German would allow Smuts to surround his forces in the first place. The second tactic, greeted with derision, was where Lettow-Vorbeck was dislodged territorially in a set of futile and time-consuming manoeuvres. Those favouring a battle of annihilation misunderstand the impossibility in gaining Lettow-Vorbeck's cooperation to stand still and receive the delivered blows.

Meinertzhagen, on the eve of the Kilimanjaro operation, offered advice on the mechanics necessary to defeat Lettow-Vorbeck in a battle of annihilation:

> Von Lettow is concentrated here and ready for a fight, but of course he's not going to risk a decisive action against vastly superior numbers. Smuts should bring him to battle and instead of manoeuvring him out of position should endeavour to surround and annihilate him no matter what are our casualties. We know the ground, we are immensely superior and our troops are fresh and eager. So why manoeuvre? I went through all of this with Smuts. His only comment was that we could not afford to risk a heavy casualty list among his South Africans.[148]

Meinertzhagen's argument proposed a tactical envelopment, whereas Smuts planned for a wider and deeper operational envelopment. Smuts planned for a massive encirclement initiated by two pincers which would meet at Kahe, trapping the Germans dislodged in the Taveta Gap. (See Map 6.1) When the actual events unfolded, Stewart partially derailed the ambitious plan due to the slothful progress of his western pincer. A further hiccup was Malleson's less-than-successful frontal attack on the Germans holding the twin hills of Latema-Reata, again demonstrating the slim chances of success in launching a frontal attack against well-prepared positions.[149]

Anderson and Strachan never stray far from the opinions of Meinertzhagen, a self-styled master of military strategy and espionage. Brian Garfield has recently exposed him as a fraud and a fabricator of stories.[150] Meinertzhagen's diary records that Smuts was determined to avoid a stand-up fight and preferred to manoeuvre and avoid a heavy casualty list. Smuts was determined not to acquire the nickname 'Butcher Smuts' back home.[151] Reluctance to incur unnecessary casualties was a common trait amongst South Africans and not particularly peculiar to Smuts. Meinertzhagen was convinced by July 1916 that Smuts would not fight an offensive action. His observations regarding the South African aversion to casualties, misunderstanding of bush warfare, and general contempt for the German askari are oft-repeated verbatim by later historians. According to Meinertzhagen, the reluctance to seek a decisive battle was costing an exorbitant amount in sickness casualties and resources:[152]

> The more I see of this little man the more I like him. He has great charm and he has already won my affection. Always cheerful, witty and prepared to make the best of things. He is, of course, no soldier, for as *Truth* said some weeks back, he is an amateur.[153] His knowledge of human nature, his eye for country, his exceptional power of imposing his will and others, his

remarkable personality, reckless disregard of difficulties and his very remarkable brain, compel one to suspect and admire him. Perhaps it is wrong to say he is no soldier. He is a bad tactician and strategist, an indifferent general, but in many ways a remarkable soldier.[154]

Meinertzhagen's overt dismissal of Smuts, who he accused of creating an entirely false impression by sending fantastic cables in which his commanders are portrayed as budding "Napoleons" when in truth Meinertzhagen believed they were nothing more than "incompetent gasbags"—dismissing their official reports as mere "flatulence"—has been taken on board by Anderson and Strachan.[155] Meinertzhagen postulates that Smith-Dorrien rather than Smuts would have brought Lettow-Vorbeck to a decisive battle early in the campaign by concentrating an overwhelming force of infantry and artillery and using his mounted troops in a wide-sweeping movement to encircle and annihilate the enemy.[156] Meinertzhagen ignores the fact that before Smuts's arrival, the British chose to disperse their forces among the frontier posts, leaving few resources for a striking force.

These authors have been selective about the secondary sources they use to bolster their case against Smuts. Strachan liberally references Charles Fendall, *The East African Force*,[157] whom he describes as writing one of two more illuminating memoirs. Strachan describes Fendall as being especially provocative about supply and administration, two areas earmarked by him as a particular weakness of Smuts. The other illuminating source is Meinertzhagen which he describes as opinionated but full of insights. Anderson ignores *The East African Force* which appears in his bibliography but prefers to reference Fendall's diary[158] to the extent of quoting tracts of Fendall verbatim to bolster his standpoint on the poor state of supply and transport under Smuts.[159] Both men hold great store in the opinions of Fendall who served as a staff officer in GEA for the duration of the campaign. Considering the extensive use made of Fendall's work, it is surprising that they overlooked the following:

> For some reason or other there was a very general idea that General Smuts was averse to fighting, that he much preferred to manoeuvre an enemy out of position to driving him out, and this with the object of avoiding a fight. This seems a wrong idea altogether. General Smuts had, above all things, a logical mind. He objected to giving the enemy the advantage of fighting in a position, or on the ground, chosen by himself. His idea was plainly to use his superior strength to make the enemy leave his chosen position; to manoeuvre him out of it, in fact, and then to use his mounted troops to intercept and force him to fight on ground of his, General Smuts', choosing.
>
> It was not the fault of General Smuts that the enemy was never placed in such a position that he would have to fight a general action to free himself, and, moreover, fight it under circumstances decidedly unpleasant for him. General Smuts' plans, on several occasions, would have resulted in placing the enemy is such a situation had it not been for want of enterprise, to call it by no harder name, on the part of his mounted brigade commanders.[160]

Fendall's opinion on Smuts's abilities may not carry much weight, for he admits that what he wrote was derived entirely from memory and from a diary he transcribed at irregular intervals. Furthermore, he did not witness combat first-hand, but gained his impressions "behind-the-scenes". However, both authors have been selective in choosing those reminiscences that bolster their opinions. Omitting Fendall's favourable opinion of Smuts has deprived readers the chance of an objective judgement based on all the facts. Fendall was not alone in his favourable opinion of Smuts. Brigadier-General S.H. Sheppard, commander of the 2nd East African Brigade, was equally complimentary.

> General Smuts was a great believer in wide turning movements, and made much use of them both strategically and tactically. They were very successful; and though, owing to the extreme difficulty of the country, we never succeeded in bringing off a Sedan, yet the enemy was frequently forced out of almost impregnable positions with heavier losses than ours.[161]

Lettow-Vorbeck correctly identified the threat of a two-pronged attack well before the operation got underway. He anticipated Van Deventer's flanking manoeuvre in good time, realising the South Africans' reluctance to launch direct assaults against entrenched positions. He opted to attack each prong in turn, using the classic advantage of concentrating in space using interior lines of communication. During the South African advance, Lettow-Vorbeck looked for opportunities to concentrate his forces and overwhelm vulnerable, isolated South African units pressing forward. However, when the battle unfolded, he could not concentrate his forces in this fashion for reasons not fully explained by him.[162]

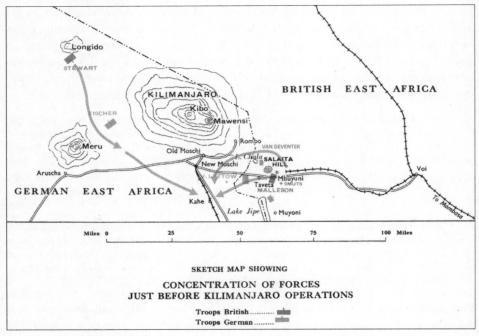

Map 6.1. Smuts's bold plan of encirclement for the Kilimanjaro operation[163]

Smuts enjoyed a 3:1 numerical superiority in manpower and artillery but only 2:1 in the all-important area of machine guns. (See Table 6.2) The machine gun dominated the battlefield, especially in the dense bush, and the Germans crewed them with the more skilled white troops.[164] Askari marksmanship was considered inferior with most of the casualties inflicted on the Allied troops attributed to machine-gun fire.[165] The force ratio favouring Smuts was not overwhelming and was the bare minimum required at the tactical level to overcome an enemy occupying a strong and well-prepared defensive position.

Table 6.2. The order of battle of the opposing forces during the Kilimanjaro operation, March 1916[166]

Unit	Commander	Rifles	Guns	Machine Guns
East Africa Force	Smuts	18,400	57	100
1st Division	Stewart	4,000	18	22
2nd Division	Tighe	4,700	19	34
SA Mounted Brigade	Van Deventer	5,900	14	28
Force Reserve	Beves	3,800	6	16

Unit	Commander	Rifles	Guns	Machine Guns
Schutztruppe	Lettow-Vorbeck	5,200	18	49
	Fischer	1,200		10
	Schulz	1,000		10
	Kraut	900		8
	Stemmermann	700		6
	Adler	600		9
	Other	800	18	6

		Rifles	Guns	Machine Guns
Force Ratio Total Force		3.54	3.17	2.04
Force Ratio Stewart/Fischer		3.33	N/A	2.20

The Germans, taking the operational defensive, could count on considerable terrain effects that offered concealment due to the surrounding bush's density. They used the months preceding the attack to strengthen their defensive positions, gaining maximum cover and excellent fields of fire.[167] The *Schutztruppen* were also eminently familiar with the terrain they defended, having occupied the positions for upwards of two years. Smuts was brand new on the job and possessed little knowledge of the commanders who reported to him, their capabilities under fire, or those of their forces they commanded. He was also unfamiliar with the extreme nature of the East African terrain, climate and diverse ecology, and the effect this would have on his campaign.[168] (See Map 6.2) However, it seems that Smuts and Smith-Dorrien were not far apart in determining the mounted troops as decisive in defeating Lettow-Vorbeck. In considering the fundamental role of mounted troops, both men severely underestimated the debilitating impact of the territory's numerous diseases on men and horses.[169]

The Attack on the Kilimanjaro Position, 5 March 1916

Stewart, commanding the western pincer, completed the concentration of his forces at Longido on the morning of 5 March 1916. His advance began a full two days before that of the 2nd Division. This would place his division well in the rear of the German defences by the time 2nd Division launched their attack.[170] (See Map 6.3) He set off for the Sheep Hills and halted there to avoid crossing the arid area stretched in front of him during the heat of the day. (See Map 6.3) Dusk saw the advance resume, and the 1st Division reached the Engare Nanyuki by 0800 on 6 March, having covered some 50 kilometres. After a cracking start, the pace of advance slowed considerably. Stewart did not reach Gerangua before 8 March even though he had encountered little opposition thus far.[171] The Germans responded to Stewart's advance by reinforcing Fischer with four more companies, bringing his strength to 250 Europeans and 1,450 askari. This reinforcement reduced the reserves available to Lettow-Vorbeck for his eastern front and provided an answer as to why his plans to counterattack vigorously never developed.[172] Stewart adopted an overcautious approach, sending his mounted troops on 9 March to reconnoitre the route ahead. He was unwilling to commit himself to a blind advance through unknown territory covered in bush. Smuts began to suspect at this early stage that Stewart's hesitancy would be the ruin of his encirclement strategy.[173] At 1500 Stewart received a telegram from Smuts urging him forward with all speed.[174] Ignoring Smuts's impassioned pleas, Stewart waited on the return of his mounted reconnaissance who duly reported that impenetrable bush covered the way ahead. Stewart set off cautiously on the morning of 10 March without his exhausted mounted troops and managed to advance five kilometres short of the Mbiriri River.[175]

The German official history is scathing in its criticism of Fischer for his failure to develop an attack against the overcautious Stewart, despite the reinforcements sent to him at a considerable cost to Lettow-Vorbeck's reserve. Boell believes that Fischer, despite suffering a numerical disadvantage, possessed sufficient amounts of modern weapons that included artillery and machine guns to overcome Stewart's larger force. What Lettow-Vorbeck needed from Fischer was to launch an aggressive attack on

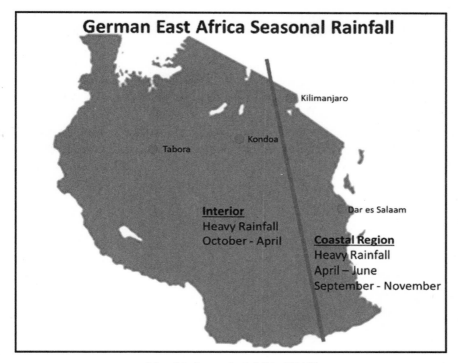

Map 6.2. Seasonal rainfall in GEA[176]

Stewart and seize the initiative, but it was evident that he lacked the determination. He divided his forces and undertook several evasive manoeuvres which yielded extraordinarily little on the battlefield. An exasperated Lettow-Vorbeck issued a direct command to Fischer on 8 March to launch an immediate and concerted attack on Stewart. Fischer's troops were exhausted with all the marching and counter-marching back and forth along the front. When Fischer eventually attacked on 10 March, he intercepted a screening force of 300 men, as the main body of Stewart's troops had already passed. Smuts was fortunate that Fischer was as incompetent as Stewart—a more resolute German commander could have inflicted a severe reversal on the British force.[177] (See Map 6.3)

Being fortunate to have escaped unscathed at the hands of Fischer, Stewart received a further message from Smuts on 11 March at 0745 urging him forward.[178] Supposedly spurred on, he set out and reached the intact road bridge at Boma Ngombe. However, his sluggish progress set him a full four days behind the planned timetable.[179] During his advance, he had seen little of the enemy. He was about to experience his first encounter. The mounted units having the lion's share of the artillery, once rested, set out to catch up with the main body at 1600 on 10 March. They encountered the Germans under Fischer en route, where the main body had passed unscathed some hours earlier. A short sharp exchange ensued which was enough to convince the mounted units to retreat into a defensive position for the night. The proximity of the Germans somehow convinced the mounted units to retreat to Gerangua. Stewart retrieved his mounted units on 12 March, which rejoined the main party, causing 1st Division a further delay of one day.[180] Smuts was convinced that there had been practically no opposition to Stewart's advance, indicating the main German forces were facing him at Latema-Reata.[181]

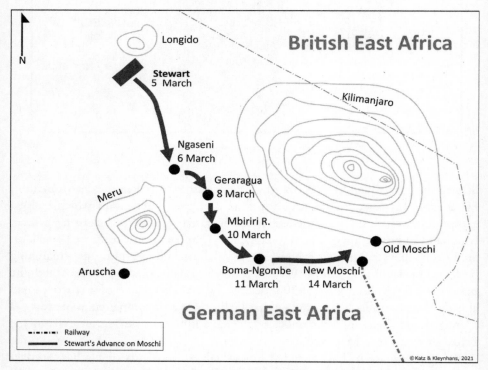

Map 6.3. Stewart's advance from the west on Kahe, 5–14 March 1916

The advance from the east set off a full two days after Stewart launched his advance. The two-day delay was at Stewart's request as his line of advance was longer and more difficult.[182] Van Deventer left Mbuyuni with the reserve force on the evening of 7 March to initiate his flanking manoeuvre to the north of Malleson's main thrust onto Salaita.[183] On the morning of 8 March, he occupied positions near Lake Chala forcing the Germans to abandon their positions at Salaita and retreat.[184] A reading of Boell reveals that although Lettow-Vorbeck was prepared to trade territory for time, his decision to sacrifice territory when confronted with Smuts's flank attack was not one he made easily. Smuts forced him to make the decision rather unwillingly.[185] Further reconnaissance established the expected, that the Germans held Taveta in some strength. Malleson's force began to bombard Salaita Hill which he captured in at 1430 on 9 March. The Germans abandoned the position after Lettow-Vorbeck considered its defence untenable in the face of Van Deventer's flanking movement.[186] Salaita, which a few weeks back saw a resounding British defeat with many casualties, fell without a fight.[187]

Van Deventer, continuing the advance, inserted himself in the rear of Taveta by 9 March. The Germans retreated out of Taveta on 10 March after a sharp skirmish, no doubt casting one eye on Van Deventer's forces in their rear.[188] The bulk of the German forces withdrew to the hills of Latema and Reata where they were determined to offer a stubborn defence. (See Map 6.4) Smuts decided to launch an immediate attack on Latema-Reata after he had conducted a personal reconnaissance. He chose a frontal attack without the aid of a turning movement owing to the difficulty of the terrain. Smuts proved his versatility in not shying away from a frontal attack where the situation demanded.[189]

The 1st East African Brigade launched its attack in the afternoon of 11 March. The assault took them to the foot of the hills before heavy enemy gunfire held them up. Malleson, suffering from dysentery and a dose of uncomfortable déjà vu, chose to report sick.[190] Tighe took over his command at 1600 and ordered more units forward into the fray. The Germans had the British pinned down for five hours with casualties mounting and subjecting them to numerous counterattacks. Lettow-Vorbeck, although determined to defend the position, had one eye cast on Van Deventer and the threat to his left flank.[191] Tighe attempted a night attack with fixed bayonets at 2000, judging that the Germans were not holding the hill in strength. A determined German counterattack flung the attack back. All that remained on the hill as night fell were pockets of British soldiers doggedly clinging on to the ground which they had held for hours.

More importantly, Van Deventer managed to advance to Spitz Hill after a brisk skirmish, placing him to the flank and rear of the German positions at Latema-Reata. (See Map 6.4) Smuts, fearing a German counterattack, and preferring to wait for the results of his turning movement, ordered Tighe to withdraw his whole force before daybreak. At dawn, Smuts realised that British units still occupied positions on the hill. He ordered an immediate advance to reoccupy, only to find that the Germans had abandoned their positions during the night.[192] Once again, the threat of Van Deventer's turning movement at Spitz Hill forced the Germans to abandon a powerful defensive position.[193] Smuts thought that Van Deventer's operational/ tactical flanking movement so crucial to the outcome of the battle that he placed himself "in close touch" with him at the expense of remaining in continuous contact with general headquarters. It is worth pondering the far more important strategic outcome had Smuts placed himself in closer proximity to Stewart and been able to positively influence his sluggish tempo.[194] Indicating the battle's ferocity, was the loss of nerve suffered by Major Georg Kraut, one of Lettow-Vorbeck's most experienced officers, who commanded the German forces defending Latema-Reata and later Kahe. He was only able to recover after a month's rest and later served with great distinction in the campaign.[195]

The hasty German retreat was an opportune moment for the two prongs to snap shut and entrap the hapless foe, but Stewart's tardiness put paid to what would have been a strategic victory. He saw his mission as twofold, firstly to draw off as many of the enemy as possible—a task he failed at miserably as the Germans ignored his advance—and secondly, to threaten the German line of retreat, which he would have better served with an early occupation of Kahe.[196] Smuts intended for Stewart to reach Kahe by 11 March, thereby cutting off the German retreat into the interior. Contrary to Smuts's expectations, Stewart languished at Boma Ngombe, 50 kilometres distant from his destination. He revealed his state of mind when he admitted to an "uneasy feeling" on receiving news on 7 March that the main force was to the east of Salaita instead of near Taveta. He felt vulnerable, stripped of his mounted units, deep inside enemy territory to the tune of 96 kilometres and a distant 240 kilometres from the nearest railhead.[197] In a disastrous change of plan, Stewart, feeling vulnerable and isolated, linked the pace of his advance to the successes of the main force.

Smuts grew increasingly frustrated at Stewart's hesitancy and sensed that the narrow opportunity to encircle Lettow-Vorbeck's forces was fast disappearing. He sent a message on the afternoon of 12 March, urging the timid Stewart forward to Kahe. Instead of making a concerted effort towards Kahe, Stewart sent the majority of his force toward Moshi, well to the north of the intended target. Heavy rain halted his faltering advance at 0130 on the morning of 14 March. Ironically, Lettow-Vorbeck was growing equally disenchanted with the performance of the commander facing Stewart. Major Eric Fischer, presented with several opportunities during Stewart's bumbling advance, failed to grab the chance to inflict damage on Stewart's muddled approach. Lettow-Vorbeck severely reprimanded Fischer and his lack of aggressive action which resulted in Fischer's suicide by gunshot to save his honour.[198]

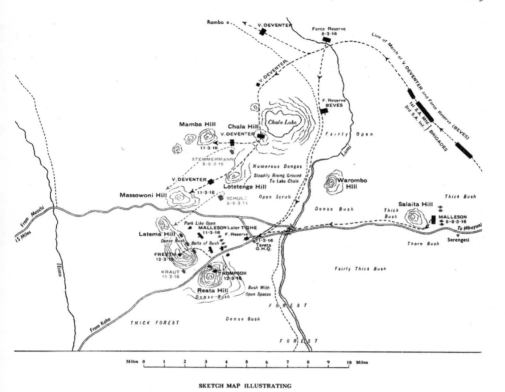

SKETCH MAP ILLUSTRATING

OPERATIONS EAST OF TAVETA

FROM MARCH 7 TO MARCH 11 CULMINATING IN ACTION AT
LATEMA AND REATA MARCH 11-12 1916.

Troops British..............
Troops German..............

Map 6.4. Advance from the west 7–12 March 1916 culminating in the battles for
Latema and Reata Hills.[199]

Despite Stewart's renewed advance, Van Deventer was first to arrive in Moshi early
on 14 March.[200] Van Deventer finally closed the pincer when he sent a motorcyclist
to Boma Ngombe to contact the hesitant 1st Division. Van Deventer also found
Moshi abandoned. The Germans had quickly retreated south along the railway out
of harm's way.[201]

Smuts's intention of encircling Lettow-Vorbeck, planned at the outset of
the operation, was frustrated by Stewart's lethargic advance.[202] Smut's flanking
manoeuvre, executed deftly by Van Deventer, managed to dislodge the Germans
from their prepared defensive positions at little cost. If Stewart had executed his

enveloping manoeuvre with the same zeal as Van Deventer, he could have reached his objective of Kahe between 10 and 12 March. The Germans would have found themselves encircled and in a precarious position. Smuts had good reason to be irate at Stewart's lacklustre performance which robbed him of a decisive strategic victory.[203] Shortly after the battle, Smuts relieved Malleson and Stewart of their commands, barely concealing his contempt at their performance. Smuts also ensured that Tighe was reassigned but was at pains to acknowledge his excellent preparation of the offensive.[204]

Lettow-Vorbeck, operating on internal lines of communication, posed a constant danger to the Allied manoeuvre wings. Had he been able to concentrate his forces into a powerful counterattack against any one of the three, Stewart, Tighe, or Van Deventer, there was a good chance of inflicting a defeat on each one in turn.[205] Smut's simultaneous advance on external lines was enough to unsettle the defenders and reduce the chance for them to concentrate an attack. Lettow-Vorbeck was unable to conduct a successful defence of Latema and Reata, robbing him of the chance to concentrate his forces against Van Deventer or Stewart.[206] Nevertheless, he came within a hairsbreadth of launching an attack on Van Deventer after the first successful defence of the Latema-Reata Hills on the night of 11 March.[207] The constant threat of outflanking and Van Deventer's threat of encirclement dissuaded Lettow-Vorbeck from launching an attack. Van Deventer's flanking movement dislodged the Germans from their defences and kept them constantly off-balance, making a concentrated counterattack untenable. Smuts's lightning operational manoeuvre failed to encircle the enemy but psychologically unhinged him.[208] Smuts managed to reclaim all of the British territory held by Lettow-Vorbeck and open up a gateway into the interior of GEA.[209] He gained much strategic territory for relatively little loss in human life—the Germans suffering 334 casualties against the 800 for the British.[210] Smuts received a well-deserved congratulatory letter from Botha via the Governor-General Sydney Buxton, recognising that "These successes have obviously only been attained by the gallantry and determination of the troops and by skilful leading of their commanders".[211] The new CIGS, Field Marshal Sir William Robert Robertson (replacing Murray in December 1915), recognised the brilliance of Smut's impressive opening operation against the Germans.[212]

CHAPTER 7

Smuts and the Conquest of German East Africa, 1916–1917

Jan Smuts, stymied by Jimmy Stewart's operational tardiness, narrowly missed an opportunity to eliminate a substantial component of Paul von Lettow-Vorbeck's Schutztruppe and end the war in German East Africa early. However, although Stewart denied him a significant strategic victory, Smuts's expeditious operational art of manoeuvre delivered the gateway through the Taveta Gap into the German colony's vast interior.[1] The British official history places his success into its proper context where contemporary British historians fail to do so.

> True. The German resistance had not been broken; but the enemy had been ousted from the most precious corner of his territory, the seizure of which relieved British East Africa from all fear of further hostile enterprise based upon it.[2]

The Germans would no longer have the opportunity of pinning their flanks against impassable mountains, nor would they be able to channel Smuts's attack through predictable passes. Smuts had opened the gateway to GEA.

Lettow-Vorbeck, numerically inferior, would now have to rely on his greater mobility and seize fleeting opportunities to concentrate in turn against Smuts's divergent advancing armies. Lettow-Vorbeck would rely on his superior mobility and knowledge of the terrain to deliver him from the encirclement battles that were sure to follow and avoid annihilation as he traded space for time. His overriding objective remained survival until the end of the war thereby attracting as many Allied resources as possible away from the main conflict in Europe. The Germans' strategic and operational mobility would come from two lateral railway lines—Tanga to Moshi and Dar es Salaam to Kigoma—which enabled them to rapidly deliver troops across the country's length and breadth. (See Map 7.1). At his disposal was a system of porters who would carry the equipment, ammunition, and stores of the Schutztruppe, giving him an unrivalled operational and tactical mobility.[3]

Smuts Eyes the Interior of GEA, March–April 1916

Smuts began his offensive on the cusp of the rainy season, and fortunately, his luck held out with the weather for the duration of the Kilimanjaro offensive.[4] However, increasing rain began to hinder supply lines, and an operational pause was necessary to restructure his forces and bring up the Voi railway line to New Moshi. Smuts grabbed the opportunity to sack the incompetent Jimmy Stewart and Wilfrid Malleson unceremoniously. Smuts respected Michael Tighe, whom he spared humiliation and relocated him to India.[5] He placed the British and imperial troops in two brigades within the 1st Division. Major-General Reginald Hoskins was appointed as the new commander of the 1st Division, and Jack Collyer replaced him in turn as chief of staff.[6] The 1st Division contained the Indian units, together with the troops from the United Kingdom, East Africa and Rhodesia.[7] The South Africans filled the ranks of the 2nd and 3rd Division commanded by Jaap van Deventer and Coen Brits respectively.[8] (See Figure 7.1) Significantly, Smuts and the British decided at this early stage for the large-scale expansion of the King's African Rifles (KAR) and the drawing of reinforcements from West Africa.[9] Doing so was admitting their particular suitability to "the peculiar conditions of East African warfare" and the South Africans vulnerability to tropical diseases and inhospitable climate.[10]

Smuts offered a logical explanation for reorganising his forces from his predecessor's two divisions to three divisions. He described his army as "a most heterogeneous army, drawn from almost all continents, and speaking a babel of languages". He designed his restructuring too secure a "smooth and harmonious" structure for the future "vigorous prosecution" of the campaign. Smuts also preferred South Africans to lead the UDF troops.[11] The South African divisions' organisation included a mounted and regular infantry brigade, each to add extra mobility to deal with the fleet-footed German askari. The infantry would act as a pinning force while the mounted units would provide operational and tactical flanking movements in the accustomed Boer manoeuvre fashion as was practised at Otavifontein in GSWA.[12] At least Smuts had found a role for the infantry formations, unlike in GSWA, where they languished behind the *Schwerpunkt* with little more than a rear-area security role. The British failed in not appointing Smuts as the overall commander to control all the different forces converging on the Germans in East Africa. Brigadier-General Edward Northey (1868–1953), commander of the Nyasa-Rhodesia Field Force, was answerable only to the Colonial Office, not even to the War Office.[13] Smuts also enjoyed little communication with the Belgians or Portuguese in coordinating operations throughout the vast territory.[14]

Ross Anderson and Hew Strachan have levelled much criticism at Smuts for the alacrity with which he undertook the next phase of operations during the heaviest period of the rainy season in East Africa. Their criticism is not restricted to Smuts's impatience but directed towards his predilection for territorial gain at the expense of

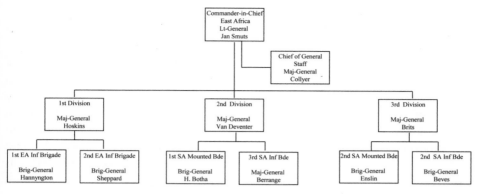

Figure 7.1. Order of battle as per Smuts's reorganised command, March/April 1916.[15]

eliminating Lettow-Vorbeck's Schutztruppe.[16] Had Horace Smith-Dorrien taken up his East African command, he had every intention of postponing the Kilimanjaro operation, or any other, until after the rains had subsided.[17] Smuts's decision to grab as much territory in the shortest timespan was well considered and not made in a political vacuum. His eye was firmly on the military and political situation in Europe, where the trench warfare stalemate meant peace could break out at any time. The Germans enjoyed little military success in 1916, in the aftermath of their decision to bleed the French forces white in a massive battle of attrition at Verdun. While the battle raged, the American president, President Woodrow Wilson (1856–1924), initiated peace feelers which he extended to all parties. The Brusilov offensive, which the Russians launched in June 1916 on the Eastern Front, broke the back of the Austro-Hungarian Army and brought Romania into the war on the Allied side.[18] The prospects of some sort of armistice were high, and like a game of musical chairs, it would behove Smuts to be sitting on as much German territory as possible should peace break out.

Stretched before Smuts lay the vast German East African territory, containing few vital physical objectives such as cities or centres. The road and communication systems were near non-existent. Dominating this immense territory were two German railway lines stretching laterally from the coast to the interior. They allowed for the speedy delivery of *Schutztruppen* to meet an attack developing anywhere from west to east. (See Map 7.1) Smuts feared that if he committed to an incorrect axis of attack, it would lead to "months of futile marching and wasted effort".[19] He realised that to conquer the large territory expeditiously would require an advance on multiple fronts and consequently identified three options. The first was a seaborne landing and then an advance from Dar es Salaam along the railway line—a similar strategy used in GSWA. Advancing along the railway line would solve some of the logistical challenges but was an obvious line of attack. Furthermore, the yearly south-easterly monsoon precluded a comfortable landing, and Smuts feared that a prolonged campaign on the coastal region would subject his forces in the interior to prolonged exposure to disease.[20]

His second option was an advance on Tabora via Mwanza, which he would have to wrest from the Germans. It was a short line of advance striking out at the main recruiting ground of the askari. This strategy would necessitate the transfer of a large portion of his forces westward, away from the centre, thereby leaving the British Uganda railway line vulnerable to continued German attacks.[21] However, the Belgians controlled considerable forces in the Lake Victoria region, and together with 2,000 British troops in the area, they would be the best choice to advance on Tabora as a combined force and rob the Germans of their prime askari recruiting aground. Smuts's lack of communication channels with the Belgians and the Portuguese left little room for cooperation and coordination. Of course, political considerations of allowing the Belgians a foothold on German territory, especially territory contested and coveted by Smuts, were at the fore.[22] GEA offered Smuts an opportunity to acquire territory at Germany's expense allowing the British a contiguous stretch of land from Cape to Cairo fulfilling Rhodes's long cherished dream. There was also Smuts's sub-imperial aim of swapping a portion of GEA territory with the Portuguese for Delagoa Bay. (See Map 2.1)

A third option was to strike against both or either one of the two German railway lines. The Tanga–Moshi railway line presented an obvious target due to its proximity to Smuts's positions in the north. It contained a significant portion (if not the majority) of the enemy forces who manned and prepared a natural defensive system along the Pare and Usambara mountains. Offensive action in this region would amount to a direct and expected assault on the waiting Germans, leading to costly and uncertain results. Levering the enemy out of these well-defended positions via costly protracted frontal assaults would still leave most of the country remaining in enemy hands even after many months of hard battle.[23] Fortunately, Smuts had the foresight to identify another option to dislodge the Germans from their strong defensive positions along the Pare and Usambara mountains. His bold plan involved a deep and unexpected thrust into the interior. (See Map 7.1).

The fourth and last option of an advance deep into the interior towards Kondoa Irangi carried risks but showed much promise to a man who favoured manoeuvrist approaches to warfare. Using Van Deventer's forces based at Arusha, a bold advance, plunging deep into the German interior, strong enough to fend off any German counterattacks, could unlock the entire German defensive system. (See Map 7.1) However, there were some powerful challenges to consider. The Germans operating on interior lines with two laterally running railways would be able to concentrate their forces quickly against such a thrust. There was also the risk of thinning out the forces facing the Germans in the Pare–Usambara area and exposing vulnerable Allied communications in the interior and at the coast.

There were obvious risks of exposing Van Deventer to a concerted German counterattack, and the risk grew greater the deeper the mounted infantry accessed the interior and distanced itself from its logistical hub. However, the benefits of such a thrust seemed to outweigh the risks. Smuts believed that Lettow-Vorbeck made a crucial mistake by retiring south along the Tanga railway with his entire fighting force, leaving the door to the interior open. Instead of falling back on Arusha and obstructing an advance into the interior, the six German companies facing Stewart chose to fall back to Kahe.[24] (See Map 6.1) There was also the added benefit of

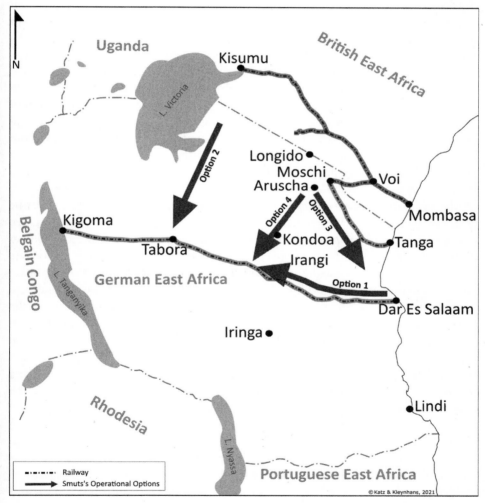

Map 7.1. Map of GEA showing the two German railway lines and the four options available to Smuts

better weather in the interior. Smuts hoped that by advancing further south and west, he would avoid the worst of the Kilimanjaro and coastal rains and thereby sidestep a complete standstill in operations. As it turned out, his hopes for kinder weather conditions proved false. Smuts was assured that the rains would not affect his advance or transport and there would be negligible risk of malaria and disease. The faulty intelligence source promising milder rainy weather inland came from "friendly Afrikaners" who had settled in the Arusha district.[25]

Smuts chose to send Van Deventer and the entire 2nd Division into the interior while keeping the other two divisions (1st and 3rd) to face the Germans manning the Pare–Usambara Mountains.[26] Van Deventer occupied Arusha at the end of March, and Smuts hoped that the thrust from there into the interior would lever the Germans out of their strongly defended positions in the Pare mountains by compelling them to meet the threat to their interior.[27] The completion of the railway link from Uganda to Moshi in April aided the operation's logistics.[28] Smuts practised manoeuvre warfare using an indirect approach over a frontal assault on well-prepared defensive positions. He ingeniously created the possibility of forcing the Germans to abandon their defences at Pare and Usambara and force them to fight on ground not of their choosing. He would also have the choice of switching forces between Van Deventer and his static arm at the Pare and Usambara mountains, reinforcing either one as the battle unfolded.[29] Contemporary British historians seem underwhelmed at Smuts's plan to take the course of least resistance.[30]

The manoeuvre aspects of deep operations (or deep battle) describe a doctrine whereby the attacker transcends mere tactical considerations of battle. Deep operations entail pinning the enemy while simultaneously advancing some forces deep into the enemy's rear operational or strategic zone. There, exercising manoeuvre in a less contested, congested and restricted space, the attacker attempts to disrupt logistics, command and control, and communication while sowing uncertainty and confusion by placing the enemy in a psychological and physical quandary. As the mobile force advances deeper into enemy territory, it may come across and have an opportunity to disrupt enemy support structures or command centres. Destroying targets throughout the operational depth of the defender reduces enemy combat effectiveness and fighting power. The psychological impact of suddenly appearing in the rear of enemy defences with the ability to advance in any direction can destroy enemy cohesion and place the enemy command structures on the horns of a dilemma.[31]

Although the Soviets in the 1930s were the first to apply a strict definition to deep operations and deep battle, empirical examples of such existed before their intellectual efforts at characterisation. One such battle, which was a precursor to and contained elements of Soviet deep battle thoughts, was Smuts's holding action in the Pare–Usambara and his simultaneous use of Van Deventer's mobile mounted infantry column to drive 345 kilometres toward Kandoa Irangi, which lay deep in

German-held territory. Smuts's conception of the operation contained the operational depth to meet the deep-battle criteria described as "the depth of penetration needed to launch a manoeuvre of operational rather than tactical significance".[32] A further relevant definition of operational depth is "that area beyond tactical depth in which both defender and attacker can achieve freedom of manoeuvre, and if gained by the attacker, provides the opportunity to destroy or disrupt the defender without engaging the majority of their defences".[33]

Smuts thought in operational terms, which was a concept not yet defined in western military thought. The notion of an operational level of war or an operational art, sandwiched between tactical and strategic considerations, would only be identified and solidified in Soviet military doctrine in the 1930s.[34] The operational level of war involves a process of tactical events, or a sequence of battles conducted to achieve a strategic objective. It recognises that in modern war, one tactical battle seldom achieves the desired strategic outcome. Contemporary historians have fallen into an anachronistic trap in accusing Smuts of not being able or willing to draw Lettow-Vorbeck into a single decisive battle of annihilation, where this was patently not possible in modern warfare. On the other hand, Smuts understood that defeating Lettow-Vorbeck would be a process rather than a single decisive event. He would conduct the campaign at the operational level orchestrating a series of battles to unlock the Schutztruppe's well-prepared defences.[35]

Toward Kondoa Irangi: Van Deventer Attacks, 1 April 1916

Van Deventer launched his attack in earnest from Arusha on 1 April. His first victims, caught by surprise by his speed of advance, were the German defenders at Lolkisale, 60 kilometres southwest of Arusha. (See Map 7.3) He surrounded the German defenders on 4 April, and in scenes that were reminiscent of the battle of Majuba in 1881, the South Africans used fire and movement combined with artillery to subdue the defenders. Contrary to long-held beliefs of Boer reluctance to launch direct assaults on well-entrenched enemy positions—this is precisely what Van Deventer arranged in the face of stiff German resistance at Lolkisale. Although the Germans held the mountain with considerable determination, Van Deventer's mounted infantry forced 17 Germans and 404 askari with two machine guns to surrender on the morning of 6 April.[36] There was a considerable haul of stores, including pack animals and ammunition. Most crucial was the intelligence gathered from documents and prisoners. Lettow-Vorbeck had instructed the garrison to hold out for as long as possible, since reinforcements would take several weeks to arrive. The South African tactical envelopment of the position caused consternation in the German ranks, leading to their premature surrender, according to Lettow-Vorbeck.[37] This information spurred Smuts on, and he ordered Van Deventer to advance with his mounted troops along the axis Ufiome, Umbulu, and Kondoa Irangi with all speed before German reinforcements arrived in strength.[38] The 2nd Division's regular infantry brigade would follow in the wake of the rapidly advancing mounted infantry.[39] (See Map 7.3)

Van Deventer advanced swiftly, encountering only sporadic resistance from a few enemy patrols, which he dispensed with, with both sides suffering some casualties. However, his main difficulties were the mounting losses of man and beast due to disease and the deteriorating climate and terrain. Communications and transport faltered as the roads and tracks became quagmires in the heavy rains.[40] Smuts's information on avoiding the worst of the weather in the interior proved false. The mounted elements of the 2nd Division occupied Ufiome on 13 April, dispersing the 20 Germans and 200 askari who retreated into the mountains. Van Deventer's exhausted mounted infantry continued the advance at a cracking pace, contacting the enemy seven kilometres outside of Kondoa Irangi on 17 April.

Lettow-Vorbeck soon came to the realisation that the considerable threat Van Deventer was developing on his left flank was indeed the South African main effort and not just a feint. Somewhat belatedly, he began to mobilise his troops to meet the developing threat at the expense of considerably thinning out his well-prepared defences ensconced in the Pare–Usambara.[41] Van Deventer's swift advance caused much consternation in the German ranks. Lettow-Vorbeck was caught by surprise and hastily assembled and sent reinforcements to Kondoa Irangi, consisting of Captain Klinghardt with 1,300 men and 10 machine guns. They would arrive too late to stop the capture of the town.[42] The German reinforcements were unable to proceed directly to Kondoa Irangi due to the harsh terrain protecting Van Deventer's left flank. Instead, they were forced to take a convoluted route making use of their railway and paths. (See Map 7.2) Van Deventer occupied Kondoa Irangi on 19 April with his remaining 600 mounted troops after a short, sharp encounter with its German defenders. The 400 German defenders suffered 20 killed and four German and 30 askari captured.[43] The defenders, in considerable disarray, retreated, suffering further casualties due to desertions.[44] The advance from Moshi to Kondoa Irangi, over 320 rain-soaked kilometres, came at a high cost, with the loss of hundreds of animals to disease and the complete exhaustion of Van Deventer's troops.[45]

Smuts decided to halt the advance and allow the 2nd Division to consolidate and replenish at Kondoa Irangi.[46] (See Map 7.3). Smuts's bold move, at a relatively small human cost, compared to what he would have had to expend on launching a frontal attack on the prepared German defences in the Pare- Usambara, had secured a commanding central position in the territory. Here, from Kandoa Irangi he could advance south and cut the Central Railway, or west and threaten Tabora, or east to threaten the coastal region and the rear of the defenders on the border. (See

Map 7.1) The South African official history considers this one of the few examples where Smuts achieved strategic surprise.[47] Charles Fendall was not impressed with Van Deventer's lunge at Kondoa Irangi, which he describes as a "wild advance". He continued with, "To allow a force to be isolated within reach of a superior force of the enemy is bad work". Fendall was equally critical of Van Deventer, describing him as "not a good man" and ignoring all orders.[48]

The British viewed Smuts's penchant for manoeuvre with a jaundiced eye. However, there were other aspects of the South African command and control, especially in the Boer-orientated mounted formations that were equally troubling to the British and the English South Africans. Reading reports from British and South African observers indicate some of the command-and-control challenges Smuts faced with his South African troops. Lack of discipline, individualism and nepotism coursed through the UDF—much as it had in the former Boer Republican armies. Colonel Marcus Hartigan, taking temporary command of the 1st South African Mounted Brigade lamented:

> How far does this story told in this report justify my efforts to avoid taking command of this [1st South African Mounted] Brigade. I was the only British born Regimental C.O. As I feared, the Dutch C.O.'s with the exception of Colonel Brits, would not carry out my orders when they did not coincide with their own ideas.[49]

Fendall, much more sympathetic to Smuts and the South Africans in his book than his diaries, often reflects on the South African lack of discipline, low regard for their horses, lackadaisical approach to orders, and a lack of tactical offensive spirit:

> There has been great friction between S.A. men and Imperial, and still greater between the Dutch and English from S.A. The S.A. troops were wanting in the spirit of discipline that leads troops to try and win a fight no matter the consequences to them. Their endurance was admirable, the real fault was the junior officers, they were totally incompetent and had no thought for their men. Senior officers were better. In the conduct of the campaign the fault has been movement without sufficient preparation.[50]

The British used to rigid discipline and red-tape-type administration found the lackadaisical approach of some of the South Africans anathema. Manoeuvre warfare, as practised by Smuts, required a directive command system that demanded high levels of initiative from subordinates. Decentralised command could and did lapse into ill-discipline and poor decision-making on occasion. The Germans using a directive command style also suffered some reverses on the battlefield due to subordinates delivering poor judgement.

All of Smuts's efforts and penchant for manoeuvre were unable to overcome the effects of weather, disease, and poor logistics. Nature halted all operations in mid-April when the territory suffered a deluge of rain, making transport impossible and flooding much of the country. Van Deventer was cut off in the interior and had to make do with supplies on hand for weeks on end, relying on foraging and porters who brought in a trickle of provisions overland from Lolkisale, a trek of some 200 kilometres. The poor weather conditions, lack of adequate rations, and the constant presence of disease steadily eroded the fighting power on the isolated 2nd Division, who remained immobile on the defensive at Kondoa Irangi. The tsetse fly found a home in all German East Africa except those areas over 1,000 metres above sea level. The correct veterinary measures could delay the onset of disease or prolong horses' lives if administered correctly and prophylactically. Strachan blames the Boer structure of decentralised command and their unwarranted powers of discretion for hindering medication to the horses. Smuts was also blamed for arrangements which found the veterinary staff "miles away from the commander in chief".[51] However, Hoskins, commanding the 1st Division, presumably using British structure and doctrine, was not immune to the ravages of disease and suffered over 50 per cent casualties due to malaria by the end of June 1916.[52] Despite all the criticism levelled at Smuts, some of it justified, his operational thrust at Kondoa Irangi placed Lettow-Vorbeck on the horns of a dilemma and unlocked the strong German defensive positions along the Pare–Usambara. When Smuts eventually attacked the Germans defending Pare–Usambara, he did so against a much-weakened German force and averted the many casualties that would have been expended in a direct assault against a well-prepared enemy.

More than Lettow-Vorbeck's spirited resistance, it was disease, malnutrition and exhaustion that tore the heart out of Smuts's army and decimated his horses and transport animals, severely curtailing his mobility.[53] The human toll was just as debilitating, with Van Deventer's chief medical officer reporting at one stage during the advance on the Central Railway that troops were "in need of a rest and change to a more salubrious climate being debilitated by continuous marching, road making, drift making, fighting and lack of food, and by malaria and dysentery".[54]

The rate of casualties due to disease and malnutrition became so alarming that the War Office ordered an investigation on 10 July 1917 into "all matters affecting the health of the troops, British and native, including followers", in what became known as the Pike Report.[55] The report contains damning conclusions about the poor conduct of the campaign's medical aspects, after making allowances for the remoteness of the theatre and inexperience of those who participated: "We cannot but feel that there is much to regret in the medical history of this campaign and that a great many of the difficulties were due to a lack of forethought, of driving power, and of expert knowledge and assistance."[56]

The Pike Report highlighted the lack of appreciation of the pressing need to provide scientific facilities for the proper diagnosis of disease and, even where such facilities existed, they were underutilised. No proper sanitary organisation scheme was devised or carried into effect until August 1917, and recommendations put forward were often ignored. The report blamed the fact that the Supply Department was not run on scientific lines. Much blame was laid at the door of the Director of Medical Services, who assumed his duties simultaneously with Smuts in January 1916. His recommendations for anti-malarial dosages were woefully inadequate, and his failure to secure anophelines in Dar es Salaam, when these had been readily available to the Germans, was disastrous.[57]

How much responsibility can be apportioned to Smuts for the medical fiasco? Anderson and Strachan lay the blame for the poor physical condition of the East Africa Force firmly on Smuts. According to them his culpability was due to a mixture of inexperience, callous disregard for his men's welfare, negligence, and a refusal to enter into a decisive battle to annihilate Lettow-Vorbeck by preferring an indirect approach to warfare. Both historians rely on the Pike Report which delivers a clue as to Smuts's responsibility. Adjutant-General Nevil Macready's comments on the Pike Report apportions responsibility across the board, stating: "Had this particular campaign been more in the public eye, a very grave scandal would have resulted, owing to the want of supervision on the part of the Commander(**s**)-in-Chief over the departments of (**their**) staff concerned." It is troubling that Anderson cites this document but adjusts the wording (leaves out the words and letters **highlighted**) to incorrectly reflect that the Adjutant-General's comments were directed solely toward Smuts rather than all the commanders-in chief who would have been Tighe, Smuts, Hoskins, and Van Deventer.[58] The inaccurate rendition of the evidence is unhelpful as it requires a considerable amount of time to unravel the falsehoods. It seems many historians have come to rely solely on secondary sources in what amounts to a culture of cross-citation.

Lieutenant-Colonel Kirkpatrick, commanding the 9th South African Infantry Regiment, felt strongly enough that there was a case for incompetence, indifference to soldiers' welfare and general negligence. In response to his charges of starvation, insufficient medical arrangements, and exposure due to insufficient clothing and equipment, Smuts set up a board of inquiry that reported on the matter in May 1917. Kirkpatrick, whose regiment of 1,200 men suffered 91 per cent casualties to disease, was emphatic that "someone must be responsible and should be brought to book".[59] Kirkpatrick's regiment suffered extreme deprivation on the march to Kondoa Iringa, with 50 per cent losses en route and after that terrible deprivations while manning the town's defences for three and a half months.[60] The board of inquiry upheld Kirkpatrick's allegations of poor administration, medical care and negligence with rations but was less emphatic of where the ultimate blame lay.

These reports leave no doubt that their ultimate findings, although scathing, were sensitive to the reputations of the personalities involved as well as the maintenance of good relations between the United Kingdom and South Africa even decades after the events had passed into history. Certainly, Smuts, who assumed overall command of the East African Force has to receive final responsibility for both the successes and failures of his command. He cannot be held responsible for the day-to-day medical arrangements behind the lines, as he was a general who led from the front and this was a burden that should have been carried by his staff under Collyer. The South African official history, written by Collyer in 1939, devotes little space in his extensive lessons-learnt section to the medical problems in GEA. Collyer, as Smuts's chief of staff, should have taken direct responsibility for the medical aspects of the campaign during the time of his tenure and decades later when writing his official history as a manual for UDF doctrine.[61]

Lettow-Vorbeck Counterattacks: The Battle of Kondoa Irangi, May 1916

Lettow-Vorbeck, sensing the significant threat that the 2nd Division posed to his lines of communication, managed to gather a force of 4,000 men culled from the Usambara defences and aided by using his railway network. He made the decision to concentrate his main forces against Van Deventer on 14 April.[62] Due to the impassable territory on the flanks of Van Deventer's advance, Lettow-Vorbeck had no option but to use his rail network to concentrate most of his forces on Kondoa Irangi.[63] (See Map 7.3) Opposing Lettow-Vorbeck were 3,000 dishevelled men of the 2nd Division who slowly gave up their advance posts as the enemy approached the outskirts of Kondoa Irangi. Using the time available while Lettow-Vorbeck concentrated his forces, Van Deventer arranged his forces in an all-around defence with an eight-kilometre perimeter. The Germans advanced on Van Deventer on 6 May, sending scouts to locate the defences. They had advanced 30 kilometres by 8 May and seized most of the dominating heights surrounding the town except for those to the south, which is where Germans focused their attack.[64]

Lettow-Vorbeck planned the opening barrage on 9 May for 1230, but the mountain battery's late arrival delayed proceedings until 1530. The cautious company commanders decided on further scouting to determine whether the South Africans occupied the southern heights in strength. These patrols were met with heavy infantry and machine-gun fire.[65] The Germans launched a determined night attack at 1930 in four separate actions, which the defending infantry met on each occasion,[66] forcing the attackers to retreat at 0315, leaving three Germans and 55 askari dead on the battlefield for the loss of two South African officers and four soldiers.[67] Once the attack had failed, Van Deventer settled into a defensive position and managed to fend off sporadic attacks that ensued in the weeks ahead.[68] Richard Meinertzhagen, present at the receiving end of the German attack, provides an insight into the working of the South African staff under Van Deventer:

His staff is not a staff as we know it. Each officer just does that particular work which comes to hand regardless of its nature, but being all very good friends and no records being kept, there is neither friction or confusion. The work gets done. Such a thing as red tape or precedents do not exist and they are distinctly efficient at this rough and ready sort of warfare. On some occasions they make possible what a normal British staff would find impossible.[69]

As opposed to the British leanings toward detailed command, the South African penchant for directive-style command was enigmatic to British observers. Here Meinertzhagen was complimentary, which ran against the tide of criticism usually levelled at the South Africans by those who found difficulty comprehending a Boer, and now a South African, way of war.

Smuts received further orders from London on 24 April instructing him to bring the whole of East Africa under British authority. The extended objective was a departure from the previous policy of securing British territory and ensuring the safety of the Uganda railway line. The British instructed him not to make any formal declaration of annexation, which was the British government's standard policy for occupied colonial territory. Smuts was not to entertain anything less than an unconditional German surrender. It is clear from these instructions exactly where the British priorities lay with the German territory's future: they were more interested in territorial gain than in the destruction of the German forces within the territory. The insistence on unconditional surrender proves the importance of controlling the territory rather than seeking an end to hostilities. British aims were in kilter with those of Smuts and both parties concurred that the speedy acquisition of territory was a priority. Smuts has received much criticism from contemporary historians such as Strachan and Anderson for making political rather than military choices at the strategic level. However, the British government not only endorsed but ultimately informed his strategy.[70]

Disease, harsh weather conditions, and insufficient supply forced Van Deventer to remain on the defensive even after inflicting defeat on Lettow-Vorbeck at Kondoa Iringa. Lettow-Vorbeck had given up on an all-out-assault on Van Deventer as being too costly and contented himself with skirmishing actions while Van Deventer's fighting power increased with every passing day.[71] He could do little more than probe the surrounding Germans for the rest of May and the greater part of June, steadily reinforcing his garrison with new arrivals. Improving weather in the middle of May allowed Smuts the opportunity to clean up the German positions along the Pare and Usambara. Smuts seized the opportunity created when Lettow-Vorbeck had weakened his forces in Pare–Usambara to assemble sufficient forces for the attack against Kondoa Irangi. His advance would run along the Central Railway parallel to Van Deventer. (See Map 7.3)

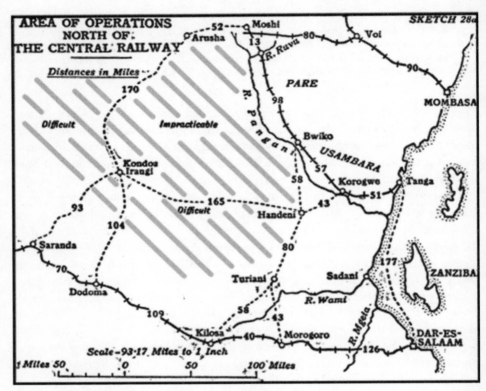

Map 7.2. The arid and rugged territory protecting Van Deventer's advance to Kondoa Irangi[72][73]

An ordnance officer gives an insightful impression of how an ordinary British officer viewed Smuts and his South Africans after gathering a few months' impression of how they operated on campaign:

> It is a strenuous campaign for those out, for Smuts spares neither man nor beast, and as one sees train after train of horses go up, it is sad to think not one of them will ever return to the Union. The men say they would prefer France, with all its bullets, and the Indians are sad because they don't get their two hours at midday. Sickness is up to 75% in some units. But it's cheering to see a bit of push from the top at last, and even the most conservative here can't help owning Smuts has a brain one doesn't often see.

> The Boer Cavalry do the loot and the rounding up. They're the most unblushing set of welshers I've struck yet, but they get a move on with their biltong and their vermin. They cannot live up to quite the same standard in the tropics as in S.A. and have been known to grouse lustily at ¼ rations here. Of course, the horses only last two months even out of fly areas, for they neglect them. My Depot staff are now alive to South African methods and treat all ranks as potential thieves.

MAP ILLUSTRATING

ADVANCE OF GENERAL SMUTS AND
GENERAL Van DEVENTER
TO
CENTRAL RAILWAY VIA PANGANI RIVER AND KONDOA IRANGI
RESPECTIVELY

Map 7.3. Van Deventer's bold advance bypassing the Schutztruppe's well-prepared defences in the Pare–Usambara Mountains[74]

The Boer has little relish for unnecessary bullets, but given a tight corner like Kondoa in May he takes a bit of dislodging. Once having been caught without entrenchments like that, they howled for the Sirhind entrenching tool which they now carry on the saddle.

One morning at six, Hawtrey of Signals burst into my tent with horror on his face. "Van Deventer's gone". I got up with a bound, collected the others, and we stormed Smuts. Apparently [Van Deventer] had gone out at 11pm and told the Cavalry to "get", and in twenty minutes their camp was empty. Secrecy, we said, was all very well, but how were we going to feed them and horse them and Signal them and ammunition them. "Easy" said Smuts! They live on the country. They've got spare horses and helios and 90 rounds a man. We explained that there wasn't any bally country to live on. It was a waterless desert, and spare horses wouldn't cover wastage with these bad horse masters, and only 3" helios wouldn't get the distance, and 90 rounds would only last the Boers one fight. We submitted that soldiering of this sort wasn't quite nice for decently bred staff officers.[75]

Fendall's impressions are also instructive after he had the opportunity to serve under and work with Smuts and his staff for five months:

[Smuts is] first class as commanding a Boer force with very little transport and no horse, quite clear headed and sound strategist in the way that his plans are good enough but he doesn't cut his coat according to his cloth, i.e. according to the capacity of his [lines of communication]. His Chief of Staff [Collyer] is much nearer a good man. In fact he is no doubt a good man but his influence is not sufficient to prevail on his chief not to try and push on without being fully prepared. He also does not seem to realize what the limitations of a line of communications are. These two practically run the whole show.[76]

Smuts's tempo in the campaign, way in advance of British-trained and -bred staff officers, caused much consternation among them. They were accustomed to a more leisurely pace, conducted within the realms of a doctrine reliant on discipline and procedure, which frowned upon individual initiative in the face of explicit orders. The relevance of Van Deventer's spearhead to Kondoa Irangi, and the operational art of a deep thrust into the enemy interior, especially the drawing away of Lettow-Vorbeck's troops from Pare–Usambara, escaped Fendall and other British officers.

The operational situation demanded rapidity in taking advantage of Lettow-Vorbeck's switch to Kondoa Irangi because the Germans could just as easily switch the forces back to meet Smuts. Smuts calculated that he had two weeks to complete the operation before German reinforcements arrived via the interior railway. The two advances, 280 kilometres apart, placed the Germans on the horns of a dilemma, making it difficult to resist given their numerical inferiority.[77] Smuts missed an opportunity to advance simultaneously with Van Deventer, instead of sequentially, which is a preferable manoeuvre doctrine recommended by Clausewitz and Jomini in overcoming an enemy who is making use of interior lines of communication.[78] However, Lettow-Vorbeck's ally—the incessant rains—precluded Smuts launching a simultaneous advance on both axes.

Lettow-Vorbeck's Intentions

Visiting 'the other side of the hill' provides insight into Lettow-Vorbeck's intentions at this stage of the campaign. Van Deventer's unexpected advance and rapid occupation of Kondoa Irangi took the Germans by surprise. Van Deventer's position threatened the Central Railway and simultaneously the encirclement of the German positions in the Pare–Usambara front. Lettow-Vorbeck decided on a counterattack on Kondoa Irangi while taking advantage of Van Deventer's poor condition and overextended lines of communication. Van Deventer, his forces severely weakened by disease and low rations, was resolute in the defence and fended off the German attack inflicting substantial losses on the Germans. The German attack came at the expense of thinning their defences facing Smuts on the Pare–Usambara.[79]

Lettow-Vorbeck gambled that leaving extensive forces threatening Van Deventer would lure Smuts to reinforce the dwindling fighting power of the defenders of Kondoa Irangi. Lettow-Vorbeck knew full well that reinforcements sent to Kondoa Irangi via the lengthy and challenging rain-swept lines of communication would suffer a 50 per cent attrition rate by the time they arrived. He hoped that nature would take a toll on the South Africans far beyond what he could inflict on them in conventional combat. Discerning Lettow-Vorbeck's intent takes reading between the lines. The losses he suffered in direct assaults against Kondoa Irangi "decided me to refrain from a general attack, and instead to damage the enemy by continuing the minor enterprises". Lettow-Vorbeck assumed that his actions around Kondoa Irangi amounted to 1,000 South African casualties, and he was content to lure more South Africans into the diseased cauldron.[80]

Leaving a substantial portion of his forces threatening Kondoa Irangi, Lettow-Vorbeck hoped to divert South African forces away from his Pare–Usambara front and his substantially reduced defences there. Smuts did not oblige and trusted that Van Deventer would hold onto his position with the troops at his disposal and the substantial infantry reinforcements making their way towards him. As he had planned, Smuts's bold drive to Kondoa Irangi using Van Deventer's mounted infantry forced Lettow-Vorbeck to respond and reinforce his position there at the expense of his well-prepared defences at Pare–Usambara. Smuts switched his emphasis and preferred to launch an attack where Lettow-Vorbeck was weakest, in the Pare–Usambara. Smuts's attack on Pare–Usambara would have the dual effect of removing the enemy from this vigorously defended enclave and diverting attention away from Van Deventer.[81] (See Map 7.3)

The Battle for the Pare–Usambara Mountains

Thus far in the campaign, Smuts had shown a keen aptitude for operational-level double envelopments and tactical double and single envelopments, in a fashion that gave justice to his mentors Botha and De la Rey's teachings. His drive into the heart of the German interior set a new bar for South African manoeuvre doctrine, if not a record for a deep drive into the enemy's operational rear.[82] His bold action and sudden switch to the Pare–Usambara front once again surprised Lettow-Vorbeck. Smuts's deep operational drive opened up possibilities for tactical outflanking manoeuvres on the well-prepared German defensive positions in the Pare–Usambara.

A narrow defensive position confronted Smuts's proposed advance, described by the railway line running through the centre and flanked on his left by the mountainous terrain of the Pare–Usambara Mountains and the Pangani River on his right. Smuts would advance in three columns, with his centre column following the railway line using the flanking columns to lever the enemy out of prepared defences along the way. Anderson is critical that Smuts, having divided his forces into three, "ignored the existing structures" but offers no explanation of why this is necessarily poor military doctrine. The German ability in the Second World War to swiftly form ad hoc *Kampfgruppen* (battle groups) designed to complete a particular task were the envy of the Allies.[83] Strachan accuses Smuts of aiming for speed and not bringing the enemy to battle, and wanting to seize Handeni and its railhead as swiftly as possible.[84]

Using the flanking technique when contacting enemy forces, Smuts forced a rapid advance southward, allowed him to advance 200 kilometres in 10 days. Meinertzhagen was highly critical of Smuts's use of flanking manoeuvres. He distinguishes between a more aggressive flank attack and "merely the throwing forward of a flank". He found the South Africans overcautious.[85] Smuts took the opportunity during a pause in his advance on 2 June, due to a blown bridge over the Pangani, to visit Van Deventer at Kondoa Irangi and plan the coordination of the two widely separated offensives. On his return on 7 June, he found the bridge repaired, allowing him to resume the advance and occupy Mombo on 9 June. Smuts encountered very little opposition along his advance route except for a few enemy rearguard actions. He discovered on 15 June that the Germans finally intended to offer resistance at Handeni, where they held a firmly entrenched position.[86] Here again, instead of conducting a direct frontal assault, Smuts preferred to send flanking columns to try and cut off the enemy's retreat. Handeni was occupied on 19 June after the Germans had beaten a hasty retreat. The next strong position on the route was Lukigura, said to be held in some strength. Again, Smuts attempted to cut off the enemy retreat with a flying column sent to outflank the position. He was able to attack the position on 24 June from three sides. Enemy losses were seven Germans killed and wounded, 14 German prisoners, and 30 askari killed, with many wounded and captured. The remaining enemy took advantage of the thick bush to make good their escape.[87]

Smuts's advance ground to a halt in front of the Nguru block of mountains, where he anticipated that a reasonable enemy force was gathering to launch a counterattack. He had also outrun his stretched logistical lines and was suffering similar debilitating attrition and exhaustion as Van Deventer's force to man and beast due to half-rations, diabolical weather, and ever-present disease. Smuts had managed to advance 320 kilometres since 22 May, having had to cut a path through dense bush for most of the way and deprived of water for the last stretch. He accomplished an arduous advance at high speed and contested by the rearguard of a wily and dangerous enemy. The rapid advance left an enclave of German territory sandwiched along the coast, which included Tanga—lightly held by the small remnants of Lettow-Vorbeck's forces previously defending the Pare–Usambara Mountains. Smuts consolidated his position 12 kilometres beyond Lukigura on the Msiha River and turned his attention to east Usambara, setting his sights on seizing Tanga.[88] Strachan labels Smuts's decision to capture Tanga and the Northern Railway "perverse" and contrary to his original decision that Tabora was crucial. Reading Smuts's dispatch reveals the reason he avoided it in the first place was that the Germans heavily defended it. The occupation of Kondo Irangi had thinned out these defenders as they had switched fronts to meet Van Deventer, making an advance in the Tanga area more attractive in the absence of defenders.[89]

Up to this stage, Smuts had deliberately avoided the defenders on the east of Usambara, hoping that they would withdraw under the pressure of his advance in the centre. In the absence of a German withdrawal, Smuts resolved the situation with a simultaneous landward advance, capturing Mwakijembe on 16 June from a seaborne landing 15 kilometres to the north of Tanga at Kwale Bay. This force managed to occupy Tanga on 7 July with little opposition. Three enemy companies remained in the vicinity, resorting to sniping and skirmishing, culminating in a determined attack on the bridge at Korogwe on 13 July. Smuts's reaction to the guerrilla-style warfare in the area was to order his forces to seize the coastal town of Pangani in a joint infantry-naval operation. Forces sweeping from Korogwe toward Pangani would clear the area of enemy activity. These measures yielded the surrender of 25 Germans and a machine gun before the remaining enemy beat a hasty retreat on 23 July, with the entire area subdued by the middle of August.[90]

Tabora and the Belgians, Northey and the Rhodesians

With all the activity in the territory's central and coastal region, Tabora remained a significant objective for the Allied forces. Tabora was an important askari recruiting centre for the Germans. The closer the Belgians got to Tabora, the more desertions the Germans experienced.[91] Smuts made the necessary arrangements with General Charles Tombeur (1867–1947), commander of the Belgian colonial military, the Force Publique, for his Belgian forces to advance on Kigali from Bukakata on Lake

Victoria. The march necessitated a 240-kilometre shift of those forces eastward—an undertaking of considerable difficulty. Smuts sent Brigadier-General Charles Crewe to the region to expedite and facilitate the arrangements. As a result of this cooperation, Belgian forces occupied Kigali on 6 May. The occupation of Kigali rendered the German positions further west untenable and allowed Colonel Phillipe Molitor (1869–1952), commander of the Belgian Brigade Nord, to reach the Kagera River on 24 June. Smuts appointed Crewe to command the Lake Force in the middle of June. Crewe proceeded to arrange a combined forward movement with the Belgian forces toward the fortified town of Mwanza to the south of Lake Victoria. After some skilful manoeuvres, the combined forces occupied the town on 14 July, with the enemy beating a retreat to Tabora.[92] The first week of August found the Belgian and British forces well south of Lake Victoria and preparing for a combined advance southward toward Tabora. A Belgian force had already crossed Lake Tanganyika and occupied Ujiji and Kigoma, the Central Railway's terminus. (See Map 7.4)

In the south-west, General Northey's force occupying Malangali was preparing to move towards Iringa, 120 kilometres further north-east. The Allies occupied most of the coastal area up to the town of Sadani, while a small column was working its way southward to the Wami River. (See Map 7.4) Smuts realised the importance of securing the entire length of the coastal regions, thus denying Lettow-Vorbeck the prospect of resupply via the German Navy.[93] The German auxiliary ship *Marie* managed to evade the blockade and land extensive supplies for the *Schutztruppen* on 16 March.[94] Van Deventer reached the Central Railway on 31 July and set about consolidating his position after outrunning his logistics. The Germans were offering scant resistance in the face of outflanking manoeuvres, preferring to keep their forces intact and trading space for time.

The Allied forces advancing on exterior lines and converging on the Central Railway in almost simultaneous fashion precluded Lettow-Vorbeck from offering stiff resistance at any one point for fear of being cut off and surrounded. The result was that Smuts forced the Germans to abandon huge tracts of land, including their main askari recruiting centre of Tabora as well as key points on the Central Railway line. The speed of the advance disallowed Lettow-Vorbeck to concentrate superior numbers at any one of the converging Allied advances, which was a significant tactic of his. Lettow-Vorbeck, by trading space for time, achieved his strategic objective of remaining in the field for as long as possible. Smuts was also able to achieve his strategic aim of conquering as much territory as possible in the shortest time space without resorting to costly frontal attacks and needless casualties.

Smuts and Van Deventer's Advance to the Central Railway

Van Deventer resumed his advance from Kondoa Irangi to the Central Railway after a short action with the enemy on 24 June. All indications pointed to the Germans

MAP TO ILLUSTRATE

STRATEGIC SITUATION AT THE END OF JULY, 1916.

Forces British...........

,,   Belgian.........

,,   German........

Map 7.4. The strategic situation at the end of July, 1916[95]

shifting forces from Kondoa Irangi to confront Smuts's advance from the Pangani River to the foot of the Nguru Mountains with his 1st and 3rd Divisions. (See Map 7.3) Smuts ordered Van Deventer's main force toward Dodoma but wanted a movement east at the same time toward Mpwapwa, closing the distance with his forces at the Nguru Mountains. (See Map 7.3) Van Deventer split his force into columns (in a similar fashion to Smuts's tactics along the Pare–Usambara) which advanced to the east and west of Kondoa Irangi as well as directly south to the Central Railway.[96] The columns at first only encountered enemy skirmishers along the way until one column reached the dense bush surrounding Mpondi on 14 July on its way to Saranda station on the Central Railway. The column dealt with the defenders via a frontal attack and occupied the town on the same day. They occupied Saranda on 31 July, cutting the Central Railway and curtailing Lettow-Vorbecks's conventional ability for swift lateral movement across the territory.

Van Deventer's central column moving south occupied Chamballa on 18 July. Van Deventer then split the column into two under Brigadier-General Manie Botha and Brigadier-General C.A.L. Berrangé to provide for outflanking manoeuvres against enemy entrenchments as both columns moved south toward the railway. It is worth noting that both Botha and Berrangé were veterans of the GSWA campaign serving under Louis Botha and by this stage of the campaign quite familiar with the developing South African way of war. Berrangé, with both columns having had several engagements, occupied Dodoma on 29 July. By the end of July, Smuts controlled 160 kilometres of the Central Railway.[97] (See Map 4.4) Louis Botha took the opportunity to pay a short visit to Smuts on 21 July 1916, where the two men spent some time discussing the campaign's direction.[98]

The time had arrived for Smuts and the 1st and 3rd Divisions to resume their advance towards the Central Railway. The direct path to the Central Railway was through the Nguru Mountains, where 3,000 of the enemy with heavy and light artillery were entrenched in the foothills. (See Map 7.3) Here too, Smuts decided to use sweeping flanking movements to threaten the enemy with envelopment, thereby levering them out of their strongly entrenched positions. Smuts opted not to fight the enemy on ground of their choosing, which they had prepared well in advance to offer the stiffest resistance—he instead opted for coercion to remove the enemy from their defences by threatening to cut them off if they hesitated to retreat. Smuts bypassed some of the resistance en route using these methods but was engaged in stubborn fighting at Matomondo on 10/11 August, resulting in 60 casualties while inflicting some loss on the enemy. It became clear that the majority of the enemy were retiring towards the Central Railway. The numerous rivers encountered, where the Germans had blown the bridges, proved more of an obstacle to the advance than any actual resistance. Some short, sharp engagements interrupted the advance at various points, but in the main, the enemy preferred to retreat in the face of outflanking actions.[99]

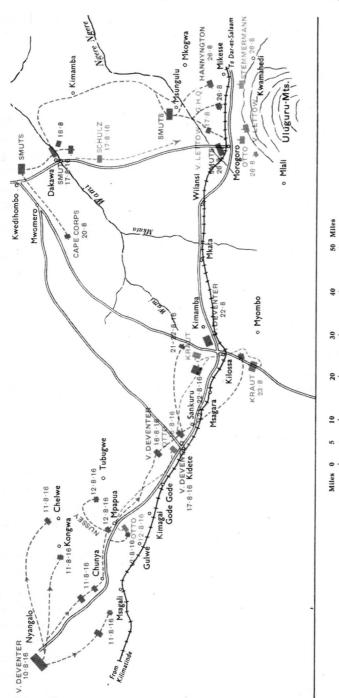

MAP ILLUSTRATING THE COMBINED

OPERATIONS of GENERAL SMUTS with GENERAL VAN DEVENTER IN SECURING CENTRAL RAILWAY

Forces British............

Forces German............

Map 7.5. Smuts and Van Deventer in a joint operation in August 1916 to secure the Central Railway line[100]

Van Deventer concentrated his 2nd Division at Njangalo and commenced his advance on 9 August. (See Map 7.5) After offering some resistance, the enemy retreated before him, resorting to skirmish actions all along the waterless 60 kilometres of terrain. The terrain—the railway ran along deep gorges in many places—was not suitable for outflanking manoeuvres. Facing 18 companies of *Schutztruppen* supported by artillery, Van Deventer often had to resort to frontal attacks to dislodge the enemy. He again engaged the enemy at Kidete station on 15 August, the action continuing until midday of the following day. Once again, when the terrain was more suitable, the enemy was driven out by an outflanking manoeuvre using the mounted troops who attacked the Germans from the rear. Van Deventer remained in constant contact with the enemy from 15 August to 22 August, driving them eastward from Kidete all along the railway line. He captured both Kilosa and Kimamba on 22 August, having advanced the last 40 kilometres through the narrow gorge containing the railway line. The nature of the terrain precluded flanking manoeuvres, and the advance was subject to enemy ambushes and rearguard actions along the entire length. The rapid advance of 350 kilometres since 9 August from Kondoa Irangi took a considerable toll on the underfed troops and diseased animals.[101] (See Map 7.3)

The Fall of Morogoro and the Advance to Kisaki

Brigadier-General William Edwards with 1,900 men including 300 South Africans, advanced from Bagamoyo to Dar es Salaam which coincided with the advances of Smuts and Van Deventer in the interior. (See Map 7.3) Two columns approached Dar es Salaam from the north, advancing southward along the coast, while the other advanced eastward along the Central Railway. Neither column met serious opposition along the march as the heavily outnumbered enemy was set upon avoiding capture. The Germans were concerned to avoid siege operations in a town containing a large German non-combatant population, and as a result, they abandoned Dar es Salaam to the advancing British columns.[102] The coastal town fell on 4 September without a fight, the occupying forces finding the railway and shipping facilities destroyed. In cooperation with the Royal Navy, Smuts decided to seize all the critical points on the coast south of Dar es Salaam.

Smuts having denied the coastal region to the Germans, forced Lettow-Vorbeck into the interior, thus precluding any resupply via the coast. The control of Dar es Salaam and the Central Railway provided Smuts with an alternative supply route into the interior. Military engineers were able to narrow the gauge of several heavy lorries, allowing them to operate on the railway line and carry 10 to 15 tons of precious supplies. Van Deventer was able to use this method to carry supplies from Dodoma to Kilosa, greatly easing his logistical burdens. Once Smuts had occupied Morogoro, the engineers applied the same treatment to that section of the line, opening the railway track for motor traffic from Dar es Salaam to Dodoma.[103] (This was a solution that could have been applied by Botha in GSWA, greatly expediting the refurbishment of the German narrow-gauge railway and the necessity of relaying the Cape gauge.) Strachan optimistically suggests that if Smuts had paused on the Central Railway and re-established his communications through Dar es Salaam before pushing forward, he would have been able to terminate his campaign north of the Rufiji River.[104]

The bulk of the enemy forces now retired to Morogoro, leaving Smuts to attempt a series of manoeuvres to bottle them up in the region with two enveloping thrusts converging on Kisaki.[105] (See Map 7.6) Lettow-Vorbeck beat a hasty retreat before the

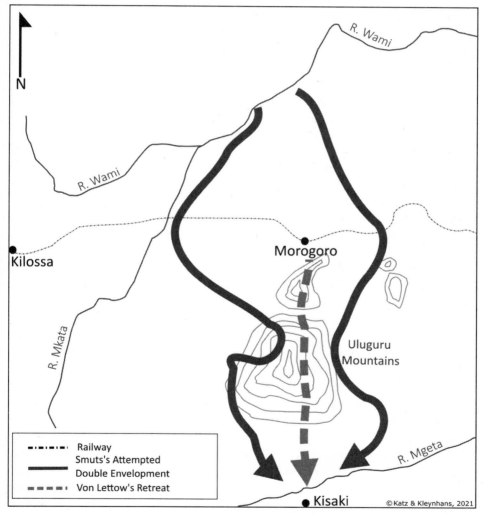

Map 7.6. Smuts's double envelopment of Morogoro, August/September 1916

jaws snapped shut, escaping with Governor Heinrich Schnee and most of his army. Smuts captured the deserted Morogoro on 26 August. Strategic logic convinced Smuts that Lettow-Vorbeck intended to make a stand at Morogoro, and had it not been for his unexpected flanking actions, the enemy would have remained lodged in his well-prepared entrenchments.[106] Lettow-Vorbeck intended to make a fight of it and contest the passage through the Uluguru Mountains. The enemy continued to show resistance with Smuts capturing Tulo on 10 September and Dutumi on 13 September. Smuts's flanking manoeuvre gave Lettow-Vorbeck no choice but to flee through the central mountains, abandoning copious quantities of ammunition, including heavy artillery ammunition. The majority of the Schutztruppe, including Lettow-Vorbeck and Schnee, retired through the mountains to Kisaki. If he could move speedily enough, Smuts hoped to bring the Germans to a decisive battle there. Approaching Kisaki on 5 September 1916, he found it covered with dense bush and thick grass three metres high and strongly defended. (See Map 7.6)

Beves and Enslin's converging attack on Kisaki was beaten back by the well-entrenched Germans. General A. Nussey of the 1st Mounted Brigade launched a further attack on 8 September but, unable to make headway, withdrew with 50 casualties. What Smuts meant to be a coordinated, simultaneous attack by the infantry and two mounted brigades, in his absence, had turned into a piecemeal effort that the 3,000–4,000 Germans defenders defeated in detail. However, Lettow-Vorbeck, once again threatened with envelopment, abandoned Kisaki on 14 September 1916. Smuts could advance no further with his exhausted troops, who had advanced 160 kilometres beyond the Central Railway and had lost extensive fighting power due to sickness and disease. The front would remain virtually the same until the end of December 1916.[107] Smuts took the opportunity to instruct the Royal Navy to occupy the remaining harbours down the GEA coast, occupying Kilwa and Lindi on 7 and 16 September 1916 respectively. Smuts controlled the entire coastline except for the Rufiji Delta.[108] Kilwa would be fundamental to his next effort to encircle the elusive Schutztruppe.

Smuts realised in early July that trapping the elusive Lettow-Vorbeck and executing a battle of annihilation was an impossible prospect considering the jungle-covered country and dense bush. It was apparent that Lettow-Vorbeck intended to retreat into the deep interior of the Iringa and Mahenge districts. Here disease made it impossible for white soldiers to operate effectively. Smuts made a surprising suggestion by motivating for the incorporation of the Belgian askari into the East African Force considering that the Belgians had no further interest in prosecuting the conflict after occupying Ruanda and Urundi.[109] He considered that the incorporation of Belgian askari into the East African Force under British command would signal his handing over command to Hoskins and his return to the Union.[110] Anderson sees this as an attempt by Smuts to escape his increasingly tricky command.[111] Giving context to Smuts's proposal was a telegram he received from Field Marshal Sir William Robert Robertson, the Chief of the Imperial General Staff (CIGS), requesting his comments on employing black troops instead of whites for future operations beyond and to the south of the Central Railway.[112] Furthermore, the CIGS agreed in principle that black troops should conduct the campaign beyond the Central Railway and that Hoskins would then assume command. Anderson states that the CIGS stipulated that this would only take place "once a decisive result had been achieved", whereas the words in the telegram read, "When the result of your present operation is seen, a definite decision will be given."[113] It also appears that the CIGS agreed with Smuts on including Belgian askari but limited them to one brigade of six battalions.[114]

After the Uluguru operations, 12,000 South Africans returned to the Union, prompting a reorganisation of the remaining South African formations in East Africa. Brits and Enslin returned to the Union on the disbandment of the South African 3rd Division and 2nd Mounted Brigade. Berrangé and his 3rd Infantry Brigade joined Van Deventer's division to become the composite 10th South African Infantry Regiment. Reinforcements from Nigeria, the King's African Rifles, and the 30th Punjabis from India made up the lost numbers. Disease had decimated Smuts's troops more than any Schutztruppe action.[115] The draft British official history cites the unsuitability of newly arriving South African recruits with an example of a reinforcement draft of South Africans arriving on 4 October 1916. Of 1,011 men arriving at Korogwe, 120 immediately fell sick, leaving 881 to march southward. The march saw a further 150 men return to Korogwe with sore feet. Only 397 eventually reached Handeni (64 kilometres from Korogwe) on 9 October, and only 328 marched onward from that point.[116]

Northey and His Advance to Iringa

Northey was not idle during Smuts and Van Deventer's rapid advance into the interior.[117] He was able to occupy Lupembe on 10 August and Iringa on 29 August. On Smuts's admission, Northey would have been able to occupy the latter much earlier had Smuts not asked him to slow down his advance until he could ascertain the enemy's line of retreat from the Central Railway. Northey's exposed advance was vulnerable to encountering General Kurt Wahle's very much intact retreating forces. By the end of September, Northey occupied positions near the Ulanga River, only a few kilometres from Smuts's forces advancing southward. Difficulties with supplies ensured the delay of Crewe's advance. The Belgians could not concentrate their forces before 22 August but managed to reach the outskirts of Tabora on 2 September, capturing the town on 19 September. Crewe reached the Central Railway at Igalulu on 26 September. Wahle's troops retreated in two columns towards Iringa, encountering Northey's and Van Deventer's patrols. The Portuguese had, in the meantime, also crossed the Rovuma River, moving northward. The sum result of all the Allied actions in GEA to date left the Germans occupying the territory to the south of the Rufiji River, being steadily hemmed in from all sides by the advancing Allied columns. Allied operations had cleared three-quarters of GEA by the first week of October 1916.[118] (See Map 7.7)

ENEMY TERRITORY OCCUPIED
AT END OF AUGUST 1916.

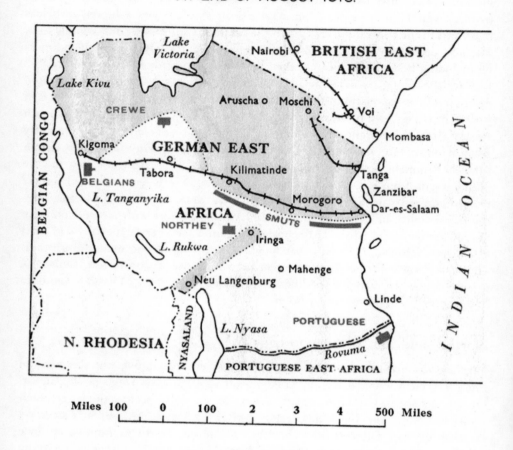

PLAN SHOWING

THE RESULTS OF THE OPERATIONS OF

GENERAL SMUTS DURING THREE MONTHS,
JUNE, JULY AND AUGUST 1916.

Enemy Territory Occupied ......

Allied Forces ....

Map 7.7. The Allied advances by August 1916 had almost divided the territory in two[119]

The troops' failing health combined with the Belgians obtaining their political objective on occupying Tabora brought the Allied advance to a halt. The draft official history describes the remaining South African troops in the field, withered by disease, as "mere cadres". Crewe in the north and Northey in the south had also reached the limit of their powers. The Belgian halt at Tabora left an unmolested force of 10 German companies, estimated at a strength of 1,200, under Major-General Wahle to the south of Tabora.[120] (See Map 7.7) The Belgians gave the impression that Wahle commanded a much-depleted force after he had suffered heavy losses on the retreat. His destination whilst retreating was possibly the Mituma Mountains. Wahle, his communications cut from Lettow-Vorbeck once Dodoma fell, acted independently of orders from headquarters. Allied intelligence incorrectly assumed that Wahle commanded a demoralised force, whereas in reality, 2,300 well-armed, undefeated Germans roamed the countryside, posing a danger to any nearby Allied troops happening along the way.[121]

Northey felt menaced by Wahle's force to his north-west flank for as long as it remained unchecked in his vicinity. He urged the South African 2nd Division to push on, but Van Deventer and his men were a spent force at the very end of their supply line, reduced to 4,752 troops and losing more to sickness and disease daily. Despite the poor state of Van Deventer's troops, Smuts directed him to secure a crucial point on the road to Iringa, the ferry over the Ruaha River at Rukwa. Elements of Van Deventer's force occupied the crossing on 27 September. The northern and southern armies achieved contact on 9 October. Nevertheless, Wahle's forces in the west and Major Georg Kraut's forces in the east converging on Iringa threatened Northey.[122] He telegraphed on 1 October that his position was critical should he not receive reinforcements from the north destined for Iringa or Muhenge. Smuts had no option but to decline and recommended retreat if necessary. However, Northey decided to make a stand at Iringa.[123]

The scarcity of supplies was one of the factors preventing reinforcement reaching Northey. Limited transport was only able to support the 2nd Division where it stood. The area around Iringa was fertile, and the possibility existed that Northey could supply reinforcements locally on arrival. On that basis, Smuts was prepared to send Northey a battalion and a further battalion to bolster him in Nyasaland.[124] The first encounter with the Germans who were heading for Iringa was on 12 October when elements of Van Deventer's forces met Wahle's vanguard in a short and sharp action. German prisoners revealed that six or seven companies with three or four guns were advancing to capture Iringa. Northey's promised reinforcements were slowly making their way to Iringa under challenging circumstances, leaving him with the prospect of having to defend the town alone. The Germans cut the telegraph line to Iringa on 22 October, and skirmishes soon took place to the south of the position. South African reinforcements began to arrive at Iringa on 23 and 25 October and a South African mounted detachment engaged the Germans 18 kilometres to the north of Iringa.[125] Prompt South African intervention had secured Northey's safety for the moment.

Last Throw of the Dice: Smuts's Advance from Mageta to the Rufiji

The *Schutztruppen* were defending the Mageta River after having abandoning Kisaki on 14 September 1916. The two sides faced each other for the remainder of the period until the end of the year. Both sides were immobile and exhausted after their exertions thus far in the campaign. The intensity of the conflict had degenerated into artillery duels and skirmishes between the two exhausted sides.[126] Beyond the Mageta was an inhospitable land covered in tropical bush, further riddled with disease, and possessing little infrastructure. A small complement of eight companies of *Schutztruppen*, comprising 100 Germans and 700 askari defended the position.[127] Facing the Germans was a force of 6,250 men, 52 machine guns, and 25 artillery pieces assembled under Smuts.[128] Such an overwhelming numerical advantage was no guarantee for success: the entire operation depended on the weather and terrain and its concomitant effects on logistics. Moreover, the terrain beyond the Mageta River could only support mules and carriers as no established road network existed.[129]

Smuts's plan was simple and pandered to his penchant for manoeuvre. He aimed to surround the defenders holding the Mageta line and swiftly establish a bridgehead across the Rufiji River. Once he had secured a bridgehead on the Rufiji, he would make an all-out effort to join Hoskins's forces advancing from their landings at Kilwa, hopefully cutting off Lettow-Vorbeck's route of retreat further into the interior.[130] Strachan describes Smuts's optimistic plan as "ridiculously ambitious, making more sense on the map than it did on the ground".[131] Beves, Brigadier-General S.H. Sheppard (1st East African Brigade), Brigadier-General F.H.G. Cunliffe (Nigerian Brigade) ,and Colonel Lyle (a mixed brigade of Nigerians and Kashmiris) formed the four columns that would advance and envelop the defenders on the Mageta and arrive at the Rufiji. The operation set to commence on 25 December was delayed to 1 January 1917 due to torrential rains.[132]

The attackers advanced rapidly, taking the defenders by surprise in many areas. Beves with his western column earmarked to cross the Rufiji as rapidly as possible, covered 48 kilometres in 24 hours, arriving at his objective at dawn on 3 January 1917.[133] The entire Cape Corps crossed the river the next day.[134] Sheppard and Lyall on the east flank stalled when they encountered thick, difficult country.[135] Beves established a firm crossing over the Rufiji on 4 January, and the possibility of a bold move by advancing to Kibambawe and cutting off the German forces retreating to the north of him existed. Beves's reason for not doing so was because the "situation was obscure". The country in front of him was difficult, unreconnoitred, and imperfectly mapped. The position of the Germans and their movements was uncertain. Vague intelligence spoke of German reinforcements from the south, and he felt it was more important to secure his crossing than risk adventures further afield. Beves stuck to his instructions and waited for orders before venturing forth from the bridgehead. However, no orders were forthcoming![136] Bolder action in undertaking his own reconnaissance and boldly advancing would have delivered a significant victory. This was a missed opportunity where Smuts, leading from the front might have added significant impetus to the operation. (See Map 7.8)

Sheppard, advancing at a more leisurely pace on the eastern flank, reached the Rufiji at Kibambawe on 5 January only to find that the Germans had destroyed the bridge. Along the way, they suffered a famous casualty when 65-year-old Captain Frederick Selous died in action on 4 January.[137] Unperturbed, Sheppard crossed the 800-metre-wide river undetected on the night of 5 January, using boats and remaining undetected by the enemy. Smuts, true to his penchant for the frontline, paid a visit to Kibambawe on 6 January, where he urged for the crossings to continue. Now fully alerted to the crossing, the Germans launched a vigorous counterattack the next day, inflicting many casualties on the Punjabis holding the position. Beves resumed his advance from his bridgehead in the interim, reaching Luhembero just eight kilometres to the south of Kibambawe in the rear of the Germans attacking Sheppard.[138] Smuts had gained his bridgehead over the Rufiji River in a rapid battle of tactical envelopment. (See Map 7.8)

However, any hope of sustaining three brigades across the Rufiji and advancing to meet Hoskins quickly dissipated when disease and poor logistics put paid to ambitious intentions once again.[139] Transport columns could no longer cope with the supply requirements as drivers succumbed to sickness and vehicles broke down in the rugged terrain. The poor state of logistics could no longer support an advance by the entire force into the interior. Smuts's administrative staff presented this unpalatable conclusion to him on 9 January in a detailed memorandum urging for troop reduction in the forward area. A needed reduction in strength by the poor supply situation dealt a fatal blow to any pursuit of a decisive result in the operation.[140] It seems incredible that Smuts's staff were unable to warn him of the logistical constraints prior to undertaking the operation, but instead served a report at the height of the operation. Once again, the ravages of disease and a poor medical and logistical system not up to the task put paid to Smuts's ambitious plans.

Smuts had fulfilled most of his primary objective in his double tactical envelopment of the *Schutztruppen* in securing a bridgehead over the Rufiji. The operation had dislodged the enemy from his prepared defences, but they were swift enough in retreat to avoid being encircled and cut off completely. Smuts also had an operational envelopment in mind where he considered that the garrison at Kilwa would advance toward his bridgehead on the Rufiji. The commander at Kilwa, Brigadier-General J.A. Hannyngton, instituted a forward movement on 10 October with the full intention of rapidly gaining ground toward the Rufiji and meeting up with Smuts's advancing forces. As a consequence of Smuts visiting Kilwa on 31 October 1916, he appointed Hoskins

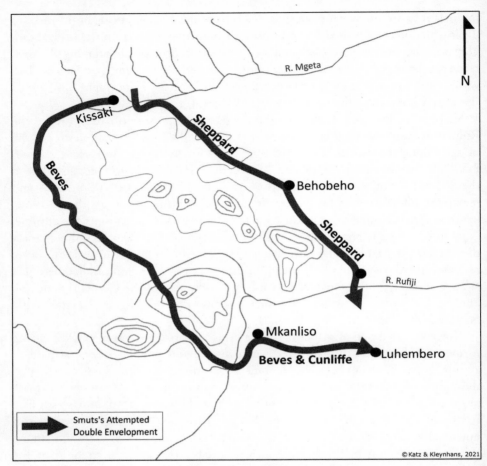

Map 7.8. The battle for the Mgeta–Rufiji gap

to command the eventual advance from Kilwa. Hoskins withstood several German attacks until that December.[141] Any hopes Smuts had possessed to press Lettow-Vorbeck further with a Portuguese invasion from northern Mozambique collapsed when the Germans routed the Portuguese, dispatching them back across the border in November/December. They would play no further role in Smuts's offensive.[142]

The advance to the Rufiji marked the end of Smuts's service in Africa. The British called on him to represent the Union of South Africa at the Imperial Conference to be held in London in 1917. The telegram from Lord Derby included:

> I cannot but regret that you should have to leave East Africa before the conclusion of the campaign in which you are now engaged, but I fully realise the larger issues at stake and your very great value of your presence at the conference.[143]

The British official history fairly sums up Smut's period of command in East Africa 1916. The conflict which the South Africans arrived at, fresh from their success in GSWA, was quite different to that which they had encountered before:

> The year of Lieut-General Smuts's command was to prove a period of long, arduous, and unsuccessful pursuit of an elusive enemy of a quality and determination no lower than his own, and was to teach lessons in tropical African warfare such as certainly had not been foreseen.[144]

Smuts formally handed over his command to Hoskins on 8 January 1917. Van Deventer and all the South Africans under him were ordered back to the Union for health reasons. The handover was effected on 17 January, and Smuts sailed from Dar es Salaam on 20 January 1917. It was almost 11 months since he had taken command of East Africa.[145]

CHAPTER 8

Epilogue: Smuts on the World Stage, 1917–1919

Jan Smuts, having crossed the political Rubicon in 1914 when he nailed his colours firmly to the imperial mast, now ended his active military service when he crossed the Rufiji River in German East Africa in December 1916. The powers recalled him to attend the Imperial War Conference (IWC) of 1917 in London on behalf of Louis Botha who was unable to leave South Africa.[1] However, as homesick as he was, he was tempted to stay in GEA to try and eliminate the Schutztruppe completely. Letters to his wife revealed that his mind was never far away from the dream of a Greater South Africa even while suffering under the stress of a difficult terrain.[2] He expressed frustration and felt this was "a great nuisance" for he would have to leave his work in GEA unfinished but that he had little choice. Furthermore, he was none too keen on the new British government under the Prime Minister David Lloyd George (1863–1945), and he particularly disliked his old adversary Alfred Milner ("the half German"), and Lord George Curzon (1858–1925), Leader of the House of Lords.[3] Although reluctant, he expected to attend the conference and return to South Africa by April or May. Bill Nasson's contention that Smuts was "lured away at the end of 1916 to join the Imperial War Cabinet", suggests more than was most probably on the cards.[4]

Ross Anderson paints a fanciful picture of a rather relieved Smuts being presented with a face-saving opportunity of leaving a far-from-settled conflict to beat a hasty retreat to London.[5] However, long before Anderson, it was the pen of H.C. Armstrong which set the tone that inspired the narrative of several contemporary historians. Armstrong, without a jot of evidence, creates the scene after Botha nominated Smuts to proceed to London:

> But Smuts might like to go. Smuts liked that sort of thing and it would be quite a good thing if someone else took over German East Africa: Smuts needed a holiday: the criticism of his handling the campaign was increasing. Smuts accepted without hesitation. He had had enough of German East [Africa].[6]

Hancock refutes the British historians' depiction of Smuts grabbing an opportunity to evacuate his position in GEA when he categorically states the case that Smuts was reluctant and showed no eagerness to go and in fact implored Botha to go there himself.[7]

Hew Strachan concedes that Smuts's GEA campaign was successful in terms of South Africa's war aims which were purely territorial. However, he criticises Smuts for continuously anticipating a short campaign, reporting great successes, and misleading the British by stating that the war in GEA was all but over. He accuses Smuts of a great fiction by depicting the campaign as a great South African feat of arms. In conquering four-fifths of the territory and nine-tenths of its infrastructure he had fought the war more as a politician than as a general: "Smuts had served the cause of imperialism rather than the Entente's war effort."[8] However, in imperial strategic terms his efforts were no small feat. For those who bothered to notice, he had delivered the life-long passion of Rhodes, and in conquering GEA he enabled a contiguous British Empire from Cape to Cairo. According to Leo Amery (1873–1955), the war cabinet secretary in Lloyd George's coalition government, the elimination of the German colonial empire and the securing of continuity of territory in East Africa was a legitimate British war aim too.[9]

Smuts's reluctance to attend the IWC went beyond sheer war weariness from his long and arduous campaign in GEA, and several bouts of malaria. South Africa's sovereignty was at threat due to the presence of certain members of the new Lloyd George Cabinet. Members of the Round Table (RT) (Milner's 'Kindergarten' in its latest guise) were pushing for an imperial federation agenda for fear of the disintegration of the British Empire.[10] The ultimate object of the Round Table was the creation of "an Imperial government constitutionally responsible to all the electors of the Empire, and with power to act directly on the individual citizens".[11] The proposed centralisation of power via some type of super-government was seen by some as a direct threat to the aspirations of the dominions who naturally sought greater independence in formulating their home and foreign policy. The First World War accelerated the nationalist desire within the dominions, and they became more self-assertive with the passing of every year of the war. Within the Round Table Lionel Curtis remained the sole dedicated proponent of federalism by 1916; he published *The Problem of the Commonwealth* in May 1916 as its sole author. Other members of the RT put all their efforts into bringing about the wartime imperial conference. Smuts effectively ruled out the federal solution and his pronouncements at a parliamentary banquet in his honour finally sealed the fate of the federalists.[12]

His speech reclaimed his concept of 'Commonwealth' that had been purloined by the Round Table for the purposes of their federalist agenda. He demolished the RT concept of the empire being one state. He believed that the British Empire was much more than a state.

> We are a system of nations. We are not a State, but a community of States and nations. We are far greater than any empire that has ever existed, and by using this ancient expression we really disguise the main fact that our whole position is different, and that we are not one State or

nation or empire, but a whole world by ourselves, consisting of many nations, of many States, and all sorts of communities, under one flag.[13]

He debunked the concept of a federal super-government, similar to the USA as an endeavour to create one nation, as an exercise in assimilation and an attempt to force its citizens into one mould. He envisaged that the Commonwealth would be something different where individual nations and communities would develop freely on the principles of self-government. Smuts saw each individual nation's culture, language, and religion safe and secure under the British flag, bound together by an allegiance to the British monarchy. Finally, he touted the idea of an annual Imperial Cabinet gathering which would formulate Commonwealth and foreign policy, which would be executed by the British government as the senior partner.[14] Responding to Smuts's speech, Lewis Harcourt wrote gleefully that "tonight was the funeral of the Round Table".[15]

Smuts also took the opportunity to explain the significance of the 'sideshow' campaigns that had been waged in the shadow of the greater catastrophe taking place on the Western Front. He would not have missed the significance of the event or the fact that he alone had relieved Germany of the greater portion of its overseas assets in the form of GSWA and GEA. He explained that Germany, prior to the war, had placed itself alongside the British communication lines via its colonies or settlements. The war had presented an opportunity to rid Germany of all its overseas assets, including its fleet, and when the time came, the United Kingdom was positioned to retain that territory which it deemed crucial to the safety and security of the empire.[16]

The Imperial War Conference, 1917

The Imperial War Conference of 20 March to 27 April 1917, dealing with the governance of the British Empire, was a series of meetings which were held concurrently with the Imperial War Cabinet on alternate days.[17] It was created in recognition of the valuable contribution of the dominions to the war effort and the need to consult with them on the conduct of the war.[18] Lloyd George felt that the time had come when the dominions ought to be consulted as to the progress and course of the war and the steps to be taken to secure victory.[19] The War Cabinet meeting, consisting of the British Cabinet and the representatives of the dominions and India, met to decide on executive measures for the conduct of the war. The IWC was presided over by Secretary of State for the Colonies, Walter Long (who succeeded Bonar Law on 10 December 1916), to discuss issues which either arose out of the war or had been accentuated by it.[20] (See Figure 8.1) This Cabinet had the power to take decisions and to give effect to them and had as its purpose the correct utilisation of the vast resources of the Empire to bring about a victorious end to the war.[21]

If Smuts had misgivings about Lloyd George, this was not reciprocated in the opinion that the latter had of the former Boer general:

> South Africa was represented by General Smuts, the gifted and versatile Dutchman. He had made a study of war and had no mean experience of it. He had just conducted a successful campaign in the vast jungles of tropical Africa, where he fought the most resourceful of all the German Generals von Lettow-Vorbeck. Smuts is one of the most remarkable personalities of his time. He is that fine blend of intellect and human sympathy which constitutes the understanding man. Although he had proved his courage in many enterprises which demanded personal valour, and although he had shown his powers in many a fight which had called for combative qualities, his sympathies were too broad to make of him a mere fighting man. His rare gifts of mind and heart strengthened those finer elements which are apt to be overwhelmed in an hour of savage temper and pitiless carnage. Of his practical contribution to our counsels during these trying years, it is difficult to speak too highly.[22]

Lloyd George considered Smuts to be essential in the task of Empire, especially in the troubled times of a destructive war. His presence, with the other participants, gave confidence to the proceedings even in the most depressing moments. Lloyd George looked upon Smuts and the other delegates as men whose minds were not "slated and stunted by years of thinking and toiling in departmental dug-outs and deep trenches". Their brains were fresh and untrammelled, and he hoped that their participation would have an "an invigorating and emancipating effect on our worn nerves and shackled minds".[23]

Lloyd George set the agenda by asking participants to enter a frank discussion as to the peace terms that would be satisfactory and beneficial to the Empire. He considered that an identification at this stage of the essentials of any satisfactory peace would give direction to the scope of the war effort needed. He set out the minimum requirements or preconditions for a peace conference. The Germans would have to vacate all the territories that they had overrun and offer compensation for the massive destruction wrought by German occupation. He fully expected that the map of Europe would have to be adjusted to take care of national aspirations and democratic freedom. He also sought the democratisation of Europe as a guarantee against future aggression by military autocrats. He spent much time in discussing the dissolution of the Turkish Empire who "have been ruling, or rather misruling, the most fertile and the most favoured lands in the world".[24] He was determined to elevate the Turkish question as an important war aim in order to "restore these famous territories to the splendour they enjoyed in the past, and to enable them once more to make their contribution to the happiness and prosperity of the world".[25]

If Smuts sought any comfort on the status of the conquered German colonies, not much emerged from Lloyd George's opening statement to the conference. He linked the final outcome of dominions over the former German colonies to the extent of the successful outcome of the war in Europe. He emphasised that partial success would put the Empire's desire for territorial possession under the spotlight as the alliance partners could not be expected to bear the brunt of the war while the Empire enjoyed an advantage in its outcome. Therefore, South Africa's wartime territorial acquisitions were not a fait accompli and the outcome depended on a favourable peace settlement.[26] During the course of the conferences, two committees were set up to deal with the territorial and non-territorial desiderata under Curzon and Milner respectively. Curzon's committee concluded that as far as the British Empire was concerned, any territorial settlement after the war must leave in British hands the German colonies and Turkish territory conquered.[27]

Amery was also prone to whispering into Lloyd George's ear on the occasion as to the importance the German colonies for the dominions.[28] This was the first time that such a demand had been formulated and this was mainly due to the instance of the dominion representatives present. A cautionary note was struck that if the Central Powers held Allied territory at the time of negotiation, this might have to be traded for territory held by the British to gain satisfactory conditions for all the Allies. The Imperial War Cabinet decided to treat the recommendations as objectives rather than definite instructions in any future negotiation, taking into consideration the demands of the other Allied nations.[29] Amery was able to report that Lloyd George seemed to have turned the corner on the colonies at a secret meeting with Churchill on 10 May 1917 where he was insistent that neither the German Colonies nor Palestine or Mesopotamia would be given back.[30]

One of the first to welcome Smuts to London was his old adversary Milner who was keen engage and introduce Smuts to other members of the Kindergarten.[31] Smuts and Milner, once bitter adversaries were seen "hobnobbing like the best of old friends".[32] Lloyd George had effectively seized power from Prime Minister Herbert Henry Asquith (1852–1928), with the support of Bonar Law (1858–1923), the Colonial Secretary, and other Conservatives in the cabinet who had lost faith in Asquith's ability to win the war. Lloyd George was open to other ideas on how to win the war beside those already unsuccessfully employed on the Western Front. There was also the question of strategic emphasis that would ensnare Smuts, who eventually threw in his lot with the 'Easterners' who favoured a strategic approach of winning the war by concentrating on removing Germany's allies from the war. This contrasted with the 'Westerners' who sought a decisive victory in France and saw all other fronts as secondary.[33]

Smuts was rapturously received in the United Kingdom by all and sundry, from politicians, industrialists, and clergy to the general population, starved of heroes and victories. Perhaps caught up in the moment and sensing the need for some good news in a dire war that had delivered only disappointment, he prematurely announced, "The campaign in German East Africa may be said to be over."[34] He was flooded with invitations and honours from notable people and institutions from all walks of British society. The British were seduced by a former enemy, who had become the fiercest defender of the imperial idea and who had delivered two clear conquests—GSWA and GEA—in a costly war that had delivered nothing more than carnage and stalemate thus far.

Figure 8.1. Group photograph of the IWC members taken in the garden of No. 10 Downing Street (Smuts bottom right). (IWM HU 81394)[35]

The War Cabinet

Smuts made a deep and lasting impression not only on his colleagues at the conference but on the British nation as well. He was encouraged to stay in the United Kingdom once the conference had ended.[36] However, according to Amery, Smuts had a "very good grip of things" and felt he could make a decisive contribution to the war effort if given a definite job. Amery felt that the War Cabinet was a bit unwieldy and that although it had managed to coordinate a general policy, it was incapable of dealing with strategy. He suggested a small committee consisting of the First Sea Lord, the Chief of Staff, Milner, and Smuts. Amery felt that Smuts and Milner were suitably qualified to effectively cross-examine the experts.[37] At this early stage Amery felt that including him in the War Cabinet would offend the other dominions.[38] He was needed there to assist at the helm of the war effort after his energetic contribution to the various committees and his obvious influence on policy and strategy. He was appointed to the British Cabinet for the remainder of the war and was involved with war direction.[39]

There was a need to determine the line the British representatives should take at the Paris Conference set down for the 4 May 1917. Smuts was tasked with ascertaining the exact French position so that the War Cabinet could determine a framework prior to the Paris Conference.[40] The result of the April visit was a document by Smuts titled, *The General and Military Situation and Particularly that on the Western Front*. In reading the document it is profitable to be aware of the contested strategy of the 'Westerners' and 'Easterners'. Smuts called for a congruency of "essential minimum war aims" and the victory considered necessary to achieve them. A consensus on these war aims had only emerged recently as a result of the Imperial War Conference. These war aims had been reduced to the destruction of the German colonial system, the dismembering of the Turkish Empire, the restoration of territory belonging to Belgium, France, Serbia, Montenegro, Rumania and some form of compensation, and a settlement that would limit or destroy the military predominance of the Germanic powers.

Smuts pointed out that the German colonial system had already been destroyed and he was at pains to stress the enormous value of this endeavour to the security of the vital communications of the Empire and that this should not be endangered at peace negotiations. He identified that a pure military solution on the Western Front seemed to be impossible under the present military circumstances. However, a measure of military success was needed to bring the Central Powers to the negotiating table. He singled out the Salonika campaign, which had failed in its original intentions, as being the least promising of all the overseas operations and especially taxing on shipping assets. In talks with Amery, Smuts suggested that if the French wanted a free hand in Greece, the British should withdraw some divisions there and send them to Palestine.[41] The Allied effort in the Balkans should either be massively bolstered to detach Bulgaria from the Central Powers, or failing that, the Allies should retire from this unprofitable front. Positions in Mesopotamia region should be consolidated, and the territory conquered defended. When it came to Palestine Smuts saw interesting political and military possibilities. Salonika should be abandoned for this front and as the Allied threat progressed toward Jerusalem and Damascus, the Turkish Empire would come under grave threat. Smuts identified this front as being second in importance only to the Western Front. He expressed his confidence that the shipping used for East Africa would soon be available for this campaign.

He considered that the Western Front had become a considerable misfortune in occupying the bulk of French and British forces on ground of Germany's choosing. The two most important armies of the Entente were locked up in a war of attrition against impregnable positions. He had no confidence that the Allies could break through the German lines on any large scale. The British Army and a large part of its war effort had become mired in an unwinnable and costly war of attrition to the extent that the British had no strategic reserve remaining uncommitted to talk of. The strategic reserve was crucial to provide against "surprises and accidents" and take advantage of opportunities. The Germans, on the other hand, possessed a huge strategic reserve that they were able to pit anywhere in Europe to tip the balance. The British had assumed more and more of the responsibility and burden from the French as the war dragged on. Smuts called for the reestablishment of a strategic reserve on the Western Front.[42]

Smuts considered that the biggest danger on the Western Front resided in a French strategy that embraced a defensive stance in facing the Germans. Several important members of the French government did not approve of the offensive being conducted by General Robert Nivelle's (1856–1924), the Commander-in-Chief of the French Army. Smuts considered this defensive policy to be tantamount to a German victory and, coupled with the U-boat campaign and the fact that the Germans held large swathes of Allied European territory, it would serve to demoralise the Entente allies. Certain French military and political sections where prepared to adopt a defensive posture until such time as the Americans arrived on the battlefield to tip the balance. As Lloyd George put it, "General Smuts was very insistent on the moral aspect of the question." Abandoning the offensive would be a fatal mistake.[43]

Smuts felt so strongly against adopting a defensive posture that he suggested the French, in the event, should take over the manning of significant portions of the British line so that a large British offensive reserve could be assembled. This reserve would be applied in offensive operations to free up the Belgium coast, freeing up Zeebrugge and Ostend, and deprive the enemy of two important submarine bases. This proposal seems to have been inspired by Field Marshal Douglas Haig (1861–1928), commander of the British Expeditionary Force, who managed to brief Smuts before his departure for France.[44] Smuts felt that an offensive in Belgium would yield more than the current French offensive which at best would free up some French territory and provide a further incentive for them to assume the defensive. Smuts felt that Russian and French inactivity would spell disaster in a situation that was already precarious.[45]

Lloyd George was sceptical of attrition-type offensives on the Western Front that lacked imagination and were hell bent of exhausting the enemy reserves. Lloyd George was a firm believer in seeking opportunities for ending the war in other sectors. In this Smuts, with considerable support of the War Cabinet, was opposed. The failure of the Nivelle offensive coupled with high French casualties led to mutinies and the dismissal of Nivelle. Marshal Philippe Pétain replaced Nivelle and the adopted a defensive strategy while the French armies recuperated and rearmed. Smuts may have not been so keen on continuing the offensive had he known of the poor morale of the French army at that stage.[46]

Smuts's considerable stature amongst the British was put to good use in October 1917 by Lloyd George who asked him to address anti-war miners in South Wales. The miners were an important source for recruitment to the army and vital to the war economy. Strikes were threatening to cripple the war effort and sow pacifist discord in an important recruitment pool. Smuts had previously managed to settle a police strike in London and a strike by 50,000 munition workers in Coventry and had gained quite a reputation in these matters.[47] Smuts proceeded to the coalfields in the afternoon after receiving a doctorate from Cardiff University. Following the advice of Lloyd George, he kept in mind his advice that the Welsh were great singers, as his motorcade made its way through the striking mobs. He stopped along the way often to make little speeches and eventually arrived at the head of the crowd and prepared to address them in an extremely tense atmosphere:

> Gentlemen, I come from far away as you know. I do not belong to this country. I have come a long way to do my bit in this war, and I am going to talk to you to-night about this trouble. But I have heard in my country that the Welsh are among the greatest singers in the world, and before I start, I want you first of all to sing to me some of the songs of your people.[48]

Smuts had managed to disarm and charm the crowd with his simple manner and their intrigue for the first statesman that they had seen from Africa. At first a lone voice began 'Land of our Fathers' and then the entire crowd joined in with fervour. When the crowd fell silent Smuts delivered:

> Well, Gentlemen It is not necessary for me to say much here to-night. You know what has happened on the Western Front. You know your comrades in their tens of thousands are risking their lives. You know that the Front is not only in France, but that the Front is just as much here as anywhere else. The trenches are in Tonypandy, and I am sure you are actuated by the same spirit as your comrades over in France. It is not necessary for me to add anything. You know it as well as I do, and I am sure that you are going to defend the Land of your Fathers of which you have sung here to-night, and that you will defend it to the uttermost and that no trouble you may have with the Government about pay or anything else will ever stand in the way of your defence of the Land of your Fathers.[49]

This settled the matter for the moment and the men were back at work the next day. This was but one of the many strike incidents that aggravated Britain's manpower difficulties and especially in 1917. The slaughter at Passchendaele and persistent labour unrest proved a considerable drain on manpower availability for the war effort.[50]

The year 1917 proved to be one of immense difficulty and disappointment for the Allies on the battlefields of Europe. The Nivelle offensive had failed and resulted in the mutiny of French troops. The British, insistent on offensive operations, had fared no better with the carnage suffered and inflicted at Passchendaele (Third Battle of Ypres) between July and November 1917. Caporetto in Italy fought during October/November 1917 registered yet another Allied disaster. The Westerners, including Smuts, had placed their faith and resources in a decisive campaign on the Western Front to no avail. Certain amongst the Easterners, including Lloyd George, believed that opportunities for decisive victory lay in knocking Turkey out of the war and controlling the Balkans. In fact, Lloyd George lamented the fact that an opportunity to overwhelm Turkey was missed in 1915 in an ill-fated campaign which would have freed up many Allied troops for cooperative offensive action with the Russians and

Rumanians deep into the Austro- Hungarian flank.[51] Lloyd George faced considerable opposition from the Westerners who felt that valuable resources applied to a 'sideshow' such as Egypt would detract from the efforts on the Western Front.

Smuts and the Offer of the Egyptian Command

Prior to the Western Front setbacks, on 23 April 1917, the War Cabinet, with the support of Edward Stanley (the Earl of Derby), the Secretary of State for War, and Field Marshal Sir William Robert Robertson (CIGS), decided that more resolute leadership needed to be injected into the command of the Egyptian Expeditionary Force. Smuts, who had stressed the strategic value of Palestine, seemed to be the ideal candidate to replace Sir Archibald Murray the Commander-in-Chief of the Egyptian Expeditionary Force, who had lost the confidence of Lloyd George by failing to capture Gaza in April 1917.[52] Lloyd George saw in Smuts a refreshing amateur military ability in contrast to the staid British military professionals who were operationally unimaginative and strategically myopic in subordinating the war effort to the quagmire of the Western Front. Lloyd George asked Smuts on 2 May 1917 to stay on in London and to undertake the High Command in Palestine.

> General Smuts was a standing disproof of the theory tenaciously held by the British War Office (despite the classic example of Oliver Cromwell to the contrary) that no one was competent to hold high military command without long training in the regular army. The career of General Smuts furnishes a practical demonstration of the absurdity. He was a lawyer by profession. But in the Boer War he was able with untrained troops to hold at bay for years the best military brains that our War Office could find to put against him, with the resources of the Empire behind them. In British East Africa he showed himself a brilliantly efficient, resourceful and energetic Commander-in-Chief of our forces. Had he consented to take in hand the Palestine campaign, I have not the least doubt that it would, under his charge, have been one of our most successful efforts.[53]

The idea of Smuts taking command in Egypt was not a new one and it seems Leo Amery[54] first raised the question directly in a letter to Smuts on 15 March 1917 in which he spoke of Smut's experience in mobile warfare and a mind free of trench warfare.[55] According to Lloyd George the enthusiasm for Smuts taking command extended through the entire War Cabinet although there was an equal amount of support for him being retained in a central position to allow for his utilisation in the higher conduct of the war.

Smuts was reluctant to accept the position unless the campaign was going to be treated as a first-class operation and not a sideshow by the War Office.[56] Smuts also sought the advice of Botha and his wife Isie on the matter.[57] In seeking Botha's advice there was a certain hesitancy by Smuts in accepting the position: "However, much I wish to do my duty South Africa comes first and I fear to do anything that would make matters difficult for you and injure my future and usefulness to my country."[58] Botha assured Smuts that he considered the offer to be a great honour for South Africa.

Botha advised that Smuts's acceptance of the command should be based on the scale of the operation and that should it be on a large scale it would be difficult to refuse. He also assured him of the security of his position back home and his continuance as a Minister without Portfolio until his return to South Africa where he would once again be offered a portfolio.[59] Smuts in reply assured Botha that he would not accept the command unless it was a "first class campaign in me and guns". He also mentioned the fact that there were strong moves to include him in the War Cabinet but that he would refuse the position due to the jealousy of the other dominions.[60]

Smuts consulted with Robertson, who dissuaded him from accepting the position based on the possibility that it might be treated as a first-class operation. Robertson was certainly not alone and was flatly opposed to Lloyd George's view that the war could be won on a front other than the Western Front. He saw Palestine as a mere sideshow and that any success Smuts achieved there would not alter the course of the war.[61] It seems that Robertson had withdrawn his support at the last moment after Smuts had secured it and that of Lloyd George a few days before and was fully prepared to go.[62] However, there seemed to be a change of heart by Robertson soon afterwards which Amery puts down to the rapidly deteriorating situation in Russia and Robertson's fears of complicating the situation in Salonika.[63]

Smuts realised that he would not have the full support of the War Office in his Palestine endeavour and without the necessary men and material he would be caught in a difficult situation. He was keen on a campaign in Turkey should efforts on the Western Front fail. He opposed Lloyd George's idea of attacking Austria through Italy and he saw little chance of success in detaching Austria. The Italian demands on Austrian territory guaranteed that Austria would remain in the war. A successful Turkish option promised to deliver the Dardanelles, keep Russia in the war and coerce Bulgaria out. No matter Lloyd George or Smuts's enthusiasm for the venture, it was impossible to convince the Westerners that these operations could amount to anything more than a sideshow.[64]

Smuts doubted that Lloyd George would be able to overcome the resistance of the War Office and as a result he would face the risk of being abandoned in Palestine. He reluctantly declined the offer on 31 May although he saw the potential of opening the Palestine Front and ending the war early:[65]

> The most careful consideration has only strengthened my first impression that the Palestine campaign will be a mistake unless at least the capture of Jerusalem is made a reasonable certainty, and all the reinforcements necessary for that purpose are assured. A limited advance, which stopped short of the capture of Jerusalem, would serve no particular purpose, and might easily be a disappointment to the public and appear as a fresh failure …[66]

Lloyd George undeterred by Smuts's rejection of the Palestine command, installed Smuts as a member of the War Cabinet. This was met with indignant protests in some quarters although it met with general approval.[67] The Colonial Secretary, Walter Long, protested that Smuts should only join for military questions and that this could be facilitated with membership of the Imperial General War Staff restricting his say on general matters concerning the dominions. However, Frederick Scott Oliver (1864–1934), a prominent Scottish political writer and a member of the Round Table,[68] was to write:

> I regard the taking in of Smuts to the War Cabinet as a most important step. So far as pure intellect goes he is the superior of any member at present on it; and by intellect I don't mean merely the power of understanding what is written ... but that curious and most rare quality of seeing into the very heart of a subject, coupled with the further and still rarer quality, in combination with the foregoing of being able to state clearly what he has seen ...[69]

If contemporary historians have expressed doubts and cast negative aspersions on Smuts's abilities as a general and a leader of men, then this must be weighed against the overwhelmingly positive opinions and confidence expressed by his peers, among whom were Botha, Lloyd George, Amery, Robertson, and several cabinet ministers.

In the meantime, following Smuts's refusal, General Edmund Allenby (1861–1936) was appointed to take Murray's place on 5 June 1917 as Commander-in-Chief of the British Forces in Egypt.[70] There remained much work for Smuts, 'the Handyman of the Empire' as he became known, as a member of the War Cabinet. He was asked to examine and report on questions of strategy and the overall direction of the war effort. His military work included visiting the various fronts to gain a first-hand impression of the battlefield and the challenges of the front. He was also engaged with social and political activities as well as issues of economic importance involving J.M. Keynes (1883–1946), the English economist, Henry Strakosch, and Thomas Lamont. His work gave him the opportunity to establish a lifelong friendship with Chaim Weizmann who invented a new simplified process for the manufacture of TNT. One of the many committees he served on was the Middle East Committee, presided over by Curzon, which assisted Allenby in his Turkish campaign.[71] The highly influential Alfred Harmsworth (Lord Northcliffe) who owned *The Times*, the *Daily Mail* and other newspapers, urged the British government to send Smuts on a special mission to the USA in order to clear up American suspicions on the effectiveness of the British war effort. He felt that Smuts carried sufficient stature in the USA as a military man, and a relative outsider to present the British case. In the event Smuts was indispensable to the War Cabinet and never made the trip.[72] However, it is instructional of the high regard he was held in certain influential circles.

Organisation of the War Effort and the Formation of the Royal Air Force

The eclectic nature to which the War Cabinet assigned Smuts various tasks is astounding. He turned down the leadership of a secret mission to Russia, believing Russia was a spent force. He was involved in the planning to protect Holland's neutrality should that be violated by Germany. As a member of the Northern Neutral Committee, chaired by Curzon, he concerned himself with the campaign in north-western Europe. He presided over numerous committees himself. He turned down the chair of the convention on Ireland, a meeting of rebels and loyalists, on the advice of Sir James Craig, later Lord Craigavon, who was a prominent Irish unionist politician, leader of the Ulster Unionist Party and the first Prime Minister of Northern Ireland. Lloyd George and Amery thought Smuts the ideal candidate to chair the convention, possessing the credentials of an old fighter against England which would win over Sinn Fein while appealing at the same time to the Unionists as a strong supporter of the United Kingdom.[73] The irony is that where his ambiguous politics proved useful to London, it sowed bitter dissent back home in South Africa. The myriad of post-war problems occupied a good proportion of his time as well as the groundwork for a league of nations. He delivered many stirring speeches which went a long way to galvanising the war effort and bolstering wavering spirits from all walks of British society.

Smuts seemed to thrive on the challenges presented to him as a British cabinet minister, far away from the divisive politics back in South Africa. He was able to tackle issues in London regarding the war effort and troubles on the British home front with an emotional detachment and a political neutrality that was just not possible in South Africa. He was also the only one on the Cabinet with military experience. Woodrow Wilson's special envoy, Colonel House, wrote of Smuts's wise and steady guidance and friendship amid the chaos of a disastrous conflict.

> He has grown to be the lion of the hour … He is one of the few men I have met in the Government who do not feel tired. He is alert, energetic and forceful.[74]

His versatility and energy knew no bounds and the War Cabinet used him for a great variety of purposes. Admiration for Smuts was not limited to the influential circles he frequented. F.S. Crafford puts it that the man in the street regarded him "as a counterpoise to elements it distrusted wholly". He goes on to say that during the dark days of 1917/18 the War Cabinet was not averse to sheltering behind the prestige of his name on several occasions.[75]

Smuts's finest work was reserved for the less prominent but equally important arrangements for coordinating and prioritising the various departments involved in the war effort. He came to realise that there was a massive wastage in effort, manpower, and resources due to the disharmonious relationship between the different departments concerned with allocating scarce resources to enable the British war machine. The demand for greater resources grew with Britain's increased commitment to the war as every month passed. The various departments acted independently of each other and guarded the resources under their control jealously acting as rivals to each other instead of a partnership of effort. The War Cabinet was the final arbitrator in ruling over disparate demands for the same scarce resources, but overloaded with work, it was hardly able to function adequately in this role. It was Smuts who suggested the establishment of a Priorities Committee and he was tasked to chair over its members, the Secretary of State for Air, the Secretary of State for War, the Minister of Munitions (Winston Churchill), the Minister of National Service, the Secretary of State for War, and the First Lord of the Admiralty. The War Priorities Committee was set up on 21 September 1917. Smuts's task was not a simple one, but he handled the committee deftly and with great success.[76]

German air raids over London had humble beginnings, the first of which took place on the night of 19/20 January 1915 with modest results. These early raids were mostly carried out by Zeppelins and the frequency and intensity gradually increased with the passing of time. There were a total of 20 raids in 1915, in which 37 tons of bombs were dropped, killing 181 and injuring 455. Aerial defences against Zeppelins were haphazard at best and divided between the Royal Navy Air Service (RNAS) and the Royal Flying Corps (RFC), with the navy engaging enemy airships approaching the coast while the RFC took responsibility once the enemy had crossed the coastline. As the frequency of the raids intensified, air defences were bolstered to meet the threat, resulting in 10 home defence squadrons being organised by February 1916. A 12-month campaign, beginning with a raid on Folkestone in May 1917, saw the enemy Gotha G.IV and R.VI Giant bombers conduct 52 raids across the country, killing 836 and wounding 1,982. The worst raid in terms of casualties took place on 13 June 1917 when 20 Gotha G.IV bombers attacked London: 162 were killed and 432 injured which included a number of children. The raids were having an adverse effect on the public morale and measures needed to be taken to restore confidence.

The problem with an effective air defence against the German air raids was the decentralised command and rivalry between the army and navy air arms which acted independently of each other. Attempts to coordinate the efforts of the army and navy through the creation of the joint Air War Committee in February 1916 came to naught and collaboration and cohesion were discarded in favour of looking after their own interests. The Admiralty demonstrated that it had no intention of allowing interference with the RNAS or its supplies. The committee had no executive power or authority and was not permitted to discuss any question of policy. Toothless and powerless in the face of two services that had their own organisations, esprit de corps, and aspirations, the committee soon collapsed with the resignations of its chairman Lord Derby and independent member Lord Montagu of Beaulieu.[77]

The military and naval air services were in competition with one another, and this extended into many spheres such as vying over the limited supply of aeroplane engines. Technical innovations, experiments, and improvements were not shared. The navy held the advantage as the senior service in attracting skills, and held a priority claim over scarce resources. Naval air missions were wedded to the needs of the navy as were the military ones wedded to the needs of the ground operations.

When it came to the defence of London against the German air raids, there was little consensus between the two arms as to how this was to be done. This resulted in the Germans being able to roam over Britain with impunity.

Curzon proposed the next step to set up a more authoritative body to improve the disjointed situation. After 21 months of the war British planes were inferior to the German rivals and they had all but lost their air superiority over the battlefields. Furthermore, each service conducted its own operations independent of each other without any intercommunication. The lack of co-operation had resulted in a competition over scarce resources and the rivalry was anything but healthy. Asquith decided to set up an Air Board in the teeth of objections and obstructions by Mr Balfour who represented the Admiralty. Curzon was appointed its chairman and it became operational on 17 May 1916, with two representatives each from the navy and army, an independent expert, and a parliamentary secretary. The committee was empowered to discuss and make representations to the Admiralty and the War Office in regard to air policy and combined operations. It was also authorised to coordinate the supply of material and the interchange of ideas and technical developments. It took nearly six months for the Air Board to issue its first report on 23 October 1916 in which it admitted the hopeless difficulties that it had encountered due to the obstinacy of the Admiralty, making any progress impossible. The Air Board's suggestion that it should take charge on behalf of both services, of invention, research, experiment, design, production, inspection, and finance, and finally production to be taken over by the Ministry of Munitions, was met with opposition by Balfour who wanted to control all these elements within the navy. After several meetings in November 1916 a set of draft conclusions emerged but had not been finally agreed upon when the resignation of Asquith overtook events.[78]

The proposals on the table were a considerable improvement on the disjointed efforts of the past. Its effect was to have the Air Board play a central role and act as an ombudsman between the naval and army services on matters of policy, production, and procurement. The Ministry of Munitions would undertake design in consultation with the ordering department, and all orders would be placed by the Air board on the Ministry of Munitions. On 19 January 191,7 the new chairman of the Air Board, Lord Weetman Cowdray, was able to report good progress in getting agreement as to the terms of the new dispensation. The new Air Board in its reconstituted format came into existence on 6 February 1917. The new format had streamlined design and production to a great extent but had not addressed a combined approach to the operational and strategic conduct of the air war. Such was the improvement of the new measures that monthly deliveries of aeroplane engines were two and a half times more than the same period in the previous year, becoming three and a half times more in the July–October 1917 period. Aircraft production had increased fourfold and was projected to be tenfold by the end of the year. However, none of these measures provided for an independent air fleet for home defence independent of the navy and army to meet the ever-increasing threat of enemy air raids over England.[79]

The inter-arm rivalry had been brought under control regarding design and production, so much so that there would soon be aircraft available in excess of the requirements of the navy and army, leaving scope for a home defence fleet. This occurred simultaneously with the government experiencing increasing pressure from all sides to put into place effective measures against the German raids. Lloyd George felt a need to examine the whole question of air power at another level over and above the measure already instituted:

> I felt that we must go far more thoroughly into the matter, with a view to ensuring the best possible use of the air weapon, alike for attack and for defence. It was a question that called for examination by a fresh and able mind, free from departmental prejudices. Fortunately such a mind was available. I asked General Smuts to investigate the problem of the air on behalf of the Cabinet.[80]

As a consequence of a secret session of the House of Commons and a resulting Cabinet meeting, a suitable solution to the problem of air power and home defence was left in the hands of Lloyd George and Smuts who were appointed reorganise the air forces, put in place a suitable air defence system, and expand the nation's air resources into an effective offensive weapon. This was to be done via a committee set up on 11 July 1917 chaired by Smuts and Lloyd George, and eventually Smuts alone when the Prime Minister backed out due to work pressure, leaving Smuts to complete this vital task.[81] The terms of reference were, "to examine (1) the defensive arrangements for Home Defence against Air Raids, and (2) the existing general organisation for the study and higher direction of aerial operations".[82]

Cowdray addressed Smuts via a memorandum on 28 July 1917 in which he stated the inevitability of an independent air service. However, he was of the view that this question was best dealt with after the war and that the Air Board should confine itself to supplying the army and navy with aircraft and controlling the distribution of aircraft to the two services. His concern was the opposition of the Admiralty to any scheme of creating an independent air service. Cowdray in seeking a permanent staff and more teeth regarding air policy for the Air Board had a view to changing the current disposition after the war but certainly maintaining the status quo during the conflict.

Lieutenant-General Sir David Henderson, the military member of the Air Board, had a different view from Cowdray and on the 19 July 1917 he submitted a memorandum clearly stating that the two air services should be combined under the control of a ministry with full administrative and executive powers. He was cognisant that the scheme would result in a temporary loss of efficiency but nevertheless pushed for the change. The official history observes the unique position of Smuts as being politically agnostic but militarily astute and "Those who came to confer with him were convinced that his one concern was to find an unprejudiced solution of the problem, and they believed that he would not make up his mind until after he had heard, and carefully weighed, every aspect. What is quite apparent is that Smuts, who was not an expert in air warfare consulted widely with experts before delivering his report.[83]

Smuts wasted no time in delivering a report to the War Cabinet on 19 July 1917 in which he addressed the defence of London. He considered homeland defence as being the more urgent and the question of creating a unified air force as being the more important. This first report dealt with home defence and the alacrity of its formulation gave testament to the grave political situation and drop in public morale brought about by the German air raids. The report identified London as an essential nerve centre and that its defence "demands exceptional measures". However, it identified the need not to prejudice operations on the various battlefields and seas and gave the fighting forces priority in this regard. The report went to great lengths in highlighting the failure to concentrate air and anti-aircraft guns against the German air formations, instead of attacking in uncoordinated penny packets.

Although the British had a numerical superiority for the purposes of home defence, they were not deployed, nor did they train to be deployed, in formation. Once airborne they did not fall under a unified command and therefore efforts to coordinate a defence fell short. London was defended by no less than four agencies, being the RNAS, RFC, Observation Corps and the anti-aircraft guns of London.[84] There was no lack of resources to meet the German air raids, but rather the problem consisted of coordinating the efforts of the four different authorities involved with air defence. The lack of organised cooperation, despite the ample availability of aircraft, ensured that the German air raids proceeded almost without serious air defence opposition. Smuts offered a simple solution, most probably influenced by Henderson, which was accepted by the War Cabinet: to institute a unified command under a first-class officer of all the home defence air fleets.[85] Available planes were combined into squadrons and properly trained to fight in formation. The air defence bubble, consisting of anti-aircraft guns and air formations, were pushed out so that German attackers were met before arriving over London. So effective were the new measures inspired by Smuts that daylight raids became too costly for the Germans and night raids became increasingly difficult.[86]

Smuts took a little longer in developing solutions to the more challenging question on air power and its ultimate organisation and direction. This was territory hotly contested by the navy and army and each had proved unwilling in the past to relinquish even a modicum of control of the assets under their command. Smuts considered the questions of the institution of an Air Ministry responsible for all air organisation and operations. He examined the possibility of a unified air service embracing the RNAS and RFC. He also examined the question of how the new air service would be able to continue to render the functions previously discharged by the RNAS and RFC in addition to new roles arising.[87] This resulted in a second and final report delivered on 17 August 1917 which contained an examination of the questions together with suitable recommendations. The official history describes this report as "the most important paper in the history of the creation of the Royal Air Force".[88] Although paying tribute to its predecessors in the form of the War Committee and Air Board, Smuts identified that the latter was really a conference rather than a board. It was a consultative association of representatives of the fighting services and the Ministry of Munitions without any technical and advisory personnel of its own. He correctly and importantly identified that the committee in this form could never formulate an independent air policy but only one subordinate to military and naval strategy.[89]

Smuts also identified that air power could be expressed as an independent means of war, and that aircraft could project the war beyond the frontlines into the heart of enemy civilian and industrial centres. This was not original thought by any means as much deliberation on the subject had already been done by the Italian Giulio Douhet (1869–1930). Douhet criticised the auxiliary use of airpower by the navy and army for reconnaissance and tactical reasons. He believed that an independent air service could be used as a full-fledged weapon of war. The effects of combat were no longer restricted to the frontlines because aircraft could fly over the lines of defence to reach targets within enemy territory. The persistent German air raids on London were proof that the age of the aeroplane as a strategic offensive weapon had arrived. Douhet advocated the use of explosive weapons, both incendiary and chemical, not only on military targets but also on the civilian population in order to affect morale and thereby reduce public support for the conflict.[90] Douhet's thinking had crystallised in the years 1911–15 long before Smuts had applied his mind to the possibilities of air power.

The War Cabinet decided on 24 August to accept Smuts's recommendations in principle that a separate service for the air be formed. The Air Organisation Committee, under Smuts, was appointed to investigate the details of the amalgamation and to prepare the draft legislation. Much depended on this committee to determine the shape and architecture of the Royal Air Force. The official history identifies Henderson as the "moving spirit" behind the activities of the committee: "Every member of the committee toiled at high pressure, but none more than Lieutenant-General Henderson, who held nothing back and whose energy burned like a flame when, as here, his heart and mind were engaged."[91] There are those who would deny or diminish the role of Smuts in the formation of the RAF and place all the accolades at Henderson's door. Doing so shows an ignorance of the levels of war, where it is apparent that Smuts was the facilitator at the strategic level and Henderson took care of the operational and tactical issues.

The opening of the German night campaign was a further cause of grave concern for the government. The War Cabinet lost no time, and, on the 5 September 1917, it requested Smuts to investigate these new raids and offer solutions as to the provision of protection of the civilian population and examine the feasibility of carrying the air war to Germany. Once again Smuts consulted the experts and with lightning speed delivered a paper to the War Cabinet on 6 September 1917. He quickly identified the impossibility of intercepting the enemy bombers at night with aircraft and he proposed that it would be more profitable to bomb the enemy airfields during the day whence the night bombers originated. The static defence could be greatly enhanced by utilising more searchlights and establishing a wire screen suspended from balloons.[92] None of the measures Smuts presented was new, but his value can be found in the expeditious and energetic manner he applied when coordinating measures that prior to his intervention had taken months to implement. Of immediate concern to the War Cabinet was the groundswell outcry for reprisals against Germany. There was much pressure on the government to launch a counterattack. It was felt that the press had engendered a feeling of insecurity in London.

War Weariness and Peace Feelers

Tentative efforts were in place towards the end of 1917 to bring the war to an end via peaceful means. Peace feelers emanated mainly from the Austrians and the Turks who were feeling the full effects of the tight Allied blockade, and in many instances, they struggled to feed sectors of the population and even the military. The Allies recognised an opportunity to detach the Austrians from the Germans. However, they were reluctant to enter premature peace negotiations directly with the Germans, having suffered a disastrous year which left the Germans in a strong military position. Russia was out of the war, Rumania defeated, the Flanders attacks beaten off and the Italian army routed. The submarine war was having a telling effect on merchant shipping and Germany was preparing for a massive offensive with the release of its divisions on the Eastern Front. Therefore, any peace efforts were directed toward prising away Germany's allies if that was at all possible.[93]

On 18 December 1917, Smuts became involved in a secret mission which amounted to an attempt by the British to detach Austria from Germany. The source of the peace initiative was Austria and Turkey who had conveyed through Switzerland that they were anxious to bring the war to an end. Smuts accompanied by Philip Kerr (Lord Lothian), private secretary to Prime Minister Lloyd George and a member of the Milner Kindergarten, travelled to Geneva on behalf of the War Cabinet to meet with Count Albert von Mensdorff-Pouilly-Dietrichstein. He was a highly regarded diplomat who, before the war, had been Austria's ambassador to London for 10 years, and during the war he was entrusted with sensitive diplomatic missions at various times aimed towards the restoration of peace. Smuts was clear that his mission was to assure the Austrians of the Allies full support in the event of them freeing " themselves from German domination and [making] a fresh start in sympathy with the British Empire". Smuts was also tasked with gathering as much information as possible without entering a discussion of general peace terms which included Germany.[94]

Smuts was sensitive to the issue of a separate peace and the pitfalls that might have transpired from any future suggestion that he had intrigued with the Austrians to bring it about. He need not have worried as any notion of a separate peace was dismissed in the strongest terms by Mensdorff before he could raise the subject. With the prospects of a separate peace out of the question, Smuts attempted to paint a picture of an alternative role that the Austrians could play in Central Europe if she discarded her subordinate role to Germany. Austria, with the backing of the Entente and a liberalisation of its subject people, could fill the power void vacated by Russia and become a counterbalance to Germany. The demise of Russia in the region opened opportunities for Austria to move closer to the Entente and disassociate itself from Germany. Mensdorff appreciated Smuts's assertions that the Allies did not seek the destruction of the Austrian Empire but would rather have them as part of the Entente and distanced from Germany. However, the prospects of a separate peace with Austria were off the table, and Smuts had to avoid Mensdorff's attempts to discuss general peace terms including Germany. At a parallel meeting with the Turks, Kerr also concluded that a separate peace with them was not possible at this juncture. However, the important point coming out of the meeting was that it was necessary for the British government to restate the terms on which it was prepared to make peace.[95]

This was not the end of Austrian peace overtures to the British and the next meeting took place in Switzerland in late February 1918 between Ottokar Czernin, Imperial Foreign Minister of Austria-Hungary, and representatives of the Foreign Office. The talks were inconclusive, and it was decided that Smuts and Kerr should once more go to Switzerland and meet with Czerin to ascertain the exact nature of the Austrian proposals. The meeting took place in Berne on 9 March 1918. Initial indications were that the Austrians had had a change of attitude and were indeed prepared to discuss a separate peace. However, Smuts soon realised that the original ardour for peace had waned somewhat due to the proximity of the German March offensive which promised much in the way of securing an advantage for the Central Powers. Once the German offensive on the Western Front was underway and early successes registered, all prospects of discussing peace disappeared.[96]

The treaty of Brest-Litovsk signed on 3 March 1918 between the new Bolshevik government of Russia and the Central Powers, ended Russia's participation in the First World War and freed up a massive contingent of reserves that the Germans could apply to the Western Front. This allowed the Germans one last throw of the dice on the Western Front before the impact of the American troop arrival in France would swing the balance in favour of the Allies. The German spring offensive, or *Kaiserschlacht* ('Kaiser's battle'), resulted in a series of German attacks along the Western Front beginning on 21 March 1918. Smuts played little role in what would become the Allies darkest hour of the war and much to his frustration he felt as if he was a mere spectator.[97] He felt that his proper place was on the firing line and on 8 June 1918 he offered to lead the Americans into battle—an offer Lloyd George deftly did not let go further than him.[98] Through a series of offensives, using Stormtrooper tactics, the Germans were able to regain a substantial part of the territory they had lost in 1916/17, causing much anxiety in the Allied camp. However, by the end of July the Germans had suffered significant casualties and eventually the Allies were able to regain the numerical advantage with the help of the newly arrived American troops. In August, the Allies launched a counteroffensive which resulted in the Germans losing all of the ground that they had taken in the spring offensive, the collapse of the Hindenburg Line, and the capitulation of Germany that November.

Expansionism Redivivus

The end of the war brought about an atmosphere of retribution among the European Allies. This was not a view shared by Smuts who believed the destruction of Germany would ultimately lead to the destruction of Europe. The Armistice did nothing to reduce Smuts's enormous workload, and he remained a member of the War Cabinet while drafting British policy at the Peace Conference and working on a memorandum for the establishment of the League of Nations. Smuts placed the establishment of the League of Nations at the centre of the conference agenda. His *League of Nations: A Practical Suggestion* was published in January 1919 and soon caught the imagination of President Wilson when it was sent to him as an expression of the British view. Once Smuts had captivated Wilson with his League pamphlet, its establishment became the central mission of both men at the conference. Towards the end of January, it was agreed that the League would be established as an integral part of the Treaty of Peace. However, despite all his efforts of ensuring an equitable peace in Europe, he was determined to secure German territory for South Africa.[99]

Smuts had entered the war in August 1914 at great political risk on the home front. South Africa's participation on the side of the United Kingdom against Germany was unpopular among vast swathes of Afrikaners. One of his main aims of waging the war was to secure further territory for South Africa. The Peace Conference after the war was Smuts's opportunity to solidify South Africa's substantial sacrifices made during the war into solid territorial gains. Unfortunately, the post-war political climate had swung against those seeking to expand the Empire as the United States, fast emerging as a dominant world power, had little patience for the United Kingdom's or its dominions territorial claims. Imperialist designs were becoming anachronistic in a rapidly changing world order. It was in these hostile waters that Smuts would attempt to swim against the anti-imperial tide and lay claim to his territorial ambitions.

At the outset Smuts's designs on the Belgian Congo and Mozambique elicited strongly worded objections from the Belgian and Portuguese governments.[100] During the war, Smuts constructed a "very secret" memorandum titled, 'The Mozambique Province and the Union of South Africa'. Interestingly, his original draft assumed the authorship of General Botha, but this was dropped in the final version. The memo clearly sets out Smuts's intention regarding the Portuguese territories and leaves little to the imagination. It states openly and brazenly at the outset, "The object of this paper is to put the case in favour of the liquidation of part of the Portuguese territories in Southern Africa, and their incorporation into the Union of South Africa." [101]

Smuts, attempting to justify his intention of what looked like a blatant land grab, offered up a myriad of reasons of why the Portuguese should forfeit their territory. These took the form of geographical, political, historical, and financial considerations. He accused the Portuguese of not duly and completely occupying the territory he coveted and that the Portuguese had lost control of this region at various times in its history. Furthermore, the Portuguese occupation was almost exclusively restricted to the coastal areas, and it was only until recently that they had occupied the hinterland. That the Portuguese had managed to venture into the hinterland was only facilitated by Boer and British initiatives in the adjacent territories. As a result, the Portuguese had accomplished very little in terms of developing and encouraging white settlement in these territories, leaving the local black population in a state of "barbarism".[102]

More importantly, the Portuguese territory of Mozambique inconveniently interfered with the Union's and Rhodesia's access to the Indian Ocean. The future development of these British territories depended on easy and unfettered access to the Portuguese ports on the Indian Ocean. The Portuguese had adopted a parasitic stance by levying tolls on British trade through the area, and without the benefit of this trade and development, "Mozambique would probably relapse to that barbarism from which it has never really emerged". The enormous disparity in development between the Portuguese and British territories was intolerable to Smuts. The Portuguese were, before the war, squandering their valuable assets to corrupt concession-hunters, who were largely German, and if the situation persisted, this would prove to be an insurmountable barrier to future development of the area.[103]

Smuts raised the spectre of a politically unstable situation in the Portuguese motherland as well as its territories in Africa. The Portuguese had faced a succession of revolutions which had unsettled the political situation in Mozambique, leading to instability and corruption. Smuts feared that a future revolt might lead to Mozambique declaring itself an independent republic. A new republic in southern Africa would pose a threat to the Union with the possibility of a rekindling the republican spirit amongst some sectors of South Africa's population. Smuts then suggested that the Union might very well "step in and take charge" in the event of a local revolution in Mozambique, to protect both South Africa's and British interests in the area. However, he preferred to pre-empt the situation and rather negotiate an amicable arrangement with the Portuguese government in advance, rather than exploit a revolutionary crisis. Smuts argued that the weak Portuguese political and financial situation precluded her from owning colonial assets. Portuguese weakness "exposed her to dangerous intrigues by other Powers". The Portuguese situation had steadily worsened since the advent of the First World War. Smuts compounded the gloomy picture by providing an annexure to the memorandum setting out the growing indebtedness of the Portuguese territory to Britain and the Union.

The memorandum proceeds lavishly in setting out Smuts's grandiose scheme for a Greater South Africa.

> It is clearly the destiny of the British Empire to develop into a conference group of great states, which will more and more absorb the scattered units at present existing. Canada is already such a great state. So also, is Australasia … The great British State in Southern Africa is far from complete and is still in process of formation. If, as a result of this war, its western and eastern flanks are completed by the addition of South West Africa and Mozambique to the Union, it would at most take only a few years before Rhodesia becomes a Province of the Union, and the British position in Southern Africa thus becomes consolidated and powerful beyond what was considered possible only five years ago.[104]

Smuts reinforced his words by attaching a visual aid in the form of a map showing the extent of his territorial ambitions for a greater South Africa. (See Map 2.1) His grand vision was for a state that incorporated the entire Portuguese territory of Mozambique and vast swathes of southern Angola. The Rovuma River defined its northern border which marked the boundary between GEA and Portuguese East Africa. His ambitious territorial scheme was not limited to generous amounts of Portuguese territory. He motivated for the inclusion of the 'Katanga Angle', a copper-rich Belgian Congo enclave jutting enticingly into Smuts's Greater South Africa. Smuts offered a more modest solution in the event that his reach exceeded his grasp. Although this solution was not on as grand a scale, it still incorporated the South West African territory and southern Mozambique running along the Kunene and Zambezi rivers respectively. Smuts was confident of the capacity of the Union to administer this huge new territory and develop it into "one of the most powerful and valuable states in the British Empire".[105]

Leaving nothing to chance Smuts then proceeded to explain the finances of the whole enterprise. The negotiations would be initiated by the more prestigious Imperial government rather than the Union. The British, via association, would include the Union in the negotiations, thus diverting attention from land-hungry South Africa. In consideration for the Mozambique territory, the Imperial government would write off the £12 million war-loan advance to the Portuguese government, and the Union government would render a sum of £5 million. In case it was seen that the Imperial government was chasing the bill on behalf of the Union, Smuts was quick to point out that in all likelihood the £12 million was unrecoverable and that, in reality, it was South Africa that would be making payment. Smuts remained unruffled in the event the Portuguese look beyond these payments and insist on an exchange of territory. He suggested that the Imperial government offer Portugal "small bits of Togoland and Cameroons [...] to be used as pawns in order to consolidate our position in an area such as Mozambique".[106]

The idea of incorporating Delagoa Bay into South African territory had developed from the days when Kruger and the ZAR sought economic autonomy from Britain by finding an independent route to the Indian Ocean. Smuts's vision took the acquisition of Portuguese territory beyond the British desire to deny the ZAR a path to economic dependence. His idea was to incorporate most of Portugal's African estate into a South African super-state stretching all the way to the equator and beyond. This more than coincidently fulfilled Rhodes's dream of a British Empire that stretched unbroken from the Cape to Cairo.

By the end of the First World War, Lourenço Marques had become integral to the economy of the Eastern Transvaal being the most used port for the export of coal from that area. As a minimum, failing a complete takeover, the South Africans wanted effective control over the harbour. The South Africans resorted to financial shenanigans and threats of building a port in Kosi Bay in northern Natal near the border to make any efforts by Portugal to acquire a loan to develop the port almost impossible. Hertzog claimed that Lourenço Marques was, "the natural harbour for the Transvaal, the [Orange] Free State and Swaziland".[107] These efforts convinced the Portuguese that the Union was attempting to destroy Portuguese interests in southern Mozambique. The Portuguese were determined to resist any further encroachment on Lisbon's sovereignty in Mozambique and saw these as not merely economic attacks, but as an assault on Portugal's national pride.[108] Due to the continuing maladministration of the Portuguese African Empire, the British Foreign Office, by 1926, began to view the eventual handover of the Portuguese colonies as inevitable and that the natural successor was to be South Africa.[109]

At a dinner speech hosted in London by Lord Selborne in 1917, Smuts defined the borders of a future South Africa and outlined his vision for expansion and the role of the white man:

> And now we are ready to go forward, and, as you know, in the last few decades enormous progress has already been made in this expansion towards the North. All our people in South Africa, English as well as Dutch, have taken part in this great movement towards the North, which is proceeding even further, and the time is coming when it will be almost a misnomer speak of 'South' Africa, because the northern limits of our civilisation will have gone so far that it will be almost impossible to use the word 'South' anymore except in reminder of our original starting-point.[110]

The notion of a civilising force is a strong thread which binds together the various, and at times disparate, characters who appear in this book. George Heaton Nicholls (1876–1959), a South African MP and member of the Native Affairs Commission, stated that "all the problems in South Africa converge upon the one vital issue behind everybody's mind, namely, how best is European South Africa to maintain itself on a huge continent, containing 140,000,000 blacks, as a white Christian civilization".[111]

The retention of GSWA by South Africa became a fundamental war aim. Smuts stated his position clearly in a speech delivered at a banquet in his honour in 1917 in London. (See Figure 8.2) He strongly expressed his reluctance to return any of the territorial gains made at the expense of Germany after the war.[112] The British on the other hand were sensitive to being accused of being "out for plunder and further territorial acquisition". The Secretary of State for Foreign Affairs suggested an alternative proposal "for the internationalisation of the former German colonies in Africa, which would have the effect of preventing the creation of a naval and military menace, while at the same time the most valuable raw materials would be available for the factories of the world, and not merely of Germany."[113] Smuts attempted to link GEA to the security of the British Empire and thus could fuse the aims of British imperialism with that of South African sub-imperialism.[114] He revealed in a letter to Deneys Reitz that he believed GSWA would once again form part of the Afrikaner heritage.[115]

Figure 8.2. Prime Minister Louis Botha's imperial ambitions in German South West Africa.[116]

Smuts's Vision of a New World Order

Smuts devoted some considerable time reflecting what format the new world order would take at the conclusion of the First World War. He shared his thoughts in a revealing memorandum written at a time when the outcome of that war was far from definite, the measure of any possible Allied victory quite uncertain, and the conditions with which the peace negotiations were to be undertaken, unknown. His focus centred around German pronouncements regarding their lost African colonies and the German colonial policy. Smuts possessed a natural tendency to elevate the African colonial question as one of the most important considerations to be dealt with in future peace negotiations. He identified the colonial question as one of the two principal issues of German war policy. (The other being Germany's territorial and economic aims in Europe.) According to Smuts, the future German colonial empire was one of the principal war aims of German imperialism.[117]

The elevation of German colonial aspirations as a fundamental part of any peace negotiation had the effect of boosting South Africa's importance at any future conference. In the memorandum, Smuts painted an ominous picture of an ambitious Germany carving out a vast colonial empire from the possessions of France, Belgium, and great swathes of Portuguese African territory. According to Smuts, the German-occupied territory in Belgium and northern France would be used as a quid pro quo to acquire their African colonial assets. Smuts concluded that Germany hoped to gain an extensive Central African empire at the peace conference even at the expense of her colonial possessions elsewhere in China and the Pacific and even South West Africa. This German *Mittelafrika* would completely dominate the strategy of the Indian and Atlantic oceans. Furthermore, its largely Muslim population would be a steppingstone to gaining influence and eventually acquiring territory in Muslim North Africa.[118]

Having painted a bleak picture of a rampant German colonisation of Africa, Smuts offered suggestions of how to thwart this threat to the British Empire in Africa. These proposals must be seen in the light of an unconquered Germany holding large portions of Belgium and French territory at the time of future peace negotiations. He insisted that the dominions could justly claim any conquered German colony adjacent to their territory. In the case of South Africa, this would be GSWA, and he was adamant that its return was non-negotiable and that he should not be asked to jeopardise its future security, peaceful development, and imperial solidarity.[119]

The situation with the other German colonies, especially that of German East Africa, was a far more complicated business. Here Smuts was insistent that peace terms should not be entertained which would endanger the future security of the Empire's communications. No lost colony should be restored to Germany where a naval or aerial base could threaten these communications. Smuts was even prepared to concede German territorial gains made in the Baltic and Black seas in exchange for

African territory. He also made the argument that if any territory had to be given back then it should be Togoland and Cameroons rather than German East Africa, which he saw as fundamental to the Empire. The retention of German East Africa would secure the maritime Red Sea route and furthermore allow for a contiguous British territory from Cape to Cairo, the dream of Rhodes fulfilled. His final suggestion provided for the international control over the colonies in tropical Africa, "which will guarantee their peaceful, non-militaristic exploitation on a common basis for the production of raw materials for the free and common use of the world".[120]

The opportunity to complete the annexation of GSWA, a process that was thwarted 30 years previously, was not without its risks. There was a significant proportion of the Afrikaner population, who, smarting after the Boer War, were more sympathetic to the Germans than to the British.[121] The decision to invade GSWA was the catalyst leading to the Afrikaner Rebellion in 1914, which severely damaged the fickle process of healing that had taken place between the Afrikaners and English since the Boer War. Botha managed to put down the rebellion successfully and go on to conquer GSWA in a campaign that was not without its fair share of military mishaps. A further risk was that the Union's annexation of the territory was not a foregone conclusion and the final decision would be deferred until after the war. In this case possession did not amount to nine-tenths of the law and physical possession did not confer automatic ownership by the Union. However, the retention of GSWA by South Africa became British policy for the reasons advanced by the 1917 committee on territorial exchanges:

> The retention and development of South-West Africa would be the final justification of General Botha and General Smuts's policy in the eyes of the majority of their compatriots. Its restoration to the Germans would be their condemnation and the vindication of the rebels. The result would be a situation fatal to the peace of South Africa and one which Germany, reinstated as a source of supply and a rallying point for all the disloyal elements in the Union, would take the fullest advantage.[122]

When victory finally arrived in 1918, Smuts's position on the War Council gave him a central role in the planning for the Paris Peace Conference. One of his tasks was to gain international recognition for the Union's sovereignty over GSWA. This was not an easy task in the face of moves to establish a supra-national organisation.[123]

Expansionism Thwarted

Complicating South Africa's claim to the territory was Wilson's position as a firm opponent of annexation of the former German colonies. Smuts would have to convince Wilson, despite the full backing he had from Lloyd George and the delegations from New Zealand and Australia, if he was to make any headway in acquiring GSWA for South Africa. Wilson was bent on prohibiting annexation and wanted the former German colonies to be administered by mandatories acting on behalf of the League of Nations. The mandate system extended to GSWA fell short of Smuts's expansionist ambition to incorporate the territory as a province of the Union. Smuts felt that the mandate system was inapplicable to GSWA as

> The German colonies in the Pacific and Africa are inhabited by barbarians, who not only cannot possibly govern themselves, but to whom it would be impracticable to apply any ideas of political self-determination in the European sense.[124]

Again Smuts expressed his desire to claim the territory of GSWA:

> Yesterday we discussed the Dominion claims to the German colonies. I hope I made a good case to South-West Africa, but I don't know. My argument was principally that it was a desert, a part of the Kalahari no good to anybody, least of all to so magnificent a body as the League of Nations! It was like a poor sinning girl's plea that her baby was only a very little one! Not that I consider our claim to South-West Africa simple or wrong.[125]

Eventually, Smuts was forced to abandon annexation and instead, in conjunction with Kerr, drafted a resolution which was eventually to become Article XXII of the League Covenant. Smuts and Kerr managed to wring out a concession that different areas had different types of mandates, thus allowing the more 'primitive areas' such as GSWA to come under virtual annexation.

The relevant portion of Article XXII reads:

> There are territories, such as South-West Africa and certain of the South Pacific Islands, which, owing to the sparseness of their population, or their small size, or their remoteness from the centres of civilisation, or their geographical contiguity to the territory of the Mandatory, and other circumstances, can be best administered under the laws of the Mandatory as integral portions of its territory, subject to the safeguards above mentioned in the interests of the indigenous population.[126]

South Africa, harbouring greater territorial ambitions, never did fully accept her mandate status over South West Africa. These ambitions drew Smuts's administrator of South West Africa, Gysbert Reitz Hofmeyr, to announce to the Empire Parliamentary Association in London in 1924 that South West Africa would be eventually annexed, and that the territory would become "a part of the Greater South Africa which is now in process of creation [sic]".[127] South African ambitions over the territory persisted for 76 years, only fading when independence was granted to Namibia in 1990. The territory that first caused the bitter internal rift leading to the 1914 Afrikaner Rebellion, would later be a constant millstone as South Africa sought its retention in the face of an increasingly hostile world.

Smuts's words to his wife from the Versailles Conference give insight into his territorial ambition and his unfounded optimism in a world that had changed forever from the one in 1914 when he first set his sights on German territory. He wrote, "German Southwest A. has been granted to us and we will shortly be at the Zambezi. What a change but parts of the programme have still to be executed. Mozambique and Rhodesia have still to come in and I am busy with that."[128] Smuts saw this dream as "a practical certainty" which ought to have been "one of the cardinal points of British Imperial policy". His territorial ambition was only slightly less than that of Rhodes before him.[129] However although the receiving of a mandate over GSWA was less than optimal, he would turn up empty-handed when it came to the long-coveted Portuguese territory of Delagoa Bay.

Smuts's expansionist intentions over GEA are a good example where the objective of South African sub-imperialism and British imperialism coincided, albeit for different and separate aims. British imperialism was desirous of removing the Germans in East Africa to form a contiguous swathe of British-held territory from the Cape to Cairo. The South Africans had a narrower strategic aim of putting into effect a land swap to acquire Delagoa Bay. In a dinner speech hosted in London by Lord Selborne in 1917, Smuts reiterated the danger of a German Central African Empire in which blacks were armed. He reminded the audience that GEA was essential as a land bridge between the southern and northern part of the British African Empire. He also took the opportunity to remind those present of the leading role South African troops had played in securing these valuable German African territories.[130]

Smuts's expressed his true intentions on invading GEA in August 1915 in a letter to Merriman. He intimated that territory could be exchanged for Mozambique to consolidate South African territory south of the Kunene and Zambezi.[131] In 1915, Harcourt touted the idea of exchanging GSWA for Mozambique with the Portuguese. Smuts turned down the proposal by preferring to exchange large swathes of GEA for Mozambique.[132] Smuts could claim that South Africa had made the principal contribution towards the conquest of GEA and therefore if she was to renounce all claims to that significant territory, it was only equitable that here claims be met in other directions. The obvious direction he was alluding to was nothing less than Delagoa Bay or the entire colony of Mozambique.[133]

The Portuguese had well-founded fears and a letter sent in 1916 by John X. Merriman, the former Prime Minister of the Cape before Union, to Botha bears this out. Merriman offered that "the best that could happen to us from our own selfish point of view would be to exchange the German territory with the Portuguese for Delagoa Bay".[134] A letter from Botha to Smuts in 1918 advising him of the course of action he should take at the forthcoming Prime Ministers' Conference implores Smuts:

> we shall perhaps never have another chance—especially the question of Mozambique. Jannie, there is no doubt about it; this is a matter which we must bring up and settle in our favour. The region must be bought out and we must pay for it.[135]

The Portuguese suffered few illusions as to the South Africa's expansionist intent and this fact is highlighted in an interesting intelligence report produced in 1917 by Major J.G.W. Leipoldt[136] on returning from Lourenço Marques by train. Leipoldt had the good fortune to share the train with some Portuguese officers and officials who expressed little sympathy for South Africa and viewed the Imperial and "especially" the Union governments with "grave suspicion". Leipoldt plied his fellow travellers with several rounds of "stimulant" encouraging "free and unreserved" conversation. The Portuguese complained bitterly that they had gained nothing and lost much during the preceding years and that, "whenever they come into contact with the Union Octopus, [it] gets its tentacles closer around them". According to Leipoldt, "the Portuguese were fully convinced that the ultimate aim was the loss to them of Portugal's most valuable colonial asset,"[137]

Smuts made clear his claim to Delagoa Bay at the Territorial Desiderata Committee 1917. It was here that he mooted the idea of exchanging territory conquered in the southern part GEA for Delagoa Bay and Beira. He referred to the secret agreement made with Germany in 1898 and suggested that this territorial settlement could be aligned with it. If the Portuguese found the proposal unattractive, he was prepared to offer a monetary consideration to supplement the deal.[138] South Africa's strategy to swap territory in GEA for Delagoa Bay began to unravel when Britain and the War Cabinet grew sensitive to land-grab accusations:

> The one difficulty we had to face was the suggestion, so freely put about by the enemy both abroad and in our midst, that the Allies, and more particularly Great Britain, were out for plunder and further territorial acquisitions.

The War Cabinet suggested that the former German colonies be "internationalised," rather than parcel out the spoils amongst the victors.[139] The irony that South Africa was thwarted in its attempt to acquire Delagoa Bay at the expense of GEA territory cannot be escaped. Smuts neglected to follow up South Africa's claim after the Territorial Desiderata Committee report in 1917 and painted himself into a corner through his suggestions of a mandate system.[140] The possibility that Smuts made the best of a difficult sitiation needs further examination. His suggestion to Wilson and Wilson's eventual acceptance that GSWA become a C Mandate may have been an exercise in masterful diplomacy. At the end of the war, the South Africans and the Portuguese were left to their own devices to negotiate over Delagoa Bay. Their efforts amounted to nought, and despite all the sacrifices and planning during the war, Smuts was left empty-handed. South Africa's failure to secure Delagoa Bay, its raison d'être for sending troops to GEA in the first place, must be counted among Smuts's failures.

Smuts failed to have GSWA incorporated into the Union and had to be satisfied with a mandate. Adding to his despair was his inability to secure Delagoa Bay at the end of the First World War. The war had deeply divided South Africans, and Botha and Smuts's power had been eroded rather than advanced by their close relationship with the United Kingdom. Botha's untimely death in 1919 accelerated Smuts's political decline. The world was rapidly changing, and the United Kingdom had lost much of its hegemony to the United States who harboured little sympathy for the territorial ambitions of Britain's anachronistic empire. Growing black nationalism and political aspirations were also beginning to challenge the unfettered idea of the spread of 'white civilisation' in Africa. South Africa's failure to incorporate black aspirations and the growing international distaste for her segregationist 'native policy' became the immovable object in the path of the irresistible desire to acquire more territory. The birth of the Union as a vehicle for territorial expansion was almost, if not quite, stillborn.

Conclusion

Bill Nasson challenged any would-be Smuts biographer to seek answers as to what Smuts amounted to, what was his essence, and how do we take his measure. Nasson's challenge coincides with the aim of this book in providing a critical and comprehensive analysis of the roles played by General J.C. Smuts and his First World War in Africa, 1914–17. The book provides fresh insights into Smuts and his generalship in the First World War in Africa. The title suggests that the study would be very much centred around 'his' experiences during the First World War in Africa. Smuts's insatiable quest for a Greater South Africa has been thoroughly investigated as the underlying and prime motivator for South Africa's involvement in the First World War. In addition, his role in shaping South Africa's war aims and the conduct of the war effort have been highlighted. The book places his generalship and conduct during the Afrikaner Rebellion, the German South West African, and German East African campaigns under the spotlight as well as a microscope. Also examined is his role as a statesman, cabinet minister and field commander leading up to and during the war years in Africa. The book delivers an insight into the essence of Smuts, albeit focused on his First World War years in Africa.

The book has referenced an extensive raft of archival documents and previously underutilised regimental histories together with the semi-official German accounts to distance itself from most previous academic and popular works on the subject. Historians attempting to accurately depict Smuts in the First World War, especially his role in GSWA and GEA, must first jump over several hurdles presented by enormous challenges in the historiography. Firstly, there is the general paucity of available secondary sources on the GSWA and GEA campaigns. Secondly, there is even less on Smuts's role in them. Thirdly, the little that historians have provided on the subject is poorly researched in many cases, and, more troubling, many works display an unwarranted extreme bias toward painting Smuts in a negative light. According to Kobus du Pisani, of all material published about Smuts in the First World War, 85 per cent is over half a century old. The few titles that have emerged after 1968 have minimal dealings on Smuts as a general on campaign in Africa in the First World War. Therefore, there is a massive lacuna in the historiography, which this book has partially filled.

This book has traced the primary roots and source of negative bias back to the efforts of Richard Meinertzhagen and Harold Courtenay Armstrong. Their work has been taken on board and influenced generations of historians. Brian Bond's exposure of Meinertzhagen as a fraud has not dissuaded contemporary historians from citing his diaries nor persuaded them to treat them with caution. It is uncertain whether Meinertzhagen manufactured the diaries covering his experiences in GEA under Smuts after and not during the events. One is obliged to approach Meinertzhagen's work with extreme caution, and he certainly does not deserve the uncritical support displayed in some historical circles. Then there is Armstrong, a self-confessed iconoclast, who has presented fanciful and sometimes imaginary events as fact in a cynical attempt to destroy Smuts's reputation. Meinertzhagen could at least lay claim to personal experience in GEA and a working knowledge of Smuts, whereas in the case of Armstrong, his diatribe amounts to nothing more than a nasty version of sensationalist journalism. Contemporary British historians have unquestioningly mirrored much of what Meinertzhagen and Armstrong have portrayed. Compounding the obfuscation is the discovery of several instances where historians have disregarded critical information in primary documentation to bolster the negative case against Smuts. This study has had to deal with flawed historical research and a culture of cross citation, which have perpetuated the many falsehoods of Meinertzhagen and Armstrong.

As an unfortunate counterpoise to the negativity created around Smuts is the hagiographic rapture with which many historians have embraced Paul von Lettow-Vorbeck. The German commander of the Schutztruppe in GEA was by all accounts a remarkable man, much admired for his resolve and skill for remaining a thorn in the British side even beyond the end of the war. However, many historians have fallen into the trap of feting him as a superhero of guerrilla warfare. The main culprits, including many mainstream historians, are American lecturers and military students from mainstream American military institutions. They regard Lettow-Vorbeck uncritically as the epitome of a resilient and resourceful guerrilla fighter who confronted and bested numerically superior Allied armies using his impressive military skills. Although there is a modicum of truth, especially when describing Lettow-Vorbeck's resilience and resourcefulness in the face of great odds, this book partially swings the pendulum back toward reality and objectivity. Lettow-Vorbeck, very much like Smuts, was a product of his nation's military doctrine, although he may have been an exceptionally gifted example of a German officer who had graduated through the German military system. There is much scope for further study in re-evaluating Lettow-Vorbeck as a general.

Voluminous primary sources available at various archives in South Africa and the United Kingdom poses a challenge to the would-be researcher. However, working through thousands of archival documents has been fundamental to the exercise of unravelling some of the misguided efforts of past and contemporary historians.

Primary documents, in many instances, offer contradictory evidence to that of Smuts's detractors who have painted him as an inexperienced and incompetent general, driven by a callous disregard for the men under his command in his unsated quest of achieving a wicked expansionist aim. Besides primary documents, this book has used first-hand accounts and regimental histories to present a more balanced and objective view of Smuts, acknowledging that Smuts possessed both human flaws as a man of his times, and flaws that transcended his times. However, what emerges after interrogating the primary sources is a rather different picture of that portrayed by historians. He was a surprisingly competent and well-liked leader of men, who chose to lead from the front, contrary to many Allied commanders of the time who preferred to command behind the lines. Smuts was brave and often suffered the same privations as his men—a common Boer trait. He was focused on and possessed a very definite set of objectives, which conformed to his lifelong pursuit of a Greater South Africa. Contrary to his portrayal as either a gifted amateur or an incompetent general, he was a great exponent and ultimately a product of his nation's manoeuvrist way of war. On his arrival in GEA, he was a veteran of many campaigns and battles.

It has been necessary to examine Smuts's early life and his environment to better understand his motives and drive in his First World War in Africa. This book delivers no surprises in reminding the reader of Smuts's enormous intelligence, colossal work ethic, capacity to multitask, and uncanny ability to grasp the most complicated ideas. Emerging from his early years, and less well understood, is his unshakeable desire to unite white South Africans within a united Greater South Africa. His quest for unity and territorial expansion presents a powerful and dominant theme running like a golden thread through his career. Smuts first made common cause with Cecil John Rhodes and Jan Hofmeyr and was comfortable with a united expanded South Africa under the umbrella of the United Kingdom. He retained the desire for a united Greater South Africa even after his break with Rhodes and defection to Paul Kruger and the Boer South African Republic (ZAR). Soon after the British had defeated the Boer Republics in the South African War, he again sought to unite South Africans in a unitary state that would incorporate massive tracts of territory to the north of its borders. Developing from the background chapter is that the concept of a Greater South Africa was at the core of Smuts's political belief system. His quest for territorial expansion was his overriding objective for entering the First World War, trumping any exercise in nation-building, loyalty to the United Kingdom, or his desire to elevate South Africa's status.

Yet another theme develops from his service as the Attorney-General and a combat general in the ZAR during the South African War. Historians have tended to minimise (if not trivialise) his wartime experience under the tutelage of the gifted Koos de la Rey and Louis Botha, discounting his service in the Boer forces as irrelevant when considering his ability to command upwards of 70,000 men in GEA.

A common theme among British and South African historians was that the total of Smuts's wartime experience, which he brought to GEA, was limited to leading 300 men at the head of a raiding party into the Cape Colony. Less obvious or ignored is that Smut gained valuable experience leading up to 3,000 men in the closing stages of the South African War. He possessed the rare gift of coherently combining political (strategic) and military (operational) leadership, shaping the nature of his generalship into the First World War. More importantly, Smuts was immersed in a very distinct Boer way of war, which inculcated a penchant for manoeuvre and an aversion to 'needless' costly frontal assaults. His style of directive command, which accompanied him to GEA, was also peculiar to the Boer way of war and distinct from the British way of war. The distinction between how the British and the Boers thought about warfare led to a conflict of military doctrine, which has manifested in how historians have portrayed Smuts's tenure in GEA. To understand the essence of Smuts's generalship is to recognise how deeply the Boer way of war was embedded in his military roots. His directive command and leadership style and manoeuvrist operational art were anathema to the British officers he commanded in GEA, and up to the present day, remain an enigma to contemporary historians.

Smuts finally realised his dream of a united South Africa with the formation of the Union of South Africa in 1910. It mattered little that this was under the auspices of his former bitter British enemies, for at his core lay the desire to create a Greater South Africa whomever the facilitator. The Act, which created the Union, also created a vehicle for its expansion by allowing for the future absorption of the High Commission Territories and Rhodesia. Smuts was a founding member of the Union Defence Force in 1912, which, at its inception, was more of an internal policing force, riven with political compromise, than an army designed to confront a first-class European power. Smuts must take responsibility that the UDF pandered to the politics of equity and compromise whereby many of its appointments were based on representation rather than ability. Importantly, Smuts embraced the concept of a modern military over the Boer commando system in that it would have structure, uniforms, discipline, and modern equipment. As a result, the Boer commandos were relegated to Rifle Associations and effectively sidelined. The Permanent Force and Active Citizen Force, trained by British instructors, incorporated many former colonial regiments, and as a result, took on a decidedly British flavour. The UDF seemed on a trajectory to becoming a colonial clone of the British Army. This book reveals that had it not been for the reactivation of the Rifle Associations—born of necessity, and crewed by the old Boer Republican commandos, to suppress the Witwatersrand miner strikes and the Afrikaner Rebellion in 1914—the UDF may have taken on a distinctly British flavour instead of the Boer manoeuvrist approach that dominated the GSWA and GEA campaigns.

For political reasons and a quest to protect reputations, the official histories have deliberately written the first phase of the GSWA campaign out of the history books. In doing so, they discarded Smuts's plan to conquer the entire territory of GSWA using only the Permanent and Active Citizen Force elements of the UDF. The Boer commandos did not feature in Smuts's original plan for the invasion of GSWA, mainly due to political reasons. An understanding of Smuts's plan shows that he intended to land at Lüderitzbucht and Walvis Bay simultaneously, and in conjunction with an advancing southern offensive, converge on Windhoek. The expunging of the original tenets of Smuts's plan for a four-prong attack converging on Windhoek has misled contemporary historians into offering erroneous notions concerning the early stages of the GSWA campaign. This book shows that Smuts's plan, contrary to what the official histories portray, and contemporary historians believe, was not cancelled on 21 August 1914.

In pursuing their notion that Smuts cancelled his plan early in the campaign before the UDF undertook any landings, historians have unwittingly removed the operational context of the UDF's defeat at Sandfontein. They have attributed the defeat at Sandfontein as an unnecessary and politically motivated tactical error due to the poor generalship of Henry Lukin or alternatively Jan Smuts. In fact, Sandfontein was a desperate operational attempt to divert German attention away from Lüderitzbucht because of the failed landings at Walvis Bay/Swakopmund called for in the Smuts plan. In a further irony, that would otherwise have remained concealed by assuming Smuts's original plan was cancelled, he can be accused of devising an overly ambitious plan given the poor state of the UDF's equipment and staff officer component. Its execution bordered on a fiasco for which Smuts must take ultimate responsibility.

The incorrect assumption that Smuts discarded his plans on 21 August 1914 has other historical consequences. The deliberate and accidental obfuscation of history has buried the different objectives Smuts and the British harboured for the occupation of GSWA. This book has revealed the resulting tense relations between South Africa and the United Kingdom surrounding the ambitious sweep of Smuts's plan compared to the limited British objectives of merely occupying the GSWA ports and disabling the wireless stations. Also revealed is the chaos experienced by the UDF at the landing grounds of Port Nolloth and Lüderitzbucht. Lack of staff work, which saw a disastrous delay of the seaborne landings at Walvis Bay/Swakopmund, was the real reason for Smuts forcing Lukin to advance to Sandfontein. The outbreak of the Afrikaner Rebellion in September/October 1914, and not a meeting of senior officers of the UDF on 21 August 1914, as some historians would have it, derailed the landings at Walvis Bay/Swakopmund and prematurely ended the Smuts plan.

Smuts seemed unconcerned and oddly indifferent that the invasion of GSWA would tear the political fabric of South Africa apart. His belief that the acquisition of GSWA would somehow be a nation-building exercise was naïve and out of kilter with his usual political astuteness. He approached the invasion of GSWA with seemingly reckless disregard for the mood of the Afrikaner nation. Once the murmurings of rebellion took root, he was slow in anticipating the treachery of Christiaan Beyers and Manie Maritz. However, with the Afrikaner Rebellion well underway, he acted decisively and ruthlessly in supressing the rebels. The Afrikaner Rebellion delivered upon Smuts and the UDF two significant windfalls which historians have tended to overlook. Firstly, Smuts played an essential part in working behind the scenes and conducting the operations, which eventually saw the rebels defeated in detail. As a result, he gained crucial operational experience during the Afrikaner Rebellion and the GSWA campaign. Historians have overlooked his experience gained during these events and insist that when he took command of GEA, his most recent military experience was the South African War. Secondly and importantly, the Afrikaner Rebellion unlocked the availability of loyal Boer commandos, who, up to that time, were languishing in the Rifle Associations. This study reveals that the Boer mounted infantry, used in the Afrikaner Rebellion, GSWA, and GEA, became the dominant component of the UDF. Strongly leaning toward the Boer way of war, the UDF's reliance on the Boer mounted infantry was decisive in shaping the future UDF manoeuvrist doctrine and directive leadership style.

The UDF increased its numbers fourfold in the second phase of the GSWA campaign, deviating from the leaner combat force envisaged in the original Smuts plan. In many ways, the increased numbers did not significantly enhance fighting power but resulted in a ponderous blunt instrument of war. Despite enjoying an overwhelming numerical advantage over the Germans, Botha at Swakopmund and Duncan McKenzie at Lüderitzbucht only advanced at a sluggish pace toward their inland objectives. Botha, much admired by the British for his military skills, seemed overcautious and bogged down by atrocious staff work, which in turn ruined his logistics and stifled his manoeuvrist instincts. Moreover, he seemed to have no combat role for the thousands of accompanying regular infantrymen, which, for lack of purpose, he relegated to the rear area defences. Placed in static positions, they sapped his limited resources and played only a minor role in the actual fighting. He would have fared better with fewer men under his command and had he placed more reliance on his mounted infantry's mobility, resourcefulness, self-sufficiency, and intuition. Historians have reduced Smuts's role as the commander of the southern front to that of a token command. In fact, his swift advance broke the logjam and unhinged the German defences before Botha who had all but stalled in the north. Smuts's forces advanced hundreds of kilometres while Botha, stuck at Trekkoppies, remained on the defensive for the duration of Smuts's advance to Gibeon. Botha only ventured forth once the Germans had given way in the south and began to withdraw in front of him.

Ironically, once Botha had captured Windhoek, he thinned out his forces substantially and was willing to face an almost numerically intact Schutztruppe which had traded space for time with very few resulting casualties. Sending back many of his superfluous men to South Africa allowed Botha to free up his logistics and restore manoeuvre to his northern front. Although Smuts was not present, this book has dealt with the last battle of the GSWA campaign where the Germans surrendered at Otavifontein in some detail. Botha conducted one of his classic enveloping manoeuvres using his regular infantry to pin down the Germans in the centre while using his mounted infantry to envelop the enemy on two wings. The two enveloping wings advanced at a rapid pace under their own logistics, intuition, and authority. The battle is a noteworthy precursor of what Smuts attempted in GEA where he used similar manoeuvrist doctrine and combined arms warfare of regular and mounted infantry. Otavifontein finds further relevance because many of the leader group and the men who participated in that battle went on to serve under Smuts in GEA. It is no exaggeration to cite the battle of Otavifontein as the coming of age of the UDF's manoeuvre and combined-arms doctrine, which would become the hallmark of Smuts's tenure as commander of the East African Force.

The unconditional surrender of all German troops in GSWA followed by South Africa's occupation of the entire territory conformed to Smuts's desire to add the territory to a Greater South Africa. Before long Smuts cast his eyes in the direction of GEA. Here again, his primary motive for accepting the command from an ailing Horace Smith-Dorrien was territorial expansion. His idea was to conquer the entire German territory and use it to barter with the Portuguese via a land swap for Delagoa Bay in southern Mozambique. His sub-imperial ambitions were not incongruous with those of the British, who desperately desired the eviction of the Germans from British territory in East Africa. The British feared that Lettow-Vorbeck's continued presence on the only piece of British real estate under German occupation would weaken their grip on the local population and ultimately their hold over East Africa.

Soon after his arrival, Smuts delivered a resounding victory at Kilimanjaro in his first battle as commander of the East African Force. His performance can be compared with the British-managed disasters at Tanga and Salaita Hill before Smuts's arrival. Kilimanjaro was an empirical example of Smuts's operational art and a validation of his penchant for manoeuvre. He not only freed British territory from German occupation after 18 months of unsuccessful British attempts, but he came close to surrounding and eliminating Lettow-Vorbeck's entire force in the Taveta Gap, coming within a hairsbreadth of destroying a rattled Lettow-Vorbeck but for the tardy conduct of Jimmy Stewart, who failed to act decisively despite Smuts's frustrated exhortations. This book goes some way to reassessing Smuts's performance in the light of historians who have either ignored this significant battle or who have portrayed his actions as reckless.

Smuts's Kilimanjaro operation came under a scathing attack by Meinertzhagen and Armstrong. They demonstrated little idea of manoeuvre warfare as practised by Smuts and would have preferred a direct assault on the entrenched German defenders rather than Smuts's attempt to unhinge their defences by bypassing them. Historians have heavily criticised Smuts's reluctance to launch a direct assault and fixate on Smuts's insistence for leading from the front. In their opinion, this placed him in unnecessary danger and left his rear headquarters without a decision-maker. Historians either do not understand or do not care for Smuts's directive command style and preference to lead from the front. They express a preference for a detailed command style of the rear-based 'chateau generals' of the Western Front. Much criticism stems from an over-reliance on the viewpoints of Meinertzhagen and Armstrong and a superficial understanding of the Smuts and the UDF's manoeuvre doctrine. Historians portray Smuts as inept and amateur when he was a gifted product and firm exponent of South Africa's military doctrine. Contemporary historians' insistence on direct frontal assaults over manoeuvre flies in the face of the many reversals suffered by the British using the same tactic in the South African War, the trenches on the Western Front, and the abortive frontal assaults at Tanga and Salaita Hill. The book exposes the paucity of knowledge surrounding Smuts and the UDF's manoeuvrist doctrine and an unfortunate tendency for historians to bolster their poor opinion of Smuts by disregarding primary documentation.

The subsequent phase of operations in GEA followed along similar lines to Kilimanjaro as Smuts continued to use a manoeuvre approach to lever Lettow-Vorbeck out of his well-entrenched positions. He conducted a further five operations from April 1916 to January 1917, which included Van Deventer's bold drive to Kondoa Irangi, the clearing of the German positions at Pare–Usambara, liberating the Central Railway, the fall of Morogoro and advance to Kisaki, and, finally, Smuts's last gambit, the advance to the Rufiji River. Van Deventer's drive to Kondoa Irangi is an example of a 'deep battle' operation, which meets many of the criteria set by later Soviet 1930s doctrine. Van Deventer's deep advance into enemy territory placed Lettow-Vorbeck on the horns of a dilemma. He was unable to ignore the South African troops placed so far in his operational rear where they threatened a multitude of objectives. As a result, he was forced to thin out his defences in the Pare–Usambara and launch a counterattack on Van Deventer at Kondoa Irangi, which, faithful to South African manoeuvre doctrine, was not a battlefield on the ground of his choosing. In the event, Lettow-Vorbeck's hastily formed counterattack failed against the well-prepared South African defences. A consequence of switching substantial forces from Pare–Usambara to Kondoa Irangi denuded Lettow-Vorbeck's defences at the Pare–Usambara and allowed Smuts an overwhelming numerical superiority in evicting Lettow-Vorbeck from his stronghold.

Kondoa Irangi provides a prime example of the operational art of manoeuvre and should form part of the syllabus of the South African National Defence Force (SANDF) army and war colleges. However, it remains forgotten in South African military circles and utterly absent from the SANDF Staff Officer's Operational Manual. The manual's authors scrambled to find the heritage and lineage of South African manoeuvre doctrine but have overlooked a genuinely South African battle which provides context and illuminates current SANDF doctrine. This book has restored the examples of South African manoeuvre warfare so long overlooked and misinterpreted by historians. Smuts's manoeuvre doctrine confounded his critics in GEA and continues to do so among contemporary historians who have little regard or doubted the existence of a South African/Union Defence Force way of war.

Despite vociferous criticism, Smuts's methods delivered the bulk of GEA territory by the time of his departure in January 1917. A question that historians need to pose is whether Smith-Dorrien or any other general would have delivered more than Smuts, with as many or fewer casualties, in as short a space of time. Contemporary historians assume too much when believing Lettow-Vorbeck would have cooperated by allowing the British to destroy him by delivering frontal assaults in a static battle of annihilation. Any adversary would have had a difficult if not impossible task in trying to fix Lettow-Vorbeck to a static defence while the German was resolved to live to fight another day and trade territory for time. Smuts's manoeuvre operations and tactics had the best chance of bringing a decisive victory, and he came close on several occasions to delivering a decisive blow. That he did not can be put down to his opponent's skill, the lethargy of some of his commanders, and the debilitating attrition suffered through disease and malnutrition. Nevertheless, had the war ended in 1916, his methods delivered up most of the territory into British hands before his departure, allowing for an important chip at the negotiating table.

Biographers of Smuts must accept his overall responsibility for the poor state of his forces' fighting power through his tenure as commander of the East African Force. His army suffered disastrous casualties due to inadequate medical facilities and an abysmal logistical system. Contemporary historians have laid the responsibility for the enormous casualties suffered through medical negligence, firmly at Smuts's door. Seeking to bolster their case, some historians have disregarded documents which have not suited their narrative. This book has restored some balance in assessing Smuts's culpability for the poor state of the forces under his command. Smuts inherited the medical facilities and systems from the British on his arrival in GEA. Smuts, leading from the front, would have relied on Jack Collyer, his chief of staff, to take care of medical arrangements. The Pike Report recognises that the medical conditions in GEA amounted to a scandal and apportions the blame equally among all the C-in-Cs in GEA, of which Smuts was one of four. There is much room for further study of the problem, which is beyond the scope of this book.

Once Smuts had delivered most of GEA territory, he was summoned by Botha to attend the Imperial Conference in London in early 1917. What was intended to be a brief sojourn in the United Kingdom turned into a protracted stay as he became a member of the War Cabinet and served on numerous committees directing Britain's war efforts. He was offered, but turned down, the command of the Egyptian front, a sure vindication of the high regard he was held by Lloyd George. He had a major role in formulating a credible air defence of the United Kingdom and played a major role in the formation of the Royal Air Force. The outbreak of peace saw him at the centre of formulating the machinery for the League of Nations. Unfortunately, he would have to settle for a mandate over GSWA instead of outright annexation as the power balance shifted from Europe to the USA while the British Empire was rapidly becoming an anachronism. South Africa's elevated status on the world stage due to the Smuts's efforts could not compensate for the paltry spoils of war he garnered at great expense nor his waning popularity among home-front Afrikaners.

In a final irony, Smuts's wily opponent Lettow-Vorbeck would enjoy a growing cult status both in Germany and overseas. This was in large measure due to him managing to battle on for a few days beyond the armistice of 11 November 1918, when he and a remaining ragtag band of *Schutztruppen* surrendered to General Jaap van Deventer on 25 November 1918. Lettow-Vorbeck returned to Germany in early March 1919 to a hero's welcome. He led the Schutztruppe veterans in their tattered tropical uniforms on a victory parade through the Brandenburg Gate, which was decorated in their honour. Smuts would return to South Africa and assume the premiership when Botha died from Spanish influenza on 27 August 1919. Smuts lacked the charisma of Botha, and he went on to suffer defeat to Hertzog and his National Party in 1924. It would be 15 years until he was again able to hold the reins of power, in 1939, when he led South Africa into the Second World War.

Appendix: Chronology of the GSWA campaign

Chronology of the German South West Africa Campaign and the Afrikaner Rebellion 1914–1915

"C" Force Beves / Central Force McKenzie	"A" Force Lukin / Southern Force Van Deventer	"B" Force Maritz / Eastern Force Berrange	"D" Force Mckenzie / Northern Force Botha	Event	Date
				Smuts finalises his plan to invade GSWA	21-Aug-14
	Port Nolloth			Lukin lands at Port Nolloth	31-Aug-1914
				General Beyers resigns from the UDF	15-Sep-1914
Luderitz				Seaborne Landing	19-Sep-1914
	Sandfontein			UDF experiences its first defeat	26-Sep-1914
				Walvis bay Landings abandoned	28-Sep-1914
X				"D" force under McKenzie abandons Walvis Bay and makes for Luderitz	30-Sep-1914
				Maritz in open rebellion	9-Oct-1914
				Martial Law Declared	14-Oct-1914
	Keimoes			Maritz attacks Keimos with German troops	22-Oct-1914
				First shots of rebellion in the TVL (Beyers) Kommissiedrif	27-Oct-1914
				De Wet defeated at Mushroom Valley by Botha	12-Nov-1914
				Kemp joins forces with Maritz in GSWA	28-Nov-1914
				Beyers dies of a heart attack	8-Dec-1914
Tschaukaib					15-Dec-1914
				Maritz and Kemp with German troops defeat UDF at Nous	21-Dec-1914

Phase I

Phase II

Date	Event				
25-Dec-2014		Walvis bay			
16-Jan-1915		Swakopmund			
25-Jan-1915	Maritz and Kemp heavily defeated on attack on Upington				
2-Feb-1915	Maritz and Kemp forces surrender at Upington				
11-Feb-1915	General Botha assumes command Northern Force	X			
22-Feb-1915			Nonidas/Husab		Garub
6-Mar-1915	Berrange sets off from Kuruman			X	
19-Mar-1915			Riet/Jackalswater		
22-Mar-1915					Dawignab
29-Mar-1915	Botha travels to Luderitzbucht to urge Mackenzie to advance on Aus				
31-Mar-1915				Hasuur	Aus
2-Apr-1915					Geitsaub
5-Apr-1915	Main railway Junction				Kalkfontein
5-Apr-1915					Kanus
7-Apr-1915					Warmbad
11-Apr-1915	Smuts Arrives to command the Southern forces			X	X
14-Apr-1915	Southern and Eastern forces meet			Kiriis West	
15-Apr-1915	Mckenzie leaves Aus			X	X
19-Apr-1915					Seeheim

Date	Keetmanshoop	Keetmanshoop/Kabus		
20-Apr-1915				
22-Apr-1915	Berseba			
26-Apr-1915			Trekkoppies	Last German offensive of the campaign
27-Apr-1915	Gibeon Station			Southern, Central, Eastern force combine
28-Apr-1915		Daberos		
5-May-1915			Karibib	Main railway Junction
12-May-1915			Windhoek	Capital of GSWA
20-Jun-1915			Omaruru	
27-Jun-1915			Otiwarango	
1-Jul-1915			Otavi	
4-Jul-1915			Tsumeb/Grootfontein	
6-Jul-1915			Namuton	
9-Jul-1915			Tsumeb	Germans surrender to Botha
Afrikaner Rebelion				
Phase I				
Phase II				

Endnotes

Introduction

1 B. Nasson, Litnet, Review of *Jan Smuts: Afrikaner sonder grense by Richard Steyn*, www.litnet.co.za/jan-smuts-afrikaner-sonder-grense-richard-steyn/ accessed 9 January 2018.

2 B. Nasson, Litnet, Review of *Jan Smuts: Afrikaner sonder grense by Richard Steyn*, www.litnet.co.za/jan-smuts-afrikaner-sonder-grense-richard-steyn/ accessed 9 January 2018.

3 K. du Pisani, 'The Smuts Biographies: Analysis and Historiographical Assessment', *South African Historical Journal*, 68.3 (2016) pp. 437–63. Kobus du Pisani has produced an impressive historiographical assessment of published Smuts biographies.

4 W.K. Hancock, *Smuts: The Sanguine Years 1870–1919* (London: Cambridge University Press, 1962) and W.K. Hancock, *Smuts: The Fields of Force 1919–1950* (London: Cambridge University Press, 1968).

5 W.K. Hancock, *Smuts: The Sanguine Years 1870–1919* (London: Cambridge University Press, 1962) p. xii.

6 N. Levi, *Jan Smuts* (London: Longmans Green & Co., 1917).

7 S.G. Millin, *General Smuts Volume I* (Safety Harbor: Simon Publications, 2001).

8 E.S. Crafford, *Jan Smuts: A Biography* (New York: Doubleday, Doron & Co. Inc, 1943).

9 *Jan Smuts: Van Boerseun Tot Wereldverhoog*, ed. by K. du Pisani, D. Kriek, and C. de Jager (Pretoria: Protea, 2017).

10 A. Grundlingh, 'The King's Afrikaners? Enlistment and Ethnic Identity in the Union of South Africa's Defence Force during the Second World War, 1939–45', *The Journal of African History*, 40.3 (1999) p. 352.

11 K. du Pisani, D. Kriek, and C. de Jager, (eds), *Jan Smuts: Van Boerseun Tot Wereldverhoog* (Pretoria: Protea, 2017).

12 R. Steyn, *Jan Smuts: Unafraid of Greatness* (Johannesburg & Cape Town: Jonathan Ball, 2015) p. ix.

13 B. Nasson, Litnet, Review of *Jan Smuts: Afrikaner sonder grense by Richard Steyn*, www.litnet.co.za/jan-smuts-afrikaner-sonder-grense-richard-steyn/ accessed 9 January 2018.

14 A. Lentin, *Jan Smuts: Man of Courage and Vision* (Johannesburg & Cape Town: Jonathan Ball, 2010).

15 Shula Marks, 'White Masculinity: Jan Smuts, Race and the South African War', in *Raleigh Lectures on History*, 2001.

16 S. Dubow, 'Smuts, the United Nations and the Rhetoric of Race and Rights', *Journal of Contemporary History*, 43.1 (2008) p. 61. See also S. Dubow, *Scientific Racism in Modern South Africao Title* (New York: Cambridge University Press, 1995) pp. 51, 52, 209.

17 M. Legassick, 'British Hegemony and the Origins of Segregation in South Africa, 1901–14', in *Segregation and Apartheid in Twentieth Century South Africa*, ed. by W. Beinart and S. Dubow (New York: Routledge, 1995).

18 Anon, *The Union of South Africa and the Great War 1918* (Nashville: Battery Press, 1924). Government Printer in Pretoria published the original book. The Battery Press is an exact facsimile of the original.

19 I. van der Waag, 'Contested histories: Official History and the South African Military in the 20th Century', in *The Last Word? Essays on Official History, in the United States and British Commonwealth*, ed. by J. Grey (Westport, Connecticut & London: Praeger, 2003) p. 34. B. Nasson, *Springboks on the Somme* (Johannesburg: Penguin, 2007).

20 J.G.W. Leipoldt, *The Union of South Africa and the Great War 1914–1918* (Pretoria: General Staff, DHQ, 1924). The first official history was in fact authored by J. Buchan, *The South African Forces in France* (London: Nelson, 1920).

21 J.J. Collyer, *Campaign in German South West Africa, 1914–1915* (Nashville: The Imperial War Museum and Battery Press, 1937).

22 J.J. Collyer, *The South Africans with General Smuts in German East Africa* (Nashville: Imperial War Museum and Battery Press, 1939).

23 C. Hordern, *Military Operations East Africa volume 1 August 1914–September 1916* (London: Her Britannic Majesty's Stationery Office, 1941).

24 Van der Waag, 'Contested histories', p. 42. The Ashanti series is described by Van der Waag as a concealed' or 'secret history' where most of the authors were unaware of their government sponsorship.

25 G. L'Ange, *Urgent Imperial Service: South African Forces in German South West Africa 1914–1915* (Rivonia: Ashanti, 1991).

26 J.A. Brown, *They Fought for King and Kaiser: South Africans in German East Africa 1916* (Rivonia: Ashanti, 1991).

27 I. Gleeson, *The Unknown Force: Black, Indian and Coloured Soldiers Through Two World Wars* (Rivonia: Ashanti, 1994).

28 Grey, 'Standing Humbly', p. 255.

29 H.C. Armstrong, *Grey Steel: A Study in Arrogance* (London: Methuen & Co., 1941). Armstrong served as a junior officer with the British 6th Division and was captured by the Turks during the siege of Kut (1915–16). There he languished until he managed to escape just before the end of the war. After the war, he was posted back to Turkey for some years, during which he was in constant touch with the Turks, including Mustafa Kemal, and watched the rise of Atatürk's New Turkey.

30 R. Meinertzhagen, *Army Diary 1899–1926* (London: Oliver and Boyd, 1960).

31 B. Gardner, *German East: The story of the First World War in East Africa* (London: Cassel, 1963).

32 L. Mosley, *Duel for Kilimanjaro: An Account of the East African Campaign* (New York: Ballantine, 1964).

33 J.R. Sibley, *Tanganyikan Guerrilla* (London: Pan Books, 1973).

34 C. Miller, *Battle for the Bundu: The First World War in East Africa* (London: Purnell, 1974).

35 E.P. Hoyt, *Guerilla: Colonell von Lettow-Vorbeck and Germany's East African Empire* (London: Macmillan, 1981).

36 B. Farwell, *The Great War in Africa, 1914–1918* (New York: W.W. Norton, 1986).

37 H.F. Trew, *Botha Treks* (London: Blackie & Son, 1936).

38 Strachan, *The First World War in Africa*. This book has been excerpted almost word for word from Strachan's magnus opus on the First World War. H. Strachan, *The First World War Volume I* (Oxford: Oxford University, 2001).

39 R. Anderson, *The Forgotten Front: The East African Campaign 1914–1918* (Gloucestershire: Tempus, 2004).

40 H. Strachan, *The First World War in Africa* (Oxford, Oxford University Press, 2004) p. 94.

41 R. Anderson, 'World War I in East Africa 1916–1918' (University of Glasgow, Department of Modern History, PhD thesis, 2001).

42 B. Nasson, Litnet, Review of *Jan Smuts: Afrikaner sonder grense by Richard Steyn*, www.litnet. co.za/jan-smuts-afrikaner-sonder-grense-richard-steyn/ accessed 9 January 2018. "[His] inability to recognise, even less to try and reconcile, his blindness towards the yawning contradiction between his grand global ambitions for an improving world ruled by human rights and human liberties, and his failure to accept that these freedoms ought to extend to all the inhabitants of his own home country."

43 J.C. Smuts, 'South Africa in Science', *South African Journal of Science*, 22 (1925) p. 17.

44 A. Samson, *World War I in Africa: The Forgotten Conflict Among the European Powers* (London: Tauris, 2013) p. 25. See also, S.B. Spies, 'The Outbreak of the First World War and the Botha Government', *South African Historical Journal*, I (1969) p. 52.

45 D.W. Kruger, *The Making of a Nation* (Johannesburg: Macmillan, 1977) p. 21.

46 A. Samson, *World War I in Africa: The Forgotten Conflict Among the European Powers* (London: Tauris, 2013) p. 38.

47 S.B. Spies, 'The Outbreak of the First World War and the Botha Government', *South African Historical Journal*, I (1969) p. 52.

48 R.C. Warwick, 'Reconcideration of the Battle of Sandfontein: The First Phase of the German South West Africa Campaign, August to September 1914' (MA Thesis, University of Cape Town, Faculty of Humanities, 2003). And R.C. Warwick, 'The Battle of Sandfontein: The Role and Legacy of Major-General Sir Henry Timson Lukin', *Scientia Militaria*, 34(2) (2006) pp. 65–92. See also I. van der Waag, 'The Battle of Sandfontein, 26 September 1914: South African military reform and the German South-West Africa campaign, 1914–1915', *First World War Studies*, DOI: 10.1080/19475020.2013.828633 (2013).

49 A. Samson, *Britain, South Africa and the East Africa Campaign, 1914–1918* (London: Tauris, 2006) p. 1. Samson's title to her book includes, 'The Union Comes of Age; which is indicative of the importance she attaches to the campaign in maturing South Africa as a nation and its standing within the Empire.

50 S. Katzenellenbogen, *South Africa and Southern Mozambique: Labour, Railways, and Trade in the Making of a Relationship* (Manchester: Manchester University, 1982) pp. 121–4.

51 I. van Der Waag, 'Rural Struggles and the Politics of a Colonial Command: The Southern Mounted Rifles of the Transvaal Volunteers, 1905–1912', in *Soldiers and Settlers in Africa, 1850–1918*, ed. by S. Miller (Leiden: Brill, 2009) p. 281. See also I. van der Waag, 'Smuts's Generals: Towards a First Portrait of the South African High Command,1912–1948', *War in History*, 18(1) (2011) p. 39.

52 I. van der Waag, 'Smuts's Generals: Towards a First Portrait of the South African High Command,1912–1948', *War in History*, 18(1) (2011) pp. 43, 44.

53 H. Strachan, *The First World War in Africa* (Oxford: Oxford University Press, 2004) p. 134.

54 H. Strachan, *The First World War in Africa* (Oxford: Oxford University Press, 2004) p. 149.

55 W.K. Hancock and J. van der Poel (eds), *Selections From the Smuts Papers III June 1910–November 1918* (London: Cambridge University Press, 1966) , p. 422.

56 H. Strachan, *The First World War in Africa* (Oxford: Oxford University Press, 2004) p. 164.

57 P.J. Yearwood, 'Great Britain and the Repartition of Africa, 1914 –1919', *The Journal of Imperial and Commonwealth History*, 18(3) (1990) pp. 317, 318.

58 W.K. Hancock, *Smuts: The Sanguine Years 1870–1919* (London: Cambridge University Press, 1962). His cooption into the War Cabinet was "constitutionally and politically anomalous" and unusual for someone who did not have a seat in the British Parliament.

59 P.J. Yearwood, 'Great Britain and the Repartition of Africa, 1914–1919', *The Journal of Imperial and Commonwealth History*, 18(3) (1990) pp. 317, 318.

60   Anne Samson is one of the few exceptions amongst the more modern researchers, after the initial work of Roger Hyam and Katzenellenbogen.

Chapter 1

1   S.G. Millin, *General Smuts Volume I* (Safety Harbor: Simon Publications, 2001) pp. 8–14

2   W.K. Hancock, *Smuts: The Sanguine Years 1870–1919* (London: Cambridge University Press, 1962) p. 5.

3   The Boer Republics came about as a result of the mass migration of Dutch-speaking inhabitants in the Cape who wished to escape direct British rule. This resulted in what became known as the Great Trek in 1835–46 and the formation of the two Boer Republics of the ZAR in 1852 and the OFS in 1854 under the Sand River Convention. The ZAR lost its independence after the British annexed it in 1877. The ZAR regained its independence in what became known as the First Anglo-Boer War in 1881. The ZAR became fully independent with the signing of the London Convention in 1884.

4   S. Trapido, 'Imperialism, Settler Identities and Colonial Capitalism: The Hundred Year Origins of the 1899 South African War', *Historia*, 53.1 (2008) pp. 47, 65. Trapido describes a "pragmatic" loyalty to the British regime by those speaking the "Queen's Dutch".

5   H.A. Shearing, 'The Cape Rebel of the South African War 1899–1902' (PhD thesis, Stellenbosch University, 2004). Shearing has produced a work which attempts to underscore the reasons why Cape Afrikaners joined the rebellion in small numbers.

6   C.M. van den Heever, *General J.B.M Hertzog* (Johannesburg: APB Bookstone, 1946), p. 10. See also L. Koorts, *D.F. Malan and the Rise of Afrikaner Nationalism* (Cape Town: Tafelberg, 2014) p. 2. General J.B.M. Hertzog and Dr D.F. Malan were born in 1866 and 1874 respectively; both lived near Smuts and were subject to the steady anglicisation of their families.

7   J. van der Poel (ed.), *Selections from the Smuts Papers Volume V September 1919–November 1934*, Letter: Smuts to Millin, 13 September 1932 (London: Cambridge University Press, 1973), p. 521. Smuts strongly criticises Millin for suggesting that the Bond was separatist in its "palmy days". He corrected her and suggested a strong British connection, especially in the post Du Toit–Hofmeyr phase.

8   H. Giliomee, 'The Beginnings of Afrikaner Nationalism, 1870–1915', *South African Historical Journal*, 19.1 (2009) p. 122. The Afrikaner Bond should not be viewed in stock nationalistic terms. Davenport describes the movement as "something wider than the nationalism of an oppressed and exclusive cultural group, but narrower than a simple patriotism".

9   J.H. Hofmeyr and F.W. Reitz, *The Life of Jan Hendrik Hofmeyr (Onze Jan)* (Cape Town: Van der Sandt, 1913), pp. 196–98. See also H. Giliomee, *The Afrikaners* (Cape Town: Tafelberg, 2003), pp. 193–227. Giliomee has a chapter 'The Queen's Afrikaners' which presents the pro-British feelings of the Cape Afrikaner during the formative years of Smuts. See also M. Tamarkin, *Cecil Rhodes and the Cape Afrikaners: The Imperial Colossus and the Colonial Parish Pump* (Johannesburg: Jonathan Ball, 1996) p. 63. Self-government created space for Afrikaner political aspirations as imperialism receded in the colony.

10   Also known as the Transvaal War of Independence.

11   M. Tamarkin, *Cecil Rhodes and the Cape Afrikaners: The Imperial Colossus and the Colonial Parish Pump* (Johannesburg: Jonathan Ball, 1996) pp. 36–8. The emergence of an Afrikaner 'political ethnic self-consciousness' began to emerge around the time of Smuts's birth. The intricacies of its manifestation are beyond the scope of this study.

12   W.K. Hancock and J. van der Poel (eds), *Selections from the Smuts Papers Volume I June 1886–May 1902*, Letter from Smuts to Murray 12 June 1886 (London: Cambridge University Press, 1966),

p. 4. Murray's comment to Smuts on returning the letter to him many years later is that he kept it because the letter stood out from the normal run of communication and the writer clearly "knew what he wanted".

13 P. Beukes, *The Romantic Smuts* (Cape Town: Human & Rousseu, 1992), pp. 7, 18–21. See also *Hancock, Selections from the Smuts Papers Volume I*, Letter from Smuts to Krige 10 December 1887, p. 6. This letter provides proof of Smuts's romantic side, an affinity for women, although the seriousness of the subject matter is beyond the years of a normal teenager

14 As quoted in S.G. Millin, *Rhodes* (London: Chatto & Windus, 1933), p. 61. Rhodes was approached by the Afrikaner Bond to lead a united South Africa under an independent flag, and he is said to have responded, "You take me either for a rogue or a fool. I would be a rogue to forfeit all my history and tradition, and I would be a fool because I would be hated by my own countrymen and mistrusted by yours."

15 Hancock, *Selections from the Smuts Papers Volume I*, Smuts Letter to publisher re: 'A study in the Evolution of Personality: Walt Whitmam, 18 May 1895', p. 53. Smuts began to formulate his ideas of holism in his study of an American poet, essayist, and journalist Walt Whitman. Smuts struggled to get the book into print, and he never published it.

16 Hancock, *Selections from the Smuts Papers Volume I*, Essay by Smuts, *South African Customs Union*, 1891, p. 15. See also Hancock, *Selections from the Smuts Papers Volume I*, Essay by Smuts, *The Conditions of Future South African Literature*, 1890, p. 41.

17 G. Tylden, *The Armed Forces of South Africa 1659–1954* (Johannesburg: Trophy Press, 1982), p. 187. Tylden does not provide a date when Smuts joined Victoria College Volunteer Rifle Corps

18 Hancock, *Selections from the Smuts Papers Volume I*, Essay by Smuts, *South African Customs Union*, 1890, p. 17. Smuts proposed a political and economic union of the British colonies, the High Commission Territories, and the Boer Republics.

19 Hancock, *Selections from the Smuts Papers Volume I*, Essay by Smuts *The Conditions of Future South African Literature*, 1892, p. 47.

20 J.C. Smuts, *Jan Smuts: Memoirs of the Boer War*, ed. by S.B. Spies and G. Nattrass (Johannesburg: Jonathan Ball, 1994), p. 19.

21 I.R. Smith, 'Jan Smuts and the South African War', *South African Historical Journal*, 41.1 (2009), p. 174.

22 As quoted in J.C. Smuts, *Jan Christian Smuts* (London: Cassel & Co., 1952), p. 32.

23 Hancock, Smuts: The Sanguine Years, p. 56.

24 P.R. Warhurst, *Anglo-Portuguese Relations in South-Central Africa 1890–1900* (London: Longmans, 1962) p. 4.

25 Smith, 'Jan Smuts and the South African War', p. 174. Smith acknowledges that Smuts held a critical view of Kruger's ZAR at that time and harboured "a Cape superiority". See also H.C. Armstrong, *Grey Steel* (London: Methuen, 1941) pp. 41, 42, 44.

26 There is considerable confusion around the nomenclature of Boers, Afrikaners, and other groups of Afrikaans/Dutch-speaking people. Trekboers were a group which left the Dutch East India Company to fend for themselves from 1657 and clashed with Khoisan and Xhosas until the British took over from 1806. Voortrekkers refer to groups which participated in the Great Trek from 1835. Burghers (citizens) or Boers (farmers) refer to all the above groups. Afrikaner is a more modern construct.

27 Hancock, *Selections from the Smuts Papers Volume I*, Essay by Smuts, *A Trip to the Transvaal: The Closing of the Drifts and other Political Questions*, 26 October 1895, pp. 77, 78.

28 Hancock, *Selections from the Smuts Papers Volume I*, Speech by Smuts Kimberley, 30 October 1895, pp. 80–92.

29 Hancock, *Selections from the Smuts Papers Volume I*, Speech by Smuts Kimberley, 30 October 1895, pp. 93–100.

30 The company was founded in 1888 by British businessman Cecil Rhodes, who was financed by the South African diamond magnate Alfred Beit and the London-based N.M. Rothschild & Sons bank.

31 S.C. Cronwright-Schreiner, *The Life of Olive Schreiner* (Boston: Little, Brown & Co., 1924), p. 275. Cronwright-Schreiner was husband to Olive Schreiner. He changed his surname to Cronwright-Schreiner when he married Olive in 1894.

32 *Mittelafrika* articulated Germany's desire prior to the First Word War to build a contiguous German African Empire from the west to the east coast of Africa straddling the equator.

33 Hancock, *Selections from the Smuts Papers Volume I*, Unpublished article 'The British Position in South Africa', June 1897, pp. 182, 183.

34 Smith, 'Jan Smuts and the South African War', p. 179. Smuts called this "Capitalistic Jingoism" which arrived with Joseph Chamberlain and the Conservative government and lasted 1895–1905. See also J.C. Smuts, *A Century of Wrong* (London: Review of Reviews, 1900), p. 54

35 Smuts, *Jan Christian Smuts*, p. 36.

36 Smuts, *A Century of Wrong*, pp. 59, 60.

37 M. Tamarkin, *Cecil Rhodes and the Cape Afrikaners: The Imperial Colossus and the Colonial Parish Pump* (Johannesburg: Jonathan Ball, 1996), p. 244.

38 P. Meiring, *Smuts the Patriot* (Cape Town: Tafelberg, 1975), p. 7.

39 R. Steyn, *Jan Smuts: Unafraid of Greatness* (Johannesburg & Cape Town: Jonathan Ball, 2015), p. 12. Steyn makes extensive use of Meiring and describes Smuts at Stellenbosch as being "fervently nationalistic"; H. Giliomee, 'The Beginnings of Afrikaner Nationalism, 1870–1915', *South African Historical Journal*, 19.1 (2009), pp. 115, 118, 120. One must be guarded when using the word 'nationalism' which was largely absent from the South African scene prior to 1870 as Afrikaners were characterised by great political apathy. In this period even the meaning of the term 'Afrikaner' was vague and shifting.

40 Hancock, *Selections from the Smuts Papers Volume I*, Article by Smuts, 'Afrikaner Rapprochement, Ons Land' 12 March 1896, pp. 103–6. Smuts lambasted Rhodes and his betrayal and his jingoism. He blamed Rhodes for dividing Cape and Republic Afrikaners. He called on colonial and Republican unity and implored, "let us lay down the corner stone of a truly united South Africa on the foundation of a pure and comprehensive national feeling."

41 M. Tamarkin, *Cecil Rhodes and the Cape Afrikaners: The Imperial Colossus and the Colonial Parish Pump* (Johannesburg: Jonathan Ball, 1996), p. 239.

42 Hancock, *Smuts: The Sanguine Years*, pp. 61–4.

43 M. Tamarkin, *Cecil Rhodes and the Cape Afrikaners: The Imperial Colossus and the Colonial Parish Pump* (Johannesburg: Jonathan Ball, 1996), p. 295. See also Smith, 'Jan Smuts and the South African War', p. 177. The main body of the Bond under Hofmeyr remained true to the ideal of amalgamating English and Afrikaner in a unified state. They remained critical of Kruger and loyal to the British connection. See also Hancock, *Selections from the Smuts Papers Volume I*, Unpublished article 'The British Position in South Africa', June 1897, p. 174. "If there is one fact on which Colonial Afrikanders are more clear than on any other, it is this: that with the Transvaal must stand or fall the cause of the Dutch Afrikanders in South Africa."

44 Hancock, *Selections from the Smuts Papers Volume I*, 'Memoirs of the Boer War', p. 624.

45 R. Hyam, *Understanding the British Empire* (Cambridge: Cambridge University Press, 2010) p. 349; Hancock, *Smuts: The Sanguine Years*, p. 133.

46 M. Samuels, *Command or Control* (London: Frank Cass & Co. Ltd, 1995), p. 8. Commonly known as the centre of gravity, Samuels defines the term in the military context as "the point of main effort" or "focus of energy".

47 Smuts, *A Century of Wrong*, "History will show convincingly that the pleas of humanity, civilisation, and equal rights, upon which the British Government bases its actions, are nothing else but the recrudescence of that spirit of annexation and plunder which has at all times characterised its dealings with our people."

48 Millin, *General Smuts*, p. 55.

49 Hancock, *Selections from the Smuts Papers Volume I*, Unpublished article 'The British Position in South Africa', June 1897, p. 149. See also J. van der Poel (ed.), *Selections from the Smuts Papers Volume V September 1919–November 1934*, Letter Smuts to Millin, 13 September 1932 (London: Cambridge University Press, 1973), p. 521. Smuts refers to the Jameson Raid as a "disaster". "It inflamed the national psychology of the Boers, made racial trust impossible, and created the very mentality of the Boer War."

50 Millin, *General Smuts*, p. 54. Smuts's version of pan-Africanism involved the spreading of white western civilisation via the hegemony of the British Empire beyond the borders of South Africa. This obviously differed substantially from the later anti-colonial and liberation pan-Africanists such as Kwame Nkrumah and Amilcar Cabral.

51 E.E. Dicey, 'Rhodes Redivivus', *Fortnightly Review*, 64, 1998, p. 605–19.

52 Millin, *General Smuts*, p. 56. Literally, Rhodes reborn.

53 Hancock, *Selections from the Smuts Papers Volume I*, Account from *South African Telegraph*, 31 August 1896, p. 143. An indication of Smuts's modest earnings for the month of August 1896 is a statement of account with the *South African Telegraph*. On average he earned £1 per submission.

54 Hancock, *Selections from the Smuts Papers Volume I*, Letter from J.I. Marais 11 August 1896, p. 142. Marais, Smuts's financial benefactor while he studied in the United Kingdom asked Smuts to supply an acknowledgement of debt in excess of £300 with 5% interest.

55 Hancock, *Smuts: The Sanguine Years*, p. 62. See also P. Beukes, *The Romantic Smuts* (Cape Town: Human & Rousseu, 1992), p. 22.

56 Hancock, *Selections from the Smuts Papers Volume I*, Letter to Hofmeyr and an article in the *Transvaal Critic*, 31 January 1897, p. 138. See also Hancock, *Smuts: The Sanguine Years*, p. 62.

57 Hancock, *Selections from the Smuts Papers Volume I*, Account from *South African Telegraph*, 31 August 1896, p. 149.

58 Hancock, *Selections from the Smuts Papers Volume I*, Unpublished article 'The British Position in South Africa', June 1897, pp. 166–76.

59 S. Dubow, 'Colonial Nationalism, the Milner Kindergarten and the Rise of "South Africanism", 1902–10', *History Workshop Journal*, 1997, p. 55. South Africanism was the belief in the principle of Anglo-Afrikaner unity within the nation. Milner's Kindergarten tried to overcome the enmities of Boer and Briton in the years after the South African War and the formation of the Union by engendering a sense of white 'South Africanism'.

60 Hancock, *Selections from the Smuts Papers Volume I*, Unpublished article 'The British Position in South Africa', June 1897, pp. 166–76.

61 Hancock, *Selections from the Smuts Papers Volume I*, Letter from Hofmeyr 15 May 1899, p. 237. Hofmeyr, somewhat prophetically, warned Smuts that he should not expect colonial Afrikaners to rush to arms en masse in a response to the outbreak of war.

62 Hancock, *Selections from the Smuts Papers Volume I*, Unpublished article 'The British Position in South Africa', June 1897, pp. 184,185.

63 C. Quigley, *The Anglo-American Establishment* (San Pedro: GSG & Associates, 1981), p. 77–9.

64 Millin, *General Smuts Volume I*, p. 29.

65 J.H. Hofmeyr and F.W. Reitz, *The Life of Jan Hendrik Hofmeyr (Onze Jan)* (Cape Town: Van der Sandt, 1913), p. 504.

66 Hancock, *Selections from the Smuts Papers Volume I*, Article in *Ons Land* 12 March 1896, p. 100.

67 Hancock, *Smuts: The Sanguine Years*, p. 62. See also Armstrong, *Grey Steel*, p. 69. There was a strong possibility that Smuts would be selected as State Secretary but age precluded him and F.W. Reitz was appointed in his stead. See also Hancock, *Selections from the Smuts Papers Volume I*, p. 189. The position of State Attorney attracted a salary of £2,500 per anum easing his financial burdens.

68 C. Headlam (ed.), *The Milner Papers South Africa 1897–1899*, Letter to Conyngham Greene 18 February 1898 (London: Cassel & Co., 1931) p. 216 Milner viewed the dismissal of Kotze as an attack on the independence of the judiciary. Headlam, *The Milner Papers*, pp. 212–16.

69 Smuts, *A Century of Wrong*, p. 60. Smuts was of the view that the strength of the Bond in the Cape Colony, after the Jameson Raid, and its increasing support of the Republics, was one of the major factors in driving Milner into a war to prevent an alliance between the Bond and the Republics.

70 Smuts, *Jan Christian Smuts*, p. 38.

71 Hancock, *Smuts: The Sanguine Years*, p. 73.

72 Hancock, *Smuts: The Sanguine Years*, p. 62. See also Armstrong, *Grey Steel*, p. 69. There was a strong possibility that Smuts would be selected as State Secretary but age precluded him and F.W. Reitz was appointed in his stead. See also Hancock, *Selections from the Smuts Papers Volume I*, p. 189. See also Smuts, *Jan Christian Smuts*, p. 38. It was Piet Grobler, Kruger's nephew and private secretary who introduced him to Kruger.

73 Headlam, *The Milner Papers*, Letter De villiers to Steyn, p. 394. It is significant that when J.H. de Villiers visited Pretoria, he avoided Kruger and called on Reitz, Smuts, and Schalk Burger who he believed wielded considerable influence. See also J. Grobler, 'The "Young Afrikaners": Jan Smuts and Piet Grobler during the Months of Storm and Stress (January–October 1899)', *Historia*, 44.1 (1999), p. 87. Kruger became increasingly reliant on Smuts and his nephew Piet Grobler. The two took over the correspondence with the British government from Reitz.

74 Van Onselen, 'Randlords and Rotgut 1886–1903: An Essay on the Role of Alcohol in the Development of European Imperialism and Southern African Capitalism, with Special Reference to Black Mineworkers in the Transvaal Republic', *History Workshop*, 2 (1976), p. 71. Ferguson was part of illicit gold dealings.

75 Hancock, *Smuts: The Sanguine Years*, p. 84.

76 Headlam, *The Milner Papers*, p. 30. The Uitlander (foreign national) grievances can be summed up as lack of franchise, unequal taxes, poor policing, and corruption in Johannesburg, and lack of educational facilities except in Dutch.

77 Hancock, *Selections from the Smuts Papers Volume I*, Letter to W.J. Leyds 30 April 1899, p. 228. Smuts makes the point that he failed to understand how Britain could insist that the ZAR make British subjects give up their allegiance to Britain and make them subjects of the ZAR.

78 Headlam, *The Milner Papers*, p. 30. In a speech delivered at his farewell banquet on 27 March 1897 he reiterated the importance of not allowing a repeat of the "dire disaster [of] the loss of the American Colonies" resulting in a "severance of another link in the great Imperial chain". See also Headlam, *The Milner Papers*, Letter to Sir George Parkin 28 April 1897, p. 42. Milner considered South Africa to be the weakest link in the imperial chain.

79 G.H.L. Le May, *British Supremacy in South Africa* (London: Oxford University Press, 1965), pp. 7, 8.

80 Smuts, *Jan Christian Smuts*, p. 47.

81 Headlam, *The Milner Papers*, Letter to Earl of Selborne, 20 March 1897, p. 37.
82 Headlam, *The Milner Papers*, Letter to Clinton Dawkins, 25 August 1897, p. 87.
83 Headlam, *The Milner Papers*, Letter to Lord Selborne, 13 October 1897, p. 100; Milner having completed half the trip was convinced that the Dutch colonials were susceptible to manipulation by the Dutch press and the Bond.
84 Headlam, *The Milner Papers*, Letter from Chamberlain 23 February 1898, p. 227.
85 Headlam, *The Milner Papers*, Letter from Selborne 22 March 1898, p. 229.
86 Hancock, *Selections from the Smuts Papers Volume I*, Conversations with E. Fraser 22 December 1898, p. 189.
87 Hancock, *Smuts: The Sanguine Years*, p. 85, 89. See also Headlam, *The Milner Papers*, Letter Conyngham Greene to Milner 15 May 1899, p. 379. Greene identified that Kruger was under pressure to concede but that the young Afrikander party led by Smuts, Piet Grobler (Kruger's confidant), Louis Esselen (son of a ZAR state secretary) and others backed by the Hollander clique were openly defiant.
88 Headlam, *The Milner Papers*, Dispatch Milner to Chamberlain, p. 391. Milner was aware that Smuts enjoyed a greater role than State Attorney through his links with prominent role players in the Cape and the OFS.
89 Headlam, *The Milner Papers*, p. 372. The Conservatives regained power in the September/October 1900 elections with a large majority in the House but a slim majority of the popular vote.
90 Headlam, *The Milner Papers*, Telegram Leyds, Berlin to Pretoria government 27 May 1899, p. 393. See also Le May, *British Supremacy*, p. 15. In the second half of 1898 Germany renounced interest in the Transvaal due to the Anglo-German agreement concluded in August in favour of a possible division of the Portuguese colonies.
91 Smuts, *Jan Christian Smuts*, p. 45.
92 Hancock, *Selections from the Smuts Papers Volume I*, Letter to Hofmeyr 10 May 1899, p. 233. Smuts believed the danger of war emanated from the Bond victories in the Cape Colony.
93 The main outcome of the London Convention was that British suzerainty over the South African Republic was amended.
94 L.S. Amery, *The Times History of the War in South Africa 1899–1900 Volume I* (London: Sampson Low, Marston & Co. Ltd, 1900), p. 262.
95 Hancock, *Smuts: The Sanguine Years*, p. 93. Milner demanded a five-year retrospective franchise. He would not entertain any bargaining. See also Headlam, *The Milner Papers*, Telegram to Chamberlain 4 May 1899, p. 353. Milner in his dispatch referred to the Uitlanders as being kept by the ZAR in the position of "helots". Milner was determined to obtain for the Uitlanders a fair share of the ZAR government. See also Headlam (ed.), *The Milner Papers*, Letter Conyngham Greene to Milner 12 May 1899, p. 378. Milner anticipated that the conference would fail, and he participated to avoid the accusation that the British made no attempt at peace.
96 Headlam, *The Milner Papers*, Dispatch Milner to Selborne 24 May 1899, p. 400.
97 Smith, 'Jan Smuts and the South African War', p. 179.
98 Armstrong, *Grey Steel*, p. 80.
99 Amery, *The Times History Volume I*, p. 274. Amery credits Smuts and Abraham Fischer with guiding Kruger. There is much evidence of Smuts working furiously behind the scenes to deliver a modification to the franchise law elaborately drawn out in clauses and sub-clauses. The handywork of a brilliant young lawyer not of an ageing curmudgeon.
100 Hancock, *Smuts: The Sanguine Years*, p. 97. Hancock is convinced that Smuts played a major role in advising Kruger at the conference. Kruger chose Smuts over Francis William Reitz, State Secretary of the ZAR, to accompany him to the conference. The probability was that it was Smuts who drafted all the counterproposals. See also Headlam, *The Milner Papers*, p. 418. The

counterproposals were designed to place numerous conditions and preconditions on the granting of the franchise which would render the process untenable. Milner saw through the ruse.

101 W.B. Worsfold, *Lord Milner's Work in South Africa* (London: John Murray Albemarle Street, 1906), p. 171.

102 Hancock, *Smuts: The Sanguine Years*, p. 97.

103 Headlam, *The Milner Papers*, Milner Diary 1 July 1899, p. 451.

104 Headlam, *The Milner Papers*, Telegram Selborne to Milner 25 June 1899, p. 445.

105 Hancock, *Smuts: The Sanguine Years*, p. 103.

106 Hancock, *Selections from the Smuts Papers Volume I*, Letter from Schreiner 6 May 1899, p. 229. Schreiner cajoled Smuts to "secure reasonable concessions". See also Hancock, *Selections from the Smuts Papers Volume I*, Letter from Hofmeyr 6 May 1899, p. 230. Hofmeyr urged Smuts to "pour oil on stormy waters".

107 Hancock, *Selections from the Smuts Papers Volume I*, Letter to Hofmeyr 9 July 1899, p. 265; Hancock, *Selections from the Smuts Papers Volume I*, Letter to Hofmeyr 10 June 1899, p. 243. Smuts made numerous appeals to Hofmeyr for Afrikaner solidarity. This is but one of many examples.

108 Hancock, *Selections from the Smuts Papers Volume I*, Letter to Hofmeyr 27 July 1899, p. 272. The franchise law was published in the *Government Gazette* on 26 July 1899.

109 Headlam, *The Milner Papers*, p. 454.

110 Hancock, *Smuts: The Sanguine Years*, p. 100.

111 Headlam, *The Milner Papers*, Telegram Chamberlain to Milner, p. 468.

112 Hancock, *Smuts: The Sanguine Years*, p. 102. Smuts did have Kruger's sanction to approach Greene. See also Armstrong, *Grey Steel*, p. 86. Armstrong doubts either Smuts's or Kruger's sincerity in the matter of these late negotiations. It was purely a scheme to delay the advent of war for as long as possible to gain political and military advantage. Armstrong places Smuts as central to this manipulation where a more sympathetic viewpoint would place him as a rather young naïve pawn in the proceedings.

113 Amery, *The Times History Volume I*, p. 321. Amery is somewhat cynical in his assessment of the genuiness of the ZAR's desire for a settlement and believed the initiative was purely a delaying tactic.

114 Headlam, *The Milner Papers*, Letter Conyngham Greene to Milner 13 March 1899, p. 325. See also Headlam, *The Milner Papers*, Letter Milner to Conyngham Greene 14 March 1899, p. 326. Milner was in agreement as to Smuts's genuineness.

115 Headlam, *The Milner Papers*, Letter Milner to Fiddes 1 April 1899, p. 331.

116 Amery, *The Times History Volume I*, p. 322.

117 Headlam, *The Milner Papers*, Letter Milner to Conyngham Greene 15 August 1899, p. 489.

118 Amery, *The Times History Volume I*, p. 330.

119 Hancock, *Selections from the Smuts Papers Volume I*, Report to ZAR government 14 September 1899, p. 274. The ZAR government added to the proposals Smuts discussed with Greene concerning suzerainty and arbitration. See also N. Levi, *Jan Smuts* (London: Longmans Green & Co., 1917), p. 44. Levi speaks of Smuts's inexperience compared with a "polished diplomat" such as Greene. Even the virulent Uitlander *Transvaal Leader* described Smuts thus, "The State Attorney, with an insight and patriotic ambition entirely honourable and creditable, approached Mr. Greene with the desire of obtaining a *modus vivendi*."

120 Headlam, *The Milner Papers*, Letter Conyngham Greene to Milner 25 August 1899, p. 491.

121 Headlam, *The Milner Papers*, p. 493.

122 J. Grobler, 'The "Young Afrikaners": Jan Smuts and Piet Grobler during the Months of Storm and Stress (January–October 1899)', *Historia*, 44.1 (1999), p. 90. In TA, FK 1117 Milner papers

(Oxford No 12) Greene – Milner 12 May 1899, p. 104. Greene informed Milner, "You have the young Afrikander War Party consisting of Smuts, Piet Grobler, Esselen … They are the dangerous combustible element in the situation."

123 Hancock, *Selections from the Smuts Papers Volume I*, Letter to Hofmeyr 22 August 1899, p. 299. See also Hancock, *Selections from the Smuts Papers Volume I*, Letter from Hofmeyr 30 August 1899, p. 305. Hofmeyr summed up Smuts's political naivety by commenting of Smuts's proposals thus: "You gave too much and at the same time asked too much—spoiling the first by the second and thereby playing into the hand of the opponent."

124 Hancock, *Selections from the Smuts Papers Volume I*, Letter to J.H. Roskill 5 October 1899, p. 299. See also Amery, *The Times History Volume I*, p. 336. Smuts had the editors of the newspapers Johannesburg *Star* and the *Leader*, together with the chairman of the Uitlander Council arrested.

125 H.H. Hewison, *Hedge of Wild Almonds: South Africa, the 'Pro-Boers' & the Quaker Conscience* (London: James Currey, 1989), p. 76. See also Hancock, *Smuts: The Sanguine Years*, pp. 105, 106.

126 Le May, *British Supremacy*, p. 28. This is a paraphrase of words spoken by Lord Salisbury.

127 Smuts, *A Century of Wrong*.

128 Smuts, *A Century of Wrong*.

129 Tylden, *The Armed Forces of South Africa*, p. 187.

130 L. Scholtz, *Why the Boers Lost the War* (London: Palgrave Macmillan, 2005), p. 17.

131 L.S. Amery, *The Times History of the War in South Africa 1899–1900 Volume II* (London: Sampson Low, Marston & Co. Ltd, 1900), p. 120.

132 Potchefstroom, Pretoria, Rustenburg, Standerton, and Marabastad

133 T.N. Dupuy, *Understanding War* (New York: Paragon House Publishers, 1987), p. 3. Moltke observed in 1867 that the increased deadliness of modern firepower demanded that the strategic offensive be coupled with the tactical defensive. This doctrine culminated in the Germans manoeuvring across the French line of communication at Metz and Sedan in the Franco-Prussian War 1870 where they took up defensive positions and forced the French to attack.

134 Parliamentary Papers, Minutes of Evidence taken before the Royal Commission on the War in South Africa Volume II (Elgin Commission), Cd 1791 (1903) p. 189, q 15056. Buller was advised by the War Office Intelligence Department that the Orange Free State would join in the war and that the Boers would enjoy a numerical superiority at the outset.

135 Scholtz, *Why the Boers Lost the War*, p. 50. Scholtz makes the case that the top Boer command echelon had no desire for territorial aggrandisement and preferred to defend the republics rather than invade British territory. Scholtz quotes the words of Frederik Rompel (parliamentary and war correspondent of the *Volkstem*) "as contrary … to the precepts of the Afrikaners regarding Christianity and civilisation".

136 Hancock, *Selections from the Smuts Papers Volume I*, pp. 322–29. Smuts highlighted the necessity of early tactical success in order to bolster and maintain the morale of the Boers. The Boers could not afford to lose any of the early battles. Smuts correctly identified all the advantages of taking the offensive and gaining the initiative.

137 G.N. van den Bergh, 'Secret Service in the South African Republic, 1895–1900', *Military History Journal of the South African Military History Society*, 3.2 (1974). This was not wishful thinking on Smuts's part. Agents had been sent by Smuts to determine the political orientation of the Afrikaners in Natal and the Cape along the proposed invasion routes.

138 Headlam, *The Milner Papers*, Letter Milner to Bertha Synge 11 February 1899, p. 303. The War Office proposed the occupation of advanced positions in Natal and the Cape Colony such as seizing bridges over the Orange River and Van Reenan's Pass in the Drakensberg. General Butler took a completely different view, and the plan was not to advance but to hang back from the frontier and to provide for an easy retirement in the face of superior numbers.

139 In a disastrous week during the South African War, dubbed 'Black Week' (10–17 December 1899), the British Army suffered three devastating defeats by the Boer Republics with a total of 2,776 men killed, wounded, and captured.

140 Royal Commission, *Minutes of Evidence on the War in South Africa Volume I*, General Sir Redvers Buller, p14963 (London, 1903), p. 172. Buller seemed to think that in the fortnight following 30 October it would have been extremely difficult for the British to have prevented the occupation of the entire Natal and great swathes of the Cape.

141 Scholtz, *Why the Boers Lost the War*, p. 17. The first-generation commanders, Generals Piet Joubert and Piet Cronjé of the Transvaal, Marthinus Prinsloo, E.R. Grobler, J.H. Olivier and C.J. Wessels of the Free State, were either overly cautious or simply incompetent.

142 T.N. Dupuy, *Understanding War* (New York: Paragon House Publishers, 1987), p. 1.

143 Smuts, *Jan Christian Smuts*, p. 49.

144 Hancock, *Selections from the Smuts Papers Volume I*, p. 562. "But however good the Boers were as raw fighting material, their organization was too loose and ineffective, and their officers too inexperienced and in many glaring cases incompetent, to make a resort to offensive tactics possible."

145 Smuts, *Jan Christian Smuts*, p. 49.

146 Hancock, *Selections from the Smuts Papers Volume I*, Letter to Botha 2 April 1900, p. 330.

147 Hancock, *Selections from the Smuts Papers Volume I*, Letter from Botha 20 May 1900, p. 333.

148 Hancock, *Selections from the Smuts Papers Volume I*, Telegraphic circular to all landrosts and Acting Special Commandant Johannesburg, undated 1900, p. 333.

149 Hancock, *Smuts: The Sanguine Years*, p. 118. The decision not to defend Pretoria came at the cost of diminishing the morale of the ordinary burgher who thought that if Pretoria was not worth defending then nothing was. See also Smuts, *Jan Smuts: Memoirs of the Boer War*, p. 39.

150 A. Jones, *The Art of War in the Western World* (London: Harrap Ltd, 1988), pp. 55, 56. A raiding strategy uses a temporary presence in hostile territory, for military, economic or political reasons or a combination thereof while a persisting strategy makes use of a protracted or permanent occupation of hostile or friendly territory.

151 Smuts, *Jan Smuts: Memoirs of the Boer War*, pp. 43, 44.

152 Hancock, *Smuts: The Sanguine Years*, pp. 120, 121.

153 Smuts, *Jan Smuts: Memoirs of the Boer War*, p. 47. Smuts obtained the bullion after overcoming some resistance from the directors of the bank by issuing a warrant for their arrest.

154 Smuts, *Jan Smuts: Memoirs of the Boer War*, p. 69. Smuts identified Botha, De la Rey, and Christian de Wet as the new breed of commanders who were imbued with ability and an offensive fighting spirit.

155 W.J. de Kock (ed.), *Dictionary of South African Biography Volume I*, (Cape Town: Tafelberg, 1968), p. 214. De la Rey acquired an in-depth knowledge of the Western Transvaal from his peacetime occupation as a surveyor and native commissioner. He was a veteran of the Basotho War (1865), Sekhukhune War (1876), First Anglo-Boer War (1880–1881), and the Jameson Raid (1896). He possessed a sound grasp of strategy and tactics. He made his mark at the battle of Modder River (November 1899) where he deployed his forces at the foot instead of the crest of the hill.

156 Smuts, *Jan Smuts: Memoirs of the Boer War*, p. 77.

157 Smuts, *Jan Smuts: Memoirs of the Boer War*, pp. 118–25.

158 Smuts, *Jan Smuts: Memoirs of the Boer War*, pp. 126–28.

159 Hancock, *Smuts: The Sanguine Years*, p. 124. Smuts effectively became De la Rey's Chief of Staff. Hancock speaks of Smuts not only learning the "technique of the game" but also the "spirit of the game" and the confidence to be audacious in execution. See also Smuts, *Jan Smuts: Memoirs of the Boer War*, ed. by S.B. Spies and G. Nattrass (Johannesburg: Jonathan Ball, 1994), pp. 130–32.

160 Smuts, *Jan Smuts: Memoirs of the Boer War*, p. 133.

161 Smuts, *Jan Smuts: Memoirs of the Boer War*, p. 174. Beyers was a contemporary of Smuts where they both received their education at Victoria College. Beyers, starting the war as an ordinary burgher, rose rapidly through the ranks to become a general. Smuts was unwilling to serve under Beyers due to an incompatibility of personality and temperament. See also D.W. Kruger and C.J. Beyers (eds), *Dictionary of South African Biography Volume III* (Cape Town: Tafelberg, 1977), p. 65. Beyers took part in suppressing the Jameson Raid but saw no action. He came to the attention of Botha due to his bravery, and outspoken and fearless criticism of incompetent officers.

162 W.J. de Kock (ed.), *Dictionary of South African Biography Volume I* (Cape Town: Tafelberg, 1968) p. 214. De Wet was an OFS Boer general and was a born leader with great military aptitude. He was a veteran of the First Anglo-Boer War. He became Commandant-in-Chief of the Western Frontier on Cronjé's surrender. He conducted a highly mobile form of manoeuvre warfare in the guerrilla phase of the Anglo-Boer War.

163 P. Kruger, *The Memoirs of Paul Kruger* (New York: The Century Co., 1902) p.264.

164 Hancock, *Smuts: The Sanguine Years*, p. 124.

165 Smuts, *Jan Smuts: Memoirs of the Boer War*, pp. 164–71.

166 Hancock, *Smuts: The Sanguine Years*, p. 125. See also Hancock, *Selections from the Smuts Papers Volume I*, Letter to Botha 23 January 1901, p. 357. Smuts commanded 800 men at this stage of the conflict. The significance of this will become apparent later in the text where British historians oft quote Smuts's inexperience of leading large bodies of men and often use the example of him initially heading up a body of 300 men when invading the Cape.

167 Smuts, *Jan Christian Smuts*, p. 65.

168 Hancock, *Selections from the Smuts Papers Volume I*, Letter to De la Rey 25 December 1900, p. 330.

169 A.W. Ward and G.P. Gooch (eds), *The Cambridge History of British Foreign Policy Volume III* (London: Cambridge University Press, 1923) p. 284.

170 It was impossible for the British to place Cape Afrikaners who were British citizens into concentration camps as they did to the Republican burghers.

171 F. Maurice (ed), *History of the War in South Africa, 1899–1902, Volume IV* (London, 1905) p 206. In attendance, Acting Transvaal President Schalk Burger and Orange Free State President Marthinus Steyn, Transvaal State Secretary Francis Reitz, Commandant-General Louis Botha and Chief Commandant Christiaan de Wet, Generals Hertzog, Viljoen, Spruyt, De la Rey, Smuts, Muller, Lucas Meyer and a number of other commandants and officers

172 F.V. Engelenburg, *General Loius Botha* (Pretoria: J.L. van Schaik Ltd, 1929) p. 53.

173 Smuts, *Jan Christian Smuts*, pp. 65, 66.

174 Hancock, *Selections from the Smuts Papers Volume I*, Letter to De la Rey 16 February 1901, p. 373.

175 Smuts, *Jan Smuts: Memoirs of the Boer War*, p. 149.

176 Hancock, *Selections from the Smuts Papers Volume I*, Letter to Botha, 27 February 1901, p. 330.

177 Hancock, *Selections from the Smuts Papers Volume I*,
Letter to N.J. de Wet 28 February 1901, p. 388.

178 Engelenburg, *General Loius Botha*, p. 264.

179 Hancock, *Selections from the Smuts Papers Volume I*, Notes of Cape Expedition, August-December 1901, pp. 407–45. Smuts found the general Cape population of Afrikaners to be receptive to the republican cause and he numbers the possible volunteers in the thousands. He was unable to recruit due to the lack of horses in the Cape where they were requisitioned for the British Army.

180 Smuts, *Jan Christian Smuts*, pp. 66, 70.

181 H. Strachan, *The First World War in Africa* (Oxford, Oxford University Press, 2004) p. 135. See also R. Anderson, 'J C Smuts and J L van Deventer: South African Commanders-in-Chief of a British Expeditionary Force', *Scientia Militaria*, 31(2) (2003) p. 125 and I. Liebenberg, 'Sociology,

278 • GENERAL JAN SMUTS AND HIS FIRST WORLD WAR IN AFRICA, 1914–1917

Biology or Philosophy of a Warrior? Reflections on Jan Smuts, Guerrilla-Being and a Politics of Choices', *Scientia Militaria*, 33(1) (2005) p. 158.

182 R. Meinertzhagen, *Army Diary 1899–1926* (Edinburgh: Oliver & Boyd, 1960); Armstrong, *Grey Steel*. Meinertzhagen and Armstrong have much that is adverse to say about Smuts's military ability or lack thereof.

183 Hancock, *Selections from the Smuts Papers Volume I*, p. 444.

184 Armstrong, *Grey Steel*, p. 106.

185 J.P. Brits (ed.), *Diary of a National Scout P.J. Du Toit 1900–1902* (Pretoria: Human Sciences Research Council, 1974), p. 29.

186 Headlam, *The Milner Papers Volume II*, p. 330.

187 Engelenburg, *General Loius Botha*, pp. 63, 64, 70.

188 Smuts, *Jan Christian Smuts*, p. 82. Steyn, De Wet and De la Rey were insistent on continuing the war.

189 Hertzog was Assistant Chief Commandant of the military forces of the Orange Free State

190 Engelenburg, *General Loius Botha*, p. 90. See also Headlam, *The Milner Papers Volume II*, p. 338. The idea of plenipotentiaries seemed to emanate from Kitchener who was anxious that the Boers get authority to make terms.

191 Smuts, *Jan Christian Smuts*, p. 82.

192 Headlam, *The Milner Papers Volume II*, pp. 337, 340. Milner complained to Chamberlain that Kitchener did not care what he gave away during negotiations. Milner complained to his staff, "I feel as if I were negotiating with Kitchener."

193 Headlam, *The Milner Papers Volume II*, p. 329. Kitchener kept an eye on conciliation and was prepared to promise self-government within two or three years. Milner and Chamberlain were determined to ensure "the Boers and their women-folk [knew] that they had been beaten in the field, and were wholly at the mercy of Great Britain". British sovereignty founded on military conquest must form the basis of peace negotiations.

194 Headlam, *The Milner Papers Volume II*, pp. 344, 345.

195 See also H. Giliomee, *The Afrikaners* (Cape Town: Tafelberg, 2003) p. 261. The private conversations between Smuts and Kitchener were viewed by some of the Boer delegates with suspicion. Giliomee also hints at the possibility that Smuts, in order to garner votes, may have promised the delegates that he would join a future military struggle should Britain find itself in trouble.

196 Smuts, *Jan Christian Smuts*, p. 84. See also Headlam, *The Milner Papers Volume II*, Letter Milner to Chamberlain 16 April 1902, p. 337. Milner identified that the least friendly of the negotiators and those wanting to continue the war were the Orange Free Staters led by Steyn and Hertzog. Kemp and De Wet were also named as diehards.

197 Hancock, *Selections from the Smuts Papers Volume I*, Vereeniging Speech 30 May 1902, p. 531.

198 Headlam, *The Milner Papers Volume II*, p. 346.

199 Headlam, *The Milner Papers Volume II*, p. 353. In a letter to Selborne on 10 May 1905, Milner expressed his regret that he yielded to the Boers over the question of black franchise, stating that this was the greatest mistake he had ever made.

200 Headlam, *The Milner Papers Volume II*, pp. 344, 345.

201 Leo Amery, together with John Buchan and Herbert Baker, were close associates of Milner's Kindergarten. The core members, some of whom feature in this document, included, Patrick Duncan, Lionel Curtis, Lionel Hichins, Richard Feetham, John Dove, Robert H. Brand, Philip Kerr, Dougal Malcolm, J.F. Perry, Hugh Wyndham, and Geoffrey Dawson. Alfred Milner (1854–1925), High Commissioner for Southern Africa and Governor of Cape Colony, in an address in 1904 revealed his views thus, "My work has been constantly directed to a great and distant end–the establishment in South Africa of a great and civilized and progressive community,

one from Cape Town to the Zambezi— independent in the management of its own affairs, but still remaining, from its own firm desire, a member of the great community of free nations gathered together under the British flag". See Headlam, *The Milner Papers Volume II*, p. 501.

202 W.J. de Kock and D.W. Kruger (eds), *Dictionary of South African Biography Volume II* (Cape Town: Tafelberg, 1972), p. 698 Sprigg replaced Schreiner as Prime Minister of the Cape in June 1900 representing the Progressives which followed a pro-British and pro-imperialist agenda. However, he took a stand when Alfred Milner ordered him to suspend the Cape constitution and defeated Milner's proposal.

203 Headlam, *The Milner Papers Volume II*, p. 403–42. The election of Jameson was a direct result of the British stripping the Cape rebels of their franchise.

204 Armstrong, *Grey Steel*, pp. 147, 149.

205 Hancock, *Selections from the Smuts Papers Volume II*, Letter to S.M. Smuts 1 June 1902, p. 4.

206 Hancock, *Smuts: The Sanguine Years*, p. 168.

207 Headlam, *The Milner Papers Volume II*, p. 428. Milner wrote to Chamberlain that "[The Boers] are far too wise to signalize their return by any open attack upon the new order of things ... But there are a hundred indirect ways, in which they are able to foment, and even to suggest dissatisfaction with the Government".

208 Le May, *British Supremacy*, pp. 36, 37.

209 Le May, *British Supremacy*, pp. 156, 157. Milner's reconstruction met with some success with his establishment of a customs union south of the Zambezi, and the single administration of the railways. He repatriated all the prisoners of war and managed to reform the police, prisons, and judicial systems. He improved the health system and enlarged the telegraphic and telephonic communications. He made inroads to improving education at schools and within agriculture. The emphasis on using English within the schools drew much resentment form a bitter Afrikaans population.

210 Headlam, *The Milner Papers Volume II*, Letter to Earl Grey 14 September 1902, p. 399. Milner was emphatic that "This would be the worst thing that could happen".

211 Hancock, *Smuts: The Sanguine Years*, p. 179.

212 Hancock, *Selections from the Smuts Papers Volume II*, Circular by Smuts to Boer leaders, 14 December 1902, p. 56. Suggestions that Smuts was overcome with depression and moribund in the wake of the war are not borne out by his resuming active politics by December of that year on the occasion of Chamberlain's imminent visit to South Africa. Smuts was soon directing Boer leaders on their conduct and strategy. See also Hancock, *Selections from the Smuts Papers Volume II*, Address to J. Chamberlain, 8 January 1903, p. 56.

213 Headlam, *The Milner Papers Volume II*, p. 432.

214 Hancock, *Smuts: The Sanguine Years*, p. 192.

215 Headlam, *The Milner Papers Volume II*, p. 380. The Boer leadership refusal was negatively portrayed in the newspapers. Milner was clearly disappointed that he could not garner the support of his former enemies who preferred to remain out of the system and free to critisise. See also Hancock, *Selections from the Smuts Papers Volume II*, Smuts to Milner, 6 February 1903, p. 82.

216 H.H. Hewison, *Hedge of Wild Almonds: South Africa, the 'Pro-Boers' & the Quaker Conscience* (London: James Currey, 1989), p. 232. Smuts's reply to Milner's invitation spoke of a need for the Boer nation for a rest from politics and a clear recognition of their government's responsibility and not a legislative council. Smuts was not enticed to take up three of the 30 seats and he rather allowed Boer stooges in his place and thereby allowed Milner to take full responsibility for the consequences of the legislative council.

217 Le May, *British Supremacy*, pp. 159–65.

218 Hancock, *Selections from the Smuts Papers Volume II*, Letter Hobhouse to Smuts, 29 May 1904, p. 166.

219 Hancock, *Selections from the Smuts Papers Volume II*, Letter Botha to Hobhouse, 13 June 1903, p. 101. This was sent by Botha but written by Smuts. See also Hancock, *Selections from the Smuts Papers Volume II*, Letter to Hobhouse, 21 February 1904, p. 56. This letter by Smuts was published without his permission. However, Hancock sees that Smuts was using Hobhouse as a conduit to the British public. See Hancock, *Smuts: The Sanguine Years*, p. 183. Hancock speaks of Smuts writing to Hobhouse with a mixture of "spontaneity and calculation". His letters were clearly designed for a bigger audience.

220 Hancock, *Selections from the Smuts Papers Volume II*, Letter Botha to Lawley, 4 July 1903, p. 112. Written by Smuts pertaining to Milner's language and education policy as well as the introduction of Chinese labour and the war debt.

221 Hancock, *Selections from the Smuts Papers Volume II*, Letter Botha to Milner, 1 June 1903, p. 97. A series of meetings were held by the leaders of the Transvaal Afrikaners between April and May 1904. This marked the beginning of the Afrikaner political organisation under Smuts and Botha.

222 T.R.H. Davenport, *South Africa: A Modern History* (Johannesburg: Macmillan, 2017) p. 238. Milners's idea of a representative government was based on a qualified franchise which favoured the admittance of urban dwellers but excluded many rural ones. This would obviously favour the more urbanised and income qualified English-speakers. See also Hancock, *Selections from the Smuts Papers Volume II*, Letter to Hobhouse, 22 August 1904, p. 180. Smuts would have none of it. "So long as we are distrusted, we don't want anything, and if we are not distrusted, why retard self-government?"

223 Headlam, *The Milner Papers Volume II*, Letter to Mr. Lyttelton 22 February 1904, p. 518.

224 Hancock, *Selections from the Smuts Papers Volume II*, Letter to Merriman, 30 May 1904, p. 171. See also Hancock, *Selections from the Smuts Papers Volume II*, Memorandum on Transvaal Constitution, January 1906, p. 215. Smuts spoke of federation in his submission for Representative Government to the Colonial Office.

225 Hancock, *Selections from the Smuts Papers Volume II*, Letter to Merriman, 15 February 1904, p. 144. See also Hancock, *Selections from the Smuts Papers Volume II*, Letter to Merriman, 17 March 1904, ed. by W.K. p. 157. Smuts went to the extent of asking his father to vacate his Cape Parliament seat in favour of Merriman, a request refused by Smuts senior.

226 Headlam, *The Milner Papers Volume II*, Dispatch Milner to Lyttelton 2 May 1904, p. 522. Milner saw the Lyttelton Constitution as a mechanism to delay responsible government until such time as the Boers were anglicised and "rejoice in membership of the British Empire" or the British element gained sufficient numbers over time to ensure loyalty.

227 N.G. Garson, '"*Het Volk*": The Botha–Smuts Party in the Transvaal, 1904–11', *The Historical Journal*, 9.1 (1966) p. 104.

228 Hancock, *Selections from the Smuts Papers Volume II*, Letter to A. Fischer, 13 October 1902, p. 38. Smuts identified very early on that "a large proportion of the moderate English are now also prepared to work with us, and if we are moderate in our future policy and do not estrange these prospective friends from us by extreme ideas, [...] I see no reason why we should not [...] achieve eventual victory". This was the blueprint for *Het Volk*.

229 Davenport, *South Africa: A Modern History*, p. 236.

230 Garson, '"*Het Volk*", p. 104.

231 Headlam, *The Milner Papers Volume II*, p. 541.

232 Hancock, *Smuts: The Sanguine Years*, p. 198.

233 Le May, *British Supremacy*, pp. 36, 37.

234 Hancock, *Selections from the Smuts Papers Volume II*, Letter to T. Lynedoch Graham, 2 August 1902, p. 25.

235 Hancock, *Selections from the Smuts Papers Volume II*, Memorandum on Transvaal Constitution presented to the Colonial Office, January 1906, p. 216.

236 Hancock, *Selections from the Smuts Papers Volume II*, Memorandum on Transvaal Constitution presented to the Colonial Office, January 1906, pp. 226, 227.

237 Hancock, *Selections from the Smuts Papers Volume II*, Letter Merriman to Smuts, 4 March 1906, p. 238.

238 Hancock, *Selections from the Smuts Papers Volume II*, Letter Smuts to Merriman, 13 March 1906, p. 242.

239 Hancock, *Selections from the Smuts Papers Volume II*, Letter Merriman to Smuts, 18 March 1906, p. 244.

240 Hancock, *Smuts: The Sanguine Years*, pp. 213–17.

241 R. Hyam, 'Smuts and the Decision of the Liberal Government to Grant Responsible Government to the Transvaal, January and February 1906', *The Historical Journal*, VIII.3 (1965) pp. 380–98. Hyam argues that the decision to grant immediate responsible government to the Transvaal was a foregone conclusion before Smuts met any of the Liberal ministers. Campbell-Bannerman, of his own accord, came to the same conclusions, independently of Smuts. He cleverly allowed Smuts to gain the impression that he had decisively influenced him. If Smuts influenced Campbell-Bannerman, we still have only Smuts's opinion for it.

242 Garson, '"Het Volk", p. 118.

243 Headlam, *The Milner Papers Volume II*, p. 532.

244 Smuts wrote a book on holism, J.C. Smuts, *Holism and Evolution* (London: Macmillan & Co., 1927). His belief in holism fuelled his desire for territorial expansion See also P. Beukes, *The Holistic Smuts: A Study in Personality* (Cape Town: Human & Rousseu, 1989). Holism is the opposite of reductionism, and is the idea that natural systems and their properties should be viewed as wholes and not a collection of parts.

245 P.R. Warhurst, 'Smuts and Africa: a Study in Sub-Imperialism', *South African Historical Journal*, 16.1 (1984) p. 83; Armstrong, *Grey Steel*, p. 61.

246 *Diario de Noticias,* 13 April 1909

247 TNA, FO 367/89/3, Telegram High Commissioner to Secretary of State, Confidential letter from Colonel A.J. Arnold, 20 June 1908. See also TNA, CO 417-455, Letter from A.J. Arnold (Mozambique Company) to High Commissioner, 11 May 1908.

248 R. Langhorne, 'Anglo-German Negotiations Concerning the Future of the Portuguese Colonies, 1911–1914', *The Historical Journal*, 16(2) (1973) p. 369.

249 Warhurst, 'Smuts and Africa', p. 83.

250 TNA, FO 367/89/2, Telegram High Commissioner to Secretary of State, 21 August 1908. See also TNA, CO 417/455, Letter from High Commissioner to Earl of Crewe , 29 June 1908.

251 Hancock, *Smuts: The Sanguine Years*, p. 246.

252 R. Hyam, *The Failure of South African Expansion, 1908–1948* (London: Macmillan, 1972) p. 15.

253 Warhurst, 'Smuts and Africa', p. 82. P.J. Yearwood, 'Great Britain and the Repartition of Africa, 1914 –1919', *The Journal of Imperial and Commonwealth History*, 18(3) (1990) p. 316.

254 M. Chanock, *Britain, Rhodesia and South Africa 1900–1945: The Unconsummated Union* (Totawa: Frank Cass & Co. Ltd, 1977), p. 10. According to Chanock, Union was brought about by the British in order to secure South Africa as part of the British political and economic world.

255 W.W.P. Selborne, *The Selborne Memorandum on the Union of South Africa 1908* (London: Oxford University Press, 1925), pp. 140, 141.

256 Hancock, *Smuts: The Sanguine Years*, pp. 250–52.

257 Secretary of State for Commonwealth Relations, *Basutoland, The Bechuanaland Protectorate and Swaziland: History of Discusssions with the Union of South Africa 1909–1939,* Cmd 8707 (London, 1952), p. 5.

258 Historical Papers Research Archive, William Cullen Library, Witwatersrand University, AD843-C1-002, Address of Lionel Curtiss to the Royal Empire Society, 'British Protectorates in South Africa', 9 February 1938, p. 2. "pending any grant of representation to natives, no native territory now administered by the Governor or High Commissioner, will be placed under the control of the new responsible Government."

259 R. Hyam and P. Henshaw, *The Lion and The Springbok: Britain and South Africa since the Boer War* (Cambridge: Cambridge University Press, 2003) p. 102.

260 Hyam, *The Lion and The Springbok,* p. 99.

261 Hyam, *The Lion and The Springbok,* p. 77. The price of unity and conciliation of the institution-alisation of white supremacy, according to L.M. Thomson, *The Oxford History of South Africa.* See Chanock, *Britain, Rhodesia and South Africa,* pp.29, 30, for a different point of view. The British saw the Cape franchise as a limited device which gave outlet to a small black minority. Government needed to be provided for the vast majority of blacks denied participation in a white-dominated system. The British preferred a system of reserves based on Cecil John Rhodes Glen Grey Act. Louis Botha, on the other hand, wished to dissolve any large gathering of blacks in the reserves and this was the sticking point of the opposing 'native policies'. See P. Lewsen (ed.), *Selections from the Correspondence of J.X. Merriman 1899–1905* (Cape Town: The Van Riebeeck Society, 1966), p. 392. See also Leonard Barnes, *The New Boer War* (London: Hogarth Press,1932) p. 228. "The cost of Boer loyalty has been met to a very slight extent by drafts on British magnanimity; the big drain has been on the material and spiritual pockets of natives. Britain has in effect fumbled about with her small change, and then, jerking her head towards the native, remarked, 'My friend will pay.'"

262 Hyam, *The Lion and The Springbok,* p. 81. See also TNA, CO 417/455, Letter High Commissioner to H.C. Sloley Resident Commissiner Basutuland, 26 May 1908. The nascent negotiotions for Union in 1908 caused considerable angst amongst the paramount chiefs of the HCT. In answer to Sloley, who was , in turn, answering Parampount Chief Letsie of Basutoland's query on the fate of his territory, Selborne expressed the sound logic of transferring control of the HCT to a future South African union or federation. However, he states, "there is an absolute obligation honour not to transfer [...] except upon conditions embodied in the South Africa Constitution Act, which guarantee [...] against any infringement of their rights."

263 Hancock, *Smuts: The Sanguine Years,* p. 254.

264 Chanock, *Britain, Rhodesia and South Africa,* p. 29.

265 It is easy to be cynical about the British concern for the welfare of blacks in the Union and in the HCT. However, evidence of British wariness of the Union's 'Native Policy' especially in regard to the HCT has breadth and depth in the primary documentation. For instance, see TNA,DO 119/956, Correspondence: Henry Lambert and Roland Bourne, July/August 1917, in which it is made quite clear that the British government did not wish the Union to undertake any militray/defence obligations in the HCT in respect of prevention or suppression of internal disturbances. It was felt that any proposal along the lines of Union intervention would have an unsettling effect on the 'natives'.

Chapter 2

1 R. Hyam, *The Failure of South African Expansion, 1908–1948* (London: Macmillan, 1972) passim.

2 S. Ferreira, *The British in Delagoa Bay in the Aftermath of the Boer War,* 'The International Impact of the Boer War' ed. by K. Wilson (New York: Palgrave, 2001) p. 169.

3   Ferreira, *The British in Delagoa Bay*, p. 179.
4   Angola, Cape Verde, Guinea-Bissau, Mozambique, São Tomé and Príncipe,
5   The National Archives United Kingdom (TNA), FO 367/236, Telegram Consul Lourenço Marques to Governor-General, 21 February 1911.
6   TNA, FO 367/236/2, Telegram Foreign Office to Admiralty, 3 March 1911.
7   National Archives Pretoria (NARSA), Jan Smuts Papers (JSP), Box 300. Personal Papers, Memorandum: The Mozambique Province and the Union of South Africa, undated. The original pencilled map where Smuts has indicated the 'A' and 'B' lines in blue. Smuts's "small" solution he indicated as 'A' while he marked his "bigger" solution as 'B' which takes the border significantly further north, wiping out the entire Portuguese presence in the region! The line (A), running along the Kunene and Zambezi rivers, represents Smuts's First World War expansionist aims, with southern Mozambique and German South West Africa forming part of an expanded Union incorporating the British HCT of Bechuanaland, Swaziland, and Basutoland. Included in the Union is Southern Rhodesia, provided as a fifth province in terms of the South Africa Act 1909.
8   TNA, FO 367/236, Colonel O'Sullivan verbal report on situation in Mozambique Company Territory, 15 March 1911.
9   TNA, FO 367/236, Telegram Governor-General to Secretary of State for the Colonies, 13 April 1911.
10 TNA, FO 367/236, Letter Foreign Office to Secretary of State for the Colonies, 18 April 1911. See also P. Henshaw, 'The "Key to South Africa" in the 1890s: Delagoa Bay and the Origins of the South African War', *Journal of Southern African Studies*, 24.3 (1998), p. 528. The 1898 Anglo-German Agreement supposedly removed the main sources of tension between these two powers in southern Africa. In return for Germany's acceptance of British paramountcy over the Transvaal, it was agreed that should the Portuguese empire collapse, Delagoa Bay and southern Mozambique would become British, while the northern half would go to Germany.
11 TNA, FO 371/972, Telegram Governor-General of Union to Secretary of State for Colonies re: Delagoa Bay, 5 October 1910.
12 Ferreira, *The British in Delagoa Bay*, p. 185.
13 Ferreira, *The British in Delagoa Bay*, p. 183.
14 TNA, FO 367/344, Correspondence surrounding Smuts's speech at Union qanquet to visiting member of the English Parliament, October 1913.
15 TNA, CO 537/569, Telegram Governor-General (Buxton) to Secretary of State for the Colonies, December 1914.
16 M. Chanock, *Britain, Rhodesia and South Africa 1900–1945: The Unconsummated Union*. (Totawa: Frank Cass & Co. Ltd, 1977) p. 66.
17 Chanock, *Britain, Rhodesia and South Africa*, p. 67.
18 NARSA, JSP, Box 189, Folio 67, J. Merriman, Botha on Swaziland, Memorandum Merriman to Smuts, December 1906 and Hyam, *The Failure of South African Expansion*, p. 18.
19 *The Milner Papers South Africa 1897–1899*, ed. by C. Headlam (London: Cassel & Co., 1931) p. 182.
20 Chanock, *Britain, Rhodesia and South Africa*, p. 51. See also TNA, CO 537/522/10, Report by C.W. Boyd on Southern Rhodesia, 1909.
21 Chanock, *Britain, Rhodesia and South Africa*, p. 52. TNA, CO 417/466, Hopwood, Dispatches: Bechuanaland Prot. and Rhodesia, 23 July 1909.
22 TNA, CO 417/502, L. Botha, Botha Swaziland, Memorandum Botha to High Commissioner, April 1911; *The Lion and The Springbok: Britain and South Africa since the Boer War* (Cambridge: Cambridge University Press, 2003) p. 98.

23 The British South Africa Company's administration of what became Rhodesia was chartered in 1889 by Queen Victoria of the United Kingdom

24 TNA, DO 116/1/8, L. Botha, Botha to Gladstone on Bechuanaland, Correspondence 1913–1926, March 1913.

25 E. Buxton, *General Botha* (New York: E.P. Dutton & Co., 1924) p. 19. A situation inherited from the Imperial government who, lacking an in-depth knowledge of the local conditions, did not always apply the best solutions.

26 P. Lewsen (ed.), *Selections from the Correspondence of John X. Merriman 1905–1924*, (Cape Town: The Van Riebeeck Society, 1969) p. 229. Merriman in a letter to Steyn 30 September 1912.

27 E.A. Walker, *A History of Southern Africa* (London: Longman, 1972), p. 545.

28 Department of Defence Force Archives (DODA), AG 14, Box 6, Biography Lukin. See also D.W. Kruger and C.J. Beyers (eds), *Dictionary of South African Biography Volume III*, (Cape Town: Tafelberg, 1977) p. 547. Lukin was born in London and was wounded in the first campaign against the Zulus at Ulundi in 1879. He served in the Basuto War of 1881 as member of the Cape Mounted Rifles (CMR). He received military training in Britain and on his return served in the Bechuana campaign of 1897. He was an artillery officer in the early stages of the South African War and later commanded the CMR. After the war he became the Commandant-General of the Cape Colonial Forces and Inspector-General of the UDF in 1912 with the rank of brig-gen. H. Arendt, *Imperialism: Part Two of the Origins of Totalitarianism* (New York: Harcourt Brace & Co., 1976). See also E.W. Nortier, 'Major General Sir H.T. Lukin, 1861–1925: The Making of a South African Hero', (MMil thesis, Stellenbosch University, 2005).

29 H.T. Lukin, *Savage Warfare: Hints on Tactics to be Adopted and Precautions to be Taken* (Cape Town: Cape Times Ltd, 1906). See also C.E. Callwell, *Small Wars: Their Principles and Practice* (London: General Staff War Office, 1906) which most probably had much influence of Lukin's military doctrine.

30 I. van der Waag, *A Military History of Modern South Africa* (Johannesburg & Cape Town: Jonathan Ball, 2015), p. 61. See also I. van der Waag, 'Hugh Archibald Wyndham: His Life and Times in South Africa, 1901–1923' (PhD thesis, University of Cape Town, 2005).

31 DODA, Diverse, Box 15, file 199, Colonial Defence Committee Memoranda on General Defence Matters, Bourne to Smuts, 8 September 1910; and Smuts to Bourne, 20 September 1910. See also Van der Waag, *A Military History of Modern South Africa*, pp. 59–72. Van der Waag succinctly captures the military thinking of the time regarding the threat perceptions to the newly formed Union.

32 DODA, Diverse Group 1, Box 31, Defensive Scheme Re Boer Uprising in Natal. There is evidence that at least in Natal some planning measures were taken in the event of a 'Dutch' uprising before Union.

33 DODA, Diverse Group 1, Box 8, The Military Situation in South Africa Department of Defence, 20 August 1910. 'Trouble with Basutoland and other Native Protectorates' was seen as more of an immediate threat than 'War with Germany' in 1910. It was decided to draw up detailed plans for Basutoland but not for an adventure into GSWA. See also Ian van der Waag, 'Military Culture and the South African Armed forces, an Historical Perspective', 2011. A paper presented at the Second South African Conference on Strategic Theory, 'On Strategy; Military Culture and African Armed Forces', co-hosted by Stellenbosch University and the Royal Danish Defence College, 22/23 September 2011. *Passim*

34 D.W. Kruger and C.J. Beyers (eds), *Dictionary of South African Biography Volume II* (Cape Town: Tafelberg, 1977) p. 421. McKenzie commanded a unit of the Imperial Light Horse during the South African War. After the war he commanded the Natal Carbineers and took part in the Bambatha Rebellion of 1906. He was a member of the Union Defence Council in 1912.

35 J. Stuart, *A History of the Zulu Rebellion 1906* (London: Macmillan & Co., 1913) pp. 90, 91, 356. Stuart refers to the lack of modern firearms among the rebels. On the other hand, he describes the Natal Mounted Regiment deploying three Maxims and a Rexer light machine gun, and two 15-pounder artillery pieces in a particular battle at Peyana against the rebel Zulus. See also P.S. Thompson, *Incident at Trewirgie: First Shots of the Zulu Rebellion 1906* (Pietermaritzburg: P.S. Thompson, 2005).

36 I. van der Waag, 'South African Defence in the Age of Total War, 1900–1940', *Historia*, 60(1) (2015) p. 134. These conferences were convened, in Pretoria, Durban, and Johannesburg, and were followed by the Imperial Conferences of 1909 and 1911.

37 I. Uys, *South African Military Who's Who 1452–1992* (Germiston: Forttress, 1992) p. 26. H.R.M. Bourne served with the 1st Royal Scots in South Africa before he was employed by the Milner administration in the Repatriation Department and then as superintendent at Machadodorp before becoming secretary for defence in 1912.

38 DODA, Diverse Group 1, Box 19, Curriculum Vitae Roland Bourne, 1910. Bourne served as a junior officer in the local militia in the United Kingdom. He served in the South African War as Regimental Transport Officer, Staff Captain on the Transport Staff and finally Chief Staff Officer to a regimental commander of a mobile column. After the war he handled various quartermanter positions. He resigned his commission in the Regular Army in 1906 to take up a position in the Transvaal Civil Service in the Colonial Secretary Office.

39 A.H. Marais (ed.), *Politieke Briewe, II: 1911–1912,* J.X. Merriman to M.T. Steyn, 16 January 1911 (Tafelberg, Bloemfontein, 1973) p 5.

40 Union of South Africa Debates, First Session of the First Parliament, 1910–1911, 1 March 1911, col. 1471–4. Smuts stated, "If [South Africa} had a scheme of defence, by which [South Africa] insured [itself] against these internal troubles which might arise in South Africa, they would have done a good day's work."

41 G. Tylden, *The Armed Forces of South Africa 1659–1954* (Johannesburg: Trophy Press, 1982) p. 5. The Cape Mounted Rifles was originally formed in 1855 to perform police duties on the Eastern Cape frontier. The unit was called upon to perform military functions more and more frequently after its formation. Members were recruited on the Silladar system where they were responsible for their own horse, equipment, rations, and arms.

42 Union of South Africa Debates, Second Session of the First Parliament, 1912, South African Defence Bill, 23 February 1911, col. 634. Any shortfall in numbers would be made up via a ballot system. A further inducement was the levy of a £1 tax for 24 years for anyone who did not volunteer for four years.

43 Union of South Africa Debates, First Session of the First Parliament, 1910–1911, 1 March 1911, col. 1475–80.

44 Union of South Africa Debates, First Session of the First Parliament, 1910–1911, 1 March 1911, col. 1475–80. See also D.B. Katz (in press), 'An Aggregation of Lion Hunters: In Search of the Boer Way of War', *International Journal of Military History and Historiography*, 2021. The article deals with the Boer lack of discipline.

45 Union of South Africa Debates, First Session of the First Parliament, 1910–1911, 1 March 1911, col. 1481, 1482.

46 Union of South Africa Debates, Second Session of the First Parliament, 1912, Second Reading of the Defence Bill, 8 March 1911, col. 638.

47 D.B. Katz (in press), 'An Aggregation of Lion Hunters: In Search of the Boer Way of War', *International Journal of Military History and Historiography*, 2021. The article deals with the Boer lack of discipline.

48 DODA, Diverse Group 1, Box 33, South African Defence Conferences 1908/1909, p. 9.

49 Union of South Africa Debates, First Session of the First Parliament, 1910–1911, T. Watt member for Dundee, 1 March 1911. col. 1483.

50 Union of South Africa Debates, First Session of the First Parliament, 1910–1911, C.P. Crewe member for Turffontein, 1 March 1911 (col. 1483). Colonel C.P. Crewe took the opposite view and saw little threat from the black population referring to them as a "danger which he did not believe existed". He went on to say that it did not exist because, "civilisation and enlightenment and fair play had done a great deal to show the native races that they were not the enemy of the whites in this country".

51 Union of South Africa Debates, First Session of the First Parliament, 1910–1911, H. Wyndham member for East London, 1 March 1911, col. 1483.

52 Union of South Africa Debates, First Session of the First Parliament, 1910–1911, Schreiner, 8 March 1911, col. 1658.

53 Union of South Africa Debates, First Session of the First Parliament, 1910–1911, Schreiner, 8 March 1911, col. 1658.

54 Union of South Africa Debates, Second Session of the First Parliament, 1912, South African Defence Bill, 23 February 1911, col. 622.

55 Union of South Africa Debates, Second Session of the First Parliament, 1912, South African Defence Bill, 23 February 1911, col. 651.

56 The term 'racial' lines in 1914 referred to the English and Afrikaners who were seen in the times as two racial groupings. The modern-day term 'racial' in the South African context usually refers to black and white groupings.

57 NARSA, JSP, Box 112, Folio 22, Report on a visit to GSWA 20–27 March 1915, pp. 2,3.

58 NARSA, JSP, Box 112, Folio 22, Report on a visit to GSWA 20–27 March 1915, p. 8.

59 DODA, AG12, Box 7, File 27, Coloured Troops World War One.

60 Union of South Africa Debates, Second Session of the First Parliament, 1912, South African Defence Bill, 23 February 1911, col. 643.

61 Union of South Africa Debates, First Session of the First Parliament, 1910–1911, Farrar and Botha, 8 March 1911, col. 1645, 1647. See also D.B. Katz (in press), 'An Aggregation of Lion Hunters: In Search of the Boer Way of War', *International Journal of Military History and Historiography*, 2021.

62 DODA, AG 14, Box 6, Biography Collyer. See also Uys, *South African Military Who's Who*, p. 48. John Johnston (Jack) Collyer was born in England and studied at Oxford. He served as a legal adviser to the Chancellor of the Exchequer from 1881. He immigrated to South Africa in 1889. Collyer attested as a trooper in the CMR in December 1899. During the South African War, he was commissioned as a lieutenant in the CMR. He was eventually appointed as the field-adjutant to Maj-Gen J.G. Maxwell, the former Military Governor of Pretoria and the Western Transvaal, a position he held until 1902. For the rest of the war, Collyer was appointed as the assistant staff officer to the commander of the Cape Colonial Forces, Col Henry Timson Lukin. When Lukin was appointed Commandant-General of the Cape Colonial Forces in 1904, Collyer was made his staff officer. Collyer remained in this office until integration into the UDF in 1912.

63 NARSA, JSP, Box 111, Memorandum: Union of South Africa, Explanatory of the South African Defence Bill, November 1911, p. 15.

64 DODA, DC Group 2, Box 47, South African Defence Bill, Smuts to Lord Gladstone, 16 November 1911.

65 Van der Waag, 'South African Defence', p. 135.

66 T.J. Stapleton, *A Military History of South Africa From the Dutch–Khoi Wars to the End of Apartheid* (Santa Barbara: Praeger, 2010) p. 114.

67 Cape Colonial Forces, the Transvaal Volunteers and the Natal Militia, and South African Constabulary.

68 Van der Waag, *A Military History of Modern South Africa*, p. 61.

69 Uys, *South African Military Who's Who*, p. 138. Col H.T. Lukin served with the Cape Mounted Rifles and was chief of the Cape Colonial Forces at the formation of the UDF. He retired in 1919, having commanded the South African Infantry Brigade and then the 9th Scottish Division in France.

70 DODA, DC Group 2, Box 47, file 1063, South Africa Defence Bill.

71 I. van der Waag, 'Smuts's Generals: Towards a First Portrait of the South African High Command, 1912–1948', *War in History*, 18(1) (2011) p. 38.

72 N. Orpen, *South African Forces World War II: East African and Abyssinian Campaigns* (Cape Town: Purnell, 1968) p. 331.

73 DODA, Diverse Group 1, Box 32, Confidential Publications, Folio 36/4, Letter from Bourne to High Commissioner, 18 September 1913. See also J.F.C. Fuller, *The Foundations of the Science of War* (London: Hutchinson & Co., 1925) p. 87.

74 Union of South Africa Debates, Second Session of the First Parliament, 1912, South African Defence Bill, 23 February 1911, col. 622. Smuts drew a distinction between the Union and South Africa. South Africa included the Union and the HCT, GSWA and Portuguese Mozambique. This reveals Smuts and his expansionist vision as well as his intention to not limit South African defence to within the borders of the Union.

75 Union of South Africa Debates, Second Session of the First Parliament, 1912, South African Defence Bill, 23 February 1911, col. 623.

76 W.A. Dorning, 'A Concise History of the South African Defence Force (1912–1987)', *Scientia Militaria*, 17.2 (1987), p. 3.

77 Union of South Africa Debates, Second Session of the First Parliament, 1912, South African Defence Bill, 23 February 1911, col. 625.

78 A.C. Lillie, 'The Origin and Development of The South African Army', *Scientia Militaria*, 12.2 (1982) pp. 10, 11.

79 NARSA, JSP, Box 111, Memorandum: Union of South Africa, Expalantory of the South African Defence Bill, November 1911, p. 9. This was in recognition that "many of these corps have served with distinction [...] and it is specially desired to find a place for the traditions and associations of the principal of these corps in the new orginisation".

80 A.C. Lillie, 'The Origin and Development of The South African Army', *Scientia Militaria*, 12.2 (1982) pp. 10, 11.

81 NARSA, JSP, Box 111, Memorandum: Union of South Africa, Expalantory of the South African Defence Bill, November 1911, p. 7.

82 R. Geyer, 'The Union Defence Force and the 1914 Strike: The Dynamics of the Shadow of the Burgher', *Historia*, 59.2 (2014).

83 Van der Waag, *A Military History of Modern South Africa*, p. 82. The Defence Council advised the Governor-General and the defence minister on general or special defence requirements of the Union.

84 N. Orpen, *South African Forces World War II: East African and Abyssinian Campaigns* (Cape Town: Purnell, 1968) p. 331. Col C.P. Crewe (Cape), Brig-Gen D. McKenzie (Natal), Gen. C.R. de Wet (OFS), Gen. S.W. Burger (TVL).

85 No provision was made for a general staff and an unsatisfactory alternative arrangement was made where the three military executive commanders, Commandant-General of the Active Citizen Force, the Inspector-General of the Permanent Force and Commandant of the Cadet corps, were placed under the direct control of Smuts, who was in turn advised by a Defence Board.

86 Union of South Africa Debates, Second Session of the First Parliament, 1912, South African Defence Bill, 23 February 1911, col. 642.

87 Union of South Africa Debates, Second Session of the First Parliament, 1912, South African Defence Bill, 23 February 1911, col. 654. Crewe worked as Director of War Recruiting for the Union for campaigns in South West, Central and East Africa, and the European theatre, from 1914

88 Van der Waag, 'South African Defence', p. 136.

89 Van der Waag, 'South African Defence', p. 137.

90 W.A. Dorning, 'A Concise History of the South African Defence Force (1912–1987)', *Scientia Militaria*, 17.2 (1987) p. 3. The group of 51 officers, which included such well-known names as J. Lewis, W.E.C. Tanner, E.T. Thackwray, P.V.G. van der Byl, A.H. Nussey, S.G. Maritz, A.J. Brink, and J.C.G. Kemp,

91 Van der Waag, 'Smuts's Generals', p. 40.

92 E.W. Nortier, 'Major General Sir H.T. Lukin, 1861–1925: The Making of a South African Hero', MMil thesis, Stellenbosch University, December 2005.

93 Van der Waag, 'South African Defence', p. 137.

94 Union of South Africa Debates, Second Session of the First Parliament, 1912, South African Defence Bill, 23 February 1911, col. 659–71. See also I. J. Van der Waag., 'Rethinking South Africa's Military Past: The Curious Case of Brig-Gen the Hon C.F. Beyers', *Inaugural Lecture Delivered 2 August 2018*. Passim

95 The diagram is based on a schematic found at NARSA, JSP, Box 111, Folio 8, Memorandum Explanatory of the South African Defence Bill, November 1911. The UDF contained structural flaws which would perpetuate differences in doctrine as well as loyalty.

96 UG 32–13, C.F. Beyers, 'Report on Mission to Attend Army Manoeuvres and Military Institutions in Switzerland, France, Germany and England', 7 December 1912.

97 G. Tylden, *The Armed Forces of South Africa 1659–1954* (Johannesburg: Trophy Press, 1982) p. 9. The PF mounted infantrymen were unlike those of the more flexible and unconventional commandos and followed British doctrine more closely such as the drill book system of march discipline. See also H.F. Trew, *Botha Treks* (London: Blackie & Son, 1936, p. 130.

98 N. Orpen, *South African Forces World War II: East African and Abyssinian Campaigns* (Cape Town: Purnell, 1968), p. 331. 456 officers and 5,481 other ranks chose to transfer to the new Active Citizen Force, in which they formed a trained nucleus in a total Active Citizen Force and Coast Garrison Force establishment of 25,155. See also G. Tylden, '"TYPES OF THE UNION DEFENCE FORCE" OF SOUTH AFRICA: From a Colour Plate Published in The Cape Times Annual of December 1913', *Journal of the Society for Army Historical Research*, 38.156 (1960) p. 150. At inception the ACF comprised most of the existing volunteers and militia units of the Cape Colony, Natal and the Transvaal. In addition, of the 28 new units half were mounted and half dismounted. The dismounted units were to be mounted if the occasion arose.

99 A.C. Martin, *The Durban Light Infantry 1854–1934* (Durban: The Regimental Asociation DLI, 1969) p.163.

100 Van der Waag, 'Smuts's Generals', p. 36.

101 NARSA, JSP, Box 111, Folio 6, Memorandum Explanatory of the South African Defence Bill, November 1911.

102 C.M. van den Heever, *General J.B.M Hertzog* (APB Bookstore, 1946) p. 138.

103 W.K. Hancock and J. van der Poel (eds) *Selections from the Smuts Papers Volume III July 1910–November 1918*, Smuts to Gillet, 19 September 1910 (London: Cambridge University Press, 1966) p. 16. See also O. Pirow, *James Barry Munnik Hertzog* (Cape Town: Howard Timmins, 1958)

p. 53. See also Van den Heever, *General J.B.M Hertzog*, pp. 134–41. Botha, writing to President Steyn, complained that 'Hertzogism' had cost the South African Party six seats in parliament.

104 Pirow, *James Barry Munnik Hertzog*, p. 59.

105 Pirow, *James Barry Munnik Hertzog*, p. 56.

106 W.K. Hancock, *Smuts: The Sanguine Years 1870–1919* (London: Cambridge University Press, 1962) p. 357.

107 Van den Heever, *General J.B.M Hertzog*, pp. 148–50; Pirow, *James Barry Munnik Hertzog*, p. 58.

108 Lewsen, *John X. Merriman*, p. 229. Merriman in a letter to Steyn 29 December 1912 questioned Botha's inability to reach an understanding with Hertzog whom he describes as not "an unreasonable [man] or a man difficult to manage".

109 Pirow, *James Barry Munnik Hertzog*, pp. 56, 57

110 Hancock, *Smuts: The Sanguine Years*, pp. 357, 358.

111 *The Transvaal Leader*, 14 January 1914; Anon, 'The Crisis: General Strike Declared – Martial Law in Force', *Rand Daily Mail*, 14 January 1914.

112 T. Boydell, *My Luck Was In: With Spotlights on General Smuts* (Cape Town: Stewart, 1948) p. 71. The imperial troops all fell under the control of Lord Gladstone. (3rd Royal Dragoons, Hussars, the Scots Fusiliers, the South Staffordshire Light Infantry, the Bedfords). Three thousand police were also used.

113 Geyer, 'The Union Defence Force', pp. 138,139. The Citizen Force Class B Reserve (Rifle Associations or commandos) were not used to suppress the industrial action of 1913.

114 Boydell, *My Luck Was In*, p. 78.

115 Trew, *Botha Treks*, p. 27. Trew makes the point that the call up of the commandos to quell the strikes afforded the opportunity to arm them and fully test their organisation as they had not been called up since the South African War.

116 Geyer, 'The Union Defence Force', pp. 139, 140.

117 Boydell, *My Luck Was In*, p. 64. These men would not have looked out of place during the South African War, and many were veterans of that conflict.

118 DODA, DC2, Box 168, File 2/7164, Correspondence, Under Secretary of Defence about pay and allowances of burghers on commando, 1914; DODA, SAMR, Box 1084, File 215/4/3, Under Secretary of Defence – District control officer Pretoria, 20 January 1914. Commandants, field-cornets, assistant field-cornets, and ordinary burghers

119 Geyer, 'The Union Defence Force', pp. 148, 149.

120 D. Reitz, *Trekking On: In the Company of Brave Men* (Edinburgh: The House of Emslie, 2012) p. 14.

121 Trew, *Botha Treks*, p. 27.

122 A. Samson, *World War I in Africa: The Forgotten Conflict Among the European Poers*. (London: Tauris, 2013) pp. 68, 69.

123 TNA, ADM 137-9, Telegram from C-in-C Cape to Governor-General, 1 August 1914.

124 S.B. Spies, 'The Outbreak of the First World War and the Botha Government', *South African Historical Journal*, 1.1 (1969) p. 47. The dominion delegates accepted the principle at the Imperial Conference 1911. The Canadian premier, Sir Wilfrid Laurier, believed that the extent of the dominion participation was a matter for each dominion to decide. This was a view held by Hertzog who believed that South Africa had a choice as to the extent of its active participation.

125 House of Commons Parliamentary Papers Online, Correspondence on the subject of Proposed Naval and Military Expedition Against German South-West Africa, Botha to Acting Governor-General, 4 August 1914. See also UG 42–16, Report of the Judicial Commission of Inquiry into the Causes and Circumstances Relating to the Recent Rebellion in South Africa, Minutes of Evidence, Louis Botha, 29 June 1916, p. 350.

126 P. van der Byl, *From Playgrounds to Battlefields* (Cape Town: Howard Timmins, 1971) p. 93.

127 Van den Heever, *General J.B.M Hertzog*, pp. 169–71.

128 UG 42–16, Recent Rebellion in South Africa, Minutes of Evidence, Louis Botha, 29 June 1916, p. 349.

129 Van den Heever, *General J.B.M Hertzog*, p. 170.

130 UG 42–16, Recent Rebellion in South Africa, Minutes of Evidence, Louis Botha, 29 June 1916, p. 350.

131 NARSA, JSP, Box 196, Folio 31, Letter from Crewe to Smuts, 3 August 1914. Crewe already identified at this early date that an expedition would depart for GSWA and he hoped to secure Delagoa "out of the scramble that will come".

132 Hancock, *Selections from the Smuts Papers, Volume III*, M.T. Steyn to J.C. Smuts, 31 July 1914, p. 184.

133 Van den Heever, *General J.B.M Hertzog*, p. 164.

134 The National Archives, London (hereafter TNA): ADM 137/9, Telegram Secretary of State for Colonies to Acting Governor-General), 6 August 1914.

135 NARSA, JSP, Box 111, Folio 18, Letter Department of Posts and Telegraphs to Secretary of Defence, German Wireless Telegraph Stations, 10 August 1914.

136 House of Commons Parliamentary Papers Online, Correspondence on the subject of Proposed Naval and Military Expedition Against German South-West Africa, Acting Governor to General Botha, 7 August 1914. The British desire to seize German colonies as 'diplomatic hostages' to be used as bargaining tools at the peace negotiations was based on the initial feeling that the war would not last long. This attitude changed rapidly into a determination not to return the German colonies in any event as they were of great strategic value in any modern future war.

137 TNA, ADM 137-9, Extract from Proceedings of Sub Committee of Imperial Defence, 5 August 1914. The sub-committee attached importance to the political effect of inviting South Africa to cooperate. See also M. Hankey, *The Supreme Command* (London: Routledge, 1961) p. 168.

138 S. Hallifax, "'Over by Christmas": British Popular Opinion and the Short War in 1914', *First World War Studies*, 1.2 (2010) p. 107.

139 H. Strachan, *The First World War* (Oxford: Oxford University Press, 2001) pp. 1012, 1013.

140 S.B. Spies, 'The Outbreak of the First World War and the Botha Government', *South African Historical Journal*, 1.1 (1969) p. 50.

141 S.B. Spies, 'The Outbreak of the First World War and the Botha Government', *South African Historical Journal*, 1.1 (1969) p. 50. This according to Malan's diary.

142 UG 46–16, Report of the Judicial Commission of Inquiry into the Causes and Circumstances Relating to the Recent Rebellion in South Africa, Correspondence between the Union and Imperial Governments regarding German South West Africa, Annexure C, p. 113.

143 House of Commons Parliamentary Papers Online, Correspondence on the subject of Proposed Naval and Military Expedition Against German South-West Africa, Secretary of State to Acting Governor-General, 9 August 1914. See also Hancock, *Selections from the Smuts Papers, Volume III*, p. 188. See also UG 42–16, Recent Rebellion in South Africa, pp.132, 133. See also UG 46–16, Recent Rebellion in South Africa, p. 31 for the proclamation that "it is quite improbable that the Government will find it necessary to call out anymore regiments of the Active Citizen Force for service outside the Union". See also S.C. 1–15, Union of South Africa Report of the Select Committee on Rebellion, Minutes of Evidence, J.B.M. Hertzog, 29 March 1915, p. 233.

144 House of Commons Parliamentary Papers Online, Correspondence on the subject of Proposed Naval and Military Expedition Against German South-West Africa, Botha to Acting Governor-General, 10 August 1914. See also NARSA, JSP, Box 111 (18), Memorandum Postmaster to Secretary for Defence, German Wireless Telegraph Stations, 10 August 1914.

145 TNA, ADM 137-9, Telephone message received by Chief Censor from War Office, 11 August 1914.

146 Lewsen, *John X. Merriman*, p. 256.

147 Trew, *Botha Treks*, p. 1.

148 DODA, AG 14, Box 6, Biography Kemp. See also *Dictionary of South African Biography Volume I*, ed. by W.J. de Kock (Cape Town: Tafelberg, 1968) pp. 420–1. Kemp was born and bred in the ZAR and was also present in suppressing the Jameson Raid. He served under Beyers in the South African War. He then served under De la Rey and became one of his ablest and most daring generals. He was one of the six who voted against the peace terms at Vereeniging. Smuts persuaded Kemp to join the UDF in 1912 as a major but he always harboured the desire to use his position to form a Boer republic when the opportunity arose. He resigned his commission on 13 September 1914 in protest of the government's war policy.

149 W.J. de Kock (ed.), *Dictionary of South African Biography Volume I*, (Cape Town: Tafelberg, 1968) pp. 513–15. Maritz was born in Kimberley and arrived in Johannesburg at the age of 19. He was not a well-educated man and joined the Transvaal Police (ZARPs) after volunteering in the Jameson Raid. He made a name in the South African War, firstly as part of an elite scout unit under Danie Theron, and then as a raider into the Cape Colony.

150 UG 42–16, Recent Rebellion in South Africa, Minutes of Evidence, Louis Botha, 29 June 1916, pp. 350, 351.

151 UG 42–16, Recent Rebellion in South Africa, Minutes of Evidence, Louis Botha, 29 June 1916, pp. 352, 351.

152 Hancock, *Selections from the Smuts Papers, Volume III*, Merriman to Smuts 8 November 1914, p. 209.

153 UG 42–16, Recent Rebellion in South Africa, Minutes of Evidence, Louis Botha, 29 June 1916, p. 352.

154 D.W. Kruger and C.J. Beyers (eds), *Dictionary of South African Biography Volume III* (Cape Town: Tafelberg, 1977) p. 66.

155 D.W. Kruger, *The Making of a Nation* (Johannesburg: Macmillan, 1977) pp. 82, 85, 86–89.

156 NARSA, JSP, Box 196, Folio 33, Letter Crewe to Smuts, 12 August 1914. Smuts consulted with Crewe on 11 August 1914 on proposals to raise four regiments. See also NARSA, JSP, Box 196, Folio 137, Letter Smuts to Duncan McKenzie, 12 August 1914. Informing McKenzie of mobilisation plans including volunteer regiments.

157 TNA, ADM 137-9, Naval Notes on Expedition to GSWA (prepared by Admiral H. Jackson), 8 August 1914. The British had formulated the rudiments of a plan very early, and these objectives as set out obviously influenced Smuts and his planning. The British plan called for an "urgent" seizure of the wireless stations at Lüderitzbucht and Swakopmund in a first phase, while giving recognition that the occupation of Windhoek was a serious military matter to be undertaken after the ports had been seized.

158 UG 42–16, Recent Rebellion in South Africa, Minutes of Evidence, Louis Botha, 29 June 1916, p. 362.

159 Samson, *World War I in Africa*, p. 70. Samson takes the view that the Union would not undertake the GSWA campaign without the approval of Parliament. This flies in the face of documentary evidence to the contrary.

160 The Union and Labour parties held 43 seats between them in the 121-seat House and thus even if the Afrikaner vote was split in half Smuts and Botha would have little trouble in garnering sufficient numbers to get them across the line.

161 Hancock, *Selections from the Smuts Papers, Volume III*, Smuts to Merriman 2 October 1914, p. 202.

162 Hancock, *Selections from the Smuts Papers, Volume III*, Poel, Smuts to Reitz 22 September 1914, p. 198.

163 UG 46–16, Recent Rebellion in South Africa, p. 30 See also S.C. 1–15, Union of South Africa Report of the Select Committee on Rebellion, Minutes of Evidence, J.B.M. Hertzog, 29 March 1915, p. 223.

164 Samson, *World War I in Africa*, p. 71.

165 DODA, DC Group 2, Box 184, Beyers resignation and Smuts reply. See also TNA, ADM 137-9, Folio 517, Telegram, Translation of Beyers resignation manifesto, Buxton to Harcourt, 20 September 1914. See also TNA, ADM 137-9, Folio 517, Telegram, Smuts reply to Beyers resignation manifesto, Buxton to Harcourt, 21 September 1914.

166 DODA, DC Group 2, Box 688, Letter Van Deventer to Smuts, 20 December 1914. Van Deventer asked Smuts to lapse the policy of volunteerism in view of the situation after the rebellion. Many commandos insisted that they need not cross the border into GSWA as volunteers. See Also DODA, DC Group 2, Box 688, Letter Smuts to Van Deventer, 11 January 1915. Smuts was reluctant to mobilise the National Reserve under power of proclamation unless there was a real threat of German invasion.

167 UG 42–16, Recent Rebellion in South Africa, Minutes of Evidence, Louis Botha, 29 June 1916, pp. 353, 354. See also TNA, ADM 137-9, Folio 538, Telegram, Report on De la Rey funeral Buxton to Harcourt, 21 September 1914. Buxton reported that Botha had a sedative effect on the crowd and was satisfied with how the funeral was conducted despite being extremely nervous before the event. Buxton and Botha seemed to think that the crisis had passed.

Chapter 3

1   D. Lloyd George, *War Memoirs of David Lloyd George* (London: Odhams Press Ltd, 1938), p. 1024.

2   S.B. Spies, 'The Outbreak of the First World War and the Botha Government', *South African Historical Journal*, I (1969) p. 52.

3   D.W. Smith, *The German Colonial Empire* (Chapel Hill: The University of North Carolina Press, 1978), pp. 53, 58, 59. New copper deposits were opened in 1907 and diamonds were discovered in 1908. GSWA showed a favourable balance of trade for the first time in 1912.

4   P. Lewsen (ed.) *Selections from the Correspondence of John X. Merriman 1905–1924*, (Cape Town: The Van Riebeeck Society, 1969) p. 256.

5   F.A. Mouton, '"The Sacred Tie": Sir Thomas Smartt, the Unionist Party and the British Empire, 1912–1920', *Historia*, 57.2 (2012) p. 12. On 18 March 1914, the Labour Party won control of the Transvaal Provincial Council; the Unionists won only two seats to the 23 of Labour.

6   Lewsen, *John X. Merriman*, p. 255. In a letter 9 July 1914 to M.T. Steyn, Merriman described at length the inroads that Hertzog and his new nationalist party were making in the OFS, Cape, and Transvaal.

7   P. Baxter, *Gandi, Smuts and Race in the British Empire* (South Yorkshire: Pen & Sword, 2017) p. 254. Smuts wrote on Gandhi's departure, "The saint has left our shores, and I sincerely hope forever."

8   W.K. Hancock, *Smuts: The Sanguine Years 1870–1919* (London: Cambridge University Press, 1962) p. 371; Lewsen, *John X. Merriman*, p. 229. Merriman in a letter to Steyn 29 December 1912 accused Botha of having an "utter incapacity for administration", a position he abdicated to Smuts from the beginning of their relationship.

9   NARSA, PM 1/1/32, File 4/95/14-4/97/14 Correspondence file, Telegram Secretary of State to Acting Governor-General, 12 August 1914. Requests for artillery alarmed the British who

encouraged the South Africans to "seize Colonies of main importance in enemy's territory, [. . .] this will probably prove tantamount to conquest of the whole". See also TNA, CAB 44–2, Operations in the Union of South Africa and German South West Africa, 11 August 1914. Union Government's requests to retain the artillery of the imperial garrison were flatly refused.

10 TNA, WO 106-47, Offensive Scheme against German South West Africa, Memorandum Acting Quarter Master General to Director general of Military Intelligence, 24 November 1902.

11 TNA, WO 106-47, Paper on Occupation of Swakopmund, 16 October 1902.

12 TNA, WO 106-47, Project for the dispatch of an Expeditionary Force to GSWA, April 1910.

13 TNA, WO 106-47, Project for the dispatch of an Expeditionary Force to GSWA, April 1910, pp. 7, 45, 47, 49.

14 TNA, WO 106-47, Memorandum Methuen to the High Commissioner Selbourne, 2 March 1909.

15 NARSA, PM 1/1/32, File 4/95/14-4/97/14 Correspondence file, Telegram Secretary of State to Acting Governor-General, 18 August 1914. "In connection with the expedition against German South West Africa British flag should be hoisted in all territories occupied successfully by His Majesty's forces and suitable arrangements made for temporary administration. No formal proclamation of annexation should however be made without previous communication with His majesty's Government."

16 NARSA, JSP, Box 196, Folio 138, Letter from Smuts to Lt-Gen Sir James Wolfe Murray, 17 August 1914.

17 TNA, ADM 137-9, Memorandum Admiralty to Secretary of State for the Colonies, 11 August 1914.

18 J.J. Collyer, *Campaign in German South West Africa 1914–1915* (London: Imperial War Museum and Battery Press, 1937) p. 157) Collyer identifies the tenets of the original Smuts plan only at the end of the official history in the lessons learnt section.

19 D.B. Katz (in press), 'An Aggregation of Lion Hunters: In Search of the Boer Way of War', *International Journal of Military History and Historiography*, 2021.

20 I. Uys, *South African Military Who's Who 1452–1992* (Germiston: Forttress, 1992) p. 18. Beves served in the South African War in the Rand Pioneer Regiment and started life in the UDF as the Commandant of Cadets.

21 DODA, DC Group 2, Box 252, Folio 17138, Lukin's Report on 'A' Force, 19 August 1915. Lukin describes his strength on 25 August 1914 as 135 officers and 2463 other ranks, 522 black troops, 12 field guns, 12 machine guns.

22 Anon, *The Union of South Africa and the Great War 1918* (Nashville: Battery Press, 1924) p. 13. See also Collyer, *Campaign in German South West Africa*, pp. 28, 29.

23 Map adapted from G. L'Ange, *Urgent Imperial Service: South African Forces in German South West Africa 1914–1915* (Johannesburg: Ashanti, 1991) p. 85.

24 TNA, ADM 137–13, Folio 50, Buxton to Harcourt, 8 October 1914. See Rayner and O'Shaughnessy, 1916, 9. The official histories make no mention of 'D' Force in their initial line-ups and Order of Battle (ORBATs). Mention of 'D' Force can be found in the work of the imbedded journalists and the primary sources. This is perhaps the reason for historians overlooking its existence. S. Monick, *A Bugle Calls: The Story of the Witwatersrand Rifles and Its Predecessors 1899–1987* (Johannesburg: Witwatersrand Rifles Regimental Council, 1989) p. 87. The regimental history identifies that the reinforcements received at Lüderitzbucht were "originally designated 'D' Force" and destined for Walvis Bay. However, the outbreak of the rebellion led to a revision of Smuts's plans.

25 Collyer, *Campaign in German South West Africa*, pp. 30,31.

26 C. von Clausewitz, *On War* (New York: Random House, 1943) p. 328.

27 Von Clausewitz, *On War*, p. 604. See M.N. Vego, *Operational Warfare: Theory and Practice* (New York, Department of the Navy, 2000) pp. 171–5.

28 Classic Prussian tactics of King Frederick the Great (1712–86) emulated and adapted by Napoleon with his corps system— concentrating a superior force the decisive point, which was usually the enemy's weakest, with the object of overwhelming them.

29 A.H. de Jomini, *The Art of War* (London: Greenhill Books, 1992) p. 102

30 Von Clausewitz, *On War*, p. 617. "It is certainly much pleasanter to march with a small army through an opulent country, than with a large army through a poor one."

31 Von Clausewitz, *On War*, New York: Random House, 1943, p. 611.

32 The figures for the force levels were derived from T.R. Ungleich, 'The Defence of German South-West Africa During World War I' (MA thesis, University of Miami, 1974) pp. 36, 37; and Anon, *The Union of South Africa and the Great War 1918* (Nashville: Battery Press, 1924) p. 13. See also Collyer, *Campaign in German South West Africa*, pp. 28, 29

33 E. Buxton, *General Botha* (New York: E.P. Dutton & Co., 1924) p. 102.

34 A. Jones, *The Art of War in the Western World* (London: Harrap Ltd, 1988) p. 12. See A. Garcia, 'Manoeuvre Warfare in the South African Campaign in German South West Africa During the First World War' (MA thesis, Humanities, University of South Africa, 2015) p. 67.

35 Collyer, *Campaign in German South West Africa*, p. 157. Collyer is highly critical of the UDF's decision to advance but ignores the fact that an advance was only anticipated once a landing at Walvis Bay/Swakopmund had been effected.

36 Jones, *The Art of War*, p. 280. A concentration in time which sometimes involves the refusing of battle and retreat of one of the forces while the other forces advance is the cornerstone of exploiting the advantages of exterior lines.

37 Jones, *The Art of War*, p. 520. Frederick the Great, a successful practitioner of concentration on interior lines, noted another disadvantage of concentration in space, applicable to the logistics of his day, when he wrote: "These kinds of wars ruin the armies by fatigue and the marches that one must have his men make."

38 Von Oelhafen, *Der Feldzug in Südwest*. The German semi-official history has not been translated into English. This poses a considerable barrier for historians with no command of the German language. The author made use of online translation services to make sense of the German text. Although the translation is cumbersome, a good general sense of the text was obtained.

39 Judicial Commission of Inquiry, Causes of and Circumstances Relating to the Recent Rebellion in South Africa, Minutes of Evidence, Evidence Louis Botha, December 1916, p. 359

40 J.H. Buchanan, 'The Danger in Reading History Backwards', *The Educational Forum*, 10.1 (2008) p. 70.

41 A. Garcia, 'Airpower in the Union of South Africa's First World War Campaign in German South West Africa', *Historia*, 62.2 (2017) p.9. The South Africans were able to field six planes of a superior quality and reliability, but this was only late in the campaign in April 1915.

42 Von Oelhafen, *Der Feldzug in Südwest*, p. 13.

43 Von Oelhafen, *Der Feldzug in Südwest*, p. 12.

44 Von Oelhafen, *Der Feldzug in Südwest*, pp. 13–15. See TNA, ADM 137–13, Folio 10, Telegram Buxton to Harcourt, 1 October 1914. The total number of field guns available to the South Africans was five batteries (two of six guns each and three of four guns each). Therefore, there were 24 in total of which Lukin fielded eight, McKenzie 12, and Botha had four earmarked.

45 Collyer, *Campaign in German South West Africa*, p. 21.

46 Collyer, *Campaign in German South West Africa*, p. 25. See TNA, ADM 137-9, Folio 459, Buxton to Harcourt, 16 September 1914. The South Africans requested help from the British in acquiring

heavy artillery pieces for the GSWA expedition. The South African artillery was in a poor state and at best improvised (three batteries of 13-pounders and two batteries of 15-pounders). The South Africans were looking for two big gun detachments (each of which would consist of 2 x 6 inch and 2 x 4.7 inch) to silence German field batteries and demolish fortifications. The British acceded to the request for more artillery but amended what was on offer to a battery of 4-inch guns and a battery of 12-pounders, which they felt was more manoeuvrable and better suited to the conditions. The South Africans gratefully accepted on 19 September 1914. See TNA, ADM 137-9, Folio 509, Buxton to Harcourt, 19 September 1914.

47 The Landwehr was part of the organised national armed force that had completed the required service and constituted the second line of defence.

48 Von Oelhafen, *Der Feldzug in Südwest*, p. 7. Oelhafen sets the number at 1,870 with a white population of 15,000. He laments the small size of the army compared to a population that grew from 4,500 since the Hottentot rebellion in 1893.

49 T.R. Ungleich, 'The Defence of German South-West Africa During World War I' (MA thesis, University of Miami, 1974), pp. 36, 37

50 J. Stejskal, *The Horns of the Beast: The Swakop River Campaign and World War I in South-West Africa 1914–1915* (Solihull: Helion & Co., 2014) pp. 50–53.

51 Stejskal, *The Horns of the Beast*, pp. 50–53. See Ungleich, 'The Defence of German South-West Africa', p. 48.

52 TNA, ADM 137–13, Folio 299, Buxton to Harcourt, Reuters Report on German proclamation, 29 October 1914.

53 Von Oelhafen, *Der Feldzug in Südwest*, p. 7.

54 Von Oelhafen, *Der Feldzug in Südwest*, p. 17.

55 Collyer, *Campaign in German South West Africa*, p. 23. The advantages of internal lines of communication meant the Germans could retreat on shortening supply lines and adequate provisions, while the UDF lines of communication would extend as they advanced. The UDF would have to bring all their supplies from Cape Town and then transport over long distances through inhospitable countryside.

56 Von Oelhafen, *Der Feldzug in Südwest*, p. 16. Coal is a superior fuel due to its energy density.

57 Collyer, *Campaign in German South West Africa*, p. 23. See E. Kleynhans, 'A Critical Analysis of the Impact of Water on the South African Campaign in German South West Africa, 1914–1915', *Historia*, 61.2 (2016). Kleynhans illuminates the fundamental role of water, its accessibility and its protection in shaping the strategic and operational conduct of the campaign. See I. van der Waag, 'African Water Histories: Transdisciplinary Discourses', ed. by J.W.N. Tempelhoff (Vanderbijlpark: North West University, 2005). Van der Waag highlights how the shortage of water impacted on the GSWA campaign.

58 Von Oelhafen, *Der Feldzug in Südwest*, p. 16.

59 Collyer, *Campaign in German South West Africa*, p. 22.

60 Von Oelhafen, *Der Feldzug in Südwest*, p. 35. The Germans felt that an attack on Beves ensconced at Lüderitzbucht would yield little result in the face of overwhelming Allied naval artillery support and an ability to bring in reinforcements enabled by overwhelming command of the seas.

61 Stejskal, *The Horns of the Beast*, pp. 50–3.

62 NARSA, 'Memorandum on the Country known as German South-West Africa'. Union Government Papers, 1915, p. 6–7. At the time the First World War began, 2,000 'Cape subjects' were living in the German territory.

63 Ungleich, 'The Defence of German South-West Africa' pp. 50–2.

64 Von Oelhafen, *Der Feldzug in Südwest*, p. 10.

65 Von Oelhafen, *Der Feldzug in Südwest*, pp. 12, 17. Some of these indigenous troops were disarmed on the approach of the UDF and others turned their weapons against the Germans, justifying the initial German suspicion as to the unreliability of the local black citizens.

66 Von Oelhafen, *Der Feldzug in Südwest*, p. 11. See TNA, ADM 137-9, Folio 566, Telegram, Buxton to Harcourt, 23 September 1914. The Germans failed to destroy the condensing plant at Lüderitzbucht, and it was found intact by the UDF. Furthermore, see TNA, ADM 137–13, Folio 344, Buxton to Harcourt, 2 November 1914, McKenzie reported on the 2 November 1914 that he secured a 1,000 gallon per hour water supply at Kolmanskop. This later proved to be optimistic as the water was of poor quality and had to be mixed in equal parts with condensed water to be usable. See TNA, ADM 137–13, Folio 625, Telegram Buxton to Harcourt, 28 November 1914.

67 Von Oelhafen, *Der Feldzug in Südwest*, p. 11.

68 Ungleich, 'The Defence of German South-West Africa', p. 52.

69 Von Oelhafen, *Der Feldzug in Südwest*, p. 10.

70 TNA, ADM 137-9, Folio 60, Telegram Acting Governor-General to the Secretary of State, 4 August 1914.

71 TNA, ADM 137-9, Folio 70, Telegram Secretary of State to Acting Governor-General, 6 August 1914. See Collyer, *Campaign in German South West Africa*, p. 6. And G. L'Ange, *Urgent Imperial Service: South African Forces in German South West Africa 1914–1915* (Johannesburg: Ashanti, 1991) p. 9.

72 TNA, ADM 137-9, Folio 86, Memo Admiral H.B. Jackson, 8 August 1914. "The seizure of the coast wireless stations at Lüderitzbucht and Swakopmund is an urgent necessity."

73 R. Warwick, 'Reconsideration of the Battle of Sandfontein:The First Phase of the German South West Africa Campaign, August to September 1914' (MA thesis, University of Cape Town, 2003) p. iv. "an urgent and impatient plan based upon political considerations, to make an immediate and highly visible impact … [a] petulant act of policy, combined with the failure to devise a sound strategic assessment based upon thorough intelligence and communication, led to the defeat of a sizeable South African detachment".

74 TNA, ADM 137-9, Folio 69, Extract from Proceedings of a Sub Committee of the Committee of Imperial Defence, 5 August 1914. See also TNA, CAB 44–2, Operations in the Union of South Africa and German South West Africa, 5 August 1914.

75 TNA, ADM 137-9, C-in-C Cape to Governor-General, Folio 33, 1 August 1914. It was suggested at this early stage that Walvis Bay be provided with guns and a garrison and that local troops be used. See also TNA, CAB 44–2, Operations in the Union of South Africa and German South West Africa, 8 August 1914. Suggesting a joint naval and military expedition.

76 TNA, CAB 44–2, Operations in the Union of South Africa and German South West Africa, 8 August 1915.

77 NARSA, PM 1/1/32, File 4/95/14-4/97/14, Minute no' 750, Correspondence file, Telegram Botha to Lord de Villiers, 15 August 1914. Botha telegrammed Lord de Villiers again on Minute no 759, 17 August 1914 speaking of 1,600 dismounted men and eight guns earmarked for Lüderitzbucht and <u>Swakopmund</u> (author's emphasis) with a further mounted force of 1,600 under Lukin to be landed at Port Nolloth supported by a further 1,000 mounted men at Upington. On Minute no 776, 20 August 1914 Lord de Villiers was informed that the dismounted forces proceeding to <u>Swakopmund</u> (author's emphasis) and Lüderitzbucht would be increased to 5,000 and to Steinkopf increased to 3,000. See I. van der Waag, 'The Battle of Sandfontein, 26 September 1914: South African Military Reform and the German South West Africa Campaign, 1914–1915', *First World War Studies*, (2013) p. 22, note 39. Van der Waag using Minute no. 759, 17 August 1914 uses the document to imply that by this stage the plans were modified despite the landings at Swakopmund being emphatically referred to by Botha on 17 August and again on 20 August.

78 TNA, ADM 137-9, De Villers to Harcourt, 17 August 1914. The plan may have been finalised on 21 August, but the Acting Governor was able to report to the British in much detail including troop numbers for the invasion of GSWA and the building of the railway from Prieska to the GSWA border. The original numbers were 1,600 dismounted troops and eight guns for Lüderitzbucht and Swakopmund and 1,600 mounted men (SAMR) and three gun batteries under Lukin destined for Port Nolloth. See TNA, ADM 137-9, Memorandum Acting Governor of Union of SA to Secretary of State for the Colonies, 20 August 1914. It was reported on 20 August that the number of troops to be dispatched to Lüderitzbucht and Swakopmund was to be increased to 5,000. This increase was obviously decided on before the meeting held by Smuts on 21 August with his commanders.

79 I. van der Waag, 'Smuts's Generals: Towards a First Portrait of the South African High Command, 1912–1948', *War in History*, 18(1) (2011) p. 50. Skinner was one of several British officers who had been attached to the UDF training units and served as the commandant of the South African Military School.

80 Union Of South Africa, *Judicial Commission of Inquiry: Causes Of and Circumstances Relating to the Recent Rebellion in South Africa* (Cape Town, 1916) p. 7. See Collyer, *Campaign in German South West Africa*, p. 27.

81 Van der Waag, 'The Battle of Sandfontein', p. 8, note 84. "Events now prescribed a smaller arc of operations extending around the southern extremities of the German territory only."

82 Collyer, *Campaign in German South West Africa*, p. 27.

83 NARSA, JSP, Box 196, Folio 34, Letter from Crewe to Smuts, 24 August 1914.

84 See NARSA, PM 1/1/32, File 4/95/14-4/97/14, Minute no 800, Correspondence file, Telegram Botha to Lord de Villiers, 25 August 1914. See Minute no. 800 2 September 1914, which complains of disembarkation delays at Port Nolloth and warns that similar delays may be expected at Lüderitzbucht and <u>Swakopmund</u> (author's emphasis).

85 W.K. Hancock and J. van der Poel (eds), *Selections from the Smuts Papers Volume III July 1910–November 1918* (London: Cambridge University Press, 1966) p. 202.

86 Hancock *Selections from the Smuts Papers Volume III*, p. 201.

87 Governor-General and High Commissioner for Southern Africa: The Viscount Gladstone (until 27 July 1914). Baron de Villiers (acting, 27 July 1914 to 2 September 1914). Sir James Rose Innes (acting, 2 to 8 September 1914). Sydney Buxton 8 September 1914 to 17 November 1920).

88 NARSA, PM 1/1/32, File 4/95/14-4/97/14, Correspondence file, Telegram Secretary of State to Acting Governor-General, 25 August 1914. Discretion was granted on whether to issue a formal demand of surrender to the German defenders before the attack.

89 W.S. Rayner and W.W. O'Shaughnessy, *How Botha and Smuts Conquered German South West* (London: Simpson, Marshall, Hamilton, Kent & Co., 1916) p. 9.

90 DODA, DC Box 252, Historical Record of the Campaign in GSWA compiled by Hugh Wyndham, p. 1. "Any plans that were formed in August 1914 […] had to be abandoned or modified suddenly to meet the grave menace which had unexpectedly arisen within the Union." Wyndham places the cancellation of the Smuts plan firmly after the outbreak of the rebellion.

91 TNA, ADM 137-9, Folio 598, C-in-C Cape to Admiralty, 29 September 1914.

92 H. Strachan, *The First World War in Africa* (Oxford: Oxford University Press, 2004) p. 69.

93 Anon, *The Union of South Africa and the Great War*, p. 13.

94 NARSA, PM 1/1/32, File 4/95/14-4/97/14, Minute no 860, Correspondence file, Telegram Botha to Buxton, 8 September 1914.

95 NARSA, PM 1/1/32, File 4/95/14-4/97/14, Correspondence file, Telegram Secretary of State to Governor-General, 9 September 1914.

96 NARSA, PM 1/1/32, File 4/95/14-4/97/14, Correspondence file, Telegram Buxton to Secretary of State, 8 September 1914. Smuts informally through Buxton called for another warship, HMS *Cumberland*, to be dispatched to the area and cover the landings at Walvis Bay.

97 Strachan, *The First World War in Africa*, p. 67.

98 Anon, *The Union of South Africa and the Great War*, p. 13.

99 TNA, ADM 137-9, Memorandum from Sir H. Jackson, 22 August 1914. Admiral H.B. Jackson was advisor on overseas expeditions planning attacks on Germany's colonial possessions at the start of the First World War.

100 TNA, ADM 137-9, Memorandum Acting Governor of Union of SA to Secretary of State for the Colonies, 30 August 1914. De Villiers was concerned that the HMS *Astraea* would be required for escorting garrison troops back to the United Kingdom leaving on 12 September with a three-week delay from that date.

101 TNA, ADM 137-9, Telegram S of S Colonies to Act Gov Union of SA, 23 August 1914. Harcourt was anxious that the build-up of forces and additional transport beyond what was initially required would cause a delay in the destruction of the wireless stations there. He urged the Acting Governor-General to seize the wireless stations without delay and not let the build-up for the land invasion interfere with the original mission. See DODA, DC Box 252, Telegram Secretary of State to Acting Governor-General, 23 August 1914.

102 TNA, ADM 137-9, Telegram C-in-C Cape Admiralty, 25 August 1914.

103 TNA, ADM 137-9, Telegram Act Gov Union to S of S Colonies, 24 August 1914.

104 TNA, ADM 137-9, Telegram C-in-C Cape Admiralty, 26 August 1914.

105 TNA, ADM 137-9, Memorandum Acting Governor of Union of SA to Secretary of State for the Colonies, 31 August 1914.

106 DODA, DC Group 2, Box 252, Folio 17138, Lukin's Report on 'A' Force, 19 August 1915. Disembarkation, according to Lukin, took more than two weeks and was not completed before 16/17 September 1914. The major delay occurred with the disembarkation of the animals that were slung twice from ship to lighter and then lighter to shore. See DODA, DC Group 2, Box 252, Letter from Secretary for Defence to unknown, 19 September 1914, which refers to the great difficulties of disembarkation. See also DODA, GSWA Group, Box 14, Methods and Points to be Observed in Embarking and Disembarking.

107 TNA, ADM 137-9, Telegram Officer Advising Gov of SA to H.B. Jackson, 2 September 1914.

108 DODA, DC Group 2, Box 252, Letter from Secretary for Defence to unknown, 19 September 1914. The letter refers to great loss of equipment for lack of care and the unsuitability of donkeys over mules. There was the problem of inferior quality equipment such as artillery harnesses.

109 TNA, ADM 137-9, Telegram C-in-C Cape to H.B. Jackson, 5 September 1914. See N. Orpen, *The History of the Transvaal Horse Artillery 1904–1974* (Johannesburg: THA Regimental Council, 1975) p. 14. The regimental history alludes to the chaos of disembarkation at Port Nolloth. It seems that it took the THA from 31 August to 9 September to fully assemble at the port before making their way to Steinkopf. See F.B. Adler, *The History of the Transvaal Horse Artillery* (Johannesburg: Regimental Asociation of the THA, 1927). The author attests to the disorganisation that accompanied the embarking at Cape Town and disembarking at Port Nolloth. See DODA, DC Group 2, Box 252, Folio 17138, Lukin's Report on 'A' Force, 19 August 1915. The move to Steinkopf began on 4 September 1914 where Lukin established his Headquarters on 10 September 1914. See also DODA Box 252, Lukin's Report on 'A' Force, 19 August 1915. Lukin reports that all troopships had arrived by 3 September 1914 and their disembarkation was not completed until 17 September 1914. See also also Mark Coghlan, *History of the Umvoti Mounted Rifles* (Durban: Just Done Productions, 2012) p. 1162. There was no luxury of a wharf in Lüderitzbucht as late as March 1914 and horses disembarking had to swim to the shore. See also DODA, AG 14, Box

13, File 2 Veterinary Services GSWA Campaign and Rebellion August 1914 to July 1915, Report by Colonel J.A.S. Irvine Smith, p. 15. Smith reports that by 17 March disembarkation of horses had improved by avoiding slinging and using of a special gangway allowing for 900 animals to be offloaded in 10 hours.

110 DODA, DC Group 2, Box 252, Joint Naval and Military Operations, Secretary of Defence, 9 September 1914.

111 TNA, ADM 137-9, Telegram S.S. for Colonies to Gov of SA, 7 September 1914.

112 TNA, ADM 137-9, Telegram Governor of Union of SA to Secretary of State for the Colonies, 8 September 1914.

113 TNA, ADM 137-9, Telegram C-in-C Cape to H.B. Jackson, 9 September 1914.

114 TNA, ADM 137-9, Telegram S.S. for Colonies to Gov of SA, 9 September 1914.

115 Nico Moolman collection of glass negatives. Thank you to Nico Moolman for allowing access to his wonderful collection of glass negatives and the use in this book of some of them.

116 TNA, ADM 137-9, Folio 426, Telegram C-in-C Cape to H.B. Jackson, 11 September 1914.

117 NARSA, PM 1/1/32, File 4/95/14-4/97/14, Minute no 868, Correspondence file, Telegram Botha to Buxton, 11 September 1914. Botha cautioned that it was unlikely the landing at Walvis Bay would be completed before 30 September 1914.

118 NARSA, PM 1/1/32, File 4/95/14-4/97/14, Minute no. 875, Correspondence file, Telegram Botha to Buxton, 12 September 1914. See TNA, ADM 137-9, Folio 434, Telegram Governor of Union of SA to Secretary of State for the Colonies, 12 September 1914.

119 Collyer, *Campaign in German South West Africa*, pp. 28,29. See TNA, ADM 137-8, Letter from Rear Admiral H.K. Hall to The Secretary of the Admiralty 15 October 1914. The harbour at Lüderitzbucht was reported as excellent and the piers, lighters and cranes were all intact. The Germans failed to destroy the facilities. The navy provided three 4.7-inch guns to protect the port from sea and land attack. It was regarded as a protected port and a secure land base.

120 TNA, ADM 137-9, Folio 472, Telegram, Buxton to Harcourt, 15 September 1914. Beyers published his manifesto on his resignation in Hertzog's newspaper. See P. van der Byl, *From Playgrounds to Battlefields* (Cape Town: Howard Timmins, 1971) p. 92 for a physical description of Maritz.

121 DODA, DC Group 2, Letter Smuts to McKenzie, 6 January 1915. Smuts stressed to McKenzie, commanding the Central Force at Lüderitzbucht, of the need to advance his forces "simultaneously" with those under Botha at Walvis Bay/Swakopmund of the Northern Force. This is strong evidence of Smuts's intention of the simultaneity of advances.

122 *Bittereinders* (Afrikaans) were those Republican Boers who fought the British to the bitter end of the South African War (1899–1902).

123 M. Maritz, *My Lewe En Strewe* (NA: NA, 1939) p. 62. Maritz first contacted the German governor in GSWA as early as 1913 seeking future assistance to secure Boer freedom.

124 Maritz, *My Lewe En Strewe*, p. 64. Smuts suspected Maritz of treachery early on and confronted him openly on the occasion of the Commandants conference in August 1914. He accused Maritz of being two-faced and said that he couldn't work out if Maritz would conduct his treachery during the day or the night. Maritz spoke to Beyers of the incident, and they agreed that Smuts was suspicious of them.

125 Stejskal, *The Horns of the Beast*, p. 34. The Free Corps was supported with one artillery battery (four guns) manned by *Schutztruppen* commanded by Captain Hausding. This formation was intended to augment the Boer Revolt and fought several actions within the Union. It was disbanded in early 1915 with the failure of the revolt. The German semi-official history puts the Free Corps at 100 Boers and 25 Germans, some of whom were of dubious fitness and militarily untrained. The Germans held De Wet's abilities as an officer in low regard. See Von Oelhafen, *Der Feldzug*

in Südwest, pp. 31, 32. See TNA, ADM 137–13, Folio 132, Telegram Navy Office Melbourne to Admiralty, Translation of secret German message intercepted, 8 October 1914, and TNA, ADM 137–13, Folio 276, Buxton to Harcourt, 27 October 1914. The Germans promised the rebels recognition by the Imperial government of an independent South Africa at war with the United Kingdom, the recognition that the rebels were a war-waging power, and the recognition of a future independent Boer free state, support for the seizing of Delagoa Bay, and granting of German citizenship to any burgher who entered German territory in the event of the rebellion failing.

126 Union Of South Africa, *Judicial Commission of Inquiry: Causes Of and Circumstances Relating to the Recent Rebellion in South Africa* (Cape Town, 1916) pp. 11–16.

127 DODA, AG14, Box 13 File 7, Slaag van Sandfontein 26 September 1914, p. 1. The after-battle report clearly states that the operational objective of 'A' Force was the capture of Warmbad and then Kalkfontein. It was "anticipated" that this would lessen the chances of an invasion from GSWA and "materially assist" the forces landing at Lüderitzbucht. See DODA, DC Group 2, Box 252, Folio 17138, Lukin's Report on 'A' Force, 19 August 1915. Lukin states his immediate objective was Warmbad.

128 Buxton, *General Botha*, p. 45. Buxton asserts that the rebellion came as a complete surprise to the South African government and that no preparations were made to meet it.

129 Hancock *Selections from the Smuts Papers Volume III*, p. 198.

130 DODA, DC Group 2, Box 252, Folio 17138, Lukin's Report on 'A' Force, Appendix A, 19 August 1915. Lukin attaches the original telegram he received from Smuts on 23 September 1914 cajoling him to move to Sandfontein and "avoid undue delay in your move to Warmbad". Smuts was anxious that Lukin would curtail the advance to Warmbad and not Kalkfontein and therefore avoid a delay of three weeks in accumulating supplies.

131 Anon, *The Union of South Africa and the Great War*, p. 14. See Collyer, *Campaign in German South West Africa*, pp. 32, 48. Collyer goes to great lengths to explain that Lukin must have expressed his reservation to DHQ on being ordered to Sandfontein. The extent of his reservation is contained in this line: "Headquarters had to request high pressure to the verge of self-sacrifice on the part of General Lukin to which he most loyally responded." Collyer cites the fact that Lukin did not receive vital intelligence that the Germans were gathering a force in proximity to him because of a bungle at DHQ. Lukin is quoted as saying that if he had received this intelligence in time, he would have been apt to withdraw from Sandfontein promptly. The fact is that Lukin should have expected a strong German response to his advance in any event and he did not provide a sufficient force forward.

132 TNA, ADM 137-9, Folio 580, Buxton to Harcourt, 25 September 1914. See Collyer, *Campaign in German South West Africa*, p. 48. Collyer has a different take on the events pertaining to the intelligence of a German threat to Sandfontein. Collyer blames a nameless staff officer at Headquarters who posted instead of telegraphed the intelligence summary to Lukin with the result that it only reached him on 7 October 1914. (Collyer was Lukin's brother-in-law.) See Van der Waag, 'The Battle of Sandfontein', p. 22. Note 84.

133 DODA, DC Group 2, Box 252, Folio 17138, Lukin's Report on 'A' Force, 19 August 1915.

134 H. Guderian, *Panzer Leader* (London: Futura Publication, 1979), pp. 105, 316. Literally, "Use a fist rather than fingers" and refers to making the use of the maximum available force and firepower at one's disposal when arriving on the field of battle, rather than arriving in penny-packets.

135 Union of South Africa, *Judicial Commission of Inquiry: Causes Of and Circumstances Relating to the Recent Rebellion in South Africa* (Cape Town, 1916) pp. 16–18. See TNA, ADM 137–13, Folio 83, Buxton to Harcourt, 10 October 1914.

136 DODA, AG 14, Box 6, Biography Brits. See also *Dictionary of South African Biography Volume III*, ed. by C.J. Beyers and J.L. Basson (Pretoria: Human Sciences Research Council, 1987), p. 107. Brits was a veteran of the South African War where he rose rapidly through the ranks to *vechtgeneraal* (combat general).

137 Union Of South Africa, *Judicial Commission of Inquiry: Causes Of and Circumstances Relating to the Recent Rebellion in South Africa* (Cape Town, 1916) pp. 19–21.

138 Collyer, *Campaign in German South West Africa*, pp. 36-49.

139 DODA, AG14, Box 13 File 7, Slaag van Sandfontein 26 September 1914, p.12. The after-battle report is equally scathing accusing Lukin of failing to set up communications from Raman's Drift to Sandfontein, the lack of forward strength, and the slow pace of advance and decision making.

140 TNA, ADM 137-9, Folio 624, Buxton to Harcourt, 29 September 1914. See NARSA, PM 1/1/32, File 4/95/14-4/97/14, Correspondence file, Telegram Buxton to Naval C-in-C Cape Station, 28 September 1914. A further indicator that the operation to Walvis Bay was abandoned was a suggestion by Smuts and Buxton that HMS *Kinfauns* remain at Walvis for a few days longer to fool the Germans that it was proposed to land a force there. This would alleviate some of the risk Beves at Lüderitzbucht faced in light of the Sandfontein fiasco and the cancellation of the Walvis Bay landing.

141 NARSA, PM 1/1/32, File 4/95/14-4/97/14, Correspondence file, Telegram Buxton to Naval C-in-C Cape Station, 28 September 1914.

142 NARSA, PM 1/1/32, File 4/95/14-4/97/14, Correspondence file, Telegram Naval C-in-C Cape Station to Buxton, 27/28 September 1914.

143 M.A. Johnston, *Ulundi to Delville Wood: The Life Story of Major-General Sir Henry Timson Lukin* (Cape Town: Maskew Miller Ltd, 1929) p 119. Lukin's biographer lays the blame for Sandfontein squarely on the treachery of Maritz and places Lukin's advance strictly in terms of the original Smuts plan which included the landings at Swakopmund.

144 NARA, JSP, Folio 36, Letter from Crewe to Smuts, 29 September 1914.

145 The first phase only came into existence on its cancellation on 29 September 1914. Before then the entire operation was planned as a single-phase simultaneous landing at the GSWA ports.

146 Van der Waag, 'The Battle of Sandfontein', p. 10.

147 TNA, ADM 137–13, Folio 32, Buxton to Harcourt, 5 October 1914. See TNA, ADM 137–13, Folio 50, Buxton to Harcourt, 8 October 1914. Buxton cites the reversal at Sandfontein and Lukin's challenges regarding water and transport, and Maritz's "unreliability" and the delays on disembarkation at the landings as "destroying all possibility of simultaneous action".

148 A. Garcia and E. Kleynhans, 'Counterinsurgency in South Africa: the Afrikaner Rebellion, 1914–1915'. *Small Wars & Insurgencies*, (2020) pp. 1–27. Passim. The authors attest to the complexity of the reasons for the Afrikaner Rebellion which went beyond the mere invasion of GSWA and included complex social and economic reasons. See also T.R.H Davenport, 'The South African Rebellion, 1914', *The English Historical Review* LXXVIII, no. 78 (1963) pp. 73–94; S.S. Swart, 'The Rebels of 1914: Masculinity, Republicanism and the Social Forces that Shaped the Boer Rebellion' (MA dissertation, University of Natal, 1997); S. Swart, '"Men of Influence" – The Ontology of Leadership in the 1914 Boer Rebellion', *Journal of Historical Sociology* 17, no. 1 (2004) pp. 1–30; S.S. Swart, 'The Five Shilling Rebellion: Rural White Male Anxiety and the 1914 Boer Rebellion', *South African Historical Journal*, 56 (2006) pp. 88–102; S.S. Swart., 'A Boer and His Gun and His Wife are Three Things Always Together: Republican Masculinity and the 1914 Rebellion', *Journal of Southern African Studies,* no. 24 (2008) pp. 737–51; A.M. Grundlingh and S.S. Swart, *Radelose Rebeellie: Dinamika Van Die 1914–1915 Afrikanerrebellie* (Pretoria: Protea, 2009).

149 TNA, ADM 137–13, Folio 238, Buxton to Harcourt, 22 October 1914. Buxton reported the situation as being most grave.

150 TNA, ADM 137–13, Folio 427, Buxton to Harcourt, 9 November 1914. This was a speech made by Smuts on the Rand to the newly formed motor brigade.

151 S.G. Millin, *General Smuts Volume I* (Safety Harbor: Simon Publications, 2001) p. 297.

152 TNA, ADM 137–13, Folio 461, Buxton to Harcourt, 12 November 1914.

153 TNA, ADM 137–13, Folio 470, Buxton to Harcourt, 12 November 1914.

154 Smuts was not alone in underestimating the danger of a rebellion. See Hancock, *Selections from the Smuts Papers Volume III*, Letter from Reitz to Smuts, 12 September 1914, p. 197. Deneys Reitz warned Smuts that there would be trouble in the Free State if troops were commandeered. However, he felt that if GSWA could be swiftly and cleanly conquered with the existing army, the matter would be seen in another light. See Hancock, *Selections from the Smuts Papers Volume III*, Letter from Smuts to Reitz, 12 September 1914, p. 198. Smuts in his reply to Reitz said that he was not afraid of a revolution or civil war and felt that the conquest of GSWA would find general approval when it once again formed part of the Afrikaner heritage.

155 N. Orpen, *Gunners of the Cape: The Story of the Cape Field Artillery* (Cape Town: CFA Regimental History Commitee, 1965) p. 81. The commandos led by Botha did not possess an organic artillery component and would have to rely for artillery support on the PF and the ACF traditional English artillery regiments. See also Mark Coghlan, *History of the Umvoti Mounted Rifles*, p. 155. Although the government sought to use mostly Afrikaner troops, use was made of bilingual units such at the Umvoti Mounted Rifles.

156 I. van der Waag, 'Rethinking South Africa's Military Past: The Curious Case of Brig Gen the Hon C.F Beyers', *Inaugural Lecture Delivered 2 August 2018*, 2018, p. 7.

157 DODA, DC Group 2, Box 1438, Secret Intelligence, Telegram Smuts to Lukin, 4 November 1914.

158 K. Fedorowich., 'Sleeping with the Lion? The Loyal Afrikaner and the South African Rebellion of 1914–15', *South African Historical Journal*, 49(1) (2003) p. 80.

159 Garcia and Kleynhans, 'Counterinsurgency in South Africa', p. 8. The British offered 30,000 Australian and New Zealand soldiers who were en route to Europe.

160 H.F. Trew, *Botha Treks* (London: Blackie & Son, 1936) p. 38.

161 Trew, *Botha Treks*, p. 54.

162 DODA, DC Group 2, Box 1438, Secret Intelligence G. This file contains a plethora of secret telegrams to and from Smuts to the various commanders fighting the rebels in October-December 1914. These telegrams/instructions are evidence of Smuts cajoling, advising and directing the commanders on the battlefield. Notably absent are any similar instructions from Botha.

163 TNA, ADM 137–13, Folio 356,372, C-in-C Cape to Admiralty, Intercepted German code, 4 November 1914.

164 Van der Byl, *From Playgrounds to Battlefields,* pp. 110, 112. Botha would remain in Pretoria to centralise control. Trains stood with steam up day and night ready to strike in any direction with a large force.

165 Garcia and Kleynhans, 'Counterinsurgency in South Africa', p. 18.

166 Van der Waag, 'Rethinking South Africa's Military Past', p. 7. See also Garcia and Kleynhans, 'Counterinsurgency in South Africa', p. 15.

167 DODA, DC Group 2, Box 1438, Secret Intelligence Incoming Telegrams, Telegram Van Deventer to Smuts, 23 October 1914. Van Deventer gives insight into the arrangements that gave the Boers their extraordinary mobility. Each two men had three horses between them. Each section had three pack horses/mules or a cart. Each platoon would have a trolley with 10 to 12 mules.

168 A.C. Martin, *The Durban Light Infantry 1854–1934* (Durban: The Regimental Asociation DLI, 1969) p. 136. The regimental history records a forced march prior to the building of the railway from Prieska to Upington of 200 kilometres in eight days. See also Fedorowich, 'Sleeping with the Lion?' p. 83.

169 Van der Byl, *From Playgrounds to Battlefields*, pp. 111, 123. The commandos were able to entrain and detrain their mounted units with extraordinary rapidity. Horses were entrained with their saddles on to save space and make for a speedy deployment.

170 Trew, *Botha Treks*, p. 3. Most of the Union secret service work was done by the police under the commissioner Col Truter. The police in the country and agents in the towns provided early indicators that an armed uprising was being planned.

171 Trew, *Botha Treks*, p. 29.

172 My gratitude to Evert Kleynhans and Tony Garcia for giving me access to a paper delivered at the South African Historical Society in 2015, 'A Critical Analysis of Union Defence Force Operations During the Afrikaner Rebellion, 1914–1915'.

173 DODA, GSWA Group, Box 15, Lukin to Botha, 12 November 1914. Brits blamed Lukin's helio operator for not taking his coordination messages. Lukin strongly denied this accusation and suggested it was Brits's helio operator's incompetence or his "want of desire to maintain communication".

174 DODA, Diverse Group 1, Box 57, Letter from Botha to Smuts, 12 November 1914; TNA, ADM 137–13, Folio 484, Buxton to Harcourt, 13 November 1914. See also Collyer, *Campaign in German South West Africa*, p. 19.

175 TNA, ADM 137–13, Folio 494, Buxton to Harcourt, 14 November 1914. See TNA, ADM 137–13, Folio 508, Buxton to Harcourt, 16 November 1914.

176 TNA, ADM 137–13, Folio 520, Buxton to Harcourt, 15 November 1914.

177 NARSA, JSP, Box 196, Folio 153 Letter Steyn to Smuts, 16 November 1914, and NARSA, JSP, Box 196, Folio 153, Letter Smuts to Steyn, 17 November 1914. See also TNA, ADM 137–13, Folio 523, Buxton to Harcourt, 17 November 1914.

178 TNA, ADM 137–13, Folio 539, Buxton to Harcourt, 19 November 1914.

179 TNA, ADM 137–13, Folio 677, Buxton to Harcourt, 2 December 1914.

180 TNA, ADM 137–13, Folio 707, Buxton to Harcourt, 7 December 1914.

181 TNA, ADM 137–13, Folio 707, Buxton to Harcourt, 8 December 1914. The remaining rebel leadership of any substance was Serfontein and Wessel Wessels.

182 TNA, ADM 137–13, Folio 707, Buxton to Harcourt, 8 December 1914.

183 TNA, ADM 137–13, Folio 558, Buxton to Harcourt, 21 November 1914.

184 TNA, ADM 137–13, Folio 567, Buxton to Harcourt, 22 November 1914. See also Collyer, *Campaign in German South West Africa*, pp. 22–5.

185 TNA, ADM 137–13, Folio 550, Buxton to Harcourt, 19 November 1914. See also Collyer, *Campaign in German South West Africa*, p. 24.

186 DODA, Diverse Group 1, Box 53, South African Police Commissioner to Secretary for Defence, 10 April 1915.

187 DODA, Diverse Group 1, Box 41, Memorandum Roland Bourne to Minister of Defence, 30 July 1917. South Africa had no concrete plan to mobilise troops on the home front in the event of strikes or further rebellion.

188 Buxton, *General Botha*, p. 195.

Chapter 4

1   H.F. Trew, *Botha Treks* (London: Blackie & Son, 1936). Lt-Col H.F. Trew was commander of General Botha's bodyguard in GSWA.

2   NARSA, JSP, Box 196, Folio 156, Letter Smuts to Crewe, 18 December 1914. In this letter Smuts confirms the appointment of Van Deventer to command the whole Orange River and the raising of six further mounted brigades for GSWA. The hand of Smuts in directing and recruiting for the campaign was everywhere.

3   NARSA, PM 1/1/32, File 4/95/14-4/97/14, Correspondence file, Telegram Naval C-in-C Cape Station to Buxton, 29 September 1914. McKenzie received instructions on 29 September to dispatch a battalion each to Port Nolloth and Lüderitzbucht.

4   DODA, AG 14, Box 6, Biography Van Deventer. See also *Dictionary of South African Biography Volume V*, ed. by C.J. Beyers and J.L. Basson (Pretoria: Human Sciences Research Council, 1987) p. 809. Van Deventer as Republican joined the Transvaal Staats Artillerie one of the two formal formations (other than the ZARPs) of the ZAR. During the South African War he served under Beyers and Smuts.

5   DODA, AG 14, Box 6, Biography Berrangé. See also *Dictionary of South African Biography Volume V*, ed. by C.J. Beyers and J.L. Basson (Pretoria: Human Sciences Research Council, 1987) p. 45. Berrangé first saw action in the Ninth Frontier War, 1877–8. He was present at the siege of Kimberley in the South African War and was captured twice during the war. He commanded the Cape Mounted Police after the South African War before entering the UDF.

6   TNA, ADM 137–13, Folio 51–53, Buxton to Harcourt, 8 October 1914. See TNA, ADM 137–13, Folio 88, Memorandum Admiral H.B Jackson, 8 October 1914. See NARSA, PM 1/1/32, File 4/95/14-4/97/14, Minute no. 994, Correspondence file, Telegram Botha to Buxton, 7 October 1914.

7   The figures have been derived from NARSA, JSP, Box 112, Folio 17, Visit of the Governor-General of Union of South Africa to German South West Africa, March 1915, p. 24; DODA, AG 1914–1921, Box 150, Total Strengths Field Force and Garrison, and J.J. Collyer, *Campaign in German South West Africa 1914–1915* (London: Imperial War Museum and Battery Press, 1937) pp. 54, 55, 63, 97. It is interesting to note that the total strength of the mobilised UDF is quoted as 49,572 including 6,016 in provincial garrison.

8   DODA, AG 1914–1921, Box 8, Folio G5/305/9199, Appointment of Botha.

9   A. Garcia, *The First Campaign Victory of the Great War* (Solihull: Helion & Co., 2019) p. 139. Garcia relegates all discussion of UDF numerical advantage as "superficial" citing other factors such as divergent advances and German lack of offensive élan. However, he does not address the superfluous nature of the infantry component of the UDF on the GSWA campaign and the consequent drain on logistics of maintaining an unnecessarily large force.

10 NARSA, PM 1/1/32, File 4/95/14-4/97/14, Minute no. 889, Correspondence file, Telegram Botha to Buxton, 14 September 1914. Botha asked for "powerful guns of heavy calibre to demolish fortifications and enemy filed batteries". Botha suggested the source of the guns to be the Royal and Cape Garrison Artillery. See NARSA, PM 1/1/32, File 4/95/14-4/97/14, Correspondence file, Telegram Secretary of State to Buxton, 17 September. The British were prepared to lend the Union a battery of 4-inch guns and a battery of 12-pounder guns with ammunition and personnel.

11 TNA, ADM 137–13, Folio 56,57, Remarks on new plan, 10 October 1914.

12 TNA, ADM 137–13, Folio 70, C-in-C Cape to Admiralty, 9 October 1914.

13 Garcia, *The First Campaign Victory*, p. 117; I. van der Waag, 'The Battle of Sandfontein, 26 September 1914: South African Military Reform and the German South-West Africa Campaign, 1914–1915', *First World War Studies* (2013) p. 14; H. Strachan, *The First World War in Africa* (Oxford: Oxford University Press, 2004) p. 67.

14 TNA, ADM 137–13, Folio 103, Buxton to Harcourt, 12 October 1914. See TNA, ADM 137–13, Folio 348, C-in-C Cape to Admiralty, 3 November 1914, where again the delay in landing at Walvis Bay and the continuation of the GSWA offensive was laid squarely on the need to suppress the rebellion and that operations would not restart until this was achieved and that there was no firm timeline when this would be achieved.

15 TNA, ADM 137–13, Folio 260, C-in-C Cape to Admiralty, 26 October 1914.

16 TNA, ADM 137–13, Folio 573, C-in-C Cape to Admiralty, 25 November 1914. See TNA, ADM 137–13, Folio 621, C-in-C Cape to Admiralty, 27 November 1914. The Royal Navy had four duties regarding the expedition to GSWA which involved the conveyance of troops to Walvis Bay, to protect Walvis Bay, to cover and protect Lüderitzbucht, and to guard the lines of communication from the Cape to Lüderitzbucht and Walvis Bay. The British were reluctant to split their forces or undertake the expedition until such time as the enemy force were dealt with.

17 TNA, ADM 137–13, Folio 649, C-in-C Cape to Admiralty, 30 November 1914.

18 TNA, ADM 137–13, Folio 651, Buxton to Harcourt, 30 November 1914.

19 TNA, ADM 137–13, Folio 710, Sir R Tower, Buenos Ayres to Admiralty, 7 December 1914. The tip-off was received from a correspondent of *The New York Times*.

20 TNA, ADM 137–13, Folio 728, India Office to Admiralty, 9 December 1914.

21 Ian van der Waag has produced a body of work dealing with the formation of the UDF. See I. van der Waag, 'Smuts's Generals: Towards a First Portrait of the South African High Command, 1912–1948', *War in History*, 18(1) (2011); I. van der Waag, 'South African Defence in the Age of Total War, 1900–1940', *Historia*, 60(1) (2015); I. van der Waag, 'Boer Generalship and the Politics of Command', *War in History*, 12(1) (2005). Another work that has merit on the formation of the UDF is T.J. Stapleton, *A Military History of South Africa from the Dutch-Khoi Wars to the End of Apartheid* (Santa Barbara, Praeger, 2010).

22 I. van der Waag, *A Military History of Modern South Africa* (Cape Town, Jonathan Ball, 2015) pp. 83, 84.

23 Stapleton, *A Military History of South Africa*, pp. 113–18.

24 Denis Santry, South Africa and the Great War in Cartoons, *The Rand Daily Mail* & *The Sunday Times*, www.facebook.com/306152646247018/photos/rpp.306152646247018/325449697650646/?-type=3&theater, accessed 3 February 2020. South Africa went to war in 1914 with two armies, mounted infantry and infantry; two doctrines; two languages, Afrikaans and English; all within one defence force. The cartoon depicts the two uniforms of the two different military types who served together in the UDF.

25 DODA, AG 14, Box 6, Biography Van Deventer.

26 A.C. Martin, *The Durban Light Infantry 1854–1934* (Durban: The Regimental Asociation DLI, 1969) p. 163. "The Commandos had not as yet mastered the form of the UDF."

27 NARSA, JSP, Box 112, Folio 17, Visit of the Governor-General of Union of South Africa to German South West Africa, March 1915, p. 15. The Governor-General general witnessed first-hand the Republican flavour of the Northern Force under Botha and commented that the commando officers, "are beginning to realise the importance of drilling". See also D.B. Katz (in press), 'An Aggregation of Lion Hunters: In Search of the Boer Way of War', *International Journal of Military History and Historiography*, 2021.

28 DODA, AG 14, Box 13, File 2 Veterinary Services GSWA Campaign and Rebellion August 1914 to July 1915, Report by Colonel J.A.S. Irvine Smith, p. 29.

29 Trew, *Botha Treks*, p. 179.

30 Collyer, *Campaign in German South West Africa*, p. 12.

31 C.E. Callwell, *Small Wars: A Tactical Textbook for Imperial Soldiers* (London: HMSO, 1896) p 27. Colonel Callwell's offered his famous description of the Boers as well-armed, educated and led

by men of knowledge and repute but "merely bodies of determined men, acknowledging certain leaders, drawn together to confront a common danger".

32 H. du Cane (ed.), *German Official Account of the War in South Africa March 1900 to September 1900*, (London: John Murray, 1906) p. 326. The Germans describe the Boer way of war as being quite unmethodical.

33 Du Cane (ed.), *German Official Account of the War in South Africa*, pp. 325–7.

34 H.F.B. Walker, *A Doctor's Diary in Damaraland* (London: Edward Arnold, 1917) p. 9.

35 A. Garcia, 'Manoeuvre Warfare in the South African Campaign in German South West Africa During the First World War', (MA thesis, Humanities, University of South Africa, 2015).

36 Collyer, *Campaign in German South West Africa*, p. 26. The doctrine applied by the UDF on the GSWA campaign was to ensure that any detachment must at least be equal in strength to any possible concentration against it. Furthermore, arrangements must be made for detachments to cooperate in the event of one being attacked.

37 H. von Oelhafen, *Der Feldzug in Südwest 1914/1915: Auf Grund Amtlichen Materials Bearbeitet* (Berlin: Safari-Verlag, 1923), pp. 19, 20.

38 Von Oelhafen, *Der Feldzug in Südwest,* p. 20.

39 Trew, *Botha Treks*, pp. 177, 178.

40 Walker, *A Doctor's Diary*, p. 135.

41 NARSA, JSP, Box 112, Folio 17, Visit of the Governor-General of Union of South Africa to German South West Africa, March 1915, p. 17.

42 DODA, AG 1914–1921, Box 150, Total Strengths Field Force and Garrison. A mere 6,016 troops remained on active duty in provincial garrison.

43 E. Buxton, *General Botha* (New York: E.P. Dutton & Co., 1924) p. 103.

44 A. Samson, 'South Africa Mobilises: The First Five Months of the War', *Scientia Militaria*, 44.1 (2016) p. 8.

45 The expeditionary force consisted of the Imperial Light Horse, Grobbelaar's Scouts, and an artillery brigade. Col P.C.B. Skinner, formerly of the Northumberland Regiment, was loaned from the British government to support Botha and during the GSWA campaign Botha asked him to set up a general staff. He was previously the commandant of the South African Military School.

46 W.S. Rayner and W.W. O'Shaughnessy, *How Botha and Smuts Conquered German South West* (London: Simpson, Marshall, Hamilton, Kent & Co., 1916), p. 164. Skinner's personal staff comprised Maj Mitchell Baker, Capt C.F. Stallard, K.C., Capt Piet v.d. Bijl, and Capt Christian. The combatant sections were 1st Imperial Light Horse (Col Ligertwood), Grobelaar's Scouts (Maj Grobelaar), Machine Gun Section (Maj Giles), and Heavy Artillery Brigade (Col Kose). The 3rd Infantry Brigade, under Col Burnside, with staff officers Maj Harvie and Capt Reginald Schwartz, consisted of 2nd Transvaal Scottish (Col Kirkpatrick), Kimberley Regiment (Col Rogers), and 1st Rhodesia Regiment (Maj Warwick, vice Col Burnside commanding the brigade), and was responsible for the area around the Whaling Station. The 4th Infantry Brigade was under the command of Col Wylie, with Maj Taylor and Capt Judd as staff officers, and this brigade consisted of 1st Durban Light Infantry (Col Goulding), South African Irish (Col Brennan), and Rand Rifles (Col Purcell).

47 TNA, ADM 123/144, General letters and proceedings Walvis Bay, Letter of Proceedings from Captain of HMS *Astraea* to C-in-C Cape Station 29 January 1915. British sea power would form an integral part of the early defence of Walvis Bay and Swakopmund, with the ship guns and the infantry cooperating in a firing scheme should the Germans approach the beachhead.

48 Rayner, *How Botha and Smuts Conquered German South West*, p. 173. See also Trew, *Botha Treks*, p. 89. The Germans were unaware that the South Africans had a wireless that could intercept all

their communication. During the campaign the South Africans were able to break the German cypher code and gain valuable intelligence. See also TNA, ADM 137–13, Folio 525 C-in-C Cape to Admiralty, 17 November 1914.

49   E. Kleynhans, 'A Critical Analysis of the Impact of Water on the South African Campaign in German South West Africa, 1914–1915', *Historia*, 61.2 (2016) Passim

50   Rayner, *How Botha and Smuts Conquered German South West*, p. 165.

51   Rayner, *How Botha and Smuts Conquered German South West*, p. 178.

52   Rayner, *How Botha and Smuts Conquered German South West*, p. 186.

53   TNA, ADM 123/144, General letters and proceedings Walvis Bay, Letter of Proceedings from Captain of HMS *Astraea* to C-in-C Cape Station 15 January 1915. The occupation of Swakopmund was unexpected and unplanned and carried out two weeks before the railway line from Walvis could be completed. Provisioning would have to be carried out by sea. The railway components were brought in by sea as no railway existed between Walvis and Swakopmund.

54   Rayner, *How Botha and Smuts Conquered German South West*, p. 183. General Botha was accompanied by the following staff: Col Collyer, Chief Staff Officer; Maj Bok, Military Secretary; Maj D. de Waal, Provost Marshal; Col Odium, Medical Staff Officer; Maj Stopford, Principal Signalling Officer; Maj Trevor, OC Headquarters Transport; Capt Esselen, ADC; Capt Louis Botha, ADC; Capt Collender, OC Topographical Section; Capt Ribbinck (in charge war dogs); Lt Wagner; Lt Cook, field telegraphs; Lt Jantje Botha. Intelligence Department: Maj Leipoldt and Lts. Nobbs and Richter (afterwards promoted captains). Bodyguard: Maj Trew, OC; Capt Fulton, and Capt Donald.

55   NARSA, JSP, Box 112, Folio 17, Visit of the Governor-General of Union of South Africa to German South West Africa, March 1915, p. 11. The eventual numbers available to Northern Force were 19,000 in total by March/April 1915.

56   Trew, *Botha Treks*, p. 91. The commanding officers of the enveloping forces had been offered compasses, but some refused them. The northern wing got lost in the thick sea mist and spent a portion of the night riding in circles. Lack of navigation skills and ill-discipline cost Botha an early victory.

57   Rayner, *How Botha and Smuts Conquered German South West*, pp. 183–191.

58   Kleynhans, 'A Critical Analysis of the Impact of Water', p.45. The poisoning of wells was part of the German military strategy. The South Africans adopted a harsh method to test the water by allowing the German prisoners to drink it as proof of its potability. Botha was convinced that the German practice was contrary to the Hague Convention while the Germans denied this. See also NARSA, JSP, Box 112, Folio 15, Botha Dispatch No. 2 covering the period 24 February to 28 March. Botha did not take kindly to the German poison tactics and sent objections directly to Franke complaining.

59   DODA, DC Group 2, Box 668, File M822, Infection of water by enemy during hostilities in S.W.A., Letter Franke to Botha 11 March 1915. Franke denied poisoning the water and called it "merely effecting a change of the natural condition of the water in order to deprive the enemy of the use of this means of existence". See also Rayner, *How Botha and Smuts Conquered German South West*, p. 191.

60   TNA, ADM 123/144, General letters and proceedings Walvis Bay, Letter of Proceedings from Captain of HMS *Astraea* to C-in-C Cape Station 15 February 1915. The senior naval officer of Walvis Bay described Botha's ailment as dysentery.

61   B. Farwell, *The Great War in Africa* (New York: W.W. Norton & Co., 1989), p. 93. See also P. van der Byl, *From Playgrounds to Battlefields* (Cape Town: Howard Timmins, 1971) p. 144. See also Trew, *Botha Treks*, p. 131. There were numerous clues that Botha was not well on the campaign and certainly far from his physical best. Trew, a member of his personal bodyguard, noted that

the general showed alarming signs of ill-health on the gruelling march to Windhoek. On the other hand, Trew noted that Smuts was the picture of health and energy on campaign.

62   NARSA, JSP, Box 197, Folio 10A, Letter Botha to Smuts, 28 February 1915.

63   W.K. Hancock and J. van der Poel (eds), *Selections from the Smuts Papers Volume III July 1910–November 1918*, (London: Cambridge University Press, 1966) p. 242. Botha and Collyer had done much in the interim to ensure a vast improvement in the disembarkation process.

64   Hancock, *Selections from the Smuts Papers Volume III*, pp. 247, 249. Smuts sent a short sharp letter to Botha assuring him that "no efforts or expense have or are being spared [to] supply your requirements and [I] deprecate contrary implications". Botha cautioned Smuts not to vent his impatience through the conventional military communication channels.

65   NARSA, JSP, Box 112, Folio 15, Botha Dispatch No. 2 covering the period 24 February to 28 March.

66   TNA, CAB 103-94. Historical Section, Comments on Official History by Jan Smuts, 18 March 1935. Smuts was at pains to correct the GEA official history which referred to a "strategy of advancing inland along existing railway lines had already been employed with success in the conquest of GSWA". Smuts replied, "As a matter of fact, the advance did not follow railway lines; both I in the South and General Botha in the North of that territory, conducted our campaigns irrespective of railway lines, and in fact completely upset the calculations of the enemy by vast turning movements, for hundreds of miles and ignored the railway system."

67   W.K. Hancock, *Smuts: The Sanguine Years 1870–1919* (London: Cambridge University Press, 1962) p. 395.

68   NARSA, JSP, Box 112, Folio 31, Secretary of Defence to H. Burton (Minister of Finance), 4 May 1915.

69   Rayner, *How Botha and Smuts Conquered German South West*, p. 165. See also I. van der Waag, 'Major J.G.W. Leipoldt, D.S.O. : A Portrait of a South African Surveyor and Intelligence Officer, 1912–1923', *Scientia Militaria*, 25.1 (1995) p. 33. Leipoldt was awarded the DSO for his services on campaign in GSWA.

70   Hancock, *Selections from the Smuts Papers Volume III*, p. 243.

71   NARSA, JSP, Box 112, Folio 17, Visit of the Governor-General of Union of South Africa to German South West Africa, March 1915, p. 17. There were no existing water holes between Swakopmund and Usakos. All water across the 130-kilometre stretch had to be transported from Swakopmund. The lack of water was exacerbated by a shortage of water bottles for drinking, and none could be spared for ablutions.

72   NARSA, JSP, Box 112, Folio 17, Visit of the Governor-General of Union of South Africa to German South West Africa, March 1915, p. 17. Buxton reports that the Germans removed the rails and the sleepers completely, however this seems unlikely to have been applied to the entire rail system. See NARSA, JSP, Box 112, Folio 22, Report on a visit to GSWA 20–27 March 1915. The Germans destroyed the 3-feet 6-inch railway by placing explosives under the joints of each pair of line. The South African engineers cut off the damaged ends and relaid the line. The Germans removed the sleepers and rails on the narrow-gauge line and here the entire railway had to be renewed.

73   P.L. Close, *A Prisoner of the Germans in South-West Africa* (Cape Town: T. Maskew Miller) p. 37. Close wrote in his diary that as a POW he suspected the German railway gauge was 3 foot 4 inches, but they found while travelling its length as prisoners, that it was the same as the South African Railways, measuring 3 foot 6 inches.

74   Walker, *A Doctor's Diary*, p. 30. See also NARSA, JSP, Box 112, Folio 17, Visit of the Governor-General of Union of South Africa to German South West Africa, March 1915, p. 7. At their peak, the railway teams could lay track at a rate of three kilometres a day using a large amount of black labour.

75 Trew, *Botha Treks*, p. 92.
76 Collyer, *Campaign in German South West Africa*, p. 27.
77 NARSA, JSP, Box 112, Folio 15, Botha Dispatch No. 2 covering the period 24 February to 28 March, pp. 12,13
78 NARSA, JSP, Box 112, Folio 22, Report on a visit to GSWA 20–27 March 1915, p. 5 See also DODA, DC Box 252, Historical Record of the Campaign in GSWA compiled by Hugh Wyndham, p. 2. The GSWA railway system consisted of two different gauges. The first was 3 feet 6 inches (the same as the South African railway) which stretched from Lüderitzbucht–Keetmanshoop–Windhoek–Karibib and extended from Seeheim to Kalkfontein. The second was a narrow gauge of 2 feet 6 inches from Swakopmund–Karibib–Tsumeb–Grootfontein.
79 TNA, WO 32-5820 Smuts Dispatch 27 October 1916, pp. 45–50.
80 W. Whittal, *With Botha and Smuts in Africa* (London: Cassell & Co., 1917) p. 33. See also Walker, *A Doctor's Diary*, pp. 29, 30. The author attributes the ability of Botha to advance solely on "the inexhaustible supply of pure water" provided by the Swakop River. "In or near the river there was always a road, there was always water for the digging, if not wells or springs, and there was always some grazing, even at Swakopmund."
81 NARSA, JSP, Box 112, Folio 15, Botha Dispatch No. 2 covering the period 24 February to 28 March.
82 Walker, *A Doctor's Diary*, p. 36. Walker gives some idea of the logistical effort. It took 11 lorries and many carts to transport everything for 7,000 men over 30 kilometres from the railhead to the advance base of Husab. These vehicles delivered 500,000 pounds per week with each lorry carrying 6,000 pounds and making the journey eight or nine times a week.
83 G. L'Ange, *Urgent Imperial Service: South African Forces in German South West Africa 1914–1915* (Johannesburg: Ashanti, 1991) pp. 60–4.
84 S. Monick, *Clear the Way: The Heritage of the South African Irish 1880–1990* (Johannesburg: South African Irish Regimental Council, 1991) p. 76. The regimental history attests to the shortage of water and food suffered by the infantry components advancing with Botha.
85 NARSA, JSP, Box 112, Folio 15, Botha Dispatch No. 2 covering the period 24 February to 28 March, p. 13.
86 Collyer, *Campaign in German South West Africa*, pp. 60, 61.
87 Collyer, *Campaign in German South West Africa*, p. 62.
88 TNA, CAB 45–112, The Campaign in GSWA, 1914–1915, Narrative of Events, p. 6. Garub was the first camp outside of Lüderitzbucht where fresh water was obtainable and was destroyed by the Germans. It was restored and eventually yielded 60,000 gallons daily. Garub is 90 kilometres from Lüderitzbucht.
89 NARSA, JSP, Box 112, Folio 17, Visit of the Governor-General of Union of South Africa to German South West Africa, March 1915, p. 5. Up until Garub was occupied no water had been found between Lüderitzbucht and Garub, marking the importance of the town as a jump-off point for the next phase of operations.
90 NARSA, JSP, Box 112, Folio 4, Letter Farrar to Smuts, Water situation at Garub, 5 March 1915.
91 NARSA, JSP, Box 112, Folio 14, Letter Farrar to Smuts, Water situation at Garub, 23 March 1915. Farrar worked on a daily allowance of 1.5 gallons per man, 8 gallons for horse or mule, and 10 gallons for an ox.
92 Hancock, *Selections from the Smuts Papers Volume III*, p. 270.
93 NARSA, JSP, Box 112, Folio 18, Botha to Smuts, 3 April 1915.
94 Hancock, *Selections from the Smuts Papers Volume III*, p. 243.
95 Hancock, *Selections from the Smuts Papers Volume III*, p. 270.
96 Hancock, *Selections from the Smuts Papers Volume III*, p. 243.

97   NARSA, JSP, Box 112, Folio 17, Visit of the Governor-General of Union of South Africa to German South West Africa, March 1915, p. 15. The two mounted brigades under Brits and Alberts would eventually be joined by a third under Myburgh. These formations gave the Northern Force under Botha a distinctively Afrikaner flavour. Each of these commanders had been active in the South African War, the rebellion and were serving MPs. Another brigade under Manie Botha, nephew of Louis Botha, would join later. The men in these brigades hailed mainly from the Orange Free State and were volunteers instead of conscripts.

98   Collyer, *Campaign in German South West Africa*, pp. 64–6.

99   Kleynhans, 'A Critical Analysis of the Impact of Water', 2016, pp. 29, 41. Kleynhans emphasises that the GSWA campaign depended on "access, availability and control of all water sources in the operational area" and also "The UDF operations were reliant on water and to some extent, water dictated the pace and scope of all military advances within GSWA".

100 A. Garcia, 'Manoeuvre Warfare in the South African Campaign in German South West Africa During the First World War' (MA thesis, Humanities, University of South Africa, 2015) p. 22. In fairness it seems Garcia was alluding to the tactical level of war, especially in the attack on Pforte/Riet.

101 There is a significant disparity between Stejskal quoting German sources and the official history regarding the number of German troops. See J. Stejskal, *The Horns of the Beast: The Swakop River Campaign and World War I in South-West Africa 1914–1915* (Solihull: Helion & Co., 2014) p. 73 and Anon, *The Union of South Africa and the Great War 1914–1918* (Nashville: Battery Press, 1924) p. 41.

102 Stejskal, *The Horns of the Beast*, p. 73 and Anon, *The Union of South Africa*, p. 41.

103 Nico Moolman collection of glass negatives.

104 Trew, *Botha Treks*, p. 105. Trew has an alarming account of the failure of the Bloemhof Commando to outflank the German position, which if true points to an incredible break in military discipline. Trew explains that the commando had encountered big game en route which they proceeded to hunt down. As a result, the commando had become considerably disorganised and failed to get together before the onset of darkness. See NARSA, JSP, Box 112, Folio 15, Botha Dispatch No. 2 covering the period 24 February to 28 March. Botha gives little explanation in his dispatch for the failure of Bezuidenhout's flank attack.

105 Collyer, *Campaign in German South West Africa*, pp. 66–9.

106 C.J. Beyers and J.L. Basson (eds), *Dictionary of South African Biography Volume V*, (Pretoria: Human Sciences Research Council, 1987) p. 145. William Richard Collins was born to a Scottish father and Afrikaans mother. He joined the civil service of the ZAR in 1897 and worked under Smuts in the office of the Attorney-General. He served on Botha's staff during the South African War.

107 Collyer, *Campaign in German South West Africa*, pp. 70, 71.

108 NARSA, JSP, Box 112, Folio 15, Botha Dispatch No. 2 covering the period 24 February to 28 March.

109 Collyer, *Campaign in German South West Africa*, pp. 71–2.

110 Collyer, *Campaign in German South West Africa*, p. 72.

111 NARSA, JSP, Box 112, Folio 18, Botha to Smuts, 3 April 1915. Botha was using all his influence to prevent the indigenous population from taking part in the war against the enemy. Interestingly, Antonio Garcia takes a different view on the importance of Windhoek as a tool for German surrender. In Garcia, *The First Campaign Victory*, p. 182. Garcia proposes that Botha considered that the *Schutztruppe* headquarters and not Windhoek was the centre of gravity of the German defence. He cites the German failure to surrender after the fall of Windhoek as proof of Botha's theory. However, it is plain from the documents that Botha expected the Germans to surrender after Windhoek had been captured. See also Collyer, *Campaign in German South West Africa*,

pp. 50, 51. Collyer identifies Windhoek as the centre of gravity of the German defence being the railway hub which enabled the rapid concentration of forces to meet an enemy threat in any direction. Without Windhoek, the Germans had to abandon the south and would have to concentrate to the north using their mounted infantry exclusively and not the railway to bring about operational mobility.

112 G.J.J Oosthuizen, 'The Military Role of the Rehoboth Basters During the South African Invasion of German South West Africa, 1914–1915', *Scientia Militaria*, 28.1 (1998) pp. 97,98.

113 Monick, *A Bugle Calls*, p. 82. The regimental historian draws attention to the "far from spectacular" role given to the infantry on campaign compared with the "paramount role" played by the mounted units.

114 Trew, *Botha Treks*, p. 168. This also goes to demonstrate the mounted infantry's reluctance to fight a pitched frontal battle, a task better suited to the British-trained and English-led infantry. See also NARSA, JSP, Box 112, Folio 17, Visit of the Governor-General of Union of South Africa to German South West Africa, March 1915, p. 4. Central Force used the infantry formations to man blockhouses that were placed at regular intervals along the railway line and manned by up to six soldiers each. The blockhouses played an important role as the railway lines were visited on occasion by German patrols and blown up.

115 NARSA, JSP, Box 112, Folio 17, Visit of the Governor-General of Union of South Africa to German South West Africa, March 1915, p. 20.

116 NARSA, JSP, Box 112, Folio 22, Report on a visit to GSWA 20–27 March 1915, p. 9.

117 Trew, *Botha Treks*, pp. 142, 154. The UDF was not totally averse to using German rolling stock and their narrow-gauge system. Once Windhoek was conquered, Sir William Hoy, who was appointed as the Director of Military Railways in 1914 and accompanied Smuts and Botha on campaign, was able to recommission some of the German trains and man one of them with a German driver and fireman. Again, with Botha's advance from Windhoek, he was able to make good use of engineers to swiftly repair blown-up bridges and use the German narrow gauge and rolling stock to aid his advance. Hoy had done some remarkable work in building many hundreds of kilometres of railway line across virgin territory on the GSWA border and beyond.

118 Trew, *Botha Treks*, p. 152. Botha apparently made good use of his scouts before launching any attack. Scouts were handpicked and took tremendous risks riding right through the enemy lines. Botha is reported to have said, "Nothing is too good for the scouts. I would be blind without them. They take great risks, and it is harder for a man to be brave when alone than in the company of others." Botha also made use of his aircraft for reconnaissance by embracing the new technology. See also TNA, ADM 123/144, General letters and proceedings Walvis Bay, Letter of Proceedings from Captain of HMS *Astraea* to C-in-C Cape Station 11 May 1915. It was reported that three of the five military aircraft had completed their trials and would immediately proceed to the front. See also TNA, AIR 1–1247–204-7–1, Report of Major Wallace on the work of the South African Aviation Corps GSWA 1915, p. 4. Wallace places Smuts at Swakopmund on 6 May 1915 where he instructed the air wing to begin reconnaissance operations against Karibib from Husab. Events overtook the instruction as Botha occupied Karibib shortly thereafter.

119 Katz, 'An Aggregation of Lion Hunters', p. 8.

120 Katz, 'An Aggregation of Lion Hunters', p. 10.

121 *The Department of Defense Dictionary of Military and Associated Terms*. Command and Control: The exercise of authority and direction by a properly designated commander over assigned and attached forces in the accomplishment of the mission.

122 Katz, 'An Aggregation of Lion Hunters', p. 15.

123 Walker, *A Doctor's Diary*, p. 40. "The Burghers are a very peculiar army, wanting in discipline in camp, yet full of dash, energy, and endurance, in the field."

124 Du Cane (ed.), *German Official Account of the War in South Africa*, pp. 324–4.

125 Collyer, *Campaign in German South West Africa*, p. 12.

126 Collyer, *Campaign in German South West Africa*, p. 78.

127 NARSA, JSP, Box 112, Folio 17, Visit of the Governor-General of Union of South Africa to German South West Africa, March 1915, p. 1. Botha was the supreme commander of the Northern and Central Forces when he took over from Col Skinner in February 1915 before the arrival of Smuts.

128 Hancock, *Smuts: The Sanguine Years*, p. 397.

129 NARSA, JSP, Box 112, Folio 17, Visit of the Governor-General of Union of South Africa to German South West Africa, March 1915, p. 2. Buxton describes the Central Force under command of Duncan McKenzie as almost entirely British and consisting of 11000 troops and considerably strengthened in artillery by the time Buxton had arrived for a visit to GSWA.

130 G. L'Ange, *Urgent Imperial Service*, p. 209. See also T.R. Ungleich, 'The Defence of German South-West Africa During World War I' (University of Miami, 1974) p. 115.

131 NARSA, JSP, Box 112, Folio 17, Visit of the Governor-General of Union of South Africa to German South West Africa, March 1915, p. 7.

132 Hancock, *Selections from the Smuts Papers Volume III*, p. 271.

133 Hancock, *Selections from the Smuts Papers Volume III*, p. 270.

134 NARSA, JSP, Box 112, Folio 18, Botha to Smuts, 3 April 1915. See also Ungleich, 'The Defence of German South-West Africa', p. 118. Smuts commanded a force of 14,300 men and 26 cannon against a German force of 800 men, two cannon and six machine guns.

135 NARSA, JSP, Box 112, Folio 22, Smuts to Botha, 5 April 1915

136 NARSA, JSP, Box 112, Folio 25, Botha to Smuts, Telegram from McKenzie, 5 April 1915.

137 Kleynhans, 'A Critical Analysis of the Impact of Water', Passim. See also G. L'Ange, *Urgent Imperial Service*, p. 211.

138 Collyer, *Campaign in German South West Africa*, pp. 50–2.

139 Collyer, *Campaign in German South West Africa*, pp. 77–9.

140 DODA, DC Box 252, Folio 17138, McKenzie's Dispatch 16 May 1915, p. 1.

141 Collyer, *Campaign in German South West Africa*, pp. 92, 93.

142 Ungleich, 'The Defence of German South-West Africa', p. 147.

143 Stejskal, *The Horns of the Beast*, pp. 95-98. The German sources show that the Germans had a numerical disadvantage as Abteilung Ritter under Maj Ritter who had 700 troops and eight guns at his disposal. The same sources place the number of UDF troops at Trekkoppies at 1,300 with one gun.

144 W. Whittal, *With Botha and Smuts in Africa* (London: Cassell & Co., 1917) pp. 35–7. See also Stejskal, *The Horns of the Beast*, p. 96. German sources indicate that the UDF deployed 12 armoured cars in GSWA of which nine were stationed at Trekkoppies.

145 Stejskal, *The Horns of the Beast*, p. 97.

146 Rayner, *How Botha and Smuts Conquered German South West*, pp. 199–202.

147 Rayner, *How Botha and Smuts Conquered German South West*, p. 119.

148 Hancock, *Selections from the Smuts Papers Volume III*, p. 244.

149 Hancock, *Selections from the Smuts Papers Volume III*, p. 254. Botha complained on 7 March 1915 that the engineers had laid only 42 kilometres of track in two months. That was far less than a kilometre a day.

150 Hancock, *Selections from the Smuts Papers Volume III*, p. 262.

151 Collyer, *Campaign in German South West Africa*, p. 95.

152 Collyer, *Campaign in German South West Africa*, p. 86.

153 DODA, DC Group 2, Box 252, Folio 17138, Mentions GSWA Campaign Commanding Officer DLI, 2 October 1917.

154 Ungleich, 'The Defence of German South-West Africa', pp. 157–9.

155 Stejskal, *The Horns of the Beast*, p. 102. The news reaching the Germans from Europe was positive if not completely factual.

156 DODA, DC Group 2, Box 252 GSWA, Botha's Dispatch No. 4 Covering the period 15 May to 18 July 1915, pp. 5, 6.

157 DODA, DC Group 2, Box 668, Botha letter to Seitz, 19 June 1915. See also Rayner, *How Botha and Smuts Conquered German South West*, p. 222.

158 DODA, DC Group 2, Box 252, Botha's Dispatch No. 4 Covering the period 15 May 1915 to 18 July 1915, p. 8; Collyer, *Campaign in German South West Africa*, p. 117.

159 Ungleich, 'The Defence of German South-West Africa', p. 147.

160 The map is an adaption of the one appearing in Garcia, *The First Campaign Victory*, p. 153

161 DODA, DC Group 2, Box 252 GSWA, Botha's Dispatch No. 4 Covering the period 15 May to 18 July 1915, pp. 18, 26. Botha was receiving information from the local population of the likely German intention to defend Kalkfeld. Botha had a detailed knowledge of the German defences there.

162 DODA, Diverse Group 1 Box 24, General Order No. 1 Col Bouwer Acting GOC Southern Force, 8 May 1915; Ungleich, 'The Defence of German South-West Africa', pp. 164–8; G. L'Ange, *Urgent Imperial Service*, p. 287; Collyer, *Campaign in German South West Africa*, p. 128. See also Von Oelhafen, *Der Feldzug in Südwest*, p. 214. The German official history overestimates the numerical superiority of the UDF in the final push at 20,000 to 35,000 men.

163 DODA, DC Group 2, Box 1434, South West African Campaign Memorandum, 1936. Collyer states that the brigades were cut down to 1,500 men and the wings each had 750 men. The previous larger bodies were too large for the relatively untrained staff, Collyer, *Campaign in German South West Africa*, p. 119.

164 DODA, DC Group 2, Box 252 GSWA, Botha's Dispatch No. 4 Covering the period 15 May to 18 July 1915, p. 7.

165 Collyer, *Campaign in German South West Africa*, pp. 122, 123, 125. Each of the six advancing brigades now had sufficient wagons to ensure supplies for two to three weeks.

166 DODA, DC Group 2, Box 252 GSWA, Botha's Dispatch No. 4 Covering the period 15 May to 18 July 1915, pp. 19, 21. The supply wagons would carry a minimum of provisions and meat was to be procured in the country covered by the advance. Each mounted brigade would be allocated 100 supply wagons, a vast improvement in numbers compared with previous operations in the campaign.

167 Collyer, *Campaign in German South West Africa*, p. 24.

168 DODA, DC Group 2, Box 252 GSWA, Botha's Dispatch No. 4 Covering the period 15 May to 18 July 1915, p. 44. The location of Brits and Myburgh's flanking forces was often ascertained using aerial reconnaissance.

169 DODA, DC Group 2, Box 252 GSWA, Botha's Dispatch No. 4 Covering the period 15 May to 18 July 1915, p. 14; Collyer, *Campaign in German South West Africa*, p. 124; G. L'Ange, *Urgent Imperial Service*, p. 287.

170 DODA, DC Group 2, Box 252 GSWA, Botha's Dispatch No. 4 Covering the period 15 May to 18 July 1915, p. 35. Botha learnt of the hasty German withdrawal from local informants and his air reconnaissance.

171 DODA, DC Group 2, Box 252 GSWA, Botha's Dispatch No. 4 Covering the period 15 May to 18 July 1915, p. 35; Stejskal, *The Horns of the Beast*, p. 105.

172 Stejskal, *The Horns of the Beast*, p. 105.

173 Collyer, *Campaign in German South West Africa*, p. 136. G. L'Ange, *Urgent Imperial Service*, p. 288.

174 DODA, DC Group 2, Box 252 GSWA, Botha's Dispatch No. 4 Covering the period 15 May to 18 July 1915, p. 52. Botha was aware that the Germans on interior lines had ample opportunity to concentrate on any one of his advancing wings. See also Garcia, *The First Campaign Victory*, p. 153 and G. L'Ange, *Urgent Imperial Service*, pp. 151–4. Both authors have overlooked the operational/strategic possibilities of the Germans successfully defending Otavifontein and forcing a South African retreat. A reading of the official German history reveals the possibilities through German eyes.

175 DODA, DC Group 2, Box 252, Letter Franke to *Schutztruppen*, 28 June 1915. Von Oelhafen, *Der Feldzug in Südwest*, p. 217. The prospect of an early peace in Europe that would save the Schutztruppe had all but disappeared.

176 Collyer, *Campaign in German South West Africa*, p. 120.

177 Von Oelhafen, *Der Feldzug in Südwest*.

178 DODA, DC Group 2, Box 252 GSWA, Botha's Dispatch No. 4 Covering the period 15 May to 18 July 1915, p. 45.

179 Von Oelhafen, *Der Feldzug in Südwest*, p. 216. The Germans were awed by the the speed of Botha's advance which they described as "extraordinary" and attributed it to excellent fodder and horse material as well as the rear area logistical network built by Botha in the preceeding month.

180 Von Oelhafen, *Der Feldzug in Südwest*, p. 222. Apparently the German reserves were not deployed to the battle as Franke had no idea of the attack on Otavifontein nor the course of the battle.

181 DODA, DC Group 2, Box 252 GSWA, Botha's Dispatch No. 4 Covering the period 15 May to 18 July 1915, p. 48.

182 DODA, DC Group 2, Box 252 GSWA, Botha's Dispatch No. 4 Covering the period 15 May to 18 July 1915, p. 50; The Germans had an opportunity to make a proper defence according to Botha. All indicators of their mediocre performance point to low morale and marginal leadership. See also Collyer, *Campaign in German South West Africa*, p. 140.

183 Von Oelhafen, *Der Feldzug in Südwest*, p. 223.

184 Stejskal, *The Horns of the Beast*, p. 105.

185 Von Oelhafen, *Der Feldzug in Südwest*, p. 216.

186 Ungleich, 'The Defence of German South-West Africa', p. 192.

187 Von Oelhafen, *Der Feldzug in Südwest*, p. 224. DODA, DC Group 2, Box 252 GSWA, Botha's Dispatch No. 4 Covering the period 15 May to 18 July 1915, p. 56. Botha was aware of his vulnerability in the centre, and he was content to wait for the slow advancing infantry to reinforce him.

188 DODA, DC Group 2, Box 252 GSWA, Botha's Dispatch No. 4 Covering the period 15 May to 18 July 1915, p. 48. Botha is at pains to explain that the truce only involved the local forces and not the Myburgh-Brits wings rapidly closing the gap to the north of the Germans. See also Rayner, *How Botha and Smuts Conquered German South West*, p. 230.

189 DODA, DC Group 2, Box 668, Letter from Seitz to Kaiser, 4 August 1915. Seitz puts the figure of *Schutztruppen* at the final surrender at 3,400. See also Collyer, *Campaign in German South West Africa*, pp. 147–51.

190 DODA, OC Records Group, Box 92, File O.R. 139, Statistics Re Casualties Rebellion, South West Africa, East and Central Africa and Europe.

Chapter 5

1 I. van der Waag, 'The Battle of Sandfontein, 26 September 1914: South African Military Reform and the German South-West Africa Campaign, 1914–1915', *First World War Studies*, http://dx. (2013). *Passim*

2 Kriegsschule ('war school') was a school where officers were educated. Kriegsakademie ('war academy') was the school for general staff, the next step, where the further education for officers and the education for the general staff (division command level) took place.
3 (Author's emphasis) This definition owes its derivation in part to the Canada Department of National Defence. The Conduct of Land Operations B-GL–300-001/FP-000, 1998.
4 J. Baily, *The First World War and the Birth of the Modern Style of Warfare* (Camberly, Strategic and Combat Studies Institute, 1996) p. 48.
5 *German Official Account of the War in South Africa March 1900 to September 1900*, ed. by H. du Cane (London: John Murray, 1906) pp. 332, 333.
6 T. Pakenham, *The Boer War* (London: Futura, 1982) p. 128. Meinertzhagen admits below that he has no understanding of manoeuvre warfare, which is not surprising, in the light of the British predisposition for the Aldershot way of war.
7 *German Official Account of the War in South Africa March 1900 to September 1900*, ed. by H. du Cane (London: John Murray, 1906) p. 333.
8 Fritz Bronsart von Schellendorf, 'Considerations Regarding a Method of Fighting for the Infantry Suited to the Present Conditions', *Royal United Services Institution Journal*, 35:162 (1891) p. 935.
9 *Infantry Training (Provisional)* (London: War Office, 1902).
10 *Infantry Training (Provisional)* p. 146). See also S. Jones, 'The influence of the Boer War (1899–1902) on the tactical development of the regular British Army 1902–1914' (PhD thesis, University of Wolverhampton, 2009) p. 51.
11 Jones, 'The influence of the Boer War', p. 43.
12 *German Official Account of the War in South Africa March 1900 to September 1900*, ed. by H. du Cane (London: John Murray, 1906) p. 337.
13 Army Council, *Field Service Regulations: Operations* (Edinburgh, His Majesty's Stationery Office, 1909).
14 *Combined Training* (London: War Office, 1905) pp. 100,1 01). See also Jones, 'The Influence of the Boer War', pp. 65, 66. See also Beca, *A Study of the Development of Infantry Tactics* (London: Geirge Allen & Unwin Ltd, 1915) pp ix, x. The author discusses the overturning of the defensive tendencies brought about by the South African War and reflected in *Infantry Training 1902*. The new training manuals reverted to "a thoroughly offensive spirit" and the author celebrates with, "it is hoped that the attack with its strong moral backing will always remain the bedrock of our training".
15 Differences in conditions between southern Africa and Europe consisted of the abnormally good visibility in Africa compared to Europe, the large distances, poor infrastructure, different weather patterns and local terrain features which included the semi-arid nature of the battlefield.
16 Schikkerling, *Commando Courageous*, p. 208; E.M. Spiers, 'The Learning Curve in the South African War: Soldiers' Perspectives', *Historia*, 55.1 (2010) p. 9; De Wet, *Three Years' War*, pp. 80, 143.
17 H.F.B. Walker, *A Doctor's Diary in Damaraland* (London: 1917), p. 9; Amery, *The Times History of the War*, p. 54.
18 Schikkerling, *Commando Courageous*, p. 208.
19 Hillegas, *With The Boer Forces*, pp. 120–3.
20 R. Meinertzhagen, *Army Diary 1899–1926*, p. 164. Meinertzhagen decribes thus, "The Dutch mounted Brigade should do us well, for the men's physique is splendid and their morale high."
21 R. Anderson, 'J.C. Smuts and J.L. van Deventer: South African Commanders-in-Chief of a British Expeditionary Force', *Scientia Miltaria*, 31(2) (2003). Anderson is less than complimentary on the UDF (Smuts) way of war differing very little from the consensus amongst British generals of the time, Meinertzhagen, or indeed most contemporary British historians.

22 D.B. Katz, (in press), 'An Aggregation of Lion Hunters: In Search of the Boer Way of War', *International Journal of Military History and Historiography* (2020) p. 2.

23 R. Meinertzhagen, *Army Diary 1899–1926* (London: Oliver & Boyd, 1960) (p 166)

24 B.H. Liddell Hart, *Strategy* (New York: 1974). See also Dupuy, *Understanding War*, pp. 6, 30.

25 M. Van Creveld, *Air Power and Maneuver Warfare* (Alabama: 1997) pp. 4–7.

26 P.J. le Riche, *General Ben Bouwer*, (Pretoria: Human Sciences Research Council, 1980) p. 67.

27 M. Samuels, *Command or Control* (London: Routledge, 1995) p. 5.

28 C.E. Callwell, *Small War: A Tactical Textbook for Imperial Soldiers* (London: 1896) p. 27; Amery, *The Times History of the War*, p. 76.

29 Waters, *The German Official Account*, p. 220; Reitz, *Commando*, p. 43.

30 S. Jones, *From Boer War to World War* (Norman: University of Oaklahoma Press, 2012) p. 25; Sternberg, *My Experiences*, p. 201. Boers were not lacking in fire control and discipline.

31 Schikkerling, *Commando Courageous*, p. 170.

32 Du Cane, *German Official Account*, 326. The Germans describe the Boer way of war as being quite unmethodical; L.S. Amery, *The Times History of the War in South Africa 1899–1900 Volume II* (London: 1900) p. 51; A.C. Doyle, *The Great Boer War* (1902), p. 359.

33 Dupuy, *Understanding War*, p. 3.

34 Amery, *The Times History of the War*, p. 77.

35 *German Official Account of the War in South Africa March 1900 to September 1900*, ed. by H. du Cane (London: John Murray, 1906) p. 325.

36 H.F. Trew, *Botha Treks* (London: Blackie & Son, 1936) p. 78.

37 G. Tylden, *The Armed Forces of South Africa 1659–1954* (Johannesburg: 1982) p. 187.

38 McKenzie, *The Dukes*, p. 74.

39 Trew, *Botha Treks*, p. 177.

40 Amery, *The Times History of the War*, p. 95.

41 H.F. Trew, *Botha Treks* (London: Blackie & Son, 1936) pp. 177, 178.

42 A. Garcia, 'Manoeuvre Warfare in the South African Campaign in German South West Africa During the First World War' (MA thesis, Humanities, University of South Africa, 2015).

43 M.R. Moyd, *Violent Intermediaries: African Soldiers, Conquest, and Everyday Colonialism in German East Africa* (Athens: Ohio University Press, 2014) pp. 88–101.

44 M.R. Moyd, *Violent Intermediaries: African Soldiers, Conquest, and Everyday Colonialism in German East Africa* (Athens: Ohio University Press, 2014) p. 102.

45 G. Adams, *King's African Rifles Soldier Versus Schutztruppe Soldier: East Africa 1917–18* (Oxford: Osprey Publishing, 2016) pp. 19–21.

46 Strachan, *The First World War in Africa*, p. 136.

47 T. Zuber, *The Battle of the Frontiers: Ardennes 1914* (Brimscombe Port: The History Press, 2009) pp. 12, 13.

48 T. Zuber, *The Battle of the Frontiers: Ardennes 1914* (Brimscome Port: The History Press, 2009) p. 14.

49 F. Halder, *Analysis of U.S. Field Service Regulations, MS No. P–133* (Historical Division, United States Army Europe, 1953). Halder defined German leadership as a capacity for independent action and a willingness to shoulder responsibility with a moral obligation to adhere to the mission and an ability to make complete clear and unambiguous decisions to establish a point of main effort.

50 Robert Citino has contributed greatly to the understanding of the German way of war. R.M. Citino, *The Path to Blitzkrieg: Doctrine and Training in the German Army, 1920–39* (Mechanicsburg: Stackpole, 1999); R.M. Citino, *Death of the Wehrmacht: The German Campaigns of 1942* (Kansas: University Press of Kansas, 2007).

51 G. Adams, *King's African Rifles Soldier Versus Schutztruppe Soldier: East Africa 1917–18* (Oxford: Osprey Publishing, 2016) pp. 22–4.

52 TNA, WO 106/310 f20, General Staff Appreciations, Future Conduct of the War 16 December 1915.

53 The Germans also occupied Nakob briefly, a border post on the northern Cape/GSWA border.

54 TNA, WO 106/310 f20, General Staff Appreciations, Future Conduct of the War 16 December 1915.

55 The National Archives United Kingdom, (TNA), War Office (WO) 106/310 f17 (1), Appreciation of the Situation in East Africa, Smith-Dorrien 1 December 1915. The railway from Mombasa to Nairobi received particular attention from the Germans.

56 Meinertzhagen, *Army Diary* pp 108, 123, 149, 153.

57 TNA, WO 141/62 f15, Colonel Malleson, Precis.

58 DODA, 3rd South African Infantry Brigade, Box 6, Report of Lieutenant-Colonel A.M. Hughes and Lieutenant-Colonel Dirk van Deventer, 26 November 1915.

59 TNA, WO 95/5345/15 f59 War Diary 130th King George's Own Baluchis, Report on the action at Mbuyuni, 14 July 1915.

60 C. Hordern, *Military Operations East Africa Volume 1 August 1914–September 1916* (London: Her Britannic Majesty's Stationery Office, 1941) p 156.

61 A.E. Capell, *The Second Rhodesia Regiment in East Africa* (Uckfield, The Naval & Military Press, 2006) p. 30. Lieutenant-Colonel Capell was was commander of the 2nd Rhodesia Regiment.

62 National Archives Record Services of South Africa Pretoria (NARSA), Jan Smuts Papers (JSP), A1 Box 390, Malleson Papers on Salaita Hill Engagement in East Africa Campaign 1916–1918, Notes on the action at Salaita, Appendix III. See also TNA, WO 106/310 f20, General Staff Appreciations, Future Conduct of the War 16 December 1915. The attack was in terms of a general vision for the theatre drawn up in December 1915.

63 Hordern, *Military Operations East Africa*, p. 230. Major-General Michael Tighe replied in response to a query from Smith-Dorrien on the 7 February that he would attack Salaita between 12–14 February.

64 J.J. Collyer, *The South Africans with General Smuts in German East Africa* (Pretoria: Government Printers, 1939) p. 52.

65 Hordern, *Military Operations East Africa,* (p 230).

66 TNA, WO 95/5345/15 f11 War Diary 130th King George's Own Baluchis, 29 March 1915. Casualties amounted to 14 killed, wounded and missing and the two machine guns had to be abandoned.

67 Hordern, *Military Operations East Africa*, pp 143, 144. See also Meinertzhagen, *Army Diary*, p 122.

68 NARSA, JSP, A1 Box 390, Malleson Papers on Salaita Hill Engagement in East Africa Campaign 1916–1918, Official report on the action at Salaita Hill 12 February 1918, Appendix II. Collyer emphasises the high expectation of a German counterattack. See also Collyer, *The South Africans with General Smuts*, p 55.

69 Ditsong War Museum Saxonwold from the German East Africa collection.

70 TNA, WO 95/5345/12 f55 War Diary 1st East African Division, Operation Order No. 2, 11 February 1916.

71 E. Paice, *Tip and Run: The Untold Tragedy of the First World War in Africa* (London: Phoenix, 2008) p 177. The South Africans began arriving on 19 January 1916.

72 Hordern, *Military Operations East Africa*, p 231.

73 NARSA, JSP, A1 Box 390, Malleson Papers on Salaita Hill Engagement in East Africa Campaign 1916–1918, Official report on the action at Salaita Hill 12 February 1918, Appendix II.

74 Collyer, *The South Africans with General Smuts*, pp. 58, 59.

75 Paice, *Tip and Run*, p. 177.

76 J.F.C. Fuller, *The Foundations of the Science of War* (Kansas: US Army Command and General Staff College Press, 1993). Fuller set out the principles of warfare in his book resulting in nine basic principles that have seen some variation over time. 1. Aim/Objective: Setting an aim with a clear set of measurable objectives. 2. Concentration: The point of maximum effort or focal point to meet the objective. 3. Offensive: Gain and maintain the initiative. Dictate the time, place, purpose, scope, intensity, and pace of operations. 4. Economy of Force: Directs bulk of resources to the primary objective and minimum of combat power on secondary objectives. 5. Surprise: Strike at a time or place or in a manner for which the enemy is unprepared. 6. Manoeuvre/Mobility: Outmaneuver the enemy using superior mobility and flexibility. 7. Security: Protect operations from enemy actions. 8. Simplicity: Avoid unnecessary complexity in preparing, planning, and conducting military operations. 9. Unity of Command: Unity of effort for every objective under one responsible commander.

77 South African National Defence Force Documentation Centre (DODA), Personnel File, P. S. Beves, Record of Service, Beves died on 26 September 1924 of complications due to the malaria he contracted while serving in German East Africa.

78 I. Uys, *South African Military Who's Who 1452–1992* (Germiston: Fortress, 1992) p. 18; Collyer, *The South Africans with General Smuts*, p. 54. Beves had served as a captain in the South African War in a regular British infantry regiment and thereafter commanded the Transvaal Volunteer Force until 1912 when he became Commandant of Cadets in the UDF.

79 NARSA, JSP, A1 Box 390, Malleson Papers on Salaita Hill Engagement in East Africa Campaign 1916–1918, Notes on the action at Salaita, Appendix III.

80 Paice, *Tip and Run*, p. 177. The South Africans began arriving in German East Africa on 14 January 1916 and would be in action at Salaita a mere four weeks later.

81 NARSA, JSP, A1 Box 390, Malleson Papers on Salaita Hill Engagement in East Africa Campaign 1916–1918, Official report on the action at Salaita Hill 12 February 1918, Appendix II.

82 P.E von Lettow-Vorbeck, *My Reminiscences of East Africa* (London: Hurst & Blackett) pp. 79, 80.

83 NARSA, JSP, A1 Box 390, Malleson Papers on Salaita Hill Engagement in East Africa Campaign 1916–1918, Notes on the action at Salaita, Appendix III.

84 Hordern, *Military Operations East Africa*, p. 230; Collyer, *The South Africans with General Smuts*, p 54. P.J. Sampson, 'The Conquest of German East', *The Nongquai Special Commemoration* (Pretoria: Argus, 1917) p. 14. "The trenches on the hill itself appear to have been devised for the sole purpose of misleading our airmen and intelligence men generally."

85 TNA, WO 95/5345/12 f42 War Diary 1st East African Division, Operation Order No. 1, 2 February 1916. The operation order estimates 200 enemy and two Maxim machine guns defending Salaita on 2 February. See also Hordern, *Military Operations East Africa*, p. 231.

86 NARSA, JSP, A1 Box 390, Malleson Papers on Salaita Hill Engagement in East Africa Campaign 1916–1918, Official report on the action at Salaita Hill 12 February 1918, Appendix II. See also TNA, WO 95/5345/12 f47 War Diary 1st East African Division, Operation Order No. 4, 6 February 1916. German strength in and around Taveta was estimated as not exceeding 3,000.

87 The table has been derived using the Collyer's figures, Collyer, *The South Africans with General Smuts*, pp. 53, 54.

88 P.J. Sampson, 'The Conquest of German East', *The Nongquai Special Commemoration* (Pretoria: Argus, 1917) p. 14. On inspecting the hill many weeks later, it was found that, "The hill was practically impregnable with concrete gun emplacements and rifle pits beautifully concealed, barbed wire entanglements and, of course, plenty of dummy trenches". J.H.V. Crowe, *General*

Smuts' Campaign in East Africa (London: John Murray, 1918) p. 56. The Germans had prepared for an all-round defence of Salaita.

89 DODA, 3rd South African Infantry Brigade, Box 6, Report of Captain Frank Douglas, 17 December 1915. References to South African tendency to dismiss the fighting qualities of 'native' troops, friend or foe are many amongst the secondary sources. This primary source gives credence to the notion that the South Africans were indeed dangerously dismissive before the battle of Salaita Hill. See also C.P. Fendall, *The East African Force 1915–1919: The First World War in Colonial Africa* (London: Leonaur, 2014) p. 40.

90 Collyer, *The South Africans with General Smuts*, pp 54, 55.

91 Collyer, *The South Africans with General Smuts*, p 55.

92 Collyer, *The South Africans with General Smuts*, p 55.

93 The Boers had entrenched their forces at the foot of the hills rather than the forward slopes, as was the accepted practice.

94 DODA, War Diary of 2nd South African Infantry Brigade, 3 February 1916, WWI GSWA, Box 77. See also Paice, *Tip and Run*, p. 180.

95 NARSA, JSP, A1 Box 390, Malleson Papers on Salaita Hill Engagement in East Africa Campaign 1916–1918, Official report on the action at Salaita Hill 12 February 1916, Appendix II; See also Hordern, *Military Operations East Africa*, p. 232; Collyer, *The South Africans with General Smuts*, p. 13. Author attests to the ineffectiveness of the artillery in silencing the German machine guns as "the enemy positions were most cunningly concealed".

96 E.S. Thompson, 'A Machine Gunner's Odyssey Through German East Africa: The Diary of E.S. Thompson, Part I. 17 January–24 May 1916', *South African Military History Society Journal*, 7.4 (1987).

97 Reference to Lettow-Vorbeck and P.J. Sampson, 'The Conquest of German East', *The Nongquai Special Commemoration* (Pretoria: Argus, 1917). "The enemy forces apparently were not on the hill at all, but in a cleverly constructed trench among the bush at the very foot of the hill. The searching bombardment of the hill by our guns, therefore had no effect, and it is doubtful if any of our shells touched the enemy's real trenches at the foot of the hill."

98 Collyer, *The South Africans with General Smuts*, p 56.

99 Hordern, *Military Operations East Africa*, p. 232.

100 TNA, WO 141/62 f6, Memorandum Colonel Malleson to Secretary of the Army, 6 July 1916.

101 DODA, War Diary of 2nd South African Infantry Brigade, 3 February 1916, WWI GSWA, Box 77. See also C. Hordern, *Military Operations East Africa Volume 1 August 1914–September 1916* (London: Her Britannic Majesty's Stationery Office, 1941) p. 230. A reconnaissance in force against Salaita was made by the 2nd Rhodesia Regiment and the 130th Baluchis and artillery elements on 3 February 1916. Paice, *Tip and Run*, p. 178. The South Africans were part of a reconnaissance undertaken 3 February and 9 February when the whole brigade took part in a demonstration in front of Salaita Hill.

102 DODA, War Diary of 2nd South African Infantry Brigade, 5 February 1916, WWI GSWA, Box 77.

103 DODA, War Diary of 2nd South African Infantry Brigade, 5 February 1916, WWI GSWA, Box 77. The purpose of this adventure was to examine roads, and locating mines. The South Africans advanced to within 700 metres of the Salaita defences. See also TNA, WO 95/5345/12 f42 War Diary 1st East African Division, Operation Order No. 8, 8 February 1916. The main purpose of the probe according to the divisional operations order was to make the road over the Njoro Drift fit for every description of vehicle. The infantry advance was meant to create a diversion in order to cover the work of the engineers and the reconnaissance parties.

104 L. Boell, *Die Operationen in Ost-Afrika* (Hamburg: Walther Dachert, 1951) p. 139. See also Paice, *Tip and Run*, p 177. See also Capell, *The Second Rhodesia Regiment in East Africa*, p. 47.

105 Capell, *The Second Rhodesia Regiment in East Africa*, p. 53.

106 P.J. Sampson, *The Conquest of German East* (Cape Town: *The Nongqai*, 1917) p. 14.

107 Hordern, *Military Operations East Africa*, p. 233.

108 Collyer, *The South Africans with General Smuts,* (p 57). Collyer admits that several platoons of the 7th SAI retired in disorder although no panic set in. See also C.P. Fendall, *The East African Force 1915–1919: The First World War in Colonial Africa* (London: Leonaur, 2014) p. 40. The author describes the South Africans as "thoroughly scared".

109 Boell, *Die Operationen in Ost-Afrika*, p. 140.

110 TNA, WO 95/5345/15 f146 War Diary 130th King George's Own Baluchis, Appendix IV, 12 February 1916. See also Collyer, *The South Africans with General Smuts*, p. 57; Fendall, *The East African Force*. The South Africans are described as being "contemptuous", going as far as to express their disgust at having to serve alongside Indian soldiers.

111 Command, Control, Communications and Intelligence. Command and Control is a system that empowers a commander to accomplish his mission by marshalling the resources, human and logistical to achieve his mission.

112 Collyer, *The South Africans with General Smuts*, p. 58.

113 Collyer, *The South Africans with General Smuts*, p. 59.

114 TNA, WO 95/5345/15 f146 War Diary 130th King George's Own Baluchis, Appendix IV, 12 February 1916. See also Hordern, *Military Operations East Africa*, (p 233).

115 TNA, WO 95/5345/12 f55 War Diary 1st East African Division, Operations against Salaita, 12 February 1916.

116 TNA, WO 95/5345/15 f146 War Diary 130th King George's Own Baluchis, Appendix IV, 12 February 1916.

117 Capell, *The Second Rhodesia Regiment in East Africa*, p. 48.

118 Thompson, 'A Machine Gunner's Odyssey'.

119 TNA, WO 141/62 f6, Memorandum Colonel Malleson to Secretary of the Army, 6 July 1916.

120 Van der Waag, *A Military History of Modern South Africa*, p. 126).

121 Boell, *Die Operationen in Ost-Afrika*, (p 141).

122 TNA, WO 33/858, M. Tighe, 'Action at Salaita Hill', Telegram Tighe to Kitchener, 16 February 1916.

123 TNA, WO 33/858, Kitchener, 'Action at Salaita Hill', Telegram Kitchener to Tighe, 18 February 1916.

124 TNA, WO 141/62 6128, Smuts Dispatch on East Africa, 20 June 1916.

125 *Selections from the Smuts Papers Volume III July 1910–November 1918*, ed. by W.K. Hancock and J. van der Poel (London: Cambridge University Press, 1966) p. 337.

126 R. Meinertzhagen, *Army Diary 1899–1926* (London: Oliver & Boyd, 1960) p. 170. Meinertzhagen provides a little more illumination on the matter recalling that Smuts had called Malleson a coward. This was not a position that Meinertzhagen disagreed with.

127 TNA, WO 32/5822, J. Smuts, 'Operations in East Africa' (Memorandum Smuts to CIGS, 23 March 1916) p. 73a. Smuts was anxious that Tighe's reassignment to the Indian Army was not be considered in the same light as Malleson.

Chapter 6

1   W.K. Hancock, *Smuts: The Sanguine Years 1870–1919* (London: Cambridge University Press, 1962) pp. 405, 406.

2 A. Samson, *Kitchener: The Man Not the Myth* (Solihull: Helion & Co., 2020) p. 203.

3 TNA, CAB 22–3, Minute by the Secretary of State for War, appended to the General Staff Appreciation, 14 December 1915. And TNA, CAB 22–3, War Committee Meeting of 15 December 1915.

4 Samson, *Kitchener*, p. 203.

5 NARSA, JSP, Box 197, Folio 174, Letter Smuts to A.B. Gillet, 2 September 1915. See also Hancock, *Smuts: The Sanguine Years*, pp. 405, 406. See also Robertson Papers, Liddell Hart Archive, King's College, WR 4/3/15, Letter Josiah Wedgwood (JCS Staff) to Prime Minister, 25 January 1916. Winston Churchill was suggested as an alternative to Smuts should Smuts refuse the appointment.

6 TNA, CAB 45-44, Private Diary of Brig-Gen C.P. Fendall January 1915–December 1918, 7 February 1916, p. 7. Fendall's first impression of the enemy strength holding the Taveta Gap was greatly exaggerated. See also TNA, WO 32-5324, conclusion of a Sub-Committee of future Operations in East Africa, 12 November 1915. The German has considerably strengthened their position with rearming from the *Königsberg*, a recruitment drive bringing their number up to 20,000, and a raiding strategy that threatened the Uganda railway.

7 TNA, WO 106–308, Note on our Future Military Policy, 28 December 1915.

8 TNA, WO 32-5325, Smith-Dorrien Appreciation on Situation in East Africa, 27 November 1915, p. 1.

9 NARSA, JSP, Box 197, Folio 174, Letter from Smuts to A.B. Gillet, J.C. Smuts, Military command of East Africa refused, 29 November 1915. Smuts refused the initial offer citing the need to support Botha and the thin majority in parliament.

10 DODA, AG 14, Box 32, File AG (7) WOI, Verslag Deur General J.C. Smuts Krygsverrigtinge in Oos Afrika, 30 April 1916, p. 1. See also TNA, WO 33-858, Secret Telegrams January 1915–February 1917, Tighe to War Office 24 November 1915. Tighe had a good idea by the end of November 1915 as to the workings of the offensive he proposed.

11 J.J. Collyer, *The South Africans with General Smuts in German East Africa* (Nashville: Imperial War Museum and Battery Press, 1939) p. 49.

12 F.B. Adler, A.E Lorch, and H.H. Curson, *The South African Field Artillery: German East Africa and Palestine 1915–1919* (Pretoria: J.L. van Schaik Ltd, 1957), p. 9. South African volunteers who served in GEA received three shillings per day compared with those who went to France and received only one shilling. Unlike in GSWA where the UDF consisted of Permanent and Active Citizen Force and commandos and volunteers, all those who served in GEA were volunteers.

13 M. Page, '"With Jannie in the Jungle": European Humor in an East African Campaign, 1914–1918', *The International Journal of African Historical Studies*, 14(3) (1981) p. 467.

14 NARSA, JSP, Box 197, Folio 89, Letter Merriman to Smuts 4 August 1915.

15 TNA, WO 106–310 Folio 20, General Staff Appreciations, Future Conduct of the War, 16 December 1915. See also TNA, CAB 22–3, An Appreciation by the General Staff on the Situation in East Africa, Lt-General A.J. Murray CIGS, 10 December 1915.

16 TNA, CAB 24–1-4, Committee of Imperial Defence: Future Operations in East Africa, 12 November 1915.

17 NARSA, JSP, Box 197, Folio 154, Letter Smuts to Merriman 30 August 1915.

18 J.H.V. Crowe, *General Smuts' Campaign in East Africa* (London: John Murray, 1918) p. ix.

19 J.C. Smuts, 'East Africa', *The Geographical Journal*, 51(3) (1918) p. 141.

20 R. Anderson, *The Forgotten Front: The East African Campaign 1914–1918* (Gloucestershire: Tempus, 2004).

21 H. Strachan, *The First World War in Africa* (Oxford, Oxford University Press, 2004) p. 94.

22 R. Anderson, 'World War I in East Africa 1916–1918' (University of Glasgow, Department of Modern History, PhD thesis, 2001).

23 R. Anderson, 'J.C. Smuts and J.L. van Deventer: South African Commanders-in-Chief of a British Expeditionary Force', *Scientia Militaria*, 31(2) (2003) p. 125. Many definitions hold that imperial troops originate from the United Kingdom, whereas colonial troops are those that originate outside the United Kingdom. See also Crowe, *General Smuts' Campaign*, p. 7. Smuts in fact commanded a polygot of troops from West, East and southern Africa, Great Britain and India, speaking a myriad of languages.

24 P.A. Pedersen, *Monash as Military Commander* (Carlton, Victoria: Melbourne University Press, 1985) p. 294

25 Anderson, 'J.C. Smuts and J.L. van Deventer', p. 125.

26 Anderson, 'J.C. Smuts and J.L. van Deventer', p. 125 quoting M.S. Buxton, Semi-Official Letter File, 12 February 1916, Smith-Dorrien to Buxton.

27 NARSA, JSP, Box 113 (8), Memorandum Simpson-Baikie to Governor-General, Smith-Dorrien, Smith-Dorrien poor health, 31 January 1915. See also TNA, WO 33-858, Secret Telegrams January 1915–February 1917, Smith-Dorrien to War Office, 31 January 1916.

28 DODA, AG 14, Box 32, File AG (7) WOI, Verslag Deur General J.C. Smuts Krygsverrigtinge in Oos Afrika, 30 April 1916, p. 1.

29 C. Hordern, *Military Operations East Africa Volume 1 August 1914–September 1916* (London: Her Britannic Majesty's Stationery Office, 1941) p. 222. The italicised sentence in the quote is my own emphasis.

30 Anderson, *The Forgotten Front*, p. 111.

31 TNA, WO 33-858, Secret Telegrams January 1915 - February 1917, GIGS to Smuts 8 February 1916.

32 R. Anderson, 'World War I in East Africa 1916–1918' (PhD thesis, University of Glasgow, Modern History, 2001) pp. 23, 24.

33 P. Lewsen (ed.), *Selections From the Correspondence of John X. Merriman 1905–1924*, (Cape Town: Van Riebeck Society, 1969) p. 275. Merriman in his *Thoughts on GEA an Expedition* 5 December 1915 before the appointment of Smuts as the supreme commander objected that South Africa was sending men to East Africa without any clear idea or objective or under whose command they fell. This was a sentiment that Smuts wished to dispel quickly after his arrival in GEA.

34 TNA, WO 32-5325, Smith-Dorrien Appreciation on Situation in East Africa, 27 November 1915, p. 3. The original document has the words underlined most probably by the recipient, the CIGS.

35 TNA, WO 32-5325, Smith-Dorrien Appreciation on Situation in East Africa, 27 November 1915, p. 3.

36 TNA, WO 32-5325, Smith-Dorrien Appreciation on Situation in East Africa, 27 November 1915, p. 4.

37 DODA, DC, Box 758, Operations in GEA, Folio D9/1973/9199, Letter Smuts to Governor-General, 26 February 1916.

38 DODA, AG 14, Box 32, File AG (7) WOI, Verslag Deur General J.C. Smuts Krygsverrigtinge in Oos Afrika, 30 April 1916, p. 1. See also TNA, WO 33-858, Secret Telegrams January 1915–February 1917, Smuts to GIGS 23 February 1916.

39 TNA, WO 32/5822, Tighe, Operations in East Africa, Memorandum Tighe to CIGS, 9 January 1916, p. 46a.

40 TNA, WO 32/5822, J. Smuts, Operations in East Africa, Memorandum Smuts to CIGS, 23 February 1916, p. 19a. See also NARSA, JSP, Box 113, Folio 10, Buxton, Launch of operations

before the rain, Buxton to Secretary of State, 31 January 1915. Again, Anderson considers that an attack before the rains was ill-advised giving only 18 days of general campaigning. Anderson fails to explore the motivation behind the decision or the fact that an early offensive was supported by Buxton and Botha for sound political and military reasons. See Anderson, 'J.C. Smuts and J.L. van Deventer', pp. 129, 130.

41 R. Anderson, 'World War I in East Africa 1916–1918' (PhD thesis, University of Glasgow, Modern History, 2001) pp. 14, 24. This is a point seemingly conceded by Anderson that inactivity and lack of an energetic commander had "sapped their effectiveness and the year was largely spent on static warfare". The same point offered by Smuts to the Governor-General as motivation for an attack prior to the rainy season is described by Anderson as being part of his "over-riding haste". See also Adler, *The South African Field Artillery*, p. 22. For an in-depth analysis of the Salaita Hill battle see D.B. Katz, 'A Clash of Military Doctrine: Brigadier-General Wilfrid Malleson and the South Africans at Salaita Hill, February 1916', *Historia*, 62 (2017).

42 TNA, CAB 45-43, An Ordinance Officer in East Africa 1914–1916, p. 349.

43 Crowe, *General Smuts' Campaign*, p. 44. Crowe goes to great lengths in describing the low morale of the troops prior to Smuts's arrival. He ascribes this to the months of inactivity and sitting on the defensive.

44 L. Boell, *Die Operationen in Ost-Afrika* (Hamburg: Walther Dachert, 1951) p. 137. The Germans correctly discounted a seaborne landing at Dar es Salaam, where in fact Smuts discarded the option.

45 TNA, CAB 24/1/12, Alexandretta and Mesopotamia Memorandum by Lord Kitchener, 16 March 1915. Kitchener ranked the conquest of German African possessions far below that of the Ottoman Empire in the Middle East.

46 DODA, DC, Box 758, Operations in GEA, Folio D8/1973/9199, Letter Smuts to Governor-General, 25 February 1916. See also J.C. Smuts, 'East Africa', *The Geographical Journal*, 51(3) (1918) p. 135. Smuts described the deluge of rain which confronted him in April may 1916 which exceeded his worst expectations. See also TNA, WO 33-858, Secret Telegrams January 1915–February 1917, GIGS to Smuts 24 February 1916.

47 J. Keegan, *The Mask of Command: A Study of Generalship* (London: Pimlico, 1999) p. 1.

48 Keegan, *The Mask of Command*, p. 2.

49 in *Oxford Dictionaries* www.oxforddictionaries.com/definition/english/generalship accessed 15 April 2015.

50 in *Collins Dictionaries* www.collinsdictionary.com/dictionary/english/generalship accessed 15 April 2015.

51 M.M. Chemers, *An Integrative Theory of Leadership*, (Mahwah NJ:, Lawrence Erlbaum Associates, 1997).

52 P.E. von Lettow-Vorbeck, *My Reminiscences of East Africa* (London: Hurst & Blackett, 1922) p. 170.

53 H.C. Armstrong, *Grey Steel: A Study in Arrogance* (London: Methuen & Co., 1941).

54 Defence Web, editor Leon Engelbrecht, http://defenceweb.co.za/index.php?option=com_content&view=article&id=603&catid=57:Book%20Reviews&Itemid=141, 20 April 2015. Armstrong served as a junior officer with the 6th Army Division and was captured by the Turks in the siege of Kut during the First World War. There he served out the rest of the war until he managed to escape. After the war he was posted back to Turkey for some years, during which he was in constant touch with the Turks, including Mustafa Kemal, and watched the rise of New Turkey. Drawing on this connection, Armstrong wrote *Turkey in Travail, Turkey and Syria Reborn, Unending Battle*, and *Grey Wolf, Lord of Arabia*.

55 Armstrong, *Grey Steel*, p. 10.

56 Armstrong, *Grey Steel*, p. 362. The quote is as follows: "and [Smuts] fell through ignorance of handling men and through pride, and because he was as arrogant as a steel blade drawn and held on guard."

57 Armstrong, *Grey Steel*, p. 243. This in a reference to, and laying the blame on, Smuts who failed to grasp, despite Botha's warnings that a dispute between two generals Lukin and Brits, allowed De Wet to escape during the Afrikaner Rebellion in the battle of mushroom valley.

58 Hew Strachan has produced one of the few works covering the entire First World War in Africa. It is also amongst the first using a 'new military history' approach and as such includes the social impact of the war, Strachan, *The First World War in Africa*. Ross Anderson studied under Strachan and has produced more of a traditional campaign history, Anderson, *The Forgotten Front*. Both authors harbour a jaded view of Smuts's abilities as a general.

59 Armstrong, *Grey Steel*, p. 251.

60 Armstrong, *Grey Steel*, p. 264.

61 Armstrong, *Grey Steel*, p. 266.

62 F.W. Beckett (ed.), *Rommel Reconsidered* (Mechanicsburg: Stackpole, 2013) pp. 4, 8.

63 Alaric Searle, *Rommel Reconsidered*, ed. by F.W. Beckett, (Mechanicsburg: Stackpole, 2013) p. 8. The author attributes the birth of the 'Rommel Myth' to the building of a West German defence contribution in the early 1950s. Contributors to facilitating the rearmament of Germany, in the face some of the German generals being tried for war crimes, were B.H. Liddell Hart and Desmond Young.

64 Armstrong, *Grey Steel*, p. 281.

65 Hancock, *Smuts: The Sanguine Years*, pp. 433–5. There are also many instances of Botha congratulating Smuts on his military achievements, leaving little doubt that he admired his leadership. See also W.K. Hancock and J. van der Poel (eds), *Selections From the Smuts Papers Volumer III June 1910–November 1918* (London: Cambridge University Press, 1966) pp. 336, 341, 352, 368, 390.

66 Hancock, *Selections From the Smuts Papers Volume III*, pp. 493–9.

67 S. Mitchell, 'Jan Smuts, Paul von Lettow-Vorbeck and the Great War in GEA', in *The Greater War: Other Combatants and Other Fronts 1914–1918*, ed. by J. Krause (New York: Palgrave Macmillan, 2014).

68 R. Meinertzhagen, *Army Diary 1899–1926* (London: Oliver & Boyd, 1960) p. 199.

69 J.F.C. Fuller, *Generalship: Its Diseases and Their Cure* (Harrisburg: Military Service Publishing Co., 1936) p. 22. "To do something that the enemy does not expect, is not prepared for, something which will surprise him and disarm him morally. To be always thinking ahead and to be always peeping round corners. To spy out the soul one's adversary, and to act in a manner which will astonish and bewilder him, this is generalship."

70 Fuller, *Generalship*, p. 24.

71 Fuller, *Generalship*, p. 9.

72 Armstrong, *Grey Steel*, p. 268.

73 Von Lettow-Vorbeck, *My Reminiscences*, pp. 123, 124.

74 Anderson, *The Forgotten Front*, p. 114. See also Strachan, *The First World War in Africa*, p. 136.

75 S. Bidwell and D. Graham, *Fire-Power: The British Army Weapons & Theories of War 1904–1945* (Barnsley: Pen & Sword, 2004) p. 140.

76 M. Samuels, *Command or Control* (London: Frank Cass & Co. Ltd, 1995), p. 177, 183.

77 Von Lettow-Vorbeck, *My Reminiscences*, pp. 38, 138; Boell, *Die Operationen in Ost-Afrika*, p. 187.

78 M.E. Page, '"With Jannie in the Jungle": European Humor in an East African Campaign, 1914–1918', *The International Journal of African Historical Studies*, 14.3 (1981) p. 467.

79 Strachan, *The First World War in Africa*, p. 136. These are of course Meinertzhagen's words quoted verbatim by Strachan, who goes on to say that he was "an indifferent general, but in many ways a remarkable soldier". See Meinertzhagen, *Army Diary*, p. 194

80 Strachan, *The First World War in Africa*, p. 135.

81 Fuller, *Generalship*, p. 20.

82 Strachan, *The First World War in Africa*, pp. 135–6.

83 DODA, DC, Box 758, Operations in GEA, Folio D31/1973/9199, Letter Smuts to Governor-General, 23 March 1916. The British favoured General Hoskins as Chief of Staff. However, they insisted he be given command of a division instead of a brigade. TNA, CAB 45-44, Private Diary of Brig-Gen C.P. Fendall January 1915–December 1918, 15 May 1916, p. 32. Fendall had quite a high opinion of Collyer.

84 TNA, CAB 45-44, Private Diary of Brig-Gen C.P. Fendall January 1915–December 1918, p. 3.

85 C.P. Fendall, *The East African Force 1915–1919* (London: Leonaur, 2014), p. 25.

86 Crowe, *General Smuts' Campaign*, pp. 4,12. Most of the staff had accompanied Smith-Dorrien from England except for the intelligence and signals officers who were GEA veterans. See also DODA, CSO, Box 36, File CSO45, Telegram Tighe to Hughes, 4 December 1914. Tighe was not averse to receiving South African staff officers while awaiting Smith-Dorrrien's srrival to GEA.

87 This table has been drawn up using Fendall, *The East African Force* and valuable input from Anne Samson and David Boyd. See also DODA, GSWA, Box 23b, Supplement to General Routine Orders, 19 May 1916.

88 Boell, *Die Operationen in Ost-Afrika*, p. 19. See also Crowe, *General Smuts' Campaign*, p. 25.

89 Von Lettow-Vorbeck, *My Reminiscences,* pp. 166–128.

90 Jan Smuts (seated in chair) with Collyer (on his right) and Van Deventer (on his left). Deneys Reitz appears at Smuts's bottom left.

91 I. Liebenberg, 'Sociology, Biology or Philosophy of a Warrior? Reflections on Jan Smuts, Guerrilla-Being and a Politics of Choices', *Scientia Militaria*, 33(1) (2005) pp. 141–70.

92 Liebenberg, 'Sociology, Biology or Philosophy of a Warrior?', p. 158.

93 My thanks to Dr Fankie Monama for drawing my attention to that point.

94 Strachan, *The First World War in Africa*, p. 135. Anderson cites Strachan in emphasizing Smuts's unsuitability for the task at hand. See Anderson, *The Forgotten Front*, p. 111.

95 J.C. Smuts, *Jan Christian Smuts* (London: Cassel & Co., 1952) p. 66.

96 W.K. Hancock and J. van der Poel (eds), *Selections from the Smuts Papers Volume I June 1886–May 1902* (London: Cambridge University Press, 1966) p. 500.

97 Hancock, *Smuts: The Sanguine Years*, pp. 107–11.

98 Crowe, *General Smuts' Campaign*, p. 2.

99 I. van der Waag, 'Military Culture and the South African Armed Forces, an Historical Perspective', A paper presented by Ian van der Waag at the Second South African Conference on Strategic Theory, 'On Strategy; Military Culture and African Armed Forces, co-hosted by Stellenbosch University and the Royal Danish Defence College, 22–23 September 2011.

100 T.R. Getz, 'Smuts and the Politics of Colonial Expansion: South African Strategy in Regard to South-West Africa (Namibia) and the League of Nations Mandate: c. 1914–1924' (MA degree, University of Cape Town), p. 38.

101 I. van der Waag, *A Military History of Modern South Africa* (Johannesburg & Cape Town: Jonathan Ball, 2015), p. 98.

102 A. Garcia, 'Manoeuvre Warfare in the South African Campaign in German South West Africa During the First World War' (MA thesis, Humanities, University of South Africa, 2015), p. 87.

103 Crowe, *General Smuts' Campaign*, p. 19.

104 DODA, Box 6, File 4/984/9199, 3rd SA Infantry Brigade, Confidential Statements and Reports re Method of Conducting the Campaign in GEA, 26 November 1915.

105 Crowe, *General Smuts' Campaign*, p. 19.

106 DODA, Box 6, File 4/984/9199, 3rd SA Infantry Brigade, Confidential Statements and Reports re Method of Conducting the Campaign in GEA, 26 November 1915, Latest information as to Enemy Numbers. See also Crowe, *General Smuts' Campaign*, p. 35.

107 DODA, Box 6, File 4/984/9199, 3rd SA Infantry Brigade, Confidential Statements and Reports re Method of Conducting the Campaign in GEA, 26 November 1915, Telegram Smith-Dorrien to Smuts, 29 January 1915.

108 DODA, Box 6, File 4/984/9199, 3rd SA Infantry Brigade, Confidential Statements and Reports re Method of Conducting the Campaign in GEA, 26 November 1915, Van Deventer/Hughes Report, 26 November 1915, p. 2. See also DODA, AG 14, Box 33, File AG(7)/WOI, Folio 149, Letter Curson to Tylden, 5 June 1962. The animal mortality rate was GSWA (8,12%) and GEA (10% monthly) over the period August 1914 to January 1916. The animal mortality rate in GEA for the period January 1916 to October 1916 was 98%. "There is no parallel instance of such colossal wastage of animals in any campaign."

109 DODA, Box 6, File 4/984/9199, 3rd SA Infantry Brigade, Confidential Statements and Reports re Method of Conducting the Campaign in GEA, 26 November 1915, Letter from Papenfus to Smuts, 17 December 1915

110 DODA, Box 6, File 4/984/9199, 3rd SA Infantry Brigade, Confidential Statements and Reports re Method of Conducting the Campaign in GEA, 26 November 1915, Van Deventer/Hughes Report, 26 November 1915, pp. 19, 20.

111 DODA, Box 6, File 4/984/9199, 3rd SA Infantry Brigade, Confidential Statements and Reports re Method of Conducting the Campaign in GEA, 26 November 1915, Van Deventer/Hughes Report, 26 November 1915, pp. 23, 24.

112 G.M. Orr, '1914–1915 in East Africa', *Journal of the United Service Institution India*, 1926, p. 72.

113 Boell, *Die Operationen in Ost-Afrika*, pp. 19–23.

114 Von Lettow-Vorbeck, *My Reminiscences*, p. 16.

115 Von Lettow-Vorbeck, *My Reminiscences*, p. 16.

116 Crowe, *General Smuts' Campaign*, p. 35. Crowe estimates the German strength at 2,309 whites, 11,621 askari, which together with the porters amounted to well over 30,000 men.

117 Boell, *Die Operationen in Ost-Afrika*, p. 28, 29.

118 TNA, CAB 45–29, Major-General G.J. Gifford Organisation of African labour in German East Africa, pp. 2, 3.

119 Adler, *The South African Field Artillery*, p. 14.

120 Boell, *Die Operationen in Ost-Afrika*, p. 7–13. See Orr, '1914–1915 in East Africa', p. 61. 16,500 carriers could deliver 1,600kg a day sufficient for 1,000 troops from 720 kilometres away. Of these 2,500 carriers were for the troops and 14,000 to sustain the carriers. See also Crowe, *General Smuts' Campaign*, p. 48. Crowe highlights the advantages of porters over the transport methods used by the Allies in GEA.

121 Boell, *Die Operationen in Ost-Afrika*, p. 15. Germans considered that the most militarily competent were the Wahehe, Wangoni, Wanjamwesi, and Wasukuma from the Tabora area. Boell makes special mention of the Manjema who originated from the Belgian Congo.

122 Boell, *Die Operationen in Ost-Afrika*, pp. 19, 29. Each company with an ammunition reserve of 18,000 rounds and food for three days was allocated 160 porters. See also Crowe, *General Smuts' Campaign*, pp. 25,38.

123 Crowe, *General Smuts' Campaign*, p. 31.

124 A.W. Lloyd, *'Jambo', or With Jannie in the Jungle* (Cape Town, n.d.). A booklet of cartoons by a South African volunteer in East Africa.

125 J.C. Smuts, *Smuts: By His Son J.C. Smuts* (London: Cassell, 1952) p. 166. See also P. van der Byl, *From Playgrounds to Battlefields* (Cape Town: Howard Timmins, 1971) p. 204. Piet van der Byl was appointed staff captain to General Smuts. He describes Salaita Hill as an almost impregnable fort with an extensive trench system and machine-gun positions with well-prepared tactical fields of fire.

126 Adler, *The South African Field Artillery*, p. 21.

127 The front of the Kilimanjaro operation stretched 200 kilometres as opposed the 760 kilometres of frontline on the Western Front.

128 TNA, WO 32/5822, J. Smuts, Operations in East Africa, Memorandum Smuts to CIGS, 15 March 1916, p. 63a.

129 DODA, AG 14, Box 32, File AG (7) WOI, Verslag Deur General J.C. Smuts Krygsverrigtinge in Oos Afrika, 30 April 1916, p. 3. Smuts gave testament to the extensive preparations for the offensive Tighe performed prior to his arrival in East Africa.

130 TNA, WO 32/5822, J. Smuts, Operations in East Africa, Memorandum Smuts to CIGS, 15 March 1916, p. 73a.

131 DODA, AG 14, Box 32, File AG (7) WOI, Verslag Deur General J.C. Smuts Krygsverrigtinge in Oos Afrika, 30 April 1916, p. 4.

132 Boell, *Die Operationen in Ost-Afrika*, p. 141. The Germans failed to identify that Van Deventer had switched from Longido to Mbuyuni despite capturing 10 South African mounted infantrymen in the vicinity of Lake Jipe on 1 March 1916. Reports from patrols confirmed the presence of South African mounted infantry in the Mbuyuni region, but incorrectly concluded that Longido was yet to be reinforced.

133 R.M. Maxwell, *Jimmie Stewart: Frontiersman* (Durham: Pentland Press, 1992), p.76.

134 Boell, *Die Operationen in Ost-Afrika*, p. 141.

135 TNA, CAB 103-94. Historical Section, Comments on Official History by Jan Smuts, 12 November 1934. Smuts corrected the official history and the impressions left by Lettow-Vorbeck that the reason for his withdrawal from the strong positions of Latema-Reata was the appearance of Van Deventer in his rear.

136 Boell, *Die Operationen in Ost-Afrika*, fn 2, p. 173.

137 TNA, WO 32/5822, J. Smuts: Operations in East Africa, Memorandum Smuts to CIGS, 6 March 1916) p. 51a.

138 TNA, WO/32/5820, Draft Dispatch from General Smuts on East African Operations, 1916.

139 Hordern, *Military Operations East Africa*, p. 238.

140 DODA, CSO, Box 36, Letter Hughes to Tighe 4 January 1916. Pretorius was recruited by Tighe before Smuts's arrival in GEA. Pretorius was awarded the Distinguished Service Order (DSO) for his role in the *Königsberg* operation when working with the navy.

141 P.J. Pretorius, *Jungle Man: The Autobiography of Major P.J. Pretorius* (Alexander City: Alexander Books, 2001) pp. 165.166. See also Boell, *Die Operationen in Ost-Afrika*, p. 166. Boell confirms the tenuous water supply at Salaita Hill.

142 P.B. Blanckenberg, *The Thoughts of General Smuts* (Cape Town: Juta & Co., 1951), pp. 175, 176.

143 Van der Byl, *From Playgrounds to Battlefields*, p. 205. He relates a sardonic remark of Smuts made while inspecting the abandoned German positions at Salaita Hill. "British generals seem to take a fortified position as a personal affront and attack it head on. We believe in going round it."

144 Hordern, *Military Operations East Africa*, p. 234. The quote is as follows: "but the repulse at Salaita had shown that strong opposition was certain on the line and that it would be wise to avoid direct attacks against German entrenched positions in the Bush."

145 Meinertzhagen, *Army Diary*, p. 166.

146 E. Paice, *Tip and Run* (London: Phoenix, 2008). Strachan rates Anderson's work as the latest and last word on the German East African campaign "overtaking" all that went before. Strachan, *The First World War in Africa*, p. 94. However, Paice does add an important new dimension by re-examining and devaluing the efforts of Lettow-Vorbeck in the light of the futility and wastefulness of his otherwise expert defence.

147 Strachan, *The First World War in Africa*, p. 137. "Moreover, for all his talk of battle, Smuts's aim was to manoeuvre rather than to fight."

148 Meinertzhagen, *Army Diary*, p. 166.

149 TNA, CAB 45-44, Private Diary of Brig-Gen C.P. Fendall January 1915–December 1918, 19 March 1916, p. 17. Fendall is scathing in his assessment of Malleson whom he describes as a writer and never a soldier. "Malleson ought never to have been sent on service except as an official war correspondent. Fendall accused Stewart of "playing the fool" and failing to make a plan to stick to the timetable. He describes Tighe as having "no head for anything but actual scrapping. At that he is first class and thoroughly enjoys it".

150 B. Garfield, *The Meinertzhagen Mystery: The Life and Legend of a Colossal Fraud* (Washington: Potomac Books, 2007).

151 Meinertzhagen, *Army Diary*, p. 166.

152 Meinertzhagen, *Army Diary*, p. 193.

153 Van der Byl, *From Playgrounds to Battlefields*, p. 210. Smuts was aware that senior British officers looked upon him as an amateur while serving as the commander in East Africa. Therefore, the label of amateurishness was not a post-war construct but a feeling present amongst most senior British officers serving under him.

154 Meinertzhagen, *Army Diary*, p. 194.

155 Meinertzhagen, *Army Diary*, p. 199. See also Strachan, *The First World War in Africa*, p. 164. Refers to Smuts consistently reporting great successes in his cables. See also R. Anderson, 'World War I in East Africa 1916–1918' (PhD thesis, University of Glasgow, Modern History, 2001) p. 27. Refers to, "Yet, despite appearances and the optimistic communiques sent to the War Office, things were not quite as they seemed". And again, on page 109 referring to "Smuts's own over-optimistic reports".

156 Meinertzhagen, *Army Diary*, p. 205.

157 Fendall, *The East African Force*.

158 TNA, CAB 45/44, War Diaries (Private): Operations in East Africa: diary of Col C.P. Fendall

159 R. Anderson, 'World War I in East Africa 1916–1918' (PhD thesis, University of Glasgow, Modern History, 2001) p. 150.

160 Fendall, *The East African Force*, p. 56.

161 S.H. Sheppard, 'Some Notes on Tactics in the East African Campaign', *The Journal of the United Service Institution of India*, 158.215 (1919) p. 146.

162 Von Lettow-Vorbeck, *My Reminiscences*, p. 110.

163 Map derived from that enclosed with Collyer, *The South Africans with General Smuts*.

164 S.H. Sheppard, 'Some Notes on Tactics in the East African Campaign', *The Journal of the United Service Institution of India*, 158.215 (1919), p. 152.

165 Collyer, *The South Africans with General Smuts*, p. 77.

166 Collyer, *The South Africans with General Smuts*, pp. 63–6. Anderson has significantly different figures in Anderson, *The Forgotten Front*, pp. 112, 114 where he numbers the Germans at 4,000 in total facing the British with over 40,000, thus giving the impression of a force ratio of 10:1. The official history Hordern, *Military Operations East Africa*, p. 235 offers figures for the Germans much closer to that of Collyer. See also TNA, WO 32/5822, J. Smuts: Operations in East Africa,

Memorandum Smuts to CIGS, 27 March 1916, p. 79a. Smuts puts the figure at 600 Europeans and 5,000 natives, 30 machine guns and a further 1,000 men if the Germans were able to concentrate. See also Boell, *Die Operationen in Ost-Afrika*, p. 142. Boell places German strength at 800 'Europeans' and 5,200 askari with 47 machine guns, five cannons of mid-calibre and five cannons of small calibre.

167 Cover offers protection from enemy fire and concealment hides the soldier from enemy view. The two are not the same and the confusion between them has led to the unfortunate demise of many a soldier.

168 Crowe, *General Smuts' Campaign*, p. 22.

169 NARSA, JSP, Box 113 Folio 6, Smith-Dorrien: On the raising of the Cape Boys unit, Memorandum Smith-Dorrien to Smuts, 28 January 1916). "both you and General Botha were as deeply impressed as I am with the necessity for using considerable bodies of Mounted Troops for the subjugation of German East Africa, and that such troops drawn from South Africa would live off the country and require little transport." This is in stark contrast to a document TNA, WO 106–310, Smith-Dorrien: Appreciation on situation in East Africa, quoted in Anderson, 'J.C. Smuts and J.L. van Deventer', p. 127 in which Smith-Dorrien is said to have requested that only frontline units be equipped with mules and the remainder motor vehicles.

170 DODA, AG 14, Box 32, File AG (7) WOI, Verslag Deur General J.C. Smuts Krygsverrigtinge in Oos Afrika, 30 April 1916, p. 5.

171 On Smuts's growing desperation with Stewart, see TNA, WO 32/5822, J. Smuts: Operations in East Africa, Memorandum Smuts to CIGS, 12 March 1916, p. 58a. and TNA, WO 32/5822, J. Smuts: Operations in East Africa, Memorandum Smuts to CIGS, 11 March 1916, p. 57a.

172 Boell, *Die Operationen in Ost-Afrika*, p. 161.

173 Meinertzhagen, *Army Diary*, p. 168. Meinertzhagen describes Smuts's strategy thus far as being "sound". This goes against the run of play of the more caustic remarks that Meinertzhagen offers on Smut's strategy of manoeuvre.

174 TNA, WO 32/5822, DCIGS: Operations in East Africa, Memorandum DCIGS to General Buller, 12 March 1916, p. 59a. Smuts warned Stewart to expidite his advance and expected him to intercept Lettow-Vorbeck. See also TNA, WO 33-858, Secret Telegrams January 1915–February 1917, Smuts to GIGS 11 March 1916. The first signs of Smuts's irritation with Stewart is contained in a telegram to the CIGS on 11 March 1916.

175 Hordern, *Military Operations East Africa*, pp. 236–9.

176 Orr, '1914–1915 in East Africa', p. 60. The map was compiled by the author from figures derived from Orr.

177 Boell, *Die Operationen in Ost-Afrika*, pp. 160–4.

178 DODA, DC, Box 758, Operations in GEA, Folio D31/1973/9199, Letter Smuts to Governor-General, 12 March 1916.

179 TNA, WO 32/5822, J. Smuts: Operations in East Africa, Memorandum Smuts to CIGS, 15 March 1916, p. 63a. Smuts expected Stewart to reach Kahe by 11 March. See also Meinertzhagen, *Army Diary*, p. 167. Meinertzhagen describes Smuts as livid with rage at the ineptitude of his British subordinates, especially Stewart.

180 Hordern, *Military Operations East Africa*, pp. 240, 241.

181 DODA, DC, Box 758, Operations in GEA, Folio D31/1973/9199, Letter Smuts to Governor-General, 12 March 1916.

182 Maxwell, *Jimmie Stewart*, p. 77.

183 DODA, WWI GSWA and EA, Box 77, War Diary of the 2nd South African Infantry Brigade, p. 15.

184 TNA, WO 32/5822, J. Smuts: Operations in East Africa, Memorandum Smuts to CIGS, 8 March 1916, p. 53a.

185 Boell, *Die Operationen in Ost-Afrika*, p. 166.

186 Von Lettow-Vorbeck, *My Reminiscences*, p. 110.

187 Meinertzhagen, *Army Diary*, p. 168. Meinertzhagen attests the strength of the German defences at Salaita and the efficacy of Smuts's turning movement in forcing its abandonment.

188 TNA, WO 32/5822, J. Smuts: Operations in East Africa, Memorandum Smuts to CIGS, 9 March 1916, p. 54a. See also DODA, DC, Box 758, Operations in GEA, Folio D31/1973/9199, Letter Smuts to Governor-General, 9 March 1916. See also DODA, GSWA, Box 44, Intelligence Summary, 13 March 1916.

189 Hordern, *Military Operations East Africa*, p. 243.

190 Meinertzhagen, *Army Diary*, p. 170. Meinertzhagen provides a little more illumination on the matter recalling that Smuts had called Malleson a coward. This was not a position that Meinertzhagen disagreed with.

191 Boell, *Die Operationen in Ost-Afrika*, p. 169.

192 TNA, WO 32/5822, J. Smuts, Operations in East Africa, Memorandum Smuts to CIGS, 12 March 1916. p. 60a. See also Hordern, *Military Operations East Africa*, pp. 246–6. See also DODA, AG 14, Box 32, File KA/WOI, Intelligence Supplement Richard Meinertzhagen, 14 July 1916.

193 DODA, WWI GSWA and EA, Box 25, Lindenken, News from enemy sources, Diary of a member of the 7 Schutzen Company, p. 4. The author describes the flanking movement of a British column of 2,000 from Longido as being the reason for retreat. See also Meinertzhagen, *Army Diary*, p. 170. Meinertzhagen is critical of Van Deventer's flanking manoeuvre, taking the view that this was a missed opportunity to annihilate the enemy via a direct assault. "We score nothing but territory."

194 Blanckenberg, *The Thoughts of General Smuts*, p. 176.

195 NARSA, JSP, Box 113, Folio 154, Meinertzhagen: Notes on the officers serving with the enemy forces in German East Africa, Intelligence Supplement No. 3, 14 July 1916.

196 Maxwell, *Jimmie Stewart*, p.78.

197 Maxwell, *Jimmie Stewart*, p.80.

198 NARSA, JSP, Box 113, Folio 154, Meinertzhagen: Notes on the officers serving with the enemy forces in German East Africa, Intelligence Supplement No. 3, 14 July 1916.

199 Collyer, *The South Africans with General Smuts*.

200 TNA, WO 32/5822, J. Smuts: Operations in East Africa Memorandum Smuts to CIGS, 15 March 1916, p. 63a and also TNA, WO 32/5822, J. Smuts: Operations in East Africa, Memorandum Smuts to CIGS, 14 March 1916, p. 61a. See also Meinertzhagen, *Army Diary*, p. 172. Stewart's conduct of the operation was described as lamentable by Smuts. He had only managed to cover an average of 6.5 kilometres per day over a period of six days in the face of little opposition. See also DODA, AG 14, Box 32, File KA/WOI, Intelligence Supplement Richard Meinertzhagen, 14 July 1916. See also TNA, WO 33-858, Secret Telegrams January 1915–February 1917, Smuts to GIGS 12 March 1916.

201 Hordern, *Military Operations East Africa*, pp. 246, 247.

202 Meinertzhagen, *Army Diary*, p. 171.

203 DODA, DC, Box 758, Operations in GEA, Folio D31/1973/9199, Letter Smuts to Governor-General, 15 March 1916. Smuts described Stewart's performance as lamentable. p. 4.

204 TNA, WO 32/5822. J. Smuts: Operations in East Africa, Memorandum Smuts to CIGS, 23 March 1916, p. 73a. Smuts was anxious that Tighe's reassignment to the Indian Army would not be considered in the same light as Stewart and Malleson. See also Meinertzhagen, *Army Diary*,

p. 175. Meinertzhagen describes a stormy interview with Stewart followed by his dismissal. Smuts refused to see Malleson at all prior to his dismissal.

205 Von Lettow-Vorbeck, *My Reminiscences*, p. 109. This was Lettow-Vorbeck's plan all along to attack first the one force and then the other in quick succession.

206 Von Lettow-Vorbeck, *My Reminiscences*, p. 112. Lettow-Vorbeck considered the Latema-Reata position to be almost impregnable, even if attacked by "greatly superior strength".

207 Von Lettow-Vorbeck, *My Reminiscences*, p. 114.

208 Boell, *Die Operationen in Ost-Afrika*, note 2, p. 173.

209 DODA, DC, Box 758, Operations in GEA, Folio D31/1973/9199, Letter Smuts to Governor-General, 23 March 1916.

210 Boell, *Die Operationen in Ost-Afrika*, p. 178.

211 DODA, DC, Box 758, Operations in GEA, Folio D31/1973/9199, Press Communiqué, 27 March 1916.

212 TNA, WO 32-5822, Operations in East Africa, Memorandum W. Robertson CIGS to Smuts, 24 March 1916, p. 75a.

Chapter 7

1 Anderson, *The Forgotten Front*, p. 114. Anderson feels that Smuts's removal of Van Deventer's mounted infantry from Stewart's command weakened the fighting power of Stewart's advance from Longido.

2 C. Hordern, *Military Operations East Africa August 1914–September 1916* (London: Battery Press and the Imperial War Museum, 1941), p. 258.

3 G. Hodges, *Kariakor: The Carrier Corps* (Niarobi: Nairobi Press, 1999). One of the few books dedicated to the hundreds and thousands of porters who served both sides and suffered immensely in the GEA campaign.

4 www.climatestotravel.com/climate/tanzania, Climates to travel, accessed 22 May 2020. Modern-day Tanzania receives an annual rainfall of 1,150mm of which is 52% falls between March and June. See also Hordern, *Military Operations East Africa*, p. 263.

5 DODA, DC, Box 758, Operations in GEA, Folio D31/1973/9199, Letter Smuts to Governor-General, 23 March 1916. Smuts was prepared to retain Tighe as a divisional commander, but the British preferred to give the position to Hoskins after Smuts insisted on Collyer as Chief of Staff. Tighe was sent to India.

6 DODA, DC, Box 758, Operations in GEA, Folio D31/1973/9199, Letter Smuts to Governor-General, 22 March 1916.

7 Hordern, *Military Operations East Africa*, p. 263.

8 Anderson, *The Forgotten Front*, p. 116.

9 The KAR was made up of black members and white leader group from a number of British African possessions. Its formation was rather small but expanded rapidly in 1917 under Hoskins's tenure.

10 TNA, CAB 45–27, East African Campaign 1914–1918, Preliminary Studies of the Operations in East Africa, p. 2; Hordern, *Military Operations East Africa*, p. 265. See also Anri. Delport, '"Boks and Bullets, Coffins and Crutches": An Exploration of the Body, Mind and Places of "Springbok" South African Soldiers in the First World War' (MA thesis, Stellenbosch University, 2015) passim.

11 TNA, WO 32-5820 Smuts Dispatch 27 October 1916, pp. 1, 2. See also DODA, DC, Box 758, Operations in GEA, Folio D31/1973/9199, Letter Smuts to Governor-General, 15 March 1916. See also TNA, WO 33-858, Secret Telegrams January 1915–February 1917, Smuts to GIGS 15 March 1916.

12 Anderson, *The Forgotten Front*, p. 116. Anderson dismisses the restructuring as an exercise in nepotism.

13 H. Strachan, *The First World War in Africa* (Oxford: Oxford University Press, 2004) p. 158. Northey was technically not under Smuts's command; nevertheless, he coordinated his movements with him.

14 Strachan, *The First World War in Africa*, p. 141.

15 J.J. Collyer, *The South Africans with General Smuts in German East Africa* (London: Imperial War Museum and Battery Press, 1939) p. 97. See also TNA, WO 32-5823, Operations in German East Africa: General Smuts Command, Telegram Smuts to CIGS, 21 September 1917. Smuts considered it safer not to count on any real cooperation from the Portuguese.

16 R. Anderson, *The Forgotten Front: The East African Campaign 1914–1918* (Gloucestershire: Tempus, 2004) p. 116. See also Strachan, *The First World War in Africa*, p. 141.

17 TNA, WO 33-858, Secret Telegrams, Folio 810, Smith-Dorrien to WO, 31 January 1916

18 D.R. Woodward, *World War One Almanac* (New York: Facts on File, 2009), pp. 101, 107, 108, 128. See also TNA, CAB 45-44, Private Diary of Brig-Gen C.P. Fendall January 1915–December 1918, 10 June 1916, p. 36. Fendall reported that "Everyone seems convinced it cannot last very long, and certainly it is quite useless the Germans going on even now". Fendall felt that German morale in GEA had collapsed and a surrender could be expected in August/September.

19 TNA, WO 32-5820 Smuts Dispatch 27 October 1916, p. 3.

20 Hordern, *Military Operations East Africa*, p. 267.

21 TNA, WO 32-5820 Smuts Dispatch 27 October 1916, p. 4.

22 Hordern, *Military Operations East Africa*, p. 267.

23 TNA, WO 32-5820 Smuts Dispatch 27 October 1916, p. 5. See also Hordern, *Military Operations East Africa*, p. 268.

24 TNA, WO 32-5820 Smuts Dispatch 27 October 1916, p. 6.

25 Strachan, *The First World War in Africa*, p. 143. The weather contradicted the predictions and rainfall was heavy in the interior. See also Collyer, *The South Africans with General Smuts*, p. 101. Hordern, *Military Operations East Africa*, pp. 269, 277. The British official history laments that "at this early stage the value of British intelligence service was under-rated". See also TNA, CAB 45–27, East African Campaign 1914–1918, Preliminary Studies of the Operations in East Africa, Intelligence, p. 9.

26 Strachan, *The First World War in Africa*, p. 142. Strachan describes van Deventer's advance as essentially Boer in conception and execution.

27 TNA, WO 32-5822, Folio 99a, Telegram Smuts to CIGS, 19 May 1916.

28 Anderson, *The Forgotten Front*, p. 118.

29 TNA, WO 32-5820, Smuts Dispatch 27 October 1916. p. 7.

30 Anderson, *The Forgotten Front*, p. 118. Anderson seems underwhelmed at Smuts's plan calling it "a bold scheme that ignored the effects of the rains and his inadequate transport".

31 P.A. Povlock, *Deep Battle in World War One: The British 1918 Offensive in Palestine* (Newport RI: Naval War College, 1997) p. 7.

32 R. Simpkin, *Deep Battle: The Brainchild of Marshal Tukhachevskii* (New Delhi: Natraj Publishers, 2012) p. 50.

33 C.L. Crow, *Tactical and Operational Depth* (Fort Leavenworth, KS: School of Advanced Military Studies, U.S. Army Command and General Staff College 1986) p. 3.

34 D.M. Glantz, *Soviet Military Operational Art: In Pursuit of Deep Battle* (New York: Frank Cass & Co. Ltd, 1991) p. 18.

35 Glantz, *Soviet Military Operational Art*, p. 19. Operational results emerge as the sum of the results of tactical combat. See also J. A. Olsen and M. van Creveld (eds), *The Evolution of Operational Art: From Napoleon to the Present* (Oxford: Oxford University Press, 2011) pp. ix, x.

36 Anderson, *The Forgotten Front*, p. 118. Anderson barely mentions this substantial tactical victory, in the face of challenging weather and logistics. See also L. Boell, *Die Operationen in Ost-Afrika* (Hamburg: Walther Dachert, 1951) p. 181. The German history reflects the low morale of the defenders in "unnecessarily" surrendering and lowering the reputation of the European component of the Schutztruppe. See also Hordern, *Military Operations East Africa*, p. 271. See also TNA, CAB 45-44, Private Diary of Brig-Gen C.P. Fendall January 1915–December 1918, 13 April 1916, p. 25.

37 P.E. von Lettow-Vorbeck, *My Reminiscences of East Africa* (London: Hurst & Blackett, 1922) p. 126.

38 Boell, *Die Operationen in Ost-Afrika*, p. 182.

39 TNA, WO 32-5820 Smuts Dispatch 27 October 1916, p. 8.

40 Hordern, *Military Operations East Africa*, p. 273.

41 Von Lettow-Vorbeck, *My Reminiscences*, pp. 126,127.

42 Boell, *Die Operationen in Ost-Afrika*, p. 182.

43 Hordern, *Military Operations East Africa*, p. 275.

44 Boell, *Die Operationen in Ost-Afrika*, p. 182. Captain Klinghardt, threatened with encirclement, retreated from the town.

45 Anderson, *The Forgotten Front*, p. 118. Anderson concedes that Smuts achieved a victory, albeit tempered by the enormous loss in animals, growing sickness of the troops, and impossible logistics.

46 TNA, WO 32-5820 Smuts Dispatch 27 October 1916, pp. 9, 10.

47 Collyer, *The South Africans with General Smuts*, p. 264.

48 TNA, CAB 45-44, Private Diary of Brig-Gen C.P. Fendall January 1915–December 1918, 15 May 1916, pp. 32, 33.

49 TNA, CAB 45-46, Report on the Operations of the 1st South African Mounted Brigade 23 October 1916–1 January 1917, Lt-Col Hartigan.

50 TNA, CAB 45-44, Private Diary of Brig-Gen C.P. Fendall January 1915–December 1918, 4 February 1917, p. 70.

51 Strachan, *The First World War in Africa*, p. 143. Strachan cites Blenkinsop and Rainey, *Veterinary Services*, pp. 407–18.

52 TNA, WO 33-858, Secret Telegrams January 1915–February 1917, Secretary of State to Smuts, 2 July 1916.

53 Collyer, *The South Africans with General Smuts*, p. 193. During the three months' advance from Kahe to the Central Railway the Allies lost 28,000 oxen. Between 15 September and 15 November 10,000 horses, 10,000 mules,11,000 oxen, and 2,500 donkeys died.

54 Collyer, *The South Africans with General Smuts*, p. 195. See also Anri Delport, '"Boks and Bullets, Coffins and Crutches": An Exploration of the Body, Mind and Places of "Springbok" South African Soldiers in the First World War' (MA thesis, Stellenbosch University, 2015) passim.

55 TNA, WO 141/31, Report on Medical and Sanitary Matters in German East Africa 1917.

56 TNA, WO 141/31, Report on Medical and Sanitary Matters in German East Africa 1917, Section 12, p. 184.

57 TNA, WO 141/31, Report on Medical and Sanitary Matters in German East Africa 1917, Section 12, pp. 187–9.

58 TNA, CAB 103-94. Historical Section, Letter G.E. Edmonds to Sir Herbert Creedy, 30 April 1937. See R. Anderson, 'J.C. Smuts and J.L. van Deventer: South African Commanders-in-Chief of a British Expeditionary Force', *Scientia Miltaria*, 31(2) (2003) p. 134.

59 TNA, CO 551–101, File 38195, Proceedings of a Court of Enquiry to Investigate and Report upon Certain Allegations made by Lt-Colonel H.J. Kirkpatrick 9th Regiment SAI, 31 July 1917, p. 248.

60 TNA, CO 551–101, File 38195, Proceedings of a Court of Enquiry to Investigate and Report upon Certain Allegations made by Lt-Colonel H.J. Kirkpatrick 9th Regiment SAI, 31 July 1917, p. 255.

61 Collyer, *The South Africans with General Smuts*, pp. 260–89.

62 Boell, *Die Operationen in Ost-Afrika*, p. 184.

63 Von Lettow-Vorbeck, *My Reminiscences*, p. 127.

64 Boell, *Die Operationen in Ost-Afrika*, p. 185. See also Von Lettow-Vorbeck, *My Reminiscences*, p. 135.

65 Boell, *Die Operationen in Ost-Afrika*, p. 185.

66 Strachan, *The First World War in Africa*, p. 144. Strachan cites the reason for the night attack as the lack of concealment during the day over open and exposed ground. German reconnaissance was inadequate and failed to identify Van Deventer's positions.

67 TNA, WO 32-5820, Smuts Dispatch 27 October 1916, pp. 12, 13. See also Von Lettow-Vorbeck, *My Reminiscences*, p. 137.

68 R. Meinertzhagen, *Army Diary 1899–1926* (London: Oliver & Boyd, 1960) p. 185. Meinertzhagen thought Van Deventer very fortunate in a close-run battle that could have led to the demise of the South Africans.

69 Meinertzhagen, *Army Diary*, p. 186.

70 TNA, WO 33-858, Secret Telegrams January 1915–February 1917, Secretary of State to Smuts, 24 April 1916. See Anderson, *The Forgotten Front*, p. 119. Anderson conceded that the British instruction fitted in well with Smuts's own territorial ambitions.

71 Von Lettow-Vorbeck, *My Reminiscences*, p. 138.

72 Hordern, *Military Operations East Africa*, p. 268.

73 National Archives Pretoria (NARSA), Jan Smuts Papers (JSP), Box 300. Personal Papers, Memorandum: The Mozambique Province and the Union of South Africa, undated. The original pencilled map where Smuts has indicated the 'A' and 'B' lines in blue. Smuts's "small" solution he indicated as 'A' while he marked his "bigger" solution as 'B' which takes the border significantly further north, wiping out the entire Portuguese presence in the region! The line (A), running along the Kunene and Zambezi rivers, represents Smuts's First World War expansionist aims, with southern Mozambique and German South West Africa forming part of an expanded Union incorporating the British HCT of Bechuanaland, Swaziland, and Basutoland. Included in the Union is Southern Rhodesia, provided as a fifth province in terms of the South Africa Act 1909.

74 Collyer, *The South Africans with General Smuts*.

75 TNA, CAB 45-43, An Ordinance Officer in East Africa 1914–1916, Letter to Colonel Jennings 30 June 1916, pp. 382, 383. See also TNA, CAB 45-44, Private Diary of Brig-Gen C.P. Fendall January 1915–December 1918, 6 April 1916. p. 24. On the Boer penchant for looting.

76 TNA, CAB 45-44, Private Diary of Brig-Gen C.P. Fendall January 1915–December 1918, 26 June 1916, p. 40.

77 TNA, WO 32-5820 Smuts Dispatch 27 October 1916, p. 14.

78 C. von Clausewitz, *On War* (New York: Random House, 1943), p. 604. See M.N. Vego, *Operational Warfare: Theory and Practice* (New York, Department of the Navy, 2000) pp. 171–5. See also A. H. de Jomini, *The Art of War* (London: Greenhill Books, 1992), p. 102.

79 Von Lettow-Vorbeck, *My Reminiscences*, pp. 138, 139.

80 Collyer, *The South Africans with General Smuts*, pp. 114, 115. See also pp. 138, 139.

81 Collyer, *The South Africans with General Smuts*, pp. 114, 115. See also Strachan, *The First World War in Africa*, p. 144 and Meinertzhagen, *Army Diary*, pp. 186–8. Strachan and Meinertzhagen are convinced that Smuts was determined to avoid a frontal clash and therefore preferred to launch

an attack in the Pare–Usumbara rather than reinforcing Van Deventer and seeking a decisive action there against the bulk of Lettow-Vorbeck's forces.

82 For perspective, in the greatest tank battle in history, the Germans at Kursk in 1943 were expected to cover 240 kilometres from two flanks, while the Schlieffen Plan of 1914 proposed a distance of 450 kilometres at its greatest extent.

83 Anderson, *The Forgotten Front*, p. 122.

84 Strachan, *The First World War in Africa*, p. 145.

85 Meinertzhagen, *Army Diary*, p. 191.

86 Boell, *Die Operationen in Ost-Afrika*, p. 192.

87 TNA, WO 32-5820 Smuts Dispatch 27 October 1916, pp. 16–20.

88 TNA, WO 32-5820 Smuts Dispatch 27 October 1916, pp. 19–21.

89 Strachan, *The First World War in Africa*, p. 144.

90 TNA, WO 32-5820 Smuts Dispatch 27 October 1916, pp. 22–24.

91 Strachan, *The First World War in Africa*, p. 154.

92 TNA, WO 32-5820 Smuts Dispatch 27 October 1916, pp. 25–28.

93 TNA, CAB 24//1/4, Committee of Imperial Defence: Future Operations in East Africa, 12 November 1915. Occupation of the coastal region was the most secure means of denying Lettow-Vorbeck resupply from the sea.

94 Boell, *Die Operationen in Ost-Afrika*, p. 179. The *Maria's* cargo, consisted of four 10.5cm field howitzers, two 7.5cm mountain cannons, six machine guns with riflescopes, four wheeled carriages for the 10.5cm cannons, 2,000 modern rifles, 5,000,000 cartridges, several thousand hand and rifle grenades as well as explosives, medical material, clothing and supplies for 2,000 Europeans and 10,000 sskari, and rations.

95 Collyer, *The South Africans with General Smuts*.

96 Collyer, *The South Africans with General Smuts*, p. 163.

97 TNA, WO 32-5820 Smuts Dispatch 27 October 1916, pp. 29–31.

98 Collyer, *The South Africans with General Smuts*, p. 161.

99 TNA, WO 32-5820 Smuts Dispatch 27 October 1916, pp. 33–7.

100 Collyer, *The South Africans with General Smuts*.

101 TNA, WO 32-5820 Smuts Dispatch 27 October 1916, p. 37,38. See also J.H.V. Crowe, *General Smuts' Campaign in East Africa* (London: John Murray, 1918) p. 197. Strachan describes Crowe "as the best English source for this phase of the operations [in GEA]". Strachan, *The First World War in Africa*, p. 163.

102 Collyer, *The South Africans with General Smuts*, p. 223.

103 TNA, WO 32-5820 Smuts Dispatch 27 October 1916, pp. 45–50.

104 Strachan, *The First World War in Africa*, p. 150.

105 Collyer, *The South Africans with General Smuts*, pp. 188–90.

106 TNA, WO 32-5820 Smuts Dispatch 27 October 1916, pp. 39–44. See also Collyer, *The South Africans with General Smuts*, p. 192.

107 Crowe, *General Smuts' Campaign*, pp. 212–20.

108 Crowe, *General Smuts' Campaign*, p. 209. See also Collyer, *The South Africans with General Smuts*, pp. 224, 241.

109 TNA, WO 106–257, East Africa History Volume IV Chapter II, Precis of Correspondence to Belgian Occupation of Tabora District. The Belgians were decidedly reluctant to hand over Tabora, campaign beyond Tabora or provide soldiers or carriers for Smuts.

110 TNA, WO 33-858, Secret Telegrams January 1915–February 1917, Smuts to CIGS, 6 July 1916.

111 Anderson, *The Forgotten Front*, p. 140.

336 • GENERAL JAN SMUTS AND HIS FIRST WORLD WAR IN AFRICA, 1914–1917

112 TNA, WO 33-858, Secret Telegrams January 1915015–February 1917, CIGS to Smuts, 28 June 1916.

113 Anderson, *The Forgotten Front*, p. 140.

114 TNA, WO 33-858, Secret Telegrams January 1915–February 1917, CIGS to Smuts, 11 July 1916. See TNA, WO 33-858, Secret Telegrams January 1915–February 1917, Smuts to CIGS, 18 July 1916. Smuts suggested the CIGS increase his request to the Belgians to 10 battalions of 600 men each.

115 TNA, CAB 44-6, Draft British Official History, Chapter 14, The Advance to the Rufiji December 1916–February 1917, p. 2. See also Collyer, *The South Africans with General Smuts*, p. 232.

116 TNA, CAB 44-6, Draft British Official History, Chapter 14, The Advance to the Rufiji December 1916–February 1917, p. 1. The Indian formations were also decimated by the hardships of making war in GEA.

117 Strachan, *The First World War in Africa*, p. 156. Strachan, without reference, writes that Northey was "the only British general in East Africa for whom the Germans confessed admiration".

118 TNA, CAB 44-4, Draft British Official History Chapter 1, p. 1.

119 Collyer, *The South Africans with General Smuts*.

120 Collyer, *The South Africans with General Smuts*, p. 232.

121 TNA, CAB 44-4, Draft British Official History Chapter 1, p. 4. See also Collyer, *The South Africans with General Smuts*, p. 232. Collyer estimates Wahle's force at not less than 2,300.

122 TNA, WO 32-5823, Operations in German East Africa: General Smuts Command, Telegram Smuts to CIGS, 21 September 1917.

123 TNA, CAB 44-4, Draft British Official History Chapter 1, pp. 6–8. See also Collyer, *The South Africans with General Smuts*, p. 233.

124 TNA, CAB 44-4, Draft British Official History Chapter 1, p. 9.

125 TNA, CAB 44-4, Draft British Official History Chapter 1, pp. 15–20.

126 Crowe, *General Smuts' Campaign*, p. 248.

127 TNA, CAB 44-6, Draft British Official History, Chapter 14, The Advance to the Rufiji December 1916–February 1917, p. 12. TNA, WO 32-5823, Operations in German East Africa: General Smuts Command, Telegram Smuts to CIGS, 27 September 1917.

128 TNA, CAB 44-6, Draft British Official History, Chapter 14, The Advance to the Rufiji December 1916–February 1917, p. 15.

129 TNA, CAB 44-6, Draft Official British History, Chapter 14, The Advance to the Rufiji December 1916–February 1917, pp. 16–19. It was estimated that the operation would require 7,350 carriers which number was not available. All that remained of the 150,000 carriers recruited at the beginning of the war was 62,234. Recruitment was curtailed by an outbreak of plague and smallpox, and a reluctance of recruits in recently liberated areas to join the Allies for fear of reprisal. The operation would have to rely on the use of light motor vehicles which were susceptible to vagaries of the weather.

130 TNA, CAB 44-6, Draft British Official History, 14, The Advance to the Rufiji December 1916–February 1917, p. 11. See also Collyer, *The South Africans with General Smuts*, p. 248.

131 Strachan, *The First World War in Africa*, p. 163; TNA, CAB 44-6, Draft British Official History, Chapter 14, The Advance to the Rufiji December 1916–February 1917, p. 20. The draft official history describes it "and it was with hope rather than with certainty of a successful result that General Smuts completed his final preparations".

132 Crowe, *General Smuts' Campaign*, p. 252. See also TNA, CAB 44-6, Draft British Official History, Chapter 14, The Advance to the Rufiji December 1916–February 1917, pp. 19–21.

133 TNA, CAB 44-6, Draft British Official History, Chapter 14, The Advance to the Rufiji December 1916–February 1917, p. 36.

134 TNA, CAB 44-6, Draft British Official History, Chapter 14, The Advance to the Rufiji December 1916–February 1917, p. 37.

135 TNA, CAB 45–19, Advance of the 1st East African Brigade to the Rufiji 2 to 4 January 1917, Extract from War Diary, 2–3 January 1917.

136 TNA, CAB 44-6, Draft British Official History, Chapter 14, The Advance to the Rufiji December 1916–February 1917, pp. 38–9.

137 TNA, CAB 45–19, Advance of the 1st East African Brigade to the Rufiji 2 to 4 January 1917, Extract from Sheppard's Diary, 2–3 January 1917.

138 Crowe, *General Smuts' Campaign*, p. 258. See also Collyer, *The South Africans with General Smuts*, pp. 252–9.

139 Collyer, *The South Africans with General Smuts*, p. 257.

140 TNA, CAB 44-6, Draft British Official History, Chapter 14, The Advance to the Rufiji December 1916–February 1917, pp. 46, 47.

141 Collyer, *The South Africans with General Smuts*, pp. 239–46.

142 Collyer, *The South Africans with General Smuts*, p. 246.

143 TNA, CAB 44-6, Draft British Official History, Chapter 14, The Advance to the Rufiji December 1916- February 1917, p. 48.

144 Hordern, *Military Operations East Africa*, p. 515.

145 Collyer, *The South Africans with General Smuts*, pp. 257, 258.

Chapter 8

1 W.K. Hancock, *Smuts: The Sanguine Years 1870–1919* (London: Cambridge University Press, 1962), p. 424

2 NARSA, JSP, Box 198, Folio 199, Letter Smuts to S.M. Smuts, 21 December 1916.

3 NARSA, JSP, Box 198, Folio 203, Letter Smuts to S.M. Smuts, 27 December 1916.

4 B. Nasson, *History Matters* (Cape Town: Penguin Random House, 2016), p. 100.

5 R. Anderson, *The Forgotten Front: The East African Campaign 1914–1918* (Gloucestershire: Tempus, 2004), p. 177.

6 H.C. Armstrong, *Grey Steel* (London: Methuen & Co., 1941), p. 275.

7 Hancock, *Smuts: The Sanguine Years*, p. 424.

8 H. Strachan, *The First World War in Africa* (Oxford: Oxford University Press, 2004), p. 165.

9 L. Amery, *The Leo Amery Diaries Volume I 1896–1929*, ed. by J. Barnes and D. Nicholson (London: Hutchinson & Co., 1980), p. 140 and again p. 141. in diary entry on 6 February 1917, "the future importance, both civil and military, of securing continuous British territory whenever we can".

10 Hancock, *Smuts: The Sanguine Years*, p. 427. Members of Milner's Kindergarten were well placed within the Lloyd George's Cabinet to feel that they could bring considerable influence to bear on decision-making. Milner was a member of the new War Cabinet, Philip Kerr (Lord Lothian) was Lloyd George's personal assistant, and there were groups of the Round Table active in every dominion.

11 Minutes of Round Table meeting, 15–18 January 1910, Lothian Papers, 11, ff. 7–11.

12 Anon, *Greater South Africa: Plans for a Better World. The Speeches of General the Right Honourable J.C. Smuts* (Johannesburg: Truth Legion, 1940). Speech delivered to the members of the House of Commons and House of Lords, 15 May 1917.

13 Anon, *Greater South Africa*, Speech delivered to the members of the House of Commons and House of Lords, 15 May 1917.

14 Anon, *Greater South Africa*, Speech delivered to the members of the House of Commons and House of Lords, 15 May 1917.

15 A. May, 'The Round Table and Imperial Federation, 1910–17', *The Round Table*, 99.410 (2010), p. 553. See also Hancock, *Smuts: The Sanguine Years*, p. 430.

16 Speech by Smuts delivered to the members of the House of Commons and House of Lords 15 May 1917.

17 Hancock, *Smuts: The Sanguine Years*, pp. 426, 427. Altogether there were 14 and 14 sessions of the War Cabinet and War Conference respectively.

18 Amery, *The Leo Amery Diaries*, Letter Amery to M. Hughes 8 January 1917, p. 139. The purpose of the Imperial War Cabinet meetings was to "lay emphasis on the full equality of status between the Dominion Prime Ministers and the Ministers here, and the right of the Dominion Ministers to have the fullest say, and to have it in good time, on the question of terms of Peace we can possibly accept when the time arrives".

19 D. Lloyd George, *War Memoirs of David Lloyd George Volume I* (London: Odhams Press Ltd, 1934), p. 1025.

20 Amery, *The Leo Amery Diaries*, p. 138. Amery had a significant hand in inserting the Imperial component into the War Cabinet meetings. He was also instrumental in setting up the agenda of foreign affairs and peace terms for these meetings. Setting the agenda was a well-oiled tactic of the Round Table in directing their point of view via discussion.

21 Lloyd George, *War Memoirs Volume I*, p. 1032.

22 Lloyd George, *War Memoirs Volume I*, p. 1034.

23 Lloyd George, *War Memoirs Volume I*, p. 1034.

24 Lloyd George, *War Memoirs Volume I*, p. 1050.

25 Lloyd George, *War Memoirs Volume I*, p. 1050.

26 Lloyd George, *War Memoirs Volume I*, p. 1052.

27 Amery, *The Leo Amery Diaries*, p. 140 and again p. 141. At a meeting with Curzon it was decided that neither GSWA nor GEA could possibly be given back to the Germans.

28 Amery, *The Leo Amery Diaries*, p. 152.

29 Lloyd George, *War Memoirs Volume I*, p. 1037.

30 Amery, *The Leo Amery Diaries*, p. 155.

31 NARSA, JSP, Box 201, Folio 106, Letter Milner to Smuts, 12 March 1917.

32 Amery, *The Leo Amery Diaries*, p. 145.

33 See also Hancock, *Smuts: The Sanguine Years*, p. 447.

34 *The Times*, 13 March 1917.

35 Front row (from left): Unknown (Minister without portfolio), Lord Milner (Minister without portfolio), Lord Curzon (Lord President of the Council), A. Bonar Law (Chancellor of the Exchequer), David Lloyd George (Prime Minister of the United Kingdom), Sir Robert Borden (Prime Minister of Canada), W.F. Massey (Prime Minister of New Zealand), **Lt-Gen. J.C. Smuts**. Middle row (from left): Sir S.P. Sinha (Member Designate of the Executive Council of the Government of Bengal), Col the Maharaja Sir Ganga Singh Bahadur (Maharaja of Bikaner, representing the Royal Princes of India), Sir J.S. Meston (Lieutenant Governor of the United Provinces, India), Austen Chamberlain (Secretary of State for India), Lord Robert Cecil (Secretary of State for Foreign Affairs), Walter Long (Secretary of State for the Colonies), Sir Joseph Ward (Finance Minister of New Zealand), G.H. Perley (Minister of the Overseas Forces of Canada), R. Rodgers (Minister of Public Works, Canada), J.D. Hazen (Minister of Marine and Fisheries, and of the Naval Service, Canada). Back row (from left): Captain L.S. Amery (Assistant Secretary, IWC), Admiral Sir John Jellicoe (First Sea Lord), Sir Edward Carson (First Lord of the Admiralty), Lord Derby (Secretary of State for War), Maj-Gen. F.B. Maurice (Director of Military Operations,

War Office), Lt-Col Sir Maurice Hankey (Secretary to the IWC), H.C.M. Lambert (Secretary to the Imperial War Conference), Maj L. Storr (Assistant Secretary, IWC), Imperial War Museum, The Imperial War Cabinet, 1 May 1917, www.iwm.org.uk/collections/item/object/205124978 accessed 20 October 2018.

36 Hancock, *Smuts: The Sanguine Years*, p. 432.

37 Amery, *The Leo Amery Diaries*, Letter Amery to Milner 24 May 1917, p. 157.

38 Amery, *The Leo Amery Diaries*, Diary entry 14 April 1917, p. 140. and again p. 149. Amery and Curzon again had a discussion over Smuts on 20 April 1917 over the possibility of including Smuts in the War Cabinet on personal grounds and not as a representative of the dominions.

39 Lloyd George, *War Memoirs Volume I*, p.1046.

40 Amery, *The Leo Amery Diaries*, Diary entry 23 April 1917, p. 150 On 24 April 1917 Smuts was asked by Hankey on behalf of the War Cabinet to give his views on the strategic situation; this was the first time he had been asked straightforwardly for guidance.

41 Amery, *The Leo Amery Diaries*, p. 150.

42 Hancock, *Smuts: The Sanguine Years*, pp. 439–43.

43 D. Lloyd George, *War Memoirs of David Lloyd George 1916–1917 Volume III* (Boston: Little Brown & Co., 1934), p. 437.

44 Hancock, *Smuts: The Sanguine Years*, p. 452.

45 Hancock, *Smuts: The Sanguine Years*, p. 450.

46 Lloyd George, *War Memoirs Volume III*, p. 437.

47 J.C. Smuts, *Jan Christian Smuts* (London: Cassel & Co., 1952), p. 202.

48 Lloyd George, *War Memoirs Volume I*, p. 814.

49 Lloyd George, *War Memoirs Volume I*, p. 815.

50 Hancock, *Smuts: The Sanguine Years,* p. 456.

51 D. Lloyd George, *War Memoirs of David Lloyd George 1917 Volume IV* (Boston: Little Brown & Co., 1934), p. 66.

52 Hancock, *Smuts: The Sanguine Years,* p. 434.

53 Lloyd George, *War Memoirs Volume IV*, p. 91.

54 Leo Amery was the principal correspondent for *The Times* in the Second Anglo-Boer War of 1899–1902. He became a commentator on military affairs. He became a member of the Milner Kindergarten and became lifelong friends with Bob Brand, Lionel Curtis, and John Buchan. He was also powerfully influenced by Cecil John Rhodes. On his return to England after the Anglo-Boer War, he worked tirelessly to build an effective Imperial union united in defence, trade and investment, and foreign affairs. He was contemptuous of Asquith's war leadership and spent the early war years on active service. When Lloyd George came to power in December 1917, Amery was made Assistant Secretary to the War Cabinet where he wielded great influence.

55 NARSA, JSP, Box 199, Folio 2, Letter Amery to Smuts, 15 March 1917.

56 Hancock, *Smuts: The Sanguine Years*, p. 435.

57 NARSA, JSP, Box 202, Folio 2, Letter Smuts to S.M. Smuts, 27 April 1917.

58 NARSA, JSP, Box 199, Folio 67, Letter Botha to S.M. Smuts, (Annexure A, Smuts to Botha, 24 April 1917), 4 May 1917.

59 NARSA, JSP, Box 199, Folio 67, Letter Botha to S.M. Smuts, (Annexure B, Botha to Smuts, 26 April 1917), 4 May 1917.

60 NARSA, JSP, Box 199, Folio 67, Letter Botha to S.M. Smuts, (Annexure C, Smuts to Botha, 1 May 1917), 4 May 1917.

61 Lloyd George, *War Memoirs Volume IV*, p. 92.

62 Amery, *The Leo Amery Diaries*, p. 158.

63 Amery, *The Leo Amery Diaries*, p. 159. Milner seems also to have dissuaded Smuts.

64 Smuts, *Jan Christian Smuts*, p. 203.

65 Hancock, *Smuts: The Sanguine Years*, p. 435.

66 Lloyd George, *War Memoirs Volume IV*, p. 93.

67 Hancock, *Smuts: The Sanguine Years*, pp. 435, 436.

68 A prominent Scottish political writer and businessman and important member of the Round Table. He and other members of the Round Table were instrumental in the removal of Asquith and his replacement by Lloyd George.

69 E.S. Crafford, *Jan Smuts: A Biography* (New York: Doubleday, Doron & Co. Inc, 1943) p. 125.

70 Lloyd George, *War Memoirs Volume IV*, p. 94.

71 Smuts, *Jan Christian Smuts*, pp. 203–8.

72 Crafford, *Jan Smuts*, p. 125.

73 Amery, *The Leo Amery Diaries*, Diary entry 19 May 1917, p. 156.

74 F.S. Crafford, *Jan Smuts: A Biography* (New York: Doubleday, Doron & Co. Inc, 1943) p. 126.

75 F.S. Crafford, *Jan Smuts: A Biography* (New York: Doubleday, Doron & Co. Inc, 1943) p. 125.

76 Crafford, *Jan Smuts*, pp. 128, 129.

77 Lloyd George, *War Memoirs Volume IV*, p. 106.

78 Lloyd George, *War Memoirs Volume IV*, pp. 106–9. See also Hancock, *Smuts: The Sanguine Years*, pp. 439–43.

79 Lloyd George, *War Memoirs Volume IV*, pp. 110–115. See also Hancock, *Smuts: The Sanguine Years*, pp. 439–43.

80 Lloyd George, *War Memoirs Volume IV*, p. 118.

81 Crafford, *Jan Smuts*, pp. 130, 131.

82 Lloyd George, *War Memoirs Volume IV*, p. 119.

83 H.A. Jones, *The War in the Air Volume VI* (London: Oxford University Press, 1937) pp. 8–11.

84 H.A. Jones, Appendix VI 'Report of Lieutenant-General J. C. Smuts's Committee, July 1817', *The War in the Air Volume V*, (London: Oxford University Press, 1935) p. 487.

85 H.A. Jones, *The War in the Air Volume V* (London: Oxford University Press, 1935) p. 43. Sir David Henderson, in a memorandum to Lt-Gen Smuts on the 16th of July, had said: 'I would suggest that the whole of our defences against air attack, observation, communication, aeroplanes and guns, should be organized under a single command. As the aeroplane is by far the most important means of defence, the commander should be an officer of the Royal Flying Corps. It is desirable that he should still be under the general command of the C.-in-C, Home forces.'

86 Lloyd George, *War Memoirs Volume IV*, pp. 119, 120.

87 Lloyd George, *War Memoirs Volume IV*, p. 120.

88 H.A. Jones, *The War in the Air Volume VI* (London: Oxford University Press, 1937) p. 11. See also Hancock, *Smuts: The Sanguine Years*, p. 438. Lloyd George in his memoirs revealed that Smuts had a claim to be called father of the Royal Air Force more than any other man.

89 Lloyd George, *War Memoirs Volume IV*, p. 121.

90 G. Douhet, *The Command of The Air* (Washington: Air Force History and Museums Program, 1998). This book was originally published in 1922 but Douhet had formulated much of his doctrine by 1915.

91 H.A. Jones, *The War in the Air Volume VI* (London: Oxford University Press, 1937) p. 13.

92 H.A. Jones, *The War in the Air Volume V* (London: Oxford University Press, 1935) p. 64.

93 D. Lloyd Geroge, *War Memoirs of David Lloyd George Volume II* (London: Odhams Press Ltd, 1936) p. 1477.

94 Lloyd George, *War Memoirs Volume II*, p. 1478. See also Hancock, *Smuts: The Sanguine Years*, pp. 465–8.

95 Lloyd George, *War Memoirs Volume II*, pp. 1478, 1479–90. See also NARSA, JSP, Box N, Folio 78. Political Notes by Smuts 1899–1950. See also Hancock, *Smuts: The Sanguine Years*, pp. 465–8.

96 Lloyd George, *War Memoirs Volume II*, pp. 1478, 1499–502. See also Hancock, *Smuts: The Sanguine Years*, pp. 465–8.

97 Hancock, *Smuts: The Sanguine Years*, p. 473.

98 Hancock, *Smuts: The Sanguine Years*, pp. 482–4.

99 A. Lentin, *Jan Smuts: Man of Courage and Vision* (Johannesburg & Cape Town: Jonathan Ball, 2010) pp. 49–59.

100 R. Hyam, *The Failure of South African Expansion, 1908–1948* (Lndon: Macmillan, 1972) p. 32.

101 NARSA, JSP, Box 300 (4) Box G, J. Smuts, Smuts Mozambique, Memorandum War Cabinet, undated; S. Katzenellenbogen, *South Africa and Southern Mozambique: Labour, Railways, and Trade in the Making of a Relationship* (Manchester: Manchester University, 1982) pp. 121, 122.

102 NARSA, JSP, Box 300 (4) Box G, J. Smuts, Smuts Mozambique, Memorandum War Cabinet, undated.

103 NARSA, JSP, Box 300 (4) Box G, J. Smuts, Smuts Mozambique, Memorandum War Cabinet, undated.

104 NARSA, JSP, Box 300 (4) Box G, J. Smuts, Smuts Mozambique, Memorandum War Cabinet, undated.

105 NARSA, JSP, Box 300 (4) Box G, J. Smuts, Smuts Mozambique, Memorandum War Cabinet, undated.

106 NARSA, JSP, Box 300 (4) Box G, J. Smuts, Smuts Mozambique, Memorandum War Cabinet, undated.

107 G. Stone, 'No Way to Treat an Ancient Ally: Britain and the Portuguese Connection, 1919–1933', *Peacemaking, Peacemakers and Diplomacy, 1880–1939: Essays in Honour of Professor Alan Sharp*, ed. by K. Hamilton and P. Salmon (Newcastle upon Tyne: Cambridge Scholars Publications, 2010) p. 13.

108 Katzenellenbogen, *South Africa and Southern Mozambique*, p. 121.

109 Stone, 'No Way to Treat an Ancient Ally', p. 10.

110 E.B. Robertson and T.C. Dawson (eds), *J.C. Smuts, Greater South Africa: Plans for a Better World*, (Johannesburg: Truth Legion, 1940) p. 19.

111 TNA, DO 35/903/3, Mr G. Heaton Nicholls address to the Study Committee of the Empire Parliamentary Association at Westminster Hall, 16 November 1938.

112 Robertson, *J.C. Smuts, Greater South Africa*, p. 25.

113 TNA, CAB 23/4/279, Minutes of a Meeting of the War Cabinet, 21, November 1917. This was in response to a suggestion made by General van Deventer that he offer surrender terms to Von Lettow-Vorbeck, bolstered by an announcement that the German colonies would not be returned to Germany after the war.

114 P.J. Yearwood, 'Great Britain and the Repartition of Africa, 1914 –1919', *The Journal of Imperial and Commonwealth History*, 18(3) (1990) p. 317.

115 NARSA, JSP Box 196(143A), J. Smuts, Memorandum Smuts to Reitz, September 1914.

116 The Great War blog, ww1blog.osborneink.com/?p=1485 accessed 10 December 2017.

117 NARSA, JSP, Private Papers Box 300, The German Colonies at the Peace Conference, undated.

118 NARSA, JSP, Private Papers Box 300, The German Colonies at the Peace Conference, undated.

119 NARSA, JSP, Private Papers Box 300, The German Colonies at the Peace Conference, undated.

120 NARSA, JSP, Private Papers Box 300, The German Colonies at the Peace Conference, undated.

121 N.G. Garson, 'South Africa and World War I', *The Journal of Imperial and Commonwealth History*, 8(1) (1979) p. 80.

122 Yearwood, 'Great Britain and the Repartition of Africa', p. 321.

123 T.R. Getz, 'Smuts and the Politics of Colonial Expansion: South African Strategy in Regard to South-West Africa [Namibia] and the League of Nations Mandate: c. 1914–1924', (MA thesis, University of Cape Town, n.d.) pp. 50–4.

124 *The South West Africa/Namibia Dispute: Documents and Scholarly Writings on the Controversy Between South Africa and the United Nations*, ed. by J. Dugard (Los Angeles: University of California, 1973) p. 38.

125 NARSA, JSP Box 206(200), J. Smuts, Smuts German South-West Africa, Memorandum Smuts to Gillet, January 1919.

126 T.R. Getz, 'Smuts and the Politics of Colonial Expansion: South African Strategy in Regard to South-West Africa [Namibia] and the League of Nations Mandate: c. 1914–1924', (MA thesis, University of Cape Town, n.d.) pp. 64, 65.

127 T. Dedering, 'South Africa and the Italo-Ethiopian War, 1935–6', *The International History Review* (2013) p. 8.

128 NARSA, JSP Box 206(145), J. Smuts, Versailles Conference, Letter Smuts to Wife, July 1919; P.R. Warhurst, 'Smuts and Africa: a Study in Sub-Imperialism', *South African Historical Journal*, 16,1 (1984) p. 86.

129 NARSA, JSP Box 300 (4), J. Smuts, Delagoa Bay, Memorandum, undated; NARSA, JSP Box 300(5), J. Smuts, Delagoa Bay, Memorandum, undated; Katzenellenbogen, *South Africa and Southern Mozambique*, pp. 122, 123. See TNA, DO 35/904/2, Rhodesia Nyasaland Royal Commissions Report, 31 July 1939.

130 Robertson, *J.C. Smuts, Greater South Africa*, p. 20.

131 NARSA, JSP Box 197 (154), J. Smuts, East Africa Exchange, Memorandum Smuts to Merriman, August 1915; I. van der Waag, 'All splendid, but horrible: The Politics of South Africa's Second "Little Bit" and the War on the Western Front, 1915–1918', *Scientia Militaria*, 40(3) (2012) p. 80.

132 Yearwood, 'Great Britain and the Repartition of Africa', p. 321; Hyam, *The Failure of South African Expansion*, pp. 27,28.

133 NARSA, JSP, Box 300 (4) Box G, J. Smuts, Smuts Mozambique, Memorandum War Cabinet, undated. See also Hancock, *Smuts: The Sanguine Years*, pp. 408, 437.

134 P. Lewsen (ed.), *Selections From the Corrospondence of John X. Merriman 1905–1924*, (Cape Town: Van Riebeck Society, 1969) p. 280; A. Samson, *Britain, South Africa and the East Africa Campaign, 1914–1918* (London: Tauris, 2006) p. 130.

135 NARSA, JSP Box 203 (28), L. Botha, Botha on Mozambique, Memorandum Botha to Smuts, February 1918.

136 John Leipoldt was promoted to the temporary rank of major on 12 March 1915 and appointed as Chief Intelligence Officer of the Union in May 1915. He was then, with effect from 20 August 1915, attached to the personal staff of Louis Botha. I. van der Waag, 'Major J.G.W. Leipoldt, D.S.O. : A Portrait of a South African Surveyor and Intelligence Officer, 1912–1923', *Scientia Militaria*, 25 (1995) pp. 12–34.

137 DODA, DC Group, Box 356, J. Leipoldt, Letter to the Adjutant General (Intelligence Report, 1917).

138 Samson, *Britain, South Africa*, pp. 138, 139; Yearwood, 'Great Britain and the Repartition of Africa', p. 321.

139 TNA, CAB/23/4, War Cabinet 279, 21 November 1917).

140 Samson, *Britain, South Africa*, pp. 147, 158.

Sources

Books

Adams, G., *King's African Rifles Soldier versus Schutztruppe Soldier: East Africa 1917–18* (Oxford: Osprey Publishing, 2016).

Anderson, R., *The Battle of Tanga, 2–5 November 1914* (Stroud: Tempus, 2001).

Anderson, R., *The Forgotten Front: The East African Campaign 1914–1918* (Gloucestershire: Tempus, 2004).

Anon, A *Study of the War in German East Africa 1914–1918* (Command and General Staff School Fort Leavenworth, 1930).

Anon, *Army Council, Field Service Regulations: Operations* (Edinburgh, His Majesty's Stationery Office, 1909).

Anon, *Combined Training* (London, War Office, 1905).

Anon, *Greater South Africa: Plans for a Better World. The Speeches of General the Right Honourable J.C. Smuts* (Johannesburg: Truth Legion, 1940).

Anon, *Infantry Training (Provisional)* (London, War Office, 1902).

Armstrong, H.C., *Grey Steel: A Study in Arrogance* (London: Methuen & Co., 1941).

Baily, J., *The First World War and the Birth of the Modern Style of Warfare* (Camberley, Strategic and Combat Studies Institute, 1996).

Barnes, L., *The New Boer War* (London: Hogarth Press,1932).

Baxter, P., *Gandhi, Smuts and Race in the British Empire* (South Yorkshire: Pen & Sword, 2017).

Beca, A., *Study of the Development of Infantry Tactics* (London: George Allen & Unwin Ltd, 1915).

Beckett, F.W. (ed), *Rommel Reconsidered* (Mechanicsburg: Stackpole, 2013).

Beukes, P., *The Religious Smuts* (Cape Town: Human & Rousseu, 1994).

Beukes, P., *Smuts the Botanist* (Cape Town: Human & Rousseu, 1996).

Beukes, P., *The Holistic Smuts: A Study in Personality* (Cape Town: Human & Rousseu, 1989).

Beukes, P., *The Romantic Smuts* (Cape Town: Human & Rousseu, 1992).

Beyers, C.J., and J.L. Basson (eds), *Dictionary of South African Biography Volume V* (Pretoria: Human Sciences Research Council, 1987).

Bidwell, S. and D. Graham, *Fire-Power: The British Army Weapons & Theories of War 1904–1945* (Barnsley: Pen & Sword, 2004).

Blackwell, L., *African Occasions: Reminiscences of Thirty Years of Bar, Bench, and Politics in South Africa* (London: Hutchinson & Co, 1938).

Blackwell, L., *Blackwell Remembers: An Autobiography* (Cape Town: Howard Timmins, 1971).

Blanckenberg, P.B., *The Thoughts of General Smuts* (Cape Town: Juta & Co, 1951).

Bourhill, J., *Return to Morogoro: With the South African Horse Through East Africa to France and Flanders 1914–1918* (Pinetown: 30 Degrees South, 2015).

Boydell, T., *My Luck Was In: With Spotlights on General Smuts* (Cape Town: Stewart, 1948).

Brits, J.P. (ed), *Diary of a National Scout P.J. Du Toit 1900–1902* (Pretoria: Human Sciences Research Council, 1974).

Brown, R., *The Secret Society: Cecil John Rhodes's Plan for a New World Order* (Cape Town: Penguin, 2015).

Buchanan, A., *The Lean Brown Men: Experiences in East Africa During the Great War* (London: Leonaur, 2008).

Buxton, E., *General Botha* (New York: E.P. Dutton & Company, 1924).

Callwell, C.E., *Small Wars: Their Principles and Practice* (London: General Staff War Office, 1906)

Callwell, C.E., *Small Wars: A Tactical Textbook for Imperial Soldiers* (London: HMSO, 1896).

Cannadine, D., *Ornamentalism: How the British Saw Their Empire* (New York: Oxford University Press, 2001).

Chanock, M., *Britain, Rhodesia and South Africa 1900–1945: The Unconsummated Union* (Totawa: Frank Cass & Company Limited, 1977).

Chemers, M.M., *An Integrative Theory of Leadership* (np, Lawrence Erlbaum Associates, 1997).

Child, D., *C. Smythe: Pioneer, Premier and Administrator of Natal* (Cape Town: Struik, 1973).

Citino, R.M., *Death of the Wehrmacht: The German Campaigns of 1942* (Kansas, University Press of Kansas, 2007).

Citino, R.M., *The Path to Blitzkrieg: Doctrine and Training in the German Army, 1920–39* (Mechanicsburg, Stackpole, 1999).

Close, P.L., *A Prisoner of the Germans in South-West Africa* (Cape Town: T. Maskew Miller).

Corvisier, A., *Armies and Societies in Europe, 1494–1789* (Bloomington: Indiana University Press, 1979).

Crafford, E.S. *Jan Smuts: A Biography* (New York: Doubleday, Doron & Co. Inc, 1943).

Cronwright-Schreiner, S.C., *The Life of Olive Schreiner* (Boston: Little, Brown & Company, 1924).

Crow, C.L., *Tactical and Operational Depth* (School of Advanced Military Studies, U.S. Army Command and General Staff College, Fort Leavenworth, Kansas, 1986).

Cruise, A., *Louis Botha's War: The Campaign in German South-West Africa, 1914–1915* (Cape Town: Zebra Press, 2015).

Davenport, T.R.H., *South Africa: A Modern History* (Johannesburg: Macmillan, 2017).

De Jomini, A.H., *The Art of War* (London: Greenhill Books, 1992).

De Kiewiet, C.W., *The Anatomy of South African Misery* (London: Oxford University, 1856).

De Kock, W.J. (ed) *Dictionary of South African Biography Volume I* (Cape Town: Tafelberg, 1968).

De Kock, W.J. and D.W. Kruger (eds), *Dictionary of South African Biography Volume II* (Cape Town: Tafelberg, 1972).

De Wet, C.R., *Three Years' War* (Johannesburg: Galago, 1986).

Dolbey, R.V. *The Bush War Doctor: The Experiences of a British Army Doctor During the East African Campaign of the First World War* (London: Leonaur, 2007).

Douhet, G., *The Command of The Air* (Washington: Air Force History and Museums Program, 1998).

Downs, H., *Chasing von Lettow-Vorbeck: The Story of Harold Downs' Great War Service in East Africa* (Lincoln: Tucann, 2012).

Doyle, A.C., *The Great Boer War* (1902).

Du Pisani, K., D. Kriek, and C. De Jager (eds) *Jan Smuts: Van Boerseun Tot Wereldverhoog* (Pretoria: Protea, 2017).

Dubow, S., *Scientific Racism in Modern South Africa* (New York: Cambridge University, 1995).

Dugard, J. (ed), *The South West Africa / Namibia Dispute: Documents and Scholarly Writings on the Controversy Between South Africa and the United Nations* (Los Angeles: University of California, 1973).

Dupuy, T.N., *Understanding War* (New York: Paragon House Publishers, 1987).

Engelenburg, F.V., *General Loius Botha* (Pretoria: J.L. van Schaik Limited, 1929).

Farwell, B., *The Great War in Africa, 1914–1918* (New York: W.W. Norton & Company, 1986).

Fendall, C.P., *The East African Force 1915–1919: The First World War in Colonial Africa* (London: Leonaur, 2014).

Friedman, B., *Smuts: A Reappraisal* (Johannesburg: Hugh Keartland, 1975).

Fuller, J.F.C., *Generalship: Its Diseases and Their Cure* (Harrisburg: Military Service Publishing Company, 1936).

Fuller, J.F.C., *The Foundations of the Science of War* (London: Hutchinson & Co, 1925).

Garcia A., *The First Campaign Victory of the Great War* (Warwick: Helion & Company Limited, 2019).

Gardner, B., *German East: The Story of the First World War in East Africa* (London: Cassel, 1963).

Garfield, B., *The Meinertzhagen Mystery: The Life and Legend of a Colossal Fraud* (Washington: Potomac Books, 2007).

Giliomee, H., *The Afrikaners* (Cape Town: Tafelberg, 2003).

Glantz, D.M., *Soviet Military Operational Art: In Pursuit of Deep Battle* (New York: Frank Cass and Company Limited, 1991).

Grey (ed), J., *The Last Word?: Essays on Official History in the United States and British Commonwealth*, (London: Praeger, 2003).

Grundlingh, A., *Fighting Their Own War* (Johannesburg: Ravan, 1987).

Grundlingh, A.M. and S.S. Swart, *Radelose Rebeellie: Dinamika Van Die 1914–1915 Afrikanerrebellie* (Pretoria: Protea, 2009).

Grundlingh, A., *War and Society Participation and Rememberance: South African Black and Coloured Troops in the First World War, 1914–1918* (Stellenbosch: Sun Media, 2014).

Guderian, H., *Panzer Leader* (London: Futura Publication, 1979).

Halder, F., *Analysis of U.S. Field Service Regulations, MS No. P–133* (Historical Division, United States Army Europe, 1953).

Hale. J. R., *War and Society in Renaissance Europe, 1450–1620* (London: Fontana Press 1985).

Hancock, W.K., *Smuts: The Fields of Force 1919–1950* (London: Cambridge University Press, 1968).

Hancock, W.K., *Smuts: The Sanguine Years 1870–1919* (London: Cambridge University Press, 1962).

Hankey, M., *The Supreme Command* (London: Routledge, 1961).

Hewison, H.H., *Hedge of Wild Almonds: South Africa, the 'Pro-Boers' & the Quaker Conscience* (London: James Currey, 1989).

Hodges, G., *Kariakor: The Carrier Corps* (Nairobi: Nairobi University Press, 1999).

Hofmeyr, J.H. and F.W. Reitz, *The Life of Jan Hendrik Hofmeyr (Onze Jan)* (Cape Town: Van der Sandt, 1913).

Hoyt, E.P., *Guerilla: Colonel von Lettow-Vorbeck and Germany's East African Empire* (London: Macmillan, 1981).

Hyam, R. and P. Henshaw, *The Lion and The Springbok: Britain and South Africa since the Boer War* (Cambridge: Cambridge University Press, 2003).

Hyam, R., *The Failure of South African Expansion, 1908–1948* (London: Macmillan, 1972)

Hyam, R., *Understanding the British Empire* (Cambridge: Cambridge University Press, 2010).

Ingham, K., *Jan Christian Smuts: The Conscience of a South African* (Johannesburg: Jonathan Ball, 1986).

Johnston, M.A., *Ulundi to Delville Wood: The Life Story of Major-General Sir Henry Timson Lukin* (Cape Town: Maskew Miller Limited, 1929).

Jones, A., *The Art of War in the Western World* (London: Harrap Limited, 1988).

Jones, H.A., *The War in the Air Volume V* (London: Oxford University Press, 1935).

Jones, H.A., *The War in the Air Volume VI* (London: Oxford University Press, 1937).

Jones, S., *From Boer War to World War* (Norman: University of Oklahoma Press, 2012).

Katzenellenbogen, S., *South Africa and Southern Mozambique: Labour, Railways, and Trade in the Making of a Relationship* (Manchester: Manchester University, 1982).

Keegan, J., *The Face of Battle* (Harmonds: Worth: Penguin 1983).

Keegan, J., *The Mask of Command: A Study of Generalship* (London: Pimlico, 1999).

Kraus, R., *Old Master* (New York: Dutton, E. P., 1944).

Kruger, D.W. and C.J. Beyers (eds), *Dictionary of South African Biography Volume II* (Cape Town: Tafelberg, 1977).

Kruger, D.W. and C.J. Beyers (eds), *Dictionary of South African Biography Volume III* (Cape Town: Tafelberg, 1977).

Kruger, P., *The Memoirs of Paul Kruger* (New York: The Century Co, 1902).

Le May, G.H.L., *British Supremacy in South Africa* (London: Oxford University Press, 1965).

Le Riche, P.J., *Memoirs of General Ben Bouwer* (Pretoria: Human Sciences Research Council, 1980).

Lentin, A., *Jan Smuts: Man of Courage and Vision* (Johannesburg & Cape Town: Jonathan Ball, 2010).

Levi, N., *Jan Smuts* (London: Longmans Green & Co., 1917).

Liddell Hart, B.H., *Strategy* (New York: New American Library, 1974).

Liebenberg B.J., S.B. Spies (eds) *South Africa in the 20th Century* (Pretoria: J.L. van Schaik, 1994).

Lloyd George, D., *War Memoirs of David Lloyd George* (London: Odhams Press Ltd, 1938).

Lloyd George, D., *War Memoirs of David Lloyd George Volume I* (London: Odhams Press Ltd, 1934).

Lloyd George, D., *War Memoirs of David Lloyd George Volume II* (London: Odhams Press Ltd, 1936).

Lloyd George, D., *War Memoirs of David Lloyd George 1916–1917 Volume III* (Boston: Little Brown & Company, 1934).

Lloyd George, D., *War Memoirs of David Lloyd George 1917 Volume IV* (Boston: Little Brown & Company, 1934).

Lloyd, A. W., *"Jambo", or With Jannie in the Jungle* (Cape Town: Central News Agency, n.d.).

Lukin, H.T., *Savage Warfare: Hints on Tactics to be Adopted and Precautions to be Taken* (Cape Town: Cape Times Ltd, 1906).

Marais, A.H. (ed), *Politieke Briewe, II: 1911–1912, J.X. Merriman to M.T. Steyn*, 16 January 1911, (Bloemfontein: Tafelberg, 1973).

Maritz, M., *My Lewe En Strewe* (NA: NA, 1939).

Martin, A.C., *The Durban Light Infantry 1854–1934* (Durban: The Regimental Asociation DLI, 1969).

Maurice, F. (ed), *History of the War in South Africa, 1899–1902, Volume IV* (London, 1905).

Maxwell, R.M., *Jimmie Stewart: Frontiersman* (Durham: Pentland Press, 1992).

Meinertzhagen, R., *Army Diary 1899–1926* (Edinburgh: Oliver & Boyd, 1960).

Meiring, P., *Smuts the Patriot* (Cape Town: Tafelberg, 1975)

Miller, C., *Battle for the Bundu: The First World War in East Africa* (London: Purnell, 1974).

Millin, S.G., *General Smuts Volume I* (Safety Harbor: Simon Publications, 2001).

Millin, S.G., *Rhodes* (London: Chatto & Windus, 1933).

Moore R. and J.P. Robinson, *Two Views of the South-West African Campaign 1914–1915* (London: Leonaur, 2013).

Mosley, L., *Duel for Kilimanjaro: An Account of the East African Campaign* (New York: Ballantine, 1964).

Moyd, M.R., *Violent Intermediaries: African Soldiers, Conquest, and Everyday Colonialism in German East Africa* (Athens: Ohio University Press, 2014).

Muth, J., *Command Culture* (Denton: University of North Texas, 2011).

Nasson, B., *Springboks on the Somme* (Johannesburg: Penguin, 2007).

Nasson, B., *WWI and the People of South Africa* (Cape Town: Tafelberg, 2014).

Nasson, B., *History Matters* (Cape Town: Penguin Random House, 2016).

Olsen, J. A. and M. van Creveld (eds), *The Evolution of Operational Art: From Napoleon to the Present* (Oxford: Oxford University Press, 2011).

Olusogo, D., *The World's War* (London: Head of Zeus, 2014).

Page, M.E. (ed), *Africa and the First World War* (London: Macmillan Press, 1987).

Page, M.E., *The Chiwaya War: Malawians and the First World War* (Oxford: Westview Press, 2000).

Paice, E., *Tip and Run: The Untold Tragedy of the First World War in Africa* (London: Phoenix, 2008).

Pakenham, T., *The Scramble for Africa* (Jeppestown: Jonathan Ball, 1997).

Pakenham, T., *The Boer War* (London, Futura, 1982).

Pedersen, P.A., *Monash as Military Commander* (Carlton Victoria: Melbourne University Press, 1985).

Pirow, O., *James Barry Munnik Hertzog* (Cape Town: Howard Timmins, 1958).

Povlock, P.A., *Deep Battle in World War One: The British 1918 Offensive in Palestine* (Naval War College Newport, 1997).

Pretorius, P.J., *Jungle Man: The Autobiography of Major P.J. Pretorius* (Alexander City: Alexander Books, 2001).

Quigley, C., *The Anglo-American Establishment* (San Pedro: GSG & Associates, 1981).

Quigley, C., *The Anglo-American Establishment from Rhodes to Cliveden* (New York, 1981).

Rainer, P.W., *African Hazard* (London: Butler & Tanner, 1940).

Rayner, W.S. and W.W. O'Shaughnessy, *How Botha and Smuts Conquered German South West* (London: Simpson, Marshall, Hamilton, Kent & Co., 1916).

Reitz, D., *Trekking On: In the Company of Brave Men* (Edinburgh: The House of Emslie, 2012).

Robertson, E.B. and T.C. Dawson (eds)., *J.C. Smuts, Greater South Africa: Plans for a Better World* (Johannesburg: Truth Legion, 1940).

Said, E.W. *Orientalism* (New York: Vintage Books, 1979).

Samson, A., *World War I in Africa: The Forgotten Conflict Among the European Power* (London: Tauris, 2013).

Samson, A., *Britain, South Africa and the East Africa Campaign, 1914–1918* (London: Tauris, 2006).

Samson A., *Kitchener: The Man Not the Myth* (Warwick: Helion, 2020).

Samuels, M., *Command or Control* (London: Frank Cass & Company Limited, 1995).

Schikkerling, R.W., *Commando Courageous* (Johannesburg: Hugh Keartland, 1964).

Schnee, H., *Deutsch-Ostafrika im Weltkriege. Wie wir lebten und kämpften* (Leipzig: Quelle & Meyer, 1919).

Scholtz, L., *Why the Boers Lost the War* (London: Palgrave Macmillan, 2005).

Searle, A., F.W. Beckett (ed), *Rommel Reconsidered* (Mechanicsburg: Stackpole, 2013).

Selborne, W.W.P., *The Selborne Memorandum on the Union of South Africa 1908* (London: Oxford University Press, 1925).

Sibley, J.R., *Tanganyikan Guerrilla* (London: Pan Books, 1973).

Simpkin, R., *Deep Battle: The Brainchild of Marshal Tukhachevskii* (New Delhi: Natraj Publishers, 2012).

Simpkins, B.G., *Rand Light Infantry* (Cape Town: Howard Timmins, 1965).

Smith, D.W., *The German Colonial Empire* (Chapel Hill: The University of North Carolina Press, 1978).

Smuts, J.C., *A Century of Wrong* (London: Review of Reviews, 1900).

Smuts, J.C., *Holism and Evolution* (London: Macmillan and Co., 1927).

Smuts, J.C., *Jan Christian Smuts* (London: Cassel & Company, 1952).

Smuts, J.C., *Jan Smuts: Memoirs of the Boer War*, eds S.B. Spies and G. Nattrass (Johannesburg: Jonathan Ball, 1994).

Spencer, H., *The Study of Sociology* (New York: D. Appleton & Company, 1896).

Stapleton, T.J., *A Military History of South Africa from the Dutch–Khoi Wars to the End of Apartheid* (Santa Barbara: Praeger, 2010).

Stejskal, J., *The Horns of the Beast: The Swakop River Campaign and World War I in South-West Africa 1914–1915* (Solihull: Helion & Company, 2014).

Steyn, R., *Jan Smuts: Unafraid of Greatness* (Johannesburg & Cape Town: Jonathan Ball, 2015).

Strachan, H., *The First World War in Africa* (Oxford: Oxford University Press, 2004).

Stuart, J., *A History of the Zulu Rebellion 1906* (London: Macmillan & Co., 1913).

Tamarkin, M., *Cecil Rhodes and the Cape Afrikaners: The Imperial Colossus and the Colonial Parish Pump* (Johannesburg: Jonathan Ball, 1996).

Thompson, P.S., *Incident at Trewirgie: First Shots of the Zulu Rebellion 1906* (Pietermaritzburg: P.S. Thompson, 2005).

Trew, H.F., *Botha Treks* (London: Blackie & Son, 1936).

Tylden, G., *The Armed Forces of South Africa 1659–1954* (Johannesburg: Trophy Press, 1982).

Uys, I., *South African Military Who's Who 1452–1992* (Germiston: Forttress, 1992).

Van Creveld, M., *Air Power and Manoeuvre Warfare* (Alabama: Air University Press, 1997).

Van den Heever, C.M., *General J.B.M Hertzog* (Johannesburg: APB Bookstone, 1946).

Van der Byl, P., *From Playgrounds to Battlefields* (Cape Town: Howard Timmins, 1971).

Van der Waag, I., *A Military History of Modern South Africa* (Cape Town: Jonathan Ball, 2015).

Vego, M.N., *Operational Warfare: Theory and Practice* (New York: Department of the Navy, 2000).

Von Clausewitz, C., *On War* (New York: Random House, 1943).

Von Lettow-Vorbeck, P.E., *My Reminiscences of East Africa* (London: Hurst & Blackett, 1922).

Von Lettow-Vorbeck, P., *Heia Safari! Deutschlands Kampf in Ostafrika* (Leipzig: Hase & Köhler, 1920).

Von Lettow-Vorbeck, P., *Mein Leben* (Biberach an der Riss: Koehlers Verlag, 1957).

Von Lettow-Vorbeck, P., *Meine Erinnerungen aus Ostafrika* (Leipzig: Hase & Köhler, 1920).

Walker, H.F.B. and A. Wienholt, *Narratives of the Great War in Africa: Personal Experiences of Two Soldiers in the East African and South West African Campaigns of the First World War* (London: Leonaur, 2013).

Walker, E.A., *A History of Southern Africa* (London: Longman, 1972).

Walker, H.F.B., *A Doctor's Diary in Damaraland* (London: Edward Arnold, 1917).

War Office (1909), *Field Service Regulations* (London: HMSO, 1909).

Ward, A.W. and G.P. Gooch (eds), *The Cambridge History of British Foreign Policy Volume III* (London: Cambridge University, 1923).

Warhurst, P.R., *Anglo-Portuguese Relations in South-Central Africa 1890–1900* (London: Longmans, 1962).

Welsh, F., *A History of South Africa* (London: Harper Collins, 2000).

Whittal, W., *With Botha and Smuts in Africa* (London: Cassell & Company, 1917).

Wilson, M. and L. Thompson (eds), *The Oxford History of South Africa 1870–1966* (Oxford: Oxford University Press, 1975).

Woodward, D.R., *World War One Almanac* (New York: Facts on File, 2009).

Worsfold, W.B., *Lord Milner's Work in South Africa* (London: John Murray Albemarle Street, 1906).

Young, F.B., *Marching on Tanga: With General Smuts in East Africa* (London: William Heinemann, 1935).

Zuber, T., *The Battle of the Frontiers: Ardennes 1914* (Brimscombe Port: The History Press, 2009).

Official and Semi-official Histories

Amery, L.S., *The Times History of the War in South Africa 1899–1900 Volume I* (London: Sampson Low, Marston & Company Ltd, 1900).

Amery, L.S., *The Times History of the War in South Africa 1899–1900 Volume II* (London: Sampson Low, Marston & Company Ltd, 1900).

Anon, *The Union of South Africa and the Great War 1914–1918* (Nashville: Battery Press, 1924).

Boell, L., *Die Operationen in Ostafrika, Weltkrieg 1914–1918* (Hamburg: Druck: W. Dachert, 1951).

Brown, J.A., *They Fought for King and Kaiser: South Africans in German East Africa 1916* (Rivonia: Ashanti, 1991).

Buchan, J. *The History of the South African Forces in France* (London: Imperial War Museum and Battery Press, 1920).

Collyer, J.J. *The South Africans with General Smuts in German East Africa* (Nashville: Imperial War Museum and Battery Press, 1939).

Collyer, J.J., *Campaign in German South West Africa 1914–1915* (London: Imperial War Museum and Battery Press, 1937).

Crowe, J.H.V. *General Smuts' Campaign in East Africa* (London: John Murray, 1918).

Deppe, L., *Mit Lettow-Vorbeck durch Afrika* (Berlin: Scherl, 1919).

Digby, P.K.A., *Pyramids and Poppies: The 1st SA Infantry Brigade in Libya, France and Flanders 1915–1919* (Rivonia: Ashanti, 1993).

Du Cane H. (ed), *German Official Account of the War in South Africa March 1900 to September 1900* (London: John Murray, 1906).

Gleeson, I., *The Unknown Force: Black, Indian and Coloured Soldiers Through Two World Wars* (Johannesburg: Ashanti, 1994).

Hordern, C., *Military Operations East Africa August 1914–September 1916* (London: Imperial War Museum and Battery Press, 1941).

L'Ange, G., *Urgent Imperial Service: South African Forces in German South West Africa 1914–1915* (Johannesburg: Ashanti, 1991).

Leipoldt, J.G.W., *The Union of South Africa and the Great War 1914–1918* (Pretoria: General Staff, DHQ, 1924).

Orpen, N., *South African Forces World War II: East African and Abyssinian Campaigns* (Cape Town: Purnell, 1968).

Von Oelhafen, H., *Der Feldzug in Südwest 1914/1915: Auf Grund Amtlichen Materials Bearbeitet* (Berlin: Safari-Verlag, 1923).

Regimental Histories

Adler, F.B. *The History of the Transvaal Horse Artillery* (Johannesburg: Regimental Asociation of the THA, 1927).

Adler, F.B., A.E Lorch, and H.H. Curson, *The South African Field Artillery: German East Africa and Palestine 1915–1919* (Pretoria: J.L. van Schaik Limited, 1957).

Capell, A.E., *The Second Rhodesia Regiment in East Africa* (Uckfield, The Naval & Military Press, 2006).

Coghlan, M., *History of the Umvoti Mounted Rifles* (Durban: Just Done Productions, 2012).

Coleman, F.L., *The Kaffrarian Rifles* (East London: The Regimental Association Kaffrarian Rifles, 1988).

Curson, H.H. *The History of the Kimberley Regiment* (Kimberley: Regimental Association, 1963).

Difford, I.D., *The Story of the 1st Battalion Cape Corps 1915–1919* (London: Forgotten Books, 2015).

Goetzsche, E., *Natal Mounted Rifles 1854–1969* (Durban: Regimental Asociation).

McKenzie, A.G., *The Dukes: A History of the Duke of Edinburgh's Own Rifles 1855–1956* (Cape Town: Regimental Council, 1956)

Monick, S., *A Bugle Calls: The Story of the Witwatersrand Rifles and Its Predecessors 1899–1987* (Johannesburg: Witwatersrand Rifles Regimental Council, 1989).

Monick, S., *Clear the Way: The Heritage of the South African Irish 1880–1990* (Johannesburg: South African Irish Regimental Council, 1991).

Orpen, N., *Gunners of the Cape: The Story of the Cape Field Artillery* (Cape Town: CFA Regimental History Commitee, 1965).

Orpen, N., *The History of the Transvaal Horse Artillery 1904–1974* (Johannesburg: THA Regimental Council, 1975).

Theses

Anderson, R., 'World War I in East Africa 1916–1918' (PhD thesis, University of Glasgow, Department of Modern History, 2001).

Crowson, T.A., 'When Elephants Clash: A Critical Analysis of Major General Paul Emil von Lettow-Vorbeck in the East African Theater of the Great War' (MA thesis, University of Kansas, Command and General Staff College, 2003).

Delport, A., '"Boks and Bullets, Coffins and Crutches": An Exploration of the Body, Mind and Places of "Springbok" South African Soldiers in the First World War' (MA thesis, Stellenbosch University, 2015).

Garcia, A., 'Manoeuvre Warfare in the South African Campaign in German South West Africa During the First World War' (MA thesis, Humanities, University of South Africa, 2015).

Garson, N.G., 'The Swaziland Question and a Road to the Sea 1887–1895' (MA thesis, University of Witwatersrand, 1955).

Getz, T.R., 'Smuts and the Politics of Colonial Expansion: South African Strategy in Regard to South-West Africa [Namibia] and the League of Nations Mandate: C. 1914–1924' (MA thesis, University of Cape Town).

Jones, S., 'The Influence of the Boer War (1899–1902) on the Tactical Development of the Regular British Army 1902–1914' (PhD thesis, University of Wolverhampton, 2009).

Moyd, M.R., 'Becoming Askari: African Soldiers and Everyday Colonialism in German East Africa, 1850–1918' (PhD thesis, Cornell University, 2008).

Nesselhuf, F.J., 'General Paul von Lettow-Vorbeck's East Africa Campaign: Maneuver Warfare on the Serengeti' (MA thesis, University of North Texas, 2012).

Nortier, E.W., 'Major General Sir H.T. Lukin, 1861–1925: The Making of a South African Hero' (MMil Thesis, Stellenbosch University, 2005).

Shearing, H.A., 'The Cape Rebel of the South African War 1899–1902' (PhD thesis, Stellenbosch University, 2004).

Stevens, H.C., 'The World War I Campaigns of Paul von Lettow-Vorbeck and T.E. Lawrence: A Comparison of Two Types of Guerrilla Warfare' (MA thesis, Ohio State University, 1973).

Swart, S. S., 'The Rebels of 1914: Masculinity, Republicanism and the Social Forces that Shaped the Boer Rebellion.' (MA dissertation, University of Natal, 1997).

Ungleich, T.R., 'The Defence of German South-West Africa During World War I' (MA Thesis, University of Miami, 1974).

Van der Waag, I., 'Hugh Archibald Wyndham: His Life and Times in South Africa, 1901–1923' (PhD thesis, University of Cape Town, 2005).

Von Herff, M. '"They Walk through the Fire like the Blondest German": African Soldiers Serving the Kaiser in German East Africa (1888–1914)' (MA thesis, McGill University, 1991).

Warwick, R., 'Reconsideration of the Battle of Sandfontein: The First Phase of the German South West Africa Campaign, August to September 1914' (MA Thesis, University of Cape Town, 2003).

Journal Articles and Book Chapters

Adgie, K.P., 'Askaris, Asymmetry, and Small Wars: Operational Art and the German East African Campaign, 1914–1918' (United States Army Command and General Staff College, 2001).

Anderson, R., 'J.C. Smuts and J.L. van Deventer: South African Commanders-in-Chief of a British Expeditionary Force', *Scientia Miltaria*, 31(2) (2003).

Andrew, C.M. and A.S. Kanya-Forstner, 'France, Africa, and the First World War', *The Journal of African History*, 19.1 (1978).

Buchanan, J.H., 'The Danger in Reading History Backwards', *The Educational Forum*, 10.1 (2008).

Citino, R.M., 'Military Histories Old and New: A Reintroduction', *The American Historical Review*, 112.4 (2007).

Coetzee, J.M., 'Blood, Flaw, Taint, Degeneration: The Case of Sarah Gertrude Millin', *English Studies in Africa*, 23.1 (1980).

Davenport T.R.H., 'The South African Rebellion, 1914.' *The English Historical Review* LXXVIII, no. 78 (1963) doi:10.1093/ehr/LXXVIII.CCCVI.73.

Dedering, T. 'South Africa and the Italo-Ethiopian War, 1935–6', *The International History Review*, 2013.

Dicey, E.E., 'Rhodes Redivivus', *Fortnightly Review*, 64, 1998.

Dorning, W.A., 'A Concise History of the South African Defence Force (1912–1987)', *Scientia Militaria*, 17.2 (1987).

Du Pisani, K. 'The Smuts Biographies: Analysis and Historiographical Assessment', *South African Historical Journal*, 68.3 (2016).

Dubow, S., 'South Africa and South Africans: Nationality, Belonging, Citizenship', *The Cambridge History of South Africa 1885–1994*, ed. by R. Ross, A. K Mager, and B. Nasson (Cambridge: Cambridge University, 2012).

Dubow, S., 'Smuts, the United Nations and the Rhetoric of Race and Rights', *Journal of Contemporary History*, 43.1 (2008).

Fedorowich, K., 'Sleeping with the Lion? The Loyal Afrikaner and the South African Rebellion of 1914–15'. *South African Historical Journal*, 49(1) (2003) doi:10.1080/02582470308671448.

Ferreira, S., *The British in Delagoa Bay in the Aftermath of the Boer War*, in 'The International Impact of the Boer War' ed. by K. Wilson (New York: Palgrave, 2001).

Garcia, A., 'Airpower in the Union of South Africa's First World War Campaign in German South West Africa', *Historia*, 62.2 (2017).

Garcia, A. and E. Kleynhans, 'Counterinsurgency in South Africa: the Afrikaner Rebellion, 1914–1915'. *Small Wars & Insurgencies*, (2020) doi:10.1080/09592318.2020.1812877.

Garson, N.G., '"Het Volk": The Botha-Smuts Party in the Transvaal, 1904–11', *The Historical Journal*, 9.1 (1966).

Garson, N.G., 'South Africa and World War I', *The Journal of Imperial and Commonwealth History*, 8(1) (1979).

Garson, N.G., 'South Africa and World War I', *The Journal of Imperial and Commonwealth History*, 8(1), 1979.

Geyer, R., 'The Union Defence Force and the 1914 Strike: The Dynamics of the Shadow of the Burgher', *Historia*, 59.2 (2014).

Giliomee, H. 'The Beginnings of Afrikaner Nationalism, 1870–1915', *South African Historical Journal*, 19.1 (2009).

Grey, J., 'Introduction', The Last Word? Essays on Official History in then United States and British Commomwealth (London: Praeger, 2003).

Grey, J., 'Standing Humbly in the Ante-chambers of Clio: The Rise and Fall of Union War Histories', *Scientia Militaria*, 30 (2000).

Grobler, J., 'The "Young Afrikaners": Jan Smuts and Piet Grobler during the Months of Storm and Stress (January–October 1899)', *Historia*, 44.1 (1999).

Grundlingh, A., 'The King's Afrikaners? Enlistment and Ethnic Identity in the Union of South Africa's Defence Force during the Second World War, 1939–45', *The Journal of African History*, 40.3 (1999).

Hallifax, S., '"Over by Christmas": British Popular Opinion and the Short War in 1914', *First World War Studies*, 1.2 (2010).

Henshaw, P., 'The "Key to South Africa" in the 1890s: Delagoa Bay and the Origins of the South African War', *Journal of Southern African Studies*, 24.3 (1998).

Henshaw, P., 'South African Territorial Expansion and the International Reaction to South African Racial Polices, 1939 to 1948', *South African Historical Journal*, 50(1) (2009).

Hodges, G.W.T., 'African Manpower Statistics for the British Forces in East Africa, 1914–1918', *The Journal of African History*, 19.1 (1978).

Howard, M. 'The Use and Abuse of Military History', *RUSI Journal*, 138.1 (2008).

Hyam, R., 'Smuts and the Decision of the Liberal Government to Grant Responsible Government to the Transvaal, January and February 1906', *The Historical Journal*, VIII.3 (1965).

Katz, D.B., 'A Clash of Military Doctrine: Brigadier-General Wilfrid Malleson and the South Africans at Salaita Hill, February 1916', *Historia*, 62 (2017).

Katz, D.B., (in press), 'An Aggregation of Lion Hunters: In Search of the Boer Way of War', *International Journal of Military History and Historiography*, 2021.

Killingray, D., 'Repercussions of World War I in the Gold Coast', *The Journal of African History*, 19.1 (1978).

Kleynhans, E., 'A Critical Analysis of the Impact of Water on the South African Campaign in German South West Africa, 1914–1915', *Historia*, 61.2 (2016).

Kleynhans, E, 'Deneys Reitz and the First World War: An Introduction to the Department of Defence Archival Holdings', *Scientia Militaria*, 44.1 (2016).

Kleynhans, E. and A. Garcia, Conference Paper delivered at the South African Historical Society, 'A Critical Analysis of Union Defence Force Operations During the Afrikaner Rebellion, 1914–1915' (2015).

Langhorne, R., 'Anglo-German Negotiations Concerning the Future of the Portuguese Colonies, 1911–1914', *The Historical Journal*, 16(2) (1973).

Legassick, M., 'British Hegemony and the Origins of Segregation in South Africa, 1901–14', *Segregation and Apartheid in Twentieth Century South Africa*, ed. by W. Beinart and S. Dubow (New York: Routledge, 1995).

Liebenberg, I., 'Sociology, biology or philosophy of a warrior? Reflections on Jan Smuts, guerrilla–being and a politics of choices', *Scientia Militaria*, 33(1) (2005).

Lillie, A.C., 'The Origin and Development of The South African Army', *Scientia Militaria*, 12.2 (1982).

Marks, S., 'White Masculinity: Jan Smuts, Race and the South Afican War', *Raleigh Lectures on History* (2001).

May, A., 'The Round Table and Imperial Federation, 1910–17', *The Round Table*, 99.410 (2010).

Mitchell, S. 'Jan Smuts, Paul von Lettow-Vorbeck and the Great War in German East Africa', *The Greater War: Other Combatants and Other Fronts 1914–1918*, ed. by J. Krause (New York: Palgrave Macmillan, 2014).

Mouton, F.A., '"The Sacred Tie": Sir Thomas Smartt, the Unionist Party and the British Empire, 1912–1920', *Historia*, 57.2 (2012).

Orr, G.M., '1914–1915 in East Africa', *Journal of the United Service Institution of India*, LVI, (1926).

Page, M., '"With Jannie in the Jungle": European Humor in an East African Campaign, 1914–1918', *The International Journal of African Historical Studies*, 14(3) (1981).

Page, M., 'The War of Thangata: Nyasaland and The East African Campaign, 1914–1918', *The Journal of African History*, 19.1 (1978).

Paterson, H., 'Jan Christain Smuts as a General in East Africa 1916: An Appraisal', *Military History Journal of the South African Military History Society*, 15.2 (2010).

Pirouet, M.L., 'East African Christians and World War I', *The Journal of African History*, 19.1 (1978).

Pretorius, F., 'Smuts se rol in die Anglo-Boereoorlog', *Jan Smuts: Van Boerseun Tot Wereldverhoog* (Pretoria: Protea, 2017).

Rathbone, R., 'World War I and Africa: Introduction', *The Journal of African History*, 19(1) (1978).

Sampson, P.J., 'The Conquest of German East', *The Nongquai Special Commemoration* (Pretoria, Argus, 1917).

Samson, A., 'South Africa Mobilises: The First Five Months of the War', *Scientia Militaria*, 44 (2016).

Schapiro, J.S. 'Thomas Carlyle, Prophet of Fascism', *The Journal of Modern History*, 17.2 (1945).

Sheppard, S.H., 'Some Notes on Tactics in the East African Campaign', *The Journal of the United Service Institution of India*, 158.215 (1919).

Smith, I.R., 'Jan Smuts and the South African War', *South African Historical Journal*, 41.1 (2009).

Smuts, J.C., 'East Africa', *The Geographical Journal*, 51(3) (1918).

Spiers, E.M., 'The Learning Curve in the South African War: Soldiers' Perspectives', *Historia*, 55.1 (2010).

Spies, S.B., 'The Outbreak of the First World War and the Botha Government', *South African Historical Journal*, 1.1 (1969).

Stone, G., 'No Way to Treat an Ancient Ally: Britain and the Portuguese Connection, 1919–1933', *Peacemaking, Peacemakers and Diplomacy, 1880–1939: Essays in Honour of Professor Alan Sharp.*, ed. by K. Hamilton and P. Salmon (Newcastle upon Tyne: Cambridge Scholars Publications, 2010).

Stratis, J.C., 'A Case Study in Leadership-Colonel Paul Emil Von Lettow-Vorbeck.' (US Army War College, 2002).

Summers, A., and R.W. Johnson, 'World War I Conscription and Social Change in Guinea', *The Journal of African History*, 19.1 (1978).

Swart, S. S., 'Men of Influence: The Ontology of Leadership in the 1914 Boer Rebellion.' *Journal of Historical Sociology* 17, no. 1 (2004) doi: 10.1111/ j.0952–1909.2004.00224.x.

Swart, S.S., 'A Boer and His Gun and His Wife are Three Things Always Together: Republican Masculinity and the 1914 Rebellion', *Journal of Southern African Studies*, no. 24 (2008) doi:10.1080/03057079808708599.

Swart, S.S., 'The Five Shilling Rebellion: Rural White Male Anxiety and the 1914 Boer Rebellion', *South African Historical Journal*, 56 (2006) doi:10.1080/ 02582470609464966.

Thompson, E.S., 'A Machine Gunner's Odyssey Through German East Africa: The Diary of E.S. Thompson, Part I. 17 January–24 May 1916', *Military History Journal South African Military History Society*, 7.4 (1987).

Trapido, S., 'Imperialism, Settler Identities and Colonial Capitalism: The Hundred Year Origins of the 1899 South African War', *Historia*, 53.1 (2008).

Tylden, G., '"TYPES OF THE UNION DEFENCE FORCE" OF SOUTH AFRICA: From a Colour Plate Published in The Cape Times Annual of December 1913', *Journal of the Society for Army Historical Research*, 38.156 (1960).

Van den Bergh, G.N., 'Secret Service in the South African Republic, 1895–1900', *Military History Journal of the South African Military History Society*, 3.2 (1974).

Van der Waag, I., 'African Water Histories: Transdisciplinary Discourses', ed. by J.W.N. Tempelhoff (Vanderbijlpark: North West University, 2005).

Van der Waag, I., 'Boer Generalship and the Politics of Command', *War in History*, 12(1) (2005).

Van der Waag, I., 'Recording the Great War: Military Archives and the South African Official History Programme, 1914–1939', *Scientia Militaria*, 44.1 (2016).

Van der Waag, I., 'Smuts's Generals: Towards a First Portrait of the South African High Command, 1912–1948', *War in History*, 18(1) (2011).

Van der Waag, I., 'The Battle of Sandfontein, 26 September 1914: South African Military Reform and the German South-West Africa Campaign, 1914–1915', *First World War Studies*, https://doi.org/10.1080/19475020.2013.828633 (2013).

Van der Waag, I., 'Contested histories: Official History and the South African Military in the 20th Century', *The Last Word? Essays on Official History, in the United States and British Commonwealth*, ed. by J. Grey (Westport, Connecticut & London: Praeger, 2003).

Van der Waag.,I., 'South African Defence in the Age of Total War, 1900–1940', *Historia*, 60(1) (2015).

Van der Waag: I., 'Military Culture and the South African Armed Forces, an Historical Perspective', 2011. A paper presented by Ian van der Waag at the Second South African Conference on Strategic Theory, 'On Strategy; Military Culture and African Armed Forces', co-hosted by Stellenbosch University and the Royal Danish Defence College (22/23 September 2011).

Van der Waag, I., 'Major J.G.W. Leipoldt, D.S.O.: A Portrait of a South African Surveyor and Intelligence Officer, 1912–1923', *Scientia Militaria*, 25(1) (1995).

Van der Waag, I., 'All Splendid, but Horrible: The Politics of South Africa's Second "Little Bit" and the War on the Western Front, 1915–1918', *Scientia Militaria*, 40(3) (2012).

Vandervort, B., 'New Light on the East African Theater of the Great War: A Review Essay of English Language Sources', *Soldiers and Settlers in Africa, 1850–1918*, ed. by S.M. Millar (n.p.: Brill, 2009).

Von Schellendorf, F.B., 'Considerations Regarding a Method of Fighting for the Infantry Suited to the Present Conditions', *Royal United Services Institution Journal*, 35:162 (1891).

Warhurst, P.R., 'Smuts and Africa: a Study in Sub-Imperialism', *South African Historical Journal*, 16.1 (1984).

Warwick, R.C., 'The Battle of Sandfontein: The Role and Legacy of Major-General Sir Henry Timson Lukin', *Scientia Militaria*, 34(2) (2006).

Wessels, A., 'Kabinetminister En Bevelvoerder: Smuts Se Militere Bydrae Tydens Die Eerste Wereldoorlog', *Jan Smuts: Van Boerseun Tot Wereldverhoog* (Pretoria: Protea, 2017).

Willan, B.P., 'The South African Native Labour Contingent, 1916–1918', *The Journal of African History*, 19.1 (1978).

Yearwood, P.J., 'Great Britain and the Repartition of Africa, 1914–1919', *The Journal of Imperial and Commonwealth History*, 18(3) (1990).

Government Publications

House of Commons Parliamentary Papers Online, Correspondence on the subject of Proposed Naval and Military Expedition Against German South-West Africa, Botha to Acting Governor-General, 4 August 1914.

House of Commons Parliamentary Papers Online, Correspondence on the subject of Proposed Naval and Military Expedition Against German South-West Africa, Acting Governor to General Botha, 7 August 1914.

House of Commons Parliamentary Papers Online, Correspondence on the subject of Proposed Naval and Military Expedition Against German South-West Africa, Secretary of State to Acting Governor-General, 9 August 1914.

House of Commons Parliamentary Papers Online, Correspondence on the subject of Proposed Naval and Military Expedition Against German South-West Africa, Botha to Acting Governor-General, 10 August 1914.

Judicial Commission of Inquiry, Causes of and Circumstances Relating to the Recent Rebellion in South Africa, Minutes of Evidence, Evidence Louis Botha, December 1916.

Parliamentary Papers, Minutes of Evidence taken before the Royal Commission on the War in South Africa Vol II (Elgin Commission), Cd 1791 (1903) q 15056.

Royal Commission, *Minutes of Evidence on the War in South Africa Volume I*, General Sir Redvers Buller, p14963 (London, 1903).

S.C. 1–15, Union of South Africa Report of the Select Committee on Rebellion, Minutes of Evidence, J.B.M. Hertzog, 29 March 1915.

Secretary of State for Commonwealth Relations, *Basutoland, The Bechuanaland Protectorate and Swaziland: History of Discusssions with the Union of South Africa 1909–1939, Cmd 8707* (London, 1952).

The Department of Defense Dictionary of Military and Associated Terms.

UG 32–13, C.F. Beyers, Report on Mission to Attend Army Manoeuvres and Military Institutions in Switzerland, France, Germany and England, 7 December 1912.

UG 42–16, Recent Rebellion in South Africa, Minutes of Evidence, Louis Botha, 29 June 1916.

UG 42–16, Recent Rebellion in South Africa.

UG 42–16, Report of the Judicial Commission of Inquiry into the Causes and Circumstances Relating to the Recent Rebellion in South Africa, Minutes of Evidence, Louis Botha, 29 June 1916.

UG 46–16, Recent Rebellion in South Africa.

UG 46–16, Report of the Judicial Commission of Inquiry into the Causes and Circumstances Relating to the Recent Rebellion in South Africa, Correspondence between the Union and Imperial Governments regarding German South West Africa, Annexure C.

Union of South Africa Debates, First Session of the First Parliament, 1910–1911, 1 March 1911, col. 1471–82.

Union of South Africa Debates, First Session of the First Parliament, 1910–1911, T. Watt member for Dundee, 1 March 1911, col. 1483.

Union of South Africa Debates, First Session of the First Parliament, 1910–1911, C.P. Crewe member for Turffontein, 1 March 1911, col. 1483.

Union of South Africa Debates, First Session of the First Parliament, 1910–1911, H. Wyndham member for East London, 1 March 1911, col. 1483.

Union of South Africa Debates, First Session of the First Parliament, 1910–1911, Schreiner, 8 March 1911, col. 1658.

Union of South Africa Debates, First Session of the First Parliament, 1910–1911, Schreiner, 8 March 1911, col. 1658.

Union of South Africa Debates, First Session of the First Parliament, 1910–1911, Farrar and Botha, 8 March 1911, col. 1645, 1647.

Union of South Africa Debates, Second Session of the First Parliament, 1912, South African Defence Bill, 23 February 1911, col. 634.

Union of South Africa Debates, Second Session of the First Parliament, 1912, Second Reading of the Defence Bill, 8 March 1911, col. 638.

Union of South Africa Debates, Second Session of the First Parliament, 1912, South African Defence Bill, 23 February 1911, col. 622.

Union of South Africa Debates, Second Session of the First Parliament, 1912, South African Defence Bill, 23 February 1911, col. 651.

Union of South Africa Debates, Second Session of the First Parliament, 1912, South African Defence Bill, 23 February 1911, col. 643.

Union of South Africa Debates, Second Session of the First Parliament, 1912, South African Defence Bill, 23 February 1911, col. 622.

Union of South Africa Debates, Second Session of the First Parliament, 1912, South African Defence Bill, 23 February 1911, col. 623.

Union of South Africa Debates, Second Session of the First Parliament, 1912, South African Defence Bill, 23 February 1911, col. 625.

Union of South Africa Debates, Second Session of the First Parliament, 1912, South African Defence Bill, 23 February 1911, col. 642.

Union of South Africa Debates, Second Session of the First Parliament, 1912, South African Defence Bill, 23 February 1911, col. 654.

Union of South Africa Debates, Second Session of the First Parliament, 1912, South African Defence Bill, 23 February 1911, col. 659–71.

Union of South Africa, *Judicial Commission of Inquiry: Causes of and Circumstances Relating to the Recent Rebellion in South Africa* (Cape Town, 1916).

Internet Sources

Beautiful World, Namib Desert, www.beautifulworld.com/africa/namibia/namib-desert/, accessed 21 March 2021.

Defence Web, editor Leon Engelbrecht, http://defenceweb.co.za/index.php?option=com_content&view=article&id=603&catid=57:Book%20Reviews&Itemid=141, 20 April 2015.

Denis, S., *South Africa and the Great War in Cartoons, The Rand Daily Mail & The Sunday Times*, www.facebook.com/306152646247018/photos/rpp.306152646247018/325449697650646/?-type=3&theater, accessed 3 February 2020.

Nasson, B., Litnet, Review of *Jan Smuts: Afrikaner sonder grense by Richard Steyn*, www.litnet.co.za/jan-smuts-afrikaner-sonder-grense-richard-steyn/, accessed 9 January 2018.

www.climatestotravel.com/climate/tanzania, Climates to travel, accessed 22 May 2020.

Newspapers

The Sydney Morning Herald, 'BOTHALAND', 13 July 1915.

The Transvaal Leader, 14 January 1914; Anon, 'The Crisis: General Strike Declared—Martial Law in Force', *Rand Daily Mail*, 14 January 1914.

Published Primary Documents

Amery, L., *The Leo Amery Diaries Volume One 1896–1929*, ed. by J. Barnes and D. Nicholson (London: Hutchinson & Co, 1980).

Hancock, W.K. and J. van der Poel (eds), *Selections from the Smuts Papers Volume I June 1886–May 1902* (London: Cambridge University, 1966).

Hancock, W.K. and J. van der Poel (eds) *Selections from the Smuts Papers Vol III July 1910–November 1918* (London: Cambridge, 1966).

Headlam, C. (ed) *The Milner Papers South Africa 1897–1899* (London: Cassel & Company, 1931).

Lewsen, P. (ed), *Selections from the Correspondence of J.X. Merriman 1899–1905* (Cape Town: The Van Riebeeck Society, 1966).

Lewsen, P. (ed), *Selections From the Correspondence of John X. Merriman 1905–1924* (Cape Town: The Van Riebeck Society, 1969).

Van der Poel, J. (ed), *Selections from the Smuts Papers Volume V September 1919–November 1934*, (London: Cambridge University, 1973).

Archival Sources

Department of Defence Documentation Centre

Adjutant General

DODA, AG 14, Box 13, File 2 Veterinary Services GSWA Campaign and Rebellion August 1914 to July 1915, Report by Colonel J.A.S. Irvine Smith.

DODA, AG 14, Box 13, File 2 Veterinary Services GSWA Campaign and Rebellion August 1914 to July 1915, Report by Colonel J.A.S. Irvine Smith.

DODA, AG 14, Box 32, File AG (7) WOI, Verslag Deur General J.C. Smuts Krygsverrigtinge in Oos Afrika, 30 April 1916.

DODA, AG 14, Box 32, File KA/WOI, Intelligence Supplement Richard Meinertzhagen, 14 July 1916.

DODA, AG 14, Box 33, File AG (7)/WOI, Folio 149, Letter Curson to Tylden, 5 June 1962.

DODA, AG 14, Box 6, Biography Berrange.

DODA, AG 14, Box 6, Biography Brits.

DODA, AG 14, Box 6, Biography Collyer.

DODA, AG 14, Box 6, Biography Kemp.

DODA, AG 14, Box 6, Biography Lukin.

DODA, AG 14, Box 6, Biography Van Deventer.

DODA, AG 1914–1921, Box 150, Total Strengths Field Force and Garrison. A mere 6,016 troops remained on active duty in Provincial garrison.

DODA, AG 1914–1921, Box 150, Total Strengths Field Force and Garrison.

DODA, AG 1914–1921, Box 8, Folio G5/305/9199, Appointment of Botha.

DODA, AG12, Box 7, File 27, Coloured Troops World War One.

DODA, AG14, Box 13 File 7, Slaag van Sandfontein 26 September 1914.

3rd South African Infantry Brigade

DODA, Box 6, File 4/984/9199, 3rd SA Infantry Brigade, Confidential Statements and Reports re Method of Conducting the Campaign in GEA, 26 November 1915.

DODA, Box 6, File 4/984/9199, 3rd SA Infantry Brigade, Confidential Statements and Reports re Method of Conducting the Campaign in GEA, 26 November 1915, Latest information as to enemy numbers.

DODA, Box 6, File 4/984/9199, 3rd SA Infantry Brigade, Confidential Statements and Reports re Method of Conducting the Campaign in GEA, 26 November 1915, Telegram Smith-Dorrien to Smuts 29 January 1915.

DODA, Box 6, File 4/984/9199, 3rd SA Infantry Brigade, Confidential Statements and Reports re Method of Conducting the Campaign in GEA, 26 November 1915, Van Deventer/Hughes Report, 26 November 1915.

DODA, Box 6, File 4/984/9199, 3rd SA Infantry Brigade, Confidential Statements and Reports re Method of Conducting the Campaign in GEA, 26 November 1915, Letter from Papenfus to Smuts, 17 December 1915.

DODA, 3rd South African Infantry Brigade, Box 6, Report of Captain Frank Douglas, 17 December 1915.

DODA, 3rd South African Infantry Brigade, Box 6, Report of Lieutenant-Colonel A.M. Hughes and Lieutenant-Colonel Dirk van Deventer, 26 November 1915.

Chief of Staff

DODA, CSO, Box 36, File CSO45, Telegram Tighe to Hughes, 4 December 1914.

DODA, CSO, Box 36, Letter Hughes to Tighe, 4 January 1916.

Secretary for Defence

DODA, DC2 Group 2, Box 168, File 2/7164, Correspondence, Under Secretary of Defence about pay and allowances of burghers on commando, 1914.

DODA, DC Group 2, Box 758, Operations in GEA, Folio D9/1973/9199, Letter Smuts to Governor-General, 26 February 1916.

DODA, DC Group 2, Box 758, Operations in GEA, Folio D8/1973/9199, Letter Smuts to Governor-General, 25 February 1916.

DODA, DC Group 2, Box 758, Operations in GEA, Folio D31/1973/9199, Letter Smuts to Governor-General, 23 March 1916.

DODA, DC Group 2, Box 758, Operations in GEA, Folio D31/1973/9199, Letter Smuts to Governor-General, 12 March 1916.

DODA, DC Group 2, Box 758, Operations in GEA, Folio D31/1973/9199, Letter Smuts to Governor-General, 15 March 1916.

DODA, DC Group 2, Box 758, Operations in GEA, Folio D31/1973/9199, Letter Smuts to Governor-General, 23 March 1916.

DODA, DC Group 2, Box 758, Operations in GEA, Folio D31/1973/9199, Letter Smuts to Governor-General, 22 March 1916.

DODA, DC Group 2, Box 758, Operations in GEA, Folio D31/1973/9199, Letter Smuts to Governor-General, 9 March 1916.

DODA, DC Group 2, Box 758, Operations in GEA, Folio D31/1973/9199, Press Communiqué, 27 March 1916.

DODA, DC Group 2, Box 688, Letter Van Deventer to Smuts, 20 December 1914.

DODA, DC Group 2, Box 688, Letter Smuts to Van Deventer, 11 January 1915.

DODA, DC Group 2, Box 668, Letter from Seitz to Kaiser, 4 August 1915.

DODA, DC Group 2, Box 668, File M822, Infection of water by enemy during hostilities in S.W.A., Letter Franke to Botha 11 March 1915.

DODA, DC Group 2, Box 668, Botha letter to Seitz, 19 June 1915.

DODA, DC Group 2, Box 47, South African Defence Bill, Smuts to Lord Gladstone, 16 November 1911.

DODA, DC Group 2, Box 47, file 1063, South Africa Defence Bill.

DODA, DC Group 2, Box 252, Telegram Secretary of State to Acting Governor-General, 23 August 1914

DODA, DC Group 2, Box 252, Lukin's Report on "A" Force, 19 August 1915.

DODA, DC Group 2, Box 252, Letter Smuts to McKenzie, 6 January 1915.

DODA, DC Group 2, Box 252, Letter from Secretary for Defence to unknown, 19 September 1914.

DODA, DC Group 2, Box 252, Letter Franke to *Schutztruppen*, 28 June 1915.

DODA, DC Group 2, Box 252, Joint Naval and Military Operations, Secretary of Defence, 9 September 1914.

DODA, DC Group 2, Box 252, Historical Record of the Campaign in GSWA compiled by Hugh Wyndham.

DODA, DC Group 2, Box 252, GSWA, Botha's Despatch No. 4 Covering the period 15 May to 18 July 1915.

DODA, DC Group 2, Box 252, Folio 17138, Mentions GSWA Campaign Commanding Officer DLI, 2 October 1917.

DODA, DC Group 2, Box 252, Folio 17138, McKenzie's Dispatch 16 May 1915.

DODA, DC Group 2, Box 252, Folio 17138, Lukin's Report on "A" Force, 19 August 1915.

DODA, DC Group 2, Box 252, Folio 17138, Lukin's Report on "A" Force, Appendix A, 19 August 1915.

DODA, DC Group 2, Box 184, Beyers resignation and Smuts reply.

DODA, DC Group 2, Box 1438, Secret Intelligence, Telegram Smuts to Lukin, 4 November 1914.

DODA, DC Group 2, Box 1438, Secret Intelligence Incoming Telegrams, Telegram Van Deventer to Smuts, 23 October 1914.

DODA, DC Group 2, Box 1438, Secret Intelligence G.

DODA, DC Group 2, Box 1434, South West African Campaign Memorandum, 1936.

DODA, DC Group 2, Box 356, J. Leipoldt, Letter to the Adjutant General (Intelligence Report, 1917).

Diverse (Group 1)

DODA, Diverse Group 1 Box 24, General Order No. 1 Colonel Bouwer Acting GOC Southern Force, 8 MAY 1915.

DODA, Diverse Group 1, Box 19, Curriculum Vitae Roland Bourne, 1910.

DODA, Diverse Group 1, Box 31, Defensive Scheme Re Boer Uprising in Natal.

DODA, Diverse Group 1, Box 32, Confidential Publications, Folio 36/4, Letter from Bourne to High Commissioner, 18 September 1913.

DODA, Diverse Group 1, Box 33, South African Defence Conferences 1908/1909.

DODA, Diverse Group 1, Box 41, Memorandum Roland Bourne to Minister of Defence, 30 July 1917.

DODA, Diverse Group 1, Box 53, South African Police Commissioner to Secretary for Defence, 10 April 1915.

DODA, Diverse Group 1, Box 57, Letter from Botha to Smuts, 12 November 1914.

DODA, Diverse Group 1, Box 8, The Military Situation in South Africa Department of Defence, 20 August 1910.

DODA, Diverse, Box 15, file 199, Colonial Defence Committee Memoranda on General Defence Matters, Bourne to Smuts, 8 September 1910.

German South West Africa

DODA, GSWA Group, Box 14, Methods and Points to be Observed in Embarking and Disembarking.

DODA, GSWA Group, Box 15, Lukin to Botha, 12 November 1914.

DODA, GSWA, Box 23b, Supplement to General Routine Orders, 19 May 1916.

DODA, GSWA, Box 44, Intelligence Summary, 13 March 1916.

DODA, OC Records Group, Box 92, File O.R. 139, Statistics Re Casualties Rebellion, South West Africa, East and Central Africa and Europe.

DODA, SAMR, Box 1084, File 215/4/3, Under Secretary of Defence – District control officer Pretoria, 20 January 1914.

DODA, WWI GSWA and EA, Box 25, Lindenken, News from enemy sources, Diary of a member of the 7 Schutzen Company.

DODA, WWI GSWA and EA, Box 77, War Diary of the 2nd South African Infantry Brigade.

DODA, WWI GSWA and EA, Box 81, War Diary of the 6th South African Infantry Regiment, 12 February 1916.

DODA, GSWA Group, Box 77, War Diary of 2nd South African Infantry Brigade, 3 February 1916.

National Archives of South Africa

Jan Smuts Papers

NARSA, JSP, Box 111 (18), Memorandum Postmaster to Secretary for Defence, German Wireless Telegraph Stations, 10 August 1914.

NARSA, JSP, Box 111, Folio 18, Letter Department of Posts and Telegraphs to Secretary of Defence, German Wireless Telegraph Stations, 10 August 1914.

NARSA, JSP, Box 111, Folio 6, Memorandum Explanatory of the South African Defence Bill, November 1911.

NARSA, JSP, Box 111, Folio 8, Memorandum Explanatory of the South African Defence Bill, November 1911.

NARSA, JSP, Box 111, Memorandum: Union of South Africa, Expalantory of the South African Defence Bill, November 1911.

NARSA, JSP, Box 111, Memorandum: Union of South Africa, Expalantory of the South African Defence Bill, November 1911.

NARSA, JSP, Box 112, Folio 14, Letter Farrar to Smuts, Water situation at Garub, 23 March 1915.

NARSA, JSP, Box 112, Folio 15, Botha Despatch No. 2 covering the period 24 February to 28 March.

NARSA, JSP, Box 112, Folio 17, Visit of the Governor-General of Union of South Africa to German South West Africa, March 1915.

NARSA, JSP, Box 112, Folio 17, Visit of the Governor-General of Union of South Africa to German South West Africa, March 1915.

NARSA, JSP, Box 112, Folio 18, Botha to Smuts, 3 April 1915.

NARSA, JSP, Box 112, Folio 22, Report on a visit to GSWA 20–27 March 1915.

NARSA, JSP, Box 112, Folio 22, Smuts to Botha, 5 April 1915.

NARSA, JSP, Box 112, Folio 25, Botha to Smuts, Telegram from McKenzie, 5 April 1915.

NARSA, JSP, Box 112, Folio 31, Secretary of Defence to H. Burton (Minister of Finance), 4 May 1915.

NARSA, JSP, Box 112, Folio 4, Letter Farrar to Smuts, Water situation at Garub, 5 March 1915.

NARSA, JSP, Box 113 (8), Memorandum Simpson-Baikie to Governor-General, Smith-Dorrien, Smith-Dorrien poor health, 31 January 1915.

NARSA, JSP, Box 113 Folio 6, Smith-Dorrien: On the raising of the Cape Boys unit, Memorandum Smith-Dorrien to Smuts, 28 January 1916.

NARSA, JSP, Box 113, Folio 10, Buxton, Launch of operations before the rain, Buxton to Secretary of State, 31 January 1915.

NARSA, JSP, Box 113, Folio 154, Meinertzhagen: Notes on the officers serving with the enemy forces in German East Africa, Intelligence Supplement No. 3, 14 July 1916.

NARSA, JSP, Box 189, Folio 67, J. Merriman, Botha on Swaziland, Memorandum Merriman to Smuts, December 1906.

NARSA, JSP, Box 196, Folio 137, Letter Smuts to Duncan McKenzie, 12 August 1914.

NARSA, JSP, Box 196, Folio 138, Letter from Smuts to Lt-Gen Sir James Wolfe Murray, 17 August 1914.

NARSA, JSP, Box 196, Folio 153 Letter Steyn to Smuts, 16 November 1914.

NARSA, JSP, Box 196, Folio 153, Letter Smuts to Steyn, 17 November 1914. See also TNA, ADM 137–13, Folio 523, Buxton to Harcourt, 17 November 1914.

NARSA, JSP, Box 196, Folio 156, Letter Smuts to Crewe, 18 December 1914.

NARSA, JSP, Box 196, Folio 31, Letter from Crewe to Smuts, 3 August 1914.

NARSA, JSP, Box 196, Folio 33, Letter Crewe to Smuts, 12 August 1914.

NARSA, JSP, Box 196, Folio 34, Letter from Crewe to Smuts, 24 August 1914.

NARSA, JSP, Box 197, Folio 10A, Letter Botha to Smuts, 28 February 1915.

NARSA, JSP, Box 197, Folio 154, Letter Smuts to Merriman 30 August 1915.

NARSA, JSP, Box 197, folio 174, Letter from Smuts to A.B. Gillet, J.C. Smuts, Military command of East Africa refused, 29 November 1915.

NARSA, JSP, Box 197, Folio 174, Letter Smuts to A.B. Gillet, 2 September 1915.

NARSA, JSP, Box 197, Folio 89, Letter Merriman to Smuts 4 August 1915.

NARSA, JSP, Folio 36, Letter from Crewe to Smuts, 29 September 1914.

NARSA, 'Memorandum on the Country known as German South-West Africa'. Union Government Papers, 1915.

NARSA, JSP Box 196(143A), J. Smuts, 'Smuts to Deneys Reitz', Memorandum Smuts to Reitz, September 1914.

NARSA, JSP Box 197 (154), J. Smuts, East Africa Exchange, Memorandum Smuts to Merriman, August 1915.

NARSA, JSP Box 203 (28), L. Botha, Botha on Mozambique, Memorandum Botha to Smuts, February 1918.

NARSA, JSP Box 206(145), J. Smuts, Versailles Conference, Letter Smuts to Wife, July 1919; P.R. Warhurst, 'Smuts and Africa: A Study in Sub-Imperialism', *South African Historical Journal*, 16.1 (1984).

NARSA, JSP Box 206(200), J. Smuts, 'Smuts German South-West Africa', Memorandum Smuts to Gillet, January 1919.

NARSA, JSP Box 300 (4), J. Smuts, Delagoa Bay, Memorandum, undated.

NARSA, JSP, A1 Box 390, Malleson Papers on Salaita Hill Engagement in East Africa Campaign 1916–1918, Official report on the action at Salaita Hill 12 February 1918, Appendix II.

NARSA, JSP, A1 Box 390, Malleson Papers on Salaita Hill Engagement in East Africa Campaign 1916–1918, Notes on the action at Salaita, Appendix III.

NARSA, JSP, Box 112, Folio 17, Visit of the Governor-General of Union of South Africa to German South West Africa, March 1915.

NARSA, JSP, Box 198, Folio 199, Letter Smuts to S.M. Smuts, 21 December 1916.

NARSA, JSP, Box 198, Folio 203, Letter Smuts to S.M. Smuts, 27 December 1916.

NARSA, JSP, Box 199, Folio 2, Letter Amery to Smuts, 15 March 1917.

NARSA, JSP, Box 199, Folio 67, Letter Botha to S.M. Smuts (Annexure A, Smuts to Botha, 24 April 1917) 4 May 1917.

NARSA, JSP, Box 199, Folio 67, Letter Botha to S.M. Smuts (Annexure B, Botha to Smuts, 26 April 1917) 4 May 1917.

NARSA, JSP, Box 199, Folio 67, Letter Botha to S.M. Smuts (Annexure C, Smuts to Botha, 1 May 1917) 4 May 1917.

NARSA, JSP, Box 201, Folio 106, Letter Milner to Smuts, 12 March 1917.

NARSA, JSP, Box 202, Folio 2, Letter Smuts to S.M. Smuts, 27 April 1917.

NARSA, JSP, Box 300 (4) Box G, J. Smuts, Smuts Mozambique, Memorandum War Cabinet, undated.

NARSA, JSP, Private Papers Box 300, The German Colonies at the Peace Conference, undated.

Prime Minister

NARSA, PM 1/1/32, File 4/95/14-4/97/14 Correspondence file,

NARSA, PM 1/1/32, File 4/95/14-4/97/14 Correspondence file, Telegram Secretary of State to Acting Governor-General, 12 August 1914.

NARSA, PM 1/1/32, File 4/95/14-4/97/14, Correspondence file, Telegram Secretary of State to Acting Governor-General, 25 August 1914.

NARSA, PM 1/1/32, File 4/95/14-4/97/14, Correspondence file, Telegram Secretary of State to Governor-General, 9 September 1914.

NARSA, PM 1/1/32, File 4/95/14-4/97/14, Correspondence file, Telegram Buxton to Secretary of State, 8 September 1914.

NARSA, PM 1/1/32, File 4/95/14-4/97/14, Correspondence file, Telegram Buxton to Naval C-in-C Cape Station, 28 September 1914.

NARSA, PM 1/1/32, File 4/95/14-4/97/14, Correspondence file, Telegram Naval C-in-C Cape Station to Buxton, 27/28 September 1914.

NARSA, PM 1/1/32, File 4/95/14-4/97/14, Correspondence file, Telegram Naval C-in-C Cape Station to Buxton, 29 September 1914.

NARSA, PM 1/1/32, File 4/95/14-4/97/14, Correspondence file, Telegram Secretary of State to Buxton, 17 September.

NARSA, PM 1/1/32, File 4/95/14-4/97/14, Correspondence file, Telegram Buxton to Naval C-in-C Cape Station, 28 September 1914.

NARSA, PM 1/1/32, File 4/95/14-4/97/14, Minute no. 750, Correspondence file, Telegram Botha to Lord De Villiers, 15 August 1914.

NARSA, PM 1/1/32, File 4/95/14-4/97/14, Minute no. 800, Correspondence file, Telegram Botha to Lord De Villiers, 25 August 1914.

NARSA, PM 1/1/32, File 4/95/14-4/97/14, Minute no. 860, Correspondence file, Telegram Botha to Buxton, 8 September 1914.

NARSA, PM 1/1/32, File 4/95/14-4/97/14, Minute no. 868, Correspondence file, Telegram Botha to Buxton, 11 September 1914.

NARSA, PM 1/1/32, File 4/95/14-4/97/14, Minute no. 875, Correspondence file, Telegram Botha to Buxton, 12 September 1914.

NARSA, PM 1/1/32, File 4/95/14-4/97/14, Minute no. 889, Correspondence file, Telegram Botha to Buxton, 14 September 1914.

NARSA, PM 1/1/32, File 4/95/14-4/97/14, Minute no. 994, Correspondence file, Telegram Botha to Buxton, 7 October 1914.

National Archives of the United Kingdom

Records of the Admiralty

TNA, ADM 123/144, General letters and proceedings Walvis Bay, Letter of Proceedings from Captain of HMS *Astraea* to C-in-C Cape Station 29 January 1915.

TNA, ADM 123/144, General letters and proceedings Walvis Bay, Letter of Proceedings from Captain of HMS *Astraea* to C-in-C Cape Station 15 January 1915.

TNA, ADM 123/144, General letters and proceedings Walvis Bay, Letter of Proceedings from Captain of HMS *Astraea* to C-in-C Cape Station 15 February 1915.

TNA, ADM 123/144, General letters and proceedings Walvis Bay, Letter of Proceedings from Captain of HMS *Astraea* to C-in-C Cape Station 11 May 1915.

TNA, ADM 137/13, Folio 10, Telegram Buxton to Harcourt, 1 October 1914.

TNA, ADM 137/13, Folio 103, Buxton to Harcourt, 12 October 1914. See TNA, ADM 137–13, Folio 348, C-in-C Cape to Admiralty, 3 November 1914.

TNA, ADM 137/13, Folio 132, Telegram Navy Office Melbourne to Admiralty, Translation of secret German message intercepted, 8 October 1914.

TNA, ADM 137/13, Folio 238, Buxton to Harcourt, 22 October 1914.

TNA, ADM 137/13, Folio 260, C-in-C Cape to Admiralty, 26 October 1914.

TNA, ADM 137/13, Folio 276, Buxton to Harcourt, 27 October 1914.

TNA, ADM 137/13, Folio 299, Buxton to Harcourt, Reuters Report on German proclamation, 29 October 1914.

TNA, ADM 137/13, Folio 32, Buxton to Harcourt, 5 October 1914. See TNA, ADM 137–13, Folio 50, Buxton to Harcourt, 8 October 1914.

TNA, ADM 137/13, Folio 344, Buxton to Harcourt, 2 November 1914.

TNA, ADM 137/13, Folio 356,372, C-in-C Cape to Admiralty, Intercepted German code, 4 November 1914.

TNA, ADM 137/13, Folio 427, Buxton to Harcourt, 9 November 1914.

TNA, ADM 137/13, Folio 428, Buxton to Harcourt, 9 November 1914.

TNA, ADM 137/13, Folio 461, Buxton to Harcourt, 12 November 1914.

TNA, ADM 137/13, Folio 470, Buxton to Harcourt, 12 November 1914.

TNA, ADM 137/13, Folio 484, Buxton to Harcourt, 13 November 1914.

TNA, ADM 137/13, Folio 494, Buxton to Harcourt, 14 November 1914.

TNA, ADM 137/13, Folio 50, Buxton to Harcourt, 8 October 1914.

TNA, ADM 137/13, Folio 508, Buxton to Harcourt, 16 November 1914.

TNA, ADM 137/13, Folio 51–53, Buxton to Harcourt, 8 October 1914.

TNA, ADM 137/13, Folio 520, Buxton to Harcourt, 15 November 1914.

TNA, ADM 137/13, Folio 525C-in-C Cape to Admiralty, 17 November 1914.

TNA, ADM 137/13, Folio 539, Buxton to Harcourt, 19 November 1914.

TNA, ADM 137/13, Folio 550, Buxton to Harcourt, 19 November 1914.

TNA, ADM 137/13, Folio 558, Buxton to Harcourt, 21 November 1914.

TNA, ADM 137/13, Folio 56, 57, Remarks on new plan, 10 October 1914.

TNA, ADM 137/13, Folio 567, Buxton to Harcourt, 22 November 1914.

TNA, ADM 137/13, Folio 573, C-in-C Cape to Admiralty, 25 November 1914.

TNA, ADM 137/13, Folio 621, C-in-C Cape to Admiralty, 27 November 1914.

TNA, ADM 137/13, Folio 625, Telegram Buxton to Harcourt, 28 November 1914.

TNA, ADM 137/13, Folio 649, C-in-C Cape to Admiralty, 30 November 1914.

TNA, ADM 137/13, Folio 651, Buxton to Harcourt, 30 November 1914.

TNA, ADM 137/13, Folio 677, Buxton to Harcourt, 2 December 1914.

TNA, ADM 137/13, Folio 70, C-in-C Cape to Admiralty, 9 October 1914.

TNA, ADM 137/13, Folio 707, Buxton to Harcourt, 7 December 1914.

TNA, ADM 137/13, Folio 710, Sir R Tower, Buenos Ayres to Admiralty, 7 December 1914.

TNA, ADM 137/13, Folio 726, Buxton to Harcourt, 9 December 1914.

TNA, ADM 137/13, Folio 728, India Office to Admiralty, 9 December 1914.

TNA, ADM 137/13, Folio 83, Buxton to Harcourt, 10 October 1914.

TNA, ADM 137/13, Folio 88, Memorandum Admiral H.B Jackson, 8 October 1914.

TNA, ADM 137/8, Letter from Rear Admiral H.K. Hall to The Secretary of the Admiralty 15 October 1914.

TNA, ADM 137/9, C-in-C Cape to Governor-General, Folio 33, 1 August 1914.

TNA, ADM 137/9, De Villers to Harcourt, 17 August 1914.

TNA, ADM 137/9, Extract from Proceedings of Sub Committee of Imperial Defence, 5 August 1914.

TNA, ADM 137/9, Folio 426, Telegram C-in-C Cape to H. B. Jackson, 11 September 1914.

TNA, ADM 137/9, Folio 434, Telegram Governor of Union of SA to Secretary of State for the Colonies, 12 September 1914.

TNA, ADM 137/9, Folio 459, Buxton to Harcourt, 16 September 1914.

TNA, ADM 137/9, Folio 472, Telegram, Buxton to Harcourt, 15 September 1914.

TNA, ADM 137/9, Folio 509, Buxton to Harcourt, 19 September 1914.

TNA, ADM 137/9, Folio 517, Telegram, Smuts reply to Beyers resignation manifesto, Buxton to Harcourt, 21 September 1914.

TNA, ADM 137/9, Folio 517, Telegram, Translation of Beyers resignation manifesto, Buxton to Harcourt, 20 September 1914.

TNA, ADM 137/9, Folio 538, Telegram, Report on De la Rey funeral Buxton to Harcourt, 21 September 1914.

TNA, ADM 137/9, Folio 566, Telegram, Buxton to Harcourt, 23 September 1914.

TNA, ADM 137/9, Folio 580, Buxton to Harcourt, 25 September 1914.

TNA, ADM 137/9, Folio 598, C-in-C Cape to Admiralty, 29 September 1914.

TNA, ADM 137/9, Folio 60, Telegram Acting Governor-General to the Secretary of State, 4 August 1914.

TNA, ADM 137/9, Folio 624, Buxton to Harcourt, 29 September 1914.

TNA, ADM 137/9, Folio 69, Extract from Proceedings of a Sub Committee of the Committee of Imperial Defence, 5 August 1914.

TNA, ADM 137/9, Folio 70, Telegram Secretary of State to Acting Governor-General, 6 August 1914.

TNA, ADM 137/9, Folio 86, Memo Admiral H.B. Jackson, 8 August 1914.

TNA, ADM 137/9, Memorandum Acting Governor of Union of SA to Secretary of State for the Colonies, 20 August 1914.

TNA, ADM 137/9, Memorandum Acting Governor of Union of SA to Secretary of State for the Colonies, 30 August 1914.

TNA, ADM 137/9, Memorandum Acting Governor of Union of SA to Secretary of State for the Colonies, 31 August 1914.

TNA, ADM 137/9, Memorandum Admiralty to Secretary of State for the Colonies, 11 August 1914.

TNA, ADM 137/9, Memorandum from Sir H. Jackson, 22 August 1914.

TNA, ADM 137/9, Naval Notes on Expedition to GSWA (prepared by Admiral H. Jackson), 8 August 1914.

TNA, ADM 137/9, Telegram Acting Governor Union to S of S Colonies, 24 August 1914.

TNA, ADM 137/9, Telegram C-in-C Cape Admiralty, 25 August 1914.

TNA, ADM 137/9, Telegram C-in-C Cape Admiralty, 26 August 1914.

TNA, ADM 137/9, Telegram C-in-C Cape to H. B. Jackson, 5 September 1914.

TNA, ADM 137/9, Telegram C-in-C Cape to H. B. Jackson, 9 September 1914.

TNA, ADM 137/9, Telegram from C-in-C Cape to Governor-General, 1 August 1914.

TNA, ADM 137/9, Telegram Governor of Union of SA to Secretary of State for the Colonies, 8 September 1914.

TNA, ADM 137/9, Telegram Officer Advising Governor of SA to H. B. Jackson, 2 September 1914.

TNA, ADM 137/9, Telegram S of S Colonies to Acting Governor Union of SA, 23 August 1914.

TNA, ADM 137/9, Telegram S. S. for Colonies to Governor of SA, 7 September 1914.

TNA, ADM 137/9, Telegram S. S. for Colonies to Governor of SA, 9 September 1914.

TNA, ADM 137/9, Telegram Secretary of State for Colonies to Acting Governor-General, 6 August 1914.

TNA, ADM 137/9, Telephone message received by Chief Censor from War Office, 11 August 1914.

Records of the Air Force

TNA, AIR 1/1247/204/7/1, Report of Major Wallace on the work of the South African Aviation Corps GSWA 1915.

Records of the Cabinet

TNA, CAB 103/94. Historical Section, Comments on Official History by Jan Smuts, 18 March 1935.

TNA, CAB 103/94. Historical Section, Comments on Official History by Jan Smuts, 12 November 1934.

TNA, CAB 103/94. Historical Section, Letter Edmonds to Sir Herbert Creedy, 30 April 1937.

TNA, CAB 22/3, An Appreciation by the General Staff on the Situation in East Africa, Lt-General A.J. Murray CIGS, 10 December 1915.

TNA, CAB 22/3, Minute by the Secretary of State for War, appended to the General Staff Appreciation, 14 December 1915.

TNA, CAB 22/3, War Committee Meeting of 15 December 1915.

TNA, CAB 23/4/279, Minutes of a Meeting of the War Cabinet, 21, November 1917.

TNA, CAB/23/4, War Cabinet 279, 21 November 1917).

TNA, CAB 24//1/4, Committee of Imperial Defence: Future Operations in East Africa, 12 November 1915.

TNA, CAB 24/1/12, Alexandretta and Mesopotamia Memorandum by Lord Kitchener, 16 March 1915.

TNA, CAB 24/1/4, Committee of Imperial Defence: Future Operations in East Africa, 12 November 1915.

TNA, CAB 44/2, Operations in the Union of South Africa and German South West Africa, 11 August 1914.

TNA, CAB 44/2, Operations in the Union of South Africa and German South West Africa, 8 August 1914.

TNA, CAB 44/2, Operations in the Union of South Africa and German South West Africa, 5 August 1914.

TNA, CAB 44/2, Operations in the Union of South Africa and German South West Africa, 8 August 1915.

TNA, CAB 44/4, British Draft Official History Chapter 1.

TNA, CAB 44/6, Draft Official British History, Chapter 14, The Advance to the Rufiji December 1916- February 1917.

TNA, CAB 45/112, The Campaign in GSWA, 1914–1915, Narrative of Events.

TNA, CAB 45/19, Advance of the 1st East African Brigade to the Rufiji 2 to 4 January 1917, Extract from War Diary, 2–3 January 1917.

TNA, CAB 45/27, East African Campaign 1914–1918, Preliminary Studies of the Operations in East Africa, Intelligence.

TNA, CAB 45/27, East African Campaign 1914–1918, Preliminary Studies of the Operations in East Africa; Hordern, *Military Operations East Africa*.

TNA, CAB 45/29, Major-General G.J. Gifford Organisation of African labour in German East Africa.

TNA, CAB 45/39, RE Corps History GEA, Diaries of Lt-Col L.N. King, 26 February 1916, 26 February 1916.

TNA, CAB 45/43, An Ordinance Officer in East Africa 1914–1916, Letter to Colonel Jennings, 30 June 1916.

TNA, CAB 45/43, An Ordinance Officer in East Africa 1914–1916.

TNA, CAB 45/44, Private Diary of Brig-Gen C.P. Fendall January 1915–December 1918, 13 April 1916.

TNA, CAB 45/44, Private Diary of Brig-Gen C.P. Fendall January 1915–December 1918, 10 June 1916.

TNA, CAB 45/44, Private Diary of Brig-Gen C.P. Fendall January 1915–December 1918, 15 May 1916.

TNA, CAB 45/44, Private Diary of Brig-Gen C.P. Fendall January 1915–December 1918, 6 April 1916.

TNA, CAB 45/44, Private Diary of Brig-Gen C.P. Fendall January 1915–December 1918, 7 February 1916.

TNA, CAB 45/44, Private Diary of Brig-Gen C.P. Fendall January 1915–December 1918.

TNA, CAB 45/44, Private Diary of Brig-Gen C.P. Fendall January 1915–December 1918, 19 March 1916.

TNA, CAB 45/44, Private Diary of Brig-Gen C.P. Fendall January 1915–December 1918, 15 May 1916.

TNA, CAB 45/44, Private Diary of Brig-Gen C.P. Fendall January 1915–December 1918, 4 February 1917.

TNA, CAB 45/44, Private Diary of Brig-Gen C.P. Fendall January 1915–December 1918, 26 June 1916.

TNA, CAB 45/44, War Diaries (Private): Operations in East Africa: diary of Col C.P. Fendall.

TNA, CAB 45/46, Report on the Operations of the 1st South African Mounted Brigade 23 October 1916–1 January 1917, Lt-Col Hartigan.

Records of the Colonial Office

TNA, CO 417/455, Letter from A.J. Arnold (Mozambique Company) to High Commissioner, 11 May 1908.

TNA, CO 417/455, Letter from High Commissioner to Earl of Crewe , 29 June 1908.

TNA, CO 417/455, Letter High Commissioner to H.C. Sloley Resident Commissiner Basutuland, 26 May 1908.
TNA, CO 417/466, Hopwood, Dispatches: Bechuanaland Prot. and Rhodesia, 23 July 1909.
TNA, CO 417/502, L. Botha, Botha Swaziland, Memorandum Botha to High Commissioner, April 1911.
TNA, CO 537/522/10, Report by C.W. Boyd on Southern Rhodesia, 1909.
TNA, CO 537/569, Telegram Governor-General (Buxton) to Secretary of State for the Colonies, December 1914.
TNA, CO 551/101, File 38195, Proceedings of a Court of Enquiry to Investigate and Report upon Certain Allegations made by Lt-Colonel H.J. Kirkpatrick 9th Regiment SAI, 31 July 1917.

Records of the Dominion Office

TNA, DO 116/1/8, L. Botha, Botha to Gladstone on Bechuanaland, Correspondence 1913–1926, March 1913.
TNA, DO 119/956, Correspondence: Henry Lambert and Roland Bourne, July/August 1917.
TNA, DO 35/903/3, Mr G. Heaton Nicholls address to the Study Committee of the Empire Parliamentary Association at Westminster Hall, 16 November 1938.
TNA, DO 35/904/2, Rhodesia Nyasaland Royal Commissions Report, 31 July 1939.

Records of the Foreign Office

TNA, FO 367/236, Colonel O'Sullivan verbal report on situation in Mozambique Company Territory, 15 March 1911.
TNA, FO 367/236, Letter Foreign Office to Secretary of State for the Colonies, 18 April 1911.
TNA, FO 367/236, Telegram Consul Lourenco Marques to Governor-General, 21 February 1911.
TNA, FO 367/236, Telegram Governor- General to Secretary of State for the Colonies, 13 April 1911.
TNA, FO 367/236/2, Telegram Foreign Office to Admiralty, 3 March 1911.
TNA, FO 367/344, Correspondence surrounding Smuts speech at Union Banquet to visiting member of the English Parliament, October 1913.
TNA, FO 367/89/2, Telegram High Commissioner to Secretary of State, 21 August 1908.
TNA, FO 367/89/3, Telegram High Commissioner to Secretary of State, Confidential letter from Colonel A.J. Arnold, 20 June 1908.
TNA, FO 371/972, Telegram Governor-General of Union to Secretary of State for Colonies re: Delagoa Bay, 5 October 1910.

Records of the War Office

TNA, WO 106/1460, Diary of Governor Heinrich Schnee 11/1917–11/1918.
TNA, WO 106/257, East Africa History Volume IV Chapter II, Precis of Correspondence to Belgian Occupation of Tabora District.
TNA, WO 106/308, Note on our Future Military Policy, 28 December 1915.
TNA, WO 106/310 Folio 20, 'General Staff Appreciations, Future Conduct of the War', 16 December 1915.
TNA, WO 106/310, Smith-Dorrien Appreciation on Situation in East Africa, quoted in Anderson, 'J.C. Smuts and J.L. van Deventer'.
TNA, WO 141/31, Report on Medical and Sanitary Matters in German East Africa, 1917.
TNA, WO 32/5325, Smith-Dorrien Appreciation on Situation in East Africa, 27 November 1915.
TNA, WO 32/5820 Smuts Despatch, 27 October 1916.

TNA, WO 32/5822, DCIGS: Operations in East Africa, Memorandum DCIGS to General Buller, 12 March 1916.

TNA, WO 32/5822, Folio 99a, Telegram Smuts to CIGS, 19 May 1916.

TNA, WO 32/5822, J. Smuts, Operations in East Africa, Memorandum Smuts to CIGS, 23 February 1916.

TNA, WO 32/5822, J. Smuts, Operations in East Africa, Memorandum Smuts to CIGS, 15 March 1916.

TNA, WO 32/5822, J. Smuts, Operations in East Africa, Memorandum Smuts to CIGS, 12 March 1916.

TNA, WO 32/5822, J. Smuts: Operations in East Africa, Memorandum Smuts to CIGS, 11 March 1916.

TNA, WO 32/5822, J. Smuts: Operations in East Africa, Memorandum Smuts to CIGS, 14 March 1916.

TNA, WO 32/5822, J. Smuts: Operations in East Africa, Memorandum Smuts to CIGS, 6 March 1916.

TNA, WO 32/5822, J. Smuts: Operations in East Africa, Memorandum Smuts to CIGS, 8 March 1916.

TNA, WO 32/5822, J. Smuts: Operations in East Africa, Memorandum Smuts to CIGS, 9 March 1916.

TNA, WO 32/5822, J.Smuts: Operations in East Africa, Memorandum Smuts to CIGS, 27 March 1916.

TNA, WO 32/5822, Operations in East Africa, Memorandum W. Robertson CIGS to Smuts, 24 March 1916.

TNA, WO 32/5822, Tighe: Operations in East Africa, Memorandum Tighe to CIGS, 9 January 1916.

TNA, WO 32/5822, Tighe: Operations in East Africa, Memorandum Tighe to CIGS, 16 March 1916.

TNA, WO 32/5822. J. Smuts: Operations in East Africa, Memorandum Smuts to CIGS, 23 March 1916.

TNA, WO 32/5823, Operations in German East Africa—General Smuts Command, Telegram Smuts to CIGS, 21 September 1917.

TNA, WO 32/5823, Operations in German East Africa—General Smuts Command, Telegram Smuts to CIGS, 27 September 1917.

TNA, WO 32/5823, Operations in German East Africa—General Smuts Command, Telegram Smuts to CIGS, 21 September 1917.

TNA, WO 32/5822, J. Smuts: Operations in East Africa, Memorandum Smuts to CIGS, 23 March 1916.

TNA, WO/32/5820, Draft Despatch from General Smuts on East African Operations, 1916.

TNA, WO 33/416, Military Report on German South West Africa 1906.

TNA, WO 33/858, Secret Telegrams January 1915–February 1917, GIGS to Smuts 8 February 1916.

TNA, WO 33/858, Secret Telegrams January 1915–February 1917, Smuts to GIGS 23 February 1916.

TNA, WO 33/858, Secret Telegrams January 1915–February 1917, GIGS to Smuts 24 February 1916.

TNA, WO 33/858, Secret Telegrams January 1915–February 1917, Smith-Dorrien to War Office 31 January 1916.

TNA, WO 33/858, Secret Telegrams January 1915–February 1917, Smuts to GIGS 11 March 1916.

TNA, WO 33/858, Secret Telegrams January 1915–February 1917, Smuts to GIGS 12 March 1916.

TNA, WO 33/858, Secret Telegrams January 1915–February 1917, Smuts to GIGS 15 March 1916.

TNA, WO 33/858, Secret Telegrams January 1915–February 1917, Tighe to War Office 24 November 1915.

TNA, WO 33/858, Secret Telegrams January 1915–February 1917, CIGS to Smuts, 28 June 1916.

TNA, WO 33/858, Secret Telegrams January 1915–February 1917, CIGS to Smuts, 11 July 1916.

TNA, WO 33/858, Secret Telegrams January 1915–February 1917, Secretary of State to Smuts, 2 July 1916.

TNA, WO 33/858, Secret Telegrams January 1915–February 1917, Secretary of State to Smuts, 24 April 1916.
TNA, WO 33/858, Secret Telegrams January 1915–February 1917, Smuts to CIGS, 6 July 1916.
TNA, WO 33/858, Secret Telegrams January 1915–February 1917, Smuts to CIGS, 18 July 1916.
TNA, WO 33/858, Secret Telegrams, Folio 810, Smith-Dorrien to WO, 31 January 1916.
TNA, WO 33/858, Kitchener, Action at Salaita Hill, Telegram Kitchener to Tighe, 18 February 1916.
TNA, WO 33/858, M. Tighe, Action at Salaita Hill, Telegram Tighe to Kitchener, 16 February 1916.
TNA, WO 95/5345/12 f42 War Diary 1st East African Division, Operation Order no. 8, 8 February 1916.
TNA, WO 95/5345/12 f42 War Diary 1st East African Division, Operation Order no. 1, 2 February 1916.
TNA, WO 95/5345/12 f47 War Diary 1st East African Division, Operation Order no. 4, 6 February 1916.
TNA, WO 95/5345/12 f55 War Diary 1st East African Division, Operation Order no. 2, 11 February 1916.
TNA, WO 95/5345/12 f55 War Diary 1st East African Division, Operations against Salaita, 12 February 1916.
TNA, WO 95/5345/15 f11 War Diary 130th King George's Own Baluchis, 29 March 1915.
TNA, WO 95/5345/15 f146 War Diary 130th King George's Own Baluchis, Appendix IV, 12 February 1916.
TNA, WO 95/5345/15 f59 War Diary 130th King George's Own Baluchis, Report on the action at Mbuyuni, 14 July 1915.
TNA, WO 106/47, Offensive Scheme against German South West Africa, Memorandum Acting Quarter Master General to Director General of Military Intelligence, 24 November 1902.
TNA, WO 106-47, Paper on Occupation of Swakopmund, 16 October 1902.
TNA, WO 106-47, Project for the despatch of an Expeditionary Force to GSWA, April 1910.
TNA, WO 106-47, Memorandum Methuen to the High Commissioner Selbourne, 2 March 1909.
TNA, WO 106/310 f17 (1), Appreciation of the Situation in East Africa, Smith-Dorrien, 1 December 1915.
TNA, WO 106/310 f20, General Staff Appreciations, Future Conduct of the War 16 December 1915.
TNA, WO 141/62 6128, Smuts Despatch on East Africa 20 June 1916.
TNA, WO 141/62 f15, Colonel Malleson, Precis.
TNA, WO 141/62 f6, Memorandum Colonel Malleson to Secretary of the Army, 6 July 1916.

Historical Papers Research Archive William Cullen Library, Witwatersrand University

AD843-C1-002, Address of Lionel Curtis to the Royal Empire Society, 'British Protectorates in South Africa', 9 February 1938.

Liddell Hart Archive, Kings College, Robertson Papers

WR 4/3/15, Letter Josiah Wedgwood (JCS Staff) to Prime Minister, 25 January 1916.

Bodleian Archives, Oxford University, Alfred Milner Papers

TA, FK 1117 Milner papers (Oxford No. 12) Greene – Milner, 12 May 1899.

Index